Friends and Fami

MW01101742

I have now finished your fascinating book! (I couldn't go walking this morning because I couldn't leave this computer!) Thank you SO much for sharing your life and giving me the opportunity to read your story. You are a true Double-Rainbow Family! What a great title!

– Jackie (Berry) Small

I couldn't stop reading! What an amazing life you are living! It is an inspiration to read about how God has been with you through it all. How are you going to continue to add on once it is published and you are still living it? Thoroughly engrossed!

– Beverly Fong

I was fascinated by the first three chapters of your story! You really paint a good picture of Grace and Ralph. They became "real" right away, which is a good thing. And I think for the first time I realized what an awful shock and tragedy your mother's death must have been for the whole family. Your story made that especially real for me.

– Brenda Loux, niece

I really am enjoying reading your book. It fascinates me because it is my history and heritage. It is a huge part of my dad's life that I love to know more about. Thanks for taking the time out of your life to tell the story so that many others can learn about our family's history. Wow! The Tribute brought tears to my eyes. What a gift you gave your father with that tribute.

– Wendy (Herstine) Weaver, niece

I'm in the process of reading your book and have enjoyed it very much. You have put much time and energy into the research of our family. My dad never talks too much about his childhood. He is very quiet and I've always been curious. What I have read has given me a lot to think about.

– Jeff Herstine, nephew

Your chapters are fantastic! You must have cried many tears, not only in your childhood, but also during writing. Wow, what a job!

– Helen (Friesen) Arlitt, sister-in-law

You have poured so much energy into your book, anyone who reads your chapters gains strength from your energy. You write so well and have truly done a good job.

– Mary Ann (Friesen) Mulligan, sister-in-law

Stunning detail.

– Todd Murray

—7

I'm reminded of the verse, "God resists the proud but gives grace to the humble." You are such a humble servant for Him that He has been able to "lift you up" and use you greatly. What a lifetime of great experiences and blessings you have had!

— *Mildred Barger*

Very interesting. I had no idea. I knew so little about you and your family. I am enjoying your chapters. You have worked hard at many things, and your secretarial training has certainly served you well.

— *Mildred (Rosenberger) Smith*

I just finished the first 20 chapters and am eager for more. It brought back so many memories and emotion about people, places, and events from the past. I was aware long ago that you had sad days as a child but did not realize how it was for all of you. And yet you always had such a caring and forgiving way. I could feel your struggle through it all.

— *Ada (Rosenberger) Spaeth*

Your story continues to be interesting reading. I feel so sad that you and your sisters missed having a happy childhood, in fact, that it was so difficult. I like the way you bring out the positive aspects of your father's personality—and even of your stepmother. That can't have been easy.

— *Mary Rempel*

I am reading your book again, starting from the beginning; it is great to see the pictures this time and read the polished version. It is fabulous and so interesting. I love the picturesque descriptions and the wonderfully written story; it is hard to put down. And I LOVE the poem at the beginning—you were meant to be an author!!

— *Willie Wood*

Great work! You are in one book accomplishing more than one goal. With the (ministry) chapter your family may feel it is a long side trip in which they have secondary interest, but you are reporting on a major chapter in your life. Therefore, in that sense it belongs in this book, which is a condensation of your life—and the journaling of events that blessed your life and allowed you to be a blessing.

— *Peter B. Wiebe*

Thank you for letting me read the preface and first chapters of your book. You have written honestly and well. I wanted somehow to go get those little girls (you and your sisters) and take care of them. Only a few books have made me feel that way. Please accept my sympathy for the loss of your dear mother. Your book is a loving tribute to her.

— *Glenda Zahller*

DOUBLE-RAINBOW FAMILY

To my dear friend Lynn,
from our Lynden days —
Lovingly,
Jane Friesen
Romans 8:37

April 19, 2011

Double-Rainbow Family

A true Mennonite story of tragedy, intrigue, and adventure

Jane Herstine Friesen

To my husband, Jake,
my children, Janet Friesen Brejda and Jared Friesen,
my grandsons, Joel and Josiah Brejda,
to our double-rainbow families,
and to the memory of my mother,
Grace Elizabeth Landis Herstine

Contents

The Families

HERSTINE FAMILY
Ralph Herstine and Grace Landis
Mildred (married Ralph Loux)
Jane (married Jacob Friesen)
Anna (married John B. Smith)
Ralph (married Janice Weisel)
Ralph Herstine and Jean Williams
Grace (married Philip Covelli)
Ruth (married David Ruch)
Thomas (married Debby Gross)

LANDIS FAMILY
Allen Landis and
Anna Yoder Ackerman
Grace (married Ralph Herstine)
Naomi (married Elvin Moser)
Alfred (married Polly Stephens)
John (married Dorothy Hillegas)
Melba
Ivan
Jean (married Franklin Marquet)
Matilda (married Ray Taylor)

WILLIAMS FAMILY
Thomas W. Williams and
Mabel Bernhardt
Mary (married Charles Minnich)
Ruth (married Walter Blose)
Griffith (married Perma Wertman)
Thomas (married Mildred Mitchell)
Ada (died in infancy)
Robert (died in infancy)
Scott (married Myrtle Holtzer)
Jean (married Ralph Herstine)
Leanna (married Kenneth Ruch)
Esther (married Edward Hillegas)
Frank (died age 11)

FRIESEN FAMILY
N. N. Friesen and Elizabeth Duerksen
Peter (married Mary Penner)
Elizabeth (died age 38)
Margaret (married Peter Schulz)
Nick (married Margaret Love)
Jacob (married Jane Herstine)
Mary Ann (married David Mulligan)
Helen (married Bertrand Arlitt)

HERSTEIN/HERSTINE Ancestors
Johannes Herstein (b. 1754, d. 1829)
and Catharine Schantz (b. 1757)
John
Magdalena
Jacob
Susanna
Catharine
Esther
Elizabeth

Intervening generations unknown

Samuel and Emma Herstine
Hannah (b. 1879, d. 1908; married
    Christian R. Wehring)
Augusta (b. 1881, d. 1932)
    Ralph Herstine
    (married Grace Landis)
Anna
Ella (married Jonas Wenhold)

Preface and Acknowledgments

Through years of nocturnal journal writing, I envisioned writing a book some day, but haunting, painful memories gave me pause. I could not conceive of putting them on paper for other eyes to see. Gradually, with encouragement from a host of friends and the enthusiastic prodding of my son and daughter, I began. And what a rewarding journey this has been.

I am grateful to my siblings who have been part of my "team" from the beginning. They each read parts of the book, shared stories, and gave permission to write details of our growing up years. They wanted a true story, not fiction. As brother Ralph told me, "You should write it as a true story because it's all true. Keep it positive. And you better get it right," he added good-naturedly. If I have failed in this, the responsibility is mine.

One of my goals for the book has been to preserve the memory and life of my mother – to give the facts and fill in the gap left by her untimely death. She was a kind and loving mother, and as I relived the story of her life I grieved and was healed in the writing. Brother Ralph delighted in telling me stories about her, as he learned them, to add to these pages. His warm friendship throughout my life has been a rich blessing and an important link to my mother's family. I also wanted to give the facts about my father's life and put those events into perspective. His kindness and love cheered many a day and reflected God's love to me in a powerful way. As sister Millie says, "Daddy was our comfort." Sisters, brothers, nieces, nephews, and aunts read some of the chapters with enthusiastic encouragement. I am grateful to each one.

I wrote for my siblings and extended family and I wrote for my children, Janet and Jared, and my grandsons, Joel and Josiah. When I read to the grandsons from a few chapters, they relished the stories about their mother and uncle. I hope some day they will enjoy reading this history of their mother's family and their mother, as she grew into the wonderful person she has become.

I am indebted to many people who told me through the years, "You should write a book." To Ruth Unrau, who urged, after she heard short pieces I wrote: "You should write a book about your stepmother!" Thank you to the writers in the Kansas and Phoenix writer's groups who critiqued my writing for over 20 years, before I attempted to write a book; to Dietrich (Dick) Rempel who gave me a job that led me into the world of publishing; and to Donna Goodrich and John Ventola who critiqued the early chapters.

I am deeply indebted to those who gave significant assistance: Mildred Barger and the late Muriel Thiessen Stackley for their excellent editorial help; to Mary Rempel, who invited me to my first Writer's Fellowship in 1973, and for copyediting the book with expertise. I am also grateful to Robert Kreider and to Muriel Thiessen Stackley for the comments for the back cover. Kudos to Nancy Miller, Graphic Designer at Hesston College (KS), for the beautiful cover. I am very pleased.

Words are not adequate to express my deep gratitude to my niece, Brenda Loux, who edited the entire manuscript for the family and formatted each chapter. This book could not have been completed without her professional and cheerful help, expertise, and patience over the past three years; and she seemed to enjoy scanning photos and designing pages.

Thank you to friends who read with enthusiasm and wonderful feedback as I wrote: Scarlett Kray, Carol Walczak, Jackie (Berry) Small, and Beverly Fong.

My husband Jake also read each chapter, finding errors and offering suggestions. His insights, wisdom, and cautions have made this a better book. How does one thank a spouse who has been patient with clutter and long hours at our table where we have our meals—and where I typed for the past 13 years? And for putting up with my rising at all hours of the night for years—to journal, jot lists, or write? Jake also provided competent computer help. I thank him for allowing me to share some of our hard times, along with the good. For all this and much more, I thank my wonderful husband, Jake.

Our children Janet and Jared read as I wrote, with keen interest and love. It is impossible to count the number of e-mails and calls they have made with helpful comments. A special thanks to Jared, who urged me to write the book and wanted all the childhood and youth stories left in, for his expert computer help, for making my website, and giving ongoing help with warmth and humor. Janet's wisdom and counsel in thinking through some of the more difficult issues were a blessing.

A heartfelt thank-you to Joel Alderfer, curator and librarian at Mennonite Heritage Center in Harleysville, Pennsylvania, for his help in researching my father's Herstine side of the family. His intimate acquaintance with our ancestor's story amazed me. My family is richer for his contribution to our story.

Thank you to Larry Kehler for the two photographs in Chapter 19, page 208. Larry was director of Information Services for Mennonite Central Committee at the time.

My deep gratitude goes to the people in my home church, Flatland Mennonite (now United), who loved us girls and took us under their wing after our mother died. Their dedicated teaching and example were a gift and guide. Many have gone on to their reward; others continue to love and support.

I am grateful to friends who allowed me to include their stories when their story became part of my story through a significant friendship. I thank Jake's sisters who read pertinent chapters and offered help and information on their family. I am deeply grateful to all those who prayed me through this journey. Special thanks to Todd (Richard) Murray who more than once prayed in our small group "that the book would write itself." Countless times I felt the power of that prayer.

Through the years as I wrote, life kept happening as God led and inspired in amazing ways. Inspiration came from my father's life as a solitary figure whom God set in a large family, which grew and grew into a resplendent double-rainbow family of brilliant hues. Psalm 68:6 says, "God sets the solitary in families." Songs and hymns of praise often fill my mind and heart for God's goodness to my father and to all of us. My deepest gratitude goes to God in Jesus Christ. This book would not have been written without my relationship with Christ, my Light and my Life.

Though others have read and helped with this book, any errors of fact or otherwise are my responsibility alone. I also apologize to anyone if my memories do not match theirs. I am grateful for each one who helped and prayed and blessed me in this endeavor. May God in Christ bless and keep each one into eternity.

J. H. F.

Sun City, Arizona
March 2011

PART I

CHILDHOOD AND YOUTH

Yesterday's Child

Just yesterday I was a little child
with sunbeams pressing on my roundish arms,
the wind my partner for a joyful dance
on a fair morning in July.

And dewdrops, flung profusely down
from cloudless skies to grace the velvet lawn,
sparkled pretentiously and unabashed,
then silently returned from whence they came.

And here and there a bird would flit and strut
in search of breakfast for a hungry brood.
No finer place on earth for me could be
than yesterday with God on that dear spot.

Yes, God came down and walked a while with me,
and warmed my soul and gave a gentle nod.
How very like Him to be close at hand
when love floods every corner of the heart.

by Jane Herstine Friesen

CHAPTER 1

A Goodly Heritage

The lines are fallen unto me in pleasant places;
yea, I have a goodly heritage.
PSALM 16:6 (KJV)

1932

My life begins with a love story. My mother and daddy were deeply in love, and they also knew and loved God through Jesus Christ. For this heritage, my life has been wonderfully blest. For over 70 years, God has shown His goodness to my family and me. For His tender love and faithfulness, I praise Him with a grateful heart. Because of this, I felt compelled to write my story of Jesus' redeeming love and grace all through my life.

When I stretch my mind back as far as I can go, this is what I remember: playing in the out-of-doors in summertime, running freely in the grassy yard with an irrepressible joy in living, and basking in the kindness and gentleness of my dear parents: Grace and Ralph Herstine. They were young and happy, and even though times were hard, my father's job at the bakery provided enough to pay the rent and food and what few other necessities we needed.

My older sister Mildred (Millie) and I enjoyed hours of play and getting underfoot in the small kitchen, watching our mother work. Baby Anna kept her busy, but she sang to us, taught us songs, and possibly read a book to us before hearing our prayers at bedtime. Peace reigned in our corner of the world and we felt secure.

But I'm getting ahead of my story. Let me go back to the summer of 1932, a most wonderful time for my mother and daddy. Though I don't know many details of their courtship, engagement, and marriage, Daddy and Aunt Naomi and others told me enough so that I am able to piece it together. I also taped an interview with Pappy and Aunt Naomi. So the details of their story are true, and as I have reflected on that special time of their lives

I imagine their feelings and conversations may have been something like recorded here.

The aroma of love filled the air. Fragrant spring blossoms, delicate lacy green, purple, yellow, and the pure white and bright pink of dogwood blooms graced the trees. June, the month of weddings, beckoned to Grace and Ralph, who had fallen deeply in love. Secretly, they planned their wedding, but an obstacle blocked their path. Grace Elizabeth Landis was 18 and from a conservative church family. Ralph Herstine was 27. They met at the Fritz's Bakery Shop in Quakertown, Pennsylvania where they both worked. He had baked, sliced and wrapped bread since he finished eighth grade at age 14 and boarded at the baker's large, three-story brick house nearby. Many years later, Grace came to work in the store as a sales clerk. She frequently ventured into the bakery to restock shelves in the small showroom and also boarded at Fritz's home and took her meals there, as did Ralph.

Ralph was very shy when Grace came to the bakery at perhaps age 17, but gradually over the next year, these two began to seek each other's company. He relished the time and conversations with this warm-hearted, good-natured girl.

My father as a boy.   *My mother, possibly 16.*

Ralph, about 5 feet 6 inches tall and slender, reminded Grace of her father with his dark, wavy hair. But Ralph sported a mustache and had clear blue eyes unlike her father's brown ones. He was thoughtful and soft-spoken.

Grace had dark eyes and brown curly hair. Her quick wit drew laughter at work and over the dinner table and Ralph admired her easy manner with customers and workers alike at the shop.

While Ralph had completed only the eighth grade in school, Grace rode the trolley every day to the neighboring city of Allentown to attend her last two years of high school. She had skipped two grades in elementary school because she was so bright, and therefore graduated at age 16. She was short, like her mother, and the rhyme next to her picture in the yearbook described her thus:

Curly hair, black eyes,
Clever brain, charming size.

Ralph's stepfather took a dim view of education, insisting that any more than eight years of school was unnecessary and it was time for Ralph to find a job. So at age 14, his shyness and homesickness caught the attention of Mrs. Fritz who secretly employed an old homespun remedy. Daddy told us that after he loosened up some Mrs. Fritz told him one day, "Ralph, I'm glad to see you're feeling more at home here. You were so shy when you came that I strained your coffee through a dishrag. And it worked!" Ralph took it in good humor and was grateful for his work "family" and for dear Mrs. Fritz who loved the Lord.

For his early years at the bakery, life droned on in the same way, year after year. He lived for weekends when he could go home to see his mother and attend church. At age 19, in April 1925, he was baptized and confirmed in the Reformed Church in Richlandtown. His one interest and hobby was cars. He knew every make and model of car that came along, and when his little nest of savings grew sufficiently, he purchased a coveted Model T Ford. He kept it immaculate and the windows shining.

When Grace came on the scene at the bakery, about 13 years after Ralph, he gradually sensed a stirring within, a keen interest in her every word, a delight in her smile, a spring in his step whenever she appeared unexpectedly in the bakery shop. What was happening to him? Could this be love? She was so young. How could he ever hope to win her hand? He didn't know.

I imagine that as they had free time at the big Fritz house or on a walk, they shared their lives with each other. Grace was encouraging and genuinely interested in him and had a way of drawing him out. She had three younger brothers, four younger sisters, and a host of cousins with whom she had played all her life. These strong family ties created a security, confidence, maturity, and unspoiled beauty that Ralph found irresistible. His own insecure nature as the only child of an unwed mother cried out for the complementary personality he found in this lovely young woman.

But his background was so lowly. Grace had shared with him about her family and he knew they regularly attended the Church of the Brethren. "My grandfather on my mother's side is John Ackerman and he's the German preacher at our church," she said. "My father, Allen, has worked on the railroad for years. He sings German solos at church and in a men's quartet. And his mother, Grandmother Landis, is the song leader, or 'lead singer' at our church, since we don't use musical instruments. Grandmother is Lutheran, like her family and my father, but because my mother and all us children attend the Church of the Brethren, Grandmother and my father decided to go there, too. Daddy didn't want to split up the family."

She turned toward Ralph with obvious interest. "What about your family?"

"My mother and I attended an Old Mennonite Church at Deep Run until I was ten, when we moved," he smiled. "They were very conservative and the women wore plain dresses and a prayer covering on their heads. The men wore plain coats with no ties."

"We wear prayer coverings, too, for church," Grace added. "My mother and the older women wear black cloth coverings."

Ralph took a deep breath and continued, "My mother, Augusta Herstine, needed a job after I was born and she found one working for an old widower, Jacob Bryan, who was an Old Mennonite."

"But what about your father?" Grace cut in.

Ralph knew it was coming, and dreaded it, but he plunged ahead. "That's the sad part," he explained, looking down. "I don't know who my father was and my mother never speaks of him. She was an unwed mother, 24 years old when I was born."

"Oh, I'm so sorry!" Grace empathized, reaching for his hand. "I can't imagine not having a father or knowing who he was!" As she looked deep into his blue eyes she saw the shame and pain in his soul. And he saw in her dark ones compassion and deep caring that soothed his wounded spirit. "But go on," she urged.

"We lived with Jacob Bryan for ten years. His house was near the church, so we could walk. My mother took me there and she attended as much as she could. Her mother had died when she and her three sisters were very young. Because she had little family and no one to help her, she was happy to have work with Mr. Bryan. When he died at age 76 Mother applied to work for another widower about 15 or 20 miles away." Grace nodded, her face showing keen interest.

Ralph continued, "I remember the day Jim Weaver came with his horse and buggy to pick us up and take us to his home at Richlandtown. I was ten years old and had to change schools. Jim is 20 years older than my mother. After many years, he married her, but I kept her maiden name. Later, I asked Mother where I should go to church and she suggested the Reformed Church because it was closest to where we lived and I could walk. When I was 19, I was baptized and confirmed there."

"What was it like growing up without a father?" Grace inquired. "Wasn't it hard?"

"Well, Jacob Bryan seemed like a father to me, but he was more like a kind grandfather. But Jim called me names and got angry at me a lot. He'd yell that I wasn't working fast enough."

"What kind of work did you have to do for him?"

"I cut up pumpkins for the animals and cleaned stalls, that kind of stuff. But Jim has a bad temper. He yells at my mother, too, and makes her cry when his coffee isn't hot enough."

"He sounds like a bad man to me!" Grace's eyes flashed. "I'm sorry he's so mean to you and your mother."

"He sure is a lot different than Jacob Bryan," Ralph reflected.

Ralph couldn't always go to church when he worked on Sundays and surely wondered what her parents would think of him. It was hard telling her about not having a father, and about his stepfather, and that the names Jim called him stung as much as the bees Jim kept in his hives. How Ralph hated working for his stepfather Jim and chafed under Jim's heavy-handed ways. Yet Ralph loved being near his gentle and kind mother. He was the apple of her eye and she looked forward to the occasional weekend that he came home.

Ralph saw that Grace was like his mother – gentle, good, wholesome, warm, and caring – and attentive to him. Could it be that she loved him too?

At some point, Grace shared with him, "When I was 13 and my sister Naomi was 12 we took care of our next-door neighbor, Mrs. Cliff, who had cancer. The Cliff children were quite small and we went there from school at noon to give the family lunch. After school we did the laundry, ironing, cooking, and helped with the children." Grace had learned how to work at home and was mature for her age and very responsible. (Remarkably, Mrs. Cliff survived the cancer in the 1920s and lived into her eighties.) Ralph was impressed and admired these qualities in Grace. She would make a wonderful mother for his children.

Grace recounted, "After high school I worked in Quakertown taking care of five children for a woman who made army uniforms. She also ran a boarding house for men who worked on the highway." Her face darkened and she shuddered at the memory. "Naomi stayed there with me for a while and we were afraid of all the men in the house. There was only one bathroom, down the hall, and no lock on our bedroom door. So we propped a chair against the door at night. The man of the house was away in the military. Later, I worked at Strunk's Funeral Home, cleaning house and taking care of the Strunk children. Cleaning their tile floors was the worst job ever."

"I'm sure glad you came to the bakery," Ralph said with feeling.

"Me, too," Grace smiled. "I like it much better."

One day Ralph asked her to a movie and she accepted. (Aunt Naomi told me they went to movies, a surprise to me, since I never knew Daddy to see a movie in my life.) He knew he was dating a wonderful girl and wondered if he was worthy of her and whether she cared for him as he did for her. In the spring of 1932 he determined to find out. His friend, Clarence Miller, and his wife Eleanor kept a close eye on him. Sometimes they double-dated. Clarence and Eleanor prodded and pushed Ralph to pop the question.

"Don't be so shy. If you don't ask her, someone else will!" Clarence warned.

"If you really love her, don't lose your chance," coached Eleanor.

And so it was that Ralph drove Grace to the shore in New Jersey one Saturday and they walked the boardwalk and enjoyed the sounds and smells of the ocean. Upon returning, I imagine them driving through the beautiful countryside where spring was in full bloom. Trees arched across the narrow dirt road and splotches of white dogwood dotted the roadside and woods. Grace exclaimed with delight at sightings of pink and purple and carpets of wildflowers along the road. Finally, as they emerged from the wooded area, Ralph stopped the car on a small knoll overlooking a sloping valley of lush farmland. This exquisitely beautiful day and landscape seemed as close to heaven as Ralph could get.

"It's beautiful here!" Grace exclaimed.

They strolled arm in arm, delighting in each other's company. Suddenly Ralph stopped and, mustering all the courage he could, plunged in.

"Grace, you must know how I feel about you. I think about you every waking minute. You are the most wonderful girl I have ever known. I love

8

you, sweet Grace Elizabeth. And I have to know, do you feel the same about me? Will you marry me?"

"Yes!" she exclaimed with eyes dancing. "Yes, to both questions. How could I not love you? You are the answer to my dreams, always so kind and caring. I would *love* to marry you!"

Ralph enfolded her in his arms and held her tight. He kissed her cheeks, her forehead, and finally her sweet red lips.

Then he stopped short. "But, dear Grace, I've been wondering, what will your parents say? They don't know me. I have never even met them. Don't you think it's time I meet them?"

For the first time, Grace's face turned serious. "I don't think they'll approve of me marrying you because I'm only 18 and you're 27. I *can't* tell them about you—or ask their permission to marry you—because I can't bear to have them say no."

"Then there's only one thing to do," Ralph said simply. "We'll elope."

"Are you serious?" Her face registered shock.

"Never been more so. Clarence and Eleanor anticipated this. They've offered to go with us to Elkton, Maryland, even *drive* us there themselves!"

"Really?" As the reality of her situation sank in, Grace caught her breath. She felt her chest tighten. How could such a wonderful moment be spoiled by this huge tug of war within her? Yet, she knew it was true. She had to decide between her parents and her beau. Could she really go against her parents like this? But she *must*. They would never understand.

"Yes, let's do it!" she cried. "I want to marry you more than anything else in the world."

"Oh, my sweetheart. I can't believe I'm hearing you say this. You have made me very happy and I will do everything I can to take care of you and protect you and be worthy of your love. Next week we can meet with the Millers and work out our plan."

"Yes," Grace snuggled closer and wound her arms around his neck. "I'm old enough, and my parents will just have to accept it!"

"Do you think we can do it in June then, next month?"

"In June," she smiled.

"Elkton's really not that far." Ralph had it all figured out. "The drive should only take two-and-a-half hours. We can get married Saturday morning and have a two-day honeymoon. Do you think Mr. Fritz would give us time off for another day or two?"

"Oh, ask him. That would be so much fun. We have vacation time coming anyway. If Clarence and Eleanor agree we can stay as long as we like."

And so it was that they drove with their friends and were married in Elkton, Maryland on June 25, 1932, by Rev. Morgan, a Methodist minister, as recorded on their marriage certificate.

The newlyweds returned the following week, all aglow and joyful. However, they knew they had to face the music sometime and decided on Friday night.

Ralph's tenderhearted, protective care for his mother in the face of angry outbursts from his stepfather had bonded him more closely to this gentle, submissive woman. This same protective concern rose within him now for his new wife, fearful lest her family be angry and reject her.

On the drive to her home in Coopersburg, Ralph asked, "How are we going to tell them, my dear wife?" Grace read apprehension on his face.

"I'll just tell them I'm Mrs. Ralph Herstine now," she said simply, but her heart thumped in her chest as they drew up to the two-story redbrick house, up on the hill on Station Avenue. "Just let me handle this," she reassured Ralph as they walked across the porch.

She opened the front door of her girlhood home and walked in, followed by her husband. The pretty, sheer, pastel flowered dress she wore for her wedding and Ralph's smart, three-piece suit should have been a dead give-away to her family.

The couple entered the living room where an assortment of sisters and brothers and her parents gathered after someone yelled, "Grace is home! And there's a man with her!" Grace stood her full 4 feet 11 inches tall, holding Ralph's hand, and announced, with a bright smile, "I'm Mrs. Ralph Herstine now, and this is my husband Ralph!"

The room grew still as the night as her siblings looked from one parent to another, waiting for a reaction. Their faces registered shock, disbelief, amazement, and finally resignation.

Her father, a soft-spoken man of few words, stood speechless. Though he felt anger, he would never express it. It was done and could not be undone.

Grace's mother, recovering her composure after the shock, spoke first. "So this is how you tell us! You surprised us. We didn't have time to make the wedding comforter and quilt for you. What will the aunties think? We'll have to work fast now to make sure you're ready for winter."

Then, swallowing her emotions, she walked to Ralph and extended her hand. "I'm glad to meet you. We didn't expect this," with a hint of disapproval in her voice.

Ralph shook her hand and smiled a shy, awkward grin, unsure of what to say. "Glad to meet you, too," he managed. Grace's oldest brother Alfred offered Ralph a chair and engaged him in small talk.

The ice broken, Grace and her sisters chatted excitedly. Ralph was thinking it would take some getting used to this big family – three brothers-in-law and four sisters-in-law all at once. But already the fun and banter – as the family and Grace brought each other up to date on news – put him at ease. He had married into a good family, he could see, one that would make up for his years as an only child.

Finally, Grace remembered, "Hey, we want someone to take a wedding picture of us before the sun goes down. Who wants to take it?" And they all marched outside.

That picture of the happy couple – Grace with a smile on her face, and Ralph with a half smile, sharp in his suit and stiff white high shirt collar – stood on the bureau of my parents' bedroom all my growing up years.

Ralph and Grace Herstine,
June 25, 1932.

Many years later, Aunt Naomi told me that her parents must have been angry that Grace and Ralph eloped, but it wasn't something they ever talked about, at least not in front of the children. For the most part they concealed their hurt, embarrassment, humiliation, and anger. They must forgive and forget and go on with life. Grace was their firstborn, their jewel. She had never given them any trouble. But she chose to marry and they would make the best of it and love and support the new couple. Ralph seemed a fine and good person. Yes, they would trust the Lord that Grace would be happy and Ralph would be good to her. And, more important, they would pray for them.

CHAPTER 2

Dark Clouds Gather

Our years come to an end like a sigh...they are
soon gone, and we fly away.
PSALM 90:9-10 (RSV)

1933–1938

When they returned from Maryland, Ralph took Grace to meet his mother. Augusta seemed very taken with Grace and gave the couple her blessing. The two women were alike in many ways—hard workers, used to serving, trained to please men, and wait on their every need and wish.

Ralph and Grace needed a place to live—their first major decision. Ralph had a room in his parents' farmhouse and it seemed the logical place. They had few possessions and needed little. They were in love and had each other and that was all that mattered. Ralph's Model T would get them back and forth the three or so miles to work each day. And the aunties' comforter arrived in time for the first cold snap of fall.

Unfortunately, Ralph's mother was not well and Ralph had no idea how sick she was. Six days after they were married, on July 1, 1932, Augusta died at age 51. (Jim Weaver died 6 years later on January 28, 1938. He was 20 years older than Augusta.) The joy of their marriage turned to shock and sadness for Ralph. But grief over his mother's death was tempered by the presence of his wife. He was thankful his mother had lived long enough to see how God answered her prayers for a wife to love and care for her son. Thus she died with peace in her heart for this one child of her love. In later years, my Landis aunts had no recollection of the cause of her death. However, Aunt Naomi remembered that she suffered from "melancholy," or depression. This is not surprising considering her hard life and the harshness of her husband.

Now Grace took over the duties of homemaker and cook for her husband and father-in-law, while continuing at the bakery. Before long she became pregnant and soon quit her job. Her first child, Mildred Louise, was born the next year on August 9, 1933, at the Weaver farmhouse with a doctor and midwife Great Aunt Hattie in attendance. Millie was named after Mildred Fritz, daughter of the baker for whom Ralph and Grace had worked. Millie had brown eyes and a head of dark curly hair like her mother. What joy this baby brought to the couple.

Eighteen months later, on February 6, 1935, I was born, named Jane Ellen after a "little old lady" they knew. I entered the world in the upstairs front room at the Landis house at Coopersburg, with Grammy Landis assisting the doctor. Pappy's sister, Great Aunt Hattie, as a nurse and midwife, worked in three counties. She was attending another birth the night I was born.

Grace enjoyed caring for her two babies, but after a time her dissatisfaction with their living conditions grew. Her father-in-law's friends, who were frequent visitors, made indecent remarks to her. When she shared her feelings with Ralph he offered, "Maybe we should look for our own place. I'm not sure we can afford it on my salary, but I'll work on it."

Aunt Naomi told me that one day when Grace was alone in the kitchen, one of the men with wild flirty eyes and a weird smile tried to grab her. Quick as a flash, Grace wrenched free from his grip and grabbed a big cast iron skillet from the stove. With a wallop she sent him staggering. Her heart pounded as she warned, "Stay away from me!" With an embarrassed grin and wave of his hand, he slunk out of the house.

Sisters, Great Aunt Ella and my grandmother, Augusta (47), 1927. Augusta died in 1932 at age 51.

When Ralph came home from work she ran into his arms and the tears flowed. She related the incident with his stepfather's unsavory friend. "Please, can we move out of this house?" she pled.

"I'll look for a place tonight," Ralph promised as he held her close, comforting her with soft whispers and kisses. "We'll move as soon as I can find something."

He learned from his stepsister, Priscilla, of a little house two doors down from their home on a lovely country road about two miles out of Quakertown. That Saturday Ralph took Grace to look at it. The landlord, Nelson Stump, a small, wiry, comical bachelor, showed them the three small rooms downstairs, three up, with a partial basement at the front and a cistern for water under the kitchen. A little pump in the kitchen would provide their water. Ralph liked the tiny unpainted garage for his Model T and the shop for tools and storage. There was even a chicken house. The rent was reasonable and Ralph felt he could afford it on his meager salary.

The acre of land with apple trees, a large plot for a garden, a hickory nut tree in front by the road, and a black walnut in back was the answer to Grace's dreams.

"This used to be a harness factory," Nelson commented. "Notice the stone foundation and the slate roof. It's solidly built. The one-room school is just up the road, and of course, the church across the street." It turned out that Nelson was a member of the little fieldstone Mennonite Church.

"And Priscilla and Levi are just up the street," Ralph reminded Grace. Priscilla was Jim Weaver's daughter from his first marriage and, therefore, Daddy's stepsister. Many years Ralph's senior, Priscilla was a kind and helpful woman whose own children were grown and married.

Grace loved it and her heart welled up in gratitude to her heavenly Father. Soon the family was settled in their new home. But Grace's life was not easy. With no electricity and only a wood and coal stove in the kitchen for warmth as well as cooking, winters were difficult. Washing diapers for two children, plus the rest of the family laundry, and hanging them in the frigid temperatures or the damp, cold cellar was a daunting task.

Before long, 21 months after I was born, Anna Kathryn made her appearance on November 2, 1936, in the upstairs room at Grammy Landis's. Great Aunt Hattie, the midwife, noted quite a difference in this birth from the other two. Perhaps Anna weighed more, but Grace's labor was longer and the delivery more difficult. Aunt Hattie feared for her dear niece, and her heart went out to her in her pain and suffering. Anna was named Anna Kathryn after Grammy Landis.

A wonderful bonus of this move was the little Mennonite church across the street. Since it was an historic peace church, like her own Church of the Brethren, Grace felt right at home with these humble believers. (She may not have been aware of the fact that the church was started years ago by a distant Landis relative.) Ralph regularly worked on Sundays at the bakery and could not go with her, but Grace took the children whenever she could.

In all her difficulties, Grace knew God was with her and was looking out for her. She had trusted God since a child, and accepted Jesus as her Savior at evangelistic meetings at the Quakertown Church of the Brethren, along with her sister Naomi. Also at this church, Grace and Naomi were baptized by immersion by their grandfather, John Ackerman. The Quakertown church was larger and had a baptistery, which theirs did not. Aunt Naomi recalled to me how moved she was that day. "I will never forget the tears in grandfather's eyes as he encouraged us to be faithful to the Lord," she said in her 80s. His tearful challenge made a deep impression on Naomi, and surely on my mother as well. I was grateful to learn of my mother's early commitment.

My great-grandparents, John and Matilda Yoder Ackerman.

Grace's love for the Lord was often expressed in song. Musically gifted, she had taught herself to play the organ in her parents' home. Her Uncle Ernest Landis, who played French horn in the Quakertown Band, gave her a few lessons as well. As a child, when Grace was too short to stand at the sink, her father made a bench for her to stand on to wash the dishes while Naomi dried. After the girls learned to read, they propped the songbook in the cupboard in front of them and sang as they worked. As Aunt Naomi told me, their mother would come by an hour or so later and exclaim, "What! You're not finished yet?" With their large family, there were many dishes and the task was made more pleasant as the girls sang. Only 13 months apart, with their birthdays both in June—Grace on the 3rd, Naomi, the 28th—the work and song time bonded the girls closely together, and they were the best of friends.

Ralph loved hearing Grace play the organ in her parents' home as the family gathered around to sing. He also loved the old Gospel songs, as she did. One of his favorites was "Trust and Obey," which he often heard Mildred Fritz sing as she made the beds for the boarders.

Me, about 2½, and Millie, almost 4. c. summer 1937.

The church across the street on Thatcher Road reminded Grace of the one in which she grew up. One day she confided to Helena Milz (who told Millie years later), "I hope I don't get pregnant again. I had such a hard time when Anna was born." Helena sympathized and hoped that Grace would get her wish.

But Grace *did* get pregnant again. And 14½ months after Anna was born, on January 16, 1938, Grace was ready to deliver her fourth child. Ralph took us girls to Grammy Landis's house the day before. When Grace's contractions began, he picked up Great Aunt Hattie to deliver the baby.

When they arrived at our house, our mother was already in pain and distress. After a time of difficult labor, Aunt Hattie realized something was very wrong. She urged Ralph, "Call the doctor to send an ambulance as soon as possible." He must have gone to a neighbor or to Priscilla's house up the street to phone. The minutes dragged by until the ambulance arrived. Grace, very weak, was rushed to the hospital 15 minutes away.

There, very early Sunday morning, baby Ralph Landis Herstine was born. Finally, Ralph and Grace had a son. But Grace was too weak to take in the news. After giving birth, she hemorrhaged badly. Though blood transfusions were administered, the long labor and her weakened condition took their toll. That night, our mother quietly slipped out of this life and into the presence of her Savior.

The nurse met my father in the waiting room with the news. "Mr. Herstine, you have a baby boy. But I am very sorry to tell you that your wife did not make it. We gave her transfusions but she was too weak." And there, before her eyes, Ralph toppled to the floor in a dead faint.

When he came to, my father was in a daze. He could not comprehend this unthinkable tragedy. The enormity of his loss—facing life with three little girls and a newborn baby son—overwhelmed him. What should have been a time of great joy for the couple was instead a time of tremendous heartbreak. Ralph felt lost and alone. How could he ever tell her parents? But tell them he must.

Early on Sunday morning, January 16, 1938, my father and Great Aunt Hattie went together to break the news to my grandparents. By this time, Aunt Naomi was married and was not home when the news came of her sister's death. But Aunt Melba, 17 at the time, shared with me, "I remember that day well. Your Daddy and Aunt Hattie came to the house early Sunday morning and told us Ralph was born but Grace didn't make it. Grammy cried loudly. She carried on quite a lot. It was such a terrible shock. Your Dad took you girls along home with him and Aunt Hattie stayed a couple of weeks to help him. Rev. George Landis, our pastor at the Brethren Church, went to see your dad that day to work out funeral arrangements."

Many years later I asked Melba, "Were we girls at the funeral?" Naomi didn't think so.

"Yes, I *know* you were all there. I helped put on your warm clothes after the service. And in later years, Rev. Landis told your brother Ralph, 'I remember your father holding you at your mother's funeral.' Ralph replied, 'That wasn't me because I was in the hospital. Daddy was holding Anna.'"

Aunt Matilda was seven and Aunt Jean, ten, and both remember being in bed and hearing their mother crying. That morning Uncle Alfred took Jean to church, just the two of them. Jean told me, "I cried like crazy when they announced that Grace died. Grammy's sister, Aunt Lizzie Jacoby, was sitting beside me. She hugged me and comforted me. It was a terrible day."

News of this tragic death spread quickly through the large extended family. Pappy Landis had ten sisters and brothers; Grammy had four living siblings. Grace's siblings were Naomi, 22; Alfred, 20; John, 18; Melba, 16; Ivan, 12; Jean, 9; and Matilda, 7. Born June 3, 1914, our mother was married at age 18 and died five years later at age 23.

Added to the anguish of Daddy's loss were the scathing words of Great Aunt Hattie: "You are to blame for her death! She should not have had so many children so close together. Now what will you do with all these children?" Her angry eyes flashed and Ralph's broken heart felt stomped into the ground.

Many years later, Aunt Melba told me that Great Aunt Hattie blamed herself for our mother's death because she knew that something was wrong and she should have asked Daddy sooner to get Grace to the hospital. In her own guilt and rush to judgment, she put blame and guilt on a sorely grieving husband.

The Landis family, c. 1936. Back row: Uncle Alfred, my mother Grace, Uncle John, Grammy, Pappy, Aunt Melba, Aunt Naomi; Front row: Aunt Matilda, Aunt Jean, Uncle Ivan.

Hattie agreed to help Daddy out and care for us until he could find someone else. We girls were told, "Your mother went to be with God in heaven." At the time, as an almost three-year-old (three weeks and one day before my birthday) and years following, I sensed that heaven was a nice place to be. Only gradually did I realize the enormity of the loss we all suffered. The thought of our mother with God in heaven became a powerful, fertile seed that would remain within me to grow and comfort and confound me through the years.

Notice of our mother's death appeared in the *Quakertown Free Press* that week of January 16, 1938 (brother Ralph's birthday). It read:

> Mrs. Grace Elizabeth Herstine, wife of Ralph Herstine, of Quakertown R. D. 3 died early Sunday morning in the Quakertown Community Hospital. She was aged 23 years, 7 months and 13 days. Born near Coopersburg, she was the daughter of Allen T. and Anna (nee Ackerman) Landis. She lived in that vicinity all of her life and was a member of the Church of the Brethren at Passer. Surviving are her husband, her parents, three daughters, and an infant son only a few days old. Four sisters and three brothers also survive. They are Mrs. Elvin Moser of Allentown; Melba, Jean, Matilda, Alfred, John and Ivan, all of Coopersburg. Funeral services were held Wednesday from the N. F. Benner funeral home, Richlandtown, and in the Brethren church at Passer. Interment was made in the Springfield cemetery, Pleasant Valley. The Rev. George Landis officiated, assisted by the Rev. W. J. Kohler.

(Cousin Marietta Landis Sawatzky sent this to me many years later when she found it among her deceased parents' papers. Her mother Marie was our mother's first cousin and best friend.)

An invitation card from the funeral home, bordered by a thin black line, is headed "In profound sorrow we announce the death of..." and states, "Yourself and family are respectfully invited to attend the funeral" at 1:30 at the funeral home and 2:15 at Passer Brethren church.

Our mother had lived and worked in Quakertown the previous seven years of her life. Many people knew her there—at the bakery, Strunks Funeral Home where she had worked, Flatland Mennonite Church, which she attended, and the Quakertown Church of the Brethren where she had been baptized. Her grandfather, John Ackerman, had preached and officiated there and the family was well known.

In spite of the bitterly cold snowy day, the Passer Church of the Brethren must have been packed with church people, neighbors, and friends from Coopersburg, plus Grace's very large Landis and Ackerman families. It is hard to imagine the sorrow and grief in the group gathered there.

My mother's funeral text was Psalm 90, which begins, "Lord, you have been our dwelling place in all generations"(KJV). I learned this many years later from Aunt Naomi, a year younger than my mother, who took this loss very hard. Aunt Naomi gave me her own Bible which had the binding broken at Psalm 90 from frequent reading for comfort over many years.

After the funeral and burial at Pleasant Valley cemetery, the family gathered at Grammy and Pappy's home. Years later, Aunt Naomi described to me the icy chill in the house when they arrived and the scene of uniform grief. "Pappy stoked the fire in the stove in the middle room to get it burning. The family stood or sat around in silence, as cold as the house. We had never experienced such grief. The circle was broken." Their beloved Grace was gone from them forever. Each one sat with their pain and wondered how they could bear it, and what would become of the three little girls and the baby boy who was too ailing to leave the hospital.

To my father, holding Anna, the sunny June day of announcing their marriage in this very room seemed long ago and far away. Grace had been so happy then, full of life and energy. The events of the past days left him stunned and hardly able to breathe. The minister's message on Psalm 90 and expressions of sympathy from the congregation gave little comfort for his aching heart.

At work, Mildred Fritz's loving empathy and kindness soothed his spirit. But grief, guilt, and his dark future stared him in the face each morning when he awoke in his empty bed.

With Aunt Hattie's busy schedule of midwifery duties, she could not continue to care for us. Grammy Landis kept us when Daddy could find no one else, even though Grammy still had young children of her own. Daddy hired a "maid" when he could find one. Thus began more than a year of living between grandparents and at home with a series of "maids" while Daddy was at work. We loved being at Grammy and Pappy's house. There we felt love and warmth, and had young aunts, Jean and Matilda, who were great playmates, and Melba to help care for us. But the times at home were strange and cold when Daddy was gone and a lonely spirit filled the house where once there was warmth and cheer. The presence of love – our loving mother – was gone. The maids usually stayed only a short time. One day the maid left before the day was over, leaving us locked alone in the house. Since we were mostly at Grammy's that first year, Melba quit high school to help care for us and help with the work. Only recently, at a family reunion, did we girls realize the great sacrifice she made on our behalf and we feel deeply indebted to her for this.

Twelve days after our mother died, Daddy had another funeral to attend – his stepfather Jim Weaver's. Our mother and Jim were laid to rest at Pleasant Valley cemetery where Augusta was buried. Daddy's entire family was gone now except for his Aunt Ella and Cousin Ethel.

Those were the days of no electricity, heating or plumbing, with Anna in diapers. Daddy could not afford conveniences on his bakery wages and probably paid the maids very little.

No one quite remembers when Baby Ralph came home from the hospital, but Aunt Naomi thinks he was about six or eight weeks old. Daddy could not leave him with a maid who might be undependable or not even present, so again he prevailed upon Grammy Landis. Upon her consent, Daddy picked up Baby Ralph at the hospital and took him to Grammy's house. When she saw him, she caught her breath, overcome with shock. Later she described her reaction, in Pennsylvania Dutch, translated, "When I saw him, my spirit left me, because I didn't know if I could bring him out of it." I am grateful to Aunt Naomi who knew these details. (Aunt Naomi wrote letters, and I phoned her with many questions during her last years. She died at age 88 on February 13, 2003.)

Grammy gave Baby Ralph much tender loving care and he surpassed us all with a strong, healthy, plump frame. In a picture taken a few years later with Anna, 14½ months older, he was as tall as his sister, and a handsome little boy.

Our mother Grace had many aunts and uncles on both sides of the family. Pappy had seven sisters, including Hattie. Great Aunt Rosa's postcard, postmarked January 22, 1938, must have been a balm to my father's wounded spirit. She wrote:

> Dear Ralph,
>
> I was so shocked to hear of your sorrow and all I can say is that you can get help only in the Lord Jesus who can fill you with His Spirit and heal your broken heart and spirit. Let him help you. Am thankful Hattie can help you out now. She helped me too.
>
> Aunt Rosa

Finding that card years later in the trunk in my parents' bedroom overwhelmed me with a sense of God's goodness and provision for my father in his hour of deep grief. It was wonderful to touch hearts with a woman I couldn't remember who cared enough for my father and obeyed the prompting of the Spirit to write that powerful message. A deeper empathy with my father welled up within me, plus gratitude to the Lord Jesus for this godly woman. She encouraged him with no trace of blame or accusation. Knowing my father's sensitivity to God and things of the Lord those early years leads me to believe that he took Aunt Rosa's words seriously and turned to Jesus with his heavy burden.

But the question remained: how would he find someone to take care of his motherless children?

Pappy Landis' family. Back row: Great Aunts Martha and Estella, Pappy, Great Aunts Lucy, Orpha, Alice; Seated: Great Aunts Hattie, Rosa, Great-grandmother Landis (nee Anna Marie Steininger), Great Uncles Rob and Ernest. Missing: Great Uncle Myron.

NOTE: From the "Report of the Thirty-Fifth Reunion of the Landis-Landes Families" held at Perkasie Park, Perskasie, Bucks County, Pa., August 7, 1954, I learned that Pappy was one of 12 children, and 11 grew to maturity. Flora died before she was a year old. Pappy's father, Alfred Fetzer Landis was 16 years old when his father died. Alfred was born December 5, 1848. He was married to Anna Marie Steininger on May 14, 1877, by Rev. Roth, at Allentown. Alfred was a sawyer at the "Sawmill" until 1885 when he bought Stauffer's Grist Mill, located about three-quarter mile east of Coopersburg and adjoining the Sawmill property. The Tumble Brook Golf Course was later built on this farm. Alfred F. was a farmer as well as a miller.(Many years later, Pappy Landis worked on this golf course which was very close to his home on Station Avenue in Coopersburg. And brother Ralph learned to play golf on this course.)

My great-grandfather Alfred belonged to the Springfield Brethren (Dunkard) Church and always dressed in the plain dress of this sect. His wife, Anna Marie, was of Lutheran faith, though she attended his church and was the "fore-singer" there (meaning leader of con-gregational singing since no musical instruments were allowed). Anna Marie was born September 6, 1858 and died January 7, 1933 at age 74. Alfred preceded her in death, having died on January 19, 1916, at age 68. Both are buried at Springfield Church of the Brethren cemetery. (p. 37 of the report).

CHAPTER 3

The Storm

Man is born to trouble as the sparks fly upward.
JOB 5:7 (RSV)

1939

March 7, 1939. Cold and wind kept us inside. I stood at the front window of Grammy and Pappy's house with my ten-year-old Aunt Jean. Watching. Waiting. Wondering. When will Daddy come with the new maid? Two hours seemed interminable to my four-year-old mind.

Finally Daddy drove up in his shiny 1937 Plymouth. When the new maid got out of the car, I stated, "I don't like her!"

Such a hasty, childish judgment sounds very prejudiced to me now, but my attitude persisted for a long time to come. First impressions are as hard to erase as crayon on a chalkboard. In contrast to our short, petite, gentle-mannered mother, Jean's large frame, loud voice and laugh, her rouge and lipstick put me off.

At first she was nice enough, but soon her harsh manner filled our hearts with fear. Nervous and easily frustrated, she amazed us by smoking cigarettes and told us she started at age 11. She'd scold in a loud voice when Daddy was at work and we cowered with fright, especially Anna, only two and still in diapers.

Daddy's unique way of finding Jean has long intrigued me. After a string of undependable maids, in desperation he put an ad in the big city newspaper at Allentown, 13 miles away. A letter arrived from Jean Williams from Slatington stating that she was interested in the job. Daddy arranged to pick her up at her older sister Ruth's house about 40 miles north.

Our life changed in a myriad of ways. Jean's angry scolding was like the fury of the thunderstorms of summer. Before long Daddy and Jean argued in the evenings before bedtime. The former peaceful, loving atmosphere of our home evaporated.

Daddy was our comfort. When he was at work, we longed for his return, and in the afternoons Millie and I watched at the window for his car to turn into the driveway. Evenings I stayed close to him, though he usually held Anna because she was the youngest and needed him most. She clung to him for comfort. Daddy helped get us ready for bed and took us upstairs. Our bedtime ritual included kneeling by the bed as he said, "Say your prayers," and we prayed together, "Now I lay me down to sleep, I pray the Lord my soul to keep, If I should die before I wake, I pray the Lord my soul to take." He gave us all a hug and kiss, then tucked all three of us into the big bed with the heavy comforter. In winter the room was so cold we could see our breath, and ice in fancy designs covered the windowpanes.

In bed, I often couldn't sleep. My mind reeled with upsetting events of the day and with many questions. The phrase, "If I should die before I wake," mystified me. Our mother had died mysteriously. Did this mean I could die too? As I grew older, I sometimes longed to be with my mother. The thought of our mother in heaven lingered in my mind and spread in my consciousness like the ripples of a stone in a pond. My thoughts turned to God, and I wondered about this powerful Being who seemed to have whisked my mother away from us. I wasn't angry with Him. I just pondered the imponderable. After upsetting evenings, I usually cried myself to sleep when everyone else seemed to be sleeping.

Sundays were different too. Instead of *taking* us to Sunday school and church across the street, the new maid walked with us the short distance and then we were on our own.

Jean's impatience, especially with Anna, made the days very long when Daddy was at work. Potty training and Anna's whimpering set her off. We learned to dread bath times every other week in the washtub in front of the black iron stove in the kitchen where Jean scrubbed our feet with a hard brush. It hurt to have our hair combed, especially for Millie with her thick, naturally curly hair, but hard on me too.

In the mornings Daddy cooked oatmeal for our breakfast after stoking the fire in the stove, our only means of heat in the six-room house. In winter, the door remained closed between the kitchen and "middle room" to conserve the heat in one room. So our days were spent with Jean in this one small room, with very little to do to occupy our time. On Daddy's time off, he tenderly took over the care of us as much as possible. Empathy showed in his eyes and voice.

We three girls were unaware of the dynamics of Daddy's relationship with Jean. Her designs were to marry Daddy and perhaps his were the same when she first came. But the "honeymoon" soon bombed and the initial romance boomeranged. Daddy hated how Jean treated Anna. He grieved and feared the worst, as he told me many years later, and felt helpless, caught in a bind. Jean tried to silence us so we would not squeal on her to Daddy or display unhappy emotions that might jeopardize her chances of marrying him.

With Anna's slow response to potty training, Jean became more severe, and Anna more terrified. When Daddy came home from work at noon, Anna stayed close to him. She clung to him as he got ready to leave and cried inconsolably. Jean grabbed her from Daddy, scolding, "Stop your crying!"

After several of these episodes, Jean had enough. One day after Daddy left, she took an onion, peeled it, and set it on the table in front of Anna. "Now, you eat that!" she shouted, "and you'll get a raw onion to eat every day until you learn not to cry when your daddy goes back to work!"

As tears streamed down her face, Anna obediently ate the onion with her tiny, two-year-old teeth. How I hated this maid! How could she do this to us? Why didn't someone come in and stop her? Millie and I were devastated by Jean's treatment of our little sister. I could not comprehend such injustice and how my daddy could allow this to continue, day after day. We girls were heartbroken longing for our mother, not realizing how heartbroken our father was as well.

Recently, I was struck by a compassionate description of the grief of little children that took me right back to our kitchen on Thatcher Road. Maria von Trapp tells of her six-year old daughter who let out a terrific wail when she learned they had left behind in Austria her favorite toy, "a ghost of a worn-out teddy bear." She writes, "The grief of a child is always terrible. It is bottomless, without hope. A child has no past and no future. It just lives in the present moment—wholeheartedly. If the present moment spells disaster, the child suffers it with his whole heart, his whole soul, his whole strength, and his whole little being. Because a child is so helpless in his grief, we should never take it lightly, but drop all we are doing at the moment and come to his aid." (Maria von Trapp, *Let Me Tell You About My Savior* [Green Forest, AR: New Leaf Press, 2000], 13-14.) In this case, Maria told about the Baby Jesus, Joseph, and Mary—as refugees who fled to Egypt—with incredible detail and the girl was enthralled and quieted. She saw how God took care of the holy family and learned that God would take care of her.

This quote is so poignant that, in retrospect, I ache again for each of us – Millie, Anna, and me, because there was no one to come to our aid, especially little Anna, because no one *knew*. And Jean could be so hard-hearted. Years later I saw that Someone *did* know – God – and His loving presence made a difference.

Sometime during that first year with Jean, when I was four, perhaps after the incident with the onions, I had an experience that is vivid to this day. That night, after a torrent of tears, God spoke to me through our memory verses from Sunday school – clues to the nature of God and my first lessons in theology: *"God is love"* and *"He careth for you"* (1 John 4:8; 2 Pet. 5:7, KJV). Awe and wonder filled my mind and a soothing peace washed over me. As I quieted down in my bed and snuggled deeper under the covers, I reflected on God's love and care for me, and my body, mind and spirit were comforted. I began to talk with God. Didn't we talk to Him every mealtime and at bedtime every night? I *knew* He was right there with me in bed and all the time. And He was LOVE. The Holy Spirit made that thought so real to me. Peace and gladness warmed me to the core as I experienced Jesus' second Beatitude for the first time, "Blessed are those who mourn, for they will be comforted" (Matt. 5:4, NRSV). This encounter with God was as real as any human interaction, but more deeply profound and life changing.

God CARED for *me* – tiny, crying me. That powerful thought, magnified by the Spirit, gave me significance and hope. I talked to God as if He were my daddy because He was *like* Daddy – loving and caring. So I asked God questions that I could never voice aloud to Daddy or anyone else. *Why? Why did our mother have to die? Why did Daddy keep this woman in the house? Would he send her away?* How I hoped so with all my heart.

In the interest of fairness, I must say that Jean was not always angry or mean to us. She was only 22 (a year younger than our mother when she died), and must have been lonely far away from her family. She had no friends in our area and seemed to enjoy our company. We had a few books in the house and sometimes she read to us. One day that first year she read us a book about Jesus. When she read that men killed Jesus, I burst into tears.

"Why are you crying?" she asked sympathetically.

"Because they killed Jesus," I sobbed. "Why did they kill him?"

Her kind tone got my attention as she explained that they were bad people. She had little understanding of theology and kept it simple. I hated that my mother had died and I loved Jesus. The thought of Him enduring such evil assaulted my sensitive spirit. Relieved that Jean didn't scold me for crying, as she often did, a feeling of warmth toward her grew inside me.

Jean solicited our help for various chores and Daddy encouraged this. He made a bench for Millie to stand on at the sink to wash dishes, as our grandfather had made for our mother. Millie was six now and expected to help. In a corner of the kitchen, a small pump brought up water from the cistern under the kitchen, and was heated in a large teakettle on the stove. I dried the dishes and we sang or talked as we worked, like our mother and Naomi did when they were small.

Millie and I were very close. Because she was older, I thought of her as my mother. It seemed to me she was always good – and smart. She almost never got in trouble with Jean. But if Jean scolded her so she'd cry, I'd cry too – rather *howl*, and Jean let up on her.

Millie, me, and Anna in our back yard, c. 1939.

Daddy had to work late at the bakery on Friday nights. That night we always washed the kitchen floor. The small kitchen loomed very large those days. Millie started at one end on her hands and knees and I at the other, and we met in the middle.

Sometimes on Friday nights Daddy took us to work with him. What a treat! We loved watching him run the big machines that sliced the loaves of bread on the long conveyor belt. Another machine wrapped the loaves. We slid on the slippery hardwood floors and stuck our fingers into large containers of whipped cream. What delicious smells wafted through the shop. The sight of donuts, éclairs, cream puffs, pecan sticky buns and funny cake, waiting for Saturday customers, made our mouths water. Daddy sometimes brought home these delicacies along with our bread.

(Years later, I found Daddy's W-2 form from the bakery dated 1944. His income for the year was $2,120, and withholding tax, $47.70. Somehow he always had enough to pay the bills, keep food on the table, and his car running.)

When summer came we played outside. How I relished those sunny days in the beautiful outdoors, with tricycle and wagon and running free. Visits to our grandparents, our "Baby Butter," as we called him, aunts and uncles, and a picnic reunion with my mother's Landis family and relatives made summer special. In spite of the hard times, we were happy children.

Later that year when I was four, I remember Jean coming in from the outhouse one day and as she came through the door, I noticed how large she was. Almost five years old, I observed innocently, "You're almost as big as the door."

Jean's eyes flashed angrily. "Don't you ever say anything like that again!" I didn't know that what I said was wrong and learned to be very careful about what I said—most of the time. Not until many years later did I realize that she had put on extra weight for a reason we would soon discover.

CHAPTER 4

A New Mother

Seventy years is all we have — eighty years if we are strong;
yet all they bring us is trouble and sorrow.
PSALM 90:10 (GNB)

1939–1940

One day, late in that year of 1939, I received a new understanding of Jean. I distinctly remember her standing by the sink in the corner of the kitchen and she seemed to be in distress or pain. She cried quietly, trying to hold in the sobs, but they erupted like bubbles in a simmering pot. Little cracks broke around the edges of my hard attitude toward her. I felt a new and strange feeling of compassion in this unusual situation. I stored the memory of her tears away and at times returned to it with wonder and sadness through the years.

In December, before Christmas, Jean's younger sister, 18-year-old Esther Williams, showed up at our house. She had a delightful personality and loved us girls and enjoyed playing with us. The atmosphere in our house changed like the calm after a storm. Christmas was special that year because of Esther. Perhaps she bought us presents, but that wasn't as important as feeling we had an advocate and a friend around.

The next thing I remember is that three days after Christmas all of us–Daddy, Jean, Esther, Millie, Anna and I–piled into the '37 Plymouth and drove to the minister's house in town. Daddy and Jean argued loudly, and when Daddy stopped the car, Esther yelled from the back seat, "Shut up and go in there and get married!" And they did.

Kindly, warm-hearted Mennonite minister, Rev. A. J. Neuenschwander, tied the knot. My mind didn't register the impact of this event at once. On our return home, Jean instructed us, "You call me Mama now. I'm your Mama now." I couldn't believe it! Inside I rebelled. *Will she be our mother forever?* That Esther had a hand in it did not occur to me. Or the fact that she had a reason to push. I felt like a little hypocrite giving Mama the kiss and hug she required at bedtime.

A week after they were married, on January 3, 1940, the doctor arrived at our house. Daddy heated water on the stove and carried lots of newspapers upstairs. The house had a mysterious air about it, a repressed excitement. After the doctor left, Daddy said we could go upstairs to the bedroom. There lay Mama, a glorious smile wreathing her face, holding a tiny baby in her arms. She told us this was our new sister, Grace Elizabeth (named after our mother!). What a happy surprise! We had no idea that a baby should not come this soon after a wedding.

We realized much later how unusual it was for Mama to agree to name her daughter after Daddy's first wife. After many years, Grace told me, "Mom told me that Daddy named me." We loved the name, as Mama obviously did and she respected our mother. While the wedding picture of Daddy and our mother stood on the bureau in their bedroom all of our lives in that house, there was no wedding picture of Daddy and Mama. It would take many more years for us to understand the deprivation and pain Mama suffered with Daddy, which she often buried inside.

Mama's enthusiasm and joy over her baby were contagious and I too was overjoyed at this newest member of our family. Mama had never been so happy in all her time with us. As I touched Baby Grace's tiny fingers and toes, I fell promptly in love with her. We oohed and aahed over the tiny features. Grace was perfect in every detail—a miracle—miracle of God's love. At almost five years old, I felt a mothering instinct that grew through the years.

(After having children of my own, a light came on for me about the day Jean cried quietly in distress in the kitchen. I realized it might have been labor pains or the heaviness of pregnancy that caused her pain. Or the emotional anguish of knowing she would soon deliver a child in her unmarried state. And Daddy, the man who made her pregnant, seemed immovable.)

The summer before, in 1939, at the Landis family picnic, Mama confided to our aunts, "When I got pregnant, Ralph promised he'd marry me, but it didn't happen yet."

The aunties got after him then, "Ralph, you need to marry Jean like you promised." But their words had no effect. The truth was, Daddy was heartbroken over how Jean treated Anna. He told me years later, after Mama died, "It hurt me so how Anna cried when I'd come home from work at noon and was ready to go back. I couldn't stand how Mom yelled at her and pulled her away from me. I cried on the way back to work. I was afraid if I said too much she would treat Anna even worse when I was gone."

"And you didn't even know about the onions," I told him. Then for the first time he heard about the raw onion Anna had to eat if she cried when he left for work. "Didn't you tell anyone about her, like the men at work?" I asked.

"Yes, I did, but what could they do?" This fear of Mama's abuse of his children fueled Daddy's reluctance to marry her.

Jean told us a few years after they were married that when Daddy came to pick her up she liked his shiny new car and thought he was very handsome. Her prince charming had come to get her and, after the nightmare of her former life, adventure beckoned. But the romance of the first weeks ended in a screeching halt and a heap of trouble and regret. Fortunately for Mama, Esther came to the rescue.

With Grace's birth our household took on a lighter, friendlier air, at least for a while. I can't recall Esther being there after Grace was born, but perhaps she was. Mama became a happy, loving mother to Grace. She often sang the old hymns of the church as she rocked Grace to sleep. "The Old Rugged Cross" was her favorite. It was a comfort to hear Mama singing hymns instead of scolding.

As we girls were growing up, but still very young for such stories, Mama told us about her past. In her isolation and loneliness, we served as companions and confidants. She confessed, "After my mother died, when I was 16, I sneaked out to a dance one night. When I snuck in up the cellar stairs, I knocked the pots and pans down the stairs. Pop caught me and gave me a beating. So I ran away and joined the circus. I slept in a tent with the snakes at my feet." Listening with rapt attention, we three recoiled inside and I wondered how this could be.

Then Mama revealed, "I had a baby boy named Richard (born 1937). He died of convulsions when he was four months old." (After she died, I found a copy of his funeral bill, which shows it cost $30.40 and she paid $4.00 down. After two $1.00 payments that year, and $1.00 in 1938, she finally paid the balance of $23.40 in January 1939.)

Every year on his birthday, Mama said, "Today Richard would be..." so and so old. She did this with others of her family, her mother, father, and brother Frank, who, I learned years later from a step-cousin, died of a broken heart at age 11 after his mother died. Mama's father "treated his wife mean," according to the cousin, "but was nice to us." In 1947, her younger sister Leanna Ruch died at age 29 from mumps complications, leaving four young boys, a huge grief to Mama. Her life had been hard, but we were too young to understand. Through the years she often sat at the kitchen table, hair uncombed, looking out the window, and she'd say, "I got the blues!"

In spite of this grieving, Mama had a warm, jolly side to her nature that blossomed whenever her family came to visit – her sisters and brothers and their families and especially her nieces in their teens and twenties. They liked to play games and laughter filled the house.

That first summer with us, Mama met Olive, who lived about a mile up the road. In nice weather Mama liked to sit on the front porch. Olive rode by on her bike and they became friends. Olive says she was present when Grace was born, though I don't recall her being there. The next summer, as Mama rocked Grace on the front porch and we played in the yard under the hickory nut tree, Olive stopped by to chat. She loved to hold Grace and soon became attached. She was 16 years old, short, petite, and pretty, and still in high school. Olive became a regular visitor and as an only child she enjoyed our family of four girls.

One day she asked if she could take Grace home for a weekend and Mama consented. After taking Grace for an occasional weekend for a few months, her possessiveness took a strange turn. As she held Grace on the porch, Grace's pretty dimples showing, Olive said to Mama, "Do you think I could

*Grace Elizabeth, about
7 months, 1940.*

take Grace home with me? I could bring her down several times a week to see you all."

"You'll have to ask her father," Mama said. Just like that. Mama had a generous and compassionate side to her nature, but this was going too far. Perhaps she was flattered that someone else loved her baby as much as she. Perhaps she felt overwhelmed with the care of four girls. Also, Mama was pregnant again. She'd soon have five to take care of, with two in diapers; and she was an immature 24-year-old.

Olive asked my father at the earliest opportunity. He said, "It's OK with me." Olive took our precious baby home to live with her that September—when Grace was nine months old and Olive was still 17 and in high school.

The house seemed strangely quiet without the baby sounds of laughter and cooing, and Grace's beautiful smile. I didn't like it one bit that Olive took my sister away. How could Mama do this? While Olive was in school, her mother, whom Grace came to call "Aunt Martha," took care of Grace. "Uncle Claude" had an income tax business in his office in the back of their large house.

Olive Hillegass, about 17.   *Esther Williams, 1937.*

The next year, on March 20, 1941, Ruth Ethel was born, 14 months after Grace. She was just as much a marvel to me as Grace had been. I loved her on the spot and as she grew I loved to play with her. She got lots of attention and Mama scolded that we were spoiling her. Ruth was named after Mama's sister Ruth (a favorite aunt on Mama's side) and Ethel for Daddy's Cousin Ethel who lived in western Pennsylvania. Cousin Ethel had two daughters the ages of Millie and me.

Meanwhile, life at Olive's became a nightmare for Grace. When both parents were drunk, they fought. As Grace grew older she dreaded the fights.

Olive treated Grace like a princess, buying her nice clothes, taking her to a roller-skating rink and a cowboy ranch of hillbilly singers who had a daily radio program. Occasionally we went to the ranch, too. At the skating rink, Grace mostly sat on the bench with the organist. At the end of the evening, Olive put pretty Grace in skates on the rink for people to admire.

When "Uncle Claude's" tax clients came to the house, Grace sang for them, "Mare's eat oats and does eat oats and little lambs eat ivy, a kid'll eat ivy too, wouldn't you?" and they gave her a quarter.

When Olive brought Grace home for several days she slept with me and I'd make up stories in bed. Her favorite was "The Peanut Man," a happy memory of which she'd speak to me for years to come. When Olive came back to pick up Grace, we often hid behind the garage. Grace did not want to go back so we'd conspire together. But someone always found us and off Grace went. Grace couldn't understand why she wasn't with her family and was confused about who her mother was. Years later she told me, "I asked Olive and everyone else I knew why Mama gave me away. But I never got an answer."

Mama holding Ruth, me, Anna, Millie, Daddy holding Grace; summer 1941.

Auntie Esther seemed to be in and out of our lives those early years and lived with us off and on and worked at the hosiery mill. One day when she came home she heard Anna crying.

"Where's Anna?" Esther demanded.

"I locked her in the cellar."

"Locked her in the cellar! What's the matter with you?" The cellar was damp and dark and unpleasant. Livid, Esther pushed the dead latch and opened the door. Anna, scared and red-eyed, ran into Esther's arms.

34

"Don't you know better than to treat a child like that?" she yelled. "What did she do to deserve that?"

"She whines and cries for nothing. She's such a daddy's baby and I get sick of it!"

"Well, you better straighten up and treat these children right!" Esther scolded.

Anna remembers, "Mama put me in the cellar way and pushed me down the stairs and locked the door. A snake was in the cellar once. It came up through the drain and I was so afraid of snakes. I cried and cried." Millie and I were devastated by these episodes and felt utterly helpless. How glad I was when Esther arrived and took charge with a vengeance.

Mama could be softhearted, but the slightest provocation could set her off. One day, when Anna was seven, Mama grabbed her by the arm and threw her across the kitchen. Anna's head hit the big iron handle of the back door. Blood poured from a cut above her eye. Scared, Mama washed and treated the wound. Then she told Anna, "You have a hole in your head. Don't tell Daddy what happened. If he asks you, tell him you fell against the stove." When Daddy came home from work and asked what happened, Anna obediently told him what Mama said.

Ruth Ethel, 1941.

At school, Anna was afraid of the teacher and cried every day. When she got home, Mama asked Millie and me if she cried at school. Anna remembers that if we said yes, she was punished, sometimes with eating raw onions. "I was always being punished," Anna says. "Mama called me dumb, so I thought I was, and I was afraid of everyone."

When Jean's older sister Ruth came to visit, she noticed Mama's treatment of Anna. Famous for her sharp tongue, Auntie Ruth lashed out, "You treat these girls too mean, especially Anna. You should be ashamed of yourself! It's time to stop that!"

(Many years later, when we were all grown and married, Helena Milz at church told Millie, "When Anna was little she was the saddest looking child that I and the others at church ever saw." I'm glad we have pictures of her with her sisters and brother where she has the sweetest smile of all. She did outgrow the whining and became as silly as the rest of us.)

Mama's changes from jolly to volatile caused me distress. I often lay awake at night after everyone else was asleep and I'd think about my mother in heaven with God, wishing I could be with her. I'd cry and ask God again, *Why? Why did our mother have to die?* For years I believed she would come back. One day, the truth dawned on me: my mother would never come back. That was a sad day indeed.

However, sometimes in bed the Spirit comforted me with the verses *"God is love"* and *"He cares for you."* Peace and joy flooded my being. I could talk to God who loved me as my father loved me. I *knew* He was LOVE! A calm security enveloped me and soon I fell asleep.

With few toys in the house, we girls were resourceful and had all kinds of play. We cut out pictures of paper children from the Sears catalog then cut out dresses to fit them. Millie drew beautiful clothes for her paper dolls and colored them with pencil crayons. She was the artist in the family and still has the collection of paper clothes.

And we girls sang. How we sang! Daddy enjoyed taking the family for rides in the car, his favorite family pastime. Mama, too, loved to go for a ride. Many times Daddy told us, "Look around at the beautiful world God made." I learned to love nature as I saw it through Daddy's eyes. Whenever we'd fuss in the back seat Daddy said, "Why don't you sing?" So sing we did. He loved to hear us sing, usually Sunday school songs. These songs of praise from the lips of children helped diffuse tension and brought peace into our car and our home.

Daddy's cousin Ethel, 18 years old, 1926.

But peace was often short lived, especially when four girls in the house and car became five. I wondered at times, *Will Grace ever come home to stay?*

36

CHAPTER 5

Life Goes On

Fill us each morning with your constant love,
so that we may sing and be glad all our life.
PSALM 90:14 (GNB)

1941–1948

As my sisters and I grew and learned to know our neighbors, our world expanded. Our house was part of a cluster of homes, like a charming little village in a picturesque setting along the north-south Thatcher Road. Behind our house, just to the east and down a gradual slope from our house, flowed the tree-lined Tohickon Creek. In summertime, I loved the cheery feeling of watching the sunrise over the small hill beyond the creek. At night it was comforting to see the big moonrise there as well. A farmhouse and buildings on the far hill gave evidence of another family I hoped to meet someday. Daddy said Bleams lived there. Many days a foggy mist hung over the creek until the sun rose high enough to melt it away. Our house was the last one before the big iron bridge crossing the creek to the south, where the creek curved on its way toward town, then made a wide arc back north. With spring rains, the creek rose high into the fields behind the house – an awesome sight – and flooded the road at the bridge.

Those early years, the big two-story brick house next door stood empty, the yard silent. Across the street from it was the small fieldstone church where we girls attended Sunday school. Tall poplars graced the churchyard and a long red horse shed, a remnant from the pre-automobile era, stood to the south of the lot. Beyond was the cemetery with its century-old grave-stones. Across from the church, on the corner of Thatcher and Erie Avenue, a dirt road leading to town, was a lovely stone farmhouse where a middle-aged couple, the Hagers, lived. Mrs. Hager baked yummy yeast loaves that she sometimes gave us and Mr. Hager owned a meat market in town.

A short distance past the brick house on our side of the road lived my father's stepsister Priscilla and husband Levi Kulp, in a nice, big double house. Priscilla grew lots of flowers and gave Mama zinnias, marigolds, and petunias in the spring. Mama enjoyed visiting with Priscilla. Her kind friendly ways always made me feel warm and safe inside. Across the road from Kulps and down a lane was the farm where Daddy walked to get our milk before breakfast several times a week. He'd take a shortcut on a path through the field. I liked going on that path for the milk when I got older, holding the nickel in my hand to pay for it.

Up the road a short distance from Priscilla's house was the one-room school we would all attend. Neat fields of tall corn and timothy hay grew along the road in summer. Trees in abundance dotted the landscape, especially along the creek and to the west. At the brick house next door two great sugar maple trees stood like sentinels and turned a spectacular red, orange, and yellow in the fall. But the empty house gave me a lonely feeling.

About the summer of 1941 a family moved into the brick house, Charles and Anna Renninger. What an exciting day! Fortunate for us, they had two boys. Richard was my age and James a few years younger. However, Mama kept a wary eye on the new neighbors at first, as she was very protective of us. But once she got to know Mrs. Renninger, Mama sometimes allowed us to play with the boys. This development added interest to our existence.

Thatcher Road, c.1977. On right: our white house, Renninger's, Priscilla and Levi's; On left: Flatland Mennonite Church.

As time went on we relished games of hide and seek, Red Rover, cowboys and Indians, and tag. In the fall we raked great piles of leaves to jump in under their magnificent, blazing maples. "Mr. and Mrs. Wren," as we came to affectionately call them, endeared themselves to us girls with their friendly, caring, and humorous natures. Mama usually got along with Mrs. Wren, but if she had a complaint, Mama told her off pronto. Mrs. Wren had a fiery temper as well and sometimes let fly at Mama. Usually complaints about whose children had done what precipitated the trouble.

We girls loved our Wednesday night visits to Grammy and Pappy Landis to see "Baby Butter," as Daddy called brother Ralph. As he grew older I enjoyed romping and playing with him. Grammy and Pappy were kind to us, and our youngest aunts, Jean and Matilda, were fun to play with. I remember playing "One potato, two potato, three potato, four..." Aunt Matilda says we played "Stone Teacher," as one person held a stone in a fist and if another guessed which hand, they advanced up the steps. It was a blessing in disguise that Ralph grew up with our mother's family, as these visits kept us bonded with them. Millie recalls fantasizing about running away to their house, about an eight-mile distance, when Mom's anger boiled over at us. Millie dreamed of living with Grammy and Pappy. I, on the other hand, often planned in bed how I would run away to the creek, walk up toward the school and climb up a very tall tree and sit there. I was sure no one would find me. Then I'd think of how hungry I'd get, and I'd miss my nice warm bed. This secret fantasy held the fascination of an escape.

Daddy disciplined us kindly when we were small. His empathy and compassion showed on his face. He told me, "Do what Mama tells you." He wanted to keep us out of trouble. So I obeyed her because I loved him and wanted to do what was right. At the table Daddy told us, "Say your prayer." Daddy folded his hands on the table before every meal and prayed silently, his lips moving. Observing this ritual day after day told me that Daddy believed in God, that God was good and loving, and I wanted to love God and be good.

Standing: Anna, me, Ralph; Seated: Millie, 1939.

Whenever we didn't want to clean our plate, Daddy recited a verse he probably learned from his mother or maybe Jacob Bryan. It went:

Do not throw upon the floor the crumbs you cannot eat,
For many a little hungry one would think it quite a treat.
For willful ways make woeful wants and I may live to say,
Oh, how I wish I had those crumbs that once I threw away.

If we fought, Daddy asked, "What does your Sunday school teacher say?" and quoted our memory verse, "Be ye kind one to another" (Eph. 4:32, KJV). His admonition stuck, but complying was not always easy. Yet, more often than not, we girls were kind to each other and as we got older, we tried to outdo one another in being generous.

The early years, as we girls rode our tricycles and scooters down the short sidewalk behind the house, I'd enjoy having Daddy sit on the back steps with us. But he often had a sad, far off look in his eyes, and deep wrinkles in his forehead, and I grieved with him.

My love for my daddy remained constant as a young girl. When he was home I spent time near him in the kitchen or outside, hanging around when neighbor men came to chat. I soaked up the adult conversation, though sometimes it was in Pennsylvania Dutch, which I couldn't understand. I liked Saturday mornings, which Daddy spent in the kitchen, washing up, shaving, reading the paper, and listening to the radio. As I hung out with him there, he'd tell tidbits of news from town, of chats with people in the grocery store, the meat market, the garage, or his job and be his happy relaxed self. I liked how he used big words like "fluctuate," and he'd say with a smile, "People are so accommodating." He'd call me "Sunshine" or "Janie Lee from sunny Tennessee." Later when we got TV, Mama sat in the front room watching it. The warmth of those memories cheered me through dreary days to come. Even though I probably said little, the deep bond of love and companionship between us grew stronger. I felt special and loved by Daddy. But when Mama was around, he was more guarded, and this I understood.

The early years Mama taught us girls a card game called "Haus and Peffer" which we hated. We suspected that she cheated as she held her cards down in her lap, and we couldn't win. We were so young. She enjoyed herself immensely. When relaxed and in a good mood, she seemed to love our company, telling us stories from her past, reading to us, or playing games with us.

After Millie went to school, and Anna and Ruth were napping, I remember some pleasant times alone with Mama. In the afternoons she made a special snack for us—little butter sandwiches. She'd cut the crusts off a slice of bread, spread it thick with butter, fold it in half and then in half again into a tiny sandwich just my size. Or she'd crumble crackers into a cup of milk, add sugar, and what a treat that was. I felt special and privileged as she shared these treats and talked to me just like I was her friend.

One day, when Grace was five, Daddy went to Olive and said, "Grace has to come home now. It's time for her to go to school." Suddenly, Olive was left without "her" child. And Grace struggled to understand her place in our home. Though she knew us from many previous visits, this permanent change was hard and confused her. She became part of our family but sometimes spent weekends at Olive's.

Grace's presence changed the dynamics of our family life. Ruthie felt deposed from her spot as the youngest who got lots of attention. Now the two girls had to share the spotlight. The weakened family bond from Grace's long absence took its toll. She felt like an outsider, a misfit. Used to Olive's undivided attention, she chafed at being one of five sisters. When Grace and Ruth fought, Mom's frustration level rose. Grace hated Mom's yelling. Grace and I still had a special relationship and slept together and were good buddies. One summer we spent a week together at Auntie Ruth and Uncle Walter's in Slatington, when Grace was five and I was ten.

Ruth, age 5, 1946.

Grace and me, c. 1947.

Millie was my best friend and mentor. I could not imagine life without Millie and Anna and we always stuck together. When Mama was mean, we'd go upstairs to talk about her. Grace and Ruth were dear to me too, though as their fights and feisty independence grew, tension resulted. Mama sternly told us older girls, "You may not hit Grace and Ruth."

When Daddy tried to discipline them, Mama got upset. One day she yelled, "Your girls are angels and mine are no good! I'll pack my things and take my girls and leave!" She packed a suitcase and off they walked down the road. Before long Daddy got in the car and went after them and brought them back. How I wished he'd let her go! "Her girls." "His girls." I hated times like this and felt sorry for the girls too.

After several episodes of this scenario, Mama left in a huff again one day. Exasperated beyond endurance, Daddy went to Mrs. Renninger next door and asked her advice. "Let her go," she counseled, "she'll come back." This time Daddy did not drive after her. Before long, up the road they came. Mama, subdued for the moment, never did that again.

Considering that Daddy had six children in eight years from two mothers, five girls under one roof, with all the complexities – and parenting being the "hardest job in the world" – it's amazing that Mama and Daddy stayed together. Their commitment astounds me, and I see God's grace at work.

In a happy mood, Daddy often teased Mama about being Welsh. His kindness to her after an argument left a great impression on me. She sometimes went to the front room, sat on a chair, and sobbed quietly. Daddy would go to her, put his arms around her and comfort her with kind whispers. I have often been grateful for this demonstration of tenderness on his part. And I'm sure Mama's heart was touched as well and some of her pain melted away.

One summer when Ralph was very young he came to stay with us for a week. What a special time for us girls! But Mama's loud scolding upset him and he was too scared to come back again for vacation. This made me sad indeed. I loved my brother as dearly as my daddy, and as we grew older this relationship blossomed into a close friendship. Our visits to the Landis grandparents and my relationship with Ralph provided a sense of comfort and security and made life more bearable. But as years went by, we didn't go as regularly on Wednesday nights. Ralph has told me how he'd watch for us at the window every Wednesday. With no phone, we never called before going so he had no idea if we'd come. As the evening wore on and we didn't show up, he was very disappointed.

Me, age 8, 1943.   *Ralph, age 10, 1948.*

Mama took her responsibility of raising us three girls seriously. But I cringed inside when she'd tell people, "I treat them all alike. I try to raise them like their mother would have." Her favoritism toward her two girls was obvious to us three older ones. Did her strictness with us grow out of pressure she felt to make us "good" in the eyes of our mother's family? Perhaps the shadow of our mother's memory and her relatives, plus our church people, made Mama determined to make us "good Christians;" hence her strict rules. But she rarely went to church herself. We felt somewhat strange buying Mama cigarettes at the gas station on the highway to town, but didn't mind the walk on a nice summer day. In those days, a young child could buy anything at all.

A strong point of Mama was her resourcefulness in a tight spot. One Friday night when Daddy was at work, we were all in bed when someone knocked on the front door. Tramps occasionally came through the neighborhood in daytime, but who was this at night? Mama got up, went down the stairs to the door and yelled, "Ralph, come down with your shotgun!" The knocking stopped. Daddy never owned a gun and there was none in the house.

As we got older, Mama read to us in bed when Daddy was gone on Friday nights. She found Thomas Herbert Russell's *The Sinking of the Titanic* in the house and read it to us for a bedtime story. She'd lie in bed in her room and we in our beds as she read. This was quite a feat with her third-grade education. Stumped on a word, she'd spell it out and Millie, a good reader by then, pronounced the word. Every so often she'd interrupt with, "Are you still awake?" We were, listening spellbound to the tragic story of this magnificent ship said to be unsinkable. The sad ending and mournful singing of "Nearer My God to Thee" sent shivers up my spine. We felt a unity with Mama in experiencing this sad, monstrous event. (I still have that tattered 1912 edition from which Mama read to us.)

Mama was a good cook, despite the fact that we had "raw fried potatoes" much too often. Her roasts and fried chicken on Sundays when her relatives came down were the best. And how I loved her fruit pies, especially peach. She canned a lot of peaches, green beans, and tomatoes. And she made the prettiest Easter eggs I have ever seen. Using Q-tips and small bottles of food color, she dabbed the eggs with little bright splotches. The greens and blues were especially beautiful, and all us girls remember her artistic gift with eggs that we cannot duplicate. Cookies were baked only at Christmas in many shapes with cookie cutters. Without icing or colored sprinkles, they were the best, dipped in milk, and as we got older, in coffee. Mama called them A.P.'s cookies. Years later Aunt Naomi gave me a cookbook from her church with an A.P.'s recipe in it! A favorite of the family was fried shredded wheat, perhaps from Daddy's background. It is delectable, made with milk and eggs mixed together as for French toast but using shredded wheat instead and eaten with milk like cereal. (Millie fondly remembers Daddy's cracker omelet that he made for us with large oyster crackers.)

Mama had experienced plenty of tragedies and she never shied away from the tragic. Sometimes I wonder if she had a morbid preoccupation with tragic events. For years she recorded in a notebook the deaths of everyone she knew—and some she didn't, recorded from the newspaper—as well as other important events and dates.

One day when we were older she read in the newspaper of a young woman who shot herself in the forehead. She called the husband and offered to take care of their three young children while his wife recuperated in the hospital. Fortunately, Peggy, the pretty dark-haired mother, recovered and Mama told us she grew bangs to hide the scar. I often wondered how she could shoot herself in the forehead and only have a scar, but we never knew the details. Mama befriended Peggy and her husband and for years they came to visit in our home.

One day after we were older and our neighbor, Richard, had learned to play the trumpet, we girls with Richard and James decided to put on a "program" on their front porch for cars passing by. Their house was across the street from the church and churchyard. When darkness fell, someone turned on the porch light and we girls sang lustily while Richard blared away on his trumpet. What a blast! All of a sudden, Grace and Ruth screamed, pointing to the churchyard. We older ones grew quiet as we watched a white "ghost" coming from the direction of the cemetery. As it crossed the church lawn, Grace and Ruth ran crying into Renninger's house. Mr. and Mrs. Renninger came out to see what was the commotion. The "ghost" drew closer and closer, and walked across the street toward us. Then, as I suspected, Mama lifted the sheet and laughed! She would not be left out of our fun, so decided to create some of her own. Mama's irrepressible love of fun sometimes carried her away, but we preferred this side of her personality. When we were all happy and having fun, Mama enjoyed her brood.

One year Anna and I both broke out in a rash and Mama called Dr. Weisel. A fatherly type, he always came to the house with his satchel. He diagnosed it as scarlatina (scarlet fever) and prescribed bed rest with no light, which could hurt our eyes. During that week or two in bed in the upstairs middle room, with shades drawn, we had no stress or chores. Mama was nice to us and I remember a special time with Anna as we "hung out" and laughed a lot. With meals served in bed, it was never more fun to be sick.

I remember the day when Mama made rice pudding and put it in a big glass bowl with small handles at each side. I loved rice pudding. It was still warm when she said, "Jane, carry this rice pudding down to the cellar to cool." As I began my perilous descent on the narrow steps, Mama said, "Now don't fall!" I was halfway down or more, with the big dish in front of me blocking my view of the stairs, when I missed a step and took a tumble. Crying and wailing, I landed with the dish and pudding splattered into smitherines and goo. Amazed that Mama did not scold me this time, I could have kissed her!

In spite of the hard times, I loved having fun and enjoying my family and became the family clown. (Ruth tells me *she* was, probably later when I became more serious.) Small and wiry, I shimmied up the doorframe in my bare feet one summer, much to Mama's amusement. When friends or relatives came to the house, she'd say, "Jane, show them how you can shimmy up the door" and, lickety-split, up I'd go, to hilarious laughter. Anna, as agile as I, learned the same trick. We girls could all be silly and crazy as monkeys, and when Mama was in a good mood, she reveled in the fun. But woe-be-tide if we pulled out all the stops at the table. She'd squelch our noise

45

with a stern look and warning, "If you don't stop laughing, you can get away from the table!" We settled down but the food went down so much better after a good laugh.

Daddy suffered from hay fever and asthma. One day he came home from the doctor and told Mama, "Dr. Weisel says I need to quit my job at the bakery and get a job outside. All the flour dust is bad for me. He says I need sunshine and fresh air." So he applied for a job with the borough, as our town was called, and soon enjoyed mowing the big lawn at the town park, driving garbage truck and snow plows in winter, and keeping the town streets in good shape. In summer he sported a bronze tan and his developing muscles improved his physique.

Through the years, while I vacillated between anger and warmth toward Mama, enjoyed the fun times and struggled to love her, Millie has told me, "I just avoided her." Yes, Millie, quiet and reserved, kept out of Mama's way. Millie had a sweet nature and many friends in school. Anna lived in mortal fear of Mama since having to eat raw onions. Anna says, "I remember crying at school a lot, especially my first year. Mama told me, 'You're dumb like me.' And I was so scared of the teacher and the lessons."

One of her most painful memories was that on Friday afternoons, when Mama was expecting her family to visit on the weekend, she kept Anna home from school. "Tell the teacher you have a headache," she coached, "and stay home to help me this afternoon." Anna dutifully obeyed. Mama always chose Anna, the easiest to control, and wrote "headache" on the excuse blank. Anna hated staying home and being forced to lie.

As Anna grew older she learned to jabber to Mama and appeared carefree as a summer breeze. They seemed like best friends. But inside, Anna's fears lurked below the surface. She says, "I acted like that because I was so scared of her."

One day, after we were all school age, Mama said to us three girls, "I'm sorry for the way I treated you girls when you were small." She looked so humble and sincere. And I'm sure she meant it. I was amazed. But we wondered if she would change. Her confession impressed me and I wanted to believe she would change, but my faith was small. At the time, we five girls didn't realize what a "handful" we were—literally.

Through the years, I've pondered Mama's unusual apology. What made her do it? Could it have been Auntie Ruth's sharp reprimands when she visited us and saw Mama yell at Anna? Or could it have been her reading of the Bible? When she and Daddy joined the Mennonite church, they were given a Bible. Mama heard us talk about how we were reading through our Bibles, as we learned at camp.

Mama surprised us one day when she said, "I'm reading through my Bible, too. Let's see who gets done first." True to her love of games, she wanted to race. While we girls read only a chapter a day, she read while we were in school. We didn't care to race her. One day she beamed, "I beat you reading my Bible. I finished today!" This seemed unfair to me, though I realized it was good she had read it. And I've wondered, was she convicted of her early treatment of us when she read Jesus' words? In Mark 10:14-16 (NKJ), He says, " 'Let the little children come to Me, and do not forbid them, for of such is the kingdom of God...whoever does not receive the kingdom of God like a little child will by no means enter it.' And He took them up in his arms, laid His hands on them, and blessed them." Or his very strong words, "It were better for him that a millstone were hanged about his neck, and be cast into the sea, than that he should offend one of these little ones" (Luke 17:2, KJV). Or perhaps it was one of Jesus' many commands to "love one another." Whatever it was, I believe the Holy Spirit spoke to her through Jesus' words and the many calls to love in the New Testament.

After we were all in grade school, Mama got a job in a cigar factory in town. It seemed a strange job for a woman. But Mama made a number of good friends there. Now we were unsupervised after school. Sometimes Grace and Ruth got into fights. When Ruth became too physical, I'd hold her wrists to restrain her, since at that point I was still bigger and stronger than she. Ruth hated Grace so much that one day she ran after her with the butcher knife in the kitchen. How tragedy was averted that day I cannot recall. Guardian angels were surely watching over us. While Ruth has often told this story through the years, she and Grace are good friends today and Grace does not feel any animosity from Ruth. Millie recalls, "I was so afraid that day of what Ruth would do."

In the winter of 1947, a great swirling blizzard dumped 26.4 inches of snow on New York City in 24 hours (according to an online *New York Times* article, dated February 14, 2006, when that record was broken by one-half inch more snow). Many states, including Ohio and Pennsylvania experienced the greatest snowstorm in memory. We girls loved it and we built an igloo in our back yard, probably with help from Richard and James. The snow was good for packing and we made blocks of snow and put a roof on our rounded igloo. Two windows had wide windowsills. On one of them I stood a small oil lamp that I got for Christmas that year. How I loved that place of play and, at times, solitude. Millie and Anna also fondly remember the fun we had in the igloo that year.

I delighted in the out-of-doors—running, climbing the tree in the front yard, jumping rope, and rambling in the fields. Mama called me a tomboy. One summer when Mr. Renninger cut the hay, he had a huge pile in the driveway before putting it up in the haymow. Renningers always had goats, and we loved the babies. That day, Mrs. Renninger I suspect, gathered the goats and us all together on top of the hay and took a picture. That picture is a treasure. No longer were the brick house and yard a lonely place. We had the time of our lives with our great neighbors in the freedom of the out-of-doors, whether wading in or sledding down to the creek, playing Hide and Seek or Red Rover, or romping in the leaves or new mown hay. God blessed all us Herstines immensely with these good neighbors.

Yes, summer was fun. But school days brought challenge and the punishment of my life.

The gang, c.1946. Back: James and Richard Renninger with goats. Front: Ruth, Grace, me with goat, Anna, and Millie with goat.

CHAPTER 6

School Days and Growing Pains

Lord our God, may your blessings be with us.
Give us success in all we do!
PSALM 90:17 (GNB)

1941–1949

At six years of age I walked the short distance to school with Millie on a beautiful fall morning. How exciting to join the big kids at Tohickon School! Our teacher, Mrs. Fluck, known as "Miss Dove" to many because of her kind, gentle nature—was married with no children. However, she became a mother to hundreds of school children through long years of teaching. Mrs. Fluck, whose family emigrated from England, kept a strict, orderly classroom, had high expectations, and tolerated no nonsense. I was in awe of her.

Each morning we alternated between reciting The Lord's Prayer or the 23rd Psalm for devotions. (After I joined church I learned that she was a member of our church. I am grateful for her godly influence in my young life and later life as well.)

My favorite part of school that first year was our Dick and Jane reader, which I quickly learned to read. But the days grew long and, as winter came on, I was often upset and had a stomachache before school. I cried at the breakfast table and Mama's cold stares bore into me. Daddy spoke softly and kindly to me, "Eat your oatmeal so you can go to school." I'd force the food down and off I went.

I was a good student, though I struggled with and disliked arithmetic. When I was in third grade Mrs. Fluck asked me to help Roberta, who was five. She could read before she came to school and was promoted to second grade, but needed help with other lessons. One day at recess a plane flew overhead and some boys said, "The world is going to come to an end today!" Hearing that, Roberta began to cry and would not stop. She repeated to Mrs.

Fluck what the boys said and wailed, "I want to be with my mother when the world ends!"

Though Mrs. Fluck assured her that would not happen, Roberta was inconsolable. Mrs. Fluck asked for a volunteer to walk her home and I volunteered. Her father, a brother to Mr. Renninger, owned the gas station where we got cigarettes for Mama on the road to town. Roberta and I walked the mile or so together, then I walked back to school. Being trusted with this responsibility boosted my confidence. (Years later, when Roberta came to the college I attended, she told me how much she appreciated my help at school and walking her home that day. I hadn't seen her in years and had forgotten the incident. She said she sometimes walked to school on that busy highway by herself when she was five; she also sold cigarettes to customers at the gas station at age seven!)

Sometimes in nice weather, when Mrs. Fluck worked with the older grades and my class had our work done, she sent us out to play in the meadow under a big tree down near the creek. How I relished these unexpected times and beautiful warm days. The great oak with its long branches hanging near the ground reminded me of the poem "Trees" by Joyce Kilmer that Mrs. Fluck had us memorize. The framed poem with a picture of a tree hung on the wall of the schoolroom. The exquisite imagery in the poem evoked an even greater love of trees in me: trees to climb, trees for shade on a hot summer day, trees whose rustling leaves sang me to sleep on a windy night. I loved the trees around our house, the big hickory nut in front and the walnut in back, the smaller maple with branches low enough to climb, and the stately maples at Renningers next door.

During winter, sinus infections, earaches, and sore throats dogged my days and kept me awake nights. The house full of smoke from Mama's cigarettes and Daddy's cigar surely aggravated or caused my respiratory problems. Auntie Esther smoked too (as well as some of Mama's relatives who visited) and times when she lived with us added unacceptable levels of secondhand smoke to our lungs. Emotional trauma also contributed to my poor health. Mama got upset if she had to get up with us at night but Daddy never complained. His kindly ministrations gave relief and comfort to body and soul. Many a night I cried with an earache, and he'd take me to the kitchen, blow cigar smoke in my ear and put in eardrops and cotton. Then he'd heat a clothes iron without the handle on the stove, or a crock pie plate, wrap it in a towel and I'd take it to bed with me. This special attention and his tender, caring spirit endeared Daddy to me even more. Feeling safe and comforted, I soon fell asleep.

My poor health continued and when I was ten, I had a tonsillectomy. Lonely and homesick in the hospital, I hardly appreciated having a girl my age named Jean in the same room, who also had her tonsils out. I fought hard when the nurse put the ether mask over my face; other nurses told my parents I screamed so loudly that they heard me way down the hall. Mama and Daddy visited me once, while Jean's parents came often. The minutes and hours dragged by. At a time like this, I longed for my mother.

Our landlord didn't own a car and often walked to our place to visit. He was a jolly, thin man who enjoyed children. He liked to stop at mealtimes to get a free meal and would joke and tease us. Nelse, as we called him, lived with an old couple. One day, after the couple died, I overheard Daddy tell Mama, "Nelse needs a new place to live. He says whoever keeps him till he dies will get his house." I worried. Would our house be taken away from us? The next thing I knew Nelse was moving in with us. I was overjoyed. My worries evaporated. We'd get to keep this beloved house forever, without paying for it.

With the bedrooms full, Nelse slept on the couch in the front room downstairs. At first it was fun having him around every day when we came home for lunch and after school. One of his favorite pastimes was rolling newspaper into long thin rolls for kindling for the stove. He liked showing us how to do it. He'd take one large sheet, fold the corners over in a certain way, then roll it on the table, drawing the paper toward him as he rolled. With a small tight end and the other one larger, it looked like a long thin cone.

Before long I began to see a change in Nelse. His jolly spirit faded and his eyes turned sad. Mama treated him like she treated us, putting food on his plate and scolding him to eat it all, whether he liked it or not. I felt immeasurably sad for him and helpless.

Then one day Nelse got sick. After a three-month siege of illness, during which time he stayed mostly on the couch, he died at age 66, on the last day of December 1945. I have wondered if he died of pneumonia. We children were told to stay in the kitchen where we played with our new toys. A somber sadness settled over the house. Daddy called the Kookers, members of our church, to come until the undertaker came. Our spirits rose as this friendly couple chatted and laughed with us in the kitchen. Daddy and Mama often depended on Helen and Clarence in times of need.

Nelse had attended church and Sunday school regularly for years in the little church across the street. After he died we got his books, most of which he had received as gifts for perfect attendance in Sunday school. As I grew older and found his books in the attic and read *The Vision of Christ* (by Rev. William Miller), I got a glimpse of Nelse's faith and was comforted. This eccentric, kind man had gone to a better place.

I knew that Mama didn't like when Daddy gave me attention, so I didn't feel as free and open with him as I may have otherwise. She seemed jealous of my good relationship with him because he was nice to me. With my dear brother living at Grammy's, crushes on boys at school filled a need for me. Mama had a rule that we couldn't date until we were out of high school, which seemed far away. This wasn't "dating" but I knew it was against her rules. I couldn't see any harm in *liking* a boy. Boys were good friends, like my brother, and showed an interest in me. For a while I had two boyfriends at the same time. They were handsome, both with dark hair and eyes and both lived at the children's home less than a mile from our house. Richard's moodiness and unpredictability probably stemmed from the fact that he was from a broken home and away from his family. Raymond, on the other hand, was the opposite – happy and carefree. His younger brother Seth was an exact look-alike with matching personality. Grace, five grades behind me, had a crush on Seth. She liked looking at the clock at the back of the room because it had Seth's name on it – "Seth Thomas!"

My friendship with Richard and Raymond brightened my life. For a time, we wrote each other notes every day. I took mine home, put them in a paper bag, and stored it in the attic away from Mama's prying eyes. She couldn't get through the small hole in the ceiling so she'd ask me to get things down or put things up. "Be careful to walk on the beams," she'd warn. "Don't step on the Sheetrock." One day I forgot and my foot came crashing through – for the first and last time. I didn't get a scolding, from either Mama or Daddy, who did the repair job.

The Quakertown Community Children's Home about a half mile down the road played an important part in our lives. The children attended our school and Sunday school for a number of years. Many were from Allentown, the big city north of us. They'd stay a few years and then, without warning, they were gone. It was hard to make friends and have to part from them abruptly and never see them again. (A number of years after Raymond and Seth left "the home," we read in the newspaper that they both died in a fiery pickup crash and I grieved for my two friends.)

The children from "the home" were so much a part of my life and as I learned of their broken homes, I grew in empathy for them. I felt happy that Daddy kept our family together and we didn't have to live at the home. Even though brother Ralph was at Grammy's, he was still in the family and had a loving home. As I reflected on this one day, I felt very grateful for Mama because Daddy did need someone to take care of us.

At school I wrote all my family's names and ages in my tablet, starting from the oldest to the youngest, from Daddy down to Ruth. At such times, I felt enveloped in a cocoon of family love. Daddy loved us. Mama took good care of us. She was always there (before the year she went to work), cooked our meals, washed and ironed our clothes, kept the house clean, with our help, and kept us together. She was our mother and she gave us Grace and Ruth. I felt a new love for her that surely God's Spirit put within me. On Mother's Day, my sisters and I picked tiny pink spring beauties for Mama in our front yard, a yearly ritual from the time we were small.

At Christmas each year, the children from "the home" had a free dinner at the ritziest place in Quakertown, Trainer's Seafood Restaurant on the 309 Highway from Allentown to Philadelphia. For several years, we girls were invited to join them. I wondered if it was because the home superintendent knew we were poor. Santa Claus came and we each received a box of candy and an orange. Mama made friends with three lovely outgoing sisters at the home, Mary, Betty and Frona, who were in high school. After they moved to Florida and married, Mama wrote to them for years. They sent pictures of themselves with beautiful palm trees. It seemed a wonderful life and I admired them – and they sure did like Mama.

When I was in fifth grade and Millie in seventh, we got an exciting new teacher named Eleanor Guri. Her parents had come from Russia. Eighteen years old and fresh out of high school, she was pretty, with blue eyes and dark, pageboy hair. Due to a teacher shortage, she was hired with the stipulation that she would continue her education with college classes evenings and weekends. Miss Guri's smile and sunny disposition, love of learning, books, and music enlivened school with fun. How amazing that she could handle all subjects in all eight grades! Her love of teaching and courage instilled in me a great respect for her and a desire to someday be a teacher like her.

But, alas, my warm fuzzy feelings were short-lived. One day on the playground my friend Janice and I were chasing Michael, a boy from the children's home. Before I knew it, just as he ran behind the girls' outhouse to escape us, I caught up with him and gave him a push. I watched in dismay as he slipped and fell in the muck. His clothes were covered with yucky mud. I felt bad about it but thought it was his fault for running that direction. Little did I know!

Our resourceful Miss Guri had set up a court to handle misdemeanors. On Friday afternoon, cases of the week were brought before the court. This court became my undoing. When court convened the next Friday, I was horrified to hear my name and the offense: "Jane Herstine pushed Michael Waltrix and he fell into the muck behind the girl's toilet." Inwardly I protested, *It was Michael's fault!* But the jury saw otherwise. Having no chance to defend myself, I looked helplessly across the room at Miss Guri. Surely this sweet lady would save me from my fate at the hands of this incompetent jury. But no, she let the process take its course. My heart pounded as I heard the "judge" read the worst punishment imaginable, "You will stand in the corner on the stage on one leg for ten minutes without touching anything."

Frozen with dread and humiliation I walked onto the stage to the corner and stood as sentenced. In defiance, I'm ashamed to admit (adding guilt to insult), I touched my thumb to the chalk tray in front of me every now and then to keep my balance. It was a matter of survival: touch the tray or crash.

When the ten minutes were up I hurried to my seat, put my head in my arms on my desk, and sobbed. I wished I could die. I was angry with Michael, angry with the jury, and angry with Miss Guri. Never in five years of school had I been punished (except for the time when a teacher slapped all of our hands with a ruler when no one would admit to stealing something, but that didn't count).

My one consolation was that it wasn't a spanking. Mama had a rule: if you get a spanking at school you'll get another one at home. None of us ever did, and I escaped, thanks to the jury.

My friend Janice Mann liked to tell me about watching wrestling on TV with her dad. We didn't have a TV those years. When Janice got a pony she invited me to come ride it. I didn't care about ponies but Mama let me go a few times after school. Janice lived just up the hill from the children's home. Through PTA meetings, Mama and her mother became telephone friends. PTA meetings were fun, with entertainment, and sometimes a play. A special one at Christmas one year was "The Little Match Girl," a fairy tale by Hans Christian Anderson about a poor girl. Millie had the honor of being the match girl! Mama must have been quite proud. Patsy Mullen and her father sometimes tap-danced together, a PTA treat.

When Daddy was in a happy mood, and peppy music came on the radio, he often danced in the kitchen with a big smile on his face. He had rhythm, and I loved how his joy in life showed in his merry eyes and dancing feet. He also liked to play "conductor" and conduct band music on the radio. His love of life and for his girls helped balance the bleaker days. (Millie remembers that when Daddy danced he'd say, "Ain't we got fun!" I say that to my husband but did not remember where it came from. I was glad for the reminder at Millie and Ralph's 50th wedding anniversary celebration! [August 24, 2008] For years, I have also enjoyed "dancing" in the kitchen to radio music!)

One evening in February our family all got into the car and ended up at Janice's house. *What are we doing here?* I wondered, as everyone piled out of the car. We never visited them. Once inside, I soon found out—a surprise birthday party for me! Janice and her mother had planned it and Mama, Daddy, and all my sisters attended. It was an amazing surprise. We never had parties at home, so this was special and a nice, friendly evening. I felt engulfed in a warm glow for many days after.

One thing I loved about school with Miss Guri was that she was a gifted, inspiring musician and played the piano beautifully. Every day we sang school songs and popular songs. Learning that Millie would like to play the piano, she began giving her free lessons after school. She also offered to teach me, but after a few lessons, Mama heard me practicing one day and snapped, "*Millie* can play the piano, but *you* can't!" *Why not?* I wondered. In a way I was relieved because I felt inadequate and didn't want to be embarrassed in front of Miss Guri if I didn't play well. *Yes, Millie is my big smart sister, so of course she can play and I can't*, I thought. She was in seventh grade and I was in fifth. Miss Guri gave Millie a wonderful gift. (Millie went on to take organ lessons, paid for by the church, and became our church organist for many years, from about age 15. When brother Ralph was old enough, he also took piano lessons and became church pianist, serving in that capacity into his sixties and beyond.)

Reading books from the library in our one-room school became a wonderful diversion when nothing was going on at home. But Mama scolded. "You always have your nose in a book! Anna helps with the work but you don't." Worse yet, she'd tell the same thing to anyone who came to the house. I chafed under her unfair criticism. Didn't I often help set the table, peel potatoes, and usually dry the dishes while Millie washed? Millie and I talked about Anna's "disappearing act" after meals, so we did the dishes. Yet here was Mama praising Anna and belittling me. I would never understand her. Why was she so hateful to me? Well, maybe Anna did help more as I sat in the middle room in a corner with my book. But life was good and I could be carefree and happy-go-lucky if I stayed out of Mama's way.

Middle row right: Miss Guri; Front row center, Millie in 8th grade, 1946.

When I was in sixth grade, the one-room schools consolidated and I was bussed to Shaw's School, several miles from home. I was glad I'd be coming back to Tohickon for seventh and eighth grades. Mrs. Kurtz, a motherly type, was our teacher for sixth that year. Millie stayed at Tohickon with Miss Guri. That year, when she was in eighth grade, a photographer took a picture of the class (partial picture shown).

What joy to be back at Tohickon with Miss Guri for seventh grade! (I forgave her for allowing me to endure that punishment, though I felt ashamed at times for having been naughty.) Our Busy Bee Club, initiated by Miss Guri, made the year especially exciting. Money-raising events helped acquire funds for a trip to New York City, 100 miles away. This was big time! Our family never traveled anywhere except to Mama's relatives and an occasional Landis family reunion in summers. (Only once did we travel to Daddy's cousin Ethel across the state. While there, Grace and I got chicken pox!)

Parents were needed as chaperones for our trip and, to my surprise, Daddy volunteered. I was thrilled. We visited the Empire State Building, the Cathedral of St. John the Divine, under construction for many years (Miss Guri was Catholic), Radio City Music Hall, and we climbed up the Statue of Liberty. For lunch we ate at Horne and Hardart's Automat. I walked past rows of food on little plates in glass compartments. All we had to do was open the door and take a plate of our choice, but I couldn't choose. There was too much and it all looked delicious. Finally Daddy said, "You better get something to eat because we have to leave soon." All I got was a small plate of macaroni and cheese, one of my favorite things Mama made. I was glad Daddy rescued me from starving on this wonderful trip.

The next year I was greatly disappointed to find that Miss Guri was gone. Our new teacher, Mrs. Kehler, looked very old. When I reported this at home, Daddy said, "She was *my* teacher when I was a boy back at Ottsville." She was a good teacher, I suppose, but such a change from the youthful Miss Guri.

For a diversion that year, I began writing stories and passed them one installment at a time to a classmate, who passed it to the next, and so on around the room. I loved to write and it was fun having others enjoy what I wrote and wait for the next episode.

Graduation Day was a special event. Mama was happy and even took a picture of me in a new white dress with my diploma. After a carefree summer, high school loomed ahead.

CHAPTER 7

Camp Adventures and Beyond

God is love.
I JOHN 4:16 (KJV)

1945–1952

When I was ten, a new adventure beckoned. Millie had attended summer camp before and this year was my turn. Our church encouraged all the children to attend Camp Men-O-Lan, about fifteen miles from our home. (*Men-O* was for Mennonite and *Lan* was for Landis, the man who donated the land.) Though I was too young to go at age ten, the church people decided that since Millie would be there, I should go too. They paid our way, so Mama consented.

The first night, as I sat on a blanket by a roaring campfire, I enjoyed singing the choruses with the campers from churches all over our district. Then the preacher spoke and I listened, spellbound. "All people on earth are sinners," he explained in effect. "We are all born in sin, and sinners go to hell when they die and burn in a lake of fire forever!" Shock and fear seized me and I couldn't believe my ears. He continued, "But God sent his Son Jesus to die on the cross so we might be forgiven," and quoted John 3:16, "For God so loved the world that He gave His only begotten Son, that whosoever believeth in Him, shall not perish but have everlasting life." "If you accept Jesus as your Savior, you can be saved and go to heaven when you die." There was much more, of course, but these gripping truths reverberated in my brain and I froze with fear.

Never had I heard anything so frightening. My imagination riveted on the vision of hellfire and brimstone forever and ever. The blazing fire before us provided the imagery. Now I saw clearly why Jesus had to die. God *made* Jesus die on the cross for the sins of the whole world. And *I* was guilty! It boggled my mind and sent shivers up my spine. My stomach ached worse than ever before. The idea of what God did to the kindest Man who ever lived, the most loving person, who loved "all the children of the world," was incomprehensible to me. This idea of God was a marked departure from my previous understanding of God as a loving Father. How could a God of love do something so terrible to His own Son and *make* Jesus get killed by bad men? I cried great heaving sobs.

I felt so bad that Jesus had to die. How I wished it wasn't true. But I couldn't get past the idea of God as LOVE to Jesus' death as a sacrifice for my sins. What had I done that was so bad anyway? From deep inside I cried out, *Please, God, no. Don't let it be true!* I felt condemned and helpless. Yet we were told God did this to save us from our sins and from hell. All we had to do was accept Jesus as our Savior.

When the minister gave the invitation, I went forward, still sobbing. The pastor prayed for us, but my heart was broken and I was inconsolable. I just wanted to go home to be with my sisters and Daddy, and for life to be like it was before. But it would never be the same. I was no longer an innocent child.

Still crying, I walked with the other girls on the dimly lit path through the woods back to the cabin. Though I loved the smells and sounds of nature, the exquisite fragrance of the damp woods, the fresh night air and friendly sounds of tree frogs croaking, tonight these escaped my senses. The darkened cabin, lit by one light bulb hanging from the ceiling, added to my gloom. I undressed and pulled my long, faded nightgown over my head as I continued to weep.

The counselor, Grace Moyer, thinking I was homesick, suggested, "How about if you get in bed with Millie?" Millie did not like anyone close to her in bed, the opposite of me, but she agreed. Craving comfort, I crawled in beside her. But I knew she wasn't happy about it and I felt rejected again. First rejected by God, whom I had talked to for years as a God of love, and now by my beloved "mother" sister Millie. Feeling overwhelmed by fright, I finally fell asleep, grateful for Millie beside me.

With the sunshine of a new day, the world looked brighter and God had a surprise in store for me. Little did I know His loving heart wept with me the night before and He had grieved at this frightening tactic to get children into His kingdom. Jesus never scared children but took them on His lap and blessed them as He said, "Of such is the kingdom of heaven." But God knew what He had planned for me in the years ahead and that I would come to understand that Christ came *willingly* to give His life. Oh, what a glorious truth! God did not force Him to die. And God was watching over me, He loved me, He delighted in me, and wanted to bless me.

Martha Burkhalter and me, age 10, 1945.

In missions class that morning, Martha Burkhalter, missionary to India, was dressed in a pretty Indian dress. "This dress is called a *sari*," she told us, "and I have a small sari for a small girl. After class the smallest girl at camp will get to wear the sari." Later, as we gathered outside, she lined up the girls, came to me and said, "You are the smallest one." What an honor! She first made a skirt with the long sari then wound the sheer cotton flowered print round and around my slight form and draped one end over my head and shoulders. Though feeling shy with this important missionary teacher, I also felt special and proud to wear the Indian dress. I'm grateful for the picture someone took of us. It shows the bow in my hair and happy smile on my face. This helped make up for the night before. It was as if Miss Burkhalter had wrapped me in a cocoon of God's love, reassuring me that all was well. God had comforted me.

I loved meal times at camp—the food, and the joyful singing as we waited in line to get into the dining hall, and again around the table. A favorite we sang over and over was "R-E-T-R-E-A-T retreat, that's a word that we think can't be beat for it has helped us solve the problems that we meet, so let us sing it, and sing it, aga-a-a-ain," and round and round it went. Classes were interesting. But every night, the campfire messages captured my imagination and I trembled inside, wondering if I'd go to hell when I died. I felt like I was being stalked by a bad dream. But it wasn't a dream. The thought was just too awful and I tried to put it out of my mind. Homesickness dogged me throughout that week.

It seems word got back to Mama that I had cried that first night. Maybe Millie sent a postcard home and wrote of it. At any rate, Mama called the camp and asked to speak to my counselor. I can imagine her saying, "What made Jane cry so at camp? I want you to come to my house so we can have a talk. Otherwise, she has to come home." Mama demanded that Grace Moyer leave camp and go to our house. How amazing to learn this story from Grace fifty years later in our college town of Bluffton, Ohio. Now married, she was Grace Frounfelker.

"I don't remember the conversation," Grace told me, "but it was very unpleasant." Grace's sweet, loving personality impressed me and she became a special role model. We corresponded after camp and again after our meeting in Bluffton (in 1995). I heard from her at Christmas until a few years before she died in 2006. (Grace wrote an inspiring book, *As A Little Child* [Herald Press, 1998], with wonderful stories of children, and Jesus' admonition for us to become like little children. She tells of her own sexual and psychological abuse as a child and how she came to healing.)

Millie remembers that the first year she went to camp, when she was almost 11, she asked Jesus to come into her heart. An invitation was given at campfire but she didn't go forward. Later she felt bad for not having done so. That night she talked with the counselor who prayed with her. She said, "I cried myself to sleep that night because I felt so bad for Jesus and how he suffered." Camp counselors told campers they should tell their parents they accepted Jesus into their hearts. So on the way home in the car Millie said to everyone, "I asked Jesus to come into my heart." Daddy was driving; Mama sat up front, and all us girls in back. "Everyone was quiet," Millie remembers. She got no affirmation or encouragement. Millie was so obedient and conscientious. I don't remember telling anyone that I accepted Christ. Anna tells that when Millie got home from camp the first year, she asked her what she did at camp. Millie said, "I asked Jesus to come into my heart." Anna said, "I want to do that, too." In her innocence, Millie said, "You can't, you're too little." But Anna invited Jesus in secretly and says she never was scared by the hellfire sermons at camp. Oh, the faith of a little child!

Through my early years, Auntie Esther either stayed with us or visited us often after she moved to town. It was fun having her around. She loved to sit with us on the glider on the front porch as we sang retreat choruses. One summer I wrote the words to songs in my notebook (which I still have) so she could learn them. She loved the choruses about Jesus. Those special times filled me with warm feelings of peace and joy.

Our front porch and yard were favorite places to sit or play in nice summer weather. Another visitor who liked to sit on the porch was Daddy's Aunt Ella. She and her common law husband, Jonas, had a son Harry and they lived in town. I remember visiting them in their basement apartment at the Jehovah's Witness Kingdom Hall. Whenever she got the urge, Aunt Ella walked the three or so miles to our house. I remember how she'd sit on the porch and be in one of two moods. In a dark, depressed, and angry mood she spewed curses and bitter talk non-stop. One day as I sat with her on the porch she shouted obscenities at a truck that went by. I was shocked and felt sorry for her. On her better days, she talked and laughed uncontrollably, like a hyena, in the best of moods. Sometimes she told stories about people she knew, usually of women with *auburn* hair and *calico* dresses, words not in our family vocabulary.

Depending on the state in which Daddy found her when he came home from work, he'd decide to take Aunt Ella to the mental hospital at Rittersville after supper. We'd all get in the car and as we went rather slowly around the sharp curve down at the bridge, she'd scream from the back seat, "Ralph! Don't drive so fast!" She was scared to death in a car. So Daddy slowed way down on curves. I remember several such sad and stressful trips to Rittersville. Many years later I asked Daddy about Aunt Ella and those trips and he told me, "I shouldn't have taken her to Rittersville. She wasn't that bad, but we didn't know what to do with people with mental problems back then." I don't remember Jonas ever having a job. He was often in bed when we visited and later died. Poor Aunt Ella died in the county home where my father was born. Her life had been very hard. We never knew what became of Harry.

More than once when I acted silly and laughed playfully, Mama warned, "Stop laughing like that or you'll get crazy like Aunt Ella!" What a scary thought! It made me sad and upset to see Aunt Ella so, and I sure didn't want to be like her. But Mama's warning rang in my ears at times and I feared and wondered, *Will I go crazy like Aunt Ella?*

What a comfort to discover Paul's words to Timothy in my Bible one day, "For God has not given us a spirit of fear, but of power and of love and of a sound mind" (2 Tim. 1:7). A sound mind! *God has given Christians a sound mind, and that means me,* I thought. I memorized and meditated on that verse and it strengthened me in times of fear and doubt.

Camp had a profound effect on Millie, Anna, and me each summer. After our week at camp in the summer of 1947, we decided to have a Bible Club for the Renninger boys and us. At our first meeting on August 26, I was elected president, Richard, vice president, and Millie, secretary. Millie, who started high school that fall, recorded the Minutes in her beautiful penmanship in my sixth grade notebook (with the camp choruses). After elections, "we sang songs and talked about the picnic we had planned." At our next meeting, Millie recorded:

> The meeting of the Bible Club was held on July 27, 1947. The meeting was opened by singing the club chorus, "Constantly Abiding." The Secretary's report was then read and approved. It was decided that the picnic should be held down at the creek if everyone was allowed to go down and if not it will be held in Renninger's yard. Richard R. will furnish the hot dogs and Jane H. pretzels and orange soda. We then said our verse for the week. Then we sang a few choruses, read the scripture, which was Psalm 1. After that we had sentence prayers in which everyone took part. A verse was then assigned for the week which was John 14:6. We sang, "Jesus Calls" and prayed the Lord's Prayer. The meeting was then adjourned.
>
> Signed, Mildred Herstine,
> Secretary

James Renninger, Anna, Grace and Ruth attended all the meetings and I am impressed that even the "little ones" took part in the sentence prayers. We learned about sentence prayers in our prayer groups at camp. Millie was 14, Richard and I, 12, Anna, 10, Grace, 7, and Ruth 6. James was somewhere between Anna and Grace.

The next Minutes record that we would meet every Tuesday at 2:00. We set a date for the picnic, but Mrs. Renninger said it would be better for August 30. Scripture was Psalm 24 and I told a story and everyone prayed. August 12, "The president made a new rule that there should be no more talking or fooling during the meeting or they would have to learn an extra verse." (Looks like it was hard to keep order!) Scripture was Psalm 23 and I read two stories. The last Minutes were of the August 19 meeting with no mention of the picnic. I suppose it went on as planned. The Bible Club summer evokes fond memories for me, and "seems like only yesterday," with the seven of us neighbor kids uniting in prayer and thoughts from the Bible. Millie, too, has good memories of the club and asked that it be included in my book.

Our little Flatland Mennonite Church with its devout believers and "warm piety" (as a minister at our seminary would describe our Eastern District churches to me many years later) was a safe haven for us Herstine girls. It was our extended family. Our Sunday school teachers were extraordinary; simple, loving folk who took God at his word, and I loved every one. I can remember being in the nursery and preschool room with Mrs. Clarence Kooker. Eleanor Frei taught the primary class; her brother Herman Frei, intermediate; and another brother, Oscar and their sister, Helena Milz, taught high school. These four from one family taught faithfully for many years. Their love of the Scriptures and for God and Jesus was contagious. Helena's husband Frank taught us in high school; but he usually taught the adult class. All classes met in the small sanctuary, except nursery/ preschool.

Mr. Kooker also took a turn teaching the high school class. Opinionated but very warm-hearted, he instructed and warned us about the dangers of the Christian life. Movies were of the devil and theatres, Satan's den. Worldly ways and entertainment must be avoided. He often led in prayer during opening exercises. His love for us was evident as he prayed for "the young people" with tears running down his cheeks. He had come to Christ later in life and knew the pitfalls of a worldly life firsthand. The memory of his tears and prayers helped keep me in the way of Christ. I have often thanked God for His faithful ones who nurtured our faith in Jesus. The influence of this "spiritual family" in our young lives was immeasurable.

When I was 13, I took catechism class with our kindly pastor, Rev. A. J. Nuenschwander, was baptized on Easter, and joined the Mennonite church. When we were small, Mama sent us for Sunday school. Then we often left the same morning to visit Mama's relatives at Slatington and Slatedale for dinner, returning after dark. As I grew older, my curiosity was piqued about what happened in church. What did they do there? Therefore, being allowed to go for the first time was a very special event, like becoming an adult. Hearing the organ was a sweet surprise and I loved the reverent spirit of worship, the beautiful prayers, and joyful hymns with four-part harmony. We girls sat with our friend, Eleanor, who sang alto. Sitting beside her I learned to follow the notes and sang alto as well, as did Millie.

In 1947, Mama and Daddy joined the church, which made me happy. I remember seeing them go forward to the railing to take Communion. Mama wore a nice dress and wide-brimmed hat. After that she seldom went except for Easter and Communion. Daddy came with us more often after he quit at the bakery. (No more Sunday work except for snow plowing in winter.) Mama felt more comfortable staying home to make dinner for her family.

Taking Communion was a significant event for me. I remember the first time I heard the words read, "This do in remembrance of Me." I was amazed that after 2000 years we, in our little church, were celebrating Jesus' Last Supper with Him and He was with us. Even today, Jesus' words fill me with awe and gratitude: "He took a piece of bread, gave thanks to God, broke it, and gave it to them, saying, 'This is my body which is given for you. Do this in memory of Me.' In the same way He gave them the cup…saying, 'This cup is God's new covenant, sealed with my blood, which is poured out for you'" (Luke 22:19-29).

An important part of joining church was receiving my own Bible from Flora Fellman, an older single woman. She was very large, with a huge, dark purple birthmark on one side of her face, and a large, protruding bottom lip the same color. She wore long dresses, unusual at the time. She had a deep love for the Lord, the church, and the young people and presented a Bible to every youth who joined the church. What a precious gift this King James Bible was to me. Like Millie before me, I started at Genesis and read through the Bible, a chapter a day. The Old Testament stories intrigued me, and I loved Jesus' words printed in red. How amazing it was to walk with Jesus on the dusty roads of Palestine and read His very own words. In my teen years, I found and underlined gems of familiar verses I had heard or memorized, such as: "You will seek Me and find Me, when you search for Me with all your heart" (Jere. 29:13) and "Your words were found and I ate them, and Your word was to me the joy and rejoicing of my heart" (Jere. 15:16); and, "Delight yourself also in the Lord, and He shall give you the desires of your heart" (Psa. 37:4).

The summer after I joined the church and received my Bible, I rededicated my life to Christ at camp. Pastor A. S. Schultz told us to write the date in our Bibles with the verse Galatians 2:20, "I am crucified with Christ, nevertheless I live; yet not I, but Christ liveth in me. And the life which I now live in the flesh, I live by the faith of the Son of God, who loved me and gave Himself for me." This became my life verse. I memorized it and took it seriously, though it was a big order and a mystery. I probably "rededicated my life to Christ" every summer for 11 years, and wondered, *What will I be some day, a missionary in Africa?*

My first camp counselor, Grace Moyer, had an older married sister, Viola Weidner. One summer Viola was the counselor in my prayer group. She told us, "Memorizing Scripture is very important. Like David said, 'Thy Word have I hid in my heart that I might not sin against thee.' It helps us resist temptation. I like to memorize Scripture while I work. One day I propped my old Bible on the wringer washing machine while I did the laundry." Her usually serious demeanor changed as she laughed, "And my Bible plopped into the water and was baptized!" She was a powerful inspiration to me.

We read together I Corinthians 13, which Viola called, "The great love chapter." She instructed, "If you have trouble loving someone, read I Corinthians 13 every day until you have it memorized."

The Lord spoke to my heart through her words. Often convicted of my lack of love for Mama, I saw this as a great idea to help me do what I wanted to do, for Jesus' sake. I took on the challenge. Though I memorized it in the King James Version, which calls love charity, contemporary versions are easier to understand. This famous chapter on the greatest gift reads like this (NKJ):

> Though I speak with tongues of men and of angels, but have not love, I have become sounding brass or a clanging cymbal. And though I have the gift of prophecy, and understand all mysteries and all knowledge, and though I have all faith, so that I could remove mountains, but have not love, I am nothing. And though I bestow all my goods to feed the poor, and though I give my body to be burned, but have not love, it profits me nothing.
>
> Love suffers long and is kind; love does not envy; love does not parade itself, is not puffed up; does not behave rudely, does not seek its own, is not provoked, thinks no evil, does not rejoice in iniquity, but rejoices in the truth; bears all things, believes all things, hopes all things, endures all things.
>
> Love never fails. But whether there are prophecies, they will fail; whether there are tongues, they will cease; whether there is knowledge, it will vanish away. For we know in part and we prophesy in part. But when that which is perfect has come, then that which is in part will be done away.
>
> When I was a child, I spoke as a child, I understood as a child, I thought as a child; but when I became a man, I put away childish things. For now we see in a mirror, dimly, but then face to face. Now I know in part, but then I shall know just as I also am known.
>
> And now abide faith, hope and love, these three; but the greatest of these is love.

As I read I Corinthians 13 every day, I knew it was a tall order. How could I ever attain to it? In a few weeks I knew it by heart and the verses often came to mind when I struggled to love Mama. Then, remembering Viola's love for memorizing, I read a chapter of Philippians every day until I memorized most of it. It became a treasure, hidden in my heart. Many passages from Paul's letters stored in my "memory bank" taught me about God's kind of love—*agape* love—with which we are to love *everyone, even our enemies.* I especially tried to apply it in my relationship with Mama. The joy of Philippians often lifted my spirits above my circumstances and at times I fairly danced through my days.

About this time, a Sunday school teacher, Helena Frei Milz, gave each one in our class a booklet called *The Game With Minutes* by Frank Laubach. It taught how to practice the presence of God by seeing how many minutes a day we could think about God. It made a difference in my life, but also showed me how often I fell short. This became a life-long exercise as the Spirit brought it to mind. (One day, over fifty years later in Hesston, Kansas, a young woman, Peggy Kaufman, told me about Father Lawrence and his book, *The Practice of the Presence of God*, the original source of the "Game with Minutes." What a treasure to read and recall the influence in my life of this saint of the 1600s. I am grateful for the many people God used to give me special books and messages.)

When we were young, someone gave us a player piano with many rolls to put in and the piano played itself. How I loved it! Later, Mama gave it away and someone gave us another piano. Though Mama had discouraged me from playing, the desire grew within me and I taught myself. I had learned the basics from the few lessons with Miss Guri. When Mama was out of the house, I'd sit at the piano and find easy songs in the hymnbook and pick out the notes. I played and sang the comforting hymns I loved until I had the music memorized. I especially loved, "Dear Lord and Father of mankind, forgive our feverish ways" and sang it as a prayer for myself, for Mama, and our family.

The hymns helped me have a right spirit toward Mama. I learned that my mother, Grace Elizabeth, taught herself to play the pump organ in her home. Though I never played as well as Millie, God gave me my mother's gift and love of hymns, as well as Daddy's love of Gospel songs. Besides, Millie was my main role model, and her gift inspired me.

Some Sunday mornings after worship I was so inspired that as I walked home from church I thought I would burst with the joy of God's presence and worship with His people. But before I reached our door my spirit sagged and sadness descended on me. I longed for my family to experience this same joy in Christ. Why didn't Mama go to church? And how could Daddy be so casual about his Christian life, if indeed he was a Christian?

I longed for our family to worship together, like the families at church. At camp we were taught to pray for and witness to family members. It was impossible for me to talk to Mama about my faith, or to Daddy for that matter, though I believed he was a Christian. But I prayed every day, morning and night, on my knees (as did Millie and Anna), for Mama to be saved, and for the missionaries around the world. But I worried. How could my small faith ever effect a change in Mama? Anxious thoughts and melancholy moments dragged me down. At times like this the promises of God in the Scriptures helped and strengthened me.

Millie, Anna and I sang together for Sunday school programs from the time we were small. During our high school years, we sang trios in church, in other churches, and conference events. We acquired a number of trio books and sang Gospel songs and hymns a cappella. At camp one summer, our pastor, Rev. Denlinger, had us sing for a radio program in the city of Allentown. Grace sang solos as she grew older and she also sang for the radio program.

Daddy drove us to the churches where we sang and after a time this annoyed Mama. She became frustrated and angry at our practicing. Sometimes as Millie played and Daddy and us girls sang around the piano, Mama banged pots and pans in the kitchen. One day we came home from school and our piano was gone.

"Where is the piano?" I asked. With a glare, Mama retorted, "I gave it away! Someone gave it to us and now someone else needs it. So forget it!"

"But we need it to practice our trios," I persisted, close to tears.

"You can practice at the church. You're always over there anyway! And that settles it!" She stomped out of the room. Millie loved to play the piano and was hurt and disgusted. But she did not say a word, as she never talked back to Mama.

When Daddy came home from work and learned about the piano he was furious. "Why do you have to give everything away?" he demanded. "We don't have money to waste, but you keep giving things away. You know the girls need the piano to practice."

But Mama stood firm. "We don't have room for it in this small place," she yelled. "Not since we got the TV. And they can practice at the church. The church says, 'Do this' 'Do that' and they do everything the church people say. They might as well live over there!" Daddy, used to Mama's irrational behavior, decided it was not worth the argument. We could practice at the church. Mama had stressed to us at times, "Don't go over to the church and talk about me." And we didn't. But we surely told them our piano was gone.

As our church activities increased, Mama saw her influence slipping and felt threatened. With encouragement and funds from the church, Millie took organ lessons with a view of becoming church organist. So she had a church key and we walked across the street to practice our trios. But Mama's attitude added to our feeling of alienation from her, and affected us girls deeply.

The Psalms became my prayer book. Prayers of lament, trust, and strong emotion instilled deep faith and confidence in my heart—trust in a God who was good and kind and always there for me. As for Mama, when I read David's strong words about his enemies, and his prayers for deliverance, I identified. (Never mind that he was talking about armies of mortal enemies in battle!) Yes, I thought of Mama as my enemy. Many a time (perhaps before I memorized the great love chapter!) I preached sermons to her on my bed at night, and my language was full of the righteous indignation of the psalmist and Jesus' words from the Gospels. I wished I could say these things out loud to her. I thank God for the dear person who told me years later that preaching these "sermons" probably helped me survive.

One year on Mother's Day, we girls made the unwise decision to sing in church, "My Mother's Old Bible Is True." We stood and sang a line or two and began to giggle. We stopped, started over, and giggled some more. We could not continue. Rev. Denlinger took it good-naturedly, smiled broadly, and said, "You girls must have had feathers for breakfast!"

We sat down, feeling mortified. But deep inside I sensed that song was incongruous with the kind of mother we lived with. Were the giggles our subconscious reaction to this inconsistency? Daddy was there that Sunday and his mild rebuke let us know that was unacceptable behavior in church.

The summer after seventh grade (August 1948), a bus picked us up for Bible school a few miles up the road at an "Old" Mennonite church. How I loved that Bible school, the only one I attended as a child. And I loved our teacher, Mary Cleverly, and the study on "Followers of Jesus"—on the disciples, the book of Acts, and the work of the Holy Spirit. (I still have my book.) God's love and Jesus' ministry through His disciples became very real to me. Our workbook had practical lessons on being a Christian at home, telling others about Jesus, and world missions. The people radiated joy and the vibrant singing, without instruments, filled the church to the rafters. I felt light and clean, aglow with a greater sense of Christ's presence and understanding of His Holy Spirit. On our final test, I got an A+.

The "Old" Mennonite women dressed differently from those at our church, with sheer white caps over their hair done up in buns. They wore "cape" dresses, with extra fabric over the bosom. This was in obedience to Paul's words to Timothy that women should dress modestly, not with fancy hairdos or jewelry, so they wore no wedding bands. Men wore plain suits for church on Sunday, with no ties. I wondered why we were all called Mennonites, yet our church was so different from theirs.

When Bible school was over, a new boy showed up at Renninger's house. When I was outside, he gave me a big smile. Richard told me that his friend's name was Marvin and that he saw me at Bible school and liked me. I was surprised and pleased, yet scared half to death. Hadn't Mama told us we couldn't date until we were out of high school? She watched us with an eagle eye and nothing escaped her notice. One day she asked me, "Why is that boy always over at Renningers'?" I pretended ignorance, but was careful if I ever went outside when he came.

Marvin was tall, with dark, wavy hair. I did not remember seeing him at Bible school since he was in Anna's class. The fact that he noticed *me* was flattering. Mama's unkind words and repression crushed my fragile self-esteem. How could I resist a beau like this? I worried, however, about Mama. I thought of the day when Priscilla from up the street visited us. Her warm, friendly manner made me happy and my face must have lit up in her presence. "Jane is getting very pretty," she said.

"Don't tell *her* that!" Mama snapped with obvious chagrin. How that hurt.

Nevertheless, my exciting, clandestine relationship with Marvin continued, as covert smiles from a distance over the fence. I tried to stay out of trouble. But one Saturday when my sisters and I were coming home from a trip to town with Daddy, we passed Marvin, hitchhiking. Daddy stopped to pick him up and he climbed in the back seat beside me. My heart pounded as he took my hand in his and held it all the way home. I feared for my life as I got out of the car and went into the house. What if Mama had seen him? But Marvin went to the neighbor's house and for the time being I was safe. With the escalation of this romance, my fears increased. I was learning that secret, stolen romance is hardly worth it. But what could I do about Marvin?

Daddy's attitude toward boyfriends was one of fun and humor, which helped balance Mama's strictness. He seldom spoke of it, but one day—when I was in seventh grade—we were in town and passed a boy from my class named Leroy. "Is that your old flame?" Daddy teased with a smile. I was surprised he knew (even though Leroy didn't seem to know I existed). When I was with Daddy, I felt okay and accepted as I was.

Back in my Sunday school class after Bible school, I asked our teacher, "What is the difference between us and the Mennonites who wear coverings?"

"They're Old Mennonites and we're New Mennonites," she said simply. That hardly satisfied my curiosity but I asked no more. It would be years before I learned the history that set us apart — and how privileged I was to have such a heritage. I would learn that my grandfather Landis's Mennonite (Anabaptist) ancestors came to this country from Switzerland seven generations before me, fleeing persecution. And Grammy Landis's people fled from Holland for the same reason, several generations before Pappy's.

The faith and simple lifestyle of our Landis relatives had a great influence on me, and reminded me of my mother's absence. Her death had gouged a gaping hole inside of me that no one could see from the outside. At age three I was not aware of it, and I cannot remember feeling a lack until Jean came when I was four. This was a hole only God could fill. My sadness opened my heart to a hunger and thirst for God that was insatiable — a need for unconditional love, faith, and hope.

To Mama's credit, she had talked with us about our mother, giving us a picture of her that we otherwise would not have had. "I only went to third grade," she told us, "and your Daddy to grade eight, but your mother graduated from high school." Mama held our mother in high esteem, and her wedding picture on the bureau in their bedroom was a constant reminder of her importance in our lives and home. Looking at her picture when I was alone in that room made me aware of my mother's presence, as if she were watching over me. My mother's influence continued through her family and the church she loved.

One thing I liked at church was the exchange pastors who came to preach a series of sermons. One pastor preached on the Holy Spirit from John chapters 13 to 16. I believe it was J. Herbert Fretz, whom I knew and liked from camp. The work of the Holy Spirit became clear and the teachings stayed with me to help me understand the mystifying third person of the Trinity called the "Holy Ghost" in the King James Bible. We learned that the Spirit is our Comforter, Advocate, and Guide.

As I grew older, positive influences abounded. I loved talking with Mrs. Renninger next door. She shared with me her love of poems and one day hauled out her scrapbooks, pasted full of poems. I loved poems too and that gave me an idea. I still have the scrapbook of poems I made.

I also loved to write, and on Thanksgiving Day in 1949 and 1951 I made a "newspaper" of family news, Thanksgiving verses, poems, a prayer from the *Upper Room* devotional, and the high school football score from the radio. In 1949 we had a neighborhood football game. The score: Anna, Ralph, and James, 24; Richard, Jane, and Ruth 36. In 1951, Grace was my "assistant editor." I wrote that, throughout the football game on the radio, "Anna and Grace lay on the floor of the upstairs bedroom with the radio occupying the bed, listening to the game. When a touchdown was scored they made it known by yelling and jumping up and down until Mama threatened to bring the radio down and turn it off. After that they meekly informed us of the concluding touchdowns." Quakertown 27, Sell-Perk 7 ended the game. I kept Mr. Renninger informed of the score as he was worked in the barn near our back yard. Thanksgiving was a nice relaxing day, with some of Mama's family visiting.

When I was about 14, I reluctantly agreed to teach the primary Sunday school class. Teaching from the teacher's manual for almost an hour as the children sat on hard benches was a challenge. Our class was in the back corner of the small meetinghouse, the adult class in the center, and children's classes surrounding them on each side and on the stage. I wished I could be in my own class. The teacher's quarterly had inspiring poems that I cut out for my scrapbook. I taught off and on, but poetry had become my special love.

One day I went to the attic to rummage through boxes of books, where I loved to look for treasures. My search was rewarded as my eyes fell on the title, *The Greatest Thing in the World* by Henry Drummond. Amazed, I opened it to discover that it was about I Corinthians 13, the great love chapter. What a delight! Then another title caught my attention, *In His Steps* by Charles Sheldon, which I also read. This classic made me aware of the importance of asking in every decision, "What would Jesus do?" I tried to make that the rule of my life. How I would need it in the days ahead!

CHAPTER 8

First Job

He knows the way that I take; when he has tried me,
I shall come forth as gold.

JOB 23:10 (RSV)

1949–1953

In the weeks following graduation from eighth grade, I felt free as a breeze, looking forward to summer fun before knuckling down to high school in the fall. Marvin's occasional appearance next door added some excitement.

We girls were becoming more independent. Weeks before, I had a taste of independence when Daddy took me to a job arranged by Kookers at a food stand at the farmer's market. At this monstrously long building, people came to sell their wares – from miles around and from Philadelphia, 40 miles away. My hours were six to midnight on Saturday night, the most crowded time of the weekend. I was terrified.

The stand was busy when I arrived, so the manager gave a few brief, confusing instructions and let me go. People lined up waiting for hot dogs, tea – you name it. All I remember is making tea for some unsuspecting soul. Then I had to make change. I panicked. I knew nothing about handling money since all I ever got was Daddy's nickel for Sunday school and a bit at Christmas to buy presents. After bungling the change with this first customer, I felt sick and helpless. I told the manager I was sick, hightailed it to Kooker's bakery stand, and asked them to call Daddy. I hated the sale building and all the commotion.

Daddy could be the kindest, most patient man I ever knew. When he picked me up, he didn't scold or put me down. He said not one word of rebuke. Empathy showed on his face, and I could have hugged him. How I loved my father and wanted to please him. But I felt like a failure for letting him down. After all, when we finished eighth grade, we were supposed to start earning. I hoped I could make it up to him somehow.

In spring Daddy planted a garden, which needed lots of attention. I liked working in it but somehow the weeds always got ahead of us. This summer I wanted to help keep it in better shape. Millie was gone to a summer babysitting job in a neighboring town and came home only on weekends.

One afternoon I headed to the garden to weed the carrots, happy as the birds chirping in the treetops. I sang Bible school and Sunday school choruses as I worked. Before long, a strange car stopped at the house. A distinguished looking gentleman in a suit got out, walked to the porch and talked with Mama. She called me to come. "This is Dr. Norman. His wife just had surgery and needs someone to help her until she gets better. Get your clothes and things you need and get ready to go with him."

What a shock! How could this be? One moment freedom, and the next catapulted into the unknown. Stunned, with heart thumping, I ran off upstairs to gather some clothes, my Bible and a tablet, then grabbed my toothbrush and a comb and stuffed them all into a paper bag. My stomach drew into a knot. Where was I going? Always shy of strangers, I wondered how I could go with this man. A doctor! And where did they live? How long would I be gone? I knew only that our friend Eleanor, from church, was his patient and he'd asked her if she knew a "nice Mennonite girl" to help them. She recommended the Herstine girls.

With Millie gone, I was next in line. Jobs were important to our parents once we left eighth grade. Saying no to Mama was not acceptable. There was no discussion. Mama sent me off as if I were leaving for a day at school. What kind of mother was she? Did she have no heart? Time stood still and I felt frantic. I reminded myself, *Jesus is with me. He said, "I will never leave you"* (Heb.13:5).

I vividly remember the ten-mile drive through beautiful countryside, with sun-splashed trees lining miles of curving, hilly road until we entered a main highway. Few words were spoken. If the doctor asked a question, I answered briefly. The farther we drove the more I felt like Hansel and Gretel going deep into the forest. How would I survive so far from home? In awe of professional people, I clammed up.

Finally we turned onto a dirt road that wound up an incline, then along a sloping meadow on a hillside that rose gradually to the base of a small mountain. (I learned later it was Haycock Mountain, which I knew from the other side.) The doctor stopped at a mailbox outside a fenced-in estate. As he turned into the evergreen tree-lined lane, I saw an evergreen nursery to the left of the drive. Up ahead and to the right a big, white house came into view, nestled into trees at the base of the mountain. Tall columns, reminding me of southern mansions, stood along the front, with a porch upstairs and down, creating an impressive sight. Unprepared for such wealth and splendor, I cried out inside, *Oh, God, help me!*

An amazing peace enveloped me as we walked toward the house, past a beautiful rock garden on the left, with colorful begonias in bloom – red, yellow, and orange-red.

I walked with the doctor across a lovely stone terrace at the side of the house and into a large, nicely furnished room. My eyes took in the piano, oriental rugs, fireplace, and well-stocked bookshelves under the windows. Never had I been in such an elegant house. The doctor led me into a room at the far end where his wife sat in bed. He introduced her as Marge and she welcomed me graciously, happy at her husband's success in his mission. Her youthful appearance surprised me. She had short dark hair and dark eyes and looked to be about 25, far younger than the doctor who was balding. The bedroom also had a fireplace, books, comfortable chairs, and bright paintings on the walls.

I tried to concentrate as Mrs. N. explained my duties. "I have a woman who does the heavy cleaning every three weeks, but I need you to do light housekeeping, laundry, ironing, helping with cooking and dishes, and taking care of the dogs. Tomorrow morning I will show you how to make the doctor's breakfast. I still need to rest a lot and I'm so glad to have you here," she finished with her warm smile. "The doctor will show you your room. I'll see you in the morning, Janie." Janie. She called me *Janie*. She seemed nice enough but I wished I could go home!

The doctor led me upstairs to a tiny plain room: walls and ceiling painted orange, bare wooden floor painted green, a bed and bureau. Situated at the back of the house, the room looked uninviting. "I'll call you at six," the doctor informed me. "Good night."

After unpacking my few belongings and getting ready for bed, I read my Bible and knelt to pray. God seemed near and I felt His love, yet a feeling of homesickness such as I'd never known engulfed me. I crawled into bed and cried myself to sleep, thinking of my family at home and wondering how I could stay in this place. Sleep finally came, and before long I heard the doctor's call, "Jane! Time to wake up!"

I dressed quickly, taking a minute to look out the windows. One overlooked the mountain woods and full-length terrace at the back of the house. The east window faced the woods, the rock garden and side terrace. What a

magnificent place! The peace and beauty of nature, the elegance, spacious-
ness, and affluence of the house and estate nearly took my breath away. I felt
like I was floating along, suspended in time, dropped down into a strange
land. Never had I been in such a house. Nor had I known people of the
Norman's social class. I felt like the little slave girl who told her mistress
about Elijah, who could heal Naaman the leper.

Was I here on a mission? If so, what was it? Well, of course, it was to help
a sick woman. Surely I could do that. As was my custom, I knelt for prayer,
"Oh, God, please help me today." But I must not be late. I hurried downstairs
to face the day.

Mrs. N. greeted me in the kitchen with her ever-ready smile. She showed
me the Revere Ware frying pan and gave me instructions. "First fry three
slices of bacon—nice and crisp," she demonstrated. "The doctor has two
eggs and bacon every day. After you break the eggs into the pan, add a table-
spoon of water and keep the lid on and the tops will cook just right." It
looked simple enough. Toast and orange juice were the easy part. I would
soon learn to cook bacon and eggs to perfection. Mrs. N. went back to bed
and the doctor came out with a smile and cheerful greeting. Cereal was fine
for me. As we ate together the doctor made conversation but I had little to
say. I was relieved when he finished his breakfast and left for work. I ached
with homesickness, but knew the Lord was near. I must be strong and do a
good job. I MUST!

Later, Mrs. N. showed me how to do the dishes and start the laundry in the
automatic machine in the corner of the kitchen by the back door. Everything
was so handy compared with our wringer washing machine in the dank
basement at home. "You'll change the sheets twice a week, and here's where
you'll find the ironing board." She opened a narrow door in the wall off the
living room, and there it was. As we changed the sheets, she showed me how
to fold the corners just right. I marveled at the cupboard full of lovely pastel
colored sheets, all nicely ironed. *This isn't so hard*, I thought.

Taking me to the "powder room" at one end of the living room, she
continued, "Here are the cleaning supplies for the toilets, which you can
check every day and keep clean. And now I'll show you how to feed the
dogs." A terrier, two dachshunds, and a boxer took some getting used to.
They followed me around and felt like a quadruple nuisance! (Sometime
later, the boxer was killed by a car on the road, so they got a young Great
Dane.) Mrs. N. retired to her freshly made bed as I began my chores.

76

My favorite part of the day became hanging wash on the lines and walking down the lane for the mail. I loved being out in nature, and nature was everywhere here. My eyes drank in the green lawn sloping to a swimming pool, and beyond that a fishpond. The mysterious, lovely mountain rose behind the house. And from the front lawn, a gorgeous view of the valley stretched out below. I breathed deeply of the fresh mountain air and marveled. What a lovely place! If I hadn't been so scared and homesick I would have thought I'd come to paradise. Was anything lacking here?

At bedtime my heart was heavy as the days and weeks loomed ahead. Homesickness engulfed me. In my room, I prayed on my knees, committing myself to God, and then cried myself to sleep.

As the week went on, I reflected on things I'd learned at Bible school, sang the songs in my heart, and prayed. How I prayed! The Apostle Paul's admonition to pray without ceasing took on new meaning. I practiced the presence of Jesus as I washed the dishes, did the laundry, ironed the sheets, fed the dogs, and took my daily walk for the mail. And God's presence felt more real to me here than at home.

The weekend came with welcome relief. The doctor drove me home late Saturday afternoon. I couldn't wait to see my family. I relished every moment with them and being at church on Sunday. I dreaded the thought of Sunday night when Daddy took me back. On the way he told me kindly, "If you don't like it there, you don't have to stay." Gratitude for his kindness welled up in me. But I knew Mama expected me to stay. Eleanor was pleased she found me a job, and the doctor's wife depended on me now. I didn't want to disappoint Daddy again and quit *this* job. I would stick out this new job if I died doing it. I assured Daddy that I wanted to continue.

My jobs went from one extreme to the other, I reflected, as I washed the dishes and ironed the pastel sheets—from a bustling, high-pressure nightmare at the market to "solitary confinement" in the most peaceful place on earth. What a contrast! I couldn't see it then, but God knew my needs and knew what He was doing. Much later I would see that He led me to the perfect spot for me.

Though only ten miles from home, it seemed like a hundred and the homesickness continued. I thought of Joseph, one of my favorite Old Testament characters, and how he must have felt after his brothers sold him into slavery in Egypt. His faith remained rock solid, and I must trust God, too. I was far better off than Joseph. But his story and life comforted me.

Gradually I got used to my new home, and the beauty and solitude of nature calmed my spirit. I loved the bright red cardinals flitting about the back yard and soon learned their song and imitated their whistle. In my free time after dinner I sat outside on the terrace for my devotions and wrote letters to friends and neighbors. Then our pastor, Rev. Denlinger, decided to have a midweek Bible study and Eleanor, who lived nearby, offered to pick me up. I was jubilant, seeing church friends and my sisters. We studied Paul's short epistles and I grew to love them. Rev. Denlinger also started a choir and we practiced after Bible study to sing Sunday mornings. This was a significant turning point in my life. Before long, I'd get away for my week at camp, which the Normans had agreed to.

One weekend at home, Richard told me that Marvin wanted my address at the doctor's. So I passed it along, feeling a slight twinge of guilt. Mail time grew exciting as I waited for a letter. When it came, my hands trembled as I tore it open. With the letter was a picture from this boy I hardly knew. I just knew he was an "Old" Mennonite and his father was a pastor. I was impressed. Having a secret admirer added excitement to the lonely hours. Maybe I would see Marvin soon on a weekend.

A new amenity at my job was a bathroom all to myself, though it had ancient fixtures compared with the modern one with shower downstairs. (The Normans' bathroom was in the new addition off their bedroom, adjoining a long dressing room with windows on two sides and closets on the other long wall—which spoke to me of a huge wardrobe and opulence unimaginable.) What a luxury to have an indoor toilet and hot running water after years of the outhouse at home and pump at the sink. Used to a Saturday night sponge bath with a foot tub, I saw no need to use the monstrous old tub on funny legs. What a waste of water! Besides, I didn't want to make noise, running water in that iron thing for the whole house to hear.

One day, weeks later, Mrs. N. went upstairs with me and asked, "Janie, don't you use the bathtub to take a bath?" Enormously embarrassed, I muttered something about washing with a washcloth at the sink. She pursued, "And you haven't cleaned your room and bathroom. They need it, so you can do that today." For weeks I had noticed the dust bunnies gathering around the edges of my room and the bathroom but never took the notion to clean up there. I followed her instructions and my daily routine till dinnertime, and then had free time. *Yes, I noticed the dirt. No, I didn't know why I waited.* I felt stupid. *Two strikes and you're out,* I told myself.

That night I had my first bath in a tub. (Or had I had one at Auntie Ruth's when Grace and I stayed for a week when I was ten and she was five? Probably.) I hated the whole thing and the dirty ring it left around the tub. Now I had to clean the tub! What an inconvenience these modern "conveniences" could be. I took as few tub baths as I could get by with.

When Mrs. N. recovered, she returned to work as the doctor's nurse in his office about seven miles away. I anticipated this day and hoped my job was over. But, no, she wanted me to stay on, week after week. She constantly praised me and loved having someone to clean up after meals, do the laundry and ironing, dust the long rows of books and the bookshelves. Now she added a new job: refinishing furniture. The first piece was a maple chair. I worked in the large room above the garage and horse stables, where they had kept their riding horses for years. I worked on these projects as time permitted. It seemed I was trapped for life!

But the maple chair turned into a lovely satin smooth beauty as I applied remover, sanded for days, then rubbed it with oil. Marge Norman was absolutely delighted. There were other chairs to do, and a handsome old, oak roll-top desk. While learning a valuable skill, I also learned about varieties of wood. Marge was always ecstatic about the results, and I soaked up the praise she gave so liberally.

The upstairs of the Normans' house had a nice guest room off the porch in front and a storage room containing a freezer, a collection of art supplies, and sewing paraphernalia, including a sewing form like Mrs. N.'s body. I learned she was an artist—a portrait painter—and all the portraits around the rooms were her originals. A self-portrait hung in their bedroom. She put up her easel again and painted, sometimes having someone sit for her. My awe grew at this many-talented, very cultured and well-read lady. Eventually, she used me as a model for a painting of someone else. I didn't know whether to feel flattered or insulted that she didn't paint me as *me*. But never mind, her praise warmed me inside. Once Mrs. N. was well, we ate lunch together in silence. She read a book while she ate. I felt like a nonperson and wished I could make myself invisible. How uncomfortable to eat with a stranger and never have anything to say to each other. But she knew I would not talk. Once when she had friends over and they admired the chairs I refinished, I spoke little, and she said, "Janie doesn't talk. She thinks it all." How embarrassing. But I honestly did not have anything to say. Weekends at home were short, from late Saturday afternoon until Sunday evening. But they were the highlight of my week when I caught up on the family and neighborhood news. An "Old" Mennonite family moved into the other side of Priscilla and Levi's double house up the road. They had a son, Ted, who Millie thought was good looking, and a daughter, Mary, a bit older than Millie. Their mother, Mrs. Crocker (not their real names), was a tiny sweet-natured woman, crippled with arthritis. Her husband was an alcoholic. One Sunday while I was at home, Millie and I stopped in to see them. Mrs. Crocker's angelic face beamed with the joy of Jesus. The radio was on and suddenly a startling voice pierced the air.

"Who's that?" I asked.

"Billy Graham, a young evangelist with Youth for Christ," they said. I was drawn to his voice and message and asked about the station and noted the time. From then on, when I could, I listened to him on the radio in the kitchen at home at 3 o'clock Sunday afternoons. One day Mama came into the room as I was listening. "What are you doing listening to that?" she demanded angrily. "Don't you have anything better to do?" I wondered, *So what's wrong with Billy Graham?* I continued to listen when she was gone, or watching TV at her usual spot in the living room. If our Mennonite neighbors thought he was good, how could he be bad? Before long, I learned that he was on television on Sunday nights. The Normans never used the living room so I had access to the TV there. My joy knew no bounds the first Sunday night I turned it on. Amazed at my good fortune I watched spellbound as the huge choir praised God with heavenly music, Cliff Barrows spoke, and George Beverly Shea sang. Then a youthful, handsome Billy appeared, and holding his Bible aloft, boomed out again and again, "The Bible says," challenging and blessing me with God's truth. If I had been at home, I could never have seen Billy Graham at all. God had engineered my circumstances in a wonderful way.

Thus began a weekly ritual of watching this praise-filled, hour-long program. Billy's messages—clear, direct, and practical—focused my attention on living for Jesus in every area of my life. Here in this lonely place I enjoyed this incredible blessing from God.

Before long, I sent for the sermons, offered each week on the program, and sent along $3.00 as a gift. My income for the week was $8.00, of which I gave $5.00 to Mama. So when I gave $3.00, I gave all I had left. But what did I need money for? My needs were few, and I had even fewer wants. However, I got careless with the receipts, putting them in my bureau drawer in the bedroom at home. One day Mama, with receipts in hand, erupted in anger.

"Why are you sending money to him? What is the matter with you? I want you to stop that. Don't you know we don't have money to throw away? If you don't stop it you can bring all your money home!"

What a predicament! I was dumbstruck. Here I am trying to follow Jesus and she treats me like a delinquent. How could she understand what these messages meant to me? Billy Graham taught clearly about sin and how to live for Christ. He taught youth to stay in the Word and obey it rather than following the crowd and seeking popularity. He actually strengthened me in my resolve to obey Mama. But how could I explain this to her?

In bed that night I cried out to God for the umpteenth time, *"Why did my mother have to die? And why did we have to get her for a stepmother?"* The years ahead promised to be dismal indeed, living with Mama's restrictions and bad temper. *"Oh, God, it's so hard living with her! How long, O Lord? How long?"*

As I cried silent tears into my pillow, suddenly a strong message impressed itself upon my awareness – a revelation – as clearly as if a voice had spoken. *"Your stepmother will not live to be 50, but your father will live to be 70!"*

Awestruck I asked, *"Oh, God, is this Your answer to me? Will this really come true?"* A deep calm and peace came over me as I lay there, silently pondering. The impression was so strong that it gave me a strange sort of comfort. It meant there were still plenty of years with Mama, but Daddy would outlive her. That thought made life more bearable. God showed me the truth of His promise, "Call to Me, and I will answer you, and show you great and mighty things, which you do not know" (Jere. 33:3). I never told anyone about this revelation, but thought about it at times through the years. I thought of it again and was amazed when Mama died at age 48. And I remembered it when Daddy died at age 71. It really had come true.

How could I ever doubt that God loved me personally? This evidence of God's love still astounds me. Jesus, the Good Shepherd, promises to take care of His sheep. His compassionate heart had comforted me with a word of knowledge in my anguish, and years later He kept His promise.

My week at camp helped break up the summer and the hymns on "The Hour of Decision" continued to inspire me all week long. One afternoon when I was alone, I went outside on the lawn in front of the house and sang my heart out to the heavens. I sang George Beverly Shea's solo, "The Love of God." I sang about the ocean filled with ink, the sky of parchment, the stalks on earth as quills, and men writing about God's endless love. The whole sky could not contain the words about this amazing love. My spirit soared and I was glad to be alive. I thought I would fairly burst with praise and joy and gratitude. God had healed my grieving spirit. God had guided me to this place because He knew it was best for me. He was true to His Word: "I know the plans I have for you" declares the Lord, "plans to prosper you and not to harm you, plans to give you hope and a future" (Jer. 29:11). What a summer this had become!As fall approached, I rejoiced that the job at Normans would soon end. Then one day Mrs. N. asked, "Would you be willing to work for us on weekends during the school year? I could pick you up Friday after school or your father could take you to the office. You can clean the rooms there, and then come home with us for Saturday. That would be a big help to me. The doctor can take you home as usual Saturday afternoon."

I was not overjoyed, but I would submit, if this was God's will. At camp every year we were taught to seek and do God's will with all our heart, not our own. I had received a book for perfect attendance at Sunday school called *Not My Will*. But I often wondered, how can I know God's will?

I told Mama and Daddy about Mrs. N.'s request. They agreed I could go on weekends. So, for the next three summers – and every weekend my four years of high school – I worked at the doctor's.

It would be years before I realized the significance of this time and place in my young life. I would come to see that it was not Mama who sent me there, but God, to draw me closer to Himself and deep into His Word. He took me to this place of beauty, solitude, and silence where I could learn to hear His voice and spend time in reflection and meditation. Jesus, the Apostle Paul, David and the Psalms, especially, impacted my life. Family became more precious than ever, neighbors sweeter, and in the beauty and quiet God was teaching me to love Mama. It was God's redeeming crucible.

I brought most of my things home that last week before school, including the letter and picture from Marvin. I buried them deep in my drawer, beneath my underwear. How could I look at his picture if it was in the attic? Surely it would be safe here. But I was wrong. One day I got home from school and Mama met me in a rage, holding out the letter and picture. "What are you doing with this in your drawer?" she boomed. "You tear it up right now and throw it away! And you stop writing to him! Do you hear me?" Anger rose in me like a geyser. *Why did she have to snoop in my things? Why didn't I put them in the attic?* Yet I knew her rule and I had broken it. How could

I stop Marvin from liking me? And how could I turn off this attraction I felt for him? This wasn't dating. It wasn't fair not to be able to have a friend. Why was she so unreasonable? But in the end, I knew I had defied her. I submitted my spirit to Jesus. I must obey Mama. Daddy said so. The Bible teaches it. But what would I say to Marvin? I would say nothing.

The first week at home I received a letter from Mrs. N. She wrote:

> I wanted to tell you once again how much I appreciate all the hundreds of things you did for me this summer. I never could have gotten all my own "extras" done if you had not been there.
>
> We are both missing you *very* much. Again, my sincere appreciation. We shall see you Friday night.
>
> Marge Norman

I should feel like a million dollars from such praise. Then why didn't I?

All the weekends of the next school year stretched on endlessly. *Okay, Lord, "I am crucified with Christ, Nevertheless I live..."* (Gal. 2:20, my life verse from camp). *Whatever You want, I'll do. But please, help me.*

Despite this disappointment, the adventure of high school beckoned – a country kid joining the town kids. That should be fun!

CHAPTER 9

High School Days

Study to show thyself approved unto God...
I TIMOTHY 2:15 (KJV)

1949–1953

High school! How exciting! I'd finally get to go to school on the bus with Millie who was two grades ahead of me. As we did dishes together each evening, Millie told me the details of her day, about her friends and the "town kids." It was clear the mysterious "town kids" were more sophisticated than us country girls. Millie seemed to have the most interesting life and friends. How I admired her.

Some years before, I said in Mama's hearing, "I want to be a teacher when I grow up."

Her swift response stopped me in my tracks. "You *can't* be a teacher! We don't have the money to send you to college, so get that idea out of your head. Why don't you take commercial and be a secretary like Millie?" What Mama said went. I took commercial.

My good friend Janice and I were inseparable: we took classes and ate lunch together, and at noon we walked up and down the nearby streets for diversion and fresh air. Early on, a nice-looking boy in my homeroom asked me for a date but I told him I wasn't allowed until I graduated. But I was surprised and pleased to have been asked.

I took my class work seriously and got good grades. But typing frustrated me no end. How could I type with no mistakes at top speed? Timed tests were standard in typing and shorthand. I wanted to do my best. I once read a statement that stayed with me: "I'll study and get ready, and then my chance will come." It inspired and motivated me. *What will I become?* I wondered. *Not a secretary, I hope!* I struggled for months with typing, but eventually mastered the Underwood manual and did well in the timed tests. And in shorthand I eventually won the coveted pin for 120 words per minute in dictation. Mrs. Becker taught typing, shorthand, and junior business training, and Miss Platoff, bookkeeping. She was nice but strict; from her I learned good posture. We had only two fellows in our commercial "section" and it was fun learning to know the students with whom I would spend the next four years.

In home economics class we learned to cook and sew. Now I could sew without Mama's disapproval. One summer Anna was teaching me to sew on our mother's treadle machine, which she had mastered. Mama came along and yelled, "What are you doing? Anna can sew but *you* can't!" Just like Millie could play piano but I couldn't. In high school I had an electric machine, which was easier. I made a royal blue gathered skirt with bolero. No matter that I sewed the zipper on the wrong side and the biggest gathers were in front. Glad that the teacher didn't make me redo it, I had a lovely addition to my limited wardrobe.

Before long I was enjoying new friends, and jolly good ones at that. A girl named Doris and I hit it off so well that she invited me to her home for a weekend and, amazingly, Mama consented. My first time overnight at a friend's house! Millie didn't even do that. Doris and I enjoyed many a laugh together at school. I was pleased to be invited to her home. She was pretty and sweet and also a Christian.

"We're going to have frozen peas!" Doris exclaimed, delighted to be able to share her favorite vegetable with me. Not sure I'd ever had them, I took her word for it. I couldn't believe it when she said to me, "Our house is a shack." What I found was quite the opposite. It was a modest bungalow, but compared with our humble dwelling, it was beautiful inside.

As we gathered at the dinner table, I blurted to Doris, "You're house isn't a shack! It's very nice!" In an awkward moment of silence her parents glanced at Doris, and then we took our places. Her father prayed a beautiful prayer and we enjoyed a wonderful meal. The peas were great. And what nice parents she had, so gracious and kind and happy.

Doris had an older sister, Grace. After dinner the girls took me upstairs. Doris laughed and said, "We'll show you how to shave your legs. We had Patty here overnight and she showed us how!" They whipped out a razor and proceeded to do it for me to show me how easy it was. *Oh, dear! What would Mama say to this? Would Millie agree to buy a razor with me?* Yes, these "town kids" had newfangled ideas. (Millie and I *did* buy a razor after that. Anna remembers that Mama always said, "If God wanted you to shave your legs he wouldn't have made hair grow on them." Remarkably, Doris and Grace showed *their* mother, and she accepted the modern fad.)

Doris sang like a songbird and often sang solos or duets with Grace. She told me, "You can come with us to church on Sunday. We go to the Assembly of God Church and we do things that are probably a little different from your church. Someone might speak in tongues—that's another language—and then someone else will interpret it."

I had read about tongues in Acts and Paul's epistles and was intrigued. *Why didn't we hear about that in our church?* I wondered. Sure enough, it happened just as she said, and I accepted it as a normal part of their worship. It seemed really special. I knew it was one of the gifts of the Holy Spirit and this sparked my interest in this Person of the Trinity even more.

Monday morning at school, Doris met me with a scowl. "Why did you say that about our house not being a shack? My father just finished remodeling it and my parents really bawled me out for telling you that!"

I felt like Charlie Brown on his worst day. *Well, why did she say that in the first place?* I wondered. Yet I felt terrible for getting her into trouble.

"I'm sorry," I said, meaning it, but the damage was done and Doris never invited me home again. I hoped she would forgive me. As time went on, it seemed the incident was forgotten, and we were still friends, but it took me a long time to forgive myself. How I wished I knew how to handle situations like this. (More than 50 years later, at our 50-year class reunion, Doris and I met and she was as warm as ever. What a joy! We had not been in touch since graduation. She later came to Arizona to a conference with her pastor husband and we had a wonderful day together on my birthday. She said she did not remember the incident from school. I praised the Lord for relieving me of this memory of guilt I had carried so long. She shared with enthusiasm her experience of receiving the gift of tongues, along with a friend, as they kept praising the Lord in a meeting.)

While in high school, still curious about tongues, I asked our pastor, "Why don't we speak in tongues like they did in Bible times?"

His curt answer surprised and disappointed me. "We shouldn't question too much." I knew not to ask him anything after that. *How can we learn if we never ask questions? And why don't we speak in tongues when the Apostle Paul said, "I wish you all spoke with tongues?"* (1 Cor. 14:5). I'd have to seek elsewhere for answers.

One very special Easter, Millie, Anna, and I sang at an Easter dawn service at a large non-Mennonite church out in the country west of town. The Easter music on a majestic pipe organ, glorious hymns of resurrection, and the message, as the sun streamed through the stained-glass windows, made the resurrection of Jesus real to me as if for the first time. I was filled with joy, awe, and the hope of eternal life as I experienced that first Easter morning of seeing Jesus alive. Fear of death receded into the background as I realized that death meant resurrection and being with Jesus forever.

The first weekend after school started, Daddy took me to Dr. Norman's office. In addition to his beautiful home, he owned a large, double two-story, redbrick house, which had several apartments and his office. Mrs. N. gave me money for my supper and I walked to a restaurant in the next block, a new experience for me. Every Friday I ordered crab cakes, applesauce, and a vegetable for my meal.

Mrs. N. asked me to dust the shelves full of bottles of vitamins, supplements and medicines in the back room just off one of the patient rooms. Between patients, the doctor stuck his head out the door to greet me with a warm smile. When the last patient left, the doctor said, "Now it's your turn."

He told me to lie down on the table, adjusted my neck and back, then put long "needles" up my nostrils with what appeared to be Q-Tips on the end with medicine that stung my sinuses. Because I was still plagued with sinus problems, the doctor said he'd give me a treatment every week. I was grateful but felt unworthy of all they did for me. He also gave me vitamins to take at their house. After the adjustment I vacuumed the offices, front waiting room and back room, while they finished their routine chores and paperwork and relaxed a bit. Then we drove the seven miles home.

As winter came, Mrs. N. gave me two gray flannel skirts and some sweaters she didn't want. I was just her size and felt in style. Millie was delighted, and wore the skirts as much as I.

In English class we were asked to write a poem for the school magazine, *The Quaker Challenge*. Excited by the assignment, as I thought about it that night in bed I prayed, asking the Lord to help me write something. The next day I wrote "The Valentine's Party," in very short order. When it made the *Challenge*, I knew the Lord had helped me. Later I wrote a poem, "Little Candles," about Christians as candles shining in the darkness, which also was published. Many of the published poems, articles, and stories were on Christian themes. An impressive number of students who wrote were

Christians, an inspiration to me. I did well in school, motivated by the verse, "Study to show thyself approved unto God, a workman that needeth not to be ashamed..." (2 Tim. 2:15).

The school year ended and summer saw me back at the Normans' full time. Mrs. N. liked to knit and one day she gave me yarn and a knitting book to choose a pattern so she could teach me. When I finished the first sweater, she gave me more yarn. Then she took me with her to the John Wanamaker department store in Philadelphia so I could pick out my own yarn. In all, I knitted five sweaters those years. Mrs. N. also played the piano, and I enjoyed hearing her play light classical music. When I was alone, I used her music to practice my favorites like "Barcarolle" by Offenbach. And I'd play my hymns from memory and sing.

Summers and winters came and went. On my 16th birthday, soon after I got home from school, a woman knocked on the door. Mama, unusually excited, her face all smiles, let the stranger in and the woman focused on me.

"Happy 16th Birthday to you!" she said. "I'm from the Welcome Wagon. Here are certificates from many of the merchants in town. Just take these in and claim your gifts. One is for a free sitting at the photographer." I was amazed, and Mama was delighted to have surprised me so. I felt a warm bond between us that came and went through the years. She hadn't done this for Millie, but it seemed like a great adventure and I would enjoy it. I picked up my gifts over the next few weeks—a yardstick, a ruler, household and personal things, many with the name of the business printed on them. I had my picture taken in a blue corduroy suit, a hand-me-down sent from Cousin Ethel across the state. I got a photo of a girl with a beaming smile. That was a special birthday because of Mama's thoughtfulness.

In the summer of 1951, Millie, Anna and I had the experience of singing in a mass choir with people from all the churches in our district. The director was Mr. Lantz from our church college in Bluffton, Ohio. We practiced in smaller groups in churches, and after one mass rehearsal, we gave the performance on a Sunday afternoon. We girls reveled in singing beautiful praise anthems with about 350 others. We sang, "The Heavens Are Telling the Glory of God," and the quiet prayer, "God be in my head and in my understanding, God be in my eyes and in my looking..." The photo of that large choir from our Eastern District Mennonite churches with so many familiar faces keeps the memory alive.

The next summer, Mrs. N. told me one day they would be gone for a week of vacation to the White Mountains in New York. She asked, "Would you mind staying by yourself and taking care of the dogs while we're gone?" I didn't mind. Mrs. K. came one day to clean. She was a friendly, motherly type who loved to talk, and we enjoyed chatting off and on as we worked and ate lunch together at noon. What a contrast to lunch with Mrs. N.

Marvin and I still communicated, mainly through Richard next door. He had a car now and, persistent fellow that he was, wanted to come see me at the doctor's. He asked for directions. Without stopping to think or pray about it, I agreed. Also, through Richard, I let him know the Normans would be gone for a week. What an opportunity to finally visit with him unhindered. My parents had also said they would visit me one day. Somehow it was arranged for them and Marvin to come on different days. Not immediately recognizing this as Temptation, my heart fairly soared.

But as the days went by, I had no peace. I knew I was being deceptive. Mama would kill me if she knew. And I knew I'd be displeasing Jesus. *What had I done?*

When the day for Marvin's visit came, I worried and prayed and watched down the lane for his car. I grew nervous and afraid to see him alone for the first time. This was all wrong, and downright dangerous! I was playing with fire. By now I understood a few things about the birds and the bees, and putting that together with Mama's past – a baby out of wedlock, Grace's birth a week after Mama and Daddy married – I could understand her obsession about boys. She wanted to spare me the kind of trouble she had gotten into.

"Please help me, Jesus! Forgive me! Show me what to do!" I cried out. I grew calmer and was able to think. I could feel Jesus' presence and prayed over and over for help. My decision was clear. Jesus would help me.

As I saw Marvin's car approaching, my heart beat wildly and my hands got clammy cold. Downhearted but resolute, I walked to the door to meet him, feeling like a total heel. *Why had I led him on like this?* He came in with a look that said, "I'm ready to take you in my arms!" But I lost no time getting to the point.

"I'm really sorry, Marvin," I blurted, "but I shouldn't have told you to come. As you know, I'm not allowed to date until I'm out of high school. My stepmother is very strict about this. I haven't had peace about your visit and ...and...I think you should go," I finished lamely.

Unable to conceal his disappointment, his face fell. He nevertheless was a gentleman and respectfully agreed to leave. *So near and yet so far*, I thought.

My heart must have been in my eyes, as his always was. Sadly, he turned to leave. We said goodbye at the door and he walked out–wrenched from my life–forever? *Will we ever date when I'm old enough?* But no matter, I had gotten the victory over a powerful temptation. We had the perfect opportunity and I said No!

A burden the size of a Mack truck rolled off my mind and I thanked the Lord for helping me. My pounding heart and shaking hands were all I had left, and the sweet memories of a love I had not sought. How sad I felt as I watched Marvin's car drive slowly down the lane. But I would obey Mama if it was the last thing I did. Hadn't she been good enough to have the Welcome Wagon come for me? I wanted to obey her even if she didn't know about it. My peace was restored with Jesus and I knew He cared.

I still saw Marvin on occasion, but now we were just plain friends. He was so decent! And several years later, when he became engaged, Millie, Anna and I received an invitation to his wedding. I was surprised and pleased. His friendship was genuine. By then Millie and I had a car and we three girls attended the wedding. Bittersweet memories surfaced, of pain–and joy. I prayed he'd be happy.

Mama and Daddy's visit to the estate took an unexpected turn. As I proudly showed them the grounds and house, they marveled at the luxury, such as they had never seen. Imagine my chagrin when my father opened the liquor closet in the bar, just off the living room, and proceeded to examine one bottle after another. Mama scolded him for snooping where he had no business, but he could not be dissuaded. And I stood cringing and tongue-tied.

After the doctor returned, he went to his liquor closet one evening to make a drink and discovered the bottles in disarray. He was furious! I never saw him so angry.

"Who was in my liquor closet?" he erupted. "Jane, did you do this?" I was petrified. How could I tell on my father?

Truthfully I answered, "No, I didn't." But he ranted on.

"Don't be silly," Mrs. N. chided. "What would Jane want in your liquor closet?" Quaking all the while, I kept as quiet as could be, afraid that guilt was smeared all over my face.

"Mrs. K. must have cleaned the closet," Mrs. N. concluded, which did little to smooth the doctor's ruffled feathers. He finally dropped the subject, much to my relief, and rearranged the bottles. What a close call! I had never gotten in trouble with them and was rankled by Daddy's indiscretion.

One day Mrs. N. asked, " Could you please stay overnight next Saturday to help me with a cocktail party we're having? I'll need you to wash dishes. The doctor will take you home Sunday morning for church," she reassured. Reluctantly, I agreed.

The night of the party I was glad to be able to hide out in the kitchen. It was long and narrow, for efficiency, with counters on both sides. After a while, friendly guests with warm smiles brought their used plates and cups and stacked them on the counters. Their kind words of appreciation made my job easier and my shyness evaporated. I'd heard that James Michener and his wife were among the guests. He was a friend of the Normans and lived across the valley on the highway. Knowing he was a famous author, I sensed this was big time and enjoyed the excitement of the evening. By midnight when the last dish was dried and put away, I was ready to drop.

Though disappointed that I hadn't seen Michener the night of the party, I met him at Christmas time. Before the Normans left for a few hours one Saturday, the doctor told me, "James Michener will come to pick up his Christmas tree today. Come with me to the nursery and I'll show you his tree." Eagerly I anticipated the famous author's arrival and felt honored as I led him to his tree. In his work clothes, he appeared as unimpressive as our few words were insignificant, yet I knew I had just met a very important man in the eyes of the literary world. (In a matter of 20 years or so, my sister Grace would become an avid reader of his thick volumes. Their size made them too daunting for me.)

Both the Normans were appreciative and affirming of me and complimented my work profusely, especially the refinishing of furniture. One day, the summer before my senior year, Mrs. N. came home with a huge oak chest of drawers, with rows of tiny drawers at the top and bigger ones at the bottom.

"Once you have the varnish off this piece, I'll have you rub white paint into the grain," she explained. "Then I want to organize the house and fill the drawers and make a file so we know where things are." These projects consumed hours, but I enjoyed working alone in the garage and aimed to please. As one year passed into another, I loosened up and talked more with Mrs. N. and the doctor and almost became myself. By the time my four years were over, I felt like a refinishing pro.

I still loved to read and write. One summer I wrote a poem called "I'll Follow In His Footsteps." I heard that a neighbor, Mrs. Crocker, was sick and wrote a lengthy one for her, of faith and caring. When I went home for the weekend Mama told me how pleased Mrs. Crocker was with my poem. To my amazement, so was Mama! She was all smiles and admiration as she spoke of it. For once I did something right. Then I wrote a poem for Eleanor from church when she was sick. She loved it. I was happy to find something Mama approved of. She began calling me "the writer of the family." Millie was the artist and drew beautiful pictures.

During our high school years and after, Anna talked to Mama constantly and bubbled with happiness. I, by contrast, often felt like a dud and had nothing to say to Mama. At times I'd get depressed about the situation at home. Mama was often cold and silent toward me and I couldn't understand her. Daddy and I got along well, but even he became crankier as the years went on. Mama seemed jealous of my good relationship with him. But what could I do about that?

Ruth hated Mama and hated Grace because, she said, "I always got blamed for everything. Do you know how many yardsticks she broke on me?"

And Grace told me, "I was always embarrassed by her. How would you like it if your friends at school heard on the radio that your mother requested a song for their 12th wedding anniversary and for her daughter Grace Herstine's 12th birthday a week later?" Yes, Mama liked to request songs from a Sunday morning sacred-songs program from Allentown.

Though I feared Mama at times, I was the vocal one and once in a while I spoke my mind with passion when provoked. I recalled the day in grade school when I came home and Mama was sitting on a chair outside cleaning a chicken she had killed for supper. She'd buy us colored chicks for Easter and butcher them when they were grown. Though I don't recall the issue that day, I told Mama how I felt.

"You're too bold!" she retorted hotly. (We older three were not supposed to "talk back." Then we were accused of being too timid.) Mama was seated on a chair, which helped level the playing field. I was taller than she for a change, and perhaps that gave me courage.

"We can't even express an opinion around here!" I shot back, looking her in the eye, and walked off. *So now I'm too bold. Once it's too timid, then too bold.* I thought of Peter and John's boldness in Acts when they told the authorities, "We ought to obey God rather than men." Was boldness such a bad thing? A sin? Reading my Bible had given me big ideas. And, yes, sometimes, courage. Other times I felt guilty about it and struggled with my conscience. In my heart I wanted to be like Jesus—loving, obedient, and kind.

My inner conflict over how to relate to Mama continued off and on through my high school years. I alternated between depressing guilt and inspiring joy, love and victory. The conditioning of our younger years held us girls in its grip. As children we had listened to "Let's Pretend" every Saturday morning on the radio. The dramatized fairy tales and wicked step-mother stories like "Cinderella" had their effect on us and we associated Mama with these stepmothers. Then Millie found a book in the attic by Gene Stratton Porter, called *Girl of the Limberlost*, who had a hateful mother. We identified with the girl's struggles.

Counteracting these negative influences were programs Daddy turned on for us on Sunday evenings when we were young. I sat glued to the radio for "The Greatest Story Ever Told from the Greatest Life Ever Lived" by Fulton Oursler. I loved Jesus' deep, rich voice. He sounded so kind and caring and wise and I loved Him so much. I especially remember the episode where He stood before Pilate and Pilate said to Him, "Your own nation and the chief priests have delivered You to me. What have You done?"

Jesus answered, "My kingdom is not of this world. If My kingdom were of this world, My servants would fight…; but now, My kingdom is not of this world" (John 18:35,36).

Through the years, Daddy listened to a series of church programs on Sundays as we got ready for church and at other times of the day. Dr. Donald Gray Barnhouse was a favorite, well-known preacher from Philadelphia. We heard Charles Fuller of the Old Fashioned Revival Hour, Jack Wertzen from Word of Life camp in the Adirondack Mountains in New York, and The Lutheran Hour, Missouri Synod. I listened intently to the inspiring messages and glorious music. And Mama had her favorite Gospel singer program. Though Mama seldom went to church, she heard Bible teaching and messages in song that surely lifted her spirits many a Sunday.

At church and Sunday school I learned the Mennonite teachings on peacemaking. I was struck by Jesus' words, "love your enemies, and pray for those who persecute you, so that you may be the children of your Father in heaven" (Matt. 5:44). This I knew I must do, but it was hard. My prayers often seemed totally inadequate. However, God was guiding in quiet ways by His Spirit and Word and I was blessed in ways I couldn't always see.

During my free time at home I loved to ride bike, especially on Sunday afternoons when nothing else was happening. One Sunday I rode up past Crocker's house. Mama had told me to stay away from Crocker's place. She never gave a reason. *What does she have against them?*

Mama and Daddy had gone for a ride in the car, a frequent Sunday pastime. As I rode home, I saw Mary in Crocker's yard. She waved and called to me, so I stopped by the side of the road and we visited a while. Suddenly, I heard a car coming. I looked up and knew at once I was in trouble. As they went slowly by, Daddy smiled at us and nodded but Mama gave me a cold stare that said, "You are disobeying me!"

Such an innocent thing we were doing—two girls having a friendly visit—but I was shaking in my boots. I gave Mary an excuse and hurried home. Not one to flinch from facing the inevitable, I put away the bike and walked into the kitchen.

"What were you doing up there talking with Mary?" Mama demanded angrily.

"We were just talking."

"I told you not to go up there! She runs around with boys."

So that was it! I couldn't believe it. Mary was out of high school. "She's old enough," I said, defending her.

Quick as a flash Mama struck me in the face with such force that I fell against the refrigerator and into a chair beside it.

Humiliated and angry, I ran upstairs and flung myself on the bed and sobbed. Mama had always told us when we graduated from high school we could date. Mary was out of high school and Mama was criticizing her for dating? It didn't make sense. *I have no freedom at all,* I reasoned, *and now I get in trouble for trying to defend Mary. Why do I always get blamed for doing nothing wrong?* I was convinced Mama hated me. I sobbed my heart out.

Suddenly, as I cried, a loud voice spoke, *"You should love her and forgive her!"* Instantly I knew who it was. No one else was in the room. Stunned, I sat up and dried my eyes. In shock and disbelief, I got up and looked in the next room, then out the open window. No one was there. The voice had to be God! I knew what I must do. *I would love Mama and forgive her.*

I went downstairs and proceeded to help Mama with supper. She had just come in from outside, and I was struck by the serene look on her face. Her anger was gone and she acted as if nothing had happened. She never said a word about the incident. My feelings vacillated between love and anger. Would I ever get it right? How I had to guard against negative thoughts and feelings—a constant temptation. God in love was trying to correct my faults—my quick temper and negative attitude toward Mama.

As I peeled potatoes and set the table, feelings of resentment wanted to crowd into my mind for the way she treated me, and for never apologizing. But it was not her way. She was just doing her duty, keeping me on the straight and narrow. God expected me to submit to Mama's authority. And didn't Jesus say in the Sermon on the Mount (Matt. 5) that we are blessed when we suffer for doing right? I reasoned that is why I suffered at times.

But then I remembered the voice in the bedroom. God had spoken to me! I heard God with my own ears, like the people in the Bible. It seemed so incredible. Never would I forget this day and the Voice in my bedroom.

Though it didn't occur to me at the time, people were praying for us, like Mr. Kooker in Sunday school, our other Sunday school teachers, and our grandparents. God heard and answered those prayers in remarkable ways to teach and guide us. (Years later, the last time I visited my grandmother Landis before she died, she said to me, "I pray for you." No one had ever told me that before and I was very blessed. She was in her 80s and I was 30 and had just had my first child. How I thank God for a praying grandmother and for her words to me.)

I also remember Grammy's vivacious talk and lilting laughter in contrast to Pappy's soft voice and smile as he sat in his favorite chair. My second home until I was four, it was a safe and happy place where we loved to go. Every year on Christmas Day we drove to Grammy's to visit and get our gifts. When we were young, we often got hand-knit mittens, sox, or a scarf. In high school, we received books. The Landis family loved to read, and their favorite author was Grace Livingston Hill. We learned to love this writer through their gifts, and as perfect-attendance gifts in Sunday school. We girls traded with each other and later bought the Livingston Hill books for each other. This amazing author had book titles like the woman in the Bible had oil and flour that never ran out. As Millie, Anna, and I devoured the Christian romances of ideal young men and women, we desired to be like the heroines. We looked forward to marriage and establishing a Christian home someday—unlike the home of our childhood.

My social life during high school was almost nil, because of working weekends and summers. And even a nearby friend like Mary was off limits. I became more introspective and withdrawn. Hard times with Mama at home depressed me. As our senior year wore on, we had pictures taken for our yearbook. I disliked mine. When I gave a picture to Grammy Landis she exclaimed, "You look like you're ready to cry!" What a stark contrast from my 16th birthday photo from the Welcome Wagon. *What is happening to me?*

At the Normans I had peace and quiet and respect. The future looked bleak and I was glum. Daddy had changed during my years away at the Normans and this troubled me. His job for the borough had turned him into a nervous, irritable shadow of himself I hardly knew. His boss pelted his employees with criticism. At home, Mama sometimes gave him the same. He'd developed the habit of stopping for a drink on his way home from work, at the Moose Lodge or at the Elks, which he joined later. I hated the smell of liquor on his breath and his lousy disposition. Where was the happy father who had called me "Sunshine" and "Janie Lee from sunny Tennessee?"

I felt devastated and in my mind I often blamed Mama. Plus I no longer had the piano to play and sing the consoling hymns I loved. Instead, Mama monopolized the front room with the TV going non-stop, which I hated. There was no place for peace and quiet except upstairs or outside. I missed the quiet at the Norman's house. *How did life get so complicated?* Another concern faced me. High school was ending and I had to find a real job.

One day at the Normans I was reading Colossians chapter 3 when verse 13 jumped at me off the page. I read it again. It was as clear as the Voice in my room. I needed a reminder, again and again. God was speaking to me about Mama. "…forgiving one another, if anyone has a complaint against another; even as Christ forgave you, so you also must do." That hit me squarely between the eyes.

"Oh, Father," I prayed. "Please forgive me. I do forgive Mama. Take away my sin of unforgiveness and help me to love her. And thank You, Jesus, for forgiving me." A wonderful peace came over me, and I thought of Mama with love. I remembered the day God showed me that He loved her as much as He loved me, an amazing revelation. I marveled again that the Creator of the universe took such a personal interest in me and made His will known to an insignificant girl from Thatcher Road.

My first years at the Normans, Mrs. N. was very affectionate and often sweet-talked the doctor. Sometimes he responded in kind, but other times he was preoccupied and ignored her. I had learned from Eleanor my first year there that he was 60 and Mrs. N. was 40. She looked more like 25. At times I felt sad for them, and wished they knew Jesus. They knew church was important to me and that I read the Bible, and I always prayed before meals. Once when she was recovering from her surgery she told me her pastor would come that evening. When he came I was reading Isaiah in my King James Bible on the patio. As he left, he said, "Do you understand what you're reading?" *How curious*, I thought, *he asked the same question that Philip asked the Ethiopian eunuch.* I probably mumbled that I did, though well aware that much of this book was way beyond me.

One weekend, the middle of March of my senior year, I went to the Normans' as usual. After the doctor left for the office on Saturday morning, Mrs. N. got up and started cooking breakfast – very unusual. Soon a family friend, John, arrived and they ate together at the breakfast nook. Mrs. N. usually stayed in bed awhile as I went about my chores. I was mildly curious and hoped this was a one-time thing. But the next Saturday and the next, after the doctor left, the scenario was repeated. John had an invalid wife who'd been bedridden for years. My concern and disgust grew as this clandestine relationship continued week after week. And they acted like I wasn't there.

One Friday night when I arrived at the back room of the office, Mrs. N. was nowhere to be seen. The doctor usually stuck his head through the door between patients to greet me. This night when he opened the door, I could hardly believe my eyes. His face was haggard and drawn, like he'd been through the mill. I suspected the worst.

I cleaned and vacuumed as usual, got my treatment, and the doctor and I walked to the car for the drive home. How I dreaded this ride, almost worse than the first one with him four years before. I sat in the front with him, and before long he dropped the bombshell.

"Marge left me this week!"

I wanted to clap my hands over my ears. Though I knew what was coming, hearing the words made it painfully real. I expressed my regrets and sympathy but what could I say? I felt at a loss for words. His suffering was intense and I ached for him. An ominous silence pervaded the car as the headlights beamed into the dark night.

On arriving at the house, I went into the kitchen. Imagine my surprise when he came in, threw his arms around me and sobbed like a baby. "What did I do wrong?" he cried, heaving and broken. "What did I do wrong?"

All I could tell him was about the secret breakfasts that had been going on for months. His mood quickly changed from grief to anger and he stormed around with contempt for this "friend" who stole his wife.

The next Saturday morning before the doctor left for the office he said, "Marge will come this morning for her things."

How I dreaded seeing her! My whole body reacted to the news. My stomach tightened and I trembled as I washed the dishes. What would I say to her? I was furious at her, and doubly angry with that scoundrel who took her away. What a horrible ending to my four years at this beautiful, peaceful place. I learned that a paradise on earth is deceiving and does not make a happy marriage.

As I vacuumed the bedroom at the front of the house I kept watching down the lane. Then I got out the ironing board to do the sheets and the doctor's shirts. But every now and then I stole to the front window. Finally I spotted her red-orange Buick coming very slowly up the drive. I hurried to the ironing board to wait for the inevitable.

I waited, and waited, suspense and anxiety building by the minute. What were they doing? I cried out to God, *Please, help me!*

Finally they came in. Mrs. N. greeted me cheerily at the ironing board. "Hi, Janie. It's so good to see you!" I melted, and the tears flowed.

Alarmed, Mrs. N. hugged me and cried, "Why are you crying, Janie? The doctor didn't hurt me. Really, I'm okay. The doctor didn't hurt me at all!"

Then why did you leave him? My mind fairly roared.

Then that wife-snatching brute whipped out his white handkerchief and gave it to me to wipe my tears, offering his sympathies as well. How dare he? I wanted to throw it back at him and scream, *"Get out! Get out of this house!"* But my words stuck in my throat, as my sobs continued, gradually subsiding.

They went about their business then, collecting her things, and in an hour they were gone. My heart ached, my emotions all in a jumble.

When I told my parents about the separation they said little. However, I am sure that Mama talked to Daddy and expressed fears about me continuing to go there on weekends.

One day Daddy said, "I think you should stop going to the doctor's."

"But he needs me to clean and do the laundry," I countered. I trusted the doctor and had no fear. But another day Daddy spoke to me sharply from the top of the stairs, "If you get into trouble over there, don't come to me!"

I was stunned and hurt. Never had he spoken to me like that. Why didn't he trust me? How could I explain? I couldn't. The doctor was my employer and my friend. He was counting on me. Quitting now would only add to his troubles. My spirit wounded, I decided to go against my parents' wishes and work weekends the two short months left before graduation. And Daddy continued to drive me to the office on Friday after school without another word about it.

I could hardly wait for graduation when I'd get a secretarial job in town and quit the job with the doctor. My parents would learn they had nothing to fear.

A really special event and highlight of my senior year occurred the week after Mrs. N. left – our senior class trip to Washington, D.C. What a boon to my sagging spirits! We girls all bought new outfits – a suit and spring "topper," so popular in the fifties – and everyone looked stylish and beautiful. The fellows wore suits and ties, handsome as could be. One of the fellows asked me to be his girl for the trip. I didn't mind telling him I wasn't allowed to date since I felt sure he was going steady with a girl from a lower class.

We left on a bus early in the morning and had several days seeing all the sights. I climbed to the top of the Washington Monument, loved the Lincoln Memorial and the Jefferson Memorial with the beautiful cherry trees in bloom surrounding the Tidal Basin. (Senior trips were always timed to coincide with the famous cherry blossoms in bloom.) We toured the Capitol, Congressional Library and government buildings and had our class picture taken in front of the George Washington mansion at Mount Vernon in Virginia, in our Sunday best. Oh the joy of escaping – for four glorious days – from the sadness at the Normans.

Even though I rarely socialized outside of school hours, our Commercial Section had become my "group." We had made it through four years of speed typing, taking rapid shorthand dictation and transcribing it into letters on the typewriter, meticulous bookkeeping, junior business training, plus history – "POD," Problems of Democracy – English, biology and the like. I enjoyed the camaraderie of the classroom with pleasant fellow classmates. It was sad to see the year come to an end, but I felt well prepared to face the work world.

My last day of school was Friday, May 22, and last day at the Normans was Saturday, May 23. I was delighted when sister Ruth consented to go with me overnight to the doctor's. In three more days I would begin my new job that Mrs. Becker found for me. Was I up to the challenge?

CHAPTER 10

Waiting

Rejoicing in hope; patient in tribulation;
continuing instant in prayer...
ROMANS 12:12 (KJV)

1953–1956

My commercial teacher Mrs. Becker referred me to Moyer's Hatchery in the country a couple of miles from home because they preferred a Mennonite girl. That sounded great to me. The Moyers were "Old" Mennonites. My first day there, Mr. Moyer made clear, "I know you're a good Christian and you won't cut your hair or wear sleeveless blouses."

Inside I squirmed. My hair was short so it was obvious I had cut it. I felt uneasy, knowing I didn't comply with their strict standards. He knew I was a "New" Mennonite and perhaps thought we were not as circumspect as his people. It was my first run-in with the deep division between our two groups (which occurred in 1847).

Of course, I wanted to comply and I was delighted to work in a place with other Christians. I had no problem letting my hair grow. I knew God had guided me and I was deeply grateful. It's just that these pious, simple people were quite different from my world and home. The submissive women wore the prescribed "bib dress" with extra fabric over the bosom, white sheer prayer coverings over their long hair done up in buns, and no jewelry. They looked so pure and holy that I couldn't help feeling in awe of them. Still shy with strangers and professional people, I prayed for help and felt reassured by the verse, "I can do all things through Christ who strengthens me" (Phil. 4: 13). I felt fortunate and safe here. I would do my best. I served as stenographer/receptionist with some bookkeeping duties. Mr. Moyer gave dictation for letters.

Millie had a job as a bookkeeper/receptionist at Donaghy-Lacey Studebaker dealer (later Oldsmobile) where she worked with Kitty McNutt for two to three years. Over dishes in the evenings she entertained me with rare stories of her day with Kitty, and Kitty's exuberant, funny quirks and talk. Later someone recommended that Millie apply at Perkasie Vulcanizing, so she switched and worked there until after she was married.

In March 1954, Millie and I bought a tan 1950 Chevy together. Before that, Daddy drove us to work; now Millie could relieve him. Her friend, Eva Haigh, taught Millie to drive and went with her for her driver's exam. She passed her test by June 5. The Kookers from church agreed to teach me. What a blessing they were! After bungling the parallel parking on my first test, I succeeded on July 17. We girls still sang trios together at churches so now we could drive ourselves. The car gave us a taste of freedom!

Mama didn't seem to care that Millie drove, but when I got my license, she was not pleased. She said nothing, but her angry stares said it all. Wanting freedom and independence were my great faults, according to her. Mama resented losing her authority. I had not asked her permission to learn to drive or to buy the car with Millie. Whenever we asked her if we could do something, she'd say, "Do what you want to, you always do anyway!" So I often followed her advice. But this was double talk that made us sad and her mad. We were not free, and making my own decisions resulted in lingering guilt. We wanted to follow Jesus and do what was right. Then why did we have such a hard time with Mama?

I loved being at home after the years at the doctor's, but life with Mama drove me to the Lord and His word—right where He wanted me. I often rehearsed I Corinthians 13 and Philippians in my mind. My years of solitude made me more introspective. The Holy Spirit brought to mind gems from my King James Bible. Especially helpful were "In quietness and confidence shall be your strength" (Isa. 30:15), and "Thou wilt keep him in perfect peace whose mind is set on thee" (Isa. 26:3).

But I felt sad about the silence between Mama and me and wished she would like me and we could be happy. She didn't know what she was missing by not going to church. I looked for ways to be helpful and noticed that the Venetian blinds were badly in need of cleaning. One nice warm day I washed them all, upstairs and down. Mama was pleased indeed. It felt good to be in her good graces.

Times with brother Ralph were a highlight of my teen years. He was a caring, gentle, fun-loving guy who made me feel special. Living with our mother's parents and growing up in her home, as he did, provided a bond with our mother that I felt deep inside. Also, Cousin Charlie, three months older than Millie, became a very important friend in my life. Charlie was a member of my mother's Church of the Brethren. After high school when he bought a car, he'd pick up Ralph and cousins Bobby and Warren on a Sunday afternoon and say, "Let's go for a drive. Where shall we go?" He recalls that invariably Ralph said, "To see the sisters!" We'd visit at our house or go on long walks or drives. Once we did a moonlight midnight hike up the back road. It was great fun getting to know Ralph and our male cousins in this way. One Sunday we all got an invitation for dinner at cousin Warren's house, a rare and special treat. Later when Ralph got a car, he brought the cousins to visit. When Charlie's call came for the draft, he registered as a Conscientious Objector (CO). He served in Alternative Service, or I-W, at the state mental hospital in Harrisburg. During those years, he and I corresponded. This was a "safe" relationship with a male who respected me and treated me as an equal. Charlie's long letters and sharing made me feel important and special. As he wrote about the terrible conditions in the hospital, his work, and his faith, I learned to know him in a deeper way. I felt great respect for him and his convictions about military service, which the Mennonite, Quaker (Friends) and Brethren churches espoused (the three historic peace churches). Charlie was fun, too, and he and I became best friends.

As time went on I began to wonder about my future. *What about the commitment I made all those years at camp for "full-time Christian service?" What does God have for me to do?* I could be a missionary teacher but Mama said I couldn't go to college because we didn't have the money. On my salary, I didn't see how I could afford it. *Well,* I consoled myself, *Millie, Anna, and I do have a ministry singing at churches and other meetings.*

We girls also attended Youth for Christ meetings in town where I met Ethel. She seemed lonely and loved to go to church meetings. She had a car and invited me to go with her to meetings here and there. Sometimes she went with us girls when we sang. In April of that year, according to my little Hallmark date book, she and I went to meetings eight times. I enjoyed having a friend to do things with, but it did seem a little much. And it was definitely too much for Mama and she called a halt.

"I don't want you to go with her anymore," she ordered. I was out of high school and this was a *girl*, but Mama didn't trust Ethel, or me. There was no discussion. Mama had taught me years before not to ask Why? I felt sad to tell Ethel goodbye, with no good explanation.

Rev. Wilmer Denlinger, our pastor in our teen years, used a game at Sunday evening meetings for the youth called "Draw Swords," with the Bible as our "sword of the Spirit " (Ephesians 6:17). He gave a Scripture reference as we held our Bibles above our heads. When he called, "Draw Swords!" we hunted for the verse as fast as we could. From memorizing the books of the Bible and much reading of the Bible I was quick on the draw.

One day Millie encouraged me with words she overheard at church. "Mrs. Kooker said she thinks you have the strongest faith of all the young people at church." Surprised and pleased, I realized that my faith had grown during my times of solitude at Normans. The Lord opened doors of opportunity for me at church. First I served as treasurer of the Sunday school, then as correspondent to *The Mennonite*, a weekly magazine. Later I was corresponding secretary for our district youth organization, which included about 25 churches. I enjoyed working with Dave Hillegas, president of the group and a young husband and father. He brought work to my home and I typed letters for him on the Underwood Millie had bought from the high school. The large district youth banquet was a tremendous highlight and inspiration. While I felt restricted at home, God had plans for me that I couldn't imagine. I would learn that His mysterious ways are "past finding out" (Job 9:10; Rom. 10:33). Dave, the youth president, invited me to attend the U.S. and Canadian youth meetings with him in Newton, Kansas in November 1954. I was amazed and excited at this opportunity. Since I was not yet 21, the age when Mama said we would "be on our own," I am quite sure I asked her if I could go. I am equally sure of her response: "Do what you want to. You always do anyway!" She knew we were not going to bad places when we went to church meetings and this must have helped to mollify her. I decided to go.

From Philadelphia, Dave and I traveled to Kansas on Amtrak. My first train ride – the longest trip I'd ever taken – took a day and most of the night. I loved eating in the dining car and watching the scenery pass by. But sleeping sitting up was another matter. The "Texas Chief," at 100 miles an hour, fairly flew from Chicago to Newton. It rumbled and rocked all night and by the time we arrived at Newton at 3:00 A.M. I had a splitting headache. A teenage couple met us and took us to our respective homes. I went to a big farmhouse in the country near Moundridge, a place I'd read of in *The Mennonite*.

It was so good to finally crawl into bed in the tiny bedroom off the kitchen. Before long I awakened to the most gorgeous sunrise I had ever seen. Shining through my east window, the big orange ball on the horizon flooded my room with light. God's presence seemed to fill the room and my heart leapt up and rejoiced in anticipation of blessings on this Lord's Day.

At breakfast, the elderly husband led in devotions before we ate, and again a hush of God's presence filled the room. This was my first experience with family devotions in a Mennonite home, and how I imagined every Mennonite family began their day. I felt like I was on holy ground, my heart full of gratitude and quiet excitement.

As we drove to church along the dirt road, I took in the wide expanse of flat Kansas farmland. Soon the imposing, white frame church came into view. I was dumbfounded at the streams of cars seeming to come out of nowhere. Wheat fields stretched to the horizon in every direction with few houses in sight, yet the cars kept coming and filled the great parking lot. This enormous building dwarfed our small church back home.

Inside, the church sanctuary was the largest I had ever seen. One hundred churches the size of mine at home would probably fit into it. During the Sunday school hour in the youth class, gracious words flowed from the lips of our teacher, Dr. Erland Waltner. (He would later become president of our seminary.) In the worship service, the dynamic pastor, Peter Dyck, preached a powerful sermon. (I learned much later that Peter was the well-known "Moses" who helped resettle Mennonites from Germany and Russia to Paraguay after World War II.) In quiet awe of this mountaintop experience, I was in my element. What a spiritual feast God had prepared for me!

The next days were filled with meetings at another large church built of white sandstone on the Bethel College campus in North Newton. Youth leaders from around the country and Canada deliberated on the business of the organization. I loved meeting these friendly, committed young people, many of them college students. It was my first time to meet Canadian young people; I was impressed with their mature, strong personalities and assertive leadership. We toured our General Conference Headquarters offices and the new mental hospital, Prairie View, an outgrowth of Conscientious Objectors' experiences with deplorable conditions in state-run facilities.

On the way home we had an exciting stop in Chicago where we visited Mennonite Biblical Seminary, which shared a campus with Bethany Church of the Brethren Seminary. We rode on the subway, and ate with friendly seminary people at a restaurant, with stimulating conversation. A stop at Pacific Garden Mission on skid row was a sad, eye-opening experience.

When I returned home I reported to our church about the trip. I recall the laughter at my descriptions and the way our people vicariously enjoyed the experience with me. How blessed I was to have such a caring church family, small though it was.

At home, our family was preparing for a momentous event. On March 30, 1955, when I was 20 and Ruth was 14, Mama presented us with a new baby brother. Now we were seven. Mama named him Thomas Martin after her brother Thomas Williams and nephew Martin Ruch. I was overjoyed! Tommy was born in the hospital and a few weeks later became so sick with breathing problems (from tobacco smoke in the house?) that he was hospitalized for a couple of weeks. I was glad when he was safely home again. Baby Tommy brought much sunshine into our home and we girls all loved him.

Brother Ralph had a paper route where he lived in Coopersburg. Auntie Esther, who was married now and lived near Quakertown, worked at a shoe factory in Coopersburg. Sometimes on her way to work she passed Ralph, riding his bike, and waved at him. But the morning of March 30 when she saw him, she stopped the car and announced, "You have a new baby brother, Ralph!" Delighted to get the news the same day by "special delivery," he was thrilled that at last he had a brother.

I enjoyed mothering Tommy and often wished Mama would be a better mother to him and stop her smoking. We all greatly enjoyed him and Mama scolded at times that we were spoiling him.

Back: Anna, 19; Ralph, 17; Grace, 15; Front: Ruth, 14; me, 20, holding Tommy, 8 mos.; Millie, 22, December 1955.

In November of 1955, youth president Dave encouraged me to go to the meetings in Kansas again, this time by car with him and three other officers – Shirley Moyer, Gerald Musselman, and Gordon Dyck. I wouldn't miss it! We drove cramped in a VW over 1200 miles, and had a hilarious time. Gordon was full of jokes and I never laughed so much in my life. Shirley and I roomed together at the home of an elderly couple in North Newton, and she and I became good friends. The stimulating meetings were an education and gave me a love for the wider church that grew in years to come. Again I gave a report to our church family.

After a time, a new fellow showed up at work. He'd walk by my office and smile at me. One day he asked me out for lunch and I accepted. The next day he took me to the swankiest restaurant in town – Trainer's Seafood Restaurant. I had never eaten there except for Christmas dinners with the children's home kids. This fellow said he was from New England, that he'd take me there and teach me to ski and show me a grand time. He talked too much and seemed so brash. After eating he drove me back to work and as we got out of the car he said, "I'll come to see you after work. Where do you live?" Though I was somewhat leery of him, like an idiot I gave him directions.

No sooner was I back in the office when the assistant manager stormed in all upset.

"Jane!" he barked, dark eyes piercing. "Do you know what you just did?"

"No," I said, mystified.

"You just went out with a married man! Not only that, but he's in trouble. He was given a job here to help him get straightened out. I followed you to the restaurant and waited outside, fearing what he might do with you. Do you realize he could have driven off with you?" This man had been a gentle, humble friend to me. Never had I seen him angry. My heart pounded.

"I didn't know," I said lamely, "or I never would have gone with him." Inside I seethed that no one had told me about this impostor and then blamed me. Feeling totally humiliated and chastised, I could hardly work that afternoon. And to think he was coming to my house after work!

At home I told Mama what had happened. "If he comes, tell him I don't want to see him," I said. She seemed pleased that I'd confided in her and sought her help to ward him off. In fact, my confession had disarmed her and she became unusually pleasant and cheerful. She was actually enjoying this interesting scenario!

Still angry and trembling, I ran upstairs to watch at the window. Soon a car drove into the driveway and the fellow got out, greeted Mama, and told her he wanted to see me. But Mama didn't follow my instructions. "Jane, come down," she called up to me, "He wants to see you." How could she do this to me?

"No," I yelled, shaking with disgust. "I don't want to see him!" But he refused to leave. He stood around, staring up at the window.

Finally I stormed outside, burning with anger and mortification, and told him off like I never told anyone in my life.

"You lied to me!" I accused. "You told me you weren't married and you are!"

"No, I'm not," he lied again. I couldn't believe his audacity.

"The manager *told me* you're married," I persisted, "and you can leave–NOW–and I never want to see you again!" Tears of rage coursed down my cheeks. His face fell and, sheepishly, he turned and got into his car and left. I never saw him again after that day. I learned that even a Christian establishment had its pitfalls.

Mortified, I wondered how I could live down this mistake at work. I cried out to God to forgive me and keep me from trouble and evil. In time, I felt the manager forgave me and I also forgave him.

After high school, I dated a few Christian fellows a short while but was not interested in getting serious. Millie and Anna had their friends or dates and Janice and I seldom saw each other. Millie and Anna had grown closer together during the years I spent at the doctor's, and at times I felt left out. Anna's close friend, Jeanette, often invited her for weekends. Sundays were lonely if Ralph didn't visit. Grace usually spent summers at Olive's, who was married and had children. Millie and Grace babysat for them, and Grace went to many pajama parties.

Life's hard lessons continued like one season follows another. One winter, on a Sunday afternoon, Millie and her date invited us sisters to go sledding with them on a big hill. It was my first time on a toboggan and the hill was long and perfect. Before long I found myself on the sled with the brother of Millie's boyfriend. He began calling me for dates and even though Millie said the guys didn't go to church, I accepted. I knew he had quit high school and realized we had little in common. Though he was a nice fellow I did not want to keep dating him but was afraid of hurting his feelings. We went out every Saturday night to a string of creative places he dreamed up–bowling, amusement parks, you name it, he knew of it. I didn't know how to share my faith with him and soon my conscience bothered me and I lost my peace. I felt like such a wimp and had no clue what to do. As the months went by, I felt trapped.

That summer, a Christ-for-Quakertown crusade was held from August 13-28. Though not held every summer, these crusades were usually a downer during my teen years. A fiery evangelist had his arsenal loaded with frightening sermons. We girls, with sensitive spirits, invariably felt convicted and at least once we walked the "sawdust trail." Then we went to a counseling room, often in tears, to be prayed for. But I found no peace or comfort.

Adding to my misery, one night the sermon was on the unpardonable sin. Blaspheming the Holy Spirit was the one sin that could never be forgiven. *What exactly is blasphemy?* I wondered. My imagination ran wild and I was afraid I had committed it. When the crusade was over, I continued to live in fear. Finally one day I took Anna into my confidence. "I think I committed the unpardonable sin."

"I think I did, too!" I couldn't believe it! How could good, sweet Anna be guilty of such a gross sin? It was unthinkable. But it was some comfort to know that if I went to hell she'd be there, too!

Finally, I decided to seek help. Mr. Moyer was a pastor and I confessed my fear to him. He went to his house next door for books on the subject, read to me from them, and reassured me, "If you had committed this sin against the Holy Spirit, you wouldn't care. The fact that you are worried about it shows that you are sensitive to the Spirit." He prayed with me and a great weight was lifted. How happy I was to share this good news with Anna.

Still struggling with how to break off my relationship with this fellow, my turmoil reached the point where one Friday night after work I changed clothes and told a sister to tell our parents that I would not be home for supper. I left the house and walked down the narrow back road toward town. I stopped by the creek that meandered through farmer Stoneback's fields. Cows looked up from nibbling grass near the road as I parted the barbed wire fence and climbed through into the pasture. I scarcely noticed the beauty of the warm fall day and countryside, but the grove of large trees felt like a safe canopy of privacy. Wandering back and forth through the grass, I cried my heart out to God. But God seemed far away and silent. After an hour or more, I knew I must go home. Then I realized I'd lost my glasses in the grass. I combed the area without success. This seemed a small thing compared with my heavy burden. Finally, still crying, I headed home.

As I arrived long after supper, Daddy met me outside by the back steps. He looked worried and tears ran down his face as he asked, "What's wrong?"

I was unprepared for this deep show of compassion. "I'm not a Christian any more!" I wailed.

Daddy said with conviction, "God loves *everyone*." We walked into the kitchen as Mama came from the front room. She said nothing but her angry stare assaulted my wounded spirit.

Daddy spoke kindly, "Get ready and I'll take you to the football game." My sisters had already gone. The fall football games at high school were in full swing and the home games were our usual Friday night activity. Anna had graduated but Grace was now a cheerleader. We all enjoyed the games. Having missed them during high school due to my job at the doctor's, I found them fun and exciting – but this night I was not in the mood. With nothing else to do, I dried my eyes and Daddy drove me to the game.

The next morning, farmer Stoneback knocked on our door and asked, "Did one of your girls lose her glasses down near the creek yesterday?" In amazement I realized that only God could have protected them and shown the farmer where they were. I had looked high and low, cows roamed the area, yet he found them – unbroken! Incredible! While I thought that God must be condemning me, I realized that this was a sign of God's love, a reminder that God was there with me the day before, heard me, and saw my tears. What a kind, compassionate heavenly Father, like my father was to me.

With this renewed assurance of God's presence, I resolved it was time to tell my beau goodbye. But I dreaded the next date. I hated to hurt this fellow and prayed earnestly for help. It took Mama to jar me into action.

That week she said to me, "Jane, why don't you marry ––––? He has a nice car!" *A nice car?!* I was jolted to reality. Car indeed! I would never marry a man for his car! I had read the book *Heirs Together* on dating. It stated that a Christian should not marry a non-Christian and had strict dating rules. I had adopted this standard and then blew it. I determined this Saturday would be our last date.

That Saturday night after we drove into our driveway, I explained that I was very sorry but I would not be dating him anymore. His anger flared and he threatened, "If you stop going with me, I'll kill myself!" What a shocking, dreadful thought!

Though worried about him, I had made up my mind and stood my ground. Praying for help, I knew Jesus was right there. When he saw he could not persuade me, I told my date goodbye and got out of the car. As I walked away, he backed out of the driveway, gunned the engine, and drove off so fast that I was sure the whole neighborhood heard him. He accelerated to a frightening speed, with tires squealing around every curve far up the road. *"Oh God!"* I cried, *"Please protect him! Forgive me, and thank You for helping me."*

With a deep sigh of relief, I headed up to bed. Finally I was free. Yet for a long time to come a burden of guilt and grief clouded my mind over that unwise relationship. I hoped and prayed for the best for him, and a few years later rejoiced when Millie told me that he had married.

At that point in my Christian life I thought that all Christians were pretty much perfect and that if I had accepted Christ then I should be perfect, too. When I sinned I could not forgive myself. I have since learned that we will never be perfect on this earth. Only Jesus is perfect. We make mistakes and fail, but God forgives us when we repent and turn away from our sin. I learned that instead of condemning me, the Spirit was calling me back to obedience, peace, and joy.

My life seemed full of contrasts. I liked when Daddy was in a happy mood. He and I still talked in the kitchen, often on Saturday mornings. He'd come home from work and share stories from up town, of interesting people and happenings. In spite of his problems at work, he loved life and his face often glowed with a sunny smile as he talked. I liked when Mama was in a good mood too, but after hard times with her, I closed up tight like a turtle that is poked and hit.

In time, Millie, Anna and I talked about getting an apartment. After looking at one and hearing the price of rent and utilities, with furniture costs in addition, we gave up. With a jolt I saw how good we had it at home. I earned $36.00 a week at the hatchery the first year. With taxes deducted, I had $30.00 clear—big bucks to me after getting $12.00 a week at the doctor's the last year (and giving some of that to Mama each week). After high school, I gave $10.00 to Mama and $5.00 to Daddy. Millie and Anna gave $10.00 to Daddy and $5.00 to Mama.

As one year led to another and life droned on at work, with all the routine details, my mind drifted to college and friends from camp who had gone to Bluffton. They wrote and asked, "When are you coming to college?" When indeed? God only knew. Mama said we didn't have the money and I couldn't afford it without savings and $15.00 left a week, less my tithe on the full amount of $36.00.

However, many good and wholesome things filled my days. In the fall of 1955, Millie and I were invited to attend Moody Bible correspondence classes in a nearby town with a couple of lay pastors, Dave, the youth organization president, and my cousin Marietta's father, Bob Landis. (Marietta's mother Marie and my mother Grace had been first cousins, and best friends.) This was the next best thing to going to Bluffton. After a weekly lecture, we did our lesson at home to be sent to Moody Bible Institute. I loved the studies and got good grades. Classes from September to June whetted my desire for college.

One summer Aunt Jean asked me to teach at their Bible school at my mother's Church of the Brethren. Walking through the unfamiliar halls and rooms filled me with a sense of my mother's presence, as though I was walking on holy ground. This church reminded me of the ache of having missed my mother's nurturing love and teaching, an ache I often pushed out of my mind. But as I taught, a strength not my own helped and comforted me. As I reflected on my mother's influence in my life, as well as her family's, my home church, camp and pastors, I realized how God had used all of these examples to guide me into a life of service.

We five sisters had many good times together. For Christmas one year Anna and I received ice skates from Mom and Daddy. Millie and Grace already had them and my little Hallmark date book says that I bought skates for Ruthie for an early birthday present. The creek below our house was a favorite place to play in summer and to skate or sled in winter.

The day after Christmas, 1955, we had a hard freeze on the creek. We girls and Richard and James next door decided to go skating. A few other friends joined us. Someone suggested playing "crack the whip." Richard took my hand and joined the end of the line of skaters. I was not a good skater and as the line turned in a fast circle, the leader swiftly "cracked the whip" in the other direction. At that point, Richard let go of my hand. I went flying – and fell plop on my face. I lay knocked out for a couple of minutes and came to with a bloody broken nose. My whole face hurt, and this time my glasses were broken.

Daddy drove me to the doctor's office. Mama accompanied us, but her silence and lack of sympathy hurt. My nose and black eye healed more quickly than my pride and I vowed never to play crack the whip again. I had to pray hard for God to help me love and forgive Mama.

Though Daddy never made rules for us, we knew Mama's rules all too well. She had made clear years before, "You can't date until you're out of high school, and *when you're 21 you'll be on your own.*" I looked forward to my twenty-first birthday.

The next year, on February 6, 1956, the magic day came. It wasn't a big deal, and I don't remember anything special about it. I didn't feel any freer than before. Life went on as usual, with our trio singing in churches, occasional youth socials, and the Moody Bible class. And I still served on the Executive Committee for our youth organization.

During my years in high school I had a crush on Paul (not his real name) from our sister church in town. After high school he went to college but by second semester was forced to quit due to a nervous breakdown. After having counseling he seemed much his old self and he started calling me to talk or ask me out. Since he didn't drive, I used our car for dates, often to hear a special speaker. Paul was a kind, gentle person, sensitive, and took his Christian life seriously. We both loved discussing Scripture and our faith. He was easy to talk with, unlike other fellows I dated. I couldn't believe this was happening. He respected me and we were equals.

But Mama didn't like Paul. From a friend she had learned about Paul's breakdown. One day Mama scolded, "Why are you going with a boy who has 'mental problems'? You should stop going with him." *Here we go again.* Would she ever allow me to have a friend without interference? I hated to defy her but I thought she was unfair.

Sometimes we double-dated and the other fellow drove. Once when Paul came to the door for me Mama slammed the door in his face and left him standing there. If he called on the phone she spoke rudely to him. Her behavior sickened me and made it very hard for me to love her. I could only hope that God had something better for me, and soon. Hadn't I committed my life to Christ to follow His will and plan for my life? What *was* God's plan for me? How could I find it? I longed to go to college where camp friends Violet Kaiser and Joanne Mill had gone.

In my third year at the hatchery, business had increased with chicks shipped by plane to Puerto Rico and delivered by truck as far away as Lancaster County. My workload increased in the office so that Mr. Moyer hired a woman to help me. Pauline Yoder was married with two young children. Her husband Dave worked in the shop. We became friends and I enjoyed her company and practical wisdom.

One day Mr. Moyer arranged a deep-sea fishing trip for the employees. I wasn't thrilled, but Pauline and David were going so why not? We spent the day at Cape May off the New Jersey coast. Together, 15 to 20 people caught an amazing 263 fish! I do not recall if I caught any, but we all got our quota. Mama was impressed with our abundant catch, and she and I spent several hours working together that evening. I told about our day and she chatted happily, genuinely enjoying beheading and cleaning the smelly, slippery fish. That is a memory I cherish of a good time with Mama, just the two of us.

During the summer of 1956, an amazing chain of events changed my life dramatically. Every summer for 11 years I attended camp at Men-O-Lan. This year was my 12th. Camp that summer was exceptional for me, with high school and college-age youth combined. Paul was there, as was cousin Marietta, a high school sophomore whom I didn't know well. That week we became good friends and I learned to know many other youth from our district who were so much fun. I felt enveloped in the warmth of human love and God's love. I relished the classes, spirited singing, and softball games. This had to be the most wonderful week of my life as I felt free to be me. Here Christ was central. Before the week was out, Paul asked me to go steady and I agreed.

One day as I waited in the chow line, a former missionary to India, Mrs. S. T. (Meta) Moyer, was behind me. Out of the blue she said, "I watched you playing softball today. You played so well. Have you ever thought of going to college?" Her great dark eyes shone in the most glowing, smiling face I had ever seen. How could she hit such a tender spot? And what did a softball game have to do with college?

"I've thought of going many times," I stammered, "but my stepmother says I can't because we don't have the money."

"Oh, that's no problem, there are scholarships available and you could get a job." She was so sure of herself that it scared me.

The dinner bell cut our conversation short, and unwilling to discuss the subject further I avoided Mrs. Moyer the rest of the week. I feared having to face Mama now that college seemed a possibility. Mama would not take kindly to losing my $10.00 a week. She had told me I could not go to college. The thought of telling her made me shudder. Yet the faint glimmer of hope was exhilarating.

The afterglow of camp warmed my heart after I returned home and back to work. But the memory of the conversation with Mrs. Moyer unsettled and excited me. Maybe I *could* go to college some day.

My parents received *The Mennonite* on the Every Home Plan and I loved to read it. With each issue, my mind was informed, my spirit inspired, my imagination stretched. The magazine took me out of my confined existence to towns around the country, to countries of missionaries, and the highest offices of our conference. I learned the names of many pastors and churches and became familiar with our work across the U.S., Canada, and the world. What a gift this was in our home. It helped shape my dreams, vision, and commitment to Christ and the church.

I had saved the April 17, 1956 issue (which I still have!) and re-read the article, "Why I Chose a Mennonite School." In that issue, pictures of 13 Mennonite college students stared at me from three pages, bright faces, some whom I had met at the meetings in Kansas. My heart ached with longing as I read their reasons for choosing their college: "Christ-centered," "the well-balanced products our schools produced," "I wouldn't miss it for the world!" "young people from scattered areas meet," "I wanted a solid Bible background," "I was impressed with the fine reputation of our missionaries." Many of these students were at Bluffton where I had friends from camp. *It's so easy for them*, I thought, *They have supportive parents.*

I was in my fourth year at the hatchery. How long would I have to wait? I cried out to God, *"O Father, will I ever be able to go to college? Please help me if it is Your will."*

Mrs. Moyer said I could go to college. Maybe it was not impossible. Yet, a stone wall seemed to block my path. Wavering between hope and resignation, I did nothing. Believing for so long that I had no rights of my own, I stayed in my rut. It would take a miracle to move me out of it.

On my lunch hour on nice days, I ate my lunch outside on a chair under a tree. I loved being out in nature and was grateful to Mr. Moyer for that chair. I kept a New Testament in my purse and a tiny devotional book, *The Secret of Inspiration* by Dr. Andrew Murray. The serene picture on the cover of a small house nestled among trees by a smooth lake, with mountains rising in the distance, spoke of peace and rest in God. I loved this little book. As I read and meditated, I sensed God's presence very near. The sweetness of his Spirit lifted me above my circumstances.

One noon as I sat reading, meditating, and praying about college, a deep peace enveloped me. A strong impression filled my mind that God was near and an assurance seized me that He had it all worked out. Filled with joy and excitement, I knew God understood and heard me. This awareness and confidence energized me as I went back to the office. I would trust God with my future.

About a month after camp, Mildred Rosenberger, from a church across town phoned to say that she and three other women were going to drive to our church conference in Winnipeg, Manitoba, Canada. They had room for one more. Would I care to go? *Would I? I would love to go!* But would Mr. Moyer give me another two weeks off? Even though I already had my vacation, I decided to ask him. He graciously consented and I was thankful that Pauline was there to fill in for me. Another trip! And this time, to Canada!

We took three days going and four coming back. What a joyful adventure this trip turned out to be with lovely Christian women – four of us single, and a fairly young widow who knew the meaning of sorrow. She shared about her loss, yet she had the most remarkable sense of humor and often had us in stitches. The fun and hilarity, sightseeing – a water-skiing show, viewing Madison, Wisconsin from atop the capitol, the drive across the new Mackinaw Bridge – added unexpected pleasures. Serious sharing from these women, older than I, gave insights and pause to my impatient spirit.

The day we arrived at conference, whom should I meet but Mrs. Moyer from camp. What a miracle that she found me in that great crowd of people and that she recognized and confronted me as if she had been expecting me.

"Oh, you're *here!*" she exclaimed. I would recognize those piercing eyes and radiant face anywhere. She put her arm around me. "I'm so glad you came! Now you have to meet the president, Dr. Ramseyer!" He was from Bluffton College, our church college in Ohio. She hustled me off before I could protest and introduced me to him as a prospective student. "She will need a job," she told him. What was this woman doing? I felt caught in a whirlwind.

"You'll have to see Carl Lehman, our business manager," he told me, with a twinkle in his eye. "He'll know if there are any jobs available." Dr. Ramseyer was a short, stocky man with gray hair and dark eyes. He had spoken at my home church once, and seemed like a stern, no-nonsense man. I felt scared of him. But today he had a kind smile and I relaxed.

I could not believe this was happening. Dumbfounded, I followed this diminutive missionary with the brisk step. She quickly found Mr. Lehman and after introductions he quizzed me on a couple of pertinent areas: school grades and work experience. "School begins in three weeks," he said, "so most of the jobs have been assigned. But I'll check when I get back to school and call you by Tuesday evening if there's anything available."

Ah, relief! All this was happening too fast. Most of the jobs were taken. *I'm too late for this year,* I thought. *Maybe next year I can go.* And so, in my mind, I put off the dreaded confrontation with Mama. For good measure, Mrs. Moyer introduced me next to the assistant to the president, Harry Yoder, a warm and jovial man.

How I enjoyed that conference. The huge auditorium filled with more Mennonites than I had ever seen. Their singing of "O Power of Love," and "For God So Loved Us," and other chorales they sang in German and English sent my spirit soaring. Cousin Marietta Landis was there with her parents, Bob and Marie. She and I paired up and spent happy hours together. On a bus tour of Winnipeg Mennonite homes I was awestruck by the beauty of luxurious homes and gardens. At one place, I met our former pastor, Rev. A. J. Nuenschwander, who had baptized me. He and his wife were as delighted as I to meet again.

Rooming at the dorm of Canadian Mennonite Bible College, I wished I could stay for the fall term. The spanking new building, with classrooms, dining hall and dorm combined, abounded with young people. The food was wonderful. My yearning for college deepened.

An important item of business at the conference was the move of our seminary from Chicago to Elkhart, Indiana. I paid close attention to the discussion, intrigued with the history of the seminary and the strong arguments of those for and against a move. Those in favor wanted to foster a closer relationship with our "Old" Mennonite counterparts at Goshen College and Biblical Seminary ten miles from the proposed new campus. The progressives expressed the hope that in years to come the schools would merge. The vote passed and I rejoiced. The seminary would move. I would love to see our two Mennonite groups join as one. Why should we be divided if we were all Mennonite Christians?

We arrived home Sunday evening and I returned to work once more. But my mind was riveted on an incredible secret: *maybe I will go to college this fall!* Would Mr. Lehman call on Tuesday? Would he find me a job? I felt expectant, but scared. What would I do if he *did* call? Excitement mounted as Monday slipped into Tuesday. I hardly knew how to pray. Mama would have my hide if I said I was leaving for college. Was my miracle really on the way?

PART II

ON MY OWN

CHAPTER 11

A Dream Fulfilled

*I press toward the mark for the prize of the
high calling of God in Christ Jesus.*
PHILIPPIANS 3:14 (KJV)

1956–1960

Tuesday evening at home the phone rang. The college business manager wanted to speak to me! Amazement and disbelief grew as I heard him explain, "I have a job for you. President Ramseyer needs a secretary and if you want the job you could work 24 hours a week and take a 12-hour class load. You could work your way through in four years if you attend summer school and work the year around. Or, without summer school, you could finish your degree in five years. Think about it and call Dr. Ramseyer collect by Friday if you accept." And that was it.

Shockwaves reverberated in my brain. My heart pounded as the news sank in. *The president!* Had I heard right? This was an offer too good to refuse. Convinced that God's hand was in this unexpected offer, I felt like He had me in a corner. Mr. Lehman said I should be there a week from Friday. I had to think fast. But how could I decide?

And then I remembered Mrs. Moyer's words to me at conference. "Everything will unfold like a beautiful bud." Her words were prophetic – awesome. She must be praying for me. And she surely had a direct line to God. (I learned years later that getting deserving students into college was part of her mission in life.) I was in awe of God's leading in the events of the past weeks.

Then reality hit like a thunderclap. The moment I dreaded had arrived. I went to Mama and told her, "I have a job offer to work my way through Bluffton College as secretary to the president. And I need to let them know by Friday." There! It was out.

Mama nearly exploded. I stayed calm, remembering her rule.

Quietly I reminded her, "I'm 21." She had told us for years that we'd be on our own then.

"I don't care if you are!" she snapped, eyes blazing.

With a heavy heart I went to my father with the exciting opportunity. "I don't see why you want to go so far from home," he began, "but it's up to you. I think you'll regret it." How discouraging. It hurt that Daddy did not support me, but I understood his background and could forgive him. At least he had said, "It's up to you."

My employer was more encouraging, though I felt guilty about leaving on such short notice. Pastor Moyer listened to my story, then responded, "I've been wanting to take some courses for my church work and give you more responsibility in the office, but if you feel this is God's will for you, I don't want to stand in the way." How glad I was for an understanding Christian employer, and humbled at how God kept opening the way for me.

Our church people were happy for me and encouraged me to accept. My brother Ralph and boyfriend Paul thought it was great. My sisters were excited for me. But Mama refused to budge and would not speak to me. Her dark stares whenever our paths crossed were a sad substitute for communication. Why did such an exciting time have to be filled with so much pain? And how could I make a decision amidst this turmoil?

Another concern was money. Would I earn enough to cover my expenses? My only savings were a Christmas club of a dollar or two a week for Christmas presents. Our church was adding an addition to bring our old building up to date and I would be unable to keep my pledge. I was now making $50.00 a week, which seemed like a small fortune, but it went out almost as soon as it came in. Tithe, $15.00, payment home, church pledge, car payment (Millie would pay it all now), and clothing. If I went to college I'd have to trust that God would work this out, too.

Friday after work I still struggled with indecision. I felt immobilized, lacking the courage to call and say, "I'm coming." Excited but afraid of the unknown, my heart pounded and my hands felt clammy and cold. I could not pick up the phone. *"Oh, God, help me!"* I cried.

No one else was home as I paced back and forth, from room to room, praying for guidance and trying to decide what to do. Suddenly I saw our next-door neighbor, Mrs. Renninger, turn into their driveway beside our house. Instantly I knew. *I must tell Mrs. Renninger!* I had completely forgotten. A long-time friend and confidant, so kind and funny and wise, she now appeared like a lifeline in my overwhelming indecision.

Renninger family: Left to right: Richard, Anna, Charles, James.

I bolted from the house and told her of the offer, my parents' reaction, and my dilemma. Indignant to think that I would pass up such an opportunity, she ordered, "You go in there right this minute and call and tell them you're coming!"

Finally, I had my answer. My burden lifted as I hurried to the phone, called Dr. Ramseyer and accepted. "I'll be there next Saturday," I finished confidently, my heart beating wildly.

How quickly things had changed since I came home from camp. So *this* was what God had planned for me! It was almost too much to comprehend. My dream would come true at last – three years after high school. A thought came to mind that I had read years before which I adopted as my goal, "I'll study and get ready, and then my chance will come." I was going to college!

But a hard week lay ahead. Mixed emotions churned inside me as I gathered the necessary things and prepared to leave my family. Mama's silence hurt. Unable to talk with her about deep feelings, I could not tell her now of the joy, anticipation, and adventure that filled my heart.

I had a part-time evening job doing filing for Rev. Sam Sprunger, the new administrator of the Children's Home. When I told him about my job offer at Bluffton I was dismayed at his response. "My brother lost his faith at Bluffton," he said. "If you lose your faith there, the whole conference is going to hear about it!" Well! I didn't know the "whole conference" knew me. I decided that God had opened this door for me and I would obey God and not Sam Sprunger.

I prepared to go in quietness, grateful for the help of Anna, who cut the sides off the length of two double sheets from her hope chest. With the fabric, she sewed pillowcases for me to go with the now twin-size sheets. I couldn't believe her kindness and generosity, and was blessed by her self-sacrificing nature. I knew so little about college that I hardly knew what I needed. That last week, I held and played with Tommy with tenderness and aching heart. How I would miss him!

What I didn't realize was that Millie stood up to Mama for me that week. Years later she told me, "I was so fed up with Mom's treatment of you that one day I said to her, 'What is wrong with Jane going to college? She's old enough.'" That was so out of character for Millie, who never spoke up to Mama. She could have gotten a slap in the face for that, as I had. But Mama never said a word, probably realizing the truth of Millie's words and knowing how respectful and quiet she always was. Hearing that from Millie warmed my heart. She added, "I remember how I went upstairs to cry a lot. And I'd pray that God would help me love Mom." Yes, we all had our ways of coping. And Millie felt deeply wounded when one of her sisters was mistreated.

Mrs. Kooker surprised me with a blue-and-white flowered bedspread and asked if she could accompany me to Bluffton. Her son, Clarence, had graduated from the college and taught elementary school there. She wanted to visit him and his wife, Mary Ann. My dear brother Ralph, who loved to travel, offered to drive me to Ohio. God provided everything I needed through these wonderful people. I was encouraged that Anna, cousin Bobby Moser, and Paul planned to come, too.

The church collected an offering for me and Alburtis Ahlum brought it to the house while I was at work. It is hard to believe that Mama refused the money and slammed the door on her. In Mama's mind, this whole thing was the church's fault. But they had nothing to do with it, except, that is, for their nurturing love and teaching through many years. I could not understand Mama's struggle to let us go. Perhaps she saw me as a difficult child with my head full of Scripture and "big ideas." Little did Mama know that God was engineering my circumstances, working out His purpose for my life.

On my last day of work, Mr. and Mrs. Moyer and Pauline had a surprise farewell for me with all the employees there. They raised joyful hymns of praise to God (I was too choked up to sing) and Pastor Moyer and others offered prayers for direction and guidance in my new life. What wonderful people! Tears filled my eyes. Deeply touched, I felt I would burst with mixed emotions – of sadness at leaving and gratitude for their love and support. There were gifts, too. Pauline and Dave gave me a beautiful plaid pleated skirt and white short-sleeved pullover sweater. I felt small and undeserving and overwhelmed. But my long-time dream was becoming reality.

After work on Friday, I packed my things into boxes and prepared to leave at 9 o'clock. Ralph and Bobby came and loaded my things into the car.

I said goodbye to everyone, struggling to keep my emotions under control. The hardest part was leaving 17-month-old Tommy whom I hated to leave. I hugged and kissed him with my heart in my throat.

Mama refused to say goodbye to me and I felt devastated. She had not spoken to me for two weeks. Once in the car, my grief and frustration erupted in tears. I calmed down and soon we picked up Mrs. Kooker, whose kindly mothering soothed my frazzled nerves. We picked up Paul in town and were off on the 13-hour drive on the Pennsylvania Turnpike and across Ohio.

The next morning at 10:00 we arrived at Bluffton in the northwest corner of the state. Tired from the long night cramped in the car and sleeping fitfully, I was scared when I set foot on the campus in this little town of about 2000. A wave of homesickness hit me as the strangeness of the place and impending parting from my family sank in. In self-pity I complained, "I'm not sure I want to be here!"

"Now see here!" Ralph reprimanded, in the most grownup voice I'd ever heard from him. "You wanted to go to college and now you're here, so straighten up! Pull yourself together!" Never had he talked to me like that. When the occasion demanded, he rose to it, and his big sister surely needed a kick in the pants that day.

Ralph's sharp words brought me up short and my moment of weakness passed. We carried my things up four flights of stairs to my room on the top floor of Lincoln Hall. As I met the girls, excitement stirred in me and I thought, *I like this place! What a friendly fun group of girls!* There were girls from camp back home—Nancy Wismer, Nancy Mill, Marilynn Weidner, Violet Kaiser—and Shirley Moyer, my traveling companion and roommate on my second trip to Kansas. What a surprise! All the girls were paired up with roommates but I, having registered late, had a room to myself. Used to my quiet room at the doctor's, I was grateful for a more private place.

We then took Mrs. Kooker to her son's house and met Clarence and Mary Ann, five years older than I. Clarence was the only person from our church that I knew of who had a college education, except for Mrs. Fluck, my grade school teacher. I knew Clarence from Sunday school and his trumpet solos at church before he left for college. Having a couple from "home" close by reassured me.

Ralph had driven 13 hours to Bluffton—with a little relief from other drivers in the car—after a full day of work the day before, and now planned to drive home with no rest. I was grateful for this brother who put himself out for me. Before I knew it, I was on my own in my new life.

Monday morning found me at my job in the administration building. The job for Dr. Ramseyer was quite a breeze, with mostly typing, compared with my former job. Donors who gave so much a year were in the Friendship Group and received a form letter, which "Prexy" (his affectionate title) typed hunt and peck, a new one for each month. In those pre-computer days, I typed the letter over again and again, personalizing each. Papers and exams for his psychology classes must be typed, and grading the multiple-choice questions also fell to my lot. If I ran out of work I helped in the secretarial pool for the registrar's office. Friendly Eileen Meyers Kehler, a fellow Quakertonian whom I knew, worked for Carl Lehman in the business office and probably put in a good word for me to Carl before he hired me.

The registrar, Richard Weaver, and I shared a tiny office in the corner of the administration building, with a door into the president's office and one into the large, open secretarial and receptionist office. Here I learned to know the secretaries—students who worked a few hours a week to help Mrs. Naas, the assistant registrar. A friendly, pleasant atmosphere prevailed. Besides 24 hours a week of work, I took 12 or 13 hours of classes a semester. Evenings found me studying in the library.

Recognizing that I had Mama to thank for this job as secretary, I stood in awe of God's leading. He used her to steer me into the commercial course in high school when I wanted to be a teacher. God knew that I could be both. He honored my obedience to Mama and made sure I got to college with a miracle only He could perform.

The second Sunday, I sang in the choir at First Mennonite Church, where Kookers attended. As an extracurricular activity, I joined the Student Christian Association and became involved in monthly deputations in the nearby city of Lima. We gave programs at the children's home, county home, and rescue mission. I sang in groups or gave devotions and felt right at home with these ministries and got to know other mission-minded kids from college. After the first meeting in October, a fellow asked me out for refreshments. I had other dates too and it felt good to date without interference.

Paul and I corresponded, but I realized this relationship would not last. Mama did not approve and college was a good out for me. She did not know he came along to Bluffton—that is, until she read it in the *Quakertown Free Press*. Mrs. Kooker sent a news item to the paper, which appeared with the headline, "Friends Accompany Miss Herstine to College in Ohio." Several people sent me the clipping which listed who went along on the trip.

One evening after supper, a few months into the school year, Mary Ann Kooker came to my room with a stack of magazines and pile of post cards. With a mischievous twinkle in her eye she said, "Now we're going to send for things for your friends."

I was mystified. But with deft efficiency she found ads in the magazines and pointed out that these would be perfect. "Who do you want to get a catalog on law school?" she inquired. I'd give her a name. She wrote out a post card. "Here's a prestigious men's school," she hooted. I gave the name of my good friend down the hall. "How about a nice young man to order a catalog for tall girls' clothes?" she grinned. I gave her a name. On and on it went. This was hilarious! But would I get in trouble? She laughed and thumbed through magazines and we wrote, chattering all the while. What a surprise to learn Clarence had such an outrageous wife!

In short order, friends accosted me about strange phone calls, a visit from a law school rep, swimming pool company, or the appearance of a tall girls catalog. The young man who received the girls' catalog glowered and voiced his disgust, but he was a friend and got over it. I had a reputation as a clown among my friends. I heard from surprisingly few students, so the rest of them didn't know or care. Those who knew me well accused me and I did not deny the truth. They took it good-naturedly and learned of Mary Ann's devious influence in my life. As for me, my Herstine silliness was never far from the surface. When a girl asked me how old I was and I told her 21 she said, "I thought you were 13!" I was a very small 21 and sometimes a silly one. (I thrived on college life, loved the food, and after a time I weighed 110 pounds, the most I've ever weighed.)

I enjoyed my studies and the stimulation of the classroom. Before long, Mary Ann asked me to help her with the junior high fellowship at church. In addition, I served as an assistant in a primary Sunday school class. My days were busy and fulfilling. Basketball games, football games, concerts, plays, and singing "The Messiah" in the college and community choral society at Christmas livened evenings and weekends. An abundance of good friends added sparkle to every day—friends in the secretary's pool at work, friends in the dorm, friends to take walks with and accompany to church. This was the life. Kookers "fixed me up" with a friend of theirs whom I dated several months, and I dated other fellows. But marriage was not on my mind. My goal was to graduate and see what God had for me next.

Because Mama had refused to speak to me before I left home, I did not go home for Christmas. I had written home faithfully since I left. My sisters wrote but I had not one word from Mama. So why should I go home to such coldness? This was not a hard decision, but friends and faculty thought it strange and perhaps felt sorry for me. I was invited to stay at Kookers part of the time or with other friends in Bluffton. Invitations for dinner came from professors and the Ramseyers – the president and his wife. I felt shy and different for staying over vacation and appreciated their kindness. Foreign students stayed as well and I grew to know them as good friends. Bluffton was beginning to feel like home. As for Mama, I could only pray God would work things out. He had promised, "All things work together for good to those who love God" (Rom. 8:28), a verse I long loved and trusted.

The next year for my birthday on February 6, my sisters sent me a camera, cookies, and cards. Their love warmed me that cold February day. But there was no word from Mama. The next day, Mary Ann Kooker had a surprise birthday party for me at their home, with friends from the dorm and games, food, and laughter. Then on February 20 a heavy package arrived in the mail from Mama. Amazement and gratitude swept over me as I unwrapped a large family Bible. Inside she had written, "Love, Mother and Daddy." I could hardly believe it, but I felt her love. On February 28, Mom's first letter arrived. How wonderful to be reconciled with her. The Bible was her way of saying, "I'm sorry" and "It's OK that you went to college." God had been at work, softening her heart. I was overjoyed.

So for Easter break in 1957, I headed for home with a group of Pennsylvania students. I loved being home with my family and Tommy. How much he had changed in seven months! I relished the time with them, the church people and neighbors, and I saw Paul. In July, I went home again for a week of vacation. During this time I broke off with Paul, realizing my life was taking me in a different direction. Mama's attitude toward me was changing and life was good. I saw a new respect and kindness in her.

Nancy Wismer and her roommate, Ann Hilty, from Bluffton, became best friends of mine. We often laughed hysterically when I was in their room. Ann was so amused at my silly Herstine ways that one day she said, "Janie, I'd like to go home with you sometime to see what kind of family you come from!" I was honored and delighted. That summer I took her along for vacation and she enjoyed my family and the neighbors as I did. (A few years later, Lorraine Lowenberg from Iowa went with me too.)

That fall, Mama sent me a letter with a clipping from the *Quakertown Free Press*. It told how my parents had helped a couple in the middle of the night. A man had pounded on our door after trying unsuccessfully to raise several neighbors. Desperate, he said his wife was about to give birth. Relieved at finding help, the man returned to his car to find his wife with the baby wrapped in a blanket. She had delivered it herself in the back seat of the car. Mama helped her and they transferred mother and child to my parents' car and rushed them to the hospital. The clipping is titled, "After 4 Boys, Bucks (County) Couple Has a Girl – A Troublemaker, Yet." It ends, "Who ever said little girls are less trouble than little boys?" What an experience for Mama and Daddy! For years after that, on the baby's birthday, Mama received a rose from the grateful couple. I was happy for her each year as she told me about the rose, a blessing that thrilled Mama.

College was a challenge and a joy. For four years I studied and worked and attended summer school to keep up with my class. I enjoyed my elementary education classes and others, like Life of Jesus and Christian Faith and Life. Mennonite History answered my questions from my growing up years about our two kinds of "Mennos" and other groups as well. I learned that the split occurred in Pennsylvania right in my home area. Our textbook had a picture of my fieldstone home church, Flatland, one of only two pictures of a church in the thick book. It said that our General Conference founder, John Oberholtzer, started one of the first Sunday schools among American Mennonites and that the official meeting was organized at Flatland in 1853. I was proud of my little church, so different from the big ones I saw in Kansas. I learned there were 33 different kinds of Mennonites (at that time), not just two, including the Amish, Hutterites – who live in communes – the conservative Holdemans, and the "Black Bumper" Mennonites – who may have cars if they paint the chrome black – of Lancaster County, Pennsylvania. Learning our history from 1450 to the present was an eye-opener.

Summer school afforded an opportunity to acquire more credits as well as delightful social life with a much smaller group of students. The first summer I lived in a house converted into a dorm, and took some meals with house parents, Eileen and Neil Kehler. Sometimes I ate in the dining hall with the other students and we planned activities or "pulled projects" on each other. Then our home economics professor, Miss Edna Ramseyer, built a beautiful Home Economics house where six students lived each semester and rotated between six household jobs. I had the good fortune of living there my next two summers and learned much from Miss Edna. First I was manager for two weeks, then laundress, assistant housekeeper, chief cook, assistant cook, and housekeeper in turn. Sometimes we girls planned parties and invited the fellows and generally enjoyed wholesome fun. Once we cooked dinner for the summer school teachers and ate in the big family room in the basement. The teachers loved it and we learned to know them in a more informal setting.

Pranks kept us on our toes or in stitches. One night the gang watched Billy Graham on the Jack Paar Show at Lincoln Hall. Afterwards, a couple of guys offered a friend and me a ride to our house in the trunk of their car, so we climbed in. But we didn't stay put. We wanted to surprise the guys by jumping out, and thought we were going slowly enough. Wrong.

When I went home for vacation that summer, I wrote a 59-verse poem about that crazy summer and sent it special delivery to one of the girls. In it, I described the ride in the trunk thus:

> From Lincoln Hall we got a ride,
> Joyce and I both in the trunk,
> But we weren't content with our first-class seat,
> And fell on the road kerplunk.

> My elbows healed, Joyce's watch was fixed,
> And the dirt in our clothes came out.
> But it's likely we'll never try that again,
> Or ever so loudly shout.

The friend who received the poem read it to the gang. We all thrived on the camaraderie, as well as serious discussions. One of the fellows, Ed Springer, sought encouragement for his hope of becoming a pastor – and he did. (Many years later our family visited his church in Hillsboro, Kansas, and heard him preach!)

Back home in Pennsylvania, many changes had taken place. A year after I left for college, Anna went to Bob Jones University in South Carolina with a friend. Then brother Ralph went to Bob Jones the next year, but it was not for him. After one semester he went back to his job at a car repair shop. While at Bob Jones, Ralph wrote me lengthy detailed letters about his trials there, especially his shyness at dinner. He continued to write after he returned home. Grace corresponded frequently as well, Millie and Anna occasionally. I cherished all the letters from family. Writing letters to them, to church people, friends, cousins, and other family back home honed my writing skills and kept me in touch.

In August of 1958, Millie married Ralph Loux of Quakertown. Now we had three Ralphs in the family – Daddy, my brother, and brother-in-law. Ralph was from Bethany, our sister church in town, where they were married.

Anna and Grace were bridesmaids and I the maid of honor. I sewed my dress at the home economics house that summer and brother Ralph drove out to pick me up.

Millie, Anna, and I were all out of the nest now, leaving Grace, Ruth, and Tommy at home. Grace graduated from high school in 1957 and worked as a secretary for lawyer Freed in town. Ruth had quit school in her sophomore year and got a job at Yingst Nursing Home where Anna had worked. And Tommy was growing up. I enjoyed him and took many of pictures of him when I went home.

In Children's Literature Class I read and loved books by Elizabeth Yates. She advised a would-be writer friend, "Write something every day, even if it's just notes on an envelope." I not only wrote letters, but poems for people and for Children's Lit Class, and papers galore for classes. On my autobiography for freshman Communications class the professor wrote, "Excellent word choice," a nice surprise. For years I have written notes on envelopes.

One day I learned that a pastor from my home district was on campus to see the Pennsylvania students. Claude Boyer, whom I knew from Men-O-Lan, was a good friend of Clarence Kooker. When I walked into the room, he greeted me warmly and as we talked he said, "You have really blossomed here at school." Also on campus that week was my former pastor, Rev. Neuenschwander, and cousin Marietta's mother, Marie Landis, both there for board meetings. Their warm friendship brought a touch of home.

Mrs. S.T. Moyer also visited at times, and once had evening devotions in our dorm. Another time I got a ride to Berne, Indiana to accept Mrs. Moyer's invitation for church and dinner in their home.

Sometimes I babysat for college profs, dean Robert Kreider, registrar Richard Weaver, our pastor, Jacob T. Friesen, and other families to supplement my income. Church people back home sometimes sent small gifts of money. One summer I bought several inexpensive new dresses, pretty and practical, that boosted my morale.

In December of 1958, my junior year, I had an exciting and scary experience as speaker for a Gospel Team Quartet. Each year two quartets toured Mennonite churches over Christmas break, one going west and one east. Paul Shelly, Bible professor formerly from Pennsylvania, asked if I would be one of the speakers. (He was a brother to Margaret Weaver where I babysat.) I prayed about it and, in fear and trembling, agreed. Professor Paul was my advisor and suggested I write out a sermon and he'd go over it and help me. What a challenge! I had taken a speech class but, disliking public speaking, I decided to claim the verse, "I can do all things through Christ who strengthens me."

I chose for my title, "Walk Even As He Walked," from I John 2:6, "He that says he abides in him ought himself also so to walk, even as he walked." Prof Paul had recently been to the Holy Land and I had attended his slide presentation. How I longed to go there myself some day. He suggested I begin by asking the audience if they ever wanted to go to the Holy Land and walk where Jesus walked. After a brief introduction, I quoted a song I loved, "I Walked Today Where Jesus Walked," as a lead in. I rehearsed my 20-minute sermon with Prof Paul and was inspired. I spoke about the source of Jesus' power – prayer, abiding in his Father, obedience, being filled with the Spirit – and fleshed these out with illustrations. I explained the characteristics of Jesus' walk – love, compassion, humility, forgiveness, service. Jesus had done so much for me; I would do this hard thing for Jesus.

The quartet consisted of my "Little Sis" Jeannette Sprunger, Miriam Mitchell, Judy Hilty, and Sarah Kratz. We, with Miss Edna as chaperone, and our driver, Marlin Gerber, drove to Pennsylvania and Ontario, Canada, on our eight-day tour. The very first service, at Sarah's church, was on a Sunday morning at Grace Mennonite in Lansdale. Our group had prayer together before we went on stage. As I sat on the high platform, looking out over the sea of faces – several hundred in the sanctuary and balcony, but they looked like a thousand – I felt small and weak. My legs quivered like jelly. I cried out to God in my heart, and He gave me strength to get through it. The girls' quartet sang beautifully. Miriam played a violin solo, "I Walked Today Where Jesus Walked." That evening we repeated the service at another church.

Monday night I felt much more comfortable when we gave our program at my newly remodeled small home church. Daddy and my sisters were there. For years I had preached to Mama on my bed in the night, now here I was "preaching" to my family and church. Years ago I could not have imagined such an astounding thing. Mama stayed home but had a yummy chocolate cake for us after the service. I was humbled to have Miss Edna and the girls – and even Mrs. Fluck – in our poor home, very lowly compared with the beautiful Home Economics house at school. The pump was still in the kitchen, the outhouse outside, and the rooms felt tiny and cramped, but it was *home*. Miss Edna and Mama got on famously and there was a lot of laughter around the table and sweetness in the room. My childhood "prison" was transformed with this noble lady and the college girls. Mama was downright proud to entertain such important guests.

On we went from one church to another. By the grace of God I got through our daunting itinerary. We did two services on Sundays, morning and evening. In Pennsylvania on New Year's Eve we had an evening service at Deep Run West (near to where my father lived till he was 10), and another at a watch-night service before midnight at Allentown, about 30 miles away (where my mother had graduated from high school). I enjoyed spending several nights at home that week.

Then it was on to Ontario, where we visited awesome Niagara Falls. Our itinerary included Niagara United Mennonite Church at Niagara-on-the-Lake, and others. I recall a couple of little old ladies coming to me after a service and thanking me for my talk. How I needed that encouragement!

Back in Ohio, we gave the program in two nearby churches; then two trips to Goshen and Berne, Indiana in April and May where we gave it three more times. Though quaking in my shoes at times, I depended on the Spirit and "preached that sermon" 17 times!

My senior year I student taught fourth grade in the city of Lima and first grade in Bluffton. I learned much from the two experienced teachers and enjoyed the students. The last day in Lima, as I finished the last lesson I would ever teach them, suddenly fruit came rolling down the aisles to the front. A fruit roll! Common in this school, the teacher secretly planned it with them for a student teacher's last day. Each student brought an apple, orange, or grapefruit and rolled them up the aisle at a signal from the teacher. Sad to part from these dear children, I wept at this expression of their kindness. My tears surprised them as much as their gift had surprised me. On the way back to college with the carload of prospective teachers, I was relieved to learn I was not the only one who cried at a fruit roll that morning.

In my junior year I wrote to my friend Muriel Thiessen (now Stackley) who had graduated and went on to seminary at Elkhart. I admired her as a missionary kid who grew up in India, and as a serious Christian. She responded, "You asked about seminary—it's busy—but, oh, Jane—it's such a rich earth to grow in and goodness knows I need to grow. People ask me what I'm studying to be and I honestly don't know—but it's such a relief to make the simple admission that whatever turns up, I want it to be dedicated to God." I identified with and was inspired by her goal and commitment.

Later, I was able to attend a "Women in Church Vocations" Conference at the seminary. Women came from Canada, our headquarters offices in Kansas, and all over the country, including women students and faculty at the seminary. A stimulating program highlighted various options for women in ministry. At that time, the pastorate was not one of them. I loved seeing the brand new campus that had sprouted since the conference in Winnipeg in 1956. I enjoyed meeting the other young women, including Muriel. I felt a tug, but could hardly consider seminary since Mama had voiced her desire for me to return home to teach.

That last year of college I struggled over what to do after graduation: please Mama and go home to teach? I had given her some hope that I might, but also thought about missionary teaching. A friend, Lois Shutt, planned to apply to teach at Silverton, Colorado in an isolated place and invited me to join her. I considered it. But I wanted to study more Bible, perhaps at a Bible school, like cousin Marietta at Philadelphia College of the Bible. I voiced that to Mildred Rosenberger from Quakertown when she was on campus. "That would be like going backwards after college," she said. "You should go to seminary."

There it was again. Was this God's leading? Though appealing, how could I justify or afford more schooling? One weekend, students interested in seminary went to Elkhart for a prospective student weekend. Knowing Mama's wish, and fearing it would create turmoil for me like the college decision, I did not go.

To my great surprise, some time after that weekend I received a letter from the seminary president, Dr. Erland Waltner who had taught that wonderful Sunday school class on my first visit to Kansas. My amazement grew as I read, "Some of your friends told me of your interest in attending seminary. The assistant to the president needs a secretary. If you are interested, you can work 20 hours a week and take a reduced class load. A Master of Religious Education degree normally takes two years, but you could do it in three. Please prayerfully consider this offer and let me know soon if you will accept."

How amazing! Another incredible open door—a job thrust into my lap! The call to seminary grew clearer and louder. *"Oh, God! Is this from You?"* I cried. *"Please, show me!"*

Apprehension once again overcame my excitement. What should I do? I prayed and then wrote home, telling my parents of the opportunity. Mama shot back a letter. "You said you were coming home when you were through and now you're thinking of going some more. Well, if you do, don't look for any more letters from me because I was so glad you were going to be home soon...Yes, well, you do what you want to. You always did. I could not say anything. The rest (of the girls) are the same. But don't look for any letters. And don't look for me in May or June" (for graduation, which my parents were planning to attend).

Crestfallen, I cried out to the Lord. Mama had been so kind to write me faithfully the past four years, and she sincerely wanted me home again. I felt torn and hated to disappoint her. As I prayed and wrestled with my thoughts, I knew what I must do. I went to Bible professor, William Keeney, for counsel. He listened as I told him about Dr. Waltner's letter and Mama's negative one.

"You have your life to live and your parents have theirs," he advised. "Do what you feel is right for you, and let them do as they wish." With grateful heart and a new confidence, I made the tough decision and wrote home that I felt it was God's will for me to go to seminary. I said that I was sorry but I wouldn't be home for a few more years. And I repeated my invitation for them to come to my graduation. I prayed Mama would understand.

During my four years of college, God had softened Mama's heart. Not only that, I believe Daddy "put his foot down" and said, "We're going." To my relief and delight, Mama and Daddy, Anna, Grace, Ruth, Ralph, and Tommy came to my graduation. God delights to bless His children and my heart rejoiced at my family's visit. But Mama seemed unhappy, and couldn't enter into activities like Daddy. I'm sure it hurt her that I was going to school yet again. Daddy was in his element, relaxed and very happy to be there. He relished visiting the town's utility facilities to compare them with Quakertown's.

In June 1960 I received my B.S. degree in elementary education. I had reached my goal. Graduation ceremonies were in the morning, then a reception for graduates and their parents at the president's home in the afternoon. Not comfortable in social settings, Mama declined to go to the reception but Daddy went with me. He beamed

Ralph, Anna, Grace, and Ruth at my graduation, 1960.

with happiness and pride as Dr. Ramseyer met us at the door and told Daddy, "Jane is a good student."

That was high praise and I felt proud to have been his secretary, this man for whom I worked four years and who made college possible for me. What a special moment to have my father hear this commendation. Daddy could see for himself that I didn't regret going to college one bit. Our parents never went to our high school graduations close to home, yet they came across two states to my college graduation.

I was grateful for each one in my family who had come. As we said our goodbyes, a wave of homesickness swept over me. Was Mama struggling with feelings of pain and sadness as well? Three more years of school lay ahead, and I would be even farther away from home than before. The tears fell as I hugged Tommy goodbye. Mama's earlier words about not writing anymore had been an empty threat. She relented and wrote me in her first letter that as they drove away, Tommy asked, "Why did Janie cry?" and she explained that I was sad they were leaving.

But that summer turned out to be special as I continued to work for Prexy. A few secretary friends were left in the office pool. Campus was empty and I missed walking to First Mennonite Church with the crowd of students every Sunday morning. But God had prepared a home for me.

Dr. Weaver and Margaret were expecting their seventh child and asked if I would live with them for the summer to help Margaret. Dr. Weaver was gone, doing research at the University of Michigan. It was good to be free of studies for the first time in four years. The carefree days slipped by with good times in the office and with the children at home in the evenings. On July 26, a baby girl was born and they named her Marsha Jane after me. Margaret had her hands full. Evenings for me were busy helping with cooking (the girls took turns too), dishes, and helping care for Marsha and little Paul, 10½ months old when Marsha arrived. The girls alternated nights sleeping with me in the family room.

A favorite pastime with the girls was going for walks. On a special walk with eight-year-old Sally, I told her all about college life and how important it was to get a college education. Bright little girl that she was, she listened with rapt attention and chatted excitedly. (When I went back to my 35th class reunion in 1995, the Weavers invited me to their home to tell my story of how I got to go to college. A few others were gathered there, among them Dean Kreider's wife Lois, as well as some of the Weaver girls, including Sally. She was a lovely young woman, married, and professor of Economics at the college. On top of that, Dr. Sally Weaver Sommer gave the commencement address that weekend! What a thrill to see and *hear* her so many years later. She commented that she remembered our walk that day and how I told her all about college.) In 2008, Dr. Sally became Dean Sally Weaver Sommer! And Dr. Paul Neufeld Weaver now teaches education at the college! All of the children have distinguished themselves in their chosen fields.

Also that summer, I went home for my Aunt Jean Landis' wedding to Franklin Marquet at the Church of the Brethren. Millie, Anna, and I sang three trios. Jean remembers that we sang, "O Perfect Love," and "Savior, Like A Shepherd Lead Us." Since our family was all together and dressed up I had someone take a picture of us with the camera my sisters had given me. By then, Millie and Ralph had a baby girl, Brenda Sue, and Tommy was five years old. I have always cherished that picture. I also took one of Grammy and Pappy Landis, one of the few I have of them smiling. It was a happy time for our family. I took a picture of Mom and Tommy – Mama looking relaxed, happy, and pretty, wearing an apron over her dress, as she always did, and Tom in his pajamas with a big smile.

My family, 1960. Back: Millie, Ralph and Brenda Loux (1), Mama (Jean), Daddy (Ralph), brother Ralph, Ruth. Front: Grace, Tommy (5), me, Anna.

Grammy and Pappy Landis, 1960.   *Tommy and Mama, c. 1960.*

As fall approached and seminary stared me in the face, I wondered about the road ahead. What would seminary be like? Where was God leading me? Would I finally sense a clear call to ministry? Or maybe find a husband? Knowing there would be lots of young men at seminary, I asked a good friend as I made a list of pros and cons for seminary, "Is 'finding a husband' a good reason to go?" With a big smile she pronounced an enthusiastic "Yes!" Though I dated quite a bit in college, I was not looking for a husband, but this might be different.

September 5 arrived, the day of my departure. Dr. Weaver offered to drive me to Elkhart and the girls wanted to go along. I packed my belongings, with more boxes now than when I arrived four years ago: student teaching picture file, school books and files, clothes, the Samsonite suitcase from my brother Ralph, and a big yellow one I bought the first year to travel back and forth to home.

Before leaving, Dr. Weaver gathered us all in the living room and told me that whenever one of their children left for a time, to camp, or a vacation with a relative, he always read Psalm 121 for them. He said he would like to do that for me. I was deeply moved as he read the familiar words I loved, "I lift up my eyes to the hills – from where will my help come? My help comes from the Lord, who made heaven and earth," ending with, "The Lord will keep your going out and your coming in from this time on and for evermore." God's presence enveloped me with special love as this family that had become my family for the summer listened quietly.

Dr. Weaver closed his Bible and said, "Let us bow for prayer." As he prayed for me in my new venture, the memory of the praying people at the hatchery four years earlier flashed into my mind. Tears flowed as I listened to this humble, godly man near whom I had worked in that tiny office for four years—who seldom said a word, except in greeting—beseech God on my behalf. He always had a smile for me and was respectful and kind. He and his dear, loving wife and seven children had blessed my life. I wept quietly and, as he finished, the girls and Margaret gathered around me with sad faces and hugs.

I dried my eyes, said last goodbyes to Margaret and the children who were staying home, and we piled into the car. The Weaver girls were usually fun, and this ride was no exception. Their happy talk and affection helped calm my jumbled emotions on this long ride to the next stage of my life. God's ways were mysterious indeed. I marveled at the big changes in my life since driving away from the house on Thatcher Road four years ago. And I wondered, *How will seminary change my life?*

Me holding Paul (11½ mos.) and Marsha Jane Weaver (1 mo.), August 1960.

Weaver family. Back: Jerry, Margaret holding Marsha, Dick holding Paul. Front: Louise, Shelly, Sally, Cynthia. August 1960.

CHAPTER 12

Two Degrees in One

Looking unto Jesus, the author and finisher of our faith...
HEBREWS 12:2 (KJV)

1960–1961

Seminary! What an awesome-sounding place! Who would have thought, when this scrawny girl was growing up on Thatcher Road that I would end up at seminary? Or when I arrived at college, that instead of four years, I would spend seven more years in school? I was amazed and grateful to God for His guidance on my path.

I arrived at Mennonite Biblical Seminary, which sprawls on a flat plain on the southern edge of Elkhart, Indiana on Labor Day, September 5, 1960 – at age 25. An unimposing but brand new campus, it was comprised of a low, U-shaped brick building housing offices, classrooms, library; and nearby, a long dorm for single students with dining hall and kitchen; and across the campus drive, a row of apartment buildings for married students. The dorm included a large student lounge with ping-pong table, the seminary guest room, and the host and hostess apartment. From my previous visit, I remembered the scholarly, peaceful atmosphere and friendly, warm people.

Someone from the office showed me my room and explained the unique living arrangement for single students – men's rooms at one end of the dorm, women's next to them, with only a swinging door between, quite a switch from college dorms.

Being the first one in the empty dorm, I was saved from a lonely evening by Ada Spaeth, a Pennsylvania friend, who invited me for supper. Her husband Harry was a student. (I suspected Ada may have turned in my name as a prospective student.) They lived in an apartment on campus. Friendship with this dear one from home, whom I looked up to as a Christian mentor, helped ease me into my new life. Other married students from my college days were there as well.

The next day I headed to the office to begin my job as secretary to the assistant to the president, Harry Martens. A minister staff person and I shared the first of a long row of offices, with my desk in a corner just inside the door. That morning, I met the quiet receptionist/accountant, Estelle, in the next office and the president's talkative secretary, Freda.

My work at first consisted of taking dictation and typing letters to special donors and prospective ones. My shorthand was a bit rusty since Dr. Ramseyer did not give dictation in my four years, though I had used it some in classes. By contrast, Harry Martens dictated long, involved letters and soon I was back in the groove. When Harry was on the road, I worked for other professors, cut stencils, and mimeographed the Mennonite church bulletin.

That first week, I met another college friend, my "Little Sis" Jeannette Sprunger, who lived with her family, returned missionaries from Congo, at the Congo Inland Mission office complex nearby, and had been in our Gospel Team Quartet at college.

One of my first days in the office, a dark-haired, good-looking young man arrived at my office door with a guarded smile. "Can you tell me where my room is?" he asked.

"Sorry, I can't help you," I smiled back. "Check at the next office." That was Estelle's responsibility. My interest was piqued with this first new student at the dorm.

Soon the women students arrived one by one, Katie Kehler, Gladys Siebert, Anne Epp, and Cay Snyder. Katie, Anne and Cay hailed from Canada and Gladys from Nebraska. Then the men poured in from various states and provinces of Canada.

Five single girls in the dorm and three times as many men beyond the swinging door promised to enliven the year. Cooking arrangements saved the school from paying a cook and ensured that we would mix. Fellows and girls were required to pair up and take turns by weeks. We planned menus, bought groceries, and cooked noon and evening meals. On Sundays, only a noon meal was served. Since I needed time to get into a routine of work and class schedule I waited a few weeks before signing up to cook. How could I go to classes, work in the office, and cook two meals a day? But I found it worked out well and helped us get to know the fellows.

We girls got acquainted quickly in our dorm and small lounge. Outnumbered by male students, we were a bit intimidated at first. One of the fellows, Jim Glenn, from my class at Bluffton, was engaged to my friend,

Irlene Gierman. Jim liked to tease me and I gave it back. It was good to have him around. Some of the fellows were outgoing and friendly, others more reserved—an interesting array of eligible bachelors.

On our first day of classes, our Old Testament professor, Dr. Jake Enz, asked us to introduce the person on our left. Seated next to me was the young man who came to my office to ask for a room. I had not met him yet but had seen him come and go in his black Plymouth with Kansas plates. Ahhh, Kansas! I thought of my two delightful trips there and was curious about him.

In class that day, when I turned to him he flashed me a beautiful smile. I asked for his name and where he was from and he said, "Jake Friesen, from Vancouver Island."

"Where's that? You're from Kansas!" I asserted. "It says so on your license plate."

His grin grew wider and his eyes danced with mischief. "I went to Bethel College in Kansas," he said, "but I'm from Vancouver Island in British Columbia." I had a vague idea that B.C. was on the west coast of Canada because Quakertonian Eileen Meyers at college had married a B.C. man. I had not heard of Vancouver Island.

I told the class, "This is Jake Friesen and he says he's from Vancouver Island, but his license plate says he's from Kansas." Jake enjoyed this immensely and his soft, dark eyes and smile disarmed me. "You need to learn your geography," he teased, somewhat insulted that I had never heard of his island.

That weekend a seminary retreat was scheduled at a Mennonite camp in nearby Michigan. Friday noon I picked up my mail after class. Happy for a letter from Millie, I went to the dorm and read it before going to lunch. As I read I was overcome with dismay and fear. Millie had a one-year-old daughter, Brenda, and had suffered from depression the past year. She was seeing a Mennonite psychiatrist, Dr. Norman Loux. In agony and disbelief I read, "Oh, Jane, I know Ralph needs a good wife and Brenda needs a good mother, but sometimes I feel like ending it all. Oh, Jane, Oh, Jane." Throughout the letter she repeated, "Oh, Jane!" She had never written like this before and I knew she was desperate.

My dear sister Millie! How could this be? Crushed by her frantic cries, revealed in every line, I sobbed and dropped to my knees by my bed. *"Oh, God,"* I cried, *"please, don't let Millie hurt herself! Please help her!"* Millie was one of the dearest persons on earth to me. I couldn't bear to see her suffer like this. I decided I must go home and help her. I would quit school, and *soon*!

Unable to eat, I decided on my course of action. I would watch for the president to return to his office after lunch and tell him about Millie and that I had to quit school. The hour dragged by—one of the longest waits of my life. Finally, close to one o'clock I went to the lounge window to watch. Thankfully, the students were busy in the dining hall, oblivious to my distress. Impatience mounted with the minutes. Where *was* Dr. Waltner? Why did he take so long? What if he didn't come? I must see him or I could not go to work. I knew he had a class that afternoon. I prayed as I watched. *"Dear God, please protect Millie and show me what to do."*

Finally I saw him. I fairly flew out of the dorm and ran to the ad building. His office door was shut. Dismayed, I hesitated, hating to disturb him as he prepared for his class. But I *must* do something fast. Gathering courage, I knocked.

"Come in," he said.

I went in crying, unable to speak, and gave him Millie's letter. I sat in the chair he offered opposite his desk. Quietly he read as I wept into my tissue. When he finished, I said, "I think I should go home. I'll have to quit school."

With deep compassion, Dr. Waltner spoke. "I read the letter very carefully. Your sister knows that going to seminary means a lot to you. She already is full of guilt. If you quit school, she will feel even more guilty. Her psychiatrist is a friend of mine. I'm sure he's doing all he can to help her and she's in good hands. Let me suggest that you send her letter to him and ask him how you might best help her."

His wise words made sense and helped calm me. Dr. Waltner and her psychiatrist were friends. This knowledge gave me a ray of hope. I agreed to Dr. Waltner's plan. Before I left, he prayed for me and for Millie and her family—a wonderfully comforting prayer of faith and trust, committing Millie into God's hands and care. Relieved, I returned to my room to write the psychiatrist. With the heaviness lifted, I decided I would go to the retreat and try to enjoy it.

The retreat helped me forget my sadness and was a balm to my spirit. Annie, Katie, Gladys, Cay and I had a lovely rowboat ride on the lake. That evening, a singspiration ended our day and I felt much lighter. Saturday I relished the good fellowship, fun, and laughter. That night at campfire was testimony time. Jake Friesen was the first to stand and speak. He told of growing up as the son of a minister and evangelist in Canada. He spoke of the church's great demands on his father, a hardship on the family during his dad's long absences. His voice grew husky as he spoke with deep emotion. I sensed some resentment toward the Mennonite church for taking his father away when they needed him. He also told of his struggles during and after high school.

His sharing was an eye opener for me. I knew nothing about a family's deprivation when a man of God is so dedicated to his work that his family suffers. There were more testimonies, but Jake's is the only one I remember. After he spoke, he left the campfire and my heart went out to him. I wanted to comfort him and felt love and deep compassion stirring within me. After the service, many of us went for boat rides on the lake. There I saw Jake in a boat. The day before, I felt Millie's deep pain; that night I felt Jake's. I could not forget this fascinating young man and his sharing.

That fall, I sent a birthday card and letter to Dr. Ramseyer at college, thanking him for the job that got me through school. Soon I had a reply, stating that he very much appreciated hearing from me. True to his hunt-and-peck method he wrote, "I am doing my own typing on this...My new secretary is working in quite well now, but we still miss you. I don't believe I ever had a secretary who could do as much work in an hour and do it as well as you did." I was pleasantly surprised. He told about things going on at school and then asked, "Do you have any plans beyond this school year? It was my understanding that you planned to go to seminary just one year. Any attractive, unmarried young men in seminary?" Was he kidding? Only a dorm full! His humor and fatherly concern warmed my heart. At college, my goal had been to get my degree, and marriage was a far-off dream.

One day I received a response from Millie's doctor reporting that her letter was very typical of the way she felt and that she was "full of repressed anger." That was a sobering thought and I prayed and sought to understand what had happened to my sister. How much did our childhood and losing our mother have to do with this? I had to trust God and Dr. Loux to help her.

At seminary, KP duty brought me together with the other fellows in the dorm, as we planned, shopped, and cooked meals together in pairs. After the library closed at 10 P.M., we all met in the kitchen for snacks of toast and jam and lively visiting. This was much more intimate than college had ever been. We began to feel like a family, calling ourselves the "brethren" and "sistern."

Since I worked all week at the office, I signed up to do dishes for evenings and Sunday noon. Imagine my surprise when Jake began signing up for Sunday noon, too. As I washed and he dried, always teasing me that I was "slow," we shared about our families, college, jobs, and the like. He worked at an apple orchard, picking apples and pruning.

As we shared from Sunday to Sunday, we were surprised at similarities in our backgrounds, such as: we each had seven in our family, both with four sisters and two brothers; we were both GC's – General Conference. We both grew up next to the church, with the school close by, one-room school for me, two-rooms for him; we each had a family dog named Tippy; we both had served in the Young People's Union of our district and made trips to Newton, Kansas for meetings. My mother was Grace Elizabeth; his mother was Elizabeth, as well as his oldest sister, who had worked for a doctor and his wife, taking care of their children during her high school years. (She continued to live with them through nurses' training, and was now a nurse in Toronto.) He also told me that Elizabeth was petite, like me. Then, too, I had roomed in the dorm at Canadian Mennonite Bible College in Winnipeg. Jake had graduated from the school! We were intrigued by these incredible similarities.

But our dissimilarities struck me as well. Jake was Russian Mennonite. His parents migrated to Canada in 1925 when his older brother Peter was nine months old. His father, N.N. Friesen, was the only one of his large family to leave Russia. (After the Revolution in 1917, during the 1920s, 16,000 Mennonites fled to Canada from Russia.) N.N. and his wife, Elizabeth, left against their will. Her family had gone to Saskatchewan and Jake's grandfather, Peter Duerksen, insisted they come, too. His wife, Maria, was very unhappy without them and cried all the time. Jake's parents reluctantly agreed to come and grandfather Duerksen bought their tickets for the boat. Not that he could afford it. He borrowed money – $300 – from relatives in Buhler, Kansas, which took him years to repay. Jake's mother made zwieback, their food for the trip – hard-baked, double rolls which keep for months. They arrived in Canada with few belongings.

Jake told me about the hardships of his family in Canada the first years: living in a chicken coop, felling trees to build a log house, bitter cold, crops that froze, finding work to feed the family. Jake's father and grandfather farmed and his father also delivered mail. He felled trees for firewood in such intense cold that he had to break ice out of the horses' nostrils so they could breathe. Later his father became a lay minister.

When Jake was four, his family moved to Vancouver Island, a much milder climate, where his father was called to pastor a small church. Being self-supporting, he farmed and drove school bus. He also checked people's eyes and ordered glasses for them from a mail-order catalog. Later "N. N.," as he was known, became an evangelist and traveled widely in British Columbia and Canada. Jake felt especially bad about his mother's hard work on the farm when his dad was gone.

Jake's own extensive travels in his young life, and variety of jobs, were so out of my realm that I could hardly imagine such adventures. During the summers in his teen years he worked as a whistle punk and chokerman in logging camps near his home and helped fight forest fires. One summer he worked at the airport as a jackhammer operator.

The Friesen family, c. 1942. Back: Elizabeth, Peter, N.N., Margaret. Front: Nick, Grandpa Gerhard Duerksen, Helen, Mother Elizabeth, Mary Ann, Jake, about 6.

For grades eleven to thirteen (in Canada, grade 13 is equivalent to the first year of college) Jake moved to the mainland to attend Mennonite Educational Institute (MEI), a Mennonite Brethren (MB) high school. There he lived with the Wiebes, a fine family who had four sons his age and older. Leaving home at this age was not easy. Later, his parents moved to the mainland and his younger sisters, Mary Ann and Helen, also attended MEI, and Jake lived at home.

After high school Jake traveled back and forth from Vancouver to Winnipeg 75 times on the Canadian Pacific Railway. As a sleeping car porter, he made beds and shined shoes. On the train 24 hours a day, he got only three and a half hours of sleep at night. He told me he got so tired one night that he fell asleep standing up. He fell down in the hall and slept until someone woke him several hours later. He worked ten days then had four days off. He'd sleep two days solid; his mother woke him only for meals.

Sunday after Sunday, Jake shared his interesting stories. One summer during college he worked in northern B.C. near the Alaskan border in construction; also in Thompson, Manitoba, helping to build a city from scratch for nickel miners at the end of the railroad. They usually built four houses a day. Another summer he took a ship to Europe and traveled around many countries by motorcycle. He attended Mennonite World Conference in Karlsruhe, Germany, and stayed at youth hostels and PAX housing projects, where peace-church conscientious objectors (COs) were rebuilding houses after World War II. How impressive!

Jake was quite proud of his Grandfather Duerksen who wrote a small book about his experiences in Russia. Jake recounted a story of his grandfather's courageous, tough leadership dealing with criminals in their village. In college, I studied about the Russian Mennonites—their persecutions through the Revolution, wars, and famine, and how they fled for their lives. Jake's story personalized it.

He said, "If Mennonite Central Committee (MCC of Akron, Pennsylvania, our relief and service agency) had not brought food in 1920, my parents would have starved to death, as thousands of people did." His family's suffering and dramatic rescue made a deep impression on me. Jake was by far the most fascinating young man I had ever met.

But of course I shared my life with Jake, too. I told about Daddy's unfortunate childhood without a father, and about Mama and her background. I said she had a baby out of wedlock and divulged my feelings regarding the circumstances of her marriage to Daddy. When I said she wasn't a Christian, he asked, "How do you know that? Maybe she is." That stopped me short.

Jake explained, "Don't you know about the prophet Hosea and how God told him to take an unfaithful wife? Even though Gomer lived an adulterous life, God told Hosea to take her back again and again. This is a picture of

Israel's wayward ways—following other gods—and of God's unconditional love for them, always calling them back." I was impressed. I had memorized I Corinthians 13 to help me love Mama, but I never associated Gomer's story with her. I had not spent much time studying the Minor Prophets. Obviously, Jake had, which gave him a different perspective for looking at my parents. It was clear that he accepted them as they were, though he never met them. Jake had studied the Bible with excellent teachers in high school and college. I admired that about him.

Jake seemed impressed that I had traveled twice to Newton and even to Winnipeg (his home for three years), that I had a teaching degree, and had worked as secretary for the president at college. As we continued to share our lives, I sensed a strong attraction growing between us.

Two months into the school year, on November 7, I began a journal of my feelings and experiences at seminary and my relationship with God. One day I wrote, "I am constantly confronted with the desire to be married, and it rules and dominates my thought life and makes me powerless in communing with God. Through an article in *HIS* magazine on thankfulness, I have been challenged to ask God to make me thankful that I am single, and to accept whatever is God's plan for me. I feel the need for being broken and emptied that I might be filled, and at the same time I realize the hard battle this will be." I longed to be close to Christ, to know His leading, and the "power of His resurrection."

Along with the fun times, serious studies occupied our time, too, with challenging chapel talks, papers to write, and practical work. I worked at the Salvation Army, with toddlers and preschoolers in Sunday school my first semester. Millie's depression still concerned me, and when I didn't get enough sleep, I tended to be too introspective and down on myself.

That week in chapel, Old Testament professor Jake Enz's message spoke clearly to me. He spoke about "what seminary students experience as a result of spending much time in studies and, therefore, introspection. We must be determined to go on with Christ who has called us," he said, "knowing His arm is around us." The Holy Spirit knew my struggles. I appreciated the timely encouragement.

Seminary life could be hard, serious, and sometimes tedious. We were getting deep into the Old and New Testaments, having to memorize what events were in each chapter of the four Gospels. Bachelor of Divinity students struggled with Greek and Hebrew. I had escaped languages in high school and college, and my course requirements spared me here as well. We were in a different world, with a vocabulary of its own. Dr. Enz urged us to buy the enormous *Young's Analytical Concordance of the Bible* (KJV), one of the best investments I ever made. (And still an indispensable resource for me.)

Dorm life offered welcome diversion. Two days before I started cooking with one of the fellows, Jake asked me to go with him to the Presbyterian Church on Sunday. I told him our girls' quartet was going to sing at the Mennonite Church, so Jake asked me for the following Sunday. I agreed. He told me much later the fellows in the dorm goaded him to ask me out, as they knew he wanted to and they believed the other fellow was after me. My Bluffton friend, Jim Glenn, especially pushed Jake.

Sunday dawned bright and beautiful. Our girls' quartet sang, "Praise Him" in church. Though it was November 13 in northern Indiana, Indian summer weather prevailed. After dinner, as Jake and I finished the dishes, out of the blue he said, "I bet you're afraid to go up in an airplane with me."

"No, I'm not," I countered. I had never flown in a plane before and it sounded like a nice adventure. Since I could not go with him to the Presbyterian Church, he had come up with an alternate plan – more daring and impressive.

Fleecy white clouds floated overhead in a bright blue sky as we drove to the Elkhart airport. The day could not have been more perfect. Jake parked the car then dropped a bombshell. "I'll go in and ask if I can take a plane up."

"But you don't have a license, do you?" I sputtered.

He astounded me further with, "No, but I used to fly some up north and I think they'll let me." What a predicament! I could not trust my life to an unlicensed pilot.

When he left, I cried out to God, *"Please don't let them let him fly the plane, Father. PLEASE!!"* Over and over I prayed until his return.

Jake rather sheepishly admitted, "They won't let me. Someone else will give us a ride." Enormously relieved, I thanked the Lord. Poor Jake ended up paying for the plane and the pilot. But he never let on that it bothered him, and we had a delightful flight over the patchwork-quilt landscape below. As we held hands in the back seat I felt quite safe and relaxed with the experienced pilot at the controls.

On the way back, Jake took me to the apple orchard where he worked. He drove right through the trees to one lone tree with apples on it. He reached out the window and picked four apples. We ate two and took two home, a thrifty snack after his high-priced date.

When we returned to the dorm, who should we find but Clarence and Mary Ann Kooker who were there for a short visit. Amazing timing! When I was at college they seemed bent on getting me married off, especially to a couple of their friends that I dated. Now they were delighted to meet Jake. They teased and voiced approval of him as I gave them a tour of the campus.

Later, describing that first date, I wrote: "Wonderful day! The plane ride was smooth as smooth can be. The city below looked so clean and pretty, like a model city under a Christmas tree...The afternoon couldn't have been more perfect. It was a lovely sunny warm day, with the smell of burning leaves in the air. Jake was very nice and gentlemanly and quite happy with the day."

Jake didn't tell me until after we were engaged that when he got back to the dorm he told an older student, Victor Fast, about our date and added, "I'm going to marry her."

"How do you know that?" Vic asked, incredulous at such a boast. "You've only dated her once."

"I know," Jake replied confidently. "But I'm going to marry her." Though I was unsure sometimes and agonized about our relationship, Jake was confident from the first date.

The next Sunday Jake took me to a concert in the afternoon, and in the evening we attended a play. That week we began studying together evenings in the library. Wednesday evening, we double-dated with John Harder and his girl, Carrie, to the opera "Rigeletto" at Goshen College. When we returned, we joined the students in the kitchen for toast and jam, our regular snack.

Later, as I crawled into bed, I discovered my bed had been short-sheeted. I went to Cay's room and, sure enough, her bed was just like mine. As we visited, she mentioned how impressed she was with the true spirit of Christian love manifested here, especially by the fellows in showing understanding of and concern for the problems of the girls. While that was true, I decided I would not take the short sheeting sitting down.

As I remade my bed and mused about a payback, a vision came to mind from my freshman year at college on fourth floor of Lincoln Hall. That fateful day, a girl named Mary Jane Rittenhouse got a bucket of water (I can't recall what prompted such a rash act) and declared that the first person coming through the door from the stairs would get it. To her horror, who should walk in but our dorm mother, Miss Edna. But it was too late. Miss

148

Edna took that bucket with a full-force, frontal attack and stood there – in shock – dripping wet. Poor Mary Jane wanted to fade into oblivion.

So I knew what I would do. The next morning as we girls were ready for breakfast – waiting for the knock on the swinging door signifying the guys were coming through to the dining hall – I had my bucket of water at the ready. (I can't recall if it was one-third or one-half full, but it was wet!) I told the girls, "The first person who comes through that door is going to get it."

The knock came and we called out, "Come on through."

To my surprise, Jake appeared first, all unsuspecting. My bucket already poised, I let fly with the water. His face registered astonishment – and shock – and he turned back to change clothes while I mopped up the water. He took the prank in stride and never seemed angry. He never admitted to the short sheeting, but I suspected him because of his mischievous nature plus his expertise in making beds as a sleeping car porter on the train. Undaunted, Jake took me with him the next Sunday to the First Presbyterian Church, which he attended. Overwhelmed by its beauty and worshipful atmosphere, I felt out of place among such well-heeled parishioners in the new, million-dollar edifice. But I liked the more formal service and the sermon was excellent. I questioned why Jake didn't attend the Mennonite church like most of the students. He said he liked a more formal church like the one his sister Elizabeth attended and took him to in Toronto. I was amazed to learn that the pastor of her church was the famous Oswald Smith, evangelist one summer at our Christ for Quakertown crusade. I remembered him for his wonderful sermons, in contrast to the scary hell-fire ones.

Jake had one suit, a nice, royal blue in which he looked very handsome. He was not the least bothered that the suit had tiny, neat patches and darning on one knee. He said he got it from a drunk in Winnipeg. I couldn't imagine it. His wearing that suit to this fancy church impressed me. He didn't care what people thought. He also had a beautiful tweed jacket to alternate with the suit.

Jake told me that his mother sewed most of his shirts and trousers. She also knit him a heavy sweater jacket with deer designs. Deer figured prominently in Jake's young life. He talked about his pet deer he had while growing up on the Island. One deer was often in the house and one day it ate his mother's bread dough rising on a stool by the stove. She did not like deer in the house.

When his mother needed fish for supper she told Jake to get one from the creek. With pitchfork in hand he'd reach into the water – where hundreds of salmon swam upstream—and scoop out a large one onto the bank. In summer he slept in a pup tent with his dog, Tippy, and spent hours in the woods with friends. A ship graveyard with five to ten ships off the coast not far from his home provided exploration fun with friends. They salvaged lead from the steps and doors of military ships and sold it.

What a long way Jake had come from his humble background to that million-dollar church!

In the afternoon that day, we went to hear "The Messiah," and in the evening we went for a ride and parked near the grocery store and talked and had devotions. Jake told me he loved me—two weeks after our first date. I liked him alright but I wasn't as sure as he was.

Back at the dorm with my journal, just as I wrote, "Jake told me he loved me," suddenly the four girls from the dorm, Katie, Gladys, Annie, and Cay burst into song outside my bedroom window:

> Tell me why, the stars do shine, Tell me why the ivy twines,
> Tell me why the sky's so blue, And I will tell you,
> Just why I love you.
>
> Because God made the stars to shine, Because God made the ivy twine,
> Because God made the sky so blue, Because God made you,
> That's why I love you."

Then they sang, "Lullaby, and good night."

It was so *beautiful*! The blending of their voices in harmony sounded angelic. And their timing couldn't have been more perfect. They had no way of knowing what Jake had told me that night. I felt God's Spirit very near. How blessed I was, enveloped and surrounded by love—God's love, Jake's love, the love of these dear sisters—four sisters here, just like my four back home. God was so good. Didn't God say in His Word, "My God shall supply all your need, according to his riches in glory" (Phil. 4:19)? He was supplying my need for love and assurance far beyond what I could ask or think.

I wrote in my journal, "(Tonight) Jake prayed that God's will be done, and if we should have to part that we would be willing to do it."

Jake and I had our differences. Adventure was his middle name, quite the opposite of my sheltered, overprotected upbringing. I let him know where I stood about things and he teased me about my "theology" and thought I was funny. It was 1960 and John F. Kennedy was running against Richard Nixon. I let it be known that if Kennedy got elected the Catholics would run the country and we evangelical Christians could be in trouble. (Back then my experience with Catholics was limited. I have since come to appreciate and love many of them and their gifted writers and leaders.) Jake laughed at my conservative views. Not only were we from different backgrounds and countries but from opposite ends of the continent as well. Should this be a barrier for us?

On Election Day, my perspective was altered as a chapel speaker said, "Just because one's candidate does not win, our country does not become chaotic; God still rules." Then Herman Enns, an older student in the dorm, had devotions after dinner in which he stated, "Kennedy is aware of a higher power, and rulers are used by God." My understanding and worldview needed adjustment.

One evening after dishes, as we sat together on the settee in the dining hall, delighting in each others' company, Jake said: "I've been wondering, would you like to – to join up with me?"

I knew what he meant. It was December 9, four weeks after our first date. But we had gotten to know each other since September, spent a lot of time together the past month, and had often discussed our relationship and how we felt about each other. I had prayed seriously about this and we had prayed together. I felt that he had the same "mental furniture" as I and was committed to Christ and His service. Especially in the past month, as our love for each other deepened, I felt the peace of Christ in my heart and in awe of Jake's tender love for me. I realized I had fallen head over heels in love. It didn't take me long to give Jake a resounding, "Yes!"

As we talked, Jake suggested, "I think we should wait until your birthday in February to announce our engagement. We might shock people if we told them now." I agreed. He went on, "How about if we get married before the next school year? This summer I can work in Thompson again. I can make more money there. We're going to need it."

I knew he was as short of funds as I. We were both working our way through school with little or no outside help. My mind whirled. Married in September! He had this all thought out. But the plan made sense.

Jake told me sweetly, "Dynamite comes in small packages." I knew nothing about dynamite and was amused at his comparison of it with my size. He also said, "My parents will be really happy that I'm getting married. My dad told me the last time I was home, 'It's time for you to get married.'" I was glad to oblige and felt blessed with the family into which I was marrying.

For Christmas vacation I went with Spaeths to Pennsylvania. Jake drove to Ontario to spend Christmas with his sisters, Elizabeth and Helen, the oldest and youngest girls. Then he planned to drive to Quakertown to meet my family. I had drawn him a map to our house on Thatcher Road. He sent me a letter saying he lost the map but not to worry because he would find me no matter where I was. Then he wrote out the directions correctly from memory. "Turn left at the Children's Home, go around a sharp curve at the big tree, then around another curve and over the bridge and your house is the first one on the right." He arrived the morning of December 28.

I knew when I fell in love with Jake that Mama would love him, too. Tanned, with a thick crop of dark hair with natural wave, and beautiful brown eyes, he was incredibly handsome. And he had a nice personality. I was right about Mama. She loved him, as did all of my family. Daddy's big smile and warm manner told me he was pleased, too.

By now Ruthie had a car and the morning after Jake arrived she drove us all over the countryside, laughing and entertaining us. That afternoon we visited Grammy and Pappy Landis and I showed Jake our church. We visited Millie and Ralph and Clarence and Helen Kooker. Millie seemed fine, but we had no chance to talk alone. The next day we took off for school, with a quick stop at the Kookers in Bluffton and made it to Elkhart by 12:30 A.M. after a very long day.

Soon we were back into school and work routine. One day Jake told me, "I'm glad you're going to seminary too, because you can help me with my work." Jake had a Bachelor of Christian Education degree from Canadian Mennonite Bible College and a B.A. degree in Philosophy (one year) from Bethel College in North Newton, Kansas, where I had attended the youth meetings. While at Bethel, Jake was youth pastor at Lorraine Avenue Mennonite Church in Wichita. He spoke highly of the pastor, George Stoneback, with whom he had worked and from whom he learned much. Rev. Stoneback resigned as pastor at the end of the school year and Jake filled in as interim pastor for the summer before seminary.

Jake told me the story of how, as a student at CMBC, he had to preach a German sermon at a church one Sunday. Afterwards the professor said to him, "I think I know what you were trying to say, but I don't think many other people understood." I could sympathize with his hesitancy about preaching.

On the last day of December 1960, my "Little Sis" from college, Jeannette Sprunger, asked if I would come to live with her and Shirley for second semester. Their mother had died of cancer during the first semester. Shirley was in high school and Jeannette was working. Their father had to return to Congo and did not want the girls left alone. He asked them who they wanted to live with them and they chose me. I was delighted. Rev. Sprunger told me, "You don't have to pay a cent to live here." I felt honored to stay with the girls, and what a wonderful saving for me on room and board. I had a small college loan to repay to Pauline Yoder's Aunt Katie (Pauline from Moyer's Hatchery days). Though I missed dorm life, I enjoyed being with the girls in their home just next to the seminary. Jake usually walked or drove me home the short distance after we studied in the library evenings.

Jake with pet deer.

We're engaged! Jake and me at my "home," May 1961.

On my birthday, February 6, Jake came to the house at 6:00 P.M. He gave me my ring saying, "A ring has no beginning and no end. It symbolizes love, and our love will be like that, having no end." What beautiful words! Was this really happening to me?

After he gave me the ring, we called my family and talked to Mama, Grace, Ruth, and Tommy. They were all pleased and excited. Jake soon left to study. Shirley had baked a birthday cake and later Jake came back. He brought a telegram from his parents, sending congratulations with the verses, Hebrews 13:20-21: "Now may the God of peace who brought up our Lord Jesus from the dead, that great shepherd of the sheep, through the blood of the everlasting covenant, make you complete in every good work to do His will, working in you what is well pleasing in His sight, through Jesus Christ, to whom be glory forever and ever. Amen." He had written his folks ahead of time to tell them we were engaged and sent them my picture.

After Jake left, the girls from the dorm arrived. Katie, Cay, Annie and Gladys sang "Happy Birthday" to me outside then came in for cake. I had told Annie our secret and now she told the others. Gladys shouted excited congratulations, practically bursting my eardrums. Later, Jeannette and I wrote letters together and carried on till quite late. I felt blessed to have Jeannette share in my happiness.

The news spread quickly through the seminary community. The next morning a married woman I barely knew told me, "I always thought Jake was the handsomest guy on campus; and not only handsome, but he has such a nice personality." Music professor Marvin Dirks commented to me about Jake's ability to take criticism or be disagreed with and said, "I really like Jake." President Erland Waltner came into my office and told me with a warm smile, "I'm happy about your engagement. I think highly of Jake. He has great potential." I wrote in my journal, "I am more convinced than ever that I didn't find him, but God sent him to me. I asked God to give me the one He had for me because His choice would be best."

When the weather warmed up, we double dated with Jeannette and her future husband, Tom Bechtel. He was from Goshen and had a motorboat and we enjoyed rides with them between Goshen and Elkhart on the Elkhart River. At the house, Tom made pizza for us with his own dough recipe.

Jake and I planned to be married in early September, and I would graduate two years later with my MRS. and my MRE (Master of Religious Education) degrees—two "degrees" in one. In the meantime, studies must be done and a wedding planned, with Jake far away in northern Canada in the summer.

CHAPTER 13

Now We Are One

And the Lord God said, It is not good that the man should be alone;
I will make him an help meet for him.
GENESIS 2:18 (KJV)

1961–1962

Sunday mornings ushered in the week with our most exciting weekly date – worship at the beautiful First Presbyterian Church. Ready to go, in my room at the back of the Congo Inland Mission house, I waited for Jake's familiar whistle outside my window. Hearing it, I peered out to see my handsome beau in his blue suit, with beautiful smile, eyes dancing and face aglow with gentleness and love. The Holy Spirit seemed to hover over us, and I saw Jesus' love reflected in Jake's face. It was a sacred moment that filled me with joy. Later, as we entered the sanctuary, another world awaited us – exalted and worshipful – with pipe organ, soloists (sometimes our own Mennonite Delia Dyck with her bell-like voice), choir, challenging sermon, inspiring prayers. In this peaceful place, the routine world of work and serious seminary studies was left behind.

But at times, guilt tugged at my heartstrings and sensitive spirit. Loyal Mennonite that I was, I wondered, Will Jake take me away from my Mennonite heritage? Why did he want to worship with the wealthy? Sometimes we attended the Mennonite church, but I knew Jake loved the Presbyterian and I wanted to please him.

Joys were tempered with struggles and sadness. Millie's depression lingered on. I pondered the meaning of "repressed anger." From my studies of psychology at college I had some understanding. Millie was always the good child, and had never expressed anger at Mama. She kept everything inside and seemed happy. Her deep depression worried me. What was she angry at? How long would she suffer with this? How would marriage change *my* life? Joy and sorrow seemed so closely interwoven. I recalled someone

155

praying in chapel, "Dear God, help us to bring our joys to you that you may sober them."

I enjoyed living with Jeannette and Shirley. One evening we played hymns together. Shirley was a great pianist and loved to play her new pieces for Jake. But this time she played accordion, Jeannette, the vibraharp, and I played piano. With my limited ability I had never played with others before (except for "Chopsticks," which Millie and I had perfected). What a joy to play hymns with these dear sisters.

That evening, Jake came over and I wrote to Millie while he read. I had recently received a nice letter from Mama and a rare one from Grammy Landis that was special. Jake received one from his father, in which he wrote, "I hope Jane will write us sometime." I needed no further invitation. I wrote to his family about wedding preparations in answer to their offers to help.

The next week, Jake was in charge of the weekly prayer meeting in the dorm in which he talked about fasting, and a discussion ensued. Two days later most of the dorm students fasted and I did too. I stayed at the office and worked until mealtimes. At noon and evening I read Old and New Testament passages. Isaiah 53 on the suffering servant Messiah focused my mind on Christ in a meaningful way. In Matthew I saw Jesus' dramatic ministry in fulfillment of this prophecy. In this, my first fast, these meditations strengthened me and alleviated hunger pangs. Jesus' words to His disciples came to mind, "I have food to eat of which you do not know...My meat is to do the will of Him who sent Me" (John 4:34).

In March, Rev. Andrew Shelly was on campus. Head of our conference Mission Board, he was a brother to Margaret Weaver and Paul Shelly from Bluffton. I knew him from camp in Pennsylvania and appreciated him for years as an inspiring preacher. Jake's dad was also a member of the Mission Board. With characteristic enthusiasm, "Andy" congratulated me on my engagement, adding, "I saw your future father-in-law recently. He's a wonderful man. You're marrying into a wonderful family!" Gratitude to God rose within me for this praise of Jake's family.

At the end of March our Old Testament class traveled to the University of Chicago. We also visited with a rabbi for two hours at a synagogue. Jake got excited about the university and told me he would like to go there, that it would be a challenge. I saw how different he was from me, fearless and daring, ready to do new things, things too big for me.

But Jake's more immediate concern was finding summer work. He wrote to the construction company in Thompson and in April received a letter of acceptance. Working June, July, and August, he hoped to clear $1000. He'd be back in time for us to drive to Pennsylvania together for our wedding the first weekend in September.

In December, my brother Ralph had become engaged to Janice Weisel, a high school friend of Ruthie's. They planned a June wedding. Anna was engaged to John Smith from Philadelphia, whom she met at Bob Jones University. They set their wedding date for August 26. What a busy summer with three weddings! Mama dreaded it already. By August she would be "all worked up." For years she talked to us about her "bad nerves." Anna and I reassured her that we would take care of everything–planning and paying for our weddings, as Millie had done. Mama reminded, "We don't have money to pay for your wedding but we will buy the cake." We never discussed such things with Daddy.

The semester passed quickly and Jake prepared to leave for Thompson. Rev. Sprunger was coming home from Congo to stay with Jeannette and Shirley. A Mennonite psychotherapist, Margaret Jahnke–who lived in an apartment across the street from the CIM–invited me to live with her for the summer. I agreed, grateful for God's provision.

Then we received another blessing. The dorm host and hostess apartment was being vacated and Jake and I were offered this responsibility for the next year. This entailed overseeing dorm life, dust mopping the dining hall and hallway, cleaning the guest room, and providing breakfast for guest speakers and visitors. We gratefully accepted the job and rent-free apartment.

In June, Jake left for Thompson. I continued in the office. Planning our wedding was made easier because my officemate, Estelle Bartel, also planned a September wedding. My desk had been moved into her office earlier in the year and we were good friends. We'd be married the same weekend, she and Herman Enns in Hillsboro, Kansas, Jake and I in Quakertown. Estelle and I spent hours discussing the details of our wedding service, shopping, and encouraging each other.

In one of Jake's first letters to me, he copied the wedding service of Vincent and Rosemarie Harding. Vincent was co-pastor of Woodlawn Mennonite Church in Chicago, part of the seminary campus, begun in 1947. He was one of the few black pastors in the Mennonite church at that time, perhaps the first, and very respected. Jake learned to know and admire Vince when he spoke at Bethel College. Somehow he got their wedding bulletin and kept it and, thanks to his great organization, was able to find it again when needed. He suggested we use their service as a pattern for ours. It had great organ music for the prelude and a beautiful worship service.

In June I rode home with Harry and Ada Spaeth to my brother Ralph and Janice's wedding. The weekend at home was pleasant. Mama and I got along well and the wedding was like a family reunion with Landis relatives. I was happy to find Millie feeling much better. She and I shopped for fabric for her matron of honor dress. She would be my only attendant. Jake and I wanted a simple, inexpensive wedding. On Sunday afternoon my family and I were invited to the Kooker's home where a surprise shower awaited me. How good it was to have Mama and Daddy and all the family present with the church people, and cousin Marietta, for a great time of fellowship.

Estelle and I shopped for our wedding gowns in South Bend where I was delighted to find a pretty window display model just my size for $35.00. It was street length organza with lace and full skirt. Jake gave feedback on plans through letters or an occasional phone call. He kept on top of everything, reminding me when to order the bulletins and the cross with rings for the top of our cake.

On August 25, Jake returned from Thompson and we left for Pennsylvania to attend Anna and John's wedding, one week before ours. We drove all night, arriving by noon the next day for the wedding that evening. Anna looked beautiful and had several bridesmaids and a lovely wedding at Bethany Mennonite Church in town.

I felt sad that Anna could not attend our wedding. John, an accountant for Slavic Gospel Association in Chicago, had to be at work the next week. Our family had scattered. Millie and brother Ralph were married and busy with their own lives. Grace, Ruth and Tommy still lived at home.

Jake and I had a week to take care of last-minute details. We were excited that Jake's father, mother, and younger sisters—Mary Ann and Helen—were coming from Canada. Jake told me, "When you meet my mother, she will kiss you." And she did. She was very quiet and shy about her English, but kind and helpful. His pastor father was friendly and talkative. They stayed with Clarence and Helen Kooker and got along like old friends. Dad enjoyed Mr. Kooker's lively conversation and his coons in a shed out back. Jake, Mary Ann, and Helen stayed at Renninger's next door. My friend Ann Hilty, from Bluffton, slept at our house. I asked Ann and Shirley Moyer (my Kansas trip friend) to help with the reception, along with sister Ruth, Jake's sister Helen, and Ralph's wife, Janice, and Mary Ann to attend the guest book.

Since a number of Jake's friends from seminary were also getting married that summer or involved in summer pastorates, he had no one to serve as best man. My brother Ralph accepted the honor. My cousin Charlie Mohr and brother-in-law Ralph Loux would serve as ushers. Charlie and his wife Grace invited us to their home for the Friday night rehearsal dinner. What a special surprise and lovely spread of delicious dishes! Jake's family and mine, along with the Kookers, enjoyed a time of wonderful fellowship.

Labor Day Bible Conference was held at Men-O-Lan camp that weekend, and that Saturday before the wedding, Jake and I, the Kookers, Jake's parents, and his sisters, attended the conference. It was a treat to have Jake Enz, our Old Testament professor from seminary, as the speaker.

By Saturday evening, all the commotion—of plans and people arriving, the Bible Conference, Mama's "nerves," and my own qualms—seemed too much. By evening I was tired and sad. Millie and Anna were gone. I was 26 now. How often I had felt like a motherless child the past 23 years. Mama meant well, but at a time like this I longed for my mother. I knew I must put these sad thoughts out of my mind. I cried out to God and a measure of calm returned.

(Later I learned that my experience was a "piece of cake" compared with Anna's before *her* wedding. After finishing classes at Bob Jones University a few weeks before, she came home and began *sewing* her gown and making preparations. She told me, "Mom was so mad and upset all the time that she yelled and yelled. I was a basket case, a total wreck. I cried and cried. It was terrible. All those details to work on and no support. John came home from Chicago a week before the wedding (to his home in Philly, 40 miles south) so we could have our blood tests and do the last minute things."

Perhaps Anna took the brunt of Mama's frustration that all three of us married in one summer. But God made it up to Anna with a wonderful husband. John had written Mama and Daddy a letter in which he expressed his love for Anna and asked for her hand in marriage. Grace had written me about it thus: "After I read the letter at noon one day at home, I cried all afternoon at work. I was so happy for Anna and you." What a tenderhearted, loving sister!)

Our wedding took place on Sunday, September 3, at 3:00 P.M. at East Swamp Mennonite Church. The day dawned hot and humid. On the way to the church, Daddy chewed gum, as he usually did in church. When we got out of the car, I asked him nicely, "Daddy, would you please not chew gum for the service?" With an obliging smile, he spit it out. I would never have thought of doing such a thing before but, after all, this was my wedding. He was in a happy mood, and loving toward me as usual. How grateful I was for Daddy and his love – for his reserved but solid support through all the years.

My pastor, Rev. Wilmer Denlinger, performed the wedding ceremony. Jake's father read Scripture, led the prayers and responsive reading of I Corinthians 13, and gave the meditation. This was not your traditional wedding, but a seminary one, with my student husband-to-be giving thoughtful input as a former pastor, accustomed to planning worship services. Sister Grace sang *four* solos, one during the prelude pieces and one after the processional. We had memorized our vows and all went well. We sang hymns, including Jake's favorite, "Joyful, Joyful, We Adore Thee." On the last hymn we sang two verses in German for the sake of Jake's parents, as well as for my Pappy Landis who sang German solos at church. Though the hymn was unfamiliar to some, this German chorale had a beautiful message – "He who would be in God confiding," which ends with, "For he who trusts in God above will own His friendship and His love."

Mr. and Mrs. Jake Friesen, September 3, 1961.

In the reception line, we received many good wishes and blessings from church friends and relatives. Warm hugs and best wishes from my Landis grandparents, aunts, and uncles especially warmed and comforted me. My mother's influence *was* present in her family.

After the reception, Jake drove me home, where I changed into my "going away outfit," and Jake went to Renningers to change and pack. When I came downstairs to leave, Mama met me in the middle room. She caught me totally off guard with a warm hug and kiss, such a contrast from the day I left for college. I was startled and strangely warmed by this unusual show of

Reception line: Jake, Aunt Melba kissing me with Kathy Landis looking on, Mom.

affection. My heart still leaps up in gratitude to God whenever I relive this moment. She *did* love me, and her kiss showed her approval and affirmation of my husband and me. She had stood beside me in the reception line where she observed others hugging and kissing me. One photo of that line showed

my mother's sister Melba planting a kiss on my cheek as Mama looks on with a smile. (I treasure that picture of the one who helped put on my warm coat after my mother's funeral and cared for me often that first year after her death.) Mama's hug and kiss was one of God's serendipities that filled me with joy.

My brother Ralph had arranged our first night for us at a motel at Center Valley, about ten miles from home. Before we got into bed we knelt to pray. I wept and looked at my husband as tears ran down his cheeks and we mingled our prayers and tears of joy.

Daddy with first grandchild Brenda Loux, 1961.

The next day we drove through the beautiful Pocono Mountains of northeast Pennsylvania where we stayed one night, then on to Elkhart via Bluffton where we stayed with Clarence and Mary Ann Kooker overnight.

Back in Elkhart, we moved into our studio apartment, unpacked gifts, and got organized. So many couples were married that summer that professors Lee and Bertha Harder led a Marriage and Family Class first semester in which they shared a wealth of information and personal stories. We read and wrote on many issues in separate notebooks. We were fortunate indeed to have this good foundation to begin our life together.

For our devotions, Jake suggested we use a commentary and chose the *Gospel of Mark* by William Barkley, a strange idea to me. But this was seminary. We took turns each night, one reading the Scripture and commentary and one praying.

We had never cooked together our first semester in the dorm, but found we were a great team in the kitchen and loved to entertain, hosting new students, friends, and seminary guests for meals.

For his practical work the first semester, Jake taught an adult Sunday school class at First Presbyterian. My major professor, Bertha Harder, assigned me to observe the children's classes there and write a report on each one. Awestruck at the large, well-equipped classrooms and outgoing, capable teachers, I felt like a little mouse sitting and observing these women who had not been to seminary—doing what I was supposed to be learning in school, a humbling education for me.

Second semester we served as leaders of the Junior High Youth Fellowship there. At our first social, a boy came up to me, slapped me on the back—hard—and said, "What grade are you in?" I introduced myself as a sponsor and, embarrassed, he quickly disappeared into the crowd of milling youth. *He thought I was in junior high?* I felt out of place and was glad when that assignment was over.

Life was full and humming with activity. As one year slipped into another, we wondered, *Where will all this study and work take us?* One more year and we'd have to decide.

CHAPTER 14

New Adventures

Having then gifts differing according to the grace that is
given to us, let us use them...
ROMANS 12:6 (NKJ)

1961–1964

For our first Christmas together, Jake and I drove to Pennsylvania to be with my family. I picked up all my boxes left in the attic, and we had a good time catching up with Tommy and the family. I loved taking pictures of Tommy when I was home and he took a great liking to Jake.

Jake and Tom, December 1961.

Tommy on the old iron bridge.

Our first separation came when my major professor, Bertha Harder, took me along to Central District Conference in Washington, Iowa to do a "demonstration school" for Sunday school teachers. I was her only student majoring in Christian Education and we had done such classes with local children, playing the story and other activities. How I missed Jake! After this four-day trip, I was dismayed to come home to a dark apartment and Jake sick in bed. Over Easter break, Jake left with the seminary men's chorus to churches in Ontario, Canada. I did not relish these forced separations.

The summer of 1962, for his practical work, Jake was assigned two churches, the north and the south, on the main street of Moundridge, Kansas. It was exciting to move to the Kansas prairies where I had gone twice before. First Church of Christian and West Zion each provided housing for six weeks. First we stayed with a widower, Jacob Wedel, who had a wonderful vegetable garden. He asked me to make his favorite borscht, a delicious beet and navy bean soup. (I made Jake's preferred cabbage borscht from his background.) Mr. Wedel loved having us and we enjoyed him. Then the south church pastor, Ralph Weber and wife Doris, left on a six-week vacation so we lived in their nice home. One church was Swiss; the other German, Prussian, Russian, with poppy seed pastry and cake all the rage.

Jake and I did the bulletins, visited the sick and elderly, worked with the youth and spent a week with them at camp—Jake as Bible teacher, me as cabin counselor—and Jake preached at church. He'd type up his sermon then have me critique it. The first Sunday I stood with him at the door and shook the hands of everyone after the service. Were there 250 or 300 in that line? No matter, when the last hand was shaken my cheeks felt frozen in a perpetual smile. I never knew a smile could hurt so much and empathized with pastors in a new way.

West Zion's pastor was Harris Waltner. His wife Christine asked me to write a half-month of devotionals for her for *Our Family Worships* booklet, as she couldn't meet her deadline. I wrote 15 devotionals, though she said my name would not appear with them. It was my first writing assignment.

Jake's sister Helen worked as a secretary for Andrew Shelly at our headquarters office in Newton, 14 miles away. We enjoyed dinner with her a few times that summer, glad for a family member close by.

A couple from church invited us to their home with large farm that boasted oil wells—oil and wheat. We learned about wheat harvest first hand, the biggest week of the year for Kansas farmers. What a lot of hoopla over wheat! (Little did we realize that one day we'd own Kansas farmland and raise our children seven miles down the road at Hesston.)

Back at Elkhart, a new school year faced us. When Jake's father was in the States for meetings of the Mission Board, he visited us and brought gifts of food. Mother canned beef, chicken, and pork, which made quick, delicious meals. Her dill pickles, dried apples, and bags of thin homemade noodles were fine treats. We also enjoyed an occasional visit from Anna and John from Chicago. Family visits were always special.

Over the years, my classes included Evangelism, Christian Education of Youth and Adults, Pastoral Care and Counseling, Psalms, and Prophets. The Seven Great Religions of the World was a favorite, taught by former missionary to China and our Dean, S. F. Pannabecker. He emphasized that the distinguishing mark of Christianity is that it is the only religion whose founder died and was resurrected. The others were mere men who died – period. We have a *living* Savior!

For Mennonite History class with Dr. Harold S. Bender, at Goshen Seminary, Jake and I together wrote a history of PAX, an alternate service for Conscientious Objectors who rebuilt bombed villages in Germany after the war. Dr. Bender's wife graded our final exams at the end of the year because he was too ill and died soon after the class ended. We attended his service at the large Goshen College Mennonite Church. The service of praise and glorious singing of "Lift Your Glad Voices" was extraordinary. I had never been to a memorial service like it.

Jake's three-year program included Greek and Hebrew, theology, and preaching. For our practical work, Bertha asked if Jake and I would team-teach with her in a Sunday school class at the Mennonite Church. I was delighted. Bertha stressed the importance of male role models for children in Sunday school and the effectiveness of husband-wife teams.

For Christmas, Bertha and I directed a drama, *Why the Chimes Rang*, by Elizabeth Apthorp McFadden. It was a moving worship experience. A man sitting beside me said after the performance that he wept as the boy came down the aisle with his gift for the Christ Child. (I loved the story and used the play later in churches in three different states.)

For Valentine's Day that year Jake and I threw a party for the dorm students. Guys and girls squeezed into our tiny apartment for a night of games, food, and laughter. With a recipe from a calendar Jake's sister Margaret and Peter Schulz sent us from their General Store at Black Creek on the Island, we cut large hearts from paper grocery sacks, made the huge meringue recipe, and shaped it into two large hearts on separate papers. We baked the hearts then

165

piled them high with large scoops of various flavors and colors of ice cream. They were beautiful and a big hit, and the night was a great success.

During that last year, Jake struggled with what to do after graduation. Not feeling called to the ministry he applied to Mennonite Central Committee (MCC) at Akron, Pennsylvania to work overseas. This did not appeal to me and I secretly hoped we could stay in the States. North American Mennonites, with Pennsylvanians taking a leading role, had saved the lives of Jake's parents and grandparents in the early 1920s during the great famine in Russia, when thousands died of starvation. Jake's father was so grateful to MCC that he often said he prayed for MCC workers in countries around the world every day. My home church had supported MCC relief projects through the years. Would we now become MCC workers? I had never envisioned this for myself. We waited, and prayed.

Near the end of the year Jake was offered a job, not in another country, but at the MCC headquarters office at Akron, 70 miles from my home. I couldn't have been happier and I knew that Mama, whom we now called Mom, would be thrilled. Jake's job was to be assistant director of Voluntary Service (VS) projects all over the United States. We prayed about it and he accepted. I sensed God's hand upon us in this first major decision of our life together.

But Mom was not in good health and had been in and out of the hospital. She did not follow her diet for diabetes, and smoking complicated her heart problems. She developed a sore on her foot, which did not heal. When Mom turned 45 on March 14, 1962, her leg was amputated above the knee. This drastic measure and change in her life added stress and new responsibilities for Daddy and my sisters.

At the time of the amputation, Grace wrote me about all the blessings she saw happening. Two weeks after the fact, following some heartbreaking days, she said that Mom "is unbelievably happy." One blessing was in the form of her roommate, Mrs. Krause, mother of Richard Renninger's wife, JoAnn. Mrs. Krause, a teacher and artist, was "always doing something and talking a mile a minute, just what the doctor ordered."

Daddy and Mom joined Flatland Church in 1947 and in 1958 took their membership to Daddy's United Church of Christ. Even so, Flatland Church still treated them as members, which was a wonderful support to all of us. They gave a financial gift for amputation expenses, and Mom loved Rev. Denlinger's visits. And, Grace reported, Tommy, age seven, was "eating much better and wants to be so big when Mom comes home that she doesn't know him." Grace confessed, "I myself have found a close relationship with God that has been lacking the last few years. At first I just couldn't get hold of myself. Then I realized that no amount of worry was going to help. That is when I started praying and ceased worrying…and when I count the blessings that have come out of it already, I know it was for a purpose."

Grace's letter included plans for Tommy's seventh birthday, which Mom was sorry to miss. Grace baked a cake to decorate, and wrote, "Mom bought him a pair of skates with which to break his neck and I got him a watch. He's just learning to tell time, and I know he'll love it. Millie and Ralph are giving him a baseball bat…and for the past few days all he can talk about is his birthday."

Grace was the major caregiver for Mom and managed the household, an emotional strain for her. Ruthie helped with cleaning, laundry, and ironing. Daddy helped some, but there was cooking to do and Tommy to look after. I felt removed from all that and was glad we could soon visit them more often.

Jake and I graduated together in May 1963, with a class of ten others. The only other woman was a Japanese friend, Umeno Nishimura, a Bluffton classmate. Three of the dorm girls, Gladys, Katie, and Cay, had graduated before us. Anna, John, and their son, little John, came from Chicago to represent our family for the occasion, a blessing to Jake and me. A heartwarming surprise came from the secretary I had left behind at the hatchery. Pauline Yoder and husband Dave sent a lovely bouquet of pink carnations in a glass snifter.

Soon after graduation we packed our belongings in the black Plymouth (they all fit!) and moved to Pennsylvania. We stayed in a room at the guest house the first weeks, then moved into an MCC house on 9th Street. Gerald and Lois Leinbach lived upstairs and Lois became Jake's secretary.

Jake began work in the VS office and I volunteered to write news stories for the summer for Information Services part time. Researching and writing MCC happenings from many countries aroused my interest in writing. My efforts were rewarded when our editor, Larry Kehler, told me one day, "You're a good writer." Larry later became editor of *The Mennonite*.

Jake's work required him to travel one-third of the time to voluntary service units all over the country. Before his first trip in summer we said our goodbyes and he walked out. I hated separations and as a wave of sadness washed over me tears filled my eyes. The door opened and in walked Jake!

"I *thought* you'd be crying! You knew I'd have to travel when I took this job," he reminded gently.

"I *know!*" I managed, between sobs, "but I'll *miss* you!" He was wonderful to come back and check on me. His sensitivity and thoughtfulness eased the pain and I soon learned to accept the inevitable.

Then, as often as he could, Jake planned the shorter trips to nearby states on weekends so I could drive with him. Other times he flew. His assignments took him to interesting places. At a college in the Appalachian Mountains of Kentucky he watched students make beautiful wooden crafts. He brought me an unusual walnut nut bowl on a stem and a wooden candleholder for four candles, which could be arranged in a square, straight line, or zigzag. One weekend we went to the VS Unit in Poughkeepsie, New York. Early the next morning we were awakened by a strange, earsplitting sound outside, close to our window. Jake identified it as a donkey, which brayed a raucous ten-minute alarm we could not shut off.

With my elementary education degree, I had a chance to make good on my word to Mom that I hoped to come home to teach. Having applied earlier to the Ephrata school system, I had an interview two days after arriving in Akron. I told the superintendent that I planned to teach only one year because I wanted to start a family. Fourth grade was my favorite and in spite of my restriction I was hired for a fourth grade class at a rural school with some conservative Mennonite children attending.

That fall, I jumped in. Parts of teaching I enjoyed, but disciplining was a trial. The children's previous teacher warned me about three unruly boys. One of them, Mike, had flunked. Though I had some rough days with all three, I won their respect and by the end of the year Mike's mother called me on the phone and said, "Last year I had to fight with Mike every day to go to school. This year I've had no problem and he's done much better because he liked you."

How I wished I'd felt as successful with others whose grades were poor. Spanking a boy at the principal's direction after he threw food around the cafeteria was one of the hardest things I did. I knew this boy had problems at home but he responded well to me in class and I hated to spank him. Still, he knew he deserved it, as I explained to him, and he cried as I used the big university paddle Grace had given me. But my prayers and compassion for him won out and I saw positive change in him.

Daddy, Mom, and Tommy came for a visit and enjoyed seeing my school. After seven years, Mom got her wish and I was thankful not to disappoint her. I loved having Mom, Daddy, and Tom visit in our home. My other siblings also came to see our home, town, and the MCC offices. We all loved charming Lancaster County with its picturesque Amish and Mennonite farms and winding roads through villages and towns.

That year, in 1964, Jake planned his visit to the Atlanta VS unit over Easter so I could go with him. On the beautiful drive through North Carolina we saw shacks of very poor blacks, still suffering the effects of slavery and share-cropping. I felt sad for them and remember exclaiming, "Maybe we could come down here and help them." I had no idea these words were prophetic.

On Easter Sunday we attended the church of Dr. Martin Luther King Sr. and heard his son preach. The air was charged with energy as this bold and powerful civil rights leader proclaimed God's word and truth. His impassioned heart and call for freedom for his people, birthed in this church, resounded across the nation and the world. His father cheered him on with, "Preach it, Son!" and the congregation added loud affirmation. We sang along with the civil rights anthem, "We Shall Overcome," as choir and congregation swayed from side to side, singing their hearts out.

Jake first heard Dr. King speak when he was a student at Bethel College and was deeply impressed. (Fast forward to 2010 Black History Week at Bethel when that very speech from 1960 was replayed for students and community, and available on the Internet for another month. Jake and I listened in awe as the silver-tongued orator told the history of oppression of people world-wide and the fight for freedom and equality for blacks. His impassioned plea for everyone to take up the cause of the poor and oppressed everywhere was met with questions from the audience about how they could help.)

Dr. King's home was behind the MCC-VS house, their back yards separated by a fence. Vincent Harding (former pastor in Chicago whose wedding bulletin gave us ideas for ours) was head of this unit. Several VS secretaries worked for King's Southern Christian Leadership Conference (SCLC). Jake met with Vince and the MCC secretaries and worked with a bright, young civil rights worker, Andrew Young, who supervised the SCLC office. In years to come, we followed Andy's rise to prominence. He pastored several churches in the South then joined King in leading the SCLC. Andy won election to the U.S. Congress in 1972, 1974, and 1976. In 1976, he became U.S. Ambassador to the United Nations but unfortunately was forced to resign after he had a personal meeting with a Palestinian leader. From 1981-89, Andy Young served as mayor of Atlanta. We were glad to see blacks gaining the opportunity to serve in high office.

Back at school, I usually read to the students for the last period of the day, as I had loved Miss Guri's reading to us in our one-room school. One of the books I chose was a favorite of mine, *Amos Fortune, Free Man*, by Elizabeth Yates. It told of the struggle of a slave to find freedom in the North. I later learned that the book was above fourth grade reading level, yet the students were absorbed with the story and became aware of and identified with the struggles of blacks.

When I was growing up, I empathized with blacks as we studied about slavery in the South. When I met Jake and told him how we grew up with Mama, his response surprised me: "You were like the slaves in the South!" Compared with the freedom he had as a boy growing up on the Island, my life looked hopelessly restricted. Perhaps this helped me empathize with the plight of black people.

My salary of $4500 came in handy to help buy a different car. For this one year only, I earned more than Jake. We got a Volkswagen from Germany through an MCC worker who bought the car, drove it for a few months, and then brought it to the States as a used car.

Glad when the school year ended, I decided teaching was not for me. I looked forward to being a mother. And before school was out, our baby was on the way. The due date was on my birthday, February 6. I was amazed that Jake had the book, *Childbirth Without Fear* on natural childbirth (by Grantly Dick-Read), and we read it together. With my mother's death after her fourth delivery, anxious thoughts sometimes crept into my mind. What was ahead for me? I was exceedingly grateful to God for this pregnancy and knew God was with me. I decided to trust Him to keep baby and me safe.

In the meantime, Jake had an awesome trip planned for us and I could hardly wait.

CHAPTER 15

Double Rainbow

The ransomed of the Lord…shall obtain joy and gladness,
and sorrow and sighing shall flee away.
ISAIAH 35:10 (KJV)

1964–1965

That summer of 1964, we took off on a fantastic trip—a real honeymoon. We had neither time nor money for one when we were wed, but this was it. Jake planned to combine visiting VS units with camping our way to British Columbia so I could visit his home and family for the first time. He bought a pup tent and received a complete route to follow from a touring service.

We set off in our VW bug and made it all the way to Anna and John's in Chicago, 718 miles, by 7:20 P.M. The next night we camped in Minnesota. Without a stove, we ate at restaurants or at campsites. I learned to eat sardine sandwiches that Jake liked. We stopped at Wisconsin Dells and a petrified forest in South Dakota, where Jake also made his first VS stop at Redfield State Hospital. After a long tour through Montana we crossed into Alberta.

Sometimes I read aloud from a book on expectant motherhood. Until now, I often had an afternoon nap, but today Jake informed me that naps were "not really necessary." After all, this was *Canada*! In Calgary we visited a dinosaur park, a zoo, and a greenhouse with beautiful tiny birds flying around, and larger caged birds. We had lunch at famous Banff National Park and drove past Lake Louise. (The scrapbook I made later, with map sections of our route, post cards, journaling, mileage and expense records, keeps the memories vivid.)

On Saturday, our fifth day, we reached British Columbia where we stopped to see the Spiral Train Tunnel on the Canadian Pacific Railway, through which Jake had traveled 75 times for his job as porter. The tunnel is in Yaho National Park, at Field. Also in the park we drove eight or so miles out of our way on a winding, climbing gravel road to see the highest falls in

Canada, third highest of North America, Takakkaw, at 1,248 feet. *Yaho* is the Indian exclamation for "It is beautiful!" and it was.

The snow-capped Canadian Rockies were awesome and the scenery in spectacular "super natural beautiful British Columbia" did not disappoint me. That night at a "full" campsite we saw a small bare spot by the side of the road just big enough for our tent and asked a ranger if we could camp there. He said, "Sure." So in Loop Creek Park at Glacier, we camped below and between glacier-topped peaks – a magnificent spot. A large black bear scrounged in the garbage as people nearby watched, and the ranger observed from inside the safety of his truck. A forest of tall evergreens surrounded us. As we set up our tent, the bear lumbered up a lane into the woods. That night was so cold I nearly froze!

On Sunday, after driving 3,271 miles, we arrived at Jake's parents' home in Aldergrove. The church Dad pastored was across the street. Mary Ann greeted us, since their parents were at a Sunday school picnic. Our welcome from them and Mary Ann was warm indeed. Their yard looked like a park with beautiful flower gardens and evergreen trees. Mother had just painted the side porch, steps and entryway a fresh coat of red. With such a red-carpet welcome, delicious turkey dinner, and Dad's lively conversation, I felt right at home. Mary Ann, having detected that I was pregnant, took me aside and shared her excitement. It was fun having such a neat sister.

After supper we went to visit Jake's grandfather Duerksen, Mother's father, who lived at a nursing home. He had lived in a room "on the yard" of Jake's family for 22 years, either in a house of his own or in a room built in the garage at Aldergrove. He took his meals with the family after his wife died when they lived on the island. Grandfather spoke mostly in German. He read to us from a German (or Russian) Testament, then Jake read Psalm 23 in German, and Dad prayed. After that we visited Jake's brother Nick's law office and Mary Ann's chiropractic office. She was three years younger than Jake but already had a thriving practice on the main road through Langley. She was very grateful to Jake for his encouragement to pursue her career.

The next day Mary Ann and Nick showed us a royal time, sightseeing and visiting a park with beautiful flowers. Then Jake went to Nick's office while Mary Ann and I shopped. We bought matching scarves to wear in Nick's brand new, open red '64 Triumph convertible. But it was much too cold in the back seat so we traded it for Dad's Studebaker. Nick stopped at a swanky grocery store for steaks and the works and we went to his apartment in Vancouver.

As Mary Ann and I were in the middle of preparing dinner, Nick received a phone call. He reported to us that their sister Elizabeth had died unexpectedly in Toronto. What a shock! Nick had the unenviable task of calling his parents with the news.

What a blow to the family, and especially sad for Mother Friesen. After dinner we drove to their house where Mother sat in the kitchen and cried as she talked about her eldest daughter.

Elizabeth had suffered for years from stomach problems yet continued in her nursing career in Toronto to the end. Mary Ann had just graduated from chiropractic school a few months earlier in Toronto, where for three years she lived with Elizabeth (and Elizabeth's good friend Isobel). They were very close and this was a terrible grief to Mary Ann. A memorial service was planned for Friday at the church across the street.

Mother and Dad had planned to take us to Vancouver Island to see the rest of the family. Though grieving, they steadfastly kept to their plan and, two days later, we left on my first ferry crossing to the Island–approximately one and one-half hour trip. We visited famous Butchart Gardens and Victoria on the southern tip and drove the beautiful coastal road to Black Creek halfway up the Island, where Jake grew up. There we visited Jake's brother Peter and wife Mary, and his sister Margaret and husband Peter and their families. (Peter and Margaret had visited us in Akron in May, as they camped their way across the country.) We did more sightseeing to Elk Falls, an amazing park with giant fir trees and waterfalls, and visited a pulp and paper mill. The island had a fairyland quality about it. I loved the ocean and the drive along the coast and was delighted when Dad stopped the car to let me pick up shells on the beach.

Now I had met all of Jake's sisters and brothers. I was glad that Jake and I had traveled to Toronto to see Elizabeth one weekend while we were in school. A devout Christian, she had been a positive influence in Jake's life and introduced him to Amy Carmichael's writings about Calvary love.

Laura Schulz went with us on the ferry back to the mainland, from Nanaimo to Vancouver. Margaret, Neil, and Carol planned to come the next day for the funeral. As Mother and I sat together on the ferry, she told me about their hardships during the early years in Canada and the story of Elizabeth's birth. I listened in disbelief to this dear grieving woman.

"When we came to Saskatchewan, I worked in the fields for homesteaders, 'stooking' (setting up sheaves of grain). On September 5 when I was ready to go to work, there were only two carrots in the house. My mother kept one and sent one along with me. I was pregnant with Elizabeth and my mother took care of little Peter. I worked all day with nothing to eat but that carrot. When I left late afternoon, I went to the farmer's house to ask directions to go home. The table was set with food for their supper but they didn't offer me anything. I was so hungry. I walked until I came to a fork in the road. I didn't know which road to take, so I prayed and God showed me how to go. I got home and Dad came home about an hour later. Soon Elizabeth was born."

My mind reeled at her incredible suffering. No food to eat in Canada! Working all day, bending, lifting, bending. Walking home an unknown way. Then delivering a baby. It sounded scandalous. Any hardships I had endured in my life seemed infinitesimal by comparison. That day, Mother's heart touched mine and I felt her pain. I was carrying my first child; she had just lost her second, born in harsh poverty.

As we ferried across the water, a brilliant double rainbow arched the sky. What a beautiful blessing of promise and hope! In the midst of grief, God surprised us with a reminder that His faithfulness remains constant in good times and bad. I loved rainbows—amazing wonders inspiring awe and joy, and my heart soared up in gratitude. But mother remained overwhelmed in grief and my heart ached for her.

At Elizabeth's Memorial Service, everything was in German except for one of the two sermons by a former student from our seminary days, Reuben Siemens. His message was very uplifting in contrast to one by a deacon, which Mary Ann said stressed only sadness. Elizabeth was cremated and her ashes flown to Vancouver where Jake picked them up at the airport.

Elizabeth's graduation from Royal Jubilee Hospital, Victoria, B.C., 1950.

Elizabeth was about two weeks from turning 38 when she died. She had graduated from Royal Jubilee Hospital in Victoria as an RN in 1950. (Years later in 2010, her sister Helen took three of Elizabeth's pins, inscribed with "RJH," to Victoria to present to the archives of the hospital along with the following list:

• Completed a three-year program at Toronto Bible College and graduated in 1953.

- Graduated from the University of Toronto in 1957 with a BS degree.
- Served as Nursing School instructor as well as with hospital administration at Mount Sinai Hospital in Toronto.
- Very dedicated and sincere – a mentor to all who crossed her path and a well respected leader of the profession.
- Born September 5, 1926 in Mayfair, Saskatchewan; died August 24, 1964.

Helen was able to see Elizabeth's file in the archives and observed that she had high grades in school.)

Early Sunday morning, Mary Ann and Mother packed us a huge lunch, including jars of raspberry concentrate from their raspberries to make drinks on our way. After breakfast and devotions with Mother and Dad, we said our sad goodbyes at 6:20. We headed south, through customs and the Peace Arch into the States. On the Canadian side, the arch reads, "May These Gates Never Be Closed;" on the U.S. side, "Peace Through Understanding." Beautiful words. Our marriage represented a joining of these two magnificent countries, as well as East and West. I now felt initiated into the family and Jake's B.C./Canadian culture. This trip was proving to be an exhilarating experience.

We crossed Washington and Oregon and headed into California. After only a few miles, we suddenly came upon a grove of awe-inspiring giant Redwoods, overwhelming in size and beauty. The campsite was full so we took a motel just outside the grove. As a long-time tree lover, I marveled at these oldest living things on earth, masterpieces of God's creation. We learned that they grow to over 300 feet tall, some reaching to 379 feet; sources claim they can be 2200 years old!

The next day along the coast we drove through more Redwood forests, then into the mountains to a VS unit. The long road to Hoopa Indian Hospital was the worst of our trip – hills and curves with no guardrails along precipitous cliffs. It was my first experience with unimproved roads of Indian reservations. How I missed the Pennsylvania guardrails! That night we slept in our tent behind the unit house. The next day Jake worked most of the day on VS business. Then we drove back through the Redwoods to Eureka where we got a campsite at Humboldt State Park on the Redwood Highway. That night at a campfire, a ranger gave interesting facts about Redwoods. He said that once a woman asked him if Redwoods ever fall. He said no. Just then they heard a big crash as a nearby Redwood fell!

For the first time, we had our own campsite with picnic table, fire-place, rail around the area, and place to park our car, with tall Redwoods all around–an exquisite spot. A nocturnal meeting with a couple of baby skunks on my way back between the restroom and our tent added excite-ment as Jake coached me on from inside the tent.

The next day, we bypassed San Francisco and got to Fresno at 5:30 P.M. where we found a large beautiful park with a zoo. After a relaxing walk, we headed to Reedley, where we saw miles of grape vineyards. In Reedley, we found the VS unit at Kings View Mental Hospital. One of the VSers took us to our lodging at the Simon Gerbers on Reed Street.

The next day we both went to staff meeting, and then Jake wrote reports while I read at the VS house. The cook brought a large bowl with three kinds of grapes to us on the porch. My fruit-loving husband was in his element. When the bowl was empty, she graciously refilled it. Most Mennonites in the area raised grapes for raisins. We learned that anyone may pick grapes to eat as long as they don't pick a basketful. After another day there, the cook gave us a bag of grapes for our trip, and Mrs. Gerber insisted we help ourselves to figs from their tree.

After a trip to Disneyland, crossing the Mojave Desert, and Hoover Dam, we arrived in Flagstaff, Arizona. We drove by unusual Joshua trees and yucca and camped with our tent near a Joshua tree. In the Arizona desert we saw Meteor Crater, Painted Desert, and Navajo Indian homes. New Mexico, too, had rock cliffs, mesas, and unusual scenery. We were impressed with the vastness of this great land and astonished at the variety and beauty of God's creation.

On the long, hot drive on Highway 54 across Kansas, we stopped at a park at Meade, spread out a blanket, and took a nap. Returning to our car we found tracts under a windshield wiper with the name 'Jacob R. Friesen' stamped on the back. I was beginning to understand why Jake said to me after we were engaged, "I'll take *your* name."

"No way!" I said. "Why would you do that?"

"Because there are too many Jake Friesens!" Yes, Jake Friesens seemed to be everywhere.

At Hesston we stayed overnight with our former housemates from Akron, Gerald and Lois Leinbach. While Jake visited the VS unit at Institute of Logopedics in Wichita, Lois and I caught up with each other. That after-noon, I felt our baby move for the first time. Absent Jake and my sisters, I was glad for a friend with whom to share this special moment. Lois was the mother of five-month-old baby boy Terry. They lived in a basement apartment on the corner of Weaver and Vesper streets. Who would have guessed that eight years later we would buy a house on the corner of Weaver and Amos, eight houses down the street?

We arrived home on September 11, 1964, after driving 8,076 miles through 24 states and two provinces. Jake was a stickler for budgeting and recording expenses. The trip cost us a mere $294.59! We used 273.6 gallons of gas and got 29.5 miles per gallon in our economical VW bug. It was a glorious four weeks, tarnished only by the unexpected death of Elizabeth at age 38.

Now we looked forward to the birth of our baby in February, four months away. Earlier, when we looked at our unfurnished MCC house before moving in, I had said, "We should buy some furniture."

"Furniture?" Jake retorted. " We can't buy furniture; we have to be ready to move!" What a jolt! MCC supplied furniture.

Looking forward to the birth of our first child, I loved living in the small town of Akron, "a city on a hill," so close to my family. One day I said to Jake, "We should buy a house here." He quickly nixed the idea.

"We can't buy a house! We have to be ready to move." Move? Where to? I was ready to stay here for life!

So, where were we moving? I wondered. *What would Jake come up with next?*

CHAPTER 16

A Special Gift

Lo, children are an heritage from the Lord.
PSALM 127:3 (KJV)

1964–1965

After we returned from our trip, Jake felt increasingly confined in his job at the office and admitted, "An 8:00 to 5:00 job is not for me." He needed a diversion. One Sunday we went for a drive through the beautiful Lancaster County countryside. As we approached the New Holland Airport Jake said, "I'd like to stop and ask about flying lessons." What a bombshell!

"Flying lessons?" I couldn't believe it.

"I'd really like to learn, and if I'd get my license you could fly with me to the VS units and I wouldn't have to fly commercially." That was no consolation. My stomach tightened and I felt scared as he walked in to check. I couldn't stand the thought. Jake returned to the car with a pleased smile. "I signed up and will have my first lesson in two days."

"Two days? That's your birthday!" I reminded in shock. "A birthday present to yourself."

Jake would be 29 on the 29th of September. When the day came, rain postponed the lesson until October 6. Thus began many evenings and week-ends of flying. In inner turmoil, I wondered, *How can he do this to me? I'm pregnant and he takes flying lessons!* It didn't seem fair – or safe. But what could I say? At times I acknowledged that flying with him to the units was a thoughtful idea. I should be grateful. Knowing my husband's determination, I decided to resign myself to the fact, though anxious thoughts persisted, forcing me to commit the matter to prayer.

Sometimes I went to the airport with Jake and read in the car. Soon it was too cold for that. In just three weeks, on October 22, he soloed. I was impressed. He spent hours in ground school classes and flew cross-country flights. I tried to keep my anxieties hidden and prayed for his safety.

178

My time and thoughts were occupied with preparing for the baby: finding things for the nursery, visiting and shopping with Jake's new secretary, Pauline, who was also expecting her first child. It was great to have a friend going through the same experience. There were church and MCC Wives baby showers. I looked forward to seeing my baby. Was it a boy or a girl? I had a growing feeling that it was a girl and hoped that it was. One day Jake dreamed we had twins, with no labor! For years Jake has claimed he never dreams. Back then I know he dreamed at least once.

I greatly enjoyed MCC Wives meetings once a month where I had learned to know many women dedicated to the cause of relief and service. These were times of fellowship and fun. Jake and I were also in a small group of church and MCC people, including Edgar and Ethel Metzler. Edgar was head of the Peace Section office of MCC (later he directed Peace Corp in many countries) and Ethel a vivacious mother and avid reader. Energetic Edna Ruth Byler began a self-help crafts store in her basement with items she collected from travels with her husband John, now deceased, to many countries where MCC sent relief supplies. She first discovered extraordinary needlework in Puerto Rico in 1946, later in the Middle East, and elsewhere. We often met in her home and I bought a lovely hand-knit cable-stitch sweater from China in her shop. Her basement store with a variety of crafts was the forerunner of the Self-Help Craft Stores, which spread all over the country and Canada, now known as Ten Thousand Villages.

As if the flying wasn't enough for Jake, in November a new adventure beckoned. The Civil Rights movement was in full swing in the South, with many northern whites involved. The summer of 1964, three Civil Rights workers were missing in Mississippi and the search for their bodies stretched on for months. Hatred, lawlessness, and violence of police and those in authority impeded the investigation. People from the churches wrote to MCC urging action. MCC decided to send someone to investigate. As assistant director of Voluntary Service, Jake was the likely person. My heart sank. Another separation.

Jake left for the Mississippi Delta on November 30 for three weeks. There he found many people without shoes. After a hard freeze, he requested shoes from the Akron office. Several bales were sent, which Jake helped distribute. He met with black leaders and learned the extent of the grinding poverty, discrimination, and injustice. I was happy he could help the people there, but not with his long absence.

When Jake called, he described the conditions and said that MCC wanted to send someone down to begin a VS unit. I sensed that he was interested and dreaded the thought. He called and wrote letters. The day came when I opened a letter and read, "How would you like to move down here?" While extremely upset, I felt guilty about my attitude. One evening when Jake called I was too choked up to talk. I just cried into the receiver. With our baby coming, I was overwhelmed with dread about a move to Mississippi. I got hold of myself and he explained the need and asked me not to worry.

Good friends were a support during this time. Doris Jean Brechbill from small group often stayed overnight with me and became a wonderful friend. At church I served on a committee to put on "Why The Chimes Rang" for Christmas and hoped Jake would make it home in time for the drama. To my great relief he arrived home on December 18.

Jake wrote a report of his findings from Mississippi, with the recommendation that someone be sent to begin a VS unit there. And as I expected, Jake said he was interested in the position.

The words of Job came to mind, "That which I feared has come upon me." I resisted with all my might–inwardly. We were expecting our baby in a month. How could I take my little one into such a dangerous situation? I expressed my concerns to Jake, but he was fearless. One day as we talked he said emphatically, "Jesus is Lord!"

Hadn't I committed my life to Christ and told Him and sang countless times, "I'll go where you want me to go, dear Lord, I'll be what you want me to be"? And now I'm feeling, *Anywhere but Mississippi, Lord!* Was this the call I had wondered about and waited for over the years? I wanted to be faithful. I thought of Matthew 19:29, which the Holy Spirit impressed on my mind and heart as a teenager and many times after. "Everyone who has left houses or brothers or sisters or father or mother or children or fields, for my name's sake, will receive a hundred-fold, and will inherit eternal life." What a powerful promise–and hard commitment.

The decision facing us would take much prayer and trusting of my heavenly Father. We would pray–and wait–again, for God's leading.

My birthday present came early in 1965–ten days early–on January 27. Our precious baby daughter, Janet Luana, was the best gift I could imagine.

What a joy to hold Janet for the first time! She stared deeply, steadily into my eyes and was so quiet and peaceful I was overcome with a sense of awe. I felt as if God had handed her to me Himself. What a tiny wisp of humanity she was at 5 pounds 11 ounces. God gave me a great love for babies ever since Grace was born and I felt so blessed to have Janet Luana, named for me—*Jane* with a t; *Lu* for Millie, whose middle name is Louise; and *Ana* for Anna as well as Mary Ann, Jake's sister.

I could hardly wait for Jake to see her. Labor had been long and hard. Jake took me to the hospital the day before about 1:30 P.M. and went back to work. He returned that night and waited for hours. The nurse told me that when she went to the waiting room and said, "Mr. Friesen," Jake really jumped. But she just went to say that I was all right. After a time, he gave up and went home and slept till morning. In 1965, the husband could not be with his wife during labor and delivery. After a long, lonely night, Janet was born at 2:02 A.M. I was "out" with anesthesia. So much for "natural childbirth." The doctor must have been half asleep because Janet's nose had a nasty bruise from the forceps.

Jake was very happy with his new baby daughter. Evenings at home found him reading a book with Janet on one side of his lap and Sparky, our little Chihuahua mongrel, on the other.

Mom was unable to come and help me because of her handicap, but she and Daddy came ten days later for my birthday. What a joy it was to see them hold and enjoy Janet!

Landis Grandparents, Grammy holding Janet, 4 months, June 6, 1965.

Daddy, Mom holding Janet, 6 months, July 25, 1965.

On February 20, Jake got his private pilot's license. This meant he could take passengers. We decided to fly to Quakertown on March 14, Mom's 48th birthday. Everyone was excited about our coming. Janet, six-and-a-half weeks old, was such a tiny "bundle," as Daddy always called the babies.

Jake rented a four-seat Cessna 172 at the New Holland Airport. As we prepared to leave, I climbed into the small plane and Jake put Janet into my arms. Just after taking off, Jake banked sharply to the right. Totally unprepared for this terrifying maneuver I cried out, "Jake! What's happening?"

Poor Jake looked rattled at my unexpected outburst. He was totally in control of the plane, of course. But as the wing on my side went down and the one on his side went up, I cringed at the swirling ground below and the irrational sensation that Baby Janet and I might fall out of the sky. Once we leveled off, I calmed down and the rest of the flight was bearable. Jake had his hard-won license and I nearly spoiled the whole thing. The engine roared and the radio crackled with loud static as Jake talked to the controller. Oh, how would I ever learn to feel safe and enjoy this tiny, noisy, cramped aircraft?

It was a great relief to touch down at the Quakertown Airport. There we saw Millie, Ralph, and Brenda, age six, Ruthie and Tommy, ten, and our neighbor Mrs. Renninger, all wanting a ride. Jake took them up, a few at a time, and buzzed our house, Renninger's, and Millie and Ralph's. The passengers loved it, despite some misgivings. Brenda remembers, "It was so different to see everything from the air, especially our house. I don't remember being scared, though I might have been a little. It wasn't the dominant impression." Tom and Ruth just enjoyed it and were not afraid. Tom remembers flying over his house and Renninger's.

Later I asked Millie, "Weren't you scared?"

"Yes, I was, but I decided to trust God and Jake." I felt ashamed. Had I trusted either of them? I decided to be brave and trust them both on the way home.

For work, Jake rented a plane and flew to VS units in Tennessee and Ohio, but I stayed home with Janet. (MCC paid the price of an airline ticket and Jake paid the extra.) Then he had a trip to Goshen, Indiana, and Chicago and I went along to visit Anna and John. I knew what to expect now, but landings sometimes unnerved me. A narrow strip of runway at Meigs Field in Chicago over the waters of Lake Michigan terrified me. And the runway at Goshen appeared far too short as we approached the fence. But Jake miraculously stopped in time, just short of it. These flights were an exercise in "praying without ceasing." I needed a lot of practice in that discipline!

As the weeks went by, we wondered when we would hear about the Mississippi job. Then one day the dreaded word came—Jake's application was approved. We were moving to Mississippi! My anxiety about flying was minimal compared with what faced me now.

During the "long hot summer" of '64, known as "Freedom Summer," the Civil Rights movement intensified as hundreds of northern students poured into the state to help with voter registration. As the races became polarized, forty churches were burned or bombed.

We read the story in *Life Magazine* of the three civil rights workers who were missing in Philadelphia, Mississippi. The search for the bodies continued as police denied involvement. Six months after the students disappeared, officials were forced to dig up a newly built dam, and there, as suspected, were the three bodies. The cover-up failed. Horrified at the details of such evil – perpetrated by police and law enforcement officials – everything in me revolted against such brutality and lawlessness. This was my introduction to the Civil Rights movement.

Rage at the treatment of blacks and compassion for these long-oppressed people of the South captured my thoughts and occupied my days. I couldn't forget the three students, one a southern black, the other two, warm-hearted northern whites in their prime. God got my attention and I sensed a call to love and serve that overcame fear. I wanted to go with Jake to do what we could. Our assignment was to be a "Christian presence" in the midst of hatred and violence – a big order. But my life verse reassured me: "I am crucified with Christ, nevertheless I live, yet not I, but Christ lives in me." I made up my mind that this was God's leading and He would be with us – and in us.

But I often wondered, *How long will we be in Mississippi? Long enough for Janet to go to school?* In five years she'd be in kindergarten. Would we still be there? How I dreaded the thought. I must trust our future to God, but the details of that future sometimes filled my mind and kept me awake nights. When I got up to feed Janet in the night, or stared at her sleeping peacefully in her bassinette during the day, my heart ached for this child of my love, and for Jake and me. We would leave everything I held dear – my family, the security of our church and MCC community, and our safe little "city on a hill." Tears, grief, and fear sometimes assailed me in moments of weakness, and I remembered Jesus who "set His face like a flint" as He went to Jerusalem to His death.

"Oh, God!" I cried. *"Please take care of us and keep us safe as we go!"* Our unknown future was in His hands.

PART III

ON THE MOVE

CHAPTER 17

We Hope You Stay Forever

The thing I greatly feared has come upon me.
JOB 3:25 (NKJ)

1965–1966

Up until now my parents said almost nothing about our move. One weekend when we went home, Mom said to me, "Why do you want to go down there? Tommy was there during the war and he said there are lots of 'niggers' down there." Tommy was her brother. It saddened me to hear her use that despicable word. But she did not speak with contempt and I knew she meant no harm by it. It was just her family's way. And she had always told us that black people were just like us, and we should respect everyone.

"I know," I responded. "That's why we're going. We want to help them." I left it at that and she said no more. I can't recall talking with Daddy about it but I'm sure he didn't want us to leave.

At Millie and Ralph's, August 15, 1965: Ralph Loux, Grace, Millie holding Janet, Jeff Herstine, Mom.

Millie and Ralph hosted a family farewell picnic at their home in August where Janet got a lot of attention and Mom seemed happy. It was a bittersweet time for me, surrounded by my family, but feeling reluctant to leave them all.

Jake, Jeff Herstine. Tom holding Janet, Brenda Loux with Sparky.

Janet, 7 mo., August 28, 1965.

Farewells at Akron provided support and assurances of prayer. We would go forth as Abraham and Sara, not knowing where we were going, except to the state of Mississippi. Once we arrived, Jake would "spy out the land" and decide on the location of our VS unit.

On the morning of September 1, excitement stirred within us as we loaded our VW bug with the necessary things. An MCC truck would bring the rest of our belongings later. I now saw the wisdom of having no furniture.

We put Janet in the car bed in the back seat, Jake got into the car, and I said, "I must call Mom to say goodbye." I ran back into the house one last time, dialed the phone, and waited.

Someone picked it up at the other end but no one answered. "Mom," I said, "Are you there?" Silence. "Mom, I called to say goodbye. We're ready to leave. Jake is waiting in the car with Janet." Nothing. I grew anxious. What was wrong? "Mom?" I said again.

Then heart-wrenching sobs flowed through the receiver. What a shock! I had no idea she felt this way. My heart went out to her, but from 70 miles away, I felt helpless.

"We'll try to come home for Christmas," I said, knowing how hollow that sounded. Mom didn't respond, just sobbed quietly. Jake was waiting. I felt a tremendous pull in two directions.

Finally Mom spoke between sobs. "I wish you wouldn't go."

Absolutely heartbroken at her unexpected reaction, I said goodbye to the woman who had raised me from age four and hurried to the car in tears. Then it hit me. *Was she thinking she would never see us again?* A sinking feeling came over me as I realized she was in poor health. She had been in and out of the hospital many times, with one leg amputated. Because of sores on her feet, the doctor told her that the other leg should be amputated, too, but her heart could not take it.

As we drove the first miles of our long journey south, I cried until I was emotionally spent. I thought about how Mom loved Jake and her new little granddaughter; could I ever again doubt her love for me? She loved me enough not to make a fuss about our decision to leave. She had held her tongue and her emotions. And then her repressed grief erupted in our last goodbye. Jake's sympathetic words and spirit soothed my jumbled thoughts and feelings. All I could do was commit Mom to the Lord. Before long I settled down to enjoy the beautiful drive. But the memory of Mom's tears and words would be heavy on my heart for a long time to come.

That first night we stopped at Aunt Matilda (my mother's youngest sister) and Uncle Ray Taylor's home in Mt. Airy, North Carolina. I was grateful for this rare visit and overnight stay. Since I was wearing pedal pushers, Aunt Matilda gave me a kind bit of advice, as my mother may have done.

"Since you're going to be a missionary down there, I think it would be better if you wore only dresses." I did not think of myself as a "missionary" nor that slacks were offensive, but I took "Tinda's" advice during our two years in Mississippi.

After a weekend in Atlanta with the VS unit, we headed for Gulfport on the coast. Our first home was at Camp Landon, our church's mission station, where we received orientation. Several couples lived and worked in what were old army barracks from World War II days. We slept in the "motel," a large room in the barracks. The first night when we came in and turned on the light we saw enormous cockroaches flying around the room! Terrifying! But if the missionaries could live with them, I could too. Invaders from pine trees surrounding the buildings, nothing could keep them out. Hurricane Betsy, predicted to deliver 100-mile-an-hour winds to the coast one night, kept us in suspense. Though the wind roared in the tall pines around our flimsy barracks, we committed ourselves to God's safekeeping and slept peacefully. Coastal buildings sustained heavy damage, though winds did not reach expected velocity, but only 80 miles per hour.

Jake soon left with Harold Regier, whom we knew from seminary, to various locations around the state to scout out the land and determine where to work: Jackson, Prentiss, Hattiesburg, and three days in the delta at Cleveland and Greenwood. He also checked out Canton, 30 miles north of Jackson, where the American Friends Service Committee (AFSC), Quakers from Philadelphia, Pennsylvania, had built a community center for blacks.

I stayed with Janet and enjoyed visits with Rosella Regier and son Stevie, the same age as Janet. Sam and Linda Guhr and Helene and George Dyck completed the missionary team. They were fine, friendly people, but those were lonely days for me and I grieved over Mom.

When Jake returned, he took Janet and me along to Cleveland, Greenwood, and Canton. The city locations did not appeal to me. Jake said, "I think we should live at Canton because the countryside and landscape remind me of where you grew up on Thatcher Road. I think you'll like it." I was comforted by his thoughtfulness and sensitivity and felt hopeful.

Valley View was ten miles from town, in an all black neighborhood. Madison County was 70 percent black. About 40% were landowners, but many lived in squalor. Six miles out of Canton, we turned from the highway onto a narrow, winding road for the last four miles to the community center. Dilapidated homes, surrounded by cotton fields, dotted the landscape.

I vividly recall the day we drove into Valley View in our VW. As the road came to a "T" Jake explained, "Here's the community center on the right, that dilapidated shack straight ahead is a grocery store, and we can rent the house at the back of this field next to the store." The house looked uninviting but I knew we could fix it up. As we drove through the area, I did like the serene-looking pastoral setting, which reminded me of home. I later learned that serene-*looking* is where the similarities ended. I also learned that the Quakers tried to find someone to serve as director of the community center without success. They asked MCC if they could find someone. But they too found no one – until Jake volunteered.

We decided to accept the invitation to Valley View Community Center. On a gorgeous fall day we said goodbye to our friends in Gulfport and drove the four-hour trip to Canton. I was excited at the prospect of settling down to this new calling, blissfully unaware of what awaited us. When we arrived on the outskirts of Canton, our new hometown, small shacks and signs of poverty greeted us. But as we entered town and drove around the courthouse of this county seat, we saw lovely tree-lined streets and beautiful homes of the more affluent whites. Then, at the A & W Root Beer stand, the deceptively peaceful atmosphere gave way to a sinister sign that proclaimed, "You are in occupied Mississippi. Proceed with caution." This unfriendly greeting sent shivers up my spine.

We drove the ten miles out of town to our new home. Though it appeared that the ranch-style house had possibilities, I hid my feelings as we drove through the field of grass toward the pink and white house on cement-block stilts. There was no driveway or garage and no trees. Tall weeds, peeling paint, and missing panes in the louvered windows greeted us as we drove to the front door. But the shock of my life awaited me inside.

"What a trashed house!" Jake groaned in disgust. "The people who built the community center and the burned church nearby used this for their headquarters. Looks like they stored their supplies here." We surveyed the assortment of pickaxes, shovels, and other tools in the kitchen. Blackened pots and pans hung on nails hammered into strips of wood on two walls. Clutter abounded and dirt covered the bare wood floors.

"What a mess!" Jake lamented. "No wonder the rent is only $10 a month. The price is right. Our landlord lives in Kentucky but his elderly parents, Rev. and Mrs. McCullough, live nearby."

The house boasted a small living room with a wide opening into the kitchen and three small bedrooms. Gratefully, I found a bathroom that worked. Every room was in shambles, but the kitchen was the most disheartening of all. Its dark, dirty-gray walls closed in on me like an approaching storm. The sink overflowed with dishes and water-filled, food-encrusted pots left there to soak. Roaches of all sizes (except the giant ones from Gulfport!) swarmed over all. Rows of cluttered shelves clung to two walls. A scraggly dog mingled with a giant cardboard box of trash. A small gas range, old refrigerator, table and folding chairs completed the dismal scene. My heart sank. *How can I live here?*

In the living room a bed was nailed to the floor in one corner. Along one wall were rows of books on low shelves, inhabited by mice. In a bedroom we found eleven mattresses stacked on a pile. One bedroom door was locked because a civil rights worker named Rick lived there. He registered people to vote. As we learned later, the dog was his as well as the dirty dishes in the sink. So were the boxes of bug-infested food on the shelves, which I discarded before I learned Rick wanted them. Jake gave him notice early on that we were renting the whole house and he would need to find another place.

Jake set up Janet's crib in the living room, to double as a playpen. "We'll soon make this place a home," Jake promised as he began carting things out of the house. He mopped the floors and made a bed for our first night. I took up the challenge. What a blessing to do it on a bright blue October day!

After getting Janet settled, I started on the kitchen. I washed the dishes, cleaned the sink, and prepared to cook our first meal. Jake suggested I see what I could find at the store. I wanted milk and a few staples. When I entered the building, the few people standing around chatting grew quiet. I introduced myself and asked the husband and wife owners if they had milk. They didn't. Nor did they have most of the things I mentioned. I looked at the meat available and bought some sausage. *What good is a store like this?* I wondered. I fought to keep a positive attitude. Back at the house I began working on dinner. When I turned on the gas stove, flames flared up a foot or more. I gasped and quickly turned it off. I tried the oven. Flames shot high and the oven filled with fire. I jumped back in fright, yelled for Jake, and the tears flowed. Overwhelmed, I cried out my pent-up emotions.

"Don't worry," Jake comforted, "we'll buy a new stove," and I knew things could only get better. Somehow he got the stove to work well enough so I could cook the meat. It was too spicy hot and sadly I realized I would never shop at that store again.

Since MCC paid for the improvements on the house we spent as frugally as possible. After buying paint, windows, a rug for Janet's room, and other supplies, we were down to 11 cents four days after moving in. Jake had a check for $145 and opened a checking account but could not cash checks yet. The next day a check came for $650 so we drove to town to deposit it and get some money. The cashier refused to give Jake cash. So he talked to the bank president, only to learn these people trusted no one from the north. Jake asked the president to call our bank in Akron, Pennsylvania. He was hesitant. It took some talking but Jake finally persuaded him to call. Since Jake had no money for the call and no local phone number, he used our credit card number from our Akron phone. Jake's incredulity grew when the banker asked Jake to make the call because he didn't know how! Jake dialed and the banker talked with someone at Akron. Finally he came back, apologetic for the inconvenience, and cashed the check. It took 45 minutes to cash a check! But God was with us. We were in business.

At the house, we tackled the horrendous job of cleanup with a vengeance and in three days Jake had Janet's room painted and a new carpet laid. Having kept her in the crib most of the time as we worked, we were so happy when I put our nine-month-old down to crawl. She squealed with delight at her new freedom. Such a happy child, Janet was a bright ray of sunshine in my dismal surroundings. How thankful I was for her presence.

Next we needed a phone, which were nonexistent for miles around. The closest one was five miles away at the Sharon Post Office, which had a white postmaster. When Jake ordered a phone, the company was less than gracious and said they had to look up the place. Two weeks later, on November 4, we got our phone. Three weeks without a phone seemed like months to be out of touch with the outside world. To the white utility men who came for the installation, we must have seemed a curiosity. Who would choose to live in such a remote and backward place? After a week in this depressing house, my shoulders ached as though I carried the weight of the world on them, literally. At first I was mystified by this unusual symptom, but as the days went on I realized it was a physical reaction to the emotional burden of the house, the circumstances, and the tremendous poverty, ignorance, and violence in this state that felt like a foreign land. A regular visitor those first weeks and months was Mr. G., a black civil rights worker from Canton. The first time I met him he sat in our living room and rambled on to Jake about the horrors of living in Madison County. He casually threw out the shocker, "Someone will probably put a bomb under your house. They did that a few years ago, you know, but it didn't go off!" How awful! I could visualize someone crawling under our house on stilts and my stomach churned.

Then Mr. G. asked, "How long you plannin' to stay here?" I held my breath, waiting for Jake's reply.

"I don't know...maybe five years."

Five years! Was he serious? I couldn't wait for Mr. G. to leave. When he did I confronted Jake.

"Did you hear what he said?" I demanded, close to tears. "A bomb under our house!"

"Don't believe it," he said evenly, trying to calm me. "He's a liar and a scoundrel!"

"And you said we may stay here five years! I thought we talked about two. I don't think I can stand to live here until Janet is ready for kindergarten. Where would she go to school?" He hadn't thought of that.

"I'm sorry. I just wanted to get him off my back. Don't worry. We probably won't be here five years." Jake talked with many people and seemed to understand everyone. I had to trust God and Jake in order to survive. Hearing Jake's viewpoint helped put things in perspective. As I settled into the task of adjusting to my new home, gradually the pain in my shoulders went away. Every day I saw progress on the house and it was exciting to fix it up and make it beautiful.

But those first weeks and months, inner struggles surfaced at unexpected times; bouts of homesickness hit at bedtime when Jake thanked God for our parents. Mom's deep sorrow at our leaving weighed on me and tears flowed from homesickness and the torture of my days in this crucible called Mississippi.

During that time, when God seemed far away, I recalled a speaker at a women's retreat at seminary. The wife of a seminary Bible professor, she told us that for a period of nine years she could not pray. I couldn't believe it. One of their sons was mentally disabled and the burden was too much for her to bear. Her husband was engrossed in his work and she felt alone. I was amazed. A Christian – wife of a seminary professor – couldn't pray? It was incomprehensible to me at the time, but now I understood. When God seemed distant and I couldn't pray, I'd remember that God promised to be with us always. I recalled verses of assurance and faith, and I *knew* God was with me, whether I felt Him or not. A favorite passage helped: "Why are you cast down, O my soul, and why are you disquieted within me? Hope in God, for I shall yet praise Him, who is the health of my countenance and my God." The comfort of the Spirit was real. And I was grateful for every letter from family and many friends assuring us of their prayers.

Moving-in day. October 15, 1965.

Little by little the house took on a civilized look. Jake painted, built lovely kitchen cabinets, bookcases, and shelves. He cut the grass, planted 11 trees with Rev. McCullough, and made a driveway. I cleaned and scrubbed, varnished, painted, and sewed lined drapes for the living room. Money for the autumn gold paint for that room came from Millie and Ralph, a great blessing. The house looked cheerful, with sunny yellow kitchen walls, yellow curtains at the windows, new stove and cabinets.

Kitchen, before. October 15, 1965.

Kitchen, after. March 1966.

By now we had a clean, roach-free home. Visiting the homes of neighbors, some with newspaper on the walls, I felt guilty for being white and "rich." People loved to come and visit to see Janet and our house. One young woman pointed to the ceiling and told her friend, "That's how my house will look someday!"

Outside, our area was very dark at night, so Jake ordered a floodlight. Installed on the telephone pole near our house, it shed light on our yard, the nearby street, and dimly on the community center across the street. The depressed area was gradually changing character—feeling safer and friendlier—and people noticed.

Jake quickly began to work at the center, along with working on our house. He met with people, organized a board for the center, and went to meetings with black leaders in Canton. In Jackson, 35 miles away, he met with and explained his work to southern whites sympathetic to the cause of equal rights.

Early on, Jake went to see the sheriff in Canton but never found him in until January 28, 1966, more than three months after we arrived. When Jake told about his work at the center, and the church program we were under, the sheriff observed, "You are very clean cut and intelligent compared with other northerners I've seen around here!" Most civil rights workers did not go to the sheriff to establish a relationship and, therefore, a stereotypical image was projected on northerners no matter how fine they were. We felt blessed to start off on a good footing with the law.

On February 2, the sheriff and chief of police came and toured the center! We felt honored. In June the sheriff and deputy came. Jake brought them to the house to meet me and see the house. I wrote in my diary, "Very nice guys." (Most black people would strongly disagree, but I was encouraged with the least bit of sanity displayed by law officers.) Their visits helped me feel safer in this hostile state.

Jake worked hard to get federal programs started. Eventually the center buzzed with a Head Start school for an impressive 234 children. They received a federal grant and the school officially opened February 28, 1966. Jake organized community meetings, taught classes for board members, typing class for adults, and he put out a mimeographed newspaper, *The Valley View Weekly News*. At first Jake wrote the articles; later he encouraged locals to write. Exciting news of progress at the center reached a local circulation, as well as northern whites, who had helped build the center along with the Quakers. Jake helped children with homework, organized a credit union, and initiated a Heifer Project for Madison County. His aim was to teach the people to run their own organizations.

Jake was a natural in cross-cultural settings. I on the other hand struggled with culture shock and was offended by people who seemed inconsiderate of us. The first night that Jake went to a meeting at the center, I put Janet to bed and was tidying up when I heard loud voices outside. A group of rowdy boys had converged on us. I sent up a quick plea for help and opened the door to see about eight schoolboys, junior high or older, *lifting up our VW*! I couldn't believe my eyes. How could Jake leave me alone like this? But, I realized, they were just boys. Feeling angry and threatened, I took charge.

"Please leave the car alone!" I called to them, in the bravest voice I could muster. "The baby is asleep and I don't want her to wake up." Much to my relief, they put the car down and left quietly.

When Jake returned and I told him of the incident, he calmly informed me, "They don't mean any harm. They like our small car and just wanted to see if they could lift it." I felt half guilty for spoiling their fun. Oh, how would I ever learn to live in this culture and accept the people as easily as Jake?

Since we had the only phone in the area, people came from miles around in emergencies and for advice. As the news spread, a steady stream of neighbors, young people, and people from the center came to use the phone. Especially troublesome were the young fellows who hung around Jake. Boo Jack and James often came during our supper hour or evenings and begged to use the phone; or they wanted a ride up town. Our house became the community house, our phone the community phone, our car the community taxi, and my husband, community servant.

Rev. W. E. L. and Classie McCullough made frequent, almost daily, visits to our home and were our staunchest supporters. They came separately, to sit and talk and share their struggles. Rev. McCullough spent many hours with Jake, always encouraging and grateful for his fine work. They longed for freedom for their people. Classie sat in our living room with Janet and me and poured out her heart and troubles.

One day Classie told me, "I passed by a man singin' in a field, choppin' (hoeing) cotton one day and I said, 'You must be mighty happy, singin' like that.' He said, 'No, Ma'm, I's jis singin' to keep from cryin'." She broke down and cried then, recalling the incident. As she sobbed, the great pathos of her people seemed to flood our living room. I felt so inadequate to comfort her or to make a ripple in this ocean of despair. But Classie was a woman of great faith. As she quieted down, she spoke of hope for her people and God's sure help.

Classie had written an article for a civil rights paper telling how black men were killed by whites, then thrown into lakes and rivers or castrated if they just looked at a white woman—lynchings, they were called. Yet at the same time, white men were raising families by black women; and they beat and killed black men over black women.

Despite all the lawlessness and harassment, blacks and white civil rights workers pressed on tirelessly. Their theme song, "We Shall Overcome," sung swaying from side to side as they held hands, inspired the movement. Whenever I sang in such a group, joy and hope welled up within me for this just cause. One verse said, "Black and white together, (repeat twice), Oh, deep in my heart, I do believe, that we shall overcome some day." It was a far-off but noble dream.

Though Madison County was 70 percent black, prior to the placement of federal registrars only 250 blacks were registered to vote. Four weeks after registration began, 6,000 blacks were registered. "Black power" was becoming a reality. This was a cause for rejoicing among blacks and civil rights workers, but it posed a threat to the white political system.

A huge billboard on the highway with a picture of MLK Jr. proclaimed, "Martin Luther King Jr. at communist training school." Such false, inflaming statements reflected the mood in the state as federal agents and civil rights groups helped register black voters after two centuries of repression.

About a year before we arrived, Larry Scott, a Quaker from Philadelphia, Pennsylvania AFSC had come to the state to lay the groundwork for rebuilding the 40 burned churches. He talked with sheriffs, business leaders, and church leaders and became a moderating influence for calming fear and anger. Quakers and Mennonites came to rebuild. After Larry left, Jake came at the request of the Quakers and continued this role as a catalyst between black and white factions. Every Thursday he met for breakfast in Jackson with concerned citizens who worked for peaceful integration. Sympathetic white leaders around the state also spoke out and worked for change and justice.

Our purpose was to be a "Christian presence" in the midst of the hostilities. We wanted to make a difference among these oppressed, poverty-stricken people who became our friends. In time, people called Jake "Nigger Jesus" because he helped them in many ways that no one ever had. Some told us, "We hope you stay forever!" One woman said, "I hope you live here till you die."

Some of the people were Christians and attended St. John's, the rebuilt church nearby. Classie McCullough was one of them. Her husband was 100 years old (he had no birth certificate) and Classie was 80. Both were still going strong. Jake sometimes attended black churches alone on Sundays, while I stayed with Janet. Usually we drove to Jackson to churches that were friendly toward northern whites. These churches, Methodist and Presbyterian, were like an oasis in the desert that first year of adjustment, and we made good friends there.

Dr. and Mrs. Beittel, white moderates from Jackson, visited us early on. Dr. B. was a former president of Tougaloo College, a fine Christian and civil rights activist. On their first visit, our house was still a mess, without paint, carpets or kitchen cabinets. The Dr. went to the center with Jake and Mrs. B. stayed with Janet and me for a friendly visit. "Why didn't you stay in a motel until you had your house fixed up?" she sympathized, incredulous that we would live in such a place.

"Jake would never do that," I said, "and we didn't have money for that." The Beittles were grandparents and such warm, kind friends. Mrs. B. always brought a treat for Janet, usually chocolate-covered graham crackers. Dr. B. became Jake's loyal supporter through rough times.

Our overseer from the American Friends Service Committee in Pennsylvania was Ezra Young, who worked for the Quakers in New Orleans. He visited us frequently for several days at a time and was a kind supporter and friend. Our administrator at Akron, Pennsylvania, Edgar Stoesz, kept in touch by letter and Jake wrote him regular detailed reports.

Soon after we arrived, we learned that there was a high incidence of violence among rural blacks—shootings, stabbings, and beatings. Almost every day we heard another depressing story. How distressed I felt one day when a pathetic looking man came in and told us his wife had stabbed him. If I thought my life was hard, how much more did these people suffer from all manner of shocking troubles and violence, often at the hands of their own family members?

While in VS, our rent, food, medical, and travel costs were paid for by MCC. We received a small monthly allowance, and 25 cents a meal per person for food. We skimped and saved and never made long-distance phone calls except when absolutely necessary.

While Mom was often on my mind and heart, I never called her. I wrote home frequently but phone calls were a luxury to be avoided. However, on November 14, I called to wish Daddy a happy birthday. For some reason I didn't speak with Mom. I can't recall why and I still regret that. She wrote us a letter or two, usually about how bad her health was, but I still didn't realize how ill she was.

On December 12, 1965, at 10 P.M., Daddy called to tell me that Mom died at 9:00 that evening. Overcome with grief, I cried as I held Janet. She cried loudly out of empathy or fright, and Jake took her and calmed her.

"I don't think we should go to the funeral," Jake stated. "I don't like the emotion." Early that year, Mom's two remaining brothers had died – Uncle Tommy and Uncle Scott. We went to one of the funerals and as we arrived on the porch of the home, Aunt Myrtle, Scott's wife, grabbed Jake and let out a scream. She held him tight and cried hysterically. She had seen Jake only on rare occasions, and he was shocked by her inappropriate behavior. I couldn't blame him for wanting to avoid a recurrence.

But Mom had been such an important part of my life and our family's life. I had no peace. I had to go! Finally, my strong urge to go overcame Jake's reluctance. We flew out of Jackson via Atlanta to Philadelphia. It was my first flight on an airliner and the plane rattled and shook so that I feared for our lives and cried out to God. Landing safely in Philly and finding Daddy and Grace waiting was a double blessing. It was wonderful to be home, despite the sad reason for coming.

At the funeral, Millie, Anna and I sang "The Old Rugged Cross," the last trio we ever sang together for a service. I had forgotten this, but sister Ruth remembers and told me, "It was her favorite hymn." The depressing funeral home setting added to my jumbled feelings of sorrow and regret.

That night I became ill with vomiting and dry heaves that did not quit. Daddy called the doctor and he and Jake picked up medicine. My last 30 years with Mom were often traumatic, but God had bonded us in love. Her sobbing when we moved, her death without my having spoken to her again, and no closure to our relationship left me in turmoil. Emotional, unresolved issues created internal pressures that I believe caused the retching that night. Plagued with guilt that our move had caused her death, I blamed myself. How could I ever forgive myself? Her words from years ago echoed in my brain, "You'll think about it when I'm gone," and I grieved over her years of suffering.

A nagging fear was that she might not have been ready to die and meet her Maker. I felt guilty for not talking to her about Jesus. It took years for me to see that I had witnessed–indirectly and directly–with my life and in letters. We girls had sung praises with the Gospel message at home through the years. She knew we were faithful in service to the church. Love was probably the greatest gift I had given her. But, I reasoned, it was such *imperfect* love!

In years to come, I reflected and journaled about Mom and saw that she had a big heart like her mother. Many years after she died I received a copy of Mom's mother's obituary. It says of my step-grandmother, Mabel Bernhardt Williams, "She was held in high esteem by her neighbors and friends, a faithful member of the Methodist church, and a graduate of Kutztown Normal School." It was good to learn what a fine mother Mom had. (Cousin Larry Williams compiled a genealogy of the family, with obituaries from the newspaper.) I learned that her mother played the piano very well and that she had been a schoolteacher, as Mom had told us.

Sometimes I've wondered if Mom would have gone to church across the street if it had been Methodist instead of Mennonite. As it was, a culture barrier stood in the way. Or was it also her obesity, or just her need to stay home and cook Sunday dinner for her visiting family and us? She was most content with her family and friends.

Many years later, our daughter Janet gave me a book in which the author says, "It is difficult to have compassion for one who is victimizing us, but once we've removed ourselves as a victim, we can find compassion. Our path, our way, is a gentle one, walked in love–love for self, love for others." (Melody Beattie, *The Language of Letting Go* [Hazelden Foundation, 1990], 38-39.) Having been "removed" from Mom physically and spiritually–first at the doctor's, then at college and seminary–I found compassion for her. Freeing myself psychologically has been a lifelong process.

The day after the funeral I felt better and the depressing thoughts lifted for the present. My family enjoyed Janet and after a refreshing but short time with everyone, I decided I was ready to head back to Mississippi.

CHAPTER 18

Mamie And the Peace Offering

When a man's ways please the Lord, He makes even his enemies
to be at peace with him.
PROVERBS 16:7 (NKJ)

1966

At Valley View, our days at times were filled with many people coming and going besides the community people. Wonderful people from around the state, MCC people, church people, our former seminary professors, Leland and Bertha Harder with their sons, and even PBS news commentator Daniel Shore came to visit the center. Once in a while I cooked for couples or larger groups. As a full-time mother I seldom went to the center for meetings. Janet and homemaking, answering the phone and writing letters, making weekly trips ten miles to Canton to do our laundry (and diapers), and to grocery shop kept me busy. Visitors provided fellowship, encouragement, and information about what was happening in the outside world. One day someone told us that people from California inquired in Canton about the "Mennonite settlement" they had heard about. We were amused. A Mennonite settlement of three!

In May 1966, we experienced one of the most dramatic events of our two-year stay in Mississippi. At 8:45 on Friday evening we heard a small knock at our door. Jake opened the door and there stood Stella, a seventh grader who lived nearby with her grandmother.

"Can you take me to my sister's?" she asked Jake, who was used to serving as taxi. The pleading look in her eyes matched the tone of her voice. Later we learned that her brother Boo Jack had tattled on her and Stella ran away from home to avoid a beating for being in a fight at school. "Yes, I'll be right out," Jake told her and she walked to our car. Her married sister lived four miles down the road.

"Do you think you should?" I asked anxiously. "I wonder if she has permission."

Jake pondered for a moment. "Yes, I think I should. Maybe it will be good for her to get away for a while. I'll be right back." And he was out the door.

My emotions churned as he drove off and the sound of the VW faded in the distance. Janet, then 15 months old, was in bed for the night. A lonely, uneasy feeling settled over the house and bored into me.

I walked to the front window and looked out. Darkness, pitch black, encircled the glow from the lone light on the telephone pole, but I could dimly see a short stretch of road and the community center. As I watched, I saw big Mamie walk by at a good clip, looking very determined. Her skin was black as the night, but I knew it was Mamie, Stella's grandma. She was tall and big-framed and always wore a kerchief around her head. Where could she be going, and why was she hurrying so? The dilapidated grocery store to the right of us near the road was closed. Must be going to see a neighbor, I reasoned, trying to shake off the sense of foreboding growing on me since Jake left. Yet, try as I might, I could not shake off the seriousness of the situation. I only hoped Jake was not in trouble.

Mamie disappeared into the darkness and I turned from the window to straighten up the house, trying to keep calm. At least Jake had said he'd be right back. Four miles up to Stella's sister's and four miles back should take ten minutes. There was nothing to worry about. Imagining trouble was only asking for it. Everything would be fine.

I had to admit I still wondered at times like this what we were doing here. Yet I *knew* what we were doing here. Jake's heart was here, in his work, and I wanted to be with him in it. Before we came, my fears had centered on the evil that whites perpetrated against blacks. I knew we'd be classed as "nigger lovers" and Jake could be killed. But he saw no reason to fear. How could we know that the first real threat to Jake's life would come, not from whites, but from a black? And a woman at that! Mamie had given me a hearty welcome the first time I met her, eight months earlier.

"Well, *hell-o*," she greeted me with a wide, somewhat toothless grin and merry eyes. "We's so glad to have you here!" And then, with obvious doubt in her tone and expression, "Do you-all really *like* it here?" Since young people flocked out of the area to northern cities, this became a common question. I assured her we did.

I liked Mamie instantly. Yet there was a certain roughness about her that made me wonder what was underneath that jolly exterior. Four grandchildren lived with her. Their mother was dead and their father was in jail for killing a man. My suspicion that she could be harsh with the children was later confirmed.

Stella seemed to get the brunt of Mamie's meanness. She was a shy girl, often sullen, with a deep sadness in her eyes. Innocent and naïve-looking, she could spawn ideas and situations that were stupid and embarrassing, though not vicious. Why did she do it? Was she really stupid and disobedient? I often wondered.

Stella's brother Boo Jack was less than a year older than she and both were in seventh grade. From the time we arrived, he was Jake's shadow, following him around, helping with odd jobs, begging for rides to town or for a deck of cards. He was amazed when he learned we kept no weapon in the house. Boo Jack had at least one bad habit: tattling on Stella to his grandma. Being a boy, he had lots of freedom, and Stella, it seemed, had almost none.

Peewee, in first grade, and Lulu, age four, completed Mamie's family. She lived in a tiny weather-beaten house on the hill, easily visible from our living room window. Seeing her bending over her washing in a big black iron kettle over a fire was an unforgettable picture, reminiscent of slave days a century ago.

The minutes stretched slowly by. I wrote letters to keep my mind occupied. From time to time I went to the window to see if Jake was coming. But every car that came went on by. I wondered what happened to Mamie. I wrote and prayed; wondered and waited. Jake must be in trouble, I thought. What could have happened? Again I went to the window. Boo Jack was going by! Feeling relieved to see someone I opened the door and called to him.

"Boo Jack, do you know where Jake is?"

"Yeah, he be coming soon now," he said, rather apologetically.

In a few minutes Jake drove up. It was only 50 minutes since he'd left, but it seemed like hours. When he came in, looking very sober, he told me his story.

"When I left with Stella I asked if she had permission to go. She said yes. I dropped her off and was halfway home when a car stopped me. Boo Jack jumped out and warned me not to go home. He said his grandma was waiting for me at our corner with her shotgun!"

"No!" I felt weak. "I saw her walk by soon after you left, walking very fast, but I didn't see a gun. I'm so glad I didn't. But how did she know?"

"Boo Jack was in our yard when we drove off. He ran home and told Mamie. She was furious and in such a rage that she grabbed her gun and swore she'd kill me. Boo Jack never expected that. He was scared. He ran across the fields to the road and stopped a car going by and hitched a ride to stop me. So I parked the car to wait and Boo Jack and the man drove back to the corner to talk with Mamie. When they stopped, she yelled, 'Don't nobody breathe!' Some of the neighbor kids were in the yard there and they were all scared. She told them to scat, which they did—fast! Then she told the man to drive her to her granddaughter's house. He agreed to on one condition—that she give him the gun."

"And she did?"

"Yes. I talked with him later and he said he was shaking like a leaf but he put the gun on the floor in front and she got in the back and they drove off. He blew his horn when they passed me, as a signal that it was safe to come home. I stopped and talked with Boo Jack too. He told me how scared everyone was. He said his grandma shot a man once." He stopped, and, as his words hung in the air, I hugged him tight and breathed a prayer of gratitude.

Then, as I slumped into a chair, all I could think of was Stella.

"If Stella was in trouble before, she's in double now," I said. That was Jake's concern too.

"Yes. She told me the fight at school started when a girl said something about her dead mother. She couldn't take that. Well, she and Mamie will come back to the house soon. And when they do, I'm going up there."

"Oh, no! Please! You can't do that!" I pleaded.

"But her grandmother is insane with rage. She could kill Stella."

"And what could you do about it? Get yourself killed, too?"

He didn't answer, but walked to the window to watch for their return.

I gave up. Jake was a grown man, clear thinking and levelheaded. He wouldn't interfere where he had no right.

When the car finally drove up the hill, it was too dark to see until Mamie's large frame and Stella's small one entered the lighted doorway of the house. The door closed. And Jake was already gone. Once more I waited, suspense growing by the minute.

When he came back he had more bad news.

"Mamie is yelling and screaming at Stella. She hit her over the head with something and they were fighting on a bed. I wish there was something I could do." He looked dejected. Beat.

We went to bed exhausted. I felt like a wrung-out dishrag. Sleep did not come easily that night.

I awoke the next morning with a vague feeling of uneasiness and, within seconds, the events of the night before flooded into my mind. I got up and from habit now went to the front window. Up on the hill, Mamie was at her big black pot doing her washing. Everything appeared normal. But even as I watched, Peewee and Lulu ran out of the house toward Mamie and she left her pot and hurried into the house. Soon she was out, yelling and waving her arms to anyone who would hear. A close neighbor ran up the hill, then the woman from the store hurried by. Another neighbor who usually kept to himself rode up on horseback. Wondering what to do, I went outside and heard Mamie yelling, *"COME ON! COME ON!"*

A young neighbor girl was running toward our house.

"What's happened?" I asked.

"Mamie says to call an ambulance. Stella took poison!"

Fear struck at my heart. Poison! Surely not!

Jake had been at our open door and before I got in the house he was dialing for an ambulance. But he needn't have, for within minutes a neighbor drove up, someone carried Stella into the car, Mamie climbed in, and they sped toward town.

I walked to the road as the woman from the store and her sister walked by. The store lady was crying and said, "See how she did that girl last night? I'd do the same thing!"

Her sister added, "She unconscious. She look like she dead."

A heavy cloud seemed to hang over the neighborhood the rest of the morning and I prayed as I never prayed before. Everyone waited. And then at noon a car drove up the hill. What a relief to see Stella walking!

Several variations of the near tragedy filtered in to us. Some said she took "adult pills." Others said they took her to the hospital for treatment and then to the doctor's office. And for once, Boo Jack didn't know the whole story. He eventually came over and told us, "The doctor didn't believe she swallowed anything or it would have done more damage." And Stella wouldn't talk.

By Monday life seemed back to normal but we still hadn't seen Mamie. She was janitor for the Head Start School at the center. At noon I took a telephone message to the center and ran into her actually talking with Jake!

"I's comin' to see you soon," she said to me, looking sheepish, but with her usual grin. "But this afternoon, I's goin' fishin'." I felt so relieved, knowing her anger was gone.

Late that afternoon, Stella and Peewee came to the house. Stella held out a dish with five small fish, cleaned, which Mamie had caught that afternoon. Stella beamed with happiness. I felt all warm inside as I accepted the peace offering.

This was not the last difficult episode with Stella, but Mamie seemed to have learned she could trust Jake, and that was heartening. For if Mamie was angry at you, you knew it and had better keep out of her way. But if she liked you and was sorry she'd been wrong, you knew that too. I didn't feel resentment toward her for wanting to shoot my husband. I knew that deeply ingrained fears and hatred from over 200 years of abuse died hard among southern blacks, as did the customs and mores the older ones still observed when with "white folks." I hoped that the younger ones would grow up to know they were entitled to self-respect and the respect of other humans, regardless of color.

The events of this weekend symbolized what we were here for. We had met the enemies of prejudice and hate, and had "overcome!"

CHAPTER 19

Gladness With Sadness

You shall go out with joy, and be led forth with peace.
ISAIAH 55:12 (NKJ)

1966–1967

Mother and Dad Friesen were concerned about our safety and felt the work was too overwhelming, so they offered to come down to help us. When Jake inquired, he learned that family members could not work in the same MCC unit, a disappointment to them and to us.

But help came in the summer of 1966 when 13 students from the north arrived in Valley View for two months to work at the center. Just before they came, the "James Meredith Freedom March" from Memphis to Jackson was scheduled to come through Canton. When Meredith was shot in the leg the second day of the march, Martin Luther King Jr. took over while Meredith recovered.

Fortunate for us, Larry and Jessie Kehler, our friends from the Akron MCC office, were visiting us with their two children at the time. Jake and Larry joined the march as it neared Canton and then attended the rally in town that evening. Jessie and I listened on the radio and heard about the clash with police and tear-gassing of 2000 marchers when they tried to set up tents at the elementary school. Jessie and I were concerned about our husbands' safety.

We were greatly relieved when Jake called to explain. "We were tear-gassed with the rest. My eyes are burning, but I'm okay. We ran into a nearby house and we're here with Martin Luther King. People got kicked and dragged and hit with rifles. It was bad!" Having Jessie with me for that unforgettable day was a great comfort and joy.

Later Jake told us, "A policeman was beating a woman and when Stokley Carmaichal saw it he ran toward the scuffle and yelled, 'I have to help that woman!'" King took off after Stokley and tackled him and they both fell down on the street near Larry and me. King shouted at Stokley, 'You can't fight violence with violence!'"

Larry, a photojournalist, took many pictures of the march, the Head Start school, and meetings at the center, documenting our work. That summer I had a reading club for children at the center library. Larry took a picture of me with smiling Kathy McCullough, discussing a book she'd read. After he returned to Akron, he used this picture for the "picture of the month" for MCC's supporting churches. I often felt like an insignificant part of the work there and this thoughtful gesture on Larry's part blessed me. Larry and Jake were long-time friends and former roommates at Canadian Mennonite Bible College in Winnipeg, and Jessie became a dear friend to me at Akron.

Reading club, Kathy McCullough and me, June 1966.

Jake and Janet with work campers, June 1966.

Before the students arrived for their work camp, Jake had assured the sheriff that the students would not be involved in demonstrations. When they came, Jake instructed the students about this restriction. However, the second weekend after the students arrived, the black community decided to boycott businesses up town, in protest of the tear-gassing. Wanting to show their solidarity with the people, the students forgot their instructions and got drawn into the demonstration. When police told them to halt or they'd be arrested, the students, "being good Quakers who do things by consensus," talked it over but could not come to a decision. When the line started moving again, as Paul Murray says, "We marched around the corner and right into jail!" This was a terribly traumatic experience for these idealistic northern young people. They owed a debt of gratitude to dear Rev. McCullough who used his house as collateral to pay their bond and get them released later that night. Jake had some fast explaining to do to the sheriff who was very angry. In the end the leader of the work camp and his wife got sent home to Philadelphia, an extremely painful day for them and us. So the students asked Jake and me to be their leaders. I attended the community meeting where Otha Williams, center chairman, welcomed the students. He eloquently praised Jake, me, and the students.

Over the next weeks, because of our little kitchen, we invited the students in small groups for dinner—lively times of games, fun, and fellowship.

After the jail incident, the students made a meaningful contribution to the work at the center and in the community. They registered voters, wrote a voter registration manual, helped tear down and rebuild a house for a family, planted trees at the center, and inspired young and old alike. They made a significant contribution to Valley View and the county and we were sad to see them go.

We said goodbye to the students in August, and in September a senior Voluntary Service couple, Gerhard and Leucille Buhler, moved to a black college thirty miles north of us. We became good friends as they often spent weekends with us. They felt confined at the school with only a small bedroom and bathroom. They'd come on Saturday, stay in our guest room overnight, then go with us to church in Jackson. They loved Janet and were grandma and grandpa to her. We played games and Leucille played the portable organ Ezra Young gave us and we sang hymns. Their friendship boosted my spirits our second year in Valley View.

Also after the students left, Jake painted our house a lovely green, and our ugly pink house looked like new.

Our landlord, Rev. McCullough, was a feisty man with a keen mind and a passion for freedom for his people. He had been a preacher in three states, and Classie, who was 80, claimed he was 100. Rev. McCullough often came to the door before we were out of bed in the morning with something urgent to discuss with Jake. He loved Jake, often calling him "son." He walked with a cane but still rode horseback, went fishing, and helped Jake plant trees around our house, which Jake dug up on his land.

Otha Williams, board chairman of Valley View Community Center, had donated the land on which the center was built. Even before our first year was out, Jake and Otha clashed over methods to achieve change for blacks. Otha was buying into the "black power" mentality of many impatient blacks. One night at a center meeting Otha lashed out at Jake, "Be quiet! You don't know what you're talking about! There are times you must fight fire with fire. I been taught, 'Just pray and God will take care of your problems.' It didn't work!" Jake was taken aback.

On August 31, 1966, Jake, Otha, and Rev. McCullough were at the store next to our house. Otha yelled at Jake, "We need to part ways! You are not needed here anymore. Larry Scott (Quaker from Philadelphia) said I can ask you to leave. I want you out!" What a shock to Jake, in front of people standing nearby and the storeowners inside.

Rev. McCullough yelled back as loudly as Otha. "You can't get him out! He came here to help us and you treat him like this. I'm so ashamed. You are in the wrong! And you can't make him leave!"

Otha refused to back down. "I'll bet you $500 I'll have him out of here in 30 days!"

"I'll bet you $500 you can't!" Both men wrote out checks and gave them to a neighbor standing there. The next week Otha continued his vicious ranting about Jake at the center.

Verbal fights were common where Otha was concerned. Once at a community center meeting he and his wife screamed at each other, then fought on the floor on stage—incredible behavior to all who watched.

Jake wrote regular detailed reports to Edgar Stoesz, our administrator in Akron. After getting the report of Otha's threats, Edgar flew down on September 6 to try to bring resolution. He met with the board for hours, usually without Jake present. After many discussions, Otha and Jake were reconciled. Otha said he forgave Jake. Jodi, the Head Start chairperson, and Otha wept as they also forgave each other. Two weeks after writing their checks, Otha and Rev. McCullough returned them. The bet was off.

But we were not out of the woods yet. Jake's problems with Otha were just beginning. Some Head Start teachers reported that they were not getting their full paycheck. Jake investigated. Some checks had been forged—and cashed—by Otha and he gave them only part of their money. Jake reported this to the Head Start board in Canton.

Otha's fury took a different turn when he learned that he was caught and Jake had reported him. In April of 1967, Otha told people, "I have a job for Jake in Greenville. It pays $1600."

"We don't need Jake in Greenville," retorted Classie McCullough. "We need him *here*!" Then Jake heard that Otha boasted that he never signed the deed for the center. He had agreed with the Quakers to donate the land as a gift. Now, while giving the impression of being a generous benefactor, he fleeced the people and claimed he owned the center. Jake talked with people at the Canton Head Start office and wrote letters to authorities of the programs. He learned that Otha had committed more violations than anyone at the center knew. Otha's anger and determination to get rid of Jake consumed him.

Jake spoke with the board of the center and to Otha about signing the deed. In April of 1967, Otha declared he would not sign the deed until Jake left. He insisted Jake must leave. Little did he know, we were already planning to leave. From the first months in Mississippi, Jake began taking a correspondence course in law. He also took a pilot proficiency test. As time went on he talked with various people about the two options for a career after we left VS. He settled on aviation and we planned to leave in the fall of 1967.

In the midst of this ruckus, Jake had a nice diversion one day. The host of a radio program, "Yankees in the Heart of Dixie," called and asked if he could interview Jake about his work. The kindly, elderly gentleman came to our home to tape the interview. He said, "Our program is on 75 stations in Alabama and Mississippi. Occasionally we have opposition, and one station cancelled last week."

He asked Jake about his background, experience, and about Mennonites and Amish.

"Where did you meet your wife?" he asked. "Do you remember the first time you met her?"

"Yes," Jake said. "We met at seminary. The first day I got there I went to the Information Office where Jane was working and she gave me directions for where to get a bed."

The man responded, "And you've been taking directions from her ever since!" Jake and he laughed jovially. Jake explained how he came to be at Valley View, and about the Credit Union, Co-op, Heifer Project, Head Start, Interact (whites and blacks working together), typing classes, and vegetable growing. We were glad for the exposure this interview gave to the work at Valley View, and for the witness and moderating influence of people like this man who cared.

Otha continued his tirade against Jake. In June, Jake's loyal shadow Boo Jack decided to take matters into his own hands. That evening, I walked with Janet in the stroller to the McCullough's with a quart of borscht. They lived a short distance past the store and down a lane. On the way back, I heard a loud commotion at the store. Otha had roared in on his truck, jumped out, and shouted, "Someone just tried to shoot me at my house!" Alarmed, I hurried home and told Jake.

Soon Boo Jack came to the house with his clothes. He asked Jake, "Can you take me up town?"

"Did you try to shoot Otha?" Jake questioned.

"Yes," he admitted. His eyes showed fear. Now he was scared and had to get away.

Jake did not scold or lecture. He waited until Otha left the store, and then took Boo Jack to safety.

That night before bed, Jake became sick with a bad headache and vomiting. Fear of the atrocity that had been averted – and the realization of the serious trouble we may all have been in if Boo Jack had succeeded in murdering Otha – affected Jake physically. We were grateful to God that Boo Jack failed in his evil plot.

Problems between Jake and Otha continued to fester. In May, Larry Scott came from the Philadelphia American Friends Service Committee (AFSC) office and met with the board and Otha. Larry was sympathetic to Otha because Otha had kept in touch with him by phone and gave his side. Dr. Beittel from Jackson stood staunchly by Jake and told Larry he did not agree with him. Nothing was resolved.

Then in July, the people decided to act. The Head Start board voted Otha out, 25-5. The Canton Head Start organization voted likewise, 4-3. The collapse of Otha's authority and rule hit him like a kick to the stomach. He stormed around outside the center shouting, "I'm mad! I'm mad! I'll lock up!"

But Otha knew when he was beat. He gave his center keys to Mamie, the janitor. Otha was sick for two days after being voted out. He told the people, "I can't eat." Rejection by his people hurt. For months, I alternated between feeling anger and compassion for this tall, fiery black man. He was big-hearted, but misguided. His role models in life had been unscrupulous white men in authority. Otha hated them; now he became like them, trying to rule his people in the same dishonest ways.

Even before Otha was voted out, Jake agreed to move his office out of the center. He handed in his keys and worked from home.

We planned to leave in August, but Jake wanted it kept secret.

I was sad things had turned so ugly for Jake after the commendable work he had done at Valley View. We had seen much progress in our area and in the state the past two years.

Many civil rights laws passed in the 1960s brought hope to integrate restaurants and public places. When we arrived, we could not have eaten in a restaurant in Canton. But now, in 1967, I ate with two black friends at a restaurant without incident, though many people stared. We were excited at the new freedom. *The Valley View Weekly News* that Jake published encouraged, "You may go to any window at the courthouse, use any restrooms and fountains at any public place." This was a revolutionary change.

A white friend, Jane Sample, who visited and wholeheartedly supported us, told me one day, "Canton has changed much in the last year. The whites are much more cooperative. I can talk to people and make them listen. And my husband got converted and joined the church! I'm involved in a lot of miracles!"

Exhilarated at being part of a movement of the Spirit of God that was so big nothing could stop it, we were encouraged. God was "releasing the captives" in the South in answer to their cries as surely as He freed the Israelite slaves from Egypt.

I was filled with gratitude for God's protection for us, and for the many small signs of His love, even in nature. One morning, eight red cardinals frolicked on the white sleet (a first) outside my kitchen window. And on one of my worst days, a brilliant double rainbow, with a faint triple one barely visible, spanned the sky.

Also, the Bluffton College faculty chose me for inclusion in the publication, *Outstanding Young Women of America*, a complete surprise. During our second year, I received an assignment to write a month of devotionals. What a joy it was to write 30 half-page devotionals for *Our Family Worships*. Jake always read them and gave suggestions and I loved discussing my writing with him. This devotional booklet went to our churches all over the U.S. and Canada. In some of the meditations, I told about our work in Mississippi.

Months after publication, a welcome letter arrived from former missionary to China, Aganetha Fast, an aunt of my major professor at seminary, Bertha Harder. She wrote, "Dear Mr. and Mrs. Jake and Jane Friesen and little Janet: I read about you in *Our Family Worships* and at once my heart was touched in gratitude and prayer for your life and work…" She wrote many things very lovingly, even though she didn't know us. My heart was warmed to think that many people were praying for us – people we did not know, but who were part of the great family of God.

But the absolute highlight of that second year was the birth of our son Jared John on May 23, 1967. Writing during my pregnancy kept me focused on Scripture and worship; thus I kept a happier frame of mind – good for my baby and me. This diversion also provided positive "therapy" for Jake and me in the midst of the unpleasantness at the center.

Since we lived about 30 miles from the hospital, the doctor told me that I was ready and could pick my day and be at the hospital at 7:00 A.M. to have labor induced. Jake and I chose Tuesday, May 23. Janet stayed with the Beittels in Jackson when Jake came to the hospital. Jared was born at 12:39 P.M., after less than six hours of labor. I had thought this one was a boy and was delighted to see Baby Jared, a tiny 6 pounds, 6 ounces, beautiful and amazing, like his sister. *Jared* is from Genesis 5:15-20, and he is listed as an ancestor of Jesus, in Luke 2:37. (The famous Enoch "who walked with God and he was not for God took him" was the son of Jared.) We named him Jared John, with his Daddy's middle name.

Janet was so excited that when I got in the car with him at the hospital the first thing she said was, "I want the new baby!"

The day after we brought Jared home from the hospital was the Buhlers' last day in Mississippi. Leucille cooked, kept Janet happy, and helped in many ways. While I was immensely grateful for her presence, help, and mothering love, it was a sad day too, as we parted from our good friends. (Incidentally, whereas I weighed 110 at college, after Jared was born I weighed a mere 87 pounds!)

Many people came to the house to see Jared. I enjoyed their visits and was happier than ever. All Janet could talk about before Jared came was "the new baby" and what she would do with him.

"I'm going to feed him Cheerios and help brush his teeth," she said, in her big sister voice. The first weeks she talked constantly about the new baby. She'd lie down on the sofa and cover herself up with a blanket, like I covered Jared. While she felt jealous at times, most of the time she loved him and played with her doll, imitating what I did with Jared.

Jake planned to take advanced aviation training in Clearwater, Florida, in the fall. On July 16, he wrote to Edgar at MCC with his reasons for leaving Mississippi. He couldn't bring himself to tell Rev. McCullough. However, the McCulloughs got wind of it and circulated a petition to keep us there. Rev. McCullough came often, telling Jake, "I appreciate your work to the highest." One day he insisted, "We have enough names to keep you here!" He sent the petition to Edgar in Pennsylvania.

Edgar wrote to Jake saying we could leave whenever we pleased. On August 5, Rev. McCullough came to the house with a letter from Edgar stating that we were leaving. His face sagged and his eyes were deep pools of sadness. Too choked up to talk, he gave Jake a big hug, and then sat down for a long time in our living room, silent, wiping his nose. We grieved with him but Jake had nothing to say.

Rev. McCullough with me and Jake.

Jake and me, Janet and Jared (2 mo.), August 1967.

Jake told no one when we were leaving. He had built a breezeway beside our house with a storage shed, from which we also distributed clothing from MCC. And he made a tic tac toe game on the concrete to play games with the neighborhood boys. One day he backed the MCC truck into the breezeway and slowly loaded boxes as we packed them. Boo Jack came every day and asked when we were leaving. All Jake would say was, "I'm not sure."

Joy and gladness mingled with the difficulties of our days the past two years. We were glad for many signs of progress. Head Start teachers and aides gave exuberant praise to the program and the children's rapid progress. Mothers with a few years of education became teachers and earned a paycheck for their families. Glowing reports often appeared in the *Weekly News*. A trainee wrote, "I get great joy out of watching and teaching the children. They are learning reading readiness, art, free choice, and science, and are getting along better with the world."

While the first year was hard for me and better for Jake, the second was much better for me because I was expecting what I believed to be a son, and at the same time writing and meditating on Scripture. But for Jake, the second year dealt him blow after blow from Otha. Now Jake was also ready to leave. In spite of that, he felt good about the programs at the center and the support of many people. He had decided the work would continue without him.

The day before we left, Rev. McCullough came and sat in the living room. He told Jake, "You did a fine work here, son, and I appreciate it to the highest. I can't sleep anymore just thinkin' of you leavin' us. What will we do without you?" His words tore us up inside.

Earlier Jake had told me, "I don't have the heart to tell McCulloughs when we're leaving. I'll just put a note on their door before we go." So we left as quietly as we had come, with no good-byes.

The next afternoon I drove the VW with Jared now, instead of Janet, in the car bed in back. I cried as I drove past girls I had come to know in reading club in summer, in my cooking class, and through their visits to our home. Jake followed later with Janet and our belongings in the pickup. I cried all the way to Jackson for the people we had come to love who would remain a part of our lives forever.

We stayed overnight with the Beittels who had graciously kept Janet while I was in the hospital with Jared. Dr. Beittel gave Jake tremendous moral support, spoke up for him, and wrote letters affirming him through the hard times at the center.

Classie McCullough wrote in her first letter to us, "I am so glad you all left like you did because it would have been too heartbreaking to meet face to face to say good-bye. I had to have my cry before." She wrote us warm and wonderful letters for 13 years.

On November 12, 1970, three years after we left, the community center burned down. (The house we lived in had burned down in July.) Rev. McCullough suspected arson.

We were amazed at how the people rallied around the cause of rebuilding, raising funds and borrowing a large sum. In a letter in May, 1971, Classie wrote, "I am real happy this morning. They started to rebuild our community center again. The community has been working very hard."

We went back for a visit that summer and saw the center, built bigger than before. Six years after we first set foot in Valley View, we saw the great transformation that had taken place among the people. We were heartened at their determination. They had learned what a center was for and how to run a Head Start program. And they learned how to work together.

How often we had swayed with the people and sung the hymn of the Civil Rights movement, "We Shall Overcome." Now we saw for ourselves this hope becoming reality.

As for us, we had begun a new life in Florida. Jake would finish his advanced aviation training in six months and apply for a job up north. That was our plan. "Man plans but the Lord guides," according to Proverbs. Would Jake land a job with the airlines, as he hoped? Not if God heard my prayers!

CHAPTER 20

Interlude

The Lord is my shepherd, I have everything I need.
He lets me rest in green grass...
PSALM 23:1-2 (GNB)

1967–1969

As we headed toward Florida, an uncertain future stared us in the face – again. Jake had often worked at the community center seven days a week, when there were meetings on the weekend. I felt a burden lift as we started off to Florida, the land of sunshine and "R and R." Mary Ann Kooker wrote us asking, "What are you doing in Florida, R&R?" It turned out to be anything but that for Jake.

Our MCC truck, loaded to the hilt, sagged dangerously low and the tires bulged as we left Jackson, towing the VW. When Jared slept in the car bed, I rode in the car with him. Whether or not that was legal, it horrifies me now.

At 11:30 that morning, we had a flat tire. Jake got it fixed at a gas station and we started off. A minute later we knew something was wrong as the truck began to shimmy. Jake stopped and saw the young man from the service station riding toward us on his bicycle; then he jumped off and *ran*.

"The nuts are loose on your tire and the tire is coming off!" he panted. He tightened the nuts and we were off, so grateful he had noticed and came after us. In the afternoon we had a lovely rain.

"The rain is good for the tires," Jake said. At 6:00 P.M. we stopped for gas and found another flat tire – the same one.

The next day was still cloudy and rainy. What a blessing! It was August and could have been very hot. At 2:00 P.M. we had our third flat tire. I thanked God for the gas station we found only a mile further. Rising heat and humidity filled the air with tiny fruit flies that gathered around Janet's sweaty face. At 5:30 we stopped at a Holiday Inn where we had our fourth flat tire! *Just one more day to go. We have to make it to Clearwater! Please, God, help us to make it.* Little Jared suffered from colic two nights in a row. And I suffered greatly with him.

On the morning of the third day, our old, bogged-down pickup clipped along at 52 miles per hour in sunny Florida. Between 1:00 and 2:00 P.M. the engine started missing.

"Doesn't sound good," Jake groaned. Then a few minutes later, "Well, I guess that's it." The overworked motor sputtered and conked out. Jake's face looked ashen as he lamented, "We almost made it! Only 15 miles to our motel, but we can use the car now to get there." Fortunately, a gas station was nearby. Always resourceful, Jake talked to the owner about leaving the truck there. He unhooked the car, and we started out in the VW. The children were tired and getting restless. I couldn't wait to get to our motel.

"Well, Honey," I said brightly. "We'll make it after all. And not very late either." The words were barely out of my mouth when we heard a terrible racket. The car sounded as if it was going crazy.

"Now what? Oh, no! Part of a tire flew off!" Jake groaned, incredulous that our troubles were not yet over. "Well, we can drive on it these last few miles. I'll just take it easy."

"That was so loud and terrifying, I thought the wheel came off!" I said. "But it sure was over fast. Thank God we're all safe!" We continued on that tire to the Holiday Inn.

"We made it!" Jake announced with relief, as he pulled into the parking lot. "I'll change that tire later – fifth one for the trip! Let's get you and the children into our motel room."

Then he called our good friend Ezra Young, who had visited us faithfully at Valley View. After he retired from his work with the Quakers in New Orleans, Ezra and his wife Jessamine moved to Florida. They lived in Dunedin, a coastal town about five miles north of Clearwater.

That afternoon, Ezra took Jake to the aviation school, then had our truck towed to his house. He was one of the most kind, gracious men I had ever met, and we finally got to meet his dear wife. They became "Grandma and Grandpa Young" to our children.

The next day the Youngs drove us to see the beach cottage they had reserved for us to rent at Indian Rocks Beach. What an amazing setting by a beautiful beach! As my eyes scanned the wide expanse of the Gulf of Mexico and the pretty, sunshine-yellow cottage, I felt ecstatic. After Valley View, it looked like Heaven.

Friendly Mrs. Holmes told us, "The rent is normally $70 a week but I'll give it to you for $50 a week." Ezra had told her of our work in Mississippi and that we were living on a shoestring. "But you know the cottage is occupied for two more weeks since you got here early."

I was overwhelmed at the unexpected blessing of this lovely cottage and exotic location by the beach. The fresh, salty ocean air filled our lungs and lifted our spirits. Ezra and Jessamine invited us to stay with them until Labor Day. We were exceedingly grateful for their generous offer.

Soon after Jake began classes at National Aviation Academy, he came home with discouraging news. "They say there's a glut of pilots in the country and when students graduate they can't find jobs. Many work at gas stations, pumping gas."

What a blow! On the other hand, I knew God would take care of us. Months before, when Jake told me he'd like to be an airline pilot, I worried. First, flying was unsafe. Second, it was a "worldly" occupation. I knew of no Mennonites who were airline pilots. Third, it would take Jake away from home too much. Scared at the prospect, I had cried out to God. *"Please, God, don't let Jake become an airline pilot!"* A strange reassurance came over me, that God had heard and would take care of us. Yes, I wanted Jake to be successful and do what made him happy. But I wanted him on the ground!

Jake took a job at the school as night watchman at the hanger, so he had classes during the day and worked at night. He had borrowed $4000 from his sister Mary Ann to cover tuition for six months. A family member who wanted to remain anonymous gave a generous amount to help us through the next months. God supplied our need through his family.

Dad Friesen, Jake, Janet and Jared, at beach cottage. October 1967.

I loved "nesting" with my children at the beach cottage in warm sunny weather. During that time, Jake's father came to see us. No family member had visited us in the two years in Mississippi so this was special. Dad's presence gave us a lift and he enjoyed the children. Every morning he went in the ocean, often with Janet or by himself. One day we took him along to look for an apartment. When we found an upstairs one at Pinellas Park for $100 a month, he said it was too expensive. But we knew it was a bargain and rented it. Seeing a church across the street on this main drag through town cheered me. I could take Janet there for Sunday school.

After we were settled in, Janet and I went one Sunday as Jake kept Jared. A lovely young couple was team-teaching the small children, reminding me of the time Jake and I taught together at Elkhart. But this couple would never know I went through seminary and had a Master's in Religious Education. We never shared about ourselves; except for a greeting, they spoke only to the children. I kept my secret and admired their gentle ways and natural gifts as teachers. I enjoyed going with Janet. When Jared began to walk, I took him too.

Before Christmas that year, Jake's sister Mary Ann came for two weeks and got a room down the street from us. She loved the children and was fun to have around. Christmas was special with Mary Ann. She relished the sunshine in our back yard and on the beach, and enjoyed hearing Janet, not yet three, "read" *Goldilocks and the Three Bears* from memory with good expression. We had read it to her so often that she knew it word for word.

When Janet was quite young, Jake bought the book, *Give Your Child A Superior Mind*, by Siegfried and Therese Englemann. It suggested making flash cards with the alphabet for children at a young age. Jake did this and Janet learned the letters, starting at age two. We had many books that Lee and Bertha Harder's boys had outgrown and Janet loved books.

Mary Ann enjoyed her stay so much that when she returned home she persuaded Jake's mother to come. Mother Friesen still grieved the loss of her oldest daughter, Elizabeth. She decided to visit Elizabeth's best friend in Toronto before she flew to Florida. Mother came for three weeks in January over Janet's third birthday.

Mother Friesen amazed me. Accustomed to poverty for many years, she was the most frugal person I knew. She came with a suitcase full of children's clothing she bought at the MCC thrift store: outfits for Jared, dresses and two lovely little coats with matching bonnets for Janet, a doll, small blankets—many useful things. She could knit, crochet, and sew anything. She altered clothes for me and remade a wool comforter she had made for Jake years ago. When we washed it at the Laundromat the cover disintegrated from age. The wool became fuzz balls of various sizes. Undeterred, Mother dried the wool then pulled it apart to make a new blanket. She also baked her wonderful zwieback for us, a small roll on top of a larger one. For

Janet's third birthday, which we celebrated with the Youngs, Mother baked a big batch of tasty little apple tarts. Janet loved her "Oma" very much.

Mother Friesen, Janet and Jared, Florida, February 1968.

Mother, quiet and soft-spoken, was self-conscious about her German accent. But she had studied English and spoke it quite well. She and I had several heart-to-heart talks and she shared about her difficult life as a minister's wife. One day I confided to her, "I sometimes feel guilty that Jake is not going into the ministry, as Dad expected."

"I'm not surprised," she admitted. "Dad talked so much about the problems in the church, I don't blame Jake for not wanting to be a minister. He heard of too many problems at home." That eased my conscience, at least for the time being. We greatly appreciated the visits from Jake's family.

Other visitors from the north were my college roommate, Nancy Wismer (now Hilty); Jim and Irlene Glenn from Bluffton and seminary (Jim, the matchmaker), and my Akron friend Doris Jean (Brechbill) Bickhart and husband Larry. Doris Jean often stayed overnight with me while Jake was in Mississippi. In December my sister Grace and husband Don came for a week to visit us and to play golf. Jake gave them the royal treatment – a plane ride over St. Pete. Auntie Grace and Uncle Donnie enjoyed the children immensely, and Janet and Jared loved the attention. It was wonderful to have these special visitors.

Jake finished school February 19–23, 1968, with exams and several Federal Aviation Administration (FAA) exams. By March 11, he completed the FAA flying exams. He received certificates for commercial, instrument, multi-engine, flight instructor, and ground instructor, as well as for flight engineer on a DC-6. What an impressive achievement!

He applied for jobs but took what he could get. His first job was at the airport paint shop in Clearwater, scraping paint off planes with chemical spray. He taught instrument flying for one day, and another day had his first trip in a twin-engine, flying executives to Texas. He earned $50 for eight hours of flying. Occasional trips came his way as relief pilot for company execs to Alabama and Texas. He was happy to find work flying after all, in addition to the paint shop job.

On April 9, 1968, the assassination of Martin Luther King Jr. shocked the nation and us. We were far removed now from the turmoil of the Civil Rights movement. I felt numb as I pondered this tremendous loss in the ongoing struggle for freedom and justice. When would this madness end? As I thought of the people back in Mississippi, twinges of guilt crowded into my mind because of our safe, peaceful existence away from all that.

On May 17, Jake took us for a plane ride over Pinellas Park and I was not afraid. Jared was almost one year old and appeared fascinated. He looked down at the land as we went up. Janet and I had flown with Jake once in Mississippi, as he flew occasionally to keep current. She was always a good little passenger. On Jared's first birthday I took a picture of our delightful son.

Jared's first birthday, May 23, 1968.

Our family at St. Petersburg airport, December 1968.

In summer, we got another financial break. Jessamine Young's sister, who lived next door to them, went north for the summer and said we could live in her house rent-free if we'd pay utilities. Plus, we were right next door to our friends. Dunedin, a lovely town along the Gulf, sported green lawn and palm trees lining the coastal drive. I loved taking the children for walks to the water's edge and marveled at God's goodness in bringing us here.

Jake's last day at the paint shop was June 28, 1968. On July 1, he began as an instructor at the St. Petersburg airport. He received $100 a week, and was promised $5 an hour for every extra hour if he taught more than 20 hours a week. However, he never got more than 19½, but at least he had a steady job. He told me that most pilots start at the bottom, as instructors.

Before Jessamine's sister returned, we moved into a nice, roomy house in a clean neighborhood on 10th Street in St. Petersburg, about a five-minute walk from the airport. In a small apartment attached to one side lived a 95-year old woman, Sadie McDonald, who enjoyed my visits with the children, and the children loved visiting her. News reports of plans to send a man to the moon prompted Sadie to scoff. She refused to believe it was possible. (By the next year, on July 20, 1969, Neil Armstrong walked on the moon, but that made no difference to Sadie!)

For me, living in Florida was like a dormant dream come true. I remembered the three girls from the children's home back at Quakertown – Betty, Mary and Frona – and the letters they wrote to Mom. Pictures of them with palm trees looked romantic and exotic. Now we were here! I could not believe my good fortune, and had no responsibilities except for the children and homemaking. I dearly loved "nesting" with my children. Having read an article in *Christian Living* magazine about the importance of nesting, I relished the time in this lovely fall climate taking walks with Janet and Jared, going to parks, and to the beach. The two of them played together well, and Janet was a good little mother to Jared. But I missed having Jake at home, as he flew for Gay Products lawn furniture company in addition to teaching.

One day on a walk, I met a young woman with a boy and a girl. She lived nearby and we enjoyed each other's company and shared recipes. She gave me my first recipe for lasagna, which she raved about. I missed the Presbyterian Sunday school since we had moved away and decided to drive back there on Sunday mornings. Both children loved the class with crafts and stories.

Feeling guilty for not attending church in Florida, I had confided my feelings to Jake's mother. She responded, "I often didn't go to church either when the children were little. It's hard with small children." I felt comforted and considered that Sunday school a gift from God.

The only time I went to church in Florida was on Mother's Day when we lived at Pinellas Park. I longed to go that day and asked Jake if he'd keep the children. (Usually he slept on Sunday mornings, after his night watchman shift.) The Presbyterian service blessed me greatly and I didn't need to go again. The only time Jake went to church was when his father was with us. They went to Ezra and Jessamine's church. Jake brought me a Presbyterian devotional booklet, which I treasured. Our life in Florida was in sharp contrast with our three years at seminary where we were immersed in spiritual study, service, and fellowship. But the peace of God reassured me that He was with us, and approving. He could see the big picture and knew where He was leading us.

Jake applied for jobs in the north and received an offer in New Jersey. He turned it down because it was for single engine planes only. Then on August 22, a letter arrived from Vincennes University in Indiana. They needed a flight instructor to begin September 1, a week away!

Jake called the university and agreed to start in February, not September. How wonderful! Jake had a job in Indiana, the state where we met. We looked for Vincennes on the map and found that, unfortunately, it was 250 miles from Elkhart. Indiana is a long state! I realized with relief that the job was not with the airlines!

Before our move, Jared needed surgery for a hydrocele (water sac). His pediatrician in Jackson found it soon after he was born and recommended surgery because it could develop into a hernia. The Florida pediatrician suggested doing it at 18 months of age because, he said, "He won't remember it." That would be in November. It was August and I dreaded the thought of leaving Jared alone in the hospital.

The same day that Jake received the letter from Vincennes, I met a friendly, exuberant Christian woman at the park. Mrs. Vander Ploeg was Christian Reformed and we visited as the children played. When I mentioned Jared's need for surgery, she told me about the children's hospital where mothers may stay all night with their children. I thanked God for leading us together that morning, grateful for His loving care for us in all our needs.

Jared had only one night in the hospital, and I slept on a big soft chair in his room. About 3:00 A.M. he woke, stood up, held the rail of his crib and jumped up and down, chattering away delightedly. I couldn't believe it! He had no pain or discomfort. Then he sat down and started "ironing" with his blue, life-size telephone that I bought for the occasion. Having watched me iron, he used the phone with a shiny metal bottom as his iron ever after.

Jake still flew occasionally for the company and enjoyed the larger plane. It was difficult for me to accept this "dangerous" occupation. But he was committed to it and I knew I must support him. I felt blessed to have this quiet interlude between his intense work in Mississippi and a permanent job in aviation up north.

Jake's job in St. Pete provided unusual experiences. On the 4th of July, he was asked to fly an advertising banner over the city. Told that the banner would tear on a concrete runway, he took off on a grass strip. The grass was so tall that the propeller caught the grass, wound it up tight, and the nose of the plane dove into the ground. Both the propeller and engine broke. Later Jake learned that the mechanic had installed an engine that was too heavy for the plane but did not record the change. Jake was okay, except for cuts above his nose and a ring on his forehead where he hit the radio knob. It was a scary experience and Jake had the rest of the day off.

One Sunday in December, Jake flew Santa Claus over St. Petersburg where he parachuted out of the airplane. I drove to the place where he was to land and the children watched with delight as he floated down. Jake found it amusing that a skinny Santa parachuted down into the center of the park where a police car picked him up. They drove to where the children waited and a fat "Santa" who was hiding in the car got out to visit with the children while the police car took the skinny Santa back to the airport.

Another strange duty was flying people over the Gulf to scatter their loved one's ashes. The first time, Jake took the tape off the box and dropped the box out of the window. To his embarrassment and dismay, some of the ashes floated into the plane. On subsequent ash drops he held the box outside the window before removing the tape around the lid.

After Christmas, Dr. S. F. Pannabecker, former dean of the seminary, and his wife, Sylvia, came to St. Petersburg. They invited us for supper at their mobile home and we enjoyed the time with them immensely. Sylvia was a kind, godly woman, spirited and wise, a spiritual mentor to me. We enjoyed learning to know them better outside of the academic setting. Dr. P. was a quiet, respected former missionary and teacher. Sylvia was vivacious and talkative, loved people, and sharing her faith in Jesus. They were an encouragement and blessing to us, as well as our children.

For New Year's Day we had the Youngs and Pannabeckers for dinner and enjoyed lively fellowship. The Youngs had been missionaries in the Middle East and the Pannabeckers in China and shared many interesting stories.

We planned to leave Florida on Janet's fourth birthday, January 27. Youngs had us over to celebrate her birthday with a farewell dinner the week before. Then we packed in earnest. The house and kitchen were furnished, and many of our things were in storage, so the move was easy.

On Sunday the 26th, I took the children to the Presbyterian Sunday school for the last time. I did not tell the couple we were moving, since I never shared personal things with them and they never inquired about us. That evening we loaded the U-Haul truck. Monday morning by 9:15 we were ready to roll. This time, we had good tires and were not overloaded. We anticipated a pleasant trip. For Janet's birthday I bought enough small gifts for her to open one every hour of the day. I tied them together with ribbon and put them in a box by our feet. She enjoyed opening each gift and looked forward to the next. Both children were happy and traveled well.

We planned to drive to Vincennes in three days. We said goodbye to St. Pete on a very warm day. The second day we ran into rain and cold. By the third morning, the soggy cold was seeping into my bones—and spirit. I longed for the Florida sunshine. Winter would be a big change for us.

Our arrival at Vincennes filled me with a strange sense of foreboding. I didn't know a soul, and there was no Mennonite church to look up. I wondered, *What will life be like here? How much will Jake be gone?*

We stopped at the university where Jake got the address of our new home. The chairman of the flight department had found us a nice house near them at 303 Eastgate Drive. As we drove up to it on this quiet street on the edge of town, my spirits rose. By contrast to the Mississippi pink house on stilts, this was a clean, roomy three-bedroom pink ranch-style house with lovely fireplace rock on the front. Our new adventure was just beginning!

CHAPTER 21

A Little Child Shall Lead Them

A soft answer turns away wrath, but a harsh word stirs up anger.
PROVERBS 15:1

1969–1971

Vincennes, a southern Indiana town of about 17,000, hugs the banks of the Wasbash River. Cloudy, rainy weather prevailed that first week and any excitement I felt about the move evaporated. I missed the Florida sunshine, the parks, the beach, the warmth. My thoughts drifted 250 miles north to Elkhart and our seminary days of study and fellowship. I longed for a church with friendly faces and people who loved Jesus.

The new house on the edge of town with a fireplace was a blessing. Jake made a roaring fire, which helped chase the chill out of the house and out of my spirits. The children quickly settled into their new room, unpacked toys, and explored their home. The large back yard with an orchard of fruit trees beyond it gave the feel of country. That first week it snowed and the children, enjoying their first snow, made a snowman.

Those first Sundays, Jake and I took turns taking Janet to visit churches. Jake chose one because of the friendly woman in the nursery. Janet loved it but Jared hated it. Not used to being away from his mommy, his eyes were pools of sadness every time we picked him up. I preferred the United Church of Christ, but we stayed at this church. In time, the pastor's wife and I became good friends. Soon we met our friendly neighbors and our children found playmates nearby. Faculty wives met once a month where I learned to know friendly young women in the flight department.

In addition to teaching, Jake began flying charter trips. One day his trip continued into the evening and I had no idea when to expect him. Darkness fell. After the children were in bed, a storm came up. Fear gripped me as hours dragged by. *Why doesn't he come? What if the plane crashed?* I couldn't bear the thought.

Finally, in tears I fell to my knees by the sofa. *"Oh, God!"* I cried. *"Please help me! Please take care of Jake and don't let him ever die or be hurt in a plane crash! Please, Father!"*

As I wept and prayed, an amazing peace swept over me. My fears melted away. God's answer was immediate, His presence tangible. I knew without a doubt that God had *heard* me and granted my request. It was as if God had spoken in an audible voice, "I will keep Jake safe always!" It *was* a "still small voice." Relief flooded my mind and I knew Jake would be all right. I loved Jake, but God loved him even more. And He loved *me*! I rose to my feet with joy and the knowledge of God's comforting presence. After that night, I still prayed for Jake's safety, but I never feared for his life again.

As time went on, Jake sometimes worked on Sundays. Feeling strange and out of place as I sat in church alone, tears flowed unbidden, especially during hymns. Trying to be inconspicuous, I wiped my eyes and prayed for God to take away the tears. Graciously, He answered. It was good to be back in church, but not alone. How my life had changed since our dates at First Presbyterian in Elkhart nine years ago. I hardly knew who I was. I'm ashamed to admit that I hated that aviation job and wondered how this had happened to us.

After a time, the strangeness eased as my friendship grew with the pastor's wife, Eleanor, who was Janet's kindergarten Sunday school teacher. One day I invited her and Mrs. N. from the nursery for tea with the children and me. Eleanor's sunny personality and caring endeared her to me. In time, we also learned to know her husband, Rev. B. He asked Jake to start a young couples and singles Sunday school class for our age group and Jake agreed. In class, Jake shared about our Mennonite nonresistance/peace stand. The people were receptive and wanted to know more about our novel beliefs.

Early that year of 1969, Grace wrote of Daddy's depression. Tommy was ten years old when Mom died. Daddy later took early retirement from work with the borough of Quakertown, thankful he didn't have to plow snow at all hours of the night anymore. He took a job driving a small school bus for special education children two days a week, Tuesday and Thursday. By then, Tommy was 14 and still needed a mother.

One Wednesday morning when Daddy got up he told Tommy, "I'm going to drive bus."

"Today is Wednesday," Tommy said. "You don't have to drive today."

But Daddy insisted and left the house. All alone, Tommy was scared. But he kept his cool and called his older brother Ralph, who had not yet left for work.

"Daddy's all confused! He went to drive bus and I told him this is Wednesday—but he went anyway. Can you stop him?"

"Yes," Ralph reassured, "I'll drive to meet him and stop him." Though Tom was shaken, he got ready for school. He was in seventh grade in the middle school in town, close to sister Millie and Ralph's house.

Ralph found Daddy and persuaded him that he didn't have to drive that day. Ralph followed up with a visit to the doctor for Daddy. He said Daddy had become disoriented since Mom's death. His early retirement aggravated the situation since his routine had been upset. The doctor said Daddy needed more structure in his life; he gave medicine and recommended counseling.

Daddy began seeing a psychiatrist, but his condition deteriorated. Grace wrote to me with shocking news. "Daddy was hospitalized and is strapped in bed with a complete nervous breakdown." This news broke my heart. I longed to be with him and wondered how I could help him. I could pray, but my faith was small after years of experience with Millie, who still struggled with depression and spent time in Day Care. At times I felt overwhelmed and helpless.

I was grateful for our children who were active and bright and cheered me. Keeping them busy with activities from my teaching file and reading to them helped us pass the time.

As if one family crisis weren't enough, in April we learned of Jake's mother's illness. After her visit to us in Florida, she had three surgeries, one in May, and two in September. We heard little and thought she was fine. Then a fourth surgery produced the dreaded diagnosis: stomach cancer. Dad wrote that the doctors didn't give much hope. Then one Sunday, Mother Friesen called to tell us she was out of the hospital. She sounded cheerful, but didn't speak of the prognosis.

Jake's family planned a reunion—a long-time dream-come-true for Mother. In June, we flew to British Columbia for two weeks. When Mother got home from the hospital, she rallied remarkably, anticipating the reunion. She could eat anything, felt great, and astonished everyone by cooking and doing the housework, preparing for the family. Dad believed she was healed in answer to prayer and told everyone so.

We stayed at Mary Ann's apartment in nearby Langley, while she roomed with Mother and Dad. I will never forget the tins of cookies she showed me in the pantry. "These are for you," she said. What a gift these delectable morsels of unusual varieties were to us, lovingly home baked. Janet had her Raggedy Ann doll along on the trip and Jared had his Timmy rag doll. The third floor apartment had a balcony and one day Jared took Timmy out and dropped him to the sidewalk below. Though we hurried down to retrieve the doll, sadly for Jared, Timmy had disappeared.

One day Mary Ann and Mother and Dad took us to famous Stanley Park for the children to play. Mother was very thin but kept up with everyone. We could only hope that Dad was right and that she was healed. The whole family, including the grandchildren, came for the reunion. A beautiful family picture still serves as a blessed memento of that gathering, with Mother and Dad and Mother's father, Grandfather Duerksen, age 92, in the center.

The Friesen family, June 1969. Top row: Raymond Friesen, Barbara Friesen, Carol Schulz, John and Marlene Unrau, Laura and Neil Schulz; middle row: Mary Ann, Margaret holding Garth, Nick holding Mark Friesen, Bertrand and Helen Arlitt, Jake holding Jared, me; front row: Peter and Margaret Schulz, Janet, Oma Elizabeth Friesen, Great Grandpa P. G. Duerksen, Opa N. N. Friesen with Phelia Arlitt, Peter Friesen with Randy Arlitt, Mary Friesen.

The same week in April that we learned Mother Friesen had cancer, Grace wrote me that Daddy started shock treatments. Millie had endured the same several years earlier and I hated the thought. It seemed cruel. (I've since learned of their great benefit for patients who suffer from extreme depression.) While Daddy was hospitalized, Tommy stayed with Millie and Ralph in town. I was grateful that Millie was well enough and able to help with Tom during this time.

This double blow—Mother Friesen's illness and Daddy's break-down—weighed heavily on my mind. Jake's silence regarding these concerns increased my feelings of sadness and isolation.

That spring, I received another devotional writing assignment, which boosted my morale and helped keep my mind off my troubles. On nice days I sat at the picnic table behind our house as the children played with friends from down the street. The lovely orchard of fruit trees bloomed just beyond our yard. I sensed God's presence in the sunshine and beauty of nature. The creative writing process while meditating on Scripture lifted my spirits.

Writing a month of devotionals was about a three-month process. I imag-ined my reading audience: families with small children, teenagers, moms and dads all over the United States and Canada. Peace and joy filled my mind as I felt connected to our Mennonite people through the medium of writing. I recalled the letter from Marion Preheim, editor of *Our Family Worships*, after I sent her samples of my first meditations in Mississippi. "Your devotionals are excellent!" she wrote. I admired Marion, a gifted college and seminary friend, and was encouraged by this affirmation.

In August, we took a trip to my family in Pennsylvania. We camped in our tent on the way to a Herstine reunion. I was relieved that Daddy was out of the hospital, appearing to be much better. It was wonderful to be "home" and see sisters and brothers, spouses, and the many nieces and nephews who swelled the family in the years we had been away. We met at Nockamixon State Park, which had a dam and big lake. One night, a loud thunderstorm woke us and a downpour sent a "river" under our tent. How we slept that night escapes my memory. The children loved camping and the trip. Time with my family and being in nature with Jake and the children rejuvenated my spirits. Best of all, Daddy reveled in having the family together.

In early September, Grace wrote that Daddy moved in with our youngest sister Ruth and her husband, Speedy. They had two daughters, April and Karlene. Also, "Tommy went to live with Anna and John in Chicago." They generously offered to take Tommy, to join their three children, John, James, and Amy. Joel came along later. Anna had her hands full, but she was a true homemaker and mother, loved to bake and was a great cook. And she loved Tommy dearly. A plus for Anna and John was their strong commitment to each other, the Lord, and the church. On the one hand, it was sad that the once bustling house on Thatcher Road stood empty and Tom and Daddy were separated. But we were all relieved and happy that Tom had a good home for his teen years. He was now in eighth grade.

Jake enjoyed his job at Vincennes University. Soon after we arrived, the flight school was moved across the Wabash River to Lawrenceville, Illinois. Gradually we learned the history of Vincennes, which boasted ancient Indian mounds, a monument to George Rogers Clark, and a "Trailblazer Train" to tour the historic section of town. It was also the boyhood home of Red Skelton. The city celebrated when Red returned for the dedication of the bridge across the Wabash, recently named for him.

That year, on July 16, 1969, the United States made history when Neil Armstrong and Edwin "Buzz" Aldrin walked on the moon, as Michael Collins orbited in the Command Module. Not owning a TV, we went to Don and Patty Marquez's house to watch the amazing event. (Recently I was inspired to read the story of Buzz Aldrin taking Communion on the moon on man's first-ever space walk. The moving story is told by Eric Metaxas in his book, *Everything You Always Wanted to Know About God [But Were Afraid to Ask]*, and in a *Guideposts* article. Metaxas talked with Aldrin and learned the story first hand.)

In September, Mother Friesen had an attack of what they said was flu. She was hospitalized October 15. As the weeks went by, she grew progressively weaker. The cancer, in remission a few short months, had returned. We kept in touch with letters and occasional phone calls. After we sent money to Mary Ann to buy flowers for her, Mary Ann called. "I got miniature pink roses for Mother and when I took them to her room, she was so happy, and said, 'I was just praying for them! Please tell them for me.'" How blest we were to have a praying mother and "Oma" for our children.

On December 6, Mary Ann called with the sad news that Mother had died. Earlier Mother told Jake on the phone, "You don't have to come home for my funeral. You were here for the reunion and you need your money. I'm glad I got to see you all in June."

Therefore, Jake did not go home and missed that time of closure with his family. Remembering Mom's death in December four years earlier, I ached for him. He said nothing, but went to work as usual. How I wished he would say something. I had to know what he was feeling.

One day I asked him, "How do you feel about your mother's death, Honey? You haven't talked about it. Don't you grieve for her?"

"I miss her presence," he admitted, "but we knew she wasn't well. Everyone has to die sometime."

We still had our mimeograph machine from Mississippi days and as Christmas approached, instead of the usual letter, I penned a poem, which Jake illustrated with simple drawings. We enjoyed positive feedback on our creation from family and friends.

303 Eastgate Drive,
Vincennes, Ind 47591
Christmas, 1969

In January of this year
(In case you didn't know)
We moved from Florida to Vincennes
In U-Haul, (car in tow).

At Vincennes University
Jake started teaching flight,
We found a lovely house to rent,
Things worked out quite all right.

VU's a junior college,
Three thousand students strong.
Vincennes is quite historical
We found out, before long.

There is a monument to Clark
(George Rogers, you recall),
And Lincoln crossed the Wabash here,
And that's not nearly all!

This year has been a good one,
We're glad that we are here.
Since Jake was free in summer,
We travelled far and near.

In June we took a great big jet
For two weeks in B.C.
How good it was for all of us,
Jake's family to see.

In August we drove to Pa.,
Camping on the way,
To visit with Jane's relatives,
But long we could not stay. ..

For we must get to Elkhart,
A wedding to attend,
Jane's college roommate, Nancy,
Few single days would spend.

How we enjoyed that week end
With friends from far and near!
And could it be? But, yes, it was
Nine years since we met here!

And now we're back in Fall's routine,
The cold winds often blow.
This week the children sure were thrilled
With five inches of snow

Altho we're far from Elkhart,
(Two-hundred fifty miles)
We've had our share of guests this year
Who always bring us smiles

(Jane's brother, Tom Herstine & sister,
Anna & John Smith & family, Chicago;
Mrs. S. F. Pannabecker, Elkhart; Nettie,
Helmut, & Roxy Bartel, formerly of
Bloomington, now Phila. Pa.; Nancy &
Peter Hilty, Cape Girardeau, Mo.; and
soon, we hope, Lucile & Gerhard Buhler,
Freeman, S.D., in V.S. at Cincinnati,O.)
(If you can make all that rhyme,
You're a lot better than I'm!)

The children like their home and friends,
They're very happy here,
And now when babysitters come
We seldom have a tear.

For Jared, we've high hopes some day,
When asked what he will be,
He said, "I'll be a pussy cat."
Which really tickled me!

He is a character indeed,
He will be three in May.
In one month Janet will be five,
She's busy all the day

With books and puzzles, dolls and toys,
Scissors, paint and glue,
And Jared doesn't miss a thing,
She tries to teach him, too.

It's time this silly rhyme should end,
But not until we say,
The news seems always bad these days,
Some bad news every day.

Good News for Modern Man is great,
The Bible now gone mod.
We're glad that Christmas brought good news
Of peace and love from God.

May this love fill your hearts and home
Is our wish now for you
And if you're ever near our house,
Come visit us, please do!

Love from all the Friesens,
Jane, Jake, Janet & Jared

MERRY   CHRISTMAS!

HAPPY   NEW   YEAR

For Christmas, Dad Friesen and Gerhard and Leucille Buhler, from our Mississippi days, arrived on Christmas Day. What a blessing they were! The Buhlers stayed two nights, but Dad was with us until January 2. He brought slides of Mother in the hospital and showed them to us one night. She looked shockingly thin, with great hollow cheeks and haunting eyes. Grief overcame me and I hurried to the bathroom to cry. Jake disliked emotion, so I hid my tears. I couldn't understand how anyone could look at her and be casual. I knew Dad grieved and missed her terribly. He had probably cried plenty already. My stomach hurt and my chest felt tight. But I knew I must pull myself together and go back to the family.

One night when Jake was flying late and the children were in bed, Dad and I sat and talked for several hours. I told about Daddy, his depression and shock treatments. I voiced concern about Jake's job, and about us not being in church work. I knew Dad's wish was to have Jake follow in his footsteps as a minister. Dad listened and then surprised me when he said, "It seems like you're afraid."

Was I? Yes, I feared being away from a safe Mennonite environment. I cringed at the ways of some of the men Jake rubbed shoulders with at work. I missed the Mennonite Church and chafed at the biblical illiteracy of people in our Sunday school class. They liked Jake and had genuine interest in the historic peace churches' teachings. Daddy's breakdown and Mother Friesen's death felt like "fires of adversity." My anxieties must have shown.

That night after Dad and I talked, he prayed with me and I felt somewhat better. I was grateful for his concern as a pastor and as my father-in-law.

While Dad was there we got an eight-inch snow, which the children loved playing in. On New Year's Eve afternoon, Dad declared, "We have to make New Year's cookies. Do you have raisins?" Jake went to get some. New Year's cookies are a tradition in Russian Mennonite homes. Dad could not envision New Year's Eve without them. I mixed up the yeast batter from a recipe in a Mennonite cookbook Leucille Buhler had given me, and Dad fried them. As he dropped the batter from a large spoon into the deep fat, they puffed up into plump raised cakes.

"Mom would say they're fried too hard," he said after the first batch. He turned down the burner a bit and continued. We rolled the cookies in sugar and enjoyed the treats. After that, New Year's cookies became part of our tradition.

In January 1970, I got my third devotional writing assignment. I enjoyed the challenge of this meaningful work. But I sorely missed having Jake doing church work. *How can he let go of his dream of us working together?* At times I felt mystified and grieved over my loss. But he was teaching a Sunday school class. Now, I wonder at my shortsightedness. However, I felt on the fringe—and aviation was not "the ministry!"

On January 21, I recorded in my little date book, "I began teaching Janet to read today." She was four years old on January 27. But I didn't keep on with the lessons. Janet was a busy little girl who still loved books, friends, and her brother Jared. In my teaching file I had a fat folder with patterns of hearts, shamrocks, pumpkins, something for every month of the year. Janet liked to trace, cut out and color the shapes.

By the end of January, the melting snow and rain had saturated the flat land around our house. One day when Janet flushed the toilet, water overflowed onto the carpet and kept on running. The problem persisted for weeks. Sometimes water ran into the hall, bedrooms, and out to the living room. Janet was terrified. Jake and another man worked on the problem and though at times it was better, there was no permanent solution as long as the ground was waterlogged. I grew sick of mopping up the wet carpet and Janet was afraid to use the toilet. We decided to move. But where?

On a lovely Saturday morning, Valentine's Day to be exact, Jake was happy to be home. "I'll stay with the children," he offered brightly, "and you go out and look for a house."

"By myself?"

"Sure," he encouraged. "You can have fun driving around and seeing what you can find." He actually trusted me to do it. What an assignment!

I started off, excited, but unsure. As I drove I prayed. "Please, help me, Father. You know just the right house for us. Please lead me to it." I felt God's presence and knew He heard me. I kept on praying. My excitement mounted as I got to the big city park on the main street into town. Across the street from the park, I felt led to turn left. Driving up a long gently sloping hill, I noticed nice homes lining both sides of the tree-lined street. They looked too fancy for us. At the top of the hill was a crossroad. Straight across and on the left hand corner, a "For Rent" sign caught my eye. I parked by the modest, older ranch-style house. The lot looked inviting with several huge trees in the yard. What a lovely place!

A sense of wonder filled me. *This is our house!* It sat diagonally on the corner lot with a big front yard. An awning at the front of the house shaded a semicircular cement patio. Close to the patio was a smaller tree, which, even without leaves, looked like a dogwood. I loved dogwood trees, plentiful in Pennsylvania. The house looked just right for us. It seemed the Lord was smiling on me, saying, "Here's your house!" I took down the phone number and drove home.

Jake was pleased to hear about the house; we all went to take a look, and Jake called to rent it.

On March 2, we moved to 1602 Audubon Drive. As a bird lover, I was delighted with the name. Friends kept the children that day and others helped us move. Soon a neighbor from the big brick house next door stopped in with a cake.

"I'm Phyllis Christopher," she smiled. "My husband Dick is District Superintendent for the United Methodist Church. We know your pastor, Ted and Eleanor," she said when I told her where we attended. I felt at home with such fine neighbors. Phyllis had three daughters, two of babysitting age. A few days later the friendly young woman from the house on the other side of us stopped in with a cake. We felt royally welcomed.

I organized the house and finished my devotionals in March. Vincennes was feeling more like home all the time. Our social life increased with visits with aviation faculty, church friends, and neighbors. With the coming of spring, we enjoyed the warm south Indiana weather. As I expected, the dogwood bloomed, along with daffodils and other flowers in our yard.

Our pastor, knowing of Jake's seminary degree, asked if Jake would fill in preaching at a small Presbyterian Church in town. Reluctantly, Jake agreed. Then he also substituted at a church in nearby Illinois. Jake was not excited about this but accepted the assignments. I called him my "flying preacher," glad that he could use his seminary training in this way. The pastor asked me to serve on the Evangelism Committee at church, and I taught the seventh grade Sunday school class a few Sundays.

In summer, Daddy came for a two-week visit. I was delighted. He and the children enjoyed many games together, and we took him sightseeing and on outings

Jake, me, Janet, 5, Jared, 3, 1970.

Ralph and Millie Loux, Brenda, 11,
Janet, 5, Jared, 3, 1970.

to parks. One Sunday we went to hear Jake preach at the church in Illinois.

Daddy liked to sit on the maple swivel rocker near the door into the kitchen. One day Jared came up behind him and affectionately put his arms around Daddy's neck. He lifted his feet off the floor and hung on. The chair tipped backwards and Daddy let out a yell. Disaster was averted as Jared let go and I came running. We were quite shook up, especially Daddy.

After Daddy left, Millie, Ralph and Brenda came for a week. I loved having family visit. They enjoyed the area and the ride on the Trailblazer Train. Though we had seen little of each other for years, we were very close in heart. As we parted, 11-year-old Brenda's tears revealed she too felt the strong family bond and the pain of separation. At times, I missed my family greatly.

Before Mother Friesen died, she anticipated Dad's needs and told him all she could think of to help prepare him for her death. She was unusually selfless and loving to the end. One day as she lay on her hospital bed, she told him, "When I am gone, you will be lonely. You should get married again. I think you should marry Jessie Isaac." Jessie was a widow in their church.

"Now you be quiet!" Dad said. "You've gone too far." However, eight months after she was gone, Dad *did* indeed marry Jessie Isaac, on August 23. He wrote to all the children beforehand asking what they thought of his intention. Though the idea was difficult for some to accept, they all gave their blessing.

Though I loved our pastor and his wife Eleanor, a clash was about to unfold that we could not foresee. Even before summer I sensed that our church was not a good fit. Jake strongly disagreed with the pastor's sermons supporting military solutions to conflicts between nations. Jake still taught about nonresistance in our Sunday school class as people asked questions. The pastor's career-age foster daughter, Sally, had joined our class. Her friendly outgoing personality added a younger fresh perspective to the class.

One Sunday morning Pastor Ted was strikingly out of character. His angry demeanor and vehement sermon astonished me. What an un-worshipful, unsettling sermon! Later in the foyer I met a soft-spoken woman from our class who immediately spoke her mind. "What was wrong with Pastor Ted today? He seemed like he was angry at someone."

The more I thought about the sermon, the more I felt the pastor was angry with *us*—at Jake for expounding on a "subversive doctrine" in his church. Then I remembered. The pastor's daughter! Jake's teaching was probably finding its way to the pastor's Sunday dinner table!

At home Jake and I discussed the sermon. "I believe he's angry at *us*," I said. "Probably Sally is going home and telling her parents what you say in class. I think he's trying to set you straight." Slowly the light dawned. Jake nodded.

"Maybe so," he conceded.

"I'd sure like to change churches," I offered. "I'd love to go to the United Church of Christ. Maybe we should leave if he's upset at us."

"Well, I'm not ready to do that just yet," Jake hedged. "I need to think about it."

From then on I did not look forward to Sunday morning. I disliked being in this predicament. A new pattern was developing between us. When Jake did not preach on Sundays, we often had heated "discussions" before church.

One Sunday morning five-year-old Janet cried at the breakfast table demanding, "Why do you two always have to argue every Sunday morning before church?" I was stunned—and contrite. I knew it was true. While Jake taught about peacemaking, we had lost the peace of Christ in our home and our church.

"We're not *arguing*," I told her, "we're just *discussing*." But guilt pricked my conscience.

Fall had come and the trees, turning shades of red, orange, and yellow, beckoned us outside. That afternoon we went for a drive through the lovely countryside. Janet's unsettling question of the morning haunted me.

"Don't you think it's time to look for another church," I asked, "if we're going to argue about church every Sunday morning?"

Jake was ready with a solution. "From now on, you can take the children and go to United Church of Christ. I'll teach our class to finish out the quarter and join you after class for worship at UCC. How does that sound?"

"That sounds great!" I said, relieved.

But I had a dilemma—my friendship with dear Eleanor. I didn't want to lose that. Her sunshiny nature soothed my aching spirit during a rough adjustment. How would I tell her we were leaving their church? Yet I knew I must.

Pondering our predicament, my mind wandered back to Mississippi days. There our enemy was the sin of racism. We never expected to meet another enemy here—civil religion and militarism, diametrically opposed, we believed, to the teachings of Jesus. The historic peace churches taught that as followers of the Prince of Peace, we must obey Jesus' command to "love your enemies," not fight them in war. Jesus said, "My kingdom is not of this world, hence would my servants fight." Mennonites, Quakers, and Church of the Brethren took Jesus' words literally. Jake's mind was clear about this. He would not change. From the sound of Rev. B.'s sermon, he was equally firm in his position. We would simply withdraw rather than confront.

For 400 years, Anabaptist Mennonites refused to participate in war, in Switzerland and later in all countries where Mennonites lived. As time went on, some young men chose to serve in the armed services, but the official stand of the church was non-participation. We knew the history of conscientious objectors (COs) and the great contribution they made in our country and Europe during and after World War II. Jake's brother Peter served as a medic in Germany and my cousin Charlie Mohr worked in a mental hospital in Pennsylvania. Hundreds of COs learned first hand of the appalling conditions and abusive treatment of mental patients in the United States. After the war, Mennonite mental hospitals were built where humane and compassionate treatment of patients prevailed. The example of the peace churches eventually revolutionized mental health care in the country. The contribution of COs was lauded in books, reports, and documentaries. But we felt at a loss to help Rev. B. understand.

Not wanting to put off the inevitable, on Monday morning I called Eleanor, explained the situation, and told her our decision. The hurt in her voice hit me as she countered, "I thought we had something going between us."

"I thought so, too," I told her. "I'm really sorry, but Ted and Jake's theology are just not compatible." I also told her of Janet's words to us at the table. "But I still want to be friends."

"And I want that too," she agreed.

Later that week she told me on the phone, "Ted didn't sleep for three nights after I told him you were leaving." I groaned inwardly and wondered if we did the right thing.

To my apology, Eleanor replied, "I feel loyal to my husband." She would not explain for him.

Sleep eluded me that night. I tossed and turned and wondered what to do. In my distress, I cried out to God for Ted and Eleanor, and for wisdom and help. Finally I got up and wrote Eleanor and Ted a letter. I expressed sorrow for hurting them and the hope that somehow our grief might be redemptive. Then I slept.

"You didn't have to write that letter," Eleanor told me when we next got together.

"I *had* to for my own peace of mind," I assured her. They were such good people and we didn't mean to hurt them. They believed as they were taught all their lives.

Two weeks later when Eleanor came for a visit, she commented, "Mennonites are too idealistic. We can't live the way Jesus taught in everything. That's for when we get to heaven." She referred to the Sermon on the Mount, which Mennonites take seriously. I didn't agree but let her have her say. We agreed to meet once a week and she always came to my home. Janet was in kindergarten at the time and Jared was three. Eleanor's four sons were in high school or junior high.

A few weeks later I invited Ted and Eleanor for supper. Jake had agreed to it. I was happy they accepted. Compassion for Pastor Ted overcame my anxiety at seeing him again.

That day, a pastoral call detained Ted, so Eleanor came alone. Waiting for him added to the suspense. When he finally arrived, we exchanged warm greetings all around and enjoyed good fellowship over borscht as though nothing had happened between us. We stayed off the subjects of theology and church issues and had a friendly, enjoyable evening.

My wounds began to heal and I hoped the same was true for them.

Later, Eleanor started a weekly prayer meeting at her church. She invited me and I accepted.

Months later, we received a surprising invitation. Eleanor said, "Ted told me 'I wish Jane and Jake would come to church this Sunday. I'm going to preach on peacemakers.' He'd really appreciate it if you would come."

I was delighted! Had Ted changed? I could hardly wait to tell Jake. He was pleased and had no problem going back to their church for a Sunday.

We listened with glad hearts as Ted preached on the text, "Blessed are the peacemakers."

"A couple of weeks ago," he began, "I was teaching the junior highs the Beatitudes from Jesus' Sermon on the Mount in Matthew 5:3-12. As I read, 'Blessed are the peacemakers, for they shall be called the children of God,' suddenly it was like a light bulb went on in my mind and I saw what I had never seen before. I saw clearly that Jesus is calling *all* his disciples—believers—to be peacemakers. War is not Jesus' way. Jesus is the Prince of Peace. His whole life was the way of peace and reconciliation—reconciling the world to God and believers to each other. He never acted with violence toward anyone. He submitted to the will of His Father, and to the hands of evil men. He really meant what He said about turning the other cheek. And on the cross Jesus prayed, 'Father, forgive them, for they know not what they do.'"

Ted was a changed man. Jake and I felt understood now. His sermon was a gift to us—an olive branch of peace. Jake and I felt humbled and grateful to be part of his "conversion" to Jesus' way of peace.

Janet's tearful question set in motion a chain of unexpected events. I believed that Jake and I were guided by the Spirit, and the verse came to mind from Isaiah, "and a little child shall lead them" (Isa. 11:6). The stress with our friends was replaced by peace, and Eleanor and I continued to meet.

I did not foresee that another move was on the horizon.

CHAPTER 22

Fires of Affliction

Though he slay me, yet will I trust him.

JOB 13:15 (KJV)

1970–1971

We loved our hilltop home, located about a quarter mile from Janet's kindergarten. In nice weather she walked down the hill and back with a friend, Beth Ann. Beth Ann's mother and I enjoyed visits over coffee. Jared had a playmate in her younger son, Timmy. God had led us to a pleasant neighborhood.

That first spring brought lush green grass and the great trees leafed out like a protective canopy around our home. Jonquils, daffodils and the blooming dogwood cheered me. Springtime and Easter heralded a new start. The children and I made Easter hat cookies, gave some to a reclusive neighbor, and took the rest along to Anna and John's in Chicago for a lovely Easter weekend. (Easter hat cookies consist of a sugar cookie with marshmallow dipped in hot milk, then in tinted coconut except for the bottom, put on cookie, decorate with icing, flowers—a pretty sight.) Anna and John's family had grown and Janet and Jared had fun with their cousins, John,

Daddy, Tom, 13, John, 5, and James, 3, Chicago, c. 1968.

James and Amy. We also were glad for time with brother Tom. Daddy and Tom had taken a bus to Chicago after Mom died and Anna and John had a great picture of the two of them with little John and James.

I loved our new church and felt more at home there, even though I didn't know a soul. Pastor Ritter's biblical sermons encouraged and blessed me and the children were happy in the nursery.

One Sunday morning, an attractive young woman with blond hair greeted me warmly in the hall. "Are you new here?" she asked.

"Yes," I smiled back. "We went to another church and my husband is still teaching a Sunday school class there. We didn't seem to fit in." I told her my name and the church name.

"I'm Sara Van Meter," she said. "We went there too for a while. But we're happier at U.C.C. We need to get together."

I warmed to the caring concern in Sara's expression and intense blue eyes. Her genuine, easygoing personality endeared her to me. We became friends and soon our families got together as well. Larry managed the Social Security office in town and enjoyed Jake. Sara was a stay-at-home mom with three children, Laura, Chris and Sally, Jared's age. Sara had a car to get around, but we had only our VW. In the spring of 1971, Jake bought an old Chevy van and fixed it up for camping and for work, leaving the '64 VW for me. With my new freedom I could shop and visit friends like Sara.

That spring, Jake learned about the university's building program and told me, "Students are building a small development of homes about six miles out near the village of Fritchton. I'd like to rent one of the homes. Let's drive out and take a look."

Move again? I was amazed. What kind of man was this that God had given me who could move at the drop of a hat? We found two completed homes and two more under construction on a little knoll.

"We can rent this one," Jake said, driving up to a blue frame house. "It's almost finished." It was beautiful, with a two-car garage (we had none on Audubon), big picture windows in the dining room and an eight-foot sliding glass door in the living room. I was still puzzled.

"Why do you want to move again when we just moved a year ago?"

"I need a house more in line with my station in life," Jake said simply. "Our kitchen and bathroom are so old, and there's no garage. It needs a lot of work."

Having grown up in a house lacking plumbing amenities entirely, I was happy when they existed at all. But a brand new house and living in the country sounded great. With Jake's position at the university and airport, I could see his self-image changing. I recalled his words to me when we were dirt poor before we were married, "I'm glad you won't want a big fancy house." Now it was he who wanted a spanking new one. Still, it was a modest rental. Jake put our name in for the house, which was ready the end of May 1971.

We moved for the tenth time (ninth for Janet) the weekend before Janet finished kindergarten. Joe, the building instructor, lived in another new house. Since he drove into town every day to work, Jake asked if he would take Janet along and drop her off for her last two days of school. He was happy to do so and Janet thought it was a lark.

Our gorgeous house had blue shag rug throughout, beautiful kitchen, three bedrooms and two baths. What luxury! It was a dream come true, with my favorite color, blue, inside and out. I thanked God for this blessing. Jake's schedule kept him busy at work but I enjoyed unpacking and settling in. Friends came to visit and see the house. Our circle of acquaintances had grown with aviation and church friends, and former neighbors from two locations. Everyone loved our new home, including our children.

About three weeks after the move, a phone call altered my peace and contentment. A woman's pleasant voice chided, "You moved! I've had such a hard time finding you! I'm from Famous Writer's School. We received your aptitude test and I'd like to talk with you about it. How can I find your house?" She was *here*—in the state! My mind reeled.

In mid-April I had filled in their aptitude test after seeing an ad in a magazine, never expecting a visit from the school in Connecticut. My heart fluttered. Warning bells went off. Dread and excitement filled my mind. What was I getting into? Jake had warned me about salespeople ever since one sold me a deluxe high chair/stroller/table and chair for Janet years ago in Akron, a wonderful purchase.

However, forgetting his admonitions, I gave directions and soon that exuberant woman was here, exclaiming profusely about our lovely house and the filmy blue curtain I was sewing for the kitchen window. As we sat at my dining room table, she jumped into her sales pitch. I listened, positively enthralled, and my excitement grew. Yet I knew I should beware.

Finally, she revealed the cost—$500—astronomical! Money was tight. We were still paying off Mary Ann for Jake's aviation school in Florida. What should I do? She wanted a decision—now!

I sent up a prayer for help. If Jake could pay $4000 for six months of aviation school, I reasoned, surely I could pay $500 for a writing course. But what would he say? Since I had no income of my own, this required *only* Jake's signature. My instincts told me he would not like it. However, this persistent woman, seeing my interest and wanting to clinch a sale, encouraged me to call him. Would he be at the airport? Could I dare to ask him to come home?

I dialed. Miraculously, he was there and not busy—my first open door. I explained to him.

"That's a lot of money," he responded, disapproval dripping from his words. I should have given up, but I couldn't. As we talked, my desire grew. I really wanted this!

"Please, can you come home and talk with her? Please? I'm really interested." Though it was the middle of the afternoon, he agreed to come. Bless his heart! I prayed, and hoped for the best.

Jake's manner was guarded as he listened. This vivacious woman overflowed with warmth and confidence, countering any objections. Jake did not warm to her, but finally he signed—against his will. We would pay the course with monthly installments. Somehow it didn't seem fair—two women against one man. But I had just enrolled in a creative writing course!

I knew I'd hear about it after the woman left, but I wasn't prepared. Jake was more than upset. "What were you thinking? Five hundred dollars! How can you be a writer when you don't read widely?"

I was devastated. But what could I say? I didn't have a comeback. The deed was done. To make matters worse, the school name was "Famous Writer's School!" Who was I to think I could become a "famous writer"? After such a discouraging remark, the whole thing looked ridiculous. I felt embarrassed and ashamed. But I had made my choice and would live with it. I cried out to the Lord in my distress, and God comforted me and reminded me of many affirming words I had heard about my writing through the years. I would trust God and go ahead. Seeing this as an opportunity to practice forgiveness, I could only hope that some day I would make Jake proud.

I knew I didn't read widely enough. Once Jake had asked me at seminary, "Do you only read things you agree with?" I worked on being more open-minded. When we lived in Akron, he took a night class at a seminary in

Lancaster in which he had to read books I considered – well, off-color. It was a course to understand people "of the world" in our culture. I tried reading one of his books but was repulsed. However, the class proved to be excellent background for Jake's job with Mississippi blacks. I felt naïve. My strong *"Come out from among them and be ye separate"* theology clashed with Jake's worldview.

Two days after signing up for the writing course, a letter came from Dean S. F. Pannabecker at the seminary asking me if I would accept the position of seminary alumni president. This pleasant surprise and affirmation boosted my self-esteem. I felt unworthy, but somewhat vindicated. I sensed God was smiling on me, blessing me to comfort my wounded spirit. But what would this require of me?

Excited, I called Dr. Pannabecker. "If I accept, will I have to travel to the seminary for meetings?"

"No," he reassured, "you can write and send out the newsletters and other business in the mail." He encouraged me warmly. I loved dear grand-fatherly Dr. Pannabecker, my former missions prof! God trusted me with this responsibility and honor. Jake and I talked it over and he approved. I called the seminary to accept. From 250 miles away, I felt connected to our alma mater again.

Before long I received four writing course textbooks in the mail plus a list of assignments. I felt ambivalent – excitement tempered with insecurity. Once I began reading the lessons, written by famous writers about how they learned to write, my enthusiasm returned. Here was inspiration and stimulation. And here were assignments to work on. I didn't care whether or not I became famous. I would write for the Lord, to bring glory to God's name. That would be my motive. I would write for the sheer joy of it! But I dearly hoped I could earn something to help repay my debt.

Over the next several years I wrote stories and articles and my first grades were Bs. Through helpful critiquing, I learned I was too wordy. One instructor wrote, "condense, condense, condense" in the margins of an assignment. I learned that *anyone* can become a writer – "write about what you know best – your own experiences." Commendation from graders – "famous writers" – kept me going.

One day, when I received my lesson in the mail, I found a sheet on which each instructor had typed my grade and their comments for the lesson they critiqued. As I read, I thought it must have been sent by mistake. My amazement grew as I drank in the glowing words of praise liberally sprinkled in with criticisms: "She writes well and with imagination."

"She works these ideas into clever little stories, the characterization of teacher and doctor comes through sharply—shows signs of able fiction styling."

"An ear for dialogue."

"Her usual fine work on four story situations. Has a sound story sense and knows what she's about."

"The Peace Offering is a superbly written account of what I take to be a true incident. (This was the story of Mamie in Mississippi who wanted to shoot Jake.) It is simply, clearly, and excitingly narrated from beginning to end—strong prose, appealing narrative style. *Mrs. F. is a writer!*" I fairly burst with joy.

I thanked the Lord for giving me the gift of writing. But what could I do with it? How could I earn doing this? I wanted to please Jake. I shared the page of comments with him. He said little or nothing. He needed to see published works—and a check. This would take time.

Before we left Vincennes I had several poems and an article published in *The Mennonite.* In years to come Jake found ways to encourage me. In 1987, he surprised me with a computer for Christmas! The key to it was in my stocking. Jared had made me a card on the computer, which read, "Have Fun Writing Books On Your Computer!" (This I framed.) Some years later, when I was offered a job as a secretary for the umpteenth time, I told Jake, "I don't want to be a secretary anymore."

His response delighted me. "You don't *have* to be a secretary anymore. *You're a writer!*" Others had appreciated and affirmed my work all along, but Jake's words were the sweetest of all.

One day, years later, Jake suggested that I keep all my published works in a notebook, which I did. I knew I would never become rich writing for Mennonite periodicals. But 30 years later I had earned about $975 from articles, stories, and poems—amazing and satisfying to me. The reward was in the writing and the joy my articles brought to people whose stories I wrote.

Now back to Vincennes. Secure in our neighborhood, Jake and I were busy one Saturday while the children played outside with their friends, Laura and Jay. Unaware of trouble brewing, we were surprised Monday morning when our neighbor, Joe, the building instructor, came to our door, visibly agitated.

"Do you know that your children wrote with magic markers on the siding of the house across the street?" he asked. "That wood exterior is the permanent siding. Now we'll have to tear it off and replace it. The students worked hard on this and they are very upset about doing it over."

I felt terrible. "How do you know who did it?" I asked.

"Janet and Laura wrote their names on the boards!" he replied dryly. Jake went with him to see the damage. We scolded the children soundly and then I took Janet, six, and Jared, four, over to Joe to apologize. Janet considered Joe her friend since she had enjoyed riding to school with him. She hated to face him after her misdeed, but he kindly accepted their apologies. In this case, we felt an apology was enough punishment.

As time went on in the blue house, I sometimes felt empty and disillusioned. Jake was flying more and more, taking occasional charter or business flights evenings and weekends. I also missed Mennonite fellowship. I had heard of a conservative church about 35 miles away. As our tenth wedding anniversary approached, September 3, 1971, I told Jake I'd like to look up that church on our anniversary. He didn't mind. I learned the location from a woman on the parking lot of a store who appeared to be Mennonite but said she was from a Holiness Church but knew where the church was—at Washington on the main highway about 35 miles east of us.

After dinner at a restaurant in Washington, we found the church. When we stopped to get the time of the morning service, the pastor came to greet us.

"I'm Tobe Slabaugh," he said with beaming face and wide grin, after we introduced ourselves. "We live right here next to the church. Come and join us for worship tomorrow and then have dinner with us." He took us over to meet his wife, Ada, a friendly, motherly woman wearing a sheer white prayer covering.

Jake and I played a game of miniature golf and my heart sang that we had found the church. No matter that it was conservative. We felt genuinely accepted by this older couple and by the people on Sunday morning. The beautiful four-part singing without instruments was reminiscent of what I'd heard in Old Mennonite churches in Pennsylvania and it lifted my spirit. Tobe's challenging biblical message blessed us. The sea of prayer coverings made me feel strangely at home, though also out of place. We had told Tobe and Ada we were General Conference Mennonites and they understood. I had never worn a prayer covering and didn't expect to start now.

Ada had a wonderful dinner for us and we enjoyed their warm fellowship. Tobe said he had only an eighth grade education and was chosen by lot years ago to be a minister. A few Sundays later, Jake said to me, "Tobe does his homework. He preaches better sermons than many ministers with a Ph.D." It was true and I was grateful for this church. Every Sunday we got invitations for dinner. We accepted unless Jake had to fly in the afternoon. When this happened, I struggled with the infringement of his job on our family time – and church fellowship time.

The end of October Jake called Hesston College in Kansas to ask about their flight program and had a long talk with the president. I was encouraged. It would be great to move back to a Mennonite community. My friend Lois Leinbach, Jake's secretary from MCC days in Akron, wrote in her Christmas letter one year, "Why don't you move to Hesston? Did you know they started a flight program at the college?" *What? A Mennonite college training pilots?* With that good news I felt more comfortable with Jake in aviation and hoped for a change. Every year Lois repeated the invitation. Then they came to visit us at the blue house. We talked about a move but the time wasn't right. Was Jake's phone call a first step?

As time went on at the blue house and Jake got busier with work and evening or weekend trips, I felt left out of his life and more upset and resentful. If I questioned his schedule, he became defensive. Disagreements and stress characterized our life together. Somehow our love language had become tangled up in our Dutch-German-Russian-Canadian Mennonite and Eastern Pennsylvanian Swiss-Dutch-German-Welsh backgrounds. Before long, inexplicable, unimaginable pain held us in bondage. Our garbled miscommunication grew out of increasing frustration, anger, and bitterness.

One day, after the worst argument of our marriage, I took stock of my life. Here we were in this beautiful house with Jake's somewhat prestigious position. He didn't make much money, though it was adequate. I was jealous of his time on the job at his "pinnacle of success." But we had lost the most important things – love and peace. My sister Grace's marriage had grown cold and troubled and later ended in divorce. This, plus news of college classmates' divorces caused me to fear, *Will our marriage end in divorce, too?* I certainly didn't want that.

My deep distress with our marriage disturbed my sleep as well as my days. One morning I awoke from a shocking dream: Jake had replaced our VW with a used Mercedes and I dreamed I was driving the Mercedes alone, diagonally across fields, headed "home" to Pennsylvania!

In my pain, I reflected on the life we'd had together, our strong love in the beginning and Jake's Dad's words to us in person as well as in many letters, "We pray for all the children and grandchildren every night." God had brought us together and God would have to work it out. I recalled the words of Job, "Though he slay me, yet will I trust Him." Family and friends loved us and cared about us.

One day in fall, soon after our argument, I looked out of the dining room picture window at the vacant field across from our house. The sight of a sea of tall dead weeds brought to mind the Garden of Eden after sin entered. The ugly, dry grass was a stark reminder of sin that entered the human race with our first parents. I felt as though I were back there in that beautiful lush Garden, cast out into a harsh and hostile, dry and barren land, out of touch with God's presence and loving fellowship. I was grieved to the depths. I cried and mourned. I saw that Jake and I were like a picture of Adam and Eve. The thought broke my heart.

A devotional I read recently helped make sense of this hard time in our marriage. It says, "...our relationships bear the bruises of not just human misunderstanding, but outright demonic attack, and in our sin, driven by pride and fear, still our faith in Christ will not fail. Jesus understands the nature of our condition and the ferocity of the contest." As in His words to Peter about "Satan has asked for you that he may sift you as wheat," Jesus says to us, "I have prayed for you." What comforting words! (Jack Hayford, *Living the Spirit-Filled Life.* [Nashville: Thomas Nelson], 2002. September 1, on Luke 22:31,32.)

During the years at the blue house, I began writing in my journal almost every night, often at 3:00 A.M. I'd awake with mind alert, insights pouring into my mind, and I'd jump out of bed. This started after the writing course saleswoman told me, "Buy a notebook. When you get an idea, jot it down. The mind is a tricky thing. If you don't write it down, you'll forget it." I took this to heart, not wanting to forget a thing. My journal became a friend, a source of comfort in which I poured out my pain to God and wrote my prayers. When the "fires of affliction" felt hot, I had to tell someone. God was my refuge and strength in the wee hours of the morning. I loved these times alone with God while the family slept. (For more than 38 years I journaled over 90 large notebooks full, and many smaller ones, of God's amazing ways and work in my life.)

One day I heard in a radio message the prayer, "Shepherd, show me how to go." I loved it and made it a regular, heartfelt prayer and it blessed me.

Music blessed me too. One day a Word Records Club ad caught my attention; Jake agreed we could join. As I ordered an occasional record, some of the most wonderfully inspiring and exalting praise music flowed into our home many hours of the day. The children loved the songs, too. I wanted positive spiritual influences for my children to feed on. I recalled that Jake told me that he was attracted to me at seminary because I was "gay and joyful." Now I was too often sad and worried. The praise music lifted my spirits.

One day, during this hard time, I put on Anita Bryant's beautiful song, "Lord, to my heart bring back the springtime, and may I warm and tender be again." As I worked in the laundry room next to the kitchen, the words of that prayer pierced my spirit and I cried my eyes out. The children played happily in the living room as I wrestled with God in my heart. "Oh, God, help me be the person You want me to be. Heal our marriage and give us YOUR love." How I wanted a warm and close relationship with Jake. I longed for the springtime of love and joy and peace. I felt guilty, inadequate, and weak—a failure as a wife. "Out of the depths I cried to the Lord, and He delivered me from all my fears."

One afternoon Jake came home from work and announced, "Today I went to see the pastor at the Methodist church. He said we could come for counseling. First we'll go separately and later, together. I had a session with him today, so you can call and make an appointment."

Feeling uneasy, my first reaction was, "He's divorced."

"Oh, you would have a hang-up about that," he retorted.

Yes, that was one of my big problems. I had too many hang-ups from my conservative, evangelical, Mennonite background. But it's who I was! However, God was working on me, leading me out into the world of other denominations. *Oh, God, help!*

My dear friend Eleanor and I still got together. The next time we met I talked with her about this pastor. She knew him and encouraged, "Maybe he would be more understanding since he's been through it." That made sense. I called and made an appointment. He told me that he did not want the divorce. He suspected his wife was cheating on him and had an investigator follow her, which confirmed his suspicions. As time went on I felt comfortable opening up to him.

Jake went once more, and then quit. Though disappointed, I continued with the pastor for more than a year and found it helpful. This was one answer to my prayer for help for our marriage. I knew that God had led Jake to this compassionate counselor. He saw that I had grown up with a repressive stepmother. One day he took the book, *Dibs in Search of Self* (by Virginia M. Axline), off his shelf and suggested, "I think you'll find this book helpful. It's about a boy who could not talk at all until he was about nine years old." Well, I talked much more than this boy, but the book proved to be helpful. I was grateful for the pastor's caring, sensitive counsel.

Jake kept in touch with Hesston College and for Thanksgiving that year he flew us in a university plane to Hesston where he served as consultant to their fledgling flight department. We stayed with our friends, Lois and Gerald, and we all enjoyed this wonderful break. On the return flight, Janet sat in front with Jake, Jared and I in back. Soon after takeoff, five-year-old Jared looked at me and said, "I love you, Mama." Then, "I want to sit on your lap." Soon he was fast asleep. This contented child in my arms seemed to mirror my feelings after being in Kansas these few days. Jake enjoyed meeting the president and dean of the college and working with Dave Forrer, head of the aviation department. Jake appeared more happy and relaxed than I had seen him in a long time. A feeling of peace engulfed me, and gratitude that Jake was committed to his marriage and family, despite the ups and downs. A sense of confidence and trust that God was answering prayer gave me hope.

That Christmas, Janet, in second grade, was "Snow Queen" in the program at school and sang a solo, as she had the year before. Her beautiful smiling face, along with three other children, appeared in the *Vincennes Sun Commercial*. She did well in school and her teacher told me, "Your Janet is a doll. I wish I had a whole roomful like her. But she's a worrier. She wants to get everything perfect." *Like her mom*, I thought. Janet was a sweet girl, sensitive and conscientious. I was proud of her, but also concerned about her perfectionism and wondered if that was part of my problem, too.

The years in Vincennes brought many changes and difficult challenges in my life. Maybe if we moved to Hesston, things would be better. Would Hesston be our next move? Or did God have more lessons for me right where we were?

Lament to My Stepmother

My mind is full of bellowing and ranting,
From morn till night it rattles in my brain.
How can I free myself from this loud clanging?
Not go insane?

This self-condemning grows from out its roots
In distant childhood steadfastly ingrained.
It contradicts the natural bent of growing,
And freedom kills.

"You'll think about it when I'm gone." How true.
And could I e'er forget what I have been?
You've bound it as a chain about my neck.
And it must break.

The past is over now and all forgiven.
The childish paths we both have traveled o'er.
In calm and stillness now you lie forever.
And I go on.

CHAPTER 23

Beauty for Ashes

To give them beauty for ashes, the oil of joy for mourning,
the garment of praise for the spirit of heaviness, that they may be
called trees of righteousness, the planting of the Lord,
that He may be glorified.
ISAIAH 61:3 (NKJ)

1972–1973

It was 1972. For the past seven years since Mom died, feelings of guilt over my relationship with her haunted me. She had chewed her fingernails and talked about her bad nerves. When I married Jake, he refused to let me use the word "nervous," though I rarely ever had. I knew that Christ helped me live above these influences. Yet sometimes I felt I was too much like this woman I never wanted to be like. Her words, "You'll think about it someday when I'm gone" and her sobs before we left for Mississippi came back to me. As someone has said, "A mother is a powerful figure, even after she is dead." That was true in a positive way of my biological mother, and mostly in a negative way of Mom.

For some time I had a growing desire for someone to pray for me about my relationship with Mom and felt it should be a woman. When Eleanor invited me to the Tuesday morning prayer meetings she told me about Jean, a new woman at their church who came to the meetings.

"Jean has a very dynamic faith," Eleanor said. "I called on her last November after her husband died of cancer. She was so serene and confident that I was amazed. I'm not sure I could take my husband's death like she did. I think you'd like to know her."

I was curious and eager to meet Jean. Eleanor agreed I could invite Sara, too. At the meeting, we gave prayer requests, had sharing and prayer time, and took the requests home. Eleanor prayed and maybe one or two others. Jean said little at the meetings and I didn't notice anything unusual about

255

her. Eleanor agreed to pray with me about Mom but each time we set a date, something interfered so I put it off.

In the weeks following, opportunities for service kept popping up, amazing me. I received a letter from Dean Pannabecker about a Seminar on Evangelism to be held at the seminary during interterm in January 1972. Contrary to his assurance that I would not need to travel to Elkhart for the alumni association, he asked if I could come and preside at the alumni banquet. This sounded exciting because of my interest in evangelism. But Elkhart was 250 miles north. And mostly male professors and pastors would be there. I felt out of the loop, out of touch with academia. And, I wondered, who would take care of the children?

Dr. Ramseyer, for whom I had worked my four years at college, was now interim president of the seminary. As I tried to decide, he phoned one day, strongly urging me to come. I was amazed, honored by his personal invitation, but could not decide.

Jake and I talked it over. "I think you should go," he said. "I'll take care of the children and you can go by bus." And so it was decided.

Grateful for the Tuesday morning prayer group, I told them about the trip and made my request. "Please pray for me and for the Seminar on Evangelism. I'm feeling scared about presiding at the alumni meeting and need your prayers."

Though I hated leaving the children, I trusted Jake to look after them. I took the bus to Indianapolis and went into the terminal for the short layover. When I returned to the bus to re-board, I found the men waiting in line for the women to board first. This seemed unusual. Near the door was a chivalrous young man who, by his example, had stopped the other men in their tracks. Then I noticed he was holding – of all things – a red-leather-covered Bible. I couldn't miss it. And I had my old King James Bible with me.

"You have your Bible with you!" I blurted.

"Yes."

"I do too," I was surprised to hear myself saying.

I took a seat and soon the young man with his Bible came to me and asked, "May I sit with you? We can have fellowship in the Word."

"Yes," I smiled, motioning for him to sit down.

Thus began two hours of incredible conversation.

After a brief introduction, he shared his testimony. "I was saved a couple of years ago from a life on drugs – LSD. When I received Christ I was baptized in the Holy Spirit, with the gift of tongues, all at once."

On hearing his startling revelation, I asked, "Were you delivered from the drug addiction too?"

"Yes, but I still have flashbacks at times." Then, sensing my concern, he continued, "If I had one on the bus, I would grab the rail (he demonstrated) and soon it would pass."

Having read articles about the Jesus People Movement spreading across the country, I was intrigued with these youth who were turning to Christ, hundreds of them getting baptized in the Pacific Ocean. I wished I could meet some, and here was one sitting beside me. He introduced himself as Jerry Mitchell.

Then I shared about my life, where I was going, and my fear of presiding at the alumni meeting at seminary with all the men. His compassion disarmed me and I felt free with him. As I shared other struggles in my life, suddenly he exclaimed, *"Now I know why I was supposed to take the bus today! I was supposed to meet you on this bus!"*

"What do you mean?"

"I was visiting my girlfriend in southern Indiana – her dad is a Pentecostal minister. He's the one who prayed for me when I was saved. He told me that I could use their car to go home (to northern Indiana). But I always pray about everything. So I asked the Lord, *'Shall I take the car or the bus?'* And the Lord said, *'Take the bus.'* I couldn't understand why He wanted me to take the bus when I had a car available. Now I know!"

I was stunned. God spoke to him directly because He wanted Jerry to meet me! This was incredible. Jerry's obedience and commitment to God's will in every detail amazed me. He spoke encouraging words of faith to me but also of his concerns. "I plan to go to college or Bible school but I'm a bit worried because I totally goofed off in high school. I want to prepare for whatever God wants me to do." I got his address and assured him I would write to him and pray for him.

At the next stop, he offered to buy my coffee and I declined. He admonished me kindly but firmly, "Never refuse a man who wants to buy you coffee!" He spoke with the maturity and authority of a father. This young man was a prince! He paid for my coffee.

Later we said our farewells and Jerry got off at his stop. Soon I realized: I had no more fear! It was completely gone, replaced with a deep peace. I felt free! I rode the last miles to Elkhart rejoicing and praising God in my spirit. I knew God was riding that bus with me, and God would be with me throughout the week.

And what a week it was! As I expected, the room was full of mostly men – pastors, students, and professors – but I was not afraid. In the opening introductions, I was asked to bring greetings as president of the Elkhart seminary alumni (Goshen seminary people were also present). In my remarks, I voiced my disappointment at the few women in the group and expressed hope that more women would attend seminary. I encouraged the men to think of bringing their wives to the meetings.

The speaker was professor John Howard Yoder – Mennonite theologian and writer, well known and respected throughout the theological world for his book, *The Politics of Jesus*.

During those incredible days I surprised myself by speaking up during discussion time. I took few notes, but at one point Dr. Yoder said something that seemed to limit God in drawing people to Christ. I knew the verses about God saving "to the uttermost all who come to God through Him (Christ)" (Hebrews 7:25), and Jesus' words, "The one who comes to me I will in no wise cast out" (John 6:37). So people can accept Christ at *any* age.

My sister Ruth's recent conversion came to mind. I told how she called me two months ago (on December 6) to tell me, "I was saved yesterday! I walked down the aisle at Faith Baptist Church at Sellersville in the morning." She was 30 years old and I was thrilled. I recorded in my journal that "my response got cheers from the men." I questioned Yoder several times and, as I recall, more than once a murmur of agreement rose from the men around the room. I was amazed that I could voice my opinion and differ with Yoder in this setting.

At coffee break, Ernst Harder – former seminary president from Montevideo, Uruguay (from 1958-1975, I learned from his daughter Margie), whom I had often read about in *The Mennonite* – came to me and extended his hand. Smiling warmly, he said, "I'd like to tell you how much I admire you."

In my journal I wrote after his words, "His eyes spoke the same message and I was amazed and touched. God was in that moment." (Years later I learned that Ernst's father, Bishop A. A. Harder baptized Jake at age 17 at United Mennonite Church, Black Creek, Vancouver Island, May 31, 1953.)

As if that weren't enough, Dr. Yoder shook my hand and said, "I want to thank you for helping us out this morning." I told him about our experience with the pastor at Vincennes and his change to pacifism. Jake had professor Yoder for a class while in seminary and sometimes quoted him to me. But I didn't always agree—in fact, at times I strongly *disagreed*! (Or was it that Jake and I disagreed about *peace* when we didn't feel it in our home?) Here I had been able to speak my mind, and he *thanked me*! It was good to meet Dr. Yoder as a fellow human being and take him off the pedestal in my mind.

Though our two seminaries had merged, there were separate alumni dinners. Our banquet was an informal group of about 15 to 20 at one table. Dr. Ramseyer was there, all smiles. I began by telling the group, "Before coming to the seminar I told my sister (Millie) in Pennsylvania, 'I don't know how I got the ability to be president of the alumni association. I guess I got it by osmosis from Dr. Ramseyer while I worked for him those four years.'" He beamed and chuckled.

During that week, I had a meaningful stay with Ada and Harry Spaeth, friends from Quakertown and seminary days. Ada and I had heart-to-heart talks, and Harry took me to the seminar. On one ride I shared my struggles from Vincennes and said, "Sometimes I've wished I could die." His response brought me up short, "Do you think you're the only one who feels that way?" This nugget, which altered my perspective, proved useful with a child years later.

I took the bus to Indianapolis where Jake met me with the car. The children were quiet and their eyes showed they were sick. I felt guilty for leaving them. Jake left them at a friend's at times and they caught colds. The highway was packed with snow and ice and, despite my objections Jake drove much faster than I was comfortable with. I prayed fervently in my heart for protection all the way home. When we turned into our street, the car slid on the sheet of ice, refusing to go up the small hill. Taking the flatter street below our house, we finally arrived very late and tired. I was back to reality, but I would never forget the wonderful trip and God's intervention. I could hardly wait to tell the prayer group all that had happened.

The next Tuesday, my friends were as amazed as I at God's leading. Prayers of thanksgiving rose for God's power and answered prayer.

But I still had an unresolved issue on my mind. I wanted prayer about Mom. Her messages recorded on my brain had gone round and round like a broken record for too many years. Eleanor could not meet with me that week, so I asked Jean Walker at the meeting. She agreed, but we set no date.

Two weeks after the trip, Jean called. "Can you come for coffee tomorrow morning? I want to return the magazine you loaned me."

"I'm scheduled to see my counselor (the minister), but if there's time I'll stop in after that."

The next morning, the pastor called to say he had a conflict. This had never happened before. I called Jean, took Jared, almost five, and went to her house.

A light powdering of snow covered the world. As we walked up the few steps to her door, the sun shone and twinkled brightly on the pure white snow. The beauty of the scene almost took my breath away. I had a keen sense of expectation and God seemed very near.

Jean greeted us with a warm smile, her dark brown eyes bright and sparkling.

I said, "I think God wants me to talk with you today." She gave me a wide-eyed, knowing look.

We talked about my trip and when I mentioned the unusual meeting with Jerry, she exclaimed slyly, *"And to think that you met him on the bus!"*

"What do you mean?"

"When you asked for prayer at our meeting, *I prayed that you would meet a Spirit-filled person and be filled with the Spirit yourself!"* Chills ran down my spine and goose bumps rose on my arms.

"So that's why God told Jerry to take the bus," I said, astounded, "in answer to your prayer!"

"Yes," Jean whispered, still in awe herself over God's direct answer.

I marveled at such power in prayer. Two strangers prayed in two locations in the state and God answered their prayers to meet my needs. God sent Jerry, filled with the Spirit, to fill me.

We got Jared settled in the dining room with crayons and coloring book and Jean and I sat at the breakfast bar in the kitchen with our coffee. I was surprised when Jean lit up a long slender cigarette, but I was so absorbed by her power with God that it didn't bother me. Then she got to the point. "First I'll tell you my story and then you can tell me yours and I'll pray for you."

I listened, enthralled, from beginning to end. Now I understood what Eleanor meant when she said Jean was a "dynamic Christian."

"I have been a Presbyterian all my life and taught Sunday school for years," she began. "I even constructed the Tabernacle with the children in my class. But I wasn't saved. My son Dan played in a band and planned to stay with the group through high school and college. But my husband moved a lot with his work and we had to move again. Dan did not want to move. He became so despondent and depressed that he ran away from home. I was devastated.

"The police searched everywhere but Dan could not be found. I was desperate and made endless phone calls. I was so frustrated that one day as I was driving down a street, I cried out loud, 'Oh, God! Show me the way!'

"Immediately, God spoke to me! He said, 'Go so many blocks this way and so many blocks that way and stop at this house.' I was amazed. I followed His instructions and went to the door of the house. A man let me in. I told him about my son and my frustration at not being able to find him. He started telling me the plan of salvation as his wife stood in a corner. I asked, 'What is she doing?'

"'She's praying for you to be saved.' After he finished explaining to me, he asked, 'Are you ready to accept Christ now?'

"I said no. So he called up some people and they came to the house. If you've never heard Pentecostals pray, it's an experience. They stood around me and they all prayed loudly at the same time. Then he asked me again, 'Now are you ready to accept Jesus?'

"Again I said no. So he gave me the address of a woman and said, 'When you get ready to accept Jesus as your Savior, go to this woman. She's an evangelist. Just tell her you want to accept Jesus.' I took the address, thanked the man, and left.

"But I had no peace. Finally one day I could stand it no longer. I went to the evangelist and asked her, 'If I accept Jesus, do I have to change churches? I love my church.'

"She told me, 'No, you can stay in your church.' So I said, 'Then, I'm ready.' She asked, 'May I put my hands on your head?' I agreed. She stood behind me and put her hands on my head. As she prayed, I saw the whole plan of salvation pass before my eyes. It was suddenly clear to me. Then I began to speak in tongues. I got the whole works at once! I was full of joy and peace and I *knew* I was saved."

She paused, and with a bright look, said, "And after that, the police found Dan in Florida!"

I was absolutely dumbfounded and overwhelmed at how God answered her cries for peace and finding her son. I expressed my amazement and gratitude to Jean for sharing her story.

"I'm ready to hear your story now," Jean invited.

Feeling at ease, I began with my mother's death, leaving my two sisters and me and a newborn son when I was three. I told of Daddy's difficulty in finding a maid to care for us, how he found Mom through an ad in the newspaper. I told of her rough treatment of us, the loud arguments with Daddy, and our fear and suffering those early years, continuing through my teen years. Jean listened intently as I told how God opened the way for me to go to college, Mom's opposition, then seminary, and how I met and married Jake. I said we moved closer to my home for two years after we were married and my relationship with Mom was good. But before we left for Mississippi, when I called to say goodbye, all she could say through her sobs was, "I wish you wouldn't go." Then she died a few months later and I was sorely grieved.

I explained, "Mom seldom went to church and we girls thought she wasn't a Christian. I really worried that she wasn't saved, and blamed myself for her death, because we moved away. She was critical of us and kept us under her thumb and put guilt trips on us girls. She'd often say, 'You'll think about it some day when I'm gone.'" The put-downs, negative messages, scolding, and shame that taunted me from time to time had to come out.

I told her, "For the past seven years I have often thought of Mom and of my guilt, the sins of my youth – the things she considered bad, anyway. I especially couldn't forget her heartbreaking sobs when we left for Mississippi – and then her death four months later, and *I never got to talk to her again!* So when she died, it was *my* turn to sob. Mama was dead – and I didn't know if she was saved."

"But," I noted, "In spite of the bad, I've also had tender thoughts of Mom – of all the good she did for me, her many kindnesses and change of heart toward me. Sometimes I can't help but feel she was a believer when she died. She had a very simple faith in Jesus. And two ministers (Mennonite and Daddy's U.C.C.) often visited and prayed with her when she was in the hospital. Do you think it is possible she was saved?"

"Yes," Jean replied. "The Spirit can reveal that to us in an instant, whether or not a loved one was saved. If the Spirit told you, then you can believe it."

That was a comfort to me. I was aware that some would not agree. My sisters could not accept that Mom was saved. She didn't go to church. She smoked. She complained and fussed and was miserable. How could she have the abundant wholeness of life that Jesus talked about? I couldn't answer that. It was a mystery. But I was comforted with the knowledge of the Spirit's revelation. I knew that all anyone needed to do was look up to Jesus in faith, as did the dying thief on the cross, and be saved in an instant.

I told Jean, "For some time I've felt a need to have someone pray for me, and I felt it should be a woman, because of my struggles with Mom."

Jean understood and nodded. "I've read that children who lose their mothers at a young age spend the rest of their lives looking for her. Did you know that?" Her compassionate eyes held mine. Her intense listening and great wisdom were a balm to my spirit.

"I've never read that, but I believe it's true. I can see it in my own experience. For years when I was young I expected my mother to come back. And I still grieve when I see a mother and her adult daughter as friends. I never had that, and I'd like you to pray for me."

"May I put my hands on your head?" she asked. I wondered if I'd speak in tongues but, unafraid, I consented. As I sat on a chair–at the dining room table where Jared sat–she stood behind me and rested her hands lightly on my head. As she prayed a beautiful prayer of cleansing, healing, and release, peace flooded my being. It was quiet and simple, like a dove of the Holy Spirit lighting on my head. As I stood, Jean hugged me warmly and I thanked her for a wonderful morning.

Jared had been quiet the whole time, but now was restless and ready to go. We walked out into the bright sunshine and dazzling snow, symbolic of my having been "washed whiter than snow." I felt like a new person. Jared was such a fun companion. How I loved this little guy!

The next morning, Jake said to me, "I slept better last night than I have for a long time."

I felt blessed and grateful. After he left for work I reflected on the meeting with Jean. The Spirit opened my eyes and suddenly I saw three similarities between Jean and Mom. They had the same name–*Jean*–and both had the same last initial–*W*, for Walker and Williams. Then I thought about how Jean had smoked while I was there and it didn't bother me. It surprised me, but I never doubted that she was saved. I had hated that Mom smoked, and I judged her as not being a Christian because of it. The third similarity was that Jean said her husband was ten years older than she. Daddy was ten years older than Mom and I thought she was too young for him and he should not have married her. In my small mind, I had been her judge. Astonished, I called Jean.

When I told her that Jake slept better than he had for a long time she said, "That's the witness of the Spirit." He felt the peace I had found.

Then I told her about the name similarity, the cigarettes, and the age difference of each Jean and her husband. She was quiet a few seconds, then said softly, "These things are not coincidence. I wondered why the Lord let me start smoking again. He delivered me from it for a year and I couldn't understand why I started again." Jean, not Eleanor, was the right person whom God had prepared to pray for me.

God's mysterious ways are amazing and "past finding out" (Job 9:10; Rom. 11:33).

Since her husband's death, Jean and her son Dan lived together in Vincennes, close to her aunts. One day she asked me if she and Dan could go with us to the Mennonite Church. I was delighted. We invited them for dinner after church and had lively conversation. I was glad Jake could meet them. Later that week Jean told me, "Dan was very impressed by the service at your church. He said he made a new commitment to Christ there. And he decided to go to college!" Jean was ecstatic. "He also said that the men's faces shone (in the men's Sunday school class) and that 'Mennonites are not redundant. Redundancy makes wrinkles on faces.'" What an astute observation from such a young man! And what a clear testimony the humble Mennonite believers had, with their simple ways and devout trust in God. I was overjoyed at Dan's commitment.

On March 14, what would have been Mom's 55th birthday, Jean gave me the devotional book, *My Utmost For His Highest* by Oswald Chambers. When I told her it was Mom's birthday she said, "And it was my husband's birthday, too." Another similarity! I loved the book and it gave much food for my soul as I used it for many years. Jean was truly a "spiritual mother" to me and I marveled at God's personal care in leading us together.

Later, impressed by a radio segment on Emily Dickinson, famous New England poet, I got several of her books from the library. I loved her poems, many about death and grief, faith and God. I especially liked "I measure every grief I meet" in which she analyzes others' grief and writes of the "piercing comfort" afforded "in passing Calvary." I became excited and inspired.

One day I thought about how I wrote poems in my youth, and how Mom liked that and asked me to write for people who were sick. Yet in all the years she was in and out of the hospital, I never wrote one for her. That made me sad. Had she been waiting for a poem and been disappointed? Perhaps she had. Now I wanted to write her a poem. However, the first poem I wrote was "Yesterday's Child" (Chapter 1), then a lament, recalling the barrage of criticism with which she pelted me through the years. (And the time when she opened the bedroom door, found me praying on my knees, and slammed the door hard.) I wrote a few shorter pieces, and finally "Song of Praise to My Stepmother." The words flowed from my pen, almost as if they were being dictated. In a very short time the poems were finished, all in the same day. Writing them was a great release for me. God was setting me free.

I sent the poems to *The Mennonite* and was pleased when "Song of Praise to My Stepmother" was printed that year, 1972, in the Mother's Day issue. (Two were published later.)

Psalm 116:1-2 expresses the deep gratitude and confidence I felt on this resolution of many years of struggle, "I love the Lord, because He has heard my voice and my supplications. Because He has inclined His ear to me, therefore I will call on Him as long as I live."

I shared my experience with my sisters and brother Ralph. They could not accept that Mom was a believer. Several years later they also came to that understanding.

In the spring of 1972, I was asked to serve on the planning committee for May Fellowship Day for Church Women United (CWU). Churches from many denominations participated in CWU, including Catholic. I enjoyed meeting with the friendly women on the committee. The program featured a panel of Vincennes University women and others on the topic, "Behold the Woman!" on women in leadership. I cringed when the committee asked me to moderate the meeting and panel discussion. I loved the topic but not a public assignment. It had been years since I spoke before a group, which I never liked. But as I read the material I resonated with the deep concerns of women worldwide caught in all kinds of bondage. I believed strongly that the Lord Jesus Christ was the supreme Liberator of women. As I prayed about it, I felt the Lord had given me this opportunity and so I accepted.

When I told the CWU committee my decision, they encouraged and assured me of their prayers. I met with four university women, a student, and a homemaker to discuss the material. Six wonderful women consented to serve, inspired by the significance of the subject. The enjoyable interviews gave me confidence. Then someone warned me that two of the university women did not get along. I disregarded that information, prayed about it, and got congenial cooperation from both. I typed out for the panel the questions I would ask. When the day came, I was scared half out of my wits. How could I face a whole church full of women? I prayed.

Another small concern, but big to me, was what to wear. On our tight budget my skimpy wardrobe had few acceptable options. Anna rescued me with a package in the mail. There was a beautiful sunny-yellow three-piece knit outfit! Though a perfect fit, it was much too long. I fussed and fumed and prayed about what to do. Afraid it would unravel if I cut it, I hemmed it with a wide hem, easily visible to the eye. Anna did not know I needed an outfit and, as she told me, the suit was from the "missionary barrel" of Slavic Gospel Association, for whom John worked and where she got most of hers and the boys' clothes. Accepting it as a gift from the Lord, I decided to forget the hem and wear it.

At the church, dear Eleanor greeted me with a hug. Still scared, I told her, "I wanted to call and ask you to pray for me."

With a hug and warm smile, she assured, "I walked over here this morning and prayed for you all the way!" What a great friend! I was ready. And when my turn came, I was filled with peace and confidence. I knew Christ was there beside me.

The large U.C.C. Church was packed with eager women, few of whom knew me. My fear gone, I felt "carried" and the panel discussion went beautifully. The women were gracious and their responses informative, stimulating, and insightful. At the appointed time I said, "It's time to call a halt." Later, I heard good comments about how smoothly it went and how the women got along well.

That same year Jake and I were invited to join a Sunday night discussion group of couples from Protestant and Catholic backgrounds. As we met twice a month, I became excited about what can be done when people from various church backgrounds, constrained by the love of Christ, band together to tackle tough problems. Some from this group helped organize a larger committee as a clearinghouse for a variety of community concerns—from the open sewer to Project Commitment. Supported by 18 churches and organizations, Project Commitment studied the six main problems of Vincennes on six consecutive Monday nights. Presentations dealt with poverty, race relations, drug abuse, mental health, mental retardation, and leisure. People became concerned for the victims of deeply ingrained social ills, and friendships were formed among clergy and laymen as we sat around tables for discussion of each topic and found ways to take action.

At Project Commitment, I decided to promote the evangelistic outreach, Key '73, a nationwide movement of the Spirit among Christians of many denominations attempting to be obedient to the Great Commission. Their goal was to visit every home in the country for Christ in 1973. Protestants and Catholics in each community were encouraged to share in two services in common, where each invited the other to a service in their church. The theme of both services was "Christ in Common." The Catholic service I attended had a wonderful sermon with much emphasis on Scripture, the Holy Spirit, and unity with other believers. Over refreshments I met a sweet little Catholic woman who said, "I have a daughter living in Phoenix who knows Mennonites (after I told her I was one). She loves them and just can't stop talking about how wonderful they are! Now I've met one!" Her loving smile and words blessed me.

Having promoted Key '73 among the Vincennes clergy, I also wrote a letter about it to the editor of *The Mennonite*. Soon a request came for me to write an article about Key '73 for the women's page in *The Mennonite*. My first assignment for publication netted me no dollars that I recall. But the privilege of sharing my love for Jesus via Key '73 with my denomination – and a few great letters in response – made it worthwhile.

As my friend Sara and I met together, I shared about my life and my love of the Scriptures with her. One day she said, "I never learned the Bible in my church growing up. Would you teach a Bible study? I really want to learn." I had put her off for some time since we attended the weekly prayer meeting together and I was still meeting with the pastor.

After May Fellowship Day, CWU leaders asked me to lead a Key '73 Bible study for them. Sensing God's call through Sara and this group, I consented. First we studied the ninth grade workbook I had taught in Bible school at the Mennonite Church we attended. It was filled with excellent facts and overview material on the entire Bible. We started with seven women and eventually had 18 at most. After the first meeting Sara exclaimed, "This is exactly what I wanted!" My best student, she drank it all in. When we finished the book, we did an inductive study of Genesis, which was rich and exciting. I shared my story with them and they shared as well. Two retired missionaries in the group added warmth and wisdom. I showed the group a book on marriage, *Cherishable, Love and Marriage* by David Augsburger, Mennonite writer (and speaker on *The Mennonite Hour* that we heard Sunday mornings before church). Sara ordered the book and later told me, "That book is my bible. I keep it on my kitchen counter and read it all the time!"

One day Sara said, "I have really grown in learning to be thankful the past year since being around Mennonites. When are you going to invite us to your church? Larry wants to go, too." I was delighted. One Sunday they attended with us and Larry, who had negative feelings about his Pentecostal upbringing, was deeply impressed with the people and sermon.

Later Sara wrote me in a letter, "Jane, I really feel more at peace with myself. I feel joyful and thankful this evening and I want to share my feelings with you. The rejuvenation of Christian growth that you fostered in me has really accelerated within the past few months. I believe Larry could say the same and that he is grateful to the Friesens for kindling a fire in him, too." My heart overflowed with joy.

She added, "Augsburger states that from its beginning, the Mennonite faith 'spread across Europe as a people's movement, a revival of personal faith in Christ.' And in a world dark and bleak with misery and hopelessness, a personal faith in Christ, shared by warm and caring people, helps one rise above the darkness to a new way of life, lightened by Christ as the Life-Giver and Burden-Bearer." How I loved Sara and praised God for her growth in Christ.

Exhilarating learning continued. From Jean Walker I learned about the charismatic movement, which was sweeping the nation. She had attended the famous Notre Dame meetings in Indiana where thousands of Christians of all persuasions—Catholic, Pentecostal, mainline Protestant, evangelicals—even Mennonites—all met in the power of the Holy Spirit. It was an awesome time to be living and I wanted to learn all I could.

But concerning "speaking in tongues," Jake told me one day, as I talked excitedly about what I was learning from Jean, "That's the kind of thing that breaks up marriages!" He felt threatened and I was saddened that he couldn't share my joy. To me it was just like Pentecost and what happened in the New Testament churches. I believed that "Jesus Christ is the same yesterday, today, and forever." Many churches were dead, by admission of their members, and needed the fresh wind of the Spirit. But the movement also caused deep divisions in churches and families. I didn't want that to happen to us. And I did not speak in tongues, so why was Jake worried? He had met Jean Walker and saw she was a normal, happy person and he liked her. I was glad for that. Perhaps Jake thought a move back to Mennonite territory would get us away from all this. Our time in Vincennes was drawing to a close.

The exciting day came at last when Jake was offered a job as chief pilot and director of the Hesston College aviation department. We were both more than ready. Hesston was seven miles south of Moundridge, where we spent the first summer of our marriage. Newton, where Jake had graduated from Bethel College, was seven miles south of Hesston. We felt that Hesston, a town of about 2000, would be a great place to raise our children. I praised God in my heart for this open door.

In June of 1973, we drove to Hesston to look for a house and stayed with Lois and Gerald, our former housemates in Akron. I prayed about the matter of a house and felt confident that God had just the right one for us. We looked at a new one in town and at a small farm three miles out in the country.

One night at 10 P.M., Lois came home excited. "I saw the mayor's daughter at the Dairy Queen and asked if her parents' house sold yet. She said no. It's at a really good location a block from the grade school and it's newly redecorated. They are building a new house near the high school and have not put their house on the market yet. Do you want me to call them?" We did.

At 10:30 that night, the mayor and his wife showed Lois, Jake, and me through the house on a half hour's notice. Neat as a pin and beautifully decorated inside, the roomy two-story house had two bedrooms upstairs with bath, a bedroom and bath down, large dining-living room, kitchen and small family room. With a full basement and attached two-car garage, it was perfect. We knew this was our house. We could hardly believe our good fortune. Our friends' excitement added to our feelings of jubilation as we all discussed this great find. God had once again answered prayer far beyond my expectations.

The next day we gave the mayor our decision. After renting for 12 years, we bought our first house for $20,000, a large sum to us. We needed $4000 down. Jake took out a loan on a life insurance policy and borrowed the rest from Railroad Savings and Loan in Newton, with mortgage payments of $163 a month. Since the mayor's new house would not be ready until December, we rented an apartment on Main Street for the interim. We headed home to Indiana after a very successful trip.

In July of 1973, we said goodbye to our many friends of the past four and one-half years. Sara had a lovely tea for me at her home for the Bible study group. They gave me a silver cross necklace and a card in which Sara had written, "To our loving and inspiring teacher." Their friendship was a rich blessing that would continue.

Our special friends, Sara, Larry, and daughter Sally helped us load the E-Z Haul and we took off west. Jake took Jared in the truck, towing the van. Janet and I drove in our 1967 Mercedes that Jake had bought at a bargain price.

Janet objected to the move and shed tears over leaving her friend Laurie who lived next door. But as we drove and talked she seemed happier. Jared had completed kindergarten and Janet was ready for third grade. Jake had his work cut out for him, managing the flight department. But what would I do?

As I drove the two-day, 700-mile trip west I had time to reflect on the years in Vincennes, the healing, growth, and friends who touched our lives. I marveled at God's goodness, keeping us together and giving us "beauty for ashes." I loved the passage from Isaiah that Jesus read in part in the Nazareth synagogue—Luke 4: "The Spirit of the Lord is upon me...to give them beauty for ashes ..." Truly God had done that for me.

I wondered what was ahead for us in Kansas. Ten thousand Mennonites from Russia had settled on the Kansas and Nebraska plains in 1874, and their churches were everywhere. How different from our move to Vincennes! God had brought me out of my comfortable Mennonite cocoon. I had grown and stretched into other denominations in the past tumultuous years. In Kansas, I'd be thrust into a sea of Mennonites—churches, two colleges, and church headquarters. With friends and acquaintances there, I anticipated an easier adjustment. But will Janet be happy? Time will tell.

Song of Praise to My Stepmother

When I was four you came to live with us,
To take the place of one I dearly loved.
And I could not accept that you would stay,
And marry Dad.

How often I rebelled and cried and prayed
And, later, preached you sermons in the night!
But often, caught off guard, I felt your love,
Your heart touched mine.

And now that you've been gone these seven years,
You'd be surprised to see the way I've come,
God gave a mother new, *she has your name —
And last initial!*

God led me to her on a snowy day,
She prayed for me, her hands upon my head.
And afterwards I knew God planned it so,
To set me free.

God gave me many mothers through the years,
To love and listen and to understand,
But I cannot deny that you *did* love,
And gave me much.

So like a child you were in many ways,
Not educated, not well read, well taught.
But you knew much of life we didn't know,
You did your part.

And oft you read to us when we were small,
Remember once you read that Jesus died?
I cried, and never could forget
He died for me.

Your life was hard, and you were bound by cords
Of devilish hell your dad beat into you.
But Jesus taught you as a little child,
And led you home.

Oh, God be praised! The way is plain indeed,
Wherein he leads those whom he calls in love.
Come, gracious God, lead me in higher paths
And keep me true.

PART IV

PUTTING DOWN ROOTS

CHAPTER 24

Coming Home

The Lord hath done great things for us; whereof we are glad.
PSALM 126:3 (KJV)

1973–1976

The first night on our way west, we stopped at a lovely motel just outside of Kansas City, where we got a room for $10.00. The next day Jake and I became separated for two hours between Topeka and Salina. Janet and I thought he was behind us, but he was up ahead. When we finally caught up, we felt badly that he and Jared waited an hour for us in the sweltering Kansas heat.

Psalm 37 became precious to me before the move, so I asked Janet to read it aloud as we drove. Then she read John 4 about the woman at the well and we shared about our favorite Bible stories. Janet said, "I like the story of Paul let down in a basket over the wall in Damascus, and the one about Jesus and the children." Her enthusiasm and enjoyment of the Bible blessed me.

I marveled again at the wide-open spaces of the Great Plains. Before harvest, golden fields of wheat waved in the wind for hundreds of miles of flat expanse. I anticipated a slower pace of life in our small agricultural town, not realizing the whirlwind of activity ahead.

A few miles from Hesston, I remarked cheerily, "A few more miles and we'll be home."

"Not *home*!" Janet corrected.

"Sure, home is where the heart is."

"My heart is still in Vincennes," she insisted.

"How long is it going to stay there?"

"Until I make up my mind."

"That's exactly right. It will stay there until you make up your mind."

Jake and I couldn't be happier than we were with this move. After more than six years of wanderings, it pleased me to hear Jake tell the college president, "It feels like we've come home." Jared was happy, too, always enjoying the present moment. I could only pray that Janet would change her mind.

That Saturday afternoon, with help from Gerald Leinbach and a neighbor, we unloaded the truck and slept in our own beds in our apartment that night. Janet and Jared romped and played that afternoon with Terry and Karen Leinbach, happy for instant playmates.

On Monday evening I took the children on a walking tour of downtown Hesston. Everything was in miniature. As we walked, I exclaimed excitedly, "Here's the tiny post office...the grocery store...bank...and general store. Here's the newspaper building, and there's the firehouse and city hall. The buildings are all so small, just right for small Hesston. And see the beautiful flowers! Oh, look, a cute little library right across the street!" Janet, as an avid reader, hurried over to check it out.

I continued my running commentary. "Look, there's a story hour notice on the door. You can go on Monday morning. What a delightful little town this is!"

The children enjoyed it all immensely and kept chirping, "It doesn't seem like we moved!" My plan was working. The junior college was at the other end of South Main — a lovely tree-lined street — less than a mile from our apartment. Jake could walk to work. Hesston was a beautiful, well-kept community.

On the way home, Janet said sweetly, "My heart came out here today!"

"Good for you!" I gave her a warm hug. She would still shed tears over Laurie at times, but she adjusted. Relieved and grateful, I slept better that night. For months after we moved, Jared included in his evening prayer, "Thank You that we could move to Kansas." God had led us here. If the children were happy, I was happier, too.

Jake visited the college and then told me he planned to go to Waco, Texas to Success Motivation, Inc. or SMI. He had used one of their motivational tapes with students at Vincennes, which worked wonders on lackluster attitudes. Reluctantly, I agreed. While there, he called to say he was buying a dealership for $4000. He had to borrow the money but was sure he'd earn it back before long by selling courses. I hardly knew what to think.

Thus began our daily listening to tapes on leadership development. He said we would use the program called "Adventures in Growth" for the children once we got settled in our house. (We did — every night at the dinner table we heard the same tape for five days. It took 13 weeks to listen to the entire course, one tape a week. Jake and I listened to one on leadership motivation every day as well, or as often as we could.)

At the college, Jake contacted donors and, two weeks after his return from Waco, bought a plane for $37,000. The flight department was taking off with its first plane!

Our life buzzed with meeting many new people – so many Mennonites – at college functions, churches we visited, on the street, at Newton seven miles away. It was exciting to connect again with people we knew from college, seminary, MCC, and other locations. I felt drawn to our General Conference headquarters so close by and stopped in to see people I knew. Jared and I had lunch with a college friend, Muriel Thiessen Stackley, along with Herta Funk and Nellie Lehn, writers and editors, all of whom worked at the offices. Jared still remembers the fun time at the Newton Train Station Depot turned into a restaurant, with these important, friendly women. For me it was a warm welcoming into the family of Mennonites I had grown up reading about in *The Mennonite* back home. It also took me back to my 3:00 A.M. arrival at that station on my first trip to Kansas in 1954.

Cramped in our small apartment, with unopened boxes stacked up and things in storage, we could hardly wait until December. After twelve years of marriage, we moved into our first house in time to get settled for Christmas. What a happy day! We didn't mind that the two-story frame house with white shingles was 40 years old – it was so *homey*! It had a nice big yard and space for a garden. The children loved their upstairs bedrooms. The location, on the corner of Weaver and Amos, couldn't be more perfect. Cattycornered across the street was the Inter-Mennonite Church (bringing together both "Old" Mennonites and General Conference Mennonites), which became our church home for the next seven years. We were two blocks from the downtown grocery store, post office, and bank. The children's school was one block east.

As we gradually learned to know our neighbors, we found them to be very friendly. Before long, I attended women's neighborhood coffees to celebrate birthdays.

The Millers had left a china cabinet in the basement full of driftwood, with no glass in the doors. After several weeks, I called Mrs. Miller, wondering if they'd want it back. She said, "It came with the house when we moved in and my husband planned to refinish it. It's been in the basement for 20 years. It's yours if you want."

If I wanted it? I had long wished for a china closet but could never have bought one. This one had character, sporting a beveled mirror and curlicue carving. We soon found that in heavy rain the basement leaked like a sieve at both ends of the house. For years the cabinet stood in shallow water and the legs had rotted on the bottom. I refinished it, glad for the experience at the doctor's during high school. Freedly Schrock, carpenter and retired college prof, sawed an inch off the legs, put glass in the doors, and it was perfect for my Pennsylvania Dutch dinnerware.

Christmas was relaxing in our cozy new home. But as fall turned to winter, temperatures plummeted and fierce winds pierced our heavy coats. A nagging fear crept into my thoughts. How would we survive our first frigid Kansas season? Jake ordered a very heavy coat from a used clothing catalog. He usually walked the mile to the college so I was grateful for this coat with a hood. But the walk home facing into the wind nearly froze his face!

In February '74, I caught a cold and bad sore throat but nursed it at home. In March, Jake flew us to Chicago where we spent the weekend with Anna and John. It was rainy and cold and Jared and I came home sick. An aching chest, sore throat, flu, and fever, and what seemed like bursitis, laid me low. My knees and wrists began to ache and grew steadily worse. Blood tests at the doctors' confirmed the diagnosis: rheumatic fever! "And," he reported, "you have an irregular heartbeat, a heart murmur, and you're anemic!" How had I gotten so run down? The doctor said rheumatic fever comes from strep throat and there was strep in my bloodstream. "We got this at an early stage since you have no red sore joints," he said, "but you will have to stay in bed for one month. I'll give you a shot of penicillin, and you'll have to have a shot every month for the rest of your life."

I did not believe it. I knew that God is the healer and I had prayed for years about my health and God took care of me. Having sold Shaklee vitamins and supplements since our Vincennes days, I knew that drugs are often over-prescribed. I also knew that people got well with proper nutrition, supplements, rest, and prayer. I talked it over with the doctor and asked if I *had* to take shots.

"No, but you'll have to take capsules at the first sign of a sore throat from now on."

I was greatly pleased and trusted this Mennonite, Dr. Loganbill, in Moundridge. But I knew I had to take better care of myself. He prescribed Inderal for the irregular heartbeat and said I would have to stay on it the rest of my life. *We'll see about that*, I thought. But I felt badly about being confined to bed for a month. Who would take care of my family?

But Jake and the children pitched in to help and my college wives group and small group women brought food and some helped clean. It was hard to accept this help since I didn't feel very sick. The penicillin and rest quickly took effect. (After a few years, I rarely got a sore throat and never needed penicillin. Four years later my heart was fine and the doctor agreed I could discontinue the Inderal. I made my health a matter of prayer and years later after a lengthy examination, my doctor told me I had no heart murmur or irregular heartbeat!)

That fall, on August 27, 1974, I began a part-time job at the Hesston Credit Union, next door to the Colonial House. My friend Lois, knowing of my writing course, recommended me to her sister who worked there. I was hired to write their monthly newsletter, but learned that writing was a small part of the job. I was disappointed to learn that most of the work consisted of typing loan forms, figuring interest, and sometimes waiting on customers. I walked the two blocks and worked six hours a day, while the children were in school. Typing numbers on loan papers soon got old, but in eight months at $2.50 and then $2.75 an hour, that job netted me $1,974.00 take-home pay. I had "paid back" my $500 writing course almost four times over!

Looking back now, those seven years at Hesston seem like a blur of jobs, school, friends, church activities, writer's fellowship, writer's conferences, retreats, and trips. And for Jake, more and more jobs and trips. He worked full-time at the college only one year, buying airplanes, teaching, writing curriculum and manuals. The next year he went to half time in order to sell his motivation courses. He sold one to the spirited, energetic college president, Laban Peachey. Since Laban knew what Jake was into, a year after we arrived he buttonholed Jake for a new job—restaurant manager!

Hesston boasted a beautiful restaurant downtown with seating capacity for 500. A large wagon wheel hung from the center of the ceiling of the main dining room. Five couples had built it years before and now donated it to the college. The Colonial House served a Friday and Saturday night German buffet in the huge basement and drew large crowds from a wide area. To keep the business going, Laban scrambled to find a manager. Knowing Jake's expertise in administration, he saw him as the right man.

"Your motivation course is great!" Laban offered. "We're in dire need of a manager for the Colonial House and you're the man!"

"No way!" Jake told Laban. "I'm no restaurant manager!"

Three weeks later Laban came back again. "We still have not found a manager. *Please!* We need someone right now. I have no doubt you can do it. You're half time with the college and you can manage the restaurant half time. We'll be on the lookout for someone, so this will be temporary." They hashed it over and Jake relented. He started at the restaurant about the same time I began at the Credit Union next door, but our paths rarely crossed.

Though Hesston seemed too small for a restaurant that size, the large farm equipment manufacturing plant – Hesston Corporation – employed about 2000 people. They came from a wide radius, including the largest city in Kansas, Wichita, 35 miles south. In the early and mid 1970s, business was booming and the town thrived. Jake learned that the corporation had two Cessna Citation business jets. Soon he had his eye on flying for the "corp." He put in his name as a relief pilot and had his first trip on August 24, a year after we moved. He flew for them eight days in September. He was in his element. Then, on October 5, he began at the restaurant. In February the next year he became executive director of the Colonial House board.

The Colonial House job kept Jake hopping. He often opened up early in the morning. He hired a chef, a head waitress, and a hostess. He often took on the role of host at noon, and sometimes over the dinner hour. He hired a business manager, Jim Graber, and the two of them frequently worked on finances in the basement office after closing. (Jake and Jim became good friends and in time Jim married Ruby and we flew in a college plane to their wedding in Oklahoma. They and their children, Troy and Sara, have been long-time special friends who farm our Hesston land to this day.)

Besides administering the college aviation program, teaching students, and flying as relief pilot, this new job took a big chunk of Jake's day. I struggled greatly with my feelings, not only as a "pilot widow" but now a "restaurant widow" as well. Though I had my own involvements, too many at times, I sorely missed having Jake at home.

With thousands of Mennonites in south central Kansas, a men's chorus had grown into the 500 Mennonite Men's Chorus. Jake somehow still had time to join and we attended their concerts. What beautiful music 500 men can make! One day at practice, Jake noticed a familiar face – his former high school principal, Bill Wiebe, from British Columbia! He was currently a church administrator at nearby Hillsboro. They got reacquainted and we had Bill and Louise at our home for dinner and a delightful visit.

In October 1974, the Kansas Russian Mennonites celebrated their centennial of the year they arrived from Russia with a weekend of events in Wichita at Century II Civic Center. Featured were a moving drama of pioneer days, speakers, music, and the 500 Mennonite Men. This pleasant way of learning the history of the Russian Mennonite heritage proved interesting to Janet and Jared as well.

Much publicity was given in local newspapers before and during the centennial. An article in THE *Newton* KANSAN quoted from the Topeka (capital of Kansas) newspaper of 100 years before stated:

> These curious religious exiles...who have created a very considerable stir in this country for a people whose lives are so passionless and whose fundamental doctrine is peace...As a body they are the most desirable immigrants, especially for a new country, that ever came to the U.S., and it is no wonder then that there is very considerable strife to secure them...They are thorough agriculturalists, sober, honest, industrious, and, as far as the results of their farming goes, aspiring. We cannot imagine, then, an equal number of immigrants so free from objectionable elements. The policy of these Mennonites going into the wilderness is not only to redeem but to transfigure it...They are a 'big card' for Kansas; they will largely advance the standard of our present crude and careless farming, and will teach our agriculturalists by example...

Learning about these pioneers, settling on virgin soil—breaking up sod as hard as concrete, creating homes out of sod in unforgiving weather conditions, bitter cold and wind in winter, and 100 degree plus temperatures in summer—filled me with empathy and awe.

I liked inviting guests for Sunday dinner, some we had known for years in other locations. I loved the fellowship around our table, always grateful for times when Jake was home. And I wanted our children to experience "extended family" with a variety of Christian friends since our own families were more than a thousand miles away.

On my fortieth birthday, February 6, 1975, two interesting events happened simultaneously, with a third thrown in for good measure. At the Colonial House that Thursday, the Grand Opening of the Pennsylvania Dutch buffet added another ethnic night to the existing German buffet. Also that day, Arlene Stika and I from the Credit Union attended meetings in Wichita and ate lunch at the nearby Next Door Restaurant. That night I planned to serve at the third event, our church's Sweetheart Supper, since Jake was tied up at the Colonial House and couldn't eat with me.

After returning from Wichita, I felt sick to my stomach, and soon was vomiting and sitting in the bathroom non-stop. My friend Elizabeth Small came to be with me. She was shocked at my condition and prayed fervently for me. By the time Jake got home I was violently ill and having dry heaves. At midnight he took me to the hospital. I told the doctor about the funny tasting coleslaw (that I ate from habit of eating all my food!). Tests confirmed food poisoning. I stayed on IVs through the next day and was released two days after the attack. While I was in the hospital, Janet made a sweet card that Jake brought to me and I felt deeply loved. It read:

> Dear Mommy,
>
> We miss you a lot. We miss your cooking and your happy voice. It is very quiet without you. Everything's fine, a dessert is in the refrigerator. But it is still very lonely without you. We are sweeping today so we can be with you tomorrow when you come home. We miss you very much. It wasn't a very good birthday present for you to get sick, was it? We are eating at the Colonial House tonight. Hope you get well soon. Love, Janet

From friends I learned what I had missed at the Sweetheart Supper. Good friends, Dick and Mary Rempel, from British Columbia, attended our church and Dick and I shared a birthday. As part of the entertainment, the song leader said, "I've always wanted to sing 'Happy Birthday' to Dick and Jane, and tonight we have that opportunity." So they sang to us in my absence, but Dick was there. Though I missed it, I savored the thought.

The food poisoning incident had an upside. The credit union's insurance agent called on the phone to record my story. Soon a check arrived in the mail for $500! Insurance paid the hospital bill and the $500 covered work lost and "pain and suffering." This windfall made it worth being sick since it paid for a trip to Pennsylvania the next summer for the children and me. I wanted them to visit my family and celebrate the Bicentennial of our country in historic Philadelphia. Since Jake worked hard to pay off debts, I liked to earn money for trips and marveled at God's provision.

Our church was known as the charismatic church in town and I was invited to events that broadened my understanding of the Holy Spirit. With my friend Elizabeth Small I went by bus to Oral Roberts University to hear famous evangelist, Kathryn Kuhlman. Tall and slender in her long white gown with long sleeves, she marched back and forth across the stage in striking style, preaching passionately. Here I saw healings and people "slain" or "resting in the Spirit" for the first time.

Elizabeth, Roberta Nickel, and I also attended a charismatic retreat in Kansas and heard an Israeli-born speaker with a powerful testimony and teaching. Together, Jake and I heard Charles and Frances Hunter in Wichita, who also had a healing ministry. A young woman in my church small group reported the healing of her leg (which had been in a brace) at our next meeting. I heard Merlin Carothers, retired chaplain of the army whose amazing book, *Prison to Praise*, blessed me. Jared and I watched Oral Roberts for a time on television. I recalled that the Kookers from my home church loved him and went to his meetings in Florida and, I believe, one of them was healed there. As time went on, I met people in town who attended Full Gospel Businessmen's Association and Women Aglow meetings as well. Hesston was full of on-fire Christians!

When our pastor, Waldo Miller, lived in Pennsylvania, he had a kidney transplant and nearly died. The family all gathered to pray for him, and his wife wept hysterically. Suddenly, she began to laugh. Waldo asked, "Why are you laughing?"

"God just told me you're healed," she said, continuing to laugh.

"Well, He hasn't told me yet!" he moaned. Before long, he realized he was miraculously healed and his family rejoiced. He was given eight years to live after the transplant but lived more than 39 years, the longest living kidney transplant patient on record for many years.

Through Waldo I subscribed to *Mennonite Renewal Services Newsletter*, the charismatic arm of the Mennonite Church, where I read stories and news of renewal all over the country. Notebooks filled up with notes from teachings of well-known leaders, such as Dan Yutzy and Nelson Litwiller, long-time missionary from South America who had a dramatic "baptism in the Spirit" late in life. A sweet and gentle spirit characterized these people and they opened the Scriptures to fresh understandings of truth and power in Christ. I soaked it all up like a sponge as my mind and heart were opened in a new way to role of the Spirit in drawing people to Christ.

God had blessed us with two wonderful children and I was deeply grateful to Him for them, for their love and affection and the joy they brought to our lives. I dreamed of owning a piano some day for the children to take lessons, so I put an ad in the Newton paper. From nine calls responding to my ad, I chose the one from a widower in Newton for $200. His wife had been a piano teacher and rode horse and buggy into the country for years to teach some of her pupils. It was a four-foot upright, and we bought it for Janet's tenth birthday on January 27, 1975.

Jake took piano lessons as a child so he gave the children their first lessons. In two weeks Janet could play all the songs in the first book. Then she and Jared took lessons from Lois Leinbach's niece, Chris, until she left for college. Maurine Regehr became their third teacher and she and I became friends. After a time, Jared balked at practicing and decided he would rather play guitar, so we bought him one for

Around the piano, November 1975.

Christmas. He and his friend Royce played at a 4-H meeting and won a blue ribbon. Janet continued with piano and did very well at the state recitals in Hutchinson. She also took clarinet lessons at school and played in the middle school band.

As the months went on I was ready for a change from typing numbers on loan forms. The Lord saw my heart and opened another door for me. One day, Pastor Waldo came into the credit union on business and spoke to me confidentially. "Jane, I need a secretary at the church. Would you consider coming to work for me?" I was not very interested but offered to do the bulletin each week. By the end of that school year I wanted to be home with the children in summer. I resigned at the credit union and agreed to work for the pastor a few hours a week, beginning September 8.

After a few weeks on the job, the pastor informed me, "The church council decided to build an office for you in the basement next to my office." After the office was ready, he had another surprise. "We discussed your job at church council meeting last night. Someone insisted that, as a seminary graduate, you should be more than a secretary. We would like you to be our unofficial assistant pastor. What do you say?"

"What would that entail?"

"I'd like you to help me with hospital visitation, and I'll make a list of other things where I could use some help. I hope you'll consider it."

"I'll pray about it." The church was small and I knew they could not afford to pay an assistant pastor. Then I learned that my college friend, Anna Juhnke, who was on the church council, was indignant that I was hired as a "secretary." She insisted on this proposal. (Anna taught English at nearby Bethel College and also taught classes on women's issues. She was not about to see a sister taken advantage of or demeaned!) I talked it over with Jake. It was fine with him, so I accepted the job.

The church, amazingly progressive, bought a new automatic mimeograph machine. No more handle to crank. Jared loved to visit me at my office across the street and was fascinated with the new equipment. Before long, the pastor asked if I would be willing to have the church phone line installed at my home because we were both out of the office much of the time. I usually worked four hours a day, if that. Since I wrote the bulletin, I could take calls at home. Jake consented. My unofficial position was never announced or made known except to the church council, and I sometimes felt like an "invisible" pastor. However, I loved the people and learned to know them better. Many came to me with special needs or concerns. Serving had its rewards. Soon I was on many committees, usually as secretary. I also began leading a weekly women's Bible study and prayer group.

Jake was still busy with all his jobs and I missed him greatly. Why did he have to have so many? Often the words of Wit Ylitalo came back to me and I realized how prophetic they had been. Wit was the pediatrician's wife whose family visited us in Mississippi a week or so over Easter. She wrote in her journal, which she later shared with me, "Time for us to leave. I have such a huge lump in my throat. Said good-bye to Jane in the kitchen and we both cried. Her life will never be easy because of her dedication, and Jake's, but it will be rewarding. Jake has recently spent time in the Mississippi delta, which is this community magnified many times over, so who knows what they will accept, and at the same time. How do you educate your own and continue this work at the same time?...Jake seems two jumps ahead of everyone, his bright dark eyes show his intelligence."

Well, we were no longer in Mississippi, but here we were in Kansas and, I mused, look at all the things Jake is doing at the same time. Part-time jobs have a way of becoming more than we expect. I was jealous of his time at the Colonial House and learned the truth of the words a woman once told me, "business and family don't mix." It seemed we were not destined to work together. Since our Florida days, I was mother and homemaker, and Jake jumped with both feet into his career. As "unofficial assistant pastor" in a traditional marriage, I felt like a half-liberated woman. At times I felt unfulfilled and lonely in the midst of many people and activities. I cried out to the Lord, *What is my purpose here, Father? Please help me!*

Mary Rempel, a writer from church, had invited me to Creative Writer's Fellowship where we wrote monthly assignments and read them for critiquing. For a family chronicle assignment, I wrote about mom and the family. After I read, "College–A Dream Fulfilled," of how I got to go to Bluffton, Ruth Unrau, who had several books published and taught business at Bethel College, said, "Jane, you amaze me! You always did everything by yourself. You should write a book about your stepmother. But you'd have to write it as a novel because no one would believe you!" Now *I* was amazed. *No one would believe my story?*

Ruth continued, "You are a better writer than one author I know who keeps turning out one novel after another that are rather superficial." I was pleased, but found it hard to believe her words. However, Ruth planted a seed that day that became like a rock in my shoe that I had to get out. For years the question persisted – how would I write my story, as truth or fiction? Through many years to come, I prayed and pondered and wrote, goaded by Ruth's words.

Ruth also urged me that day to give my college story to Robert Kreider, dean at Bluffton when I was there. He lived in North Newton now and I was pleased to reconnect with my amazing, brilliant former History of Civilization prof. After reading it he told me, "I think Bluffton would like to have this story." They did, and published it in their October 1976 newsletter. I was reminded of the time I babysat and stayed overnight in Kreider's home. I was deeply moved by his humble prayer before breakfast the next morning, and his tenderness with his children, reminding me of Daddy's kindness to me when I was their age. Dean Kreider had served with MCC in Europe in food relief and resettling Mennonites from Russia after the war, recounted in his book, *My Early Years* (Pandora Press and Herald Press, 2002).

Friends and acquaintances worked at our Mennonite headquarters seven miles away at Newton. One day a college friend, Jeannie Zehr, editor of the women's mission magazine, asked me to write an article for her about missionary kids. Later I did a second one on widowhood and grief and one called "Mission At My Doorstep." For the first two I interviewed many people and sent out questionnaires. I enjoyed working on these projects and meeting many "missionary kids" and widowed women who shared their struggles and stories.

Jake enjoyed his great variety of jobs, college, restaurant, and trips. Hesston Corporation, started and owned by Mennonites, flew mercy flights for people in crises, such as a man in our church waiting for a kidney transplant. Jake was warned that if a kidney became available in Oklahoma City, Gerald would be flown there on a moment's notice.

One night around midnight the phone rang. Jake rushed back into the bedroom, "A kidney is available for Gerald! I have to go right away!" He jumped into his clothes and took off like lightning in our Mercedes. About a mile from the airport, the car broke down. He ran the last mile and arrived before the passengers! Always "two jumps ahead of everyone," Jake was never late if he could help it. Promptness was a trait drilled into him in his youth. The patient got his transplant but lived only a year and a half longer. Jake's over-zealousness for the patient cost him a broken block on the Mercedes that took over a month to repair.

Another hair-raising day, with Jared the culprit, sent Jake scrambling. He set the alarm for a 4:00 A.M. flight to Iowa and Dallas. But first he had to drive 35 miles to Wichita to get the plane and fly it to Newton to pick up the passengers. That morning he jumped out of bed and switched on the light. I saw that the clock said 6:20, not 4:00. Shocked, he hurried to the bathroom, turned around and fairly thundered, "Jane! I'm terribly late!" I was up as he jerked on his trousers without his underwear. Repressing the urge to laugh as he re-dressed, I asked if I should make coffee for the thermos. He said yes, then changed his mind, "No, there's no time!"

I made it anyway as he hurriedly shaved. "Look up Beechcraft Aircraft in Wichita in the phone book and call line service and tell them to get the Baron out and put the key in it." And he was off, five minutes after waking. The kitchen clock said 6:25 when he left! I called Wichita and was on my knees thanking God and praying for Jake when the phone rang at 7:30. He had made it to Newton. "Has anyone called yet?" he asked. They had not. He had made it to Wichita and back in an hour and beat the passengers. If anyone can make it in a pinch, Jake can!

Later Jake questioned Jared and learned he had fiddled with the alarm clock the night before. Many years later Jared revealed that he took the clock out to the street to play with a friend. "I liked the nice ring it made when the alarm went off," he said, "and I put it under a car. Phil (Simpson) and I pretended it was a bomb. Then I put the clock back in the bedroom." I was appalled. What a game for a little Mennonite boy! Jared told me as an adult, "I only remember playing with it once." Yes, after one of Jake's lectures, the children did not want to repeat the same offense.

In June of 1975, we left on a wonderful three-week family vacation, driving through the western states and beautiful British Columbia to visit Jake's family. As we drove the mountainous roads of B.C., I thought of Mary and Dick Rempel's son, Harvey, who was biking with a friend all the way from Kansas to relatives in B.C. Concerned about the two-lane treacherous highway with hills and curves, I prayed for their safety as we drove.

At Aldergrove, we met Jake's stepmother, Jessie, for the first time and made a trip to Vancouver Island. We enjoyed a memorable day in court with Uncle Nick Friesen and I took a picture of the children with Judge Nick in his robe. Returning through Yellowstone Park, we stayed overnight in a cabin and watched Old Faithful geyser spout, a marvel I had long wished to see. The children loved the trip, enjoyed Jake's family, and we came home refreshed. I made a scrapbook journal to document the details with pictures, brochures, and maps.

On July 2, we received the shocking news that after making it safely to B.C., Harvey Rempel had drowned there in a lake. Invasive weed had been allowed to grow in the public swimming area and Harvey, not being able to see it, became caught in it and was exhausted when he finally extricated himself. I couldn't believe it. What an enormous tragedy! I dreaded facing my dear friends. When I saw them the first time I could not speak. A flood of tears spoke my pain as these grieving parents and I embraced. Their loss was incalculable. Harvey, a brilliant student, had just graduated from high school and planned to enter college in the fall. Harvey had two younger sisters, Nadine and Nelda, who babysat our children. Before the service, our Writer's Fellowship provided a lunch for the family in their home. Our church family and many friends suffered with them in their deep sorrow.

Easter, 1976, was a festive time for us. Jake's father and Jesse came to celebrate Easter and Dad's 75th birthday. Dad, still in good shape, tilled our garden and our widow neighbor's with her tiller. He dug around the 50 blooming tulips I had planted. He walked with Jared to school and taught him how to "march." "We always had to march in school in Russia," he told us. "I still remember Lenin's teachings that we learned at school." How remarkable to know this man who lived during Lenin's godless reign in Russia! Janet was in middle school then, about a half mile from home, and rode her bike.

Jessie knitted afghans for the children for a previous Christmas; on this trip she brought pillows to match. We took sightseeing trips to historic Mennonite sites, churches, and towns, as well as the Eisenhower Museum at Abilene. For Dad's birthday we ate at the Pennsylvania Dutch buffet at the Colonial House in Hesston, then came home for cake with our British Columbia friends, Dick and Mary Rempel. Saturday night we ate at the German buffet with all the familiar foods Dad and Jessie liked. Jake was still very involved at the Colonial House. He had trained a new manager who needed ongoing help and encouragement. Jake filled in for him (with no pay) when he was sick for three weeks just before Dad came. Jessie had brought along a round loaf of traditional Russian Easter bread called *Paska*. On Easter she put on the icing and colored sprinkles.

Jessie sometimes played the piano for us. As an accomplished pianist in Russia, she grew up with a grand piano in her home. During the Revolution, the Russian Red Army took everything from them. In Canada, she was asked to play in church for "The Messiah" a number of years; but she had no piano at home on which to practice. She devised an ingenious solution. Propping up her book, she practiced on the kitchen table. Unlike Jake's parents, Jessie had come from a wealthy family. The Revolution, with war, abuse, and resulting poverty, and then the move to Canada, took their toll on Jessie. But her faith in God sustained her, and her kind loving ways were a blessing to us.

Dad delighted in their time with us, and years later wrote about it in one of his two books: "The children were happy to see us. Janet came to me repeatedly, especially in the evening, hugged me and said, 'Opa, I love you.' Jared, the eight-year-old, was never without his afghan, made by Grandma."

Dad still worked as a part-time pastor at age 75. He wrote, "Granddaughter Janet, 10, gave up her room so we could have privacy, with a bed for each of us…for two weeks I was not reminded of congregational responsibilities. I observed nature, woke up to spring, heard larks singing, and watched squirrels frisking about." Since Jake had frequent trips and the children were at school, Dad, Jessie, and I spent days shopping, eating lunch out, sightseeing, and visiting. Our time together resulted in deeper bonding and love. What a blessing family can be!

And another family blessing was in the offing.

CHAPTER 25

The Tribute

Let us, your servants, see your mighty deeds; let our
descendants see your glorious might.
PSALM 90:16 (GNB)

1976–1977

In July 1976, the children and I flew to Pennsylvania to see my father and family and to celebrate the Bicentennial, paid for with the $500 insurance payment. At a stopover in Chicago we saw Anna and John and the children briefly at O'Hare Airport, then flew on to Philly.

For two weeks Daddy chauffeured us around to places I wanted to see. We saw the house where he lived until he was ten, the nearby church at Deep Run, and the school he attended at Ottsville. We drove the beautiful, historic Delaware River road where he loved to take us as children. Janet and Jared especially liked the visit to Philly with Auntie Grace along to see the Liberty Bell, Independence Hall, and the "most historic room in the nation," where the Declaration of Independence was signed. We went to see Pappy Landis, Aunt Melba, and Uncle Ivan at the Landis homestead, and visited often with my sisters, brothers, and families. Tommy had moved home with Daddy from Chicago a few years before. He was now married and had a two-month old son, Thomas Michael, so we met the newest members of the family. One day Renningers took us to Nockamixon Dam and lake. Renningers hadn't changed a bit, except in age, since I grew up next door to them. Their friendly interest and humor made them as comfortable as family. I was sorry that Jake could not be with us. With his heavy responsibilities, he preferred to work. (He helped at the Colonial House until October 31, when a new manager began.)

I wanted to attend Deep Run East (Old) Mennonite Church for one service, where Daddy went with his mother until he was ten. I had marveled a few years before, when God called John Duerksen, husband of a friend from Writer's Fellowship in Kansas, to serve as interim pastor of this church. I hoped Daddy would visit the church and connect with them. John and Ruth Duerksen were lovely people. Since Daddy suffered from depression and loneliness when they moved to Pennsylvania, I told Pastor John about Daddy and asked if he would call and invite him to church. He did, and Daddy attended a few times but refused their invitation for dinner. John reported that Daddy was "shy and withdrawn."

We did attend Deep Run, and I was so blessed to be there with Daddy and the children. After the service, Ruth greeted me warmly with a hug and kiss. John prayed briefly for me about a family concern. As he ended, the tears in his eyes showed his deep compassion. I was touched by their love.

Daddy also took us to the cemetery where my mother, Grace, and step-mother, Jean, were buried. I had not been there in 11 years, since Mom died. I took pictures of the gravestones of my parents and Daddy's parents, Augusta and James Weaver, who I never knew. This way I had a record of births and deaths. I also took pictures of Daddy and the children by the gravestones to remember this day. I observed again that Daddy was married to my mother, Grace, the same month and year (June 1932) that his mother died. And I saw that he lost his wife, Grace, and his stepfather, Jim, the same month and year (January 1938). His younger years were full of grief. But Daddy enjoyed these days to the full with the children and me. It did my heart good to see him relaxed and happy.

Daddy with Janet and Jared at Pleasant Valley Cemetery, July 1976.

The weather was beautiful, and this visit to the hilltop cemetery by the lovely old stone church evoked a poignant sense of family history and continuity. I remembered the verse, "Lord, you have been our dwelling place in all generations," from Psalm 90, the text for my mother's funeral service 38 years ago. The mother I never knew but who had blessed my first three years with tender love and care was buried here. And here lay the mother I struggled to love and who cared so much. I had lost two mothers without being present with them, snatched away without saying "goodbye," or "I love you." Yet God had "taken me up," as the psalmist says, and took care of me. My thoughts turned to my remaining parent. *How long will Daddy be with us?* Wanting to make each day count, I relished every moment with the children and him. In November, Daddy would be 71 years old.

Back home in Kansas, a recurring thought crossed my mind, like a premonition. *Might Daddy get cancer?* Uncle Elvin Moser was suffering with liver cancer and Daddy was concerned. He felt close to Uncle Elvin, husband to my mother's oldest sister, Naomi. I had a growing feeling of tenderness toward Daddy and wanted to write something for his birthday on November 14. Our time at home in July had stirred many memories within me of my childhood and his loving care for me when I was sick. Many good memories surfaced. I recalled that Erlene Unruh, of Writer's Fellowship, had written a beautiful tribute to her father about his hands. That gave me an idea.

One day I sat down to write. I wrote and wrote and wrote, ending up with seven typed pages of my good memories of Daddy. Thoughts flowed and along with the good, the Lord helped me put into perspective those things that had been painful in his life. I called it *Tribute to My Father, Ralph Herstine*, and concluded it as follows:

> Daddy, if you have ever blamed yourself because of Mom's treatment of us,
> and suffered guilt and remorse over that,
> let me remind you of the Old Testament story of Joseph.
> His brothers hated him and wanted to get rid of him and sold him as a
> slave into Egypt.
> And when, years later, they came to Egypt to buy corn and found that
> their brother, Joseph, was ruler of the land and they were at his mercy,
> He kindly forgave them and told them with conviction,
> "It was not *you* who sent me to Egypt, but *God* brought me here
> in order that our people would have food to eat during the
> seven years of famine."
>
> The story of Joseph and his trust in God through years of loneliness and
> suffering has been a great comfort to me all through my life.
> And I am confident that it was not *you* who brought Mom to us, but *God*,
> for a reason we will not fully understand in this life.
> God does not make a mistake, He is wise and all-knowing, and He is LOVE.
> God bless you on your birthday and in the days and years ahead.
> May Jesus' love grow sweeter and your faith stronger is my prayer for you.

Through the years, God had given me understanding of the events of Daddy's life, the circumstances of his marriage to Mom, and insights into his personality and hers. The incomprehensible events of my childhood took on meaning and significance as the life, teachings, and sufferings of Christ became clearer through the New Testament.

I knew how withdrawn and unsociable Daddy could be at times, and how he felt inferior in some ways. He had not kept up the house for years, and Mrs. Renninger voiced her negative feelings about him when I visited with her. That made me sad. I sent him the tribute with a letter requesting that he take it along when he went to each one in the family, as he often did for dinner. I asked him to let them read it. Then I asked him to take it to Mr. and Mrs. Renninger next door for them to read. They had lived side by side with Daddy for 36 years! Lastly, I asked him to take it to John and Ruth Duerksen at Deep Run. He followed through, with results beyond what I could image. Seeds planted in the tribute bore fruit.

Glowing reports came back to me. Daddy appreciated the tribute tremendously. It had transformed him and his outlook on life. He usually called Anna, in Chicago, and me once a month. This time, when he called after his birthday, he was positive and full of news. The next time he called he said, "I took the tribute to the Renningers last night and Mrs. Renninger read it to Charlie, and I stayed from 7 until 11 o'clock! We had a wonderful visit." My spirit rejoiced, as I doubted that he had ever visited in their home before.

Daddy continued, "Tommy read the tribute and said Doris Dietz (a neighbor) wants to read it. All the others in the family read it, and (brother) Ralph's mother-in-law and sister-in-law want to read it, too. They all think it's great! And the other Sunday I told my minister at the door, 'You're doing a wonderful job! I want to congratulate you!'"

To me he said, "I like to spread cheer and make people happy!" Daddy had come alive! I couldn't stop thanking the Lord. "I also took the Tribute to John and Ruth Duerksen. Ruth read it aloud while I was there." The memories opened the way for him to talk freely about his life and they had a good visit. His self-image changed from negative to positive through the praise and love in the tribute.

Later, Millie said on the phone, "Daddy sure has changed. When I asked him to go to Brenda's (high school) basketball game Tuesday night, he went. That's a first! The next time he came, he asked when her next game was because he wanted to go!" Brenda, a star athlete in high school, played hockey, basketball, and softball. With a powerful arm as a pitcher, she was chosen Most Valuable Player three consecutive years in softball. A shelf full of trophies in their living room spoke of her athletic prowess. I was overjoyed to hear that Daddy finally took an interest in her games.

Daddy also talked about the tribute on the phone with Anna, who had a copy. She wrote me about their conversation and how she told him, "That's a priceless gift!" He responded, "You bet!" She made my day with, "I'm glad you're able to be so open with him because it's doing him a world of good. It's bringing back the gentleness and softness to his life. He seems so content compared with the stormy years previously. He's always cheery now when he calls, thanks to you!" My astonishment kept growing and I kept praising the Lord. Having heard that whenever we receive praise we should immediately give it back to the Lord in our heart, I did just that. I was getting lots of practice praising Him.

Sister Grace wrote me an epistle, mentioning "the transformation in Daddy," and trying to figure it out. She had read that approval has to come from within to be effective. "When I witness what has happened to Daddy's mental health as a result of your poem...the approval obviously didn't come from within himself, but from you (outside). This has puzzled me ever since I've seen the change in Daddy. He remains very happy these days...It's a wonderful change and I'm very happy for him."

I had also sent a copy of the tribute to Jake's parents. Dad was pleased and wrote, "I am sure you lifted him spiritually by doing that. Some people at his age feel that their life was a failure. And you reminded him of many good things."

Daddy had one living relative with whom he rarely kept in touch – his Cousin Ethel Smith who lived across the state. I began to correspond with her a few years earlier when he was depressed and I found her to be a dear person who loved the Lord Jesus. The tribute went to her as well, and she sent me a beautiful, lengthy response.

In part she wrote: "Your tribute to Daddy is so very wonderful; your love, I sensed, expressed in each line. It is written with such "Beauty;" with "Love" so pure and genuine. You've always loved him especially much." She said she wrote to him at Christmas and "To my great amazement he wrote three pages on both sides. And before I answered he wrote another one saying he hoped he had not offended me. He was waiting for a letter. He writes a very interesting letter – I've enjoyed them. He wrote, 'I have wonderful children and good sons-in-law as well as daughters-in-law; all treat me wonderfully and respect me.' Praise the Lord! He mentioned Tommy's baby boy. It is good that your Dad finds pleasure in and through the little fellow. God is good."

Since my teacher from first to third grade, Mrs. Fluck, was a member of our church, I sent her a copy of the tribute as well. She wrote expressing appreciation for "the privilege of letting me read it. It's beautiful, Jane, and I'm sure it was quite a blessing and satisfaction to him to know of your deep feelings for his love and devotion to his family...This has given me a much clearer picture of your Dad, as I always thought of him as very reserved, quiet, non-talkative, and somewhat unconcerned. Later I found him more outgoing and liked to talk as I talked more to him..." (Mrs. Fluck later painted a picture of our house, church, and community for me, and one for Anna.)

My dear friend Ruth Duerksen from Daddy's childhood church wrote, "We had a nice visit with your father a week ago and read your very interesting, well-written and very loving tribute...That was a very lovely thing to do and he certainly appreciates it. He was quite a different person to visit with this time than ever before and he had so many good things to say about his family."

Proverbs 23:24 says, "The father of the righteous will greatly rejoice, and he who begets a wise child will delight in him." I reflected that our mother in heaven must be rejoicing that her children knew and loved the Lord, and her husband greatly rejoiced in their children. And Mom must be happy as well at this turn of events with all her seven children.

At Christmas that year Daddy sent us a Christmas card, which read, "To my wonderful daughter and son-in-law"! He had never sent us a card before, though he did write letters about once a month in the years after Mom died. As a result of all the praise lavished on him in the tribute, and warm responses from family and friends, he was freed up to praise others. My cup was running over at the way God led and used the tribute in Daddy's life.

Uncle Elvin Moser, Aunt Naomi's husband, died in December. In January 1977, Daddy began complaining of stomach pain. After several weeks of this he went to his doctor who simply gave him pain medication. When he called me that month he sounded worried. "I sure hope it's not liver cancer like Uncle Elvin had," a foreboding thought which I tried to quell.

Daddy's discomfort continued through February. By March, he could not keep food down. The doctors suspected a blockage. I sensed something serious was going on and recalled the thoughts that crossed my mind as I worked on the tribute: *What if he gets cancer? Daddy may not be with us long anymore. The time to write something is now.*

In mid-March Millie called with a report. "Daddy is in the hospital. They did X-rays of his liver and a biopsy of his stomach. He can't keep food down and is very weak. His vital signs are very low." It sounded grim. Was he ready to die?

As we waited for results of the tests, I called brother Ralph to suggest that he ask his pastor, who was also his employer, to visit Daddy to talk with him to make sure he was trusting Christ for his salvation. They visited him together and Pastor Linford Rotenberger explained the plan of salvation and said, "You can know that you are saved." Though he probably believed in Jesus all his life, Daddy prayed to accept Christ as his Savior. After our uncertainty about Mom when she died, it was comforting to be sure Daddy was ready to meet the Lord. I was grateful for brother Ralph and Pastor Linford, who both cared deeply about Daddy. (Pastor Linford was pastor at our mother's church, the Church of the Brethren, so Daddy had a special tie with that church.)

That same morning Daddy had surgery for the double hernia he had endured for many years. Ralph reported that when they came to his room, he was sitting up reading the paper. Daddy's pastor from the United Church of Christ had been there the night before and asked Daddy if he was optimistic. He said he was. Pastor John Duerksen also visited Daddy. He had not only *one* pastor, but *three*, visiting and praying for him. God was supplying all his spiritual needs.

Later, when Millie visited him she said, "Jesus forgives our sins." And Daddy responded, "Yes, *all* of them!" Millie rejoiced at his confident words.

Then came the fateful day when Grace called me from Millie's. "I'm sorry to have to tell you this, but Daddy has stomach cancer. It's in all his organs, so it's too extensive to operate. The doctor said he has about three months to live." I was shocked, devastated. That meant he had until the middle of June! Surely something could be done. But there was nothing. I felt numb. The children and I prayed for Daddy at mealtimes and bedtime.

My sisters and Ralph called me almost daily with updates. Millie called a few days after the first call to say, "They made a small incision and put a tube in his stomach and closed him up. Daddy told me, 'I hope I improve now.' He still doesn't know the diagnosis."

On her next call, Millie reported, "The doctor told Daddy today that he would not recover. He had suspected cancer and wanted to know the truth. Daddy took it well. Ralph and Tommy were with him and Tom started to cry. Ralph struggled to keep back the tears. Daddy said, 'It's no use to cry; that's the way it is.'" Accustomed to accepting life as it came, he now resigned himself to his death.

Millie, sensitive and caring, said, "Pray that he doesn't linger long and suffer." I made phone calls to request special prayer for him and decided I must go home. I called Anna in Chicago. They planned to drive home the next week. We decided to overlap our visits a few days to stretch out our time with Daddy. How thankful I was that the Holy Spirit prompted me to write that tribute four months earlier. I could not have known, but God knew, how little time Daddy had left.

Jake and I made arrangements for the children's care and I flew home April 15 for a week. How I wished Jake could go, too, but his responsibilities took priority. Daddy was in a nursing home in Richlandtown. Anna and her family stayed at his house a few miles away and I could sleep there, too.

An intense week stretched ahead, probably my last with my earthly father. How could I give him up? My mind and heart filled with memories and gratitude, with anxiety and pain as my plane soared over the eastern half of the continent.

I recalled my visit with Daddy in July. One day he told me, "I listen to the Christian radio station all day long. One night when I couldn't sleep, I got up at 1:30 and called the station to ask for two requests, 'My Hope Is Built' and 'Higher Ground.' I waited up until 3:00 when they finally played them. I really like 'Trust and Obey', too."

That triggered another memory from years ago when he worked at the bakery for Mr. Fritz. "When I boarded at Fritz's house, Mildred Fritz always sang 'Trust and Obey' while she worked in the bedrooms. I'll never forget that. Mildred (the owner's daughter who ran the business) encouraged your mother and me in our friendship but we felt Grace's parents would not like her to marry me because she was so young. So we went to Maryland." No wonder they named their first child Mildred! Mildred, who never married, must have been a special person to my mother and Daddy. As a devout woman, she had probably been praying for them, and for Daddy after our mother's death. (Later I learned that Mildred was still living. One day Millie and I had the privilege of visiting her together at the nursing home in Coopersburg. She lived into her nineties.)

I recalled that in July Daddy told me he had attended a large hymn sing in a nearby town with a combined choir from many churches. He kept the program on the kitchen table with his Bible. In the program were printed the words to "Higher Ground." It seemed to be his heartfelt prayer. He read his Bible more after he was alone, facing the unknown. It was the Bible the Flatland Mennonite Church gave him and Mom when they joined the church, the same Bible which Mom had "beat us" reading through. Daddy's deep interest in spiritual things comforted me. And now his life was drawing to a close.

I breathed a silent prayer as my plane circled and landed in Philadelphia. "Thank you, Father, for Daddy and for his life. I commit him to you. Please take care of him and make me a blessing in the days I have with him."

Anna and John met me at the airport. We stopped first to see John's parents and then headed north 40 miles to Quakertown and nearby Richlandtown. It was good to be with family. But my heart was in my throat as we drove into the parking lot at Zohlman Nursing Home in the village Daddy and his mother moved to when he was ten. Now he was back at age 71, struggling with the ravaging effects of the disease he had dreaded. Into my mind flashed the verse, *All things work together for good to those who love God* (Rom. 8:28), and *We are more than conquerors through Him who loved us* (Rom. 8:37). I prayed God would help us all get through this victoriously. With aching heart, I walked with Anna to Daddy's room.

CHAPTER 26

A Father's Love

*As a father is kind to his children, so the Lord is kind
to those who honor him.*
PSALM 103:3 (GNB)

1977

As Anna and I entered Daddy's room in the nursing home, I was shocked at his appearance. He sat in a chair in the corner looking gaunt and exceedingly sad. I could hardly stand it. I gave him a hug and his first words to me were excruciatingly painful, "It's all over."

I wanted to scream, "No! No! No!" Instead I prayed, "Please God, help us get through this." I knew I must be cheerful. He talked little and seemed angry and bitter. I noticed the tube coming from under his gown, inserted into his stomach and into a transparent plastic bag on the floor, my first experience with this medical solution to a blockage. Then I realized that whatever he ate or drank came out through the tube. He got no nourishment. The occasional horrible screams and groans from the hall and other rooms were unnerving. I hated that he had to be in a place like this. But there was no way anyone could take care of him at home. I cried inside to see him in this pathetic condition. Anna had been there several days before I arrived.

I asked him some questions and made small talk about my trip and the family back in Kansas. After a while he said to me with his heart in his eyes, "You'll never know what this means to me to have you here."

His words warmed my heart. "I *had* to come, Daddy," I said. "I love being here with you."

Before I came I proposed to the family that we have an anointing service and ask Rev. Duerksen from Deep Run East Church to officiate. The family agreed. Rev. D. consented, then made clear that anointing does not always mean physical healing. "But," he told me, "*there is always spiritual healing!*"

This was a comfort. We scheduled it for Saturday evening, the day after I arrived.

Mom's death 12 years before had precipitated so much guilt, remorse, and unanswered questions about her salvation, that with Daddy I did not want to take chances. Through the years, I received greater understanding about the tragedies and pain of Mom and Daddy's lives. *The Gift of Inner Healing* by Ruth Carter Stapleton (sister of President Jimmy Carter) provided insights about healing of hurts.

In her sequel, *The Experience of Inner Healing*, I read about the effects of being born out of wedlock, as Daddy had been. Ruth writes, under "Influences Before Birth," of John the Baptist's mother Elizabeth greeting Mary, and how the unborn John "leaped for joy" in Elizabeth's womb. She says this shows how deeply affected we can be before birth and contrasts that with the emotional scarring of an unwanted unborn child. She states that the unborn child of an unwed mother experiences a "barrage of shocks," such as "the stream of negative emotions flowing through the mother's body to the child as she experiences the shame of confession to parents, the threat of abortion, the fear of exposure, the painful trauma of giving birth to an unwanted child. This can have an incalculably destructive effect on the emotions of the unborn infant." (Ruth Carter Stapleton, *The Experience of Inner Healing*. [Waco, Texas: Word Books, 1977], 21-22.)

As I've reflected on Mom's pregnancy with Grace that first year at our house, I realized that Grace would have experienced the same negative emotions and "barrage of shocks" from Mom's frustration with us, her arguments with Daddy, the embarrassment and shame she must have felt with the Landis family and neighbors, fear of being put out. For nine months Mom lived with the uncertainty of *Will Ralph marry me or not?* This was a sad beginning for Grace.

In spite of Daddy's unfortunate beginning, I often saw him as a warm, happy, even joyful, person, who loved his family, Jesus, and the church, in the way he was able. (I have his book, *Love of Life* by Jack London, in which he wrote "In the year of our Lord, A.D. 1922" when he was 17, and on the cover in large print, "Property of Ralph Herstine." It must have been special to him. He had no other books that we knew of, except his Bible.) His love of life and family had inspired me with a happy, positive outlook. My desire to make his last days on earth special consumed me.

Adding to the crisis with Daddy, on Saturday afternoon Anna and John got a call from John's father that his mother had suffered a bad stroke. This was a shock. We had just been with her the day before and she was full of life. John left immediately for Philadelphia and Anna stayed for the anointing service. My heart went out to them in this double tragedy. Yet John, full of faith and hope, was grateful for God's perfect timing, and that he was here instead of in Chicago. Now he could support his father as Anna supported Daddy.

When the Duerksens came to Daddy's room that evening, all of the family except Grace had gathered. We told them about John's mother's stroke and the pastor offered encouragement to Anna. Then he explained the purpose and background of an anointing service and read from James 5:14-15. We all joined hands around Daddy's bed. Rev. Duerksen laid hands on him and prayed, committing Daddy into God's care and for God's will to be done in his life. He prayed for healing in this life and the next as God saw fit. Then he anointed him with oil. As our family trusted Daddy to the Lord in this way, I felt deep peace and joy.

Then Daddy said to the pastor, motioning to the foot of the bed, "That's my youngest son, Tommy. Pray that he will grow up to have a strong faith." Tom sobbed loudly and left the room. When he returned, Daddy said, "I didn't mean to make you cry, Tommy." Rev. D. went to him and talked with him. Tom had regained control and thanked the pastor for coming.

Tom and Daddy had been very close, since Tom, born 14 years after Ruthie, grew up as an only child. Also, he and Daddy lived alone several years after Mom died. Daddy's illness was very hard for Tom to take. Hearing Daddy's concern for his spiritual welfare touched a raw nerve. I was glad when Tom rejoined us.

Rev. D. said to Daddy, "I'm sure you have had a very good life in many ways, and many good memories."

"Yes," Daddy agreed.

"Be thankful for that," he encouraged. Then he talked to Anna. He prayed for John's mother, that "if she be taken, may there be many good memories." Anna was impressed and related this to John when he called to say that his mother would not recover. In three days they took her off the respirator.

After Daddy's anointing, his appearance and spirit changed dramatically. The bitterness and despondency I saw when I came vanished. His peaceful face and clear, deep-blue eyes spoke of the peace of God within, testimony to God's answer to prayer. God was comforting our family in preparation for

Daddy's death. How I loved this man who had endured so many hardships, yet loved life so much.

Early on Sunday I wrote in my journal, "I realized this morning something that I can tell Grace and Ruth and Tom – that I am thankful now that Mom was our stepmother because if she had not come, we would not have these two extra sisters and brother in our circle. I love them and am glad for them – for what each of them has added to the family. Praise God for healing, for time to heal of past hurts, injustices, sins."

After church on Sunday I went to Daddy's room and told him about the sermon. "The pastor talked about Jesus' personal return and of death as an open door, like going from one room into another, without trauma. We don't have to be afraid of it. Are you afraid, Daddy?"

"No," he said simply, "I'm not afraid of death." It was wonderful to hear this coming from Daddy's lips and I knew it came from his heart. He hated being handicapped like this, burdened with every movement, feeling so tired, having the tube and no appetite. *Life is so wearying to him*, I thought. Yet he did not complain.

He said to me again, "You just don't know what it means to me to have you here. You'll never know. You'll never know." I leaned over and hugged him, struggling to hold back the tears. These were precious words to me.

"I think in a way I do know, Daddy, because I know how much you meant to me when I was small."

"I know, I know," he said, and our hearts meshed with the memories of those early difficult years and our deep empathy for each other in suffering.

"And, Daddy," I continued, "I wondered if you wouldn't like to go home soon and not linger here?"

"Yes," he agreed.

"We can pray that way sometime," I said, and prayed God would lead me in His timing before I left for Kansas the end of the week.

That afternoon I called Jake. Janet answered and sounded happy. "I worked on three leather projects yesterday," she said, "and I'm finishing my saddle today." She was a horse lover and was saving money from her *Grit* newspaper route to buy a pony. The children's motivation course gave her ideas, which I didn't entirely agree with. Jared was doing math and said he had a fun time at his friend James Reimer's house. Jake sounded relaxed and gave me the latest news, and I updated him on Daddy.

Monday morning when I visited Daddy, we talked about the anointing service and I asked if he was worried about Tom.

"No," he said. "Tommy's a good boy. He helps a lot. He mows for me and does a lot of other things and I can't pay him."

"Well, didn't you give him money for the mini-bike?"

"Oh," he said, "and the motorcycle – $500 – and he never paid it back. But I don't hold anything against him. I forgive him." And I thought he added softly, "Because of my Lord and Savior Jesus Christ." His speech was a bit slurred at that point, but his words made sense.

When I came back after lunch a woman who Daddy formerly knew as Schaeffer and her husband were visiting him. She introduced herself as his former neighbor. "I've known your father since he moved to Richlandtown with his mother years ago. We lived at the end of their lane. We are members at United Church of Christ and heard Ralph was here." It was heartwarming to meet someone who knew Daddy in the distant past, since he was ten, and who knew his mother and stepfather.

That evening Ruthie and her two girls, April and Karlene, came. Ruthie always livened things up. She shared news of the cousins. Scotty (Ruch) had a miraculous conversion, and Marty, his brother, was finishing Bible school. These two, plus their older brother David, had been orphaned when young and grew up at the Milton Hershey School in Pennsylvania.

I wrote in my journal, "A really different thing tonight: Daddy smiled several times!" I told him, "You look good tonight," and he responded, "Do I?"

Anna asked eight-year-old Karlene, "Do you want to get in bed with Grandpa?" A big smile spread over Daddy's face and he said she could if she wanted. But Anna was teasing. It blessed us all to see his face light up several times with a smile.

The next morning the doctor came to see him while I was there. In the afternoon, Millie came and Daddy got a bad coughing spell. I lifted him up and turned him over a bit and patted his back. Badly frightened, we called for the nurse. How thankful I was that we were both there at the time. In his weakened condition, he could not have called for a nurse.

At mealtimes, Daddy picked at his food and ate little. Hardly able to bear this, I usually fed him. Before supper he said, "Why don't you stay to see what I have to eat?" I was happy to oblige, glad that he asked me to stay.

That day Ruthie and the girls came to Daddy's house for supper where Anna and her children—John, James, and Amy—and I ate and slept. Ruthie enlarged on the story of Scotty's conversion. "Scotty was stabbed eight to ten times in the back by a gang of guys about ten years ago. His lungs were punctured and he almost died. Recently he was driving past the VFW where that happened and a strong feeling came over him. He thought, 'God saved my life back then so I would be saved,' and he felt cleansed. He pulled over to the side of the road and stopped. He cried and worshiped and prayed." I was moved and thankful for Scotty's experience of God's grace.

Ruth continued, "The next Sunday Scotty went to Faith (Baptist) Church, where I go, so he could go forward. Then he played on their softball team. While playing another Baptist church in Lansdale, he met a fellow from the Hershey School who invited him to his church, so he joined there." We all marveled at this change in Scotty's life.

"I got goose bumps telling about it," Ruthie said.

"I have them, too," I chimed in.

"I think Scotty got saved because Marty was praying for him," Ruth added. This incredible news lifted our spirits during this sad time. Then the conversation turned to Daddy.

Ruthie had another tidbit to share. "A nursing student had to interview a dying patient and she chose Daddy. He told her he appreciated talking with her and thanked her. I thought Daddy would be terrible suffering like this and complain all the time. But instead, he's just great!"

Hearing this from her was music to my ears. This youngest sister had engaged in loud arguments with Daddy for many years (Mom too!). The rest of us would never have thought of talking to Daddy or Mom like that. When she was little and Daddy tried to discipline her, Mom scolded him. So Ruth learned she didn't have to obey Daddy. Mom was hard on her and Ruth often rebelled. When Daddy lived with her family while Tom was in Chicago, Daddy gave her a hard time and after two years Ruth asked him to leave. (Ruth had enough problems with her husband, and later divorced him.) Ruth and Grace both had hard feelings toward Daddy for how he treated their mother, especially the last year of her life, and I was grieved as well. It was heartening to see that Ruth had softened toward Daddy.

After supper at the house when we all went to see Daddy, his pastor, Rev. Dieffenderfer, was there. He counseled Anna about John's mother, "When a patient is so far gone, the doctors know when to take them off the machines, and there is no need to feel guilty. Others whose lives may be saved may need the respirator." He prayed a beautiful prayer of thanksgiving, for love of family and the support that gives.

But Anna was quite torn up about John's mother, empathizing deeply with her husband. It was hard for her to be separated from him those days. We stopped at the 7-Eleven Store on the way home and there we met Pastor Dieffenderfer again, whom we liked and respected. Anna needed reassurance and she talked with him about her concern for the children, wondering if they should go to the funeral. "It's important for the children to grieve, too," he said, "so they should be at the funeral." Anna appreciated his counsel.

That week Daddy said to me, "I pray for Ruthie." I never heard him say he prayed for anyone before and I saw how much he loved her. As someone once told me, praying for someone is the most loving thing we can do for another. It was clear he had forgiven her and I was grateful for this glimpse into his heart. God was doing a wonderful work in his life—and hers—healing and restoring. While I had also felt grievously disappointed in Daddy at times, it was easy for me to forgive him because of his kindness and love to us girls when we were small. (Grace and Ruth did not have the same experience as motherless children.) One of my all-time favorite verses is, *"Love covers a multitude of sins"* (James 5:20; I Pet. 4:8; Prov. 10:12). Repetition in Scripture means: Pay attention! The Holy Spirit inspired three writers to pen this powerful teaching. (Later I acquired a wonderful book, *To Forgive Is Divine*, by Father Robert DeGrandis, which I love.)

On Wednesday I met a nurse in the hall who asked about the books and New Testament I had left in Daddy's room. "I'm a Christian, too," she said, when I told her the books were mine.

"My mother had breast cancer and we read James 5," she told me with shining eyes. "We called the elders of the church to anoint her and she was healed. My mother was with my aunt when she was dying. Suddenly, my aunt sat up in bed and said, 'I see a light and I see…' and she named relatives who had died before her. My mother became a Christian through that experience." I thrilled to hear this.

I told her I'd read Dr. Elisabeth Kubler-Ross' book, *On Death And Dying*, while Daddy was sick. "I heard her speak," she said. "She's a wonderful person. She's going to seminary now because of hearing her patients' testimonies of their faith in Christ." I marveled at these encouraging conversations with believers here. God was holding me in the palm of His hand; and I felt the prayers of many people.

When I returned to Daddy's room he asked, "Where were you so long?"

"I met a Christian nurse in the hall and she wanted to talk." I told him my conversation with her and added, "I've heard of many people who tell of seeing their loved ones in near-death experiences and then come back to tell of it. Just think, you'll soon get to see your mother and our mother, Grace!"

"That will be wonderful!" he said with hope and joy in his voice.

I recalled asking Daddy when I was young, "What was our mother like?" and his reply, "She was very good natured." It must have been a huge shock to him to learn that his new maid Jean, and second wife, differed greatly from gentle, nurturing Grace. I must have asked him a lot of questions because once he told me, "You think too much." But I was glad I learned this about my mother.

Daddy had no requests for his funeral except that he wanted a viewing. Millie knew he wanted the Scripture used at Uncle Elvin's funeral, Isaiah 60:19,20: "The sun shall no longer be your light by day, nor for brightness shall the moon give light to you; But the LORD will be to you an everlasting light…and the days of your mourning shall be ended."

Daddy was growing weaker and slept more and more. He seemed to be asleep at 12:10 noon when his food tray had not come, so I left. Later when I returned, he chided me. "Why did you leave without waking me and helping me? I heard you sneak out and talk to Adam (his roommate)."

"I didn't sneak out," I defended, but he repeated it, and I insisted that I hadn't.

He smiled then with a light in his eyes and said, "I was just teasing you."

"Actually, Daddy, I wanted to give your tribute to Rev. Dieffenderfer before he left for lunch." I had told his pastor about the tribute, since I felt he hardly knew Daddy, and asked if he wanted to read it. He did. I wanted him to have a good picture of Daddy's life to help with funeral planning.

I rejoiced at Daddy's next words, "You did more than your share this week in helping me." His affirmation was a wonderful gift.

Brother Ralph's appearance that afternoon made me glad. Daddy told him how I had "sneaked out" at lunch. So Ralph asked, "Are you behaving yourself?"

Daddy laughed and said, "She's a good girl." I enjoyed this visit with my brother who did not grow up in our home. His caring, gentle ways blessed me. He was so much like Daddy at his best.

At supper Daddy asked me to stay while he ate and I was more than happy to oblige. When I was leaving he said, "Thank you for staying."

I hugged and assured him, "That's okay, Daddy. I love you."

He responded, *"I love you, too!"* That was the first time I ever heard those words from him! How they blessed my soul, and how I praised Jesus in my journal that night.

John (Smith) had come back up to Quakertown to be with Anna and the family. Thursday morning he got a call that his mother died at 12:20 midnight. So he left again for Philly. This was a hard time for Anna.

When I helped Daddy out of bed at noon he said, "I forgot to tell you what happened this morning. When I got out of bed I fell on the floor and bumped my head on the cabinet. I tried to get up but I couldn't, so I called the nurse. I didn't make it to the bathroom in time, so she had to clean up the floor." Now they put the sides up on the bed so he could not get out without help. He was slipping fast.

Thursday afternoon I shopped for nightshirts for Daddy at Saul's, the clothing store in Quakertown. When I mentioned to the clerk that Daddy was dying of cancer but was "ready to go," he said, "Sometimes we think we are but when the time comes we're not. If we're a good Christian we're ready." Here it was again, a Christian at "the Jewish store" – so many men and women everywhere who knew the Lord. I told him, "Daddy is a Christian."

Daddy had shopped for years at the Quakertown stores, for Mom and himself, since she shopped only occasionally, except at the Farmer's Market. Daddy enjoyed talking with the various clerks and people at the service station, meat market, and Cassel's Grocery. As he used to say with a big smile when I lived at home, "People are so accommodating."

As I drove to Daddy's house, the realization hit that this was my last full day with him. Overcome with grief, I wept on the way back to the nursing home. I dried my eyes and prayed for help.

When I came to his room he asked if a man waited on me at the store and I told him of our conversation. As we visited, I sewed name labels on the three new shirts. Anticipating our parting the next day, near suppertime I said, "Daddy, I'd sure like to stay longer if I could."

"I know you would. You always liked it at home. You always liked home." It was true. No matter how bad things were, it was always home, and I loved my family.

I told him, "If you're still here in summer I may come back with Janet and Jared." But in my heart I hoped he wouldn't linger that long. It would be hard for them to see him in this condition.

When I left, a flood of emotion swept over me and I cried as I drove. Daddy's tenderness, love, and total helplessness tore me up. At the house, a thousand memories of "Home" flooded my mind, all the good and dear times and people. Though there had been tough times, wonderful warm times also abounded – and so much love! As I entered the empty, lonely house, waves of tender love washed over me. I understood clearly that God's grace and presence had sustained our family through all the years. And I saw that from Daddy's "solitary," humble beginnings with a single mother, God had "set him in a (large) family" (Psa. 68:6). I thanked God for Daddy and all the good memories, and a deep peace settled over me.

That evening Grace, Ruth, April, Karlene, Tom, Anna, and I visited Daddy. Later John and his dad came in, having driven up from Philly. As John's dad talked calmly about his wife who had died that morning, Ruthie let the tears run down her face, unembarrassed. Though she seemed tough at times, she had a tender heart.

Anna told Daddy, "Mrs. Renninger (our next door neighbor) told me that Mr. Treffinger (long-time funeral home director) said he enjoyed talking with you so much at Arner's Restaurant (where Daddy ate breakfast almost every morning)." The restaurant people had sent Daddy a card. They were like family to him.

A while later, Daddy requested, "Grace, do me a favor and ask Mr. Treffinger to come visit for an hour sometime." Daddy considered him another friend. Grace worked for Lawyer Freed in town and knew the townspeople as Daddy did. She took care of his business and advised him on various matters and he depended on her.

Later we all congregated at Millie and Ralph's home to discuss and clarify matters regarding Daddy. Anna stopped in for a few minutes and said to Grace, "John's dad said a couple of times about you, 'She sure is good looking!'" (Indeed, Grace was known as the "pretty one" in the family by some who freely spoke their thoughts. Besides that, to me she had a perfect figure. She was a cheerleader in high school, had personality plus, and got good grades. Sometimes I envied her, but I knew her life had not been easy. She struggled with feelings of not being loved because Mom and Daddy "gave her away" to the neighbor, Olive, from nine months until she was five years old. Though she usually treated Daddy well outwardly, she carried some hard feelings toward him.)

As we talked, Tom and Grace agreed to whatever the family decided concerning the funeral and other matters. Then Grace said, "I've come to realize that I do love Daddy." I was glad to hear this.

That evening Ruth told me, "The day before Mom died, she sat up in bed calling Tommy and Scott" (her brothers who preceded her in death early in the same year Mom died). Grace said that the last week when Mom was delirious, she often called out their names. Millie told me that Mom had also called her name and it was so hard to visit her. At other times she called Anna.

Brother Ralph told me how hard it was for them to have Daddy at their house every Saturday. Lonely and depressed, he came uninvited and stayed for the day. Ralph and his wife Janice often resented his visits. Ralph added, "Later that changed completely, and we enjoyed having him. Wendy especially liked Daddy and sent a message to him in the hospital. Daddy told me, 'Yes, Wendy always liked me.'" Ralph continued, "Daddy used to tease the children and it meant a lot to them to have him there." It warmed my heart to hear of Jeff, Wendy, and my namesake Janie (Linda Jane) enjoying their grandfather when my own children were so far away.

Whenever I went to Quakertown I stayed with Millie and Ralph and helped Millie with outside work. They had many big trees around their house and over the winter sticks accumulated on the lawn. Though I was sleeping at Daddy's house, I told Millie I would gather sticks and branches for her on Friday morning so they could mow. I loved the physical exercise and the weather was great. Then I planned to visit Daddy and leave for Philly at 11:30 A.M. Since I had only a week with Daddy, I usually spent the whole day with him.

Thursday morning I told Daddy, "Tomorrow morning I'll be in a little later because I'm going to pick up branches for Millie." I was astonished when he began to cry. He had not cried since I came and I felt like a heel. I certainly did not mean to upset him.

"I think Grace loves me the most," he wept. Why would he say this? Was he trying to play one of us off against another? I saw how lonely he was and that he craved visits from his children. Grace had been at the hospital many hours when he had surgery and had visited him frequently. The others went as much as they could. Daddy seemed to measure our love by how much time we spent with him.

"I'm sorry, Daddy. I'll work as fast as I can and will still get here early," I assured him, convinced I could do both and not shortchange him.

The next morning I went out early and worked like a house afire. Arriving earlier than usual at the nursing home, I met Daddy as the nurse wheeled him into his room from his shower. He looked surprised and pleased. Daddy knew I loved him very much. We talked about the past and I read Scripture to him. Though I dreaded leaving him, I had a plan.

A year earlier, I attended a meeting with Janet at the retirement home in Hesston. After the girls' mission and service group gave their program, we visited with the residents. A man introduced himself to me as Jacob Boehr and told me his story. He was 94 years old. When his wife was dying of cancer five years earlier, he asked her how she wanted to die.

He told her, "You have a choice. Do you want to be in a wheel chair and in bed all the time or do you want to go 'home?' We can pray about it and God will answer and take you home." He reminded, "Jesus said, 'Ask and ye shall receive' and 'where two or three are gathered together, there I am.'"

She said, "Pray for me to go home." They prayed and Jacob "knew the day she began to die." Three weeks later she was gone, with no pain, but with great peace. As I listened to Jacob's story, I felt that I was in the presence of a true friend of God. God was so real and personal in his life. I believed God sent him to me that night for a purpose. I would never forget his story.

Daddy listened intently as I told him Jacob's story. Then I said, "You have a choice too, Daddy. Do you want me to pray for you to go home rather than linger and suffer?"

"Yes, you can pray for me," he said.

I put one hand on his shoulder and held his hand. I had prayed for others, in Bible studies, in my home, and over the phone, but this was the most poignant prayer of my life. The words flowed forth as I ushered my father into the presence of our heavenly Father. I thanked God for Daddy's life and love and asked Him to please take Daddy home soon to heaven. Suddenly, I choked up, overcome with emotion as I realized this was probably my last goodbye. As I said "Amen" tears ran down my cheeks and involuntarily I stroked Daddy's face gently with my hands.

He looked at me and I was struck again by his clear blue eyes. He said kindly, "You don't have to do that."

"It's just so hard seeing you here like this," I said. "Remember how you took care of me when I was sick in the night with ear aches?"

"I know, I know."

"I came because I wanted to take care of you like you took care of me. We all feel like this, Daddy. We feel sad, even Ruthie, though she doesn't show it like the rest. Your illness has brought greater unity and cooperation to the family." Then I added brightly, "If I don't see you here again, I'll see you over yonder. You can come to meet me when I come." And he smiled a faint smile.

As I was leaving he said, "Have a good trip back." I walked back to his bed and said I would. Those were his last words to me. As I exited the building and went to Daddy's car I was struck by his courage. His facing death with courage and peace gave me strength and comfort. God's Spirit sustained Daddy and all of us.

In the bright April sunshine, my heart sang in the midst of sorrow and wonder – wonder at the God who loved us, and Jesus who died so that some day we would be with God and our loved ones forever in the great Resurrection. For Daddy, that day was soon to come.

CHAPTER 27

Graduation to Glory

Death is swallowed up in victory.
But thanks be to God, who gives us the victory
through our Lord Jesus Christ.
I CORINTHIANS 15:54,57 (NKJ)

May 1977

Brother Ralph drove me to Philadelphia and Anna, John, and John's dad took me to the airport for my flight home via Columbus, Dayton, St. Louis, and Kansas City to Wichita by 8:00 P.M.

The family had fared well in my absence. Saturday Jake and Jared went to the church district men and boys' retreat until Sunday noon. Janet had her friend Karen over for the afternoon and overnight.

A busy week lay ahead with the Mission Aviation Seminar at the college, which Jake helped organize. Representatives came from all the Christian schools with aviation programs around the country, including LeTourneau in Texas, Mission Aviation Fellowship in California, and Trinity Western College in British Columbia. Speakers inspired aviation students with stories of mission pilots and challenged them with Christ's call to missions. A highlight for our family was having former missionary pilot Ralph Borthwick in our home for dinner and overnight. He had flown for Jungle Aviation and Radio Service (JAARS), the flying arm of Wycliffe Bible Translators in the Amazon region of South America. He had also taught flying at Trinity Western College. A delightful guest, he shared experiences and miracle stories of flying in some of the most primitive and inaccessible areas of the world. Many more stories were in the book, *Into The Glory*, by Jamie Buckingham, which Ralph sent us later as a gift. It chronicles the work of JAARS pilots on several continents. We enjoyed the inspiration and hair-raising stories.

Many activities that week kept me from dwelling on Daddy. Sunday night I talked with Anna on the phone. She and John stayed on to help John's dad after his wife's funeral. Anna said, "Last Tuesday already Daddy told me, 'I'm giving up. I'm not getting out of bed anymore. I'm not eating. You can tell Jane I'm giving up.'"

Anna had asked, "How do you think that will make her feel?"

"Well, you don't have to say it like that then." Not surprised at the news, I knew Daddy's heart was set toward his heavenly home.

Monday afternoon Millie called at 3:30. "Daddy died at 4:00 today (EDT—one-half hour earlier). The nursing home called Ralph and said Daddy was not good and he should come. By the time he got there, Daddy was gone." Millie added, "Mr. Treffinger came to visit Daddy last week. They didn't talk about the funeral but just visited, like they used to do at the restaurant." We were sad that none of us could be with him when he died, yet we knew that Jesus was there. He did not die alone. What a blessed hope! Daddy had graduated to glory! He had gone "into the glory," like the book title.

Jared got home from school first that afternoon and I told him, "Grandpa Herstine died today."

He cried, greatly disappointed. "But I wanted him to be healed. I prayed for him to be healed."

"I did, too, and I'm sorry he didn't get well," I said, "but sometimes our bodies are so worn out that they can only be healed in heaven. Grandpa is in heaven with Jesus now and he has no more pain. We can thank God that he took him home so quickly." And Jared was comforted. Later, Janet, too, was saddened by the news but she was not as attached to Daddy as Jared, who had gone with me more often to see him.

Again I made plans to go "home" without my family.

The viewing at Treffinger Funeral Home turned out to be a meaningful, joyful time. The family arrived early and we gathered around the coffin. Daddy looked so natural, so peaceful, as if he were sleeping. I had often thought Daddy was handsome and he still looked so to me.

The first person I recall coming in was Uncle Alfred, my mother Grace's oldest brother. He said, "How are you doing?" with his heart in his eyes. His look of empathy and compassion caught me off guard and the tears flowed briefly as he hugged me. The fact that he was my mother's brother and had suffered through the loss of his sister—my mother—had created an unspoken bond between us. I didn't know him well, but I knew his deep love for family included us girls.

Many people shared memories of Daddy or bits of news. Oscar Frei, my former Sunday school teacher and dear friend told me, "Twelve people from Arner's Restaurant were planning to visit your father tonight at the nursing home. They were so surprised to learn he died. They called him 'Pop.' One of the men who works with me kept saying he wanted to see his 'buddy,' and finally saw him Sunday night (the night before he died). He teased your dad about not giving the nurses a hard time – like he gave the waitresses at the restaurant – and made your dad laugh." This warmed my heart. Daddy had so many good friends at that restaurant his last years of living alone.

Funeral director Mr. Treffinger told brother Ralph that it was easier making Daddy look like himself because he knew him so well. At the restaurant, Daddy always sat at the counter to eat, so he was always with other people like Mr. Treffinger.

Many neighbors, friends, church people, and family came to visit and express their sympathy and memories of Daddy. I could not remember a time when I felt so loved for who I was and for who we were as a family. Who ever said viewings are morbid? This viewing was anything but that. It provided a beautiful time for the family to receive comfort and encouragement in a setting of informality and humor.

Former next-door neighbor, James Renninger, told me that when he told his father that Daddy had died, Mr. Renninger had tears in his eyes. I was thankful Daddy had taken the tribute for them to read and that they had a special visit.

Pappy Landis, my mother's father, sat in the front row of chairs where he received each one of us siblings in turn and gave us his blessing. At age 86 he was in fairly good health. He looked good, better than I ever remembered seeing him. Often somber and quiet, his face glowed with warmth and life. Never openly affectionate, he surprised me with a warm hug and held my hand all the while he talked. He reminded me of the Old Testament patriarchs with his words, "God bless you and Jake and the children" and went on and on with his blessings. What a gift!

Pappy told me, "Our pastor, Rev. Rotenberger (Church of the Brethren), brought me Communion this afternoon, but I'm still Lutheran." He was proud of his Lutheran heritage. "The whole family went to the Church of the Brethren and I didn't want to split up the family, so I went there, too. I sang in a men's quartet and sang German solos."

He went on, "The Bible says we will live three score and ten years. But the Lord gave me sixteen years of grace. I asked the Lord what He has for me to do yet. Every night I pray and ask the Lord why I have these sixteen years of grace." I loved getting this glimpse into my grandfather's heart. I believe our kind and faithful God kept him alive to bless us motherless girls and Ralph in the loss of our father.

"You girls always meant so much to me. I liked when you came to play at our house when you were little." Then his thoughts turned to Grammy, "Grammy suffered so much the last years." Yes, her tiny frame succumbed to osteoporosis at age 82, three years before, but her faith burned brightly until the end. My heart filled with praise for my godly grandparents.

When everyone had left except our family, we stood around feeling a little lost. We went to the coffin one last time and as I stood there with Tommy, I reached in and stroked Daddy's hand. "How can you do that?" Tommy said. He couldn't believe I would touch a corpse, but to me, it was the physical remains of someone I loved, and who gave me life. His life and love had demonstrated to me the Father's love. God loved us all so much and said, "I will be a Father to you, and you shall be My sons and daughters" (2 Cor. 6:18). Gratitude for Daddy's tender love to me as a young child and throughout my life flooded my being. Memories of his hands clasped in prayer at each meal – those hands that worked hard for us all those years – were special to me. Touching them was for me a warm, appropriate farewell.

Daddy had died on May 2, 1977 at age 71 years, 5 months, and 18 days. He had outlived Mom by almost 12 years. I remembered the revelation from years ago that Mom would not live to be 50 but Daddy would live to be 70. I was amazed that it had come true. God spoke to me in my grief as a child, and comforted me with this knowledge.

Before I arrived "home," the family had met with Rev. Diefenderfer to plan the funeral. As they concluded he said, "I am so amazed at your family and how you work together so well and get along. Many families like yours fight and hate one another." When I heard this, I remembered Daddy's teaching that we "love one another." It had borne fruit. Though I was not present for the funeral planning, the pastor had a copy of the tribute as my contribution.

May 5, 1977, dawned bright and beautiful in southeastern Pennsylvania. Stepping outside into the morning sun, I inhaled deeply of the spring air. Temperatures in the 70s promised a perfect day. Spring arrived early that year adorning trees and flowers in a glorious array of color: pink and white dogwood, yellow daffodils, pink magnolias, sweet-smelling lilacs. And everywhere lacey green leaves sprouted on thousands of trees awakening to the new season. My heart rejoiced and I felt enveloped in God's love.

Though Millie, Anna, and I had sung at Mom's funeral, we had not even thought of singing at Daddy's. It would be too emotional, and the pastor probably didn't know we sang together for seven years. The family gathered at the United Church of Christ in Richlandtown to celebrate Daddy's life and home-going memorial service. We walked in together to the front rows. When we were seated, the organist played, "All the Way My Savior Leads Me."

Rev. Diefenderfer read the comforting words – "I am the resurrection and the life" (John 11:25); "But now is Christ risen from the dead" (I Cor. 15:20); "O death, where is thy sting?...your labor is not in vain in the Lord" (I Cor. 15:55-58); and the text Daddy wanted, "Your sun shall no longer be your light by day, for the LORD will be your everlasting light, and the days of your mourning shall be ended" (Isa. 60:19-20).

As we sang "My Hope Is Built," Daddy's favorite hymn, I cried hard, glad for the noise of the music to drown out my sobbing. "It Is Well With My Soul" comforted and calmed me down. Along with grief, I felt joy that Daddy was safe at last with Jesus.

In his remarks, Rev. Diefenderfer said, "Ralph lived his life in the sight of God, as Joseph did. He shared with a broad spectrum of people and with many emotions. Joseph had an enduring faith. Joseph knew 'the Lord is with me' when his brothers sold him into slavery, through his trials in Potiphar's house, and in prison.

"Moses was a quiet man. His brother had to speak for him, yet Moses was always present as a source of strength and authority. He was always out in front where the people could see him. Ralph was also a quiet man, but he was present with his family.

"Our faith allows us to be in despair, even to be angry at God. That's okay. Tragedy struck Ralph twice in the death of his wives." The pastor gave a beautiful perspective to life – the Israelites and Daddy's, comparing Daddy's life to the Israelites and to the patriarchs.

He talked about the context of Isaiah 60, explaining the times in which the people of God lived. Then he returned to Joseph. I was gratified that he had the tribute with him in the pulpit. He said, "As Jane wrote in her tribute to her father" and he read from the last page about Joseph forgiving his brothers. He read how it was God who brought Joseph to Egypt and how it is God who leads and guides in all the circumstances of our lives and who guided Daddy in his life.

Such a poignant message gave great beauty and dignity to Daddy's life, and lifted it to a higher plane – the "higher plane" Daddy longed for and sang about in the song "Higher Ground."

Later I was blessed to meet Richard with Mr. and Mrs. Renninger, our long-time, loving next-door neighbors. Then I saw Rev. Rotenberger who told me, "I visited your father last Thursday and read to him from I Peter about 'our inheritance in the heavens.' He really seemed to grasp hold of it and wanted to go home to be with the Lord." I was so grateful for brother Ralph's pastor and his words.

The church had many wide steps leading up to the sanctuary. As I started down, then turned around, I saw Grace coming out of the church alone. On her face was a look of bewilderment and distress. I rushed to her and asked, "Grace, what's *wrong?*"

"We never knew how to love each other!" she cried in anguish.

"But I think we do love each other as a family," I said, surprised at her words.

She agreed, with feeling, *"Oh, yes!"* What could she have meant? That she and Daddy didn't know how to love each other, and she felt the loss? But he had said to me, "I think Grace loves me the most!" Grace had struggled to feel loved by her parents since they "gave her away" as a baby, and that pain persisted throughout Daddy's life, and many years later.

We drove to the cemetery at the Springfield Church at Pleasant Valley, where my two mothers were buried. There I met Rev. and Mrs. Duerksen from Deep Run and introduced them to my mother's two sisters, Aunts Naomi and Melba.

"I see a resemblance between you and your aunts," Mrs. Duerksen said to me.

"But Mom always said I was a Herstine," I countered, "and Millie and Anna were Landises." However, Naomi and Melba agreed that I did look like my mother.

"Millie is the image of your mother," said Naomi, "but you look like her, too." Interesting how Mom had defined me in many ways. It pleased me immensely to learn this from my aunts.

After the burial, we went to a third church, my home church, Flatland Mennonite, where I grew up, and directly across the street from the Renningers. Here Mrs. Renninger and women from the church provided us with a fine lunch. It was a great time of fellowship around the tables. I sat between Aunt Naomi and Rev. Diefenderfer. Rev. D. told me he really struggled with his sermon because he knew that others in the family did not all share the same feelings I had for my father, which he read in the tribute. But I believed the Holy Spirit led him in his appropriate remarks for all of us.

Across from me were brother Ralph and his wife, Janice. Aunt Naomi told incidents about the family and our mother. "When your mother got her first glasses, at maybe age eight or ten, she fell off a plank across a stream and lost her glasses. Grammy had to get her new ones. And Grace and I were both confirmed in the Lutheran Church, where Pappy belonged. But later at the Brethren Church we accepted Jesus as our Savior. We were baptized at the Quakertown Brethren Church because they had a baptistery under the pulpit and our church didn't." Aunt Naomi continued, "Grandfather John Ackerman, Grammy's father, was the German minister and he baptized us. After he baptized me he thanked me with tears in his eyes and I saw how important baptism was to him. That made a big impression on me."

Then she recalled the night Ralph was born. "That night your Dad brought you three girls up to our house and took Aunt Hattie down to your house. She was midwife for over 1000 babies in three counties, you know. Aunt Hattie knew something was wrong when Grace was in labor. They drove to the hospital in much snow and Ralph was born and your mother received a blood transfusion. But it was too late. The next morning your dad drove to Grammy's and told them Grace had died. He took it very hard and got so discouraged when the housekeepers didn't stay. We all felt very bad for him."

Many times throughout my life I felt like a motherless child, and I'd sing the spiritual, "Sometimes I Feel Like A Motherless Child." Surely Millie, Anna, and Ralph felt the same. But we knew that God was watching over us. That day as we listened to our mother's sister, our strong bond with the Landis family was powerful and real to me.

Naomi continued, "Your dad always brought you back to Grammy's when a housekeeper left. Melba was 17 and going to Allentown high school. But there was so much confusion at home that she couldn't study and Grammy needed her help. So she quit high school and helped care for you girls and baby Ralph." I had not known this. How indebted I felt to Aunt Melba for her sacrifice. I went on to finish high school, college, and seminary, and she never finished high school. Those were hard days for everyone in the family.

After lunch, we siblings met at Daddy's house. We sorted through everything, each choosing special keepsakes, in preparation for selling the house. We shared stories, and Ruthie "took the cake" with her rare memories.

"Remember the time I fell on the bike and bit my tongue off? It was only hanging by a membrane! And the time Grace and I sat on the back of the car before Daddy backed out of the driveway and Grace fell off? Grace yelled and Daddy stopped just in time or he would have run over her! That was close!" Then she laughed her famous hearty laugh.

"And remember the day we were supposed to bring Renninger's goats in from the field on a very hot day? Mr. and Mrs. Renninger were at work and they told Richard to be sure to bring them in so they wouldn't die. Well, we were playing and forgot. And the goats died and got bloated. So we took them into the barn and tied them up as if they died there. Renningers never said a word, but they couldn't understand how that happened." Again she laughed loudly. How we all laughed that day. We rarely were all together, and after the strain of the past months, the sadness lifted and it was good to laugh.

Ralph told me, "What bothers me the most now is that you and Anna might not come home as much anymore." I assured him that I still wanted to come to see him and all of the family.

Before I left for Kansas, Grace called me to say goodbye. I listened with joy as she said, "I enjoyed so much being with all the family at one time. It 'put me in my place' in relation to the rest of the family." She kept telling us the past days that Daddy always said to her, "Stay in your place." "Well," she continued to me, "now I've found it!"

Anna shared with me that she had a good visit with Grace who said, "It's so great to be a part of this family. Some families fight so, but our family loves each other. I'm happier now than I've ever been."

My heart felt light as I headed back to Kansas. When I changed planes in Chicago and re-boarded, I discovered seven people from our Mennonite headquarters offices in Newton, flying home after meetings in the city. Jacob T. Friesen, my former pastor at Bluffton, was among them, as well as Heinz Janzen, our executive secretary and a member of our small group. The others were all familiar to me and they greeted me warmly. Heinz sat in the empty seat beside me for a while and I shared about Daddy and the funeral. How good it was to have a friend—and long-time pastor—to visit with on what could have been a lonely flight after such an intense time. The

Lord provided a whole delegation of friends to travel with me. "The Lord is my shepherd, I have everything I need."

Arriving home the day before Mother's Day, I looked forward to celebrating with the family. Janet had not forgotten her goal of buying a pony and greeted me excitedly. "Mommy, Mr. Davis, the sixth-grade teacher, has a show pony for sale for only $200, and a gelding he'll practically give away free!" I hated to throw cold water on her dream, but we lived in town and had no place to keep a pony, let alone *two* ponies. I didn't approve, but Jake did not discourage her. What were we in for now?

CHAPTER 28

A Mother's "Nightmare"

*Delight yourself also in the Lord, and He shall give you
the desires of your heart.*
PSALM 37:4 (NKJ)

1977–1979

After my intense week away, Mother's Day soothed my mind and heart.
Being with Jake and the children provided a wonderful respite after the
emotional roller coaster of the past months. I was eager to share about my
time in Pennsylvania. Not prepared for all the sympathy at our church in
Hesston, I asked to go to First Mennonite in Newton and Jake agreed.

Our church, the former old United Methodist, had a bell tower with a bell
that was rung every Sunday morning. Jake rang the bell for several weeks
when the regular bell-ringer was gone. One Sunday he asked Jared and Janet
if they would like to ring it. Thinking they were not quite strong enough,
they both pulled with all their might. The bell turned over and wound up
the rope. As the children watched anxiously, Jake climbed to the tower and
fixed it.

In stark contrast to that white frame building, First Mennonite had a
large stately sanctuary, which boasted lovely stained-glass windows, opened
that morning to let in the cool fresh spring air. Having arrived early, we
enjoyed bird song until the majestic strains of the pipe organ prelude
began. We noted that the service was broadcast every Sunday morning. The
reverent worship ministered peace to me. Afterwards, warm greetings from
a surprising number of familiar faces made us feel at home. Both of the children were pleased to see their classroom student teachers.

Dinner at the Colonial House with two other families provided fun and
fellowship. Mrs. Fred Stucky, who had seen us in church that morning, came
to our table to meet us. When I introduced Jake as "Jake Friesen" she looked

puzzled and said, "Jake Friesen gave a dialog sermon with our pastor last Sunday."

Jake laughed and said, "I'm the *real* Jake Friesen." She laughed then, too, and I explained that my husband was Jacob J. and that Jacob T., the one she heard, had been my pastor when I was in college. "The Mennonite Game" is a favorite pastime in Mennonite territory or on meeting other Mennos anywhere: "Who is your family? Are you related to so and so?"

The next order of business that day was seeing *the ponies*. I was still hesitant about this, but Mother's Day put me in a positive mood. From the beginning I felt uneasy listening to the motivation course for children as the woman's persuasive voice explained in detail how to get your heart's desires. "First you figure the cost. Second, list all the obstacles and roadblocks to attaining your dream. Third, list how to overcome the obstacles." Just like that. In my mind it was akin to giving them the keys to the car. But Jake was strong on teaching the children self-motivation. After listening to that course, Janet had asked Jake, "Daddy, can we get a horse?" Not wanting to disappoint her, Jake stalled for time.

I jumped in, "You *can't* have a horse! We live in town and have no place to keep it." I hoped that settled the matter. But Janet persisted. She and her father figured on paper. "You'll need a barn with a foundation," he counseled, listing costs, hoping to convince her she couldn't afford it on her $5.00 a week Grit income.

When I returned from Pennsylvania I found, written large across the top of the May calendar in the kitchen, "Pony, Pony, Pony, Pony, Pony." She had won Jake over. As he told me, "Maybe a pony would be good for her. It can keep her out of trouble." With him gone so much I worried, *Can I handle this by myself?* I knew absolutely nothing about horses, and now it was about to happen.

That evening we drove to Mr. Davis's house. Janet was obviously happy riding the pretty red Welsh show pony with a striking blaze (white stripe down her face). I had to admit that Wendy was handsome.

"My daughter won lots of ribbons showing Wendy," Mr. Davis said, "but now she wants a horse. She'll sell her to you for $200. And if you want June Bug, the two-year-old stallion, you can have him for free."

"I have $200 in savings from my *Grit* newspaper route," Janet offered, and we all laughed at her enthusiasm.

"We'll have to talk it over and let you know," Jake told Mr. Davis.

Considering how this pony had practically fallen into her lap for the exact amount she had saved, I relented and suggested the farm closest to town where an older man, Mr. Sommerfeld, kept his ponies. They charged $8.00 a month for pasture, stable, and corral, which seemed like a song. Janet could ride the mile on her bike to feed, groom, and ride Wendy. Feed at $7.00 for 100 pounds should last several months. With her $20-a-month income, it looked as though she could swing it.

Then she announced, "I want Wendy *and* June Bug because one pony by itself will get lonely!" She had learned her goal-setting lessons well. In the end, we agreed she could have both.

A week after Janet rode the pony of her dreams, I went to Writer's Fellowship on Saturday afternoon. When I returned, we were the owners of two ponies, happy in their new pasture. Janet was ecstatic. She had planned and saved for two years and was now 12 years old. Feeling pride at her determination, patience, and good fortune at achieving her goal, I decorated with crepe paper streamers and fixed a special supper with a sign by her plate, which read, "Congratulations, Janet!"

Overjoyed, her warm, "Thank you, Mommy" and shining eyes melted any reservations I had left. I could handle it.

With camping conditions in Kansas less than ideal, we had sold our van. One weekend we camped with friends and a gale blew out the Coleman stove umpteen times. Another time, a deluge of rain and a river under our tent sent us packing. However, we could still camp with our tent and Mercedes. Later I bought a rusty old Opel for $200 for errands when Jake used the Mercedes. A man from church fixed the worst of the rust quite reasonably. With the ponies, that Opel became a necessity.

The first week with the ponies Janet insisted she had to get a bit at the feed mill in Newton and the forgotten saddle from the Davis's. They had told Janet she could borrow it. Not too happy, I drove her and Jared, age 10, to Davis's place and into their *curved* driveway. No one was home. With many errands to do, and feeling crabby from the prospect of a return trip, I looked into the rearview mirror and backed up *straight* and we hit something with a sudden hard thud. I had backed into the deep, wide ditch beside the driveway! To my great consternation, I had forgotten about the curve.

The engine died with the abrupt thud and refused to start. We got out and looked helplessly at the sight. My little yellow Opel's front end stuck up crazily on the bank. Cars drove by slowly and people stared. Janet, humiliated at our dilemma, hid in the shrubs at the side of the house. I asked God to forgive my bad attitude and prayed for help. God graciously answered. Almost immediately a young man drove into the driveway. He asked kindly, "Do you want me to call the police for you?"

"The police?" I groaned. "I think I need a tow truck!"

"Oh, they won't come out for just any miscellaneous thing. The police have to call them." This pony business was teaching me more than I bargained for.

"Okay, please call them for me." I thanked him. He said he lived a few blocks away and he'd go and call. While we waited–and waited–for the police, the Davises came home, oozing sympathy for us–so we got the saddle after all.

Then Mrs. Davis disclosed, "I was so afraid when we first moved in here that I would back into the ditch." Kansas is so flat that deep ditches line both sides of rural roads to drain the water in a downpour.

Soon Mr. Davis admitted, "Last week I backed into a ditch and one of my wheels came off. I had to have a tractor pull me out." Well! I didn't feel so bad after all. Mr. Davis explained, "It's fortunate you had both wheels in the ditch because if one had been on the driveway and one in the ditch the car may have rolled over." I cringed, grateful for the Lord's protection.

The tow truck driver joked, "Couldn't you find a better place to park?" Before long the car was out and we drove off to a chorus of "goodbyes" from children who had gathered to watch. Feeling repentant for my bad mood earlier, I counted my blessings aloud to the children: "Everything turned out all right after all. Insurance will pay the $10.50 for the tow truck, there was no damage to the car–not even a bent tail pipe–and we didn't turn over and get hurt!"

Jared chimed in, "And we wouldn't have gotten the saddle if we hadn't gone in the ditch!" Bless his heart! We told Jake of our escapade and, though he chided me a bit, he didn't rub it in.

Unfortunately, my trials had just begun. The following week Janet and I bought two 50-pound sacks of grain and took them to the farm. As we carried a heavy bag into the corral, Wendy met us, sniffed the sack and tore it open with her strong jaws. Grain poured onto the ground. Wendy stuck her head into the sack and munched delightedly. Janet began to cry and yelled, "Mama! She'll get foundered!"

"What's that?"

"Her hooves will grow very long and never stop!" Horrors! Janet had read many books. Could I trust her knowledge? By then June Bug was eating grain on the ground. Double trouble. With her hands, Janet scooped up grain on the ground and put it into the sack as I held it.

In a panic, we somehow lugged the bag to the gate. Wendy followed and pinned us against it. She was a 500-pound pony and we were each less than 100 pounds! When we finally got the sack out the gate and into the car, we stood there shaking from fright. Jake would hear about this! But I couldn't believe his nonchalant attitude when we told him. "It looks like you handled it well and you're gaining experience!"

Janet showed me ugly pictures of curved-up, several-feet-long hooves that had put fear into her; but there was no way we would have let those ponies eat all that grain.

Three days after the scare with the feed, Wendy got her first shoes. This was hilarious! But not for the man who did the job. All went well until the fourth hoof. Wendy had had it. Every time the man lifted up her hind leg, she'd lift up the other leg and leave him holding her heavy hind end. How could a pony be so unbelievably mischievous? The man, infuriated after ten or more tries, tied her face with a rope and yanked–hard! "Hold this," he instructed, as he handed us the rope ends, "and talk to her." The job he expected to be a cinch took two hours.

One day when Jake was home, Janet and Jared walked to the feed mill on Main Street, half a block from our house, to buy a block of salt. We watched from the window as they carried the 50-pound block a few steps, set it down, then carried it some more. Janet beamed when her father came and carried it home with one hand, above his shoulder.

"The man asked where we wanted it," she told us, "and was surprised when we held out our small hands. We should have taken the wagon."

A week after she got the ponies, Janet found a paper in the horse section of the encyclopedia on which she had written several years before, "I want a red Welsh pony."

But Wendy tried her patience. One day when Jake was gone, Wendy barged through the fence to the ponies in the next pasture and got an ugly, bloody, five-inch gash down her long blaze. The vet put in ten stitches, handed me a can of yellow wound spray with the incredible words, "Spray this on once a day and take out the stitches when it's healed. Just grab her by the ear," he said, "and she'll hold still." Was he kidding? Five-foot-one-inch me hold a 500-pound pony by the ear?

The first time I tried, Janet tied Wendy to a post. I sprayed. Wendy went wild, tore the rope, and bounded away. Never again! Fortunately, Mr. Sommerfeld, the kindly old gentleman who boarded his ponies there, offered to spray her for us. What a relief!

Janet enjoyed sharing her ponies with friends, and in fall rode Wendy in the fall festival parade. She devoured books on horsemanship and took riding lessons. She groomed and exercised ponies at a nearby stable. She was paid a check after the sale of a pony, which she had groomed and "finished." At age 13 she had become a respectable horsewoman.

Winter presented a challenge and on bitter cold days we usually drove her to feed the ponies.

After Christmas, Jake's sister Mary Ann and husband Dave Mulligan, and sons, Sean and Dean, came for a visit from British Columbia. Janet had a great time, sharing her ponies with the boys. She also sewed stuffed animals for them for Christmas – Snoopy for Dean, and Sean's favorite, Paddington Bear. (She made many clothes for herself too, especially tops and blouses.) Dave owned Hesston Corporation farm machinery for his large farm and enjoyed touring the factory.

In spring, Janet again enjoyed her ponies and in May even I was overjoyed when her yearlong secret prayer was answered. Wendy was pregnant.

Another need for prayer arose a few days before school ended. Janet woke up with severe pain in her side. I took her to the hospital at 4:00 A.M. where she was diagnosed with appendicitis. The small Moundridge Hospital, unable to accommodate too many patients at once, scheduled surgery for noon since they were waiting for a woman to deliver a baby. After several hours of waiting, a shot eased Janet's pain. The nurse marveled at her calm demeanor. The hospital administrator, who was also a chaplain, prayed with her. Our pastor, Waldo Miller, came and also prayed for Janet. He asked if she was scared. She said no. Later the anesthetist commented, "Janet was a very calm little girl for having surgery." I had heard the same thing after her tonsillectomy in Vincennes. How grateful I was for answered prayer. She came home on Saturday.

On Sunday morning, Mr. Sommerfeld stopped by to see her. "You've got an extra pony at the farm," he reported. "A little filly was born last night!" She had been praying that Wendy and June Bug would mate and have a filly.

Her faith amazed me. She named the filly Bambi and we all enjoyed the beautiful surprise.

The fence at the farm needed repair and the horses on the other side lured Wendy to break out again and again. Sometimes June Bug followed. Wendy often crossed the creek. Janet's pasture was quite small and soon tall ugly weeds replaced the grass. Though she gave them plenty of hay, the ponies preferred the green pasture. One day Jared helped Janet graze the ponies outside of their bare pasture. The children took their lunch along and while they were busy with the ponies, the geese ate their lunch!

Janet with Wendy and Bambi, June 1978.

Though the owner of the farm tried repairing the fence, by the end of the second summer Janet had chased ponies in the hottest weather—40 days with the temperature above 100 degrees—and her patience ran out. With a surprisingly philosophical attitude, she told us one day, "I've decided to sell the ponies. They broke out again and I'm tired of chasing after them. It's so hard to get them back in." Having learned some valuable lessons, she had another dream waiting—a horse. Adept at overcoming obstacles now, she knew that in time she could make her dream come true. Jake put an ad in the newspaper September 5. The next day a family from near Wichita bought Wendy and Bambi for $250.

Janet later sold June Bug for $100 to Dr. and Mrs. Vernon Yoder who had a small farm near Hesston. (Dr. Yoder was a Mennonite psychiatrist whom I had interviewed for my last article in my writing course, called "Coping With Anger," which also dealt with depression.) He invited Janet to come and ride June Bug any time and showed her how he was training the pony. He had a big white horse which Janet rode one day. He praised her ability and control of the horse when it ran away. "That's the kind of horse you would like to have, isn't it?" he asked. She agreed.

In March of 1979 we bought 11 acres of land with a large pond for $1275 an acre (reduced from $1500 an acre) in anticipation of Janet getting a horse. She bought Chief, not realizing the short time she would have with him. I don't recall any nightmares with Chief, and the "nightmares" with Wendy and June Bug seem like a joy to me now.

Summer temperatures above 100 degrees presented other problems for us. Our only window air conditioner, in the small family room downstairs, also cooled our bedroom. But the children's rooms upstairs were unbearably hot, so they often slept on sleeping bags in the living room. In 1978 Jake decided to build two bedrooms in the basement for summer use. Janet and Jared worked with him on the rooms.

One Saturday morning in May Janet asked, "Can we have a picnic today?"

"I have Writer's Fellowship today with a salad luncheon, our last meeting till fall."

Janet, resigned and obedient as usual said, "Oh, all right."

However, Jared protested loudly. "Why don't you quit Writer's Fellowship? *I hate that!*"

Since Jake was gone so much I had also disliked giving up my Saturday afternoons, even if it was only once a month. Besides, I often felt out of place there, feeling I was not a serious enough writer. So I told Jared, "I *am* planning to quit. Today is my last meeting. I never knew you felt that way."

"I *always* felt that way! Why don't you quit today? Why do you have to go *today?*"

"Because Mary Rempel is speaking and she's my friend and I want to hear her."

"Okay," he finally agreed.

When I got home hours later, I told Jared, "When Mary learned I was quitting, she said, 'But you're a *writer!*'"

Jared responded with characteristic eleven-year-old candor, "You can still *write*, but you don't have to *fellowship!*" And he jumped on me, held on, lifted his feet and kept hugging me, exclaiming, "That was your *last* Writer's Fellowship!" Well, did I feel loved, or what?

While I was gone, Jake and the children got much work done on the basement rooms. He built a bed in each room and put mattresses on them. Later he bought doors and we cleaned and painted the floors. The rooms were also a great place for guests. And we did have our picnic after all, since the next day was Mother's Day.

I often read to the children, and this year read *Run Baby, Run* by Nicky Cruz, *The Cross and the Switchblade* by David Wilkerson, and *Shadow Of The Almighty* by Elizabeth Elliott. I was inspired and the children loved the stories of God's amazing ways.

Another activity of the children at Hesston was Bible Memory at Whitestone Mennonite Church. Both Janet and Jared attended the first years, but in the fall of 1977 Jared quit. In November Janet begged her brother to accompany her. *"Please! Just this once?"* He went back and was hooked. He came home all enthused, ready to continue.

With shining eyes he told me, "I even remembered which verse I learned last (spring) when the teacher asked me. It was 'Though your sins are like scarlet they will be as white as snow' and she knew where to start me out." Janet learned 500 verses, earned a New Testament, and became a helper with the other children.

While the farm economy boomed our first years in Kansas, a serious downturn by 1977 prompted Hesston Corporation to sell two of their Cessna Citation jets. In April of 1978 they sold the last one and purchased twin engine Cessnas. Jake lost interest in the job, wanting to resign; but he stayed on and flew their twin engines while hunting for another job. As his co-worker pilot friend Dave Forrer told me, "Once you fly the fast ones (jets) you're never satisfied flying the others."

That same week, Jake called his brother Nick to talk about finding a job in British Columbia. And I wondered, *What are we in for now—another move?*

CHAPTER 29

Looking North

Enlarge the place of your tent.
ISAIAH 54:2 (NKJ)

1977–1979

As the farm economy fell into recession, Jake grew restless, ever looking northward. One day Nick told Jake, "When a pilot job was advertised in the post office here in B.C., more than 1000 pilots applied!" I gave up hope of ever moving to Canada, at least for the time being. However, Jake kept writing letters and sending out resumes.

Jake still administered the college aviation department halftime, his fifth year in that capacity. He signed a new contract, but only until December. President Laban Peachey asked the Federal Aviation Administration (FAA) office in Wichita for a written evaluation of the flight department and received a letter which said in part,

> ...we find that the school curriculums are of superior quality.
>
> Mr. Jake Friesen, Director, has demonstrated himself to be an excellent flight school manager, is highly thought of, and works very well with the personnel of this office. He has developed a well-qualified staff of flight instructors and the results of their work are directly reflected in the school graduates who completed their flight tests for pilot certificates or ratings during 1977.
>
> Our records reveal that 12 private, 9 commercial, 14 instrument rating, and 11 flight instructor flight tests were conducted and that all of the graduates passed the appropriate flight check on the first attempt. This is highly complimentary of the course content as well as quality of instruction given. The FAA records do not reveal any noncompliance (violations) of FAA regulations or accidents involving the college aircraft or personnel.

I was proud of Jake for this excellent commendation. He listened daily to his motivation tapes, which stressed setting goals in all areas of life – vocation, marriage and family, financial, social, mental, and spiritual.

In May 1978, I quit my job at church as secretary and "unofficial assistant pastor." Phone calls over the dinner hour and evenings, often with bulletin announcements, had increased dramatically. Jake voiced his disapproval and I didn't blame him. Having been involved in so many small groups, Bible studies, and church committees, I needed a change. Plus I wanted the summer free with the children. Before I resigned I prayed that God would find a new secretary, and was delighted when a young woman wanted the job.

In July, Jake flew us in the college "R.G." (retractable gear) Cessna to British Columbia. What an exciting adventure for us! In western Kansas we flew to 11,000 feet to rise above the clouds, from which we could see a gorgeous display of clouds for miles and miles. It reminded me of the anthem we sang in the Lantz Chorus from Psalm 19, "The heavens are telling the glory of God!" Later, the clouds made huge splotchy patterns on the ground. On this two-day trip, we stopped overnight at Douglass, Wyoming. The next day we had some rain, crossed our first range of mountains and then through the Rockies between peaks at 6500 feet. Storms brewed south of us and dark clouds hovered overhead at times. Snow-capped peaks and formidable, rugged mountains all around and below us were "breathtakingly beautiful if it weren't so scary," I wrote in my journal. By 12:45 P.M. we left the mountains behind and I breathed easier above the flat terrain.

Flying at 9500 feet, with rain at times, we reached Porthill, Idaho, at 3:15 P.M. When we landed, a man told Jake to follow the road through the valley to Porthill Customs. The Customs official added, "This is the prettiest little airstrip I've ever seen." And indeed it was very beautiful, with green farmland all around and towering mountains reaching toward the sky just ahead on the British Columbia side.

At Creston we stayed with Jake's sister Mary Ann and Dave Mulligan and their boys, Sean and Dean. On our visit a few years before, Jake helped Dave build forms for the foundation of their house. Now we enjoyed their lovely new home with sunken living room. Dave was a big alfalfa farmer and had Hesston Corporation equipment. He took us to the dehydration plant where the alfalfa was made into pellets after being dried in a huge cylinder dryer made in Kansas. Creston is in a big valley, and as we drove around the area, the mountains to the west were an ominous reminder of our two-hour trip ahead over solid mountainous terrain. I began dreading the trip.

"RG" trip: Dave Mulligan, Jake with Jared, Mary Ann with Dean (front) and Sean, Janet. Porthill, Idaho (south of B.C.), July 1978.

Monday morning the Mulligans took us to the airstrip and I snapped a picture of them with Jake, Janet, and Jared by the plane. When we took off, terror gripped me. I cried out to Jake as we climbed up toward the first mountain. "What do you want me to do?" he asked, exasperated. "Turn around and go back?"

"No!" I said, and the tears flowed. Janet, sitting in back with me, held my hand, "calm and cool as a cucumber." I prayed and hoped for the best, while trembling inside.

From time to time I plied Jake with questions. "Does this plane have only one engine?"

"Yes."

"What if the engine goes out?" What a morbid thought, yet I had to get it out!

"There are always valleys below that we can glide into," he reassured. After a while Jake's confidence rubbed off on me. All went well until we approached two mountain peaks in the distance.

"Aren't we too close to those peaks?" I questioned, as they loomed closer and closer. He laughed and assured me we had plenty of room. Confident of his course he kept straight ahead. I felt foolish indeed when we flew between the peaks with miles to spare. I calmed down and by the time we reached the coast I was fine – and relieved!

When we landed, Jake's brother Nick, wife Margaret, and sons Mark and Garth were there to greet us. When I voiced my fears and Jake's response about valleys down below, Nick said, "Many small planes have crashed in those mountains and were never found." Pilots and lay people alike told us the same story. Just as I thought, my fears were not unfounded. However, we had a good plane and a good pilot. God had protected us and I would trust Him to get us home safely.

Over the next days, Jake had medical exams and met with aviation officials to apply for a Canadian pilot's license. We enjoyed time with Jake's father and Jessie and the family. One day, as we were discussing Russia, Dad told us, "When the Mennonites went to Russia they had to promise not to preach or proselytize the Russian people. I believe that is why they had so much trouble and had the judgment of God on them. Because of this they learned to keep their faith to themselves and not trust outsiders, and to never speak of the Lord."

Dad continued, "The Mennonite Brethren (a more evangelistic group that began in Russia) were scared when the Russian Mennonites joined with the Pennsylvania Mennonites because they knew the Pennsylvania Mennonites were fine Christians. I was very impressed with them at the world conference in Kitchener (Ontario, 1960) and at the conference in Bethlehem (Pennsylvania, 1983)—with their simplicity and strong biblical faith." It was gratifying to hear this high praise for my fellow believers back home. Dad and I were on the same wavelength.

Thursday morning Dad took us to see Terry Norr, director of the flight department at Trinity Western College. Terry was on the phone getting a report on a plane crash of two Trinity students who were going to Africa. Another plane crash! This was fearsome territory for pilots, I concluded.

Then we met with Ralph Borthwick who had been at the aviation conference in Hesston and stayed in our home. He taught aviation at Trinity. He held us spellbound again with stories of his experiences. "I once flew on a Catalina water bombing plane, scooping up 10,000 gallons of water in twelve seconds. We dumped it on a fire in a clump of tall cedars and a whirlwind came up and knocked the plane for a loop. A ten-foot piece of the wing broke, just held together by fabric. The pilot told me to take over and fly. He was not a Christian and was white as a sheet. When we landed he told me, 'We could have been killed in that plane.' I told him, 'Yes, we could have, but I'm ready to die.' He said, 'Nobody wants to die.' And I said, 'No, but the Bible says it is appointed unto man once to die and after that the judgment. We can go to one of two places, heaven or hell.' The fellow said nothing, but three weeks later he was killed in a mid-air collision while searching for a helicopter that crashed. Pilots in two Catalinas from two different companies were so intent on their search that they didn't see each other and collided." I had just about had my fill of crash stories!

Terry Norr invited us to his home for Friday evening. He lived just over the border in Washington. He sounded encouraging. "You will have no problem getting a job," he told Jake, "and with good pay, too—water bombing, hauling fisherman on the Island, or fire spotting." We were not thrilled with the prospects.

Nevertheless, Jake visited a water bombing company and talked with the chief pilot. "Apply in January," he advised. "We choose our pilots then for the May to August season."

Later Jake told me, "I'd be a co-pilot for the first six years before I could qualify as captain." I shuddered at the thought.

We visited brother Nick and Margaret again where Jake told of the various job possibilities. I added what Ralph Borthwick experienced with water bombing and the whirlwind. As we said goodbye, Nick said to me, "I'll find something better for Jake than water bombing. I can see it upsets you." How glad I was to know he understood that I was fearful, and grateful for his kindness and caring.

A week after we arrived, we were ready to take off as heavy cloud cover blanketed the area. A radar controller in Vancouver guided our little craft, from sea level, on two 360-degree turns to gain altitude as we approached 6500-foot mountain peaks. It was a great relief when we finally cleared what seemed like several hundred feet of clouds into clear blue sky, with no peaks in sight. I wrote, "What a blessing to have the controller call the shots as we obey. Why can't we learn to rely on God with the same trust and obedience for our lives?" I sensed the Spirit speaking to me, grateful for a loving heavenly Father.

Heading south over the Washington border, cruising at 11,000 feet, we saw and took pictures of majestic Mt. Baker at 10,778 feet, rising east of Lynden, Washington. Jake's parents lived directly north of Lynden at Aldergrove, B.C. (about three and one-half miles). I couldn't help but wonder, *Where will we live someday if Jake lands a job up here?*

Soon the clouds disappeared and we headed back to Creston over Washington's hundreds of miles of spectacular snow-capped mountains. And I was not afraid. God had gotten through to me with the lesson of the radar controller. After another night with Mary Ann and Dave, we left for home. An awesome trip, it left us with perplexing uncertainties. Yet I felt a surprising peace about our future.

Back in Hesston we looked forward to a special event in July – Mennonite World Conference (MWC), held every seven years in a different country. This event brought together many branches of Mennonites from many countries (and 54 groups in Lancaster County, Pennsylvania in 2010!), Amish, and this year, Baptists from the Soviet Union with Mennonite roots. Only the Baptist Church was allowed to register in Russia; all other groups had to join them or close.

The first evening, Convention Hall in Century II, Wichita, was packed. An overflow crowd filled Concert Hall – with 7000 registered. The mayor of Wichita greeted us with "Welcome to Wichita" in a number of languages and drew warm applause. For such a small denomination, the roll call of 44 nations was impressive. The six Russian delegates received spontaneous, enthusiastic applause. (Thirty-eight nations would be represented on the General Council to plan the next meeting in seven years.)

MWC president, Million Belete of Ethiopia, brought a stirring message on "Christ Establishing the Kingdom." "The Mennonites have carried out Jesus' Great Commission, and that is why we can have such a meeting with so many nations represented," he said. "The Bible has been translated into 1600 languages. The greatest miracle is the Incarnation – God with us, walking and talking with us. This is incomprehensible to us. Good Friday was the Coronation Day in establishing the kingdom. The second birth – regeneration – is the only way to become a member of the kingdom. Jesus says, 'Come to me, all of you who are tired from carrying heavy loads; take my yoke and put it on you.'"

The next night the six Russians spoke – two in English, the others with an interpreter. They sang a Russian hymn and received a standing ovation. It was a moving experience to hear believers from behind the iron curtain of atheistic Communist Russia. That faith burned so brightly in many believers in that dark land inspired the audience with joy and hope. One of the Russians referred to divisions over baptism, "It doesn't matter how we are baptized. Only Jesus' blood can save us, and all the water in the world can't make anyone a Christian." The audience laughed and applauded with warm appreciation. (Mennonite Brethren immerse; General Conference and (Old) Mennonite Church sprinkle or pour.)

Conference concluded on Saturday night in a stadium, to accommodate a larger crowd. In 109-degree heat, one side of Cessna Stadium at Wichita State University was packed with 16,000 Mennonites. As we climbed the bleachers and took a seat, whom should I discover beside me but Ernest Moyer, my former employer at the chick hatchery in Quakertown! We were both amazed, as was his wife Verna when she joined us minutes later. Among those thousands of people, God had led us to that seat – one of His surprising serendipities! We enjoyed a time of catching up and sharing about our families. Millie's husband Ralph Loux worked at the hatchery then as bookkeeper, and Millie told me the Moyers would be at the conference. That night a large choir from Taiwan and the 500 Mennonite Men sang. What an awesome experience this conference had been, with thousands locally and from around the world blessed. I was grateful our children could be present.

In August, Jared and I had an adventure on Amtrak to Chicago and Philadelphia. Sister Anna had sent us box tops and coupon from a Kellogg's cereal offer of a free trip for a child. This was too good to pass up. Janet still had her ponies to care for and planned to spend a week at Camp Mennoscah. She would stay with friends or have the next-door neighbor, Rose, look after her when Jake was gone. But I was sorry she couldn't go, too.

Jared was extremely excited about his first train ride. He took along a sleeping bag and we traveled light. We left at 10:25 at night and after the novelty wore off, Jared sprawled into the aisle on the floor and slept peacefully on the rocking, clacking train. We arrived in Chicago Friday morning where Anna and John picked us up for a day with them.

Saturday our train was almost three hours late. At 5:00 P.M. we left for Philadelphia and Grammy's Ackerman's (her maiden name) reunion on Sunday afternoon, or so we thought. During the night the electricity went out on the train, which meant no lights or air conditioning. Stifling heat and fumes like burning rubber wafted through the doors, left open at each end of the car for ventilation. We slept fitfully and each time I woke I almost choked on the heavy exhaust. Candles on the floor lined the hall in one car to light the way to the restrooms. Some passengers waited three hours to be served in the dining car. We all received forms to register complaints.

We were too late for the Ackerman reunion, but were thankful to have arrived safely. We could still attend the Landis reunion the next weekend. Grace picked us up at the train station in Philadelphia and took us to seminary friends, Helmut and Nettie Bartel, for dinner by the pool at their huge old stone house that Helmut was restoring, with former servants' quarters on the third floor.

Jared and I stayed with Millie and Ralph at Quakertown and had a full schedule of people to see. One day we visited Pappy Landis, with Aunt Naomi there. I interviewed them about the family as Jared taped the conversation.

Another day we visited my former first to third grade teacher, Florence Fluck, who studied painting after she retired. At her lovely old stone home we saw her studio and picked up the painting I commissioned her to paint of our home and neighborhood on Thatcher Road. The little fieldstone church, one-room school, neighbors' houses, bridge, and creek mingled on canvas with bright yellow-orange-red trees of autumn. Mrs. Fluck donated all monies for her paintings to missions. We carried this unframed 16 × 20-inch painting home with us on the train. Mrs. Fluck was a member of our church and president of the Richland Historical Society "Little Red School House" for many years. The next day Millie and Brenda took us to the historic school at Richlandtown where Mrs. Fluck taught painting classes. I took pictures of her, along with Millie, Brenda, and Jared. That was a special time for Jared and Brenda – to experience a schoolroom of yesteryear, with everything just as Millie and I remembered it.

Sunday at the Landis reunion I won the prize for traveling the farthest and Jared won for being the youngest. He enjoyed every minute of this adventure and I loved seeing all the Landises.

On the train ride back to Kansas, which took exactly 24 hours, we crept so slowly on the high wooden bridge over the Mississippi River at St. Louis that I hoped the bridge would hold. From the window I got pictures of the Gateway Arch. Again we experienced crazy, hair-raising happenings. The emergency brake kept going on, which we learned goes on when the wheels don't touch the track! Finally they cut the brake cable. After dark, the air hose came loose and the train stopped abruptly at 10:15. Someone had piled rubber tires on the tracks! We learned "firsthand" of the unbelievable hazards of rail travel. We were very happy to see Jake at the Newton depot at 3:00 in the morning.

Back home, on Jake's birthday, September 29, 1978, he had an interview at FlightSafety International in Wichita to begin teaching in Cessna Citation (jet) simulators. He then took classes and began teaching part time on October 14. After his experience on Citations, this was a natural and kept him proficient in the jet. Nighttime schedules became routine as Jake taught pilots from all over the country and the world – one from the Mercedes factory in Germany.

In November, he flew Lyle Yost, president of Hesston Corporation, to Kansas City to a Future Farmers of America meeting where he sat beside Kansas Senator Dan Glickman and heard President Jimmy Carter speak.

Over Thanksgiving week we were blessed with a visit from Jake's oldest brother, Peter, and Mary from Vancouver Island. They bought us the game of crokinole and we enjoyed showing them around the area. Then in January 1979, Millie, Ralph, and Brenda came for a week during a terrible blizzard; they enjoyed a free night in a hotel in Kansas City as a result. O'Hare Airport in Chicago was closed and Wichita was socked in. Millie was so amazed that, though they could not see the ground at Wichita, the pilot landed safely on the runway. Niece Brenda says, "I remember that after we took off (at Kansas City) and got up through the clouds, the sun was shining on them and it was beautiful. Then as we landed, we were in thick clouds and as soon as we got out of the clouds we were on the ground!" We loved showing our families the unique sights of Kansas and taking them to the Colonial House to eat. These visits were a special bonding experience and the children loved the time with relatives.

For a while after our trip to British Columbia, my concern and prayers centered on a possible job for Jake in that treacherous terrain. As time passed, I thought he had given up. Then one day I found him writing yet another letter of application. I was struck with the thought, *He needs only one job, and if God wants us to move there, God can provide it!* In faith, I committed the matter to God. I still did not want Jake to fly in those mountains, and especially not water bombing!

God saw my fears and my need and graciously provided me with a new and wonderful friend and prayer partner "for such a time as this." Our next move was only a prayer away.

CHAPTER 30

An Amazing Answer

But my God shall supply all your need according to
his riches in glory by Christ Jesus.
PHILIPPIANS 4:19 (KJV)

1979–1980

January 1979 brought us blizzards and freezing cold winds. The end of that month, at our church business meeting, Jake was elected moderator for a second, one-year term. Retired after five years of directing the college aviation program, he now spent more time teaching at FlightSafety International. He also still flew for Hesston Corporation on their twin-engine Cessnas.

Over the Christmas holidays, a great tragedy had befallen Bob and Janine Stahly, from our church. Their daughter Stephanie was married to Jim, the son of Sam and Linda Guhr, whom we knew from our mission station at Gulfport, Mississippi, in the sixties. Both couples lived at Newton. Stephanie and Jim were Mennonite Voluntary Service workers in the Phoenix area. They left in a small plane on December 20 headed for Kansas for Christmas with a pilot from Phoenix and a friend from New York. But their plane mysteriously disappeared and they were never heard from again.

Search for the plane was discontinued after a week due to snow in the Arizona mountains, the wooded terrain, and exhausted pilots. For the next six months, people in many churches prayed for the families and for the plane to be found. Finally, on June 30, a hunter found remains of the plane on a mountain at St. Johns, Arizona. Authorities confirmed it was the lost Piper Comanche. Jake was asked to fly the family members and pastor of the Guhrs, Leonard Wiebe, to Phoenix in a Hesston Corporation plane for a memorial service and to bring back belongings found at the site. A memorial service was held at Sunnyslope Mennonite Church in Phoenix and at Newton as well.

In late winter Jake bought two old "clunker" cars, which Jared and he worked on at the corporation hangar in Newton. With a little help from the Corp airplane mechanic, Wayne Manske, Jake and Jared enjoyed this project immensely. They took a good engine out of a dilapidated Plymouth Valiant and installed it into a Dodge Dart. The engine of the Dodge had seized up from being run dry, but otherwise the car was in fine shape. Wayne was a character and Jared enjoyed the camaraderie and Wayne's antics. Jake sold the car in April to Stan Roth who had a small business at the airport selling airplanes. (Later Stan bought corporate jets to refurbish. Slowly, this grew into a thriving company, employing many people, including both Jake and Jared.)

In April, Jake flew to British Columbia for a week to look for work. He celebrated Easter and his father's 78th birthday there, and returned without a job prospect. After our trip there earlier, both children seemed excited about a move closer to Oma and Opa and the family.

But Jared loved Hesston and had a couple of friends who, along with him, liked to rummage in the dumpster at the telephone company a block down our street. From there they scrounged old telephones and wires and used them for whatever struck their fancy. Jared and a friend Mark (not his real name) hooked up phones for Jake's desk in the den and in our bedroom. It seemed a useful hobby.

Since fourth grade, Jared's favorite hangout was his clubhouse that he and Jake had built in the rafters of the garage. Using lumber from a huge wooden crate from the Colonial House, and rug pieces from there for the floor, he had a cozy place where he and his friends often slept, sometimes even in the heat of summer. He strung a wire and wired outlets for a lamp and a small record player he found at a yard sale. He and Janet painted the walls green inside, the ceiling black, with some white tiles added – grade school castaways. He made a "secret codebook," a chain and rope ladder, and had a trap door with a padlock. The back "door" – just a hole – led to the "balcony" on the rafters. He sometimes begged me to come up to the clubhouse, quite a feat for his not-so-nimble mom.

One day our next-door neighbor, Rose, called me and explained that Jared and Mark were doing something with the telephone hookup at the side of our house. I learned they were tapping into our phone line to hook up a telephone! Mark's uncle, an electrician, had taught Mark, and he was teaching Jared. I was appalled to learn they had tried to tap into other houses as well. We put an abrupt stop to this mischief. Mark also showed Jared the loot he shoplifted from stores. He was not a good influence. After I had a talk with Jared – and his Sunday school lesson focused on bad companions one Sunday – he decided to end his relationship with Mark. This loss of a friend was a sad learning experience.

With a growing economy, Hesston continued to boom. The town built an 18-hole golf course, a major deal for a city with a population of about 2000. Soon fancy homes sprang up around it, a lovely addition with a bike path where we liked to ride. After a search, a former big-city golf pro was hired, creating some excitement in this small community.

Imagine our surprise when the golf pro's wife, Betty, began showing up at our little Inter-Mennonite Church on Sunday mornings. My friend Elizabeth, the first to befriend her, raved to me about her. "Betty is a fantastic Christian! You have to meet her!" Betty always sat at the front of the church and raised her arms during praise songs. Sunday after Sunday she walked out as soon as the service was over and I didn't meet her. A tall, attractive blonde, meticulously groomed and well dressed, Betty seemed out of my social class (a carry-over from working at the doctor's my high school years?). I felt bad about my attitude and asked God to help me overcome these feelings.

One day I called Betty and invited her to go with me to hear a special speaker at the college. Later that day she shared her testimony with me about her dramatic conversion to Christ as an adult and a healing after having been flat on her back for two years. I was amazed at how God had worked in her life.

"I used to hate cleaning house, but now I enjoy it because I'm so thankful the Lord healed me," she said, and related her earlier trials. "My husband was an alcoholic while he was golf pro at a country club with more than 100 millionaires. After I was saved, I got so fed up with his drinking and coming home late every night. So one night I put a note in his bathroom saying I wanted a divorce, and I went to bed."

Betty's heritage is part Cherokee and part Creek Indian, as well as Caucasian. Her handsome, sensitive face, with high cheekbones, reflected pain at the memory of that night. She continued, "When Dean came home and read the note, he was so upset that he got down on his knees by his bed and asked God to forgive him and change him, and he asked Jesus to become his Lord and Savior."

Betty's somber face broke into a radiant smile. "Jesus saved him, and I found a new husband the next morning! We have both really changed. After he became a Christian, he quit drinking and stayed on five more years at the country club. But he ran into differences with the board due to his change of standards and lifestyle and was asked to leave. Losing his job was a huge blow to Dean. He was out of work for six months before we moved to Hesston."

Betty told me she was saved in 1970 at a Kathryn Kuhlman meeting. She went to many meetings to learn all she could and received the baptism in the Holy Spirit. Dean accepted Christ in 1971. Later, Oral Roberts, a friend from the country club, prayed with Dean and he received the baptism in the Spirit as well. Five years later the couple moved to Hesston. "This job was an answer to prayer," Betty glowed. "I know the Lord brought us to Hesston." Totally captivated, I drank it all in.

"Since coming here, I've spent most of my time reading the Word," she said. "I always read it a lot after I was saved, but here I didn't know anyone. I also started journaling here. I was lonely for friends and family, but God drew me into a close relationship with Himself. I've been so overwhelmed by His great love for me and for others. I just want to share His love with everyone." How refreshing! No trivial small talk with her. She was all heart and soul, passionate about Jesus. And she still is.

Later Betty told me, "When I was saved, I was not instantly set free from addictions. I was still in bondage to cigarettes and sleeping pills and I had a severe case of psoriasis since I was 12. One day God spoke to me and said, *'You deal with symptoms, but I deal with roots. I put an ax to the root. When the root is gone, you'll know it.'* I had prayed for years to be set free. We moved to Hesston in 1977 and it was there where the healings came all at once, about a year after we moved. The insomnia, anxiety attacks, and addiction to cigarettes were gone, plus the psoriasis." I felt privileged to hear her story and was deeply moved.

Concerning her back, Betty said, "In Oklahoma I had two disks removed from my back, but I still had back pain. When I went to a doctor in Wichita, he took X-rays and said I had all my disks. I told him I had two removed. He contradicted me and kept saying they were all there. Dean was with me and repeated that two disks had been removed. The doctor showed us the X-rays and we knew God had replaced them through prayer!"

"How did you happen to choose our church?" I asked her.

"Because it was the only charismatic one in town," she smiled. Yes, Pastor Waldo Miller was unashamedly charismatic, freed up by the Holy Spirit, as was Betty.

Sometime later, Betty was asked to tell her story to our women's circle at church. Men were invited so Jake went with me. In a packed room, all sat in rapt attention as Betty shared her unusual testimony. Looking stunning in a smart light blue suit, with abundant blonde hair newly coiffed, she told the painful story of Dean's job loss, his unfaithfulness, and alcoholism. She shared about her confinement flat on her back for two years, how God changed their lives, and of the miraculous healings the year before. Everyone was touched by her story of salvation and deliverance through Christ. It could be said of Betty that "out of her flowed rivers of living water" in exuberant praise, freedom, and deep love for Jesus. Like the woman at the well, she had personal experience with Jesus, the Miracle Worker. God gave Betty a ministry of prayer and teaching that continues to this day (age 80 in 2010).

As Jake and I became better acquainted with Betty and Dean as a couple, we appreciated their serious commitment. We met regularly with them and our friends, Jim and Ruby Graber, at a restaurant, and later at our home as a small group to discuss Jake's motivation material and Zig Ziglar's book, *See You At the Top.*

Knowing of Betty's dramatic answers to prayer, I began phoning her when I had a need. One day I called her with a bad migraine. She prayed, and instantly the headache was gone! I was so amazed. Whenever I called with a request, Betty prayed at length over the phone. Love and compassion flowed through the receiver like a healing balm. Never too busy, her prayers "covered all the bases."

Jake told me sometime after we were married, "You are a person who needs soothing." I had never heard that before but realized that Millie, Anna and I, from our traumatic childhood experiences, were alike in this respect. When we lived at Akron, Pennsylvania, Jake told me, "Whenever we go home to your parents, you get depressed." Betty's loving friendship and prayers did more than soothe, they encouraged and "strengthened my hand in God." Betty taught me by example to trust the Lord in every detail. After I knew her for a year or so, Jake said to me one day, "You've changed." I knew he meant for the better. Her influence calmed me and I was less anxious. I thanked Betty and the Lord that Jake recognized my more cheerful, calm outlook.

Betty explained that I also met her need for friendship and deep sharing of spiritual things. For several years I led a weekly women's Bible study group where we sang, shared spiritual journeys and prayer requests, and prayed for each other. About 12 women from various churches attended. Each woman was special in her own way, and Betty, with her gift of intercessory prayer, made a great addition to the group.

On March 9, 1979, we bought 11 acres of land with a large pond. Then in May, a friend told me they wanted to sell some of their farmland and wondered if we might want to buy 20 acres. Jake worked out a deal with them and the bank at $2000 an acre. With all of his hard work the last six years, we had prospered. Besides, from his SMI courses he had learned how to become financially independent. We had borrowed money for the 11 acres and now got a loan for $36,000 more. Another man farmed the 20 acres for us and we got a third of the profits from the wheat, alfalfa, or soybean crops each year. Oil and mineral rights on the property were not ours until 20 years later. Old oil wells littered the surrounding area for many miles, but most pumped slowly, with scant supplies of oil. Our land had no wells on it.

After school was out in May, we left on a camping trip with the Mercedes and our tent to Albuquerque, New Mexico, to visit Ezra and Jessamin Young from our Mississippi and Florida days. Though Jessamine was bedfast, Ezra ate out with us at times and gave us sightseeing tips. We took a tram up Sandia Mountain Summit, had dinner there, and watched hang gliders take off close up. Another day we saw Sandia Mountain Cave on the side of stone cliffs.

On the way home we visited the Puye Cliff Dwellers site, then tented at Sand Dunes National Monument in Colorado. Mountain-size dunes that piled up from blowing sand were trapped against the Rocky Mountains. Janet and Jared climbed three-fourths of the way up a very large dune. A stop at Boot Hill and the Wax Museum in Dodge City, Kansas, concluded our trip agenda.

When we returned, a big project awaited me. The siding of our house, exactly like on the house I grew up in, consisted of what at home we called "shingles" – white chalky squares that I never liked much. Ours had taken on a dull gray appearance, so I decided to tackle the job of painting garage and house. Jared and I began on June 25 and over the next two months I cleaned whole sections and Janet, Jared, and I painted as time allowed. Finally, exactly two months later, on August 25, Jake completed the project, doing the highest parts in about an hour and a half. What a sense of accomplishment we had, along with a spanking white house to enjoy.

That summer (1979), Janet, age 14, took driver education through school for three weeks in July. (In Kansas, a permit allows young people to drive alone only to work or school until they are 16. Since Kansas is a rural state, young people learn to drive on the farm at a younger age to help with the work.) Then on September 11, Janet began as a bus girl at the Colonial House at minimum wage, $2.90 an hour. Now she could save in earnest for a horse.

An interesting diversion fell to my lot the previous winter and I reveled in the project. Jake's father wrote in German the story of his life in Russia and Canada. Jake's sister Helen translated it and I volunteered to type it, so Dad sent the manuscript in several installments. He called it *Recollections of My Childhood and Life*. After editing, retyping, proofreading, and correcting for nearly a year, I ended up with 82 pages.

At times, I thought about finding another job. Since coming to Kansas I had a dream of someday working at our church headquarters offices in Newton. Several college and seminary friends worked there, but I wasn't sure what I could do. I asked Mary Rempel's husband Dick one day about a job for me at the offices. He was manager of Faith and Life Press, but I didn't realize that the press was a separate entity. Within two months he offered me a job as copy editor/proofreader. His wife Mary worked part-time at home in that capacity and my friend, Edna Dyck, worked for him in the office.

In October 1979, I finished work on Dad's book and asked Mary if she would proofread it for me. As it turned out, Dick told me he had a job for me *the day before* I gave Dad's book to Mary. He said I could begin the next Monday, October 22. I had no idea what I was getting into. Jake was gone on a trip and I needed someone to talk to. I accepted the job with excitement and trepidation. I called Betty. She prayed and a peaceful calm came over me.

Monday morning I went to work and had the grand tour of the offices and press. Dick stressed the importance of accuracy and that I would be responsible for any mistakes, a sobering thought. Edna began teaching me the ropes. She introduced me to the massive *Chicago Manual of Style* with, "Anything you need to know you'll find in here – punctuation, capitalization, grammar, whatever. But I'm willing to help you, too." Her desk next to mine gave me reassurance and easy access to this experienced pro. I knew I had much to learn but had no idea how much.

On Wednesday of that week I stopped to see Mary to go over Dad's manuscript. Page by page she showed me a slew of corrections, mostly punctuation and all kinds of details. As she talked, my courage evaporated. I was absolutely dumbfounded! For years I had typed letters in offices and wrote umpteen term papers. And I never knew I should be so picky. But this was a *book*! I saw Mary as a professional and myself as an amateur. Anxiety and fear gripped me about my new job. Why had I accepted it? How could I ever learn to do this so perfectly?

As Mary tells me now, she had no intention of making me feel inferior, and I knew that. It's just that I was inexperienced and green as a cucumber, and I *was* inferior to her in this profession.

Mary sensed my feelings and asked, "Is this too discouraging for you?" Too embarrassed to admit the truth, and not wanting to offend her after all her work, I told her no. I left her home that day with a profound respect for her and her profession, and with a huge prayer concern to share with Betty!

In that pre-computer era, I either re-typed or slaved away with correction tape or white out on my typewriter, making all those corrections. A Mennonite printer that Dad knew in B.C. printed several hundred books directly from my pages, and Dad was very happy.

After my humbling experience with Mary, I copyedited at work with doubts about my ability and speed. It would be months before I gained confidence with the job. Worried that I was too slow, I often skipped coffee break. The heavy responsibility of perfection weighed on my mind. Even so I loved it. I worked part-time from 9 A.M. to 1 P.M, and was home when the children returned from school.

At work, I was in awe of writers and editors on our floor and thought that editors were infallible until Edna told me, "Editors make mistakes, too." I was surprised. Why did I always hold other people up as perfect?

For months, Edna and I worked on revisions of preschool and kindergarten Sunday school curriculum. Then one day a book of peace stories for children by Cornelia (Nellie) Lehn, Children's Education Director, was assigned to me. Her office was across the room from my desk and I was honored to be trusted with her book. After meticulously reading over several sets of proofs, I sent the book to press. Some time later I was told, to my great distress and horror, that it had eleven mistakes ("typos")! Feeling contrite, I apologized to Nellie. She looked at me in surprise and said, "Do you think you are responsible for them? Others of us read it, too, and we also missed them." Relief and gratitude flooded my mind for her kindness and lack of blame, and I took on more books with renewed courage.

Working in the offices of the Commission on Education, seeing people from all departments at coffee breaks, and attending chapel twice a week was stimulating and inspiring. Dedicated Christians in home and foreign missions, voluntary service, victim offender program, women's ministry, and other areas inspired me with their commitment.

Liz Yoder was our editor and I sometimes found things she overlooked. I kept a list and then went over it with her. Usually she agreed that something needed fixing. One day as we worked together she paused, looked at me with a big smile, and admitted, "I do the macro-editing and you do the mini-editing!" I felt affirmed and gratified for my effort.

One day, long-time missionaries to India, Lubin and Tillie Jantzen, came with friends for a tour of our offices. Commission on Education executive secretary, J. R. Sprunger, showed them around. When he came to my desk he introduced me and said, "Jane is a copy editor and I'm intrigued with that because they have to read word for word, and they are the third person to read the manuscript." Actually there are often many more, but he said, "There's the writer, the editor, and then the copy editor. As Dick Rempel always says, 'God makes very few copy editors, but the ones He makes are very special.'" Dick had never said that to me, but it sounded beautiful and warmed my heart. Copyediting is demanding and painstaking but also rewarding.

One book I worked on was *New Way of Jesus* by my former seminary professor, William Klassen, by whom I felt intimidated in school. One day Liz said that when she told him I copyedited his book he said, "Give her a big hug for me!" I breathed a "Thank you, Lord!"

Then I was asked to copy edit the revision of *Smith's Story of the Mennonites*. This weighty tome by C. Henry Smith was our textbook for Mennonite History in college and seminary. I jumped at this exciting opportunity. Reading through many sets of proofs, chapter by chapter, took months. The book chronicles 500 years of Anabaptist history in countries of Europe, Russia, and North and South America up to World War II and after. (Anabaptists were "rebaptizers" who did not believe in infant baptism but in a voluntary commitment to Christ by adults. Over 10,000 were martyred for their faith through several centuries.)

A new year (1980) arrived with still no sign of a job in Canada. Jared had many friends from church, the neighborhood, and school. But he got into more and more mischief in school with two friends. In seventh grade now, they goofed off, thinking school was a lark. One day we received a letter from the principal stating that Jared had not turned in his math assignments for several weeks. If he did not catch up, he would flunk math. This wake-up call prompted Jake to insist Jared make up the work. With Jake and Janet's help, he soon got caught up. We were all gratified when he got an A on his math test. And on his report card in March he came up from an F to a B, a great relief!

I recalled the good report at my first parent-teacher conference from Jared's first grade teacher. She had said, "Jared is very quiet, but not shy, he's conscientious and gauges himself so he gets his work done on time." Great! But by the end of that year, both teachers reported being "exasperated at how slowly he worked. He acts like he's here to have a good time!" He learned to know the children and loosened up. Did his attitude have something to do with the fact that when he left for school Jake or I would say, "Have fun"? These were Jake's standard words, as Jake enjoyed himself greatly in his jobs and relating to people.

Janet had brought home reports of Jared's behavior with his middle school friends and disrespect for teachers when he was in sixth grade and I was concerned. How had this come about? One day I said to Jake, "I think it would be good for us to move closer to your family for Jared's sake. He needs to get away from his friends here." Jake kept applying. Sometimes a sister or brother called him with openings, to no avail.

On March 12 at work, we celebrated the 200th anniversary of the Sunday School in the U. S. and I was asked to write something about my early memories to share in chapel. Though reluctant because those memories were connected to my mother's death, I accepted and wrote out a page. It was unclear whether or how I would share this. On the way to the office that morning, I was detained due to an accident involving a van with 11 Hesston College nursing students having hit a truck. (Later I learned a man was killed.) Arriving as the chapel bell rang three times, I ran upstairs and found everyone seated in several rows in a semicircle. John Gaeddert, our executive secretary, came to me and asked me to read my experience. First, a brief history of the Sunday School and the GC history was shared, which led into mine about Flatland. The accident, having been late, and the subject of my material left me shaken. With churning emotions and shortness of breath, I read how the last kind thing my mother did for me before she died was to lay out clothes for Sunday school for my two sisters and me, before she went to the hospital on a Saturday night, and that my brother was born that night. I told how our wonderful teachers taught faithfully for many years and had a big impact on my life. With great difficulty, I got through it. Afterward, a young man I never saw before, Sid Sprunger, came to me and asked if my brother lived. He said that his sister was killed in a car accident a month ago in Ohio and the family was concerned about his five-year-old niece who was left. He said, "As I listened to you I thought *There's a girl who made it without her mother!*" He appreciated my sharing and I felt it was worth the trauma. I told him I've had a good life, even though it's hard sometimes. My sharing that day was one of the hardest things I had ever done.

In April, along with people from Writer's Fellowship and from work, I attended a Writer's Conference in Wichita. Famous author Richard Foster, from Friends University in Wichita, and his editors from Harper and Row spoke in turns about the process of writing and editing Foster's book *Celebration of Discipline.* What a treat to get an inside look at a writer and editor relationship and hear this fascinating story! An editor from Fleming H. Revell Company also spoke. Anyone who attended could write a story of less than 3000 words for a contest. Recalling Ruth Unrau's words to me to write about my stepmother, I did so. I called it "God's Healing Love." LaVonne Platt from our writer's group won the contest. But I shared my story with a number of people and got helpful feedback. That was the beginning for my book.

On April 26, 1980, Janet bought Chief, a fine appaloosa. She could still ride her bike to the 11 acres. Jake and the children had erected a fence along the road. Then Jake built a shelter for the horse. He had a well dug and put in a pump.

Jake agreed that Jim Graber could put sheep on our land, since they had a big operation of several hundred head. Though there was a large pond on the place, in summer it dried up almost completely. Besides, as Psalm 23, the shepherd's Psalm, indicates – "he leads me beside *still* waters" – sheep will not drink from running water. A small stream flowed into and flooded the pond in rainy weather.

One very hot day Jim brought out a large water tank while Janet and Jared were there. They came home with an amusing story. "Jim got so hot that he suddenly jumped into the water tank with his clothes and shoes on!" Janet exclaimed.

"He even dunked his head under the water!" laughed Jared. Our children enjoyed Jim and Ruby like family. Jim, a free spirit, loved the farm and he and Ruby worked tirelessly at farming the land, their sheep operation, and Jim's accounting business. In addition, Ruby worked full-time as a nurse.

Jim says of those years, "That was a very hard time for us. Farm prices were so low during the recession that we could not make ends meet. We were on food stamps and still sometimes hardly had enough food. It really helped us out when you bought the 20 acres and let us farm it."

At first, Jim brought a few sheep at a time to our land. Then the end of May, Jake helped him move almost 100 sheep—four truck loads of 45 ewes and 49 lambs. We had 164 sheep there by now, an interesting development. The day of the move, Jared was camping with his Bible school class for the weekend.

As spring turned to summer in 1980, Jake and I wondered how much longer we would have to wait for a job in Canada. Having waited for two years since our trip to the coast in the Cessna "RG," I sometimes doubted it would ever happen.

Then one day, June 26 to be exact, while Jake was on a trip to Arizona and California, I received an exciting call. Learning Jake was not home, the caller said, "I'm John Caruso from Kaiser Resources in Vancouver. Jake applied for a job with us. Please have him call me back." And the friendly voice was gone.

An electric reaction gripped me, "This is it!" It seemed like God was telling me, "This is Jake's job!" After seven years in Hesston, we had put down fairly deep roots. Was I ready for this? Excitement and apprehension filled my mind. *Will we be moving to Canada?*

I had to call Betty! I explained and she prayed a wonderful prayer. What a comfort to hear, "Father God, if this is Your will for them, open the way. If not, then shut the door!" Confident that God heard and would take charge, I could hardly wait for Jake's return the next day.

Jake talked with Mr. Caruso, the chief pilot, at some length. We both felt this was God's leading. Two days later, Jake called back and scheduled an appointment for an interview on Tuesday, July 8.

"Let's make this a vacation trip," Jake proposed. Since my job as copy editor was part-time and my schedule flexible, I had no problem getting off. *Soon I might be quitting*, I thought. When we moved last time, Janet had objected. This time Jared complained, "I don't want to move!" How would he take it if Jake got the job?

On July 2 we drove to Denver for a flight to Seattle. From there we took a rental car two hours north to Vancouver. Amazed at the change in climate from over 100 degrees in Kansas, I nearly froze in the cold rainy weather. We took a ferry to Vancouver Island and stayed with Jake's brother Peter and Mary. Sunny weather returned and we went salmon fishing on Peter's boat, with no luck that day. We visited beautiful Elk Falls in a majestic forest of giant Douglas Fir trees. We also enjoyed time with the other relatives.

The next week Jake had his interview. He flew in the simulator, studied, took an exam, and had a second interview at Kaiser. He learned that Edgar Kaiser was the grandson of the famous maker of Kaiser Frazer cars and, in California, Kaiser aluminum, steel, and shipbuilding. I was amazed at this prestigious company and job, a far cry from water bombing. Since others were applying for the same position, Jake doubted he would get the job. I prayed and felt at peace.

"If I get the job," Jake told me, "the cost of living in the U.S. is much less than in Canada. We can live over the border and the children can still be in the U.S. school system." That sounded good.

From my work at our church institutions and *The Mennonite*, I knew of the Glendale Mennonite Church at Lynden near the Canadian border. "Let's drive to Lynden and see the church there," I suggested. Dad and Mother went with us and we found it easily in the country. Noting that the parsonage beside the church looked empty, an idea struck me. "Maybe we could live here until we find a house." Though premature, it was a tantalizing thought—a ready-made home in this peaceful, beautiful countryside, and right beside the church. Lush green dairy farms with neat homes dotted the landscape.

"That might work," Jake agreed.

We flew back to Denver and drove to our General Conference sessions at Estes Park in the Rockies. John Caruso had told Jake to call him when we got to Denver. We checked into our motel room and Jake called. From the conversation, I knew immediately the job was his. And so did Jared. He began to cry and howl so loudly that I quickly ushered him into the bathroom and closed the door. He simply would not be comforted.

"I don't want to move! I want to stay in Hesston!" he wailed pitifully. Excited for Jake but heartbroken over Jared, I felt torn. What a dilemma!

We attended the conference meetings then headed home. We had to work fast. It was July 15. Jake said we must move on July 30! What an amazing answer to prayer! God had answered "exceedingly abundantly above all we could ask or think." Instead of water bombing in a small plane, Jake would fly a jet again.

As we shared the news, Betty and others prayed for us, and two days after we got home our house sold without advertising it. Jake told the realtor and he had a buyer. We bought it for $20,000 seven years before and sold it for $37,000. Then we learned that three other couples who were friends of ours wanted it.

Betty and the Bible study friends also prayed for Jared and our move. What a blessing to have such prayer support. We grieved for Jared but trusted he would adjust. He bought film and took many pictures of his friends, greatly enjoying his last two weeks with them. Janet had good friends, too, but she loved British Columbia and was ready to move. She would leave Chief at Hershbergers to sell and hoped to buy a horse in Washington.

When I told my friend Helen Hershberger in the Bible study about the vacant parsonage at Lynden, my amazement grew. "My cousin Katherine is a member there. I'll give you her phone number and you can call about renting the parsonage." Soon we had a verbal agreement to rent the parsonage for three months and I marveled at God's guidance. The pastor had left but they were interviewing a candidate. We'd have to find a house soon.

Dick Rempel accepted my resignation at work, and when I told Mary we were moving she said, "I need more work." The Lord had worked out all the details and Mary could pick up the slack.

Many friends came to visit as the news of our move spread. One day a former aviation student, Jim Roupp, stopped by for the first time. He sat at our kitchen table and talked excitedly. "I sure hate to see you all leave Hesston," he said. "I couldn't believe all the things Jake can do!" he rambled on, as all four of us sat there amazed. "He ran the college aviation program, flew for the Corp, and then one day I went into the Colonial House and there was Jake Friesen, the manager! Then one Sunday I went into a church in Moundridge and there was Jake Friesen preaching, and I thought, *Man! Is there anything Jake cannot do? He's a Jake of all trades!*" What a thrill to hear this young man share his appreciation for our husband and dad.

God had blessed us immeasurably the past seven years at Hesston. His grace and love through hundreds of people and our church nurtured all of us. We had gathered countless memories to cherish. Jared always especially loved our little church across the street. And he loved sitting in his red wagon on the street corner under the street light after dark. I prayed fervently that God would turn this loss into good for him.

So many people expressed sadness at our move. Myrtle Friesen, our elderly church organist and dear friend, told me, "Your children are extraordinary! They are always so polite and they act as if we [older people] are there." We had them in our home for dinner on a number of occasions and had enjoyed dinner in their home as well. Her husband, Peter, an artist, had made the frame for Mrs. Fluck's painting of my girlhood home. Myrtle surprised me even more by asking if we were taking a church in Washington. Another friend, Anna Juhnke, asked if I was going be a pastor there!

We worked fast and had farewells with various groups, friends, and our church. What a blessing to have a moving van for this 2,386-mile move – our mileage when we drove in 1975. Two women packed efficiently in one day. Kaiser paid for the packers and the move.

All went smoothly on loading day until it came time to load my Opel near the back of the truck. Driving up the steep ramp with limited power, the man failed again and again. Darkness fell. A small crowd had gathered under the streetlight on the corner – neighbors, the children's friends, and ours. Finally a group of men helped push and the Opel went in to cheers from the crowd. We said last goodbyes and gathered our final things into the Mercedes. That's when Jake discovered his shoes for the trip had been picked up and put on the truck by mistake. Jake wanted to get an early start, so as the workers continued to load, we started off to western Kansas at 10:30 P.M. with Jake in his slippers. We arrived at the Goodland Motel at 3:30 A.M. more than ready to fall into our beds.

Before I drifted off to sleep I marveled again at God's amazing answer to our prayers. My heart overflowed with gratitude and praise. Here we were off on another adventure, to live near Jake's family in Canada. But I wondered, *What will Jake's job entail? How much will he be gone?* We could not foresee the unbelievable surprise – and tremendous jolt – just ahead!

PART V

FARAWAY PLACES
AND RETURN

CHAPTER 31

"O Canada!"

*And you shall remember the Lord your God, for it is He who gives you
the power to get wealth, that He may establish His covenant...*
DEUTERONOMY 8:18 (NKJ)

1980–1981

The Great Northwest beckoned as highways led us through wide-open spaces and varied, spectacular scenery, buoying our spirits so that even Jared was happier. Our little Chihuahua mongrel, Sparky, slept, tranquilized, under Jake's seat all the way. After two days of driving in slippers, Jake bought new shoes that night in Douglas, Wyoming. The third night we slept in Butte, Montana.

The next day, in Washington, a white powdery substance appeared by the sides of the road, increasing as we drove. The moderate temperature ruled out snow. Soon we recognized the powder as Mount St. Helens ash. Before long, drifts lined the roadsides. A van, parked with open hood, revealed an engine choked with thick dust. Other vehicles suffered a similar fate. Twenty-three miles east of Ritzville, we stopped to take pictures and scooped ash into an empty "fiddle faddle" snack box for an unusual souvenir. At Ritzville, about 150 miles as the crow flies from Mount St. Helens, we encountered zero visibility in spots as the wind whipped the ash into a blur of dust.

The volcanic eruption on May 18, 1980 – 500 times as powerful as the atomic bomb dropped on Hiroshima in 1945 – hurled a billowing cloud of ash 60,000 feet into the air. It was now August 2 – two and one-half months later – and we felt fortunate to see firsthand the eerie lingering effects of this historic eruption. The blast blew more than 1000 feet off the top of the mountain, destroying everything in its path for 155 square miles.

The ash – a light gray, very fine powder – displayed in a small jar, served as a conversation piece in our home for years to come. Jared decided to send some in the mail to his friends Phil Simpson and Matt Schreiner in Kansas.

That night we relaxed at a lovely motel on the shore of Moses Lake. Sparky enjoyed running with the children on the big lawn. No swimming this night – the pool was filled with Mount St. Helens ash!

The next day, Sunday, we completed our 2,165-mile trip by 2:00 P.M. at our Ferndale motel, a few miles from Lynden. First Jake called Ed Flack, church trustee, to get a key for the house. Ed offered to show us the empty parsonage. Ed and Jane's daughter, Barbara Bloomquist, invited us for that evening. Their daughter Tami, Janet's age, won Janet's friendship by taking her horseback riding. Jared played with Tami's two younger brothers, Todd and Thomas, and sister, Traci.

Monday morning we anticipated the arrival of the United Van Lines truck. Jake left at 6:15 to fly at Vancouver. Promptly at 8:00 the trucker called from Bellingham and picked us up at our motel with the truck and a car. Jared rode in the truck. Awed by his first time in an 18-wheeler, he marveled, "The truck was so big and I sat up so high that on the freeway it seemed like we'd hit the overpasses as we went under!"

At the parsonage, Jake's brother Nick (five years older) came to oversee the unloading. I was grateful for his support as the garage filled up with boxes and paraphernalia, and the necessary things and more boxes went into the house.

Jake's job required that he live within a 45-minute drive of the airport at Vancouver. In the parsonage on Loomis Trail Road we were three and one-half miles south of the Canadian border. The drive to Vancouver took 30 to 45 minutes, depending on traffic. God had opened the way beautifully for us, but finding a house within that radius proved to be a challenge.

The first night in the parsonage, Tami stayed overnight with Janet. A number of Hesston people had relatives here, so we already felt somewhat connected. Word spread quickly in the small church next to us about the new occupants of the parsonage, and the friendly people made us feel welcome.

The Lord certainly plopped us down in the right place for Janet. She discovered that the man across the street had many cows and – of all things – *forty* horses! She wasted no time meeting Mr. Crabtree, sharing her love of horses, and offering to help round up the cows, sometimes enlisting Jared's help. Mr. Crabtree let her ride his horses. One day she told me, "I found the perfect mare for $600!" But she had not sold Chief back in Kansas. Even so, she glowed with happiness.

The first week Jake drove to Vancouver every day, Monday through Friday. In his time off he found a good realtor and we began looking at a string of houses on the country roads. None were suitable.

On Thursday, Mount St. Helens erupted again. The next afternoon, having learned the coast was ten miles away I took Janet and Jared to the beach at Birch Bay. How I loved being by the ocean, even if rocks covered the beach. There we could go to fill our lungs with the fresh, salty air.

On Sunday, Jake had a day trip so the children and I walked to church down our short sidewalk. Though people were friendly, I really missed Jake. After church, Pearl and Linferd Goertz came to the house with a big bouquet of flowers. Linferd was tall, with a friendly smile and firm handshake. Pearl, white-haired, short and cute, with face wreathed in smiles, breezed in like a ray of sunshine. "You're from Kansas!" she giggled. "We are, too—from Hillsboro (45 minutes from Hesston)! Welcome to Washington and Glendale Church!" Pearl, the wonderful church organist, sensitive and caring, became a special friend to me. That evening I began reading *Tom Sawyer* to Jared, a nice diversion for both of us. Janet kept busy with the horses, a friend, or writing letters to friends in Kansas.

How different life was for us here, moving from a bustling town full of people and churches and a college to the quiet pastoral countryside, from green or golden wheat fields to the lush green pastures of dairy farms in the Northwest rain forest area. Flowers abounded in gardens, window boxes, and hanging planters in town. The beauty and peace of nature quieted and refreshed my mind and spirit.

After the next week at home, Jake flew to Delaware on Sunday morning for two weeks of training on the Hawker airplane. While there, he had a bombshell delivered to him over the phone from Mr. Caruso. "I'm sorry to tell you that Kaiser Coal has been sold, and the Hawker plane you were hired to fly will go with it. So we won't have a job for you after November when the sale is final."

"So what does that mean for me?" Jake queried.

"The worst that can happen is that we'll send you back to Hesston."

"I *can't* go back to Hesston," Jake lamented. "I don't have a job there!"

"We'll see what we can do," John answered.

Kaiser Coal was only part of the Kaiser operation in B.C. and Kaiser owned another plane. But would they still need Jake?

Though Jake's precarious position at work concerned us, we went forward in faith looking for a house. Monday, September 1, we visited several in the morning, with no success. Jake was getting discouraged. We drove to the border town of Blaine, in the most northwest corner of the U.S. Janet cried tears of disappointment. "I hate Blaine and I don't want to live here!" But Jared loved it. Though it was much closer to the Vancouver Airport, Jake and I were not impressed. Here, where the beautiful Peace Arch Park divides the two countries, streams of cars, 18-wheelers, campers, and buses daily drove through customs.

"Border towns are not the most desirable place to live," Jake concluded. "I think the Lynden area is better for us." Janet beamed. Having just left Hesston, she hated to think of leaving Lynden so soon, with new friends and horses a major consideration for her. Lynden's population was 3,975, almost twice the size of Hesston.

Tuesday Jake came home from work encouraged. "My salary will be $34,000 instead of $28,500. It's $2800 a month, so maybe we can afford a higher priced house than I thought. How about if we look at the Jameses' place?" I couldn't believe it. The Jameses' house was the most beautiful one around, with a price tag to match – $125,000 with seven and one-half acres.

When we had come to look at the church and town in July with Dad and Jessie, Jake bought a newspaper in Lynden in which I saw a picture of this house. Described as having tall timbers and a creek, I read it to the others in the car that day and said, "This is our house!" The price tag told me otherwise. When we drove by it on Loomis Trail Road, Janet saw the pasture with white board fence in front and said, "I want to live there!" Jake had promised her that we would live in the country and she could have a horse. I was delighted to find it was still available, though I knew it was out of our class.

That afternoon, Jake called Ron, our realtor, and he showed us the Jameses' house.

"We're not interested in all the land," Jake said, "and the price is too high for us."

"If the Jameses sell five acres," Ron responded, "that would bring the price to $90,000."

"We'd consider that," Jake affirmed. Hope rose within me.

This beautiful house, sporting a lovely chandelier visible from the road through the picture window, tantalized me every time we drove by. Situated about a mile from the church on Loomis Trail Road, the location was perfect. The large pasture in front and along one side and attractive white-board fence would be a dream come true for Janet. Through the pasture and past the tall cedars in back were a deep ravine and the creek.

We loved seeing this wonderful house. The 2,960 square foot multi-level boasted a large formal living room, formal dining room, and kitchen on one floor, three large bedrooms and two baths above the large family room with big stone fireplace in the daylight basement downstairs, which also had a bedroom, bath, and laundry room.

Standing by the large picture window in the living room, I spied two snow-capped mountain peaks, jutting above smaller ones, straight north in British Columbia. This *had* to be a British Columbian's house! In the dining room, two large picture windows looked east and south on the tall pines, the pasture, back yard, and fenced-in garden. Also in the dining room hung the elegant chandelier. In addition to the three floors, a huge 800-square-foot unfinished basement had plenty of room for storage and Jared's large model train table.

As we walked outside in the back yard a small voice seemed to say, "This is your house!" I had prayed for God to help us find the house that *He* wanted us to have. Could this be it? Already the price sounded better. I knew that God is the God of the impossible.

In this berry country, thousands of acres of strawberries and raspberries stretched for miles along country roads. Blueberries added to the variety. This house was surrounded by berries—strawberry fields beside the yard to the West and South, hundreds of acres of raspberries across the street, and to the East a family from church had a good-sized blueberry patch. We waited while the Jameses sought a buyer for the four and a quarter acres planted in strawberries. That same day, Jake called Jim Graber at Hesston about selling our 11 acres there.

Janet was hopeful we could buy the house where she could keep a horse. One day at Crabtree's, she got kicked in the chest by a stud and had the wind knocked out of her. Unable to speak, she could not call Mr. Crabtree. She sat at a safe distance from the stalls and after a time, he came looking for her. By then she had recovered enough to explain what happened. How surprised and upset she became as he beat the horse that had kicked her. Another time a mare named Bars bucked and ran wild as she rode her. Mr. Crabtree praised her for her handling of Bars. "When you move to your house," he told her, "you can keep Bars there to ride."

School began for the children on September 3, our 19th wedding anniversary. Jared dreaded it. The night before, he cried at bedtime thinking of his friends and school back in Hesston. "You don't like it here either, do you?"

he sobbed. "You and I could go back to Hesston and let Janet and Dad stay here." I cringed. How long would he cry for Hesston?

"Some things I like and some I don't," I hedged, "but I'm not going to mope about them. And I do like it here."

He wiped his tears and prayed, "Please help me be able to go back to Hesston for part of the school year – and help us be able to move back."

His palpable apprehension and longing made my heart ache. "Think of school as an adventure," I said cheerily. "Can you think of it that way, and hold that in your mind because I love you?" I could tell that I had connected. He smiled and nodded and went to sleep.

The next morning at breakfast our devotional reading titled "Be Confident!" blessed us all. My own heaviness lifted as Jared left for the bus in a happy mood. I prayed for Janet and Jared throughout the day.

To my consternation, both children came home *unhappy*! Jared had missed the bus and Janet had a bad headache, but otherwise she had a good day. *Oh, God, help!* (Neither Jared nor I remember how he got home that day, so his trauma is forgotten. Praise the Lord!)

How I wished that our anniversary could be happier. When Jake got home from Kaiser he heard about the children's day at school, and then suggested, "Let's all go uptown to Milt's Pizza to celebrate our anniversary." As I sat down at the table across from Jake, the pained and drawn expression on his face and in his eyes totally shocked me. Never had I seen him look so bad – tired, discouraged, and beaten.

"Are you worried about losing your job?" I queried, as the children compared notes on their day at school.

That was not his main concern. "I just feel so bad for Jared." I saw a side of him I had not seen before – deep suffering and compassion at the intense grief of his son. My heart went out to both of them. And what if Jake lost his job? What a predicament! We had to trust that the Lord would take care of us. We agreed it would take time for Jared to adjust.

Happier news arrived that very night. Realtor Ron came with a first contract on the Jameses' place. Ron, tall and blonde, was a friendly young man, a warm and genuine Christian. (With a name like DeBoer, we supposed he was Dutch Reformed, the predominant denomination in Lynden and the county.) But all was not good news. Ron revealed, "A couple from Seattle has earnest money on the house and will buy it – if their house sells. However, if you sign this contract, you'll be next in line." We signed.

At bedtime, Jared cried again. "I hate riding the bus, and I hate that cemetery by the 'Welcome to Lynden' sign." That morbid entrance to town only added to his depression. "I still want to go back to Hesston!"

"Where would you stay?" Jake asked. "With Jim and Ruby?"

"Or at Phil's?" I said. "His older brother left, so they may have room."

"We'd sure miss you," Jake said.

"Couldn't Janet go back with me?" Jared's voice and dark brown eyes pleaded.

"Then we'd be really lonely!" Jake responded. We prayed with him and I had to trust that the children would both find good friends and be happier here. This was our most painful anniversary ever.

That night in bed sleep eluded me for a long time. I prayed and resolved to fast the next day until Jared got home from school.

The next day Jared went to school happy. I fasted and prayed as I went about my work and wrote letters. At about 3:15 that afternoon the phone rang. Surprise and joy rose within me as Dick Rempel, my former boss at Faith and Life Press, asked, after preliminaries, "Would you be willing to finish the project you started on *Story of the Mennonites*? The second proofs are ready, and no one else wants to do it."

Would I? I didn't have to think twice. "I would *love* to finish it!"

"Great! I'll send them to you UPS. Would you also do the massive index?"

"Yes, I'll be happy to." We had a friendly chat and he told me it was 107 degrees in Newton (on September 4), while we enjoyed days in the 70s. When I hung up, I could have turned summersaults and praised the Lord for this work to do.

Jared came home from school happy and there were no tears that night— another occasion to praise our heavenly Father. I broke my fast at suppertime with a lighter heart.

In the evening Realtor Ron came again with a contract. "You are first in line for Jameses' house!" he beamed. "The Jameses are thoroughly turned off by the Seattle people. They made a ridiculously low offer and then came to Jameses' house to try to buy it through them. They want the riding lawn mower free and almost everything but the kitchen sink!" Jake and I were relieved.

When we went to bed I was so excited that I told Jake I had to get up and record the day while it was fresh in my mind. I wrote, "I am overcome with the awareness of Jesus' love and presence…and feel unworthy—of the grace of Dick's sending *Smith* to me, and of our good fortune at getting such a beautiful house..." (next to Frank and Katherine Fast, cousin to Helen Hershberger). Actually, the house wasn't ours yet at all, but in my heart I believed God wanted us to have it. My joy at the house overshadowed my concern about Jake's job. I committed that to the Lord and felt certain that in time God would work that out, too.

Despite Jake's work schedule, we got together with his Dad and Jessie as we could, at their condominium at Abbotsford for borscht and zwieback or vereneke (delicious cottage cheese pockets), and a game or two of crokinole or checkers, or they visited us at the parsonage. A trip to Canada was always a treat, often along the border road, which had a parallel road in the States, with only a shallow ditch between. In the distance rose the majestic, snow-capped Canadian Rockies. Nearby, the flat coastal delta stretched for miles, with crops and berry fields tended mostly by turbaned East Indians.

The national anthem, "O Canada," stirred us with pride. British Columbia truly was beautiful. We loved to visit Stanley Park in Vancouver, with its stately, old trees. We also visited Queen Elizabeth Park with colorful varieties of flowers, and a high walking bridge from which to see the glorious landscape.

Since Jake had registered the children in Canada soon after they were born, they had dual citizenship. While we lived in Washington, Jake applied for their Social Insurance cards. I was the lone non-Canadian in the family.

On September 10, Jake came home, all aglow. "Would you believe, today John (Caruso) fired two of the pilots on the Gulfstream II (G-II), the overseas plane, and promoted me to that plane!" What astounding news and miraculous answer to prayer! God had not only protected his job but gave him a promotion. We were absolutely amazed. God wanted us *here*!

"He also told me I'll have to go to Savannah, Georgia—where the Gulfstream factory is located—for two more weeks of school; and when I get back, I'll get a raise!"

God was blessing us incredibly in answer to all the prayers. Betty and others back at Hesston were still praying for us and wrote wonderful letters. Before we moved, I wondered if I could get along without my calls to Betty for prayer. Then the Lord impressed on me, "Your prayers are as valid as hers." I knew she had "strengthened my hand in God," as David experienced from his friend Jonathan.

While we waited for the extra land to sell, another problem arose: a prospective pastor was coming to preach a trial sermon on September 14, with a vote on the 16th. We could be under pressure to vacate the parsonage much sooner than expected.

Pastoral candidate James Hollywood came with his wife Patricia, and James preached a fine sermon. I liked him immediately. In the afternoon they came to look at the house. James had just graduated from seminary in Oregon and was recommended to the church by Elmer Friesen. Elmer, a Mennonite and professor at the seminary, was an occasional speaker at Lynden since the pastor left a year ago. The Hollywoods were a lovely young couple. He had dark wavy hair and a friendly, outgoing personality. She was tall with long reddish blonde hair, friendly but more reserved.

We all wondered, *if he gets the job, will we be out in time?* We explained the situation and hoped for the best. The vote passed and the Hollywoods planned to move *soon*. As a temporary solution, a couple from church arranged to put their camper on the church grounds for the Hollywoods until we moved. How we wished the Jameses would hurry!

On September 19, a beautiful double rainbow arched the sky above the church and Jared took a picture. He was becoming quite a photographer. Though he struggled with adjusting here, he often sang cheerfully around the house and he enjoyed Sunday school and church. He liked to sing, to a variation of the tune, "Blest Be the Tie that Binds:" "Me froggie, he am a queer bird, he ain't got no tail almost hardly; he runs and he jumps, when he jumps he sits down on the place where he ain't got no tail, almost hardly at all." I much preferred this to tears.

On October 1, the land finally sold. Then we learned the Jameses' new house may not be ready until November. More waiting! October 3 we went to the bank to sign papers. Not possessing financial acumen, I was amazed that the bank agreed to give us such a large loan. I saw this as confirmation from the Lord that this was our house. Of course, Jake's good salary had something to do with it! We learned that our monthly payments would be $760, which seemed obscene after $163 at Hesston. As Jake and I sat at the desk, the banker pushed the papers across the desk to me with a friendly warning, "Don't look at the figure at the bottom." So how could I not? Shocked at the enormous interest charge—$210,000 over 30 years—my courage evaporated. I thought, *This house isn't $90,000 at all, but $300,000!* However, I signed, trusting the rest to God. God had opened the door, and we would walk through. The bank owned the house but it was ours to live in.

That same afternoon, Hollywoods arrived from Seattle. They had dessert with us and we shared with them the latest on the house. They graciously accepted the wait. We helped unload their belongings into the house. Now we were cramped indeed, with our boxes and theirs. In the evening our realtor called from Hesston saying he had a buyer for our 11 acres. Amazing timing! We asked $1500 an acre, a good help with our house payment.

As we endured an embarrassingly long wait, James and Patricia lived in the tiny cramped camper. We tried to make up for it by inviting them for occasional meals and snacks or they stopped in to chat and water her plants. The move delay had an upside, providing us valuable time together to get acquainted quickly. Their friendship blessed our children as well.

One day James shared with our family about his miraculous conversion in Vietnam. Through a chaplain, he had accepted Christ and received the baptism in the Holy Spirit with the gift of tongues all at once. I'd heard similar stories from Jean Walker at Vincennes and Jerry Mitchell on the bus, and now James. Jesus was still the Baptizer in the Spirit, as John had prophesied of Him: "I indeed baptized you with water, but He will baptize you with the Holy Spirit" (Mark 1:8).

James told of growing up in Seattle in a 50 percent African American neighborhood. His mother was a faithful Presbyterian. In high school he worked at a gas station. He kept a pistol with him at all times, since some of the attendants had been murdered in the restroom! We listened in horror as he told his chilling tale.

"One day I offered to demonstrate to a friend that the gun was safe because I kept the safety on. I pointed the gun through the window and pulled the trigger. Nothing happened. So I held it and while I was showing him the safety, the gun went off and shot me in the neck." His dark eyes spoke of the gravity of the situation. "The doctor told me later that the bullet entered just a fraction of an inch from my jugular vein."

James continued, "I realized later that God had spared my life for a purpose. While I was in Vietnam I sensed a clear call to the ministry. I told the Lord that if He would save my life again, I'd go to seminary. So here I am!" We were amazed and glad that God had protected him. My heart warmed to this young charismatic pastor and we became good friends.

When we finally got a moving date of October 31, everyone rejoiced. After four weeks in a camper, the Hollywoods got their parsonage. And the Jameses threw in the smaller of the two riding lawn mowers free without our asking.

During our first months in Washington, we saw Jake's father and step-mother regularly and, occasionally, other members of the family. For moving day, Peter and Mary came from the Island to help. Church members pitched in with pickups and muscle power. We were blessed with a beautiful warm day. When we arrived at the front door of our new home with Peter and Mary, Mary insisted that Jake carry me over the threshold, and we have a picture to prove he did. I had made a great many bierrocks (a bun with hamburger and cabbage filling I learned to make at Hesston) to serve the workers.

We moved in on Halloween to a myriad of lovely signs of God's blessing. I had bought a couple of cacti at garage sales and on October 31, the Thanksgiving cactus bloomed white, the Christmas cactus bloomed red, and the Easter lily (left on the back step of the parsonage) had two lilies! On top of that, in the afternoon, God sent a rainbow above the hill just to the north of us! And Peter and Mary bought a lovely large plant for the foyer. When I showed Jared the flowers, he said, "They're happy! The flowers are happy to be in this house!" That made us happy, too.

However, one problem with the house made me *un*happy: it appeared conspicuously rich looking. Janet and I were especially sensitive about that. A girl from church made comments to Janet about it on the bus, so she hated riding the bus and got a stomachache every day she rode it. Now *she* was unhappy here, too, complaining, "I wish I was finished with school so I could go back to Hesston." I cringed. She also felt a lot of pressure from non-Christians at school.

One day a boy asked Jared at church, "Are you rich?" Jared said he didn't know and asked me, "Are we?" How could we answer such a question? The children must have heard such talk at home. We did not own the house anyway. The bank did. I kept reminding myself that God had led us here and gave us the house and we would share this gift with others.

From our poverty backgrounds, plus our life-altering Mennonite Central Committee service in Mississippi, Jake and I believed in living a simple, frugal lifestyle, in accord with traditional Mennonite teachings. As Jake earned bigger and better salaries, the temptations and push to attain the "American Dream" were ever present. Had we fallen into this rut? Even

Jake's Dad said to me reproachfully the first time he visited us at the new house, "You have a very big house!" I felt blamed unfairly, and knew he would never say that to Jake. I prayed God would forgive him and help me love him anyway. He had lived very frugally for 80 years and I could understand how he felt.

Though at times I struggled with guilt and the big mortgage payment, I was convinced that God had led us every step. He was the One who had opened the doors, showing to us His abundance and that it is not His desire for His children to live in want, poverty, or inferiority. Didn't Jesus say in the Sermon on the Mount, "Seek first the kingdom of God…and *all these things* (the necessities of life) shall be added to you" (Matt. 6:33)? And, James 1:17, which I learned as a small child in Sunday school, says: "Every good gift and every perfect gift is from above…"

After we were settled, and everything in place we had an open house and invited the whole church of about 60 members. From comments I'd heard, I knew people itched to see the house. We had a house full of chattering people, got better acquainted as we showed the house, and enjoyed refreshments with our new friends.

Before long, true to his word, Mr. Crabtree brought Bars over in his horse trailer. The first afternoon she jumped the fence and ran home. So Jake and Janet put an electric wire above the fence and Mr. Crabtree brought her back. She stayed penned up until she got used to her new home. When Jake was gone, Janet groomed and rode Bars. Jared and I kept each other company. A good companion, he taught me to play chess. He made a nifty diagram of the "men" and was patient with me. I rejoiced that our children were happy at home. As long as I could forget what others thought, I could be content in the reality of God's care for us.

On December 4, 1980, we got what they called a "northeaster," a two-day blizzard that closed school Thursday and Friday, no mail delivery three days, and no church on Sunday. Jake and Jared helped a neighbor dig out his wife's car, shoveling through high drifts for almost a quarter of a mile before the snowplow came. Church neighbors got together for food, Sunday school lesson, and fellowship; and the children all enjoyed the snow.

Jake's job gave him ten days off a month. That December Jared lamented, "I still hate it here! And I hate when Dad's gone for a week. At Hesston he was gone only for a day or so and here he's always gone for a week!" Jake actually was gone for longer trips at Hesston also, but Jared was too busy with friends and his life to notice. Here he definitely missed his father.

Jared complained, "The kids at school are always looking for lacquer to sniff to get high on. Boy, they're dumb! Why do they do that? The kids at Hesston never did that. We had drug and alcohol and smoking education at Hesston but we never have it here." This appalled and saddened me. Life in the real world, without Jesus, is tough.

One Sunday afternoon, Jared came to me and asked, "Why did Jesus have to die?"

Surprised and pleased at his question, I explained, "He died to take away our sins, and the Bible says He died to deliver us from the power of darkness – of Satan – and give us life and light in God's kingdom" (1 Peter 2:4-9). Something he heard that morning caused Jared to reflect on the deeper issues of faith and I was glad we could discuss them.

In February 1981, Edgar Kaiser bought the Denver Broncos for $40 million. That kept Jake busy, flying Mr. Kaiser to Broncos games, in addition to business trips around the country and the world. He saw firsthand the lifestyle of the rich and famous.

Our family life continued in our usual routines. Jake flew trips, I proofread Smith, and made the index, we entertained people, and had rich experiences. Janet rode and groomed Bars and shared her with friends – Michelle next door and Tricia Hollywood. School was still a difficult trial for Jared and he spouted off one day, "I hate school in that condemned building! It's so different from Hesston and I still want to go back!"

"But next year you'll be in the brand new high school. That will be a lot better."

"I don't want to go to that new school," he insisted, "It's a stupid-looking building." He could not be appeased. The day came when his depression evoked the pitiful words, "I wish I could die!" I groaned, but the Lord had prepared me for this.

"I felt the exact same way when we lived at Vincennes," I told him. "When I said that to a seminary friend at Elkhart, he asked, 'Do you think you're the only one who feels that way?' " He had jarred me out of my self-pity.

Surprised by my admission and the friend's response, Jared laughed. "Lots of people feel that way," I said, "but you can be happy if you make up your mind to be." He agreed. His bubble of despair burst, at least for the present. Still, I hated that this poor child lived on Tums that school year to alleviate his perpetual stomachache. I prayed for him to find a friend and was delighted when he told me about his friend Danny, a Catholic boy. I thanked God for Danny, who Jared sometimes invited to come and play. Once I invited his mother and mentally disabled sister to come along for the day, including lunch. That very day my washing machine flooded the laundry room and hall before I discovered it. Danny's mother gladly helped mop up. At lunch, I prayed at the table as usual before we ate.

On the first snow of winter, Danny said to Jared at school, "Your friend is sending his dandruff down on us."

Mystified, Jared responded, "My friend?"

"Yes," Danny smiled. "God!" We both enjoyed that humorous observation and commentary on our faith.

By March 1981, Jared still had not changed his mind about the move. One morning our devotional was on forgiveness and after reading it I asked him, "Are you angry at God?"

"Not at *God! At you and Dad!*" At least he was honest, and he didn't *act* angry with us!

Janet had her own struggles and told me one day, "I think I'm getting wild here. The kids are so different from Hesston. I want to go to Hesston for spring break, and I'm going whether you and Dad say I can or not!" Her attitude jarred me.

We discussed her friends at school. The numerous Dutch Reformed churches had their own schools, so their students attended their high school. *Surely there are other Christian kids at the public school*, I thought. I began praying for a Christian friend for Janet.

Then Jared said he wanted to go to Hesston for spring break, too. When Jake was home one evening, we had a family conference. We discussed the alternatives and decided that Jake, Jared, and I would drive to Hesston in the summer. Janet agreed that if she went for spring break she could stay during the summer and work on a raspberry picker. Jared reluctantly accepted the plan.

But it was only April, and in Jared's mind summer was a long way off. A few days later, Jake left at 6:00 A.M. on a trip to California. That morning, the usual gray drizzle seemed to close in on me. All winter these drizzly days followed in succession. Kansas boasted more sunny days than any other state and I had prepared myself beforehand to accept the rain. With the Lord's help, I had kept a surprisingly positive attitude. Coming down to the family room, I found Jared dressed, shoulders sagging, looking enormously dejected, and staring out the picture window. "Jared, what's *wrong*?" I asked and put my arms around him.

The tears flowed and he cried, "I just miss Hesston so much and think about it all the time. I have *friends* in Hesston." These heart-shattering words pierced my sensitive mother spirit and I wanted to cry with him. He continued through his tears, "I want to go back to graduate with my eighth grade class. Can't I go back just for graduation?"

"I'll check on it," I promised, and he got ready for school. He had a glimmer of hope to hold on to and I was spurred into action. First I told Jake of our conversation.

Later, Jake and I wrote a letter to the Hesston principal, Kermit Gingerich; then one day I phoned him. "Jared has to take exams here before he could graduate," Kermit explained, "and one of them is chemistry. Has he had that?" He had not.

One evening as the four of us drove in the car, we discussed the pros and cons, trying to help Jared decide. Janet spoke up, "Chemistry is very hard, Jared. I don't think you could pass the exam without having taken the class." Jared listened to the voice of experience. We provided him with a choice. Now it was up to him. In the end, he saw the wisdom of staying and chose to graduate at Lynden.

Later he reminisced with me, "I was in Mrs. Boesker's science class and she always has you do retakes of exams if you fail. I always got A's in her class, usually without a retake. I was in the "WOW Club!" I was proud of him. Hesston had been such a homey, family place to him. By contrast, the school here felt cold and impersonal. I knew that character is forged in the school of suffering and trusted God to bring good out of this for him.

On April 11, 1981, we celebrated Jake's Dad's 80ᵗʰ birthday with a surprise party at their condo's large basement room four days before his birthday. The whole family came and everyone brought food; I made the turkey since we lived close by. Dad was totally surprised and pleased to have all the family there. How glad we were to be present for this special event.

Janet flew to Kansas for nine days and returned a new person. She looked happy and terrific in new clothes and a becoming haircut. Helen had taken her daughter Joan and Janet shopping. Hesston provided a tonic she sorely needed. She shared with me, "After a youth meeting I came back to Joan's and when I was alone in her bedroom, I prayed and rededicated my life to the Lord."

"And at a Bible study Don Sauerwein led, he told about the night his cows got out. He couldn't get them that night so he prayed for God to send angels to stand guard around them so they wouldn't run off. The next day a neighbor called and told him she saw his cows all together in a circle. When they tried to run a certain direction, they acted like they ran into something and were turned back!" We were both amazed. I thanked God with a grateful heart for His leading.

When she left for Hesston I prayed for a Christian friend for her. Again, on April 28, I prayed in my journal for a good Christian friend and asked the Lord to help us open our home to young people who our children would enjoy. The very next day, Janet came home from school all excited. "There's a really nice new girl at school from Florida—and she's a Christian! Her name is Melody and she invited me to go to Grace Baptist Church with her this evening." I nearly burst with joy. What a quick answer to prayer! And Melody was such a lovely name.

Thus began our friendship with the Sloans—Melody, Ellaina, Sharleen, and their mother Lynn. Lynn brought Janet home that night at 10:00 and they stayed until 11:30. The children enjoyed each other and Lynn and I had a great visit. From then on, Janet often attended youth meetings on Wednesday nights at Grace Baptist in town. Sometimes we had the Sloans for dinner on Wednesdays before youth meeting. Lynn's husband promised to join them in Lynden, a promise he did not fulfill, and she later endured an unwanted divorce. Then Janet met Sue, another Christian who became a close friend.

The same day Janet met Melody, April 29, Helen Hershberger called to tell us Chief had sold for $750, a year after Janet bought him. Now Janet had money to buy a new horse. She found an ad in the paper and on May 9 bought Tico Prince Piute, an appaloosa gelding, for $600. She kept busy grooming and riding Tico and sharing him with friends who came to ride.

May 12 was a red-letter day for me. After reading and re-reading Smith's Story umpteen times and making the Index, I was invited to a tea for Herta Funk, a co-worker at the Newton office, at Nellie Lehn's home over the border in B.C. Nellie was children's editor. There Edna Dyck presented me with a copy of the revised book, hot off the press the week before. It was a gift from Dick Rempel, Faith and Life Press manager and good friend. I felt royally rewarded and enjoyed great fellowship that afternoon.

On the morning of June 12, a few days before school was out, Jake and I drove separately to Jared's graduation since Jake had an early trip. In contrast to this event, Hesston had a formal evening graduation where the girls wore beautiful new dresses. After Jake left, not seeing a familiar face in that crowd on the bleachers, a feeling of loneliness and sadness engulfed me. In an instant I felt the weight of the ordeal this school year had been for Jared with the grief of separation from friends and friendly teachers in the town he loved. As I drove home in the rain I wept a few minutes for what my son had missed. Then the comfort of the Spirit and assurance of God's care for Jared filled me. Praise and thanksgiving welled up inside me for the blessings God had poured out on us. In addition, we'd soon be on our way to Hesston.

That summer, Janet joined a discipleship class with Janice, wife of the Baptist youth pastor Paul. With this wonderful mentoring, she began taking personal daily devotions seriously

When school was out and the berries ripe, Janet picked 1,654 pounds of strawberries in June. In July she worked on a raspberry picker. A tractor pulled the picker through the rows, and little plastic fingers shook off the berries onto a conveyor belt. The pickers had the unsavory job of picking out leaves and worms from the belt–with gloves on, of course. Janet has always hated raspberries. In August she and I picked blueberries at our neighbors' field.

On July 7, 1981, we took Jared for a couple of wonderful, carefree weeks at Hesston. Jake and Jared helped Grabers on the farm and I shucked corn with Ruby and cleaned out her basement laundry room full of wet sheepskins, which I hung out on lines, then washed the floor. Jared had great times with his friends and raised no objections about returning to the Northwest.

That fall, our children had the privilege of beginning the school year in a fine new building. Jared liked it in spite of himself, "got his second wind," turned around that year, made new friends, and got good grades.

One day Jake showed me a catalog and noted, "Computers are the coming thing; in a few years everyone will have a home computer. I'm going to order this TRS-80 Color Computer from Radio Shack for the kids." A novelty, it arrived on November 3, 1981. Jared worked through the manual, teaching himself all there was to know. It became a great diversion for him and he helped teach the rest of us.

During the years at Lynden, the children and I attended concerts and programs of famous Christians, such as Evie Carlson. Janet attended a David Meece concert in Canada, and a Dino (pianist) one in Lynden and bought me a record signed by Dino. She heard Josh McDowell and "Second Chapter of Acts" in Seattle with the Baptist youth and came home enthused. Janet loved contemporary Christian music and initiated me. Jake's stepmother Jessie came to our house overnight one night so she and I could hear Norma Zimmer at Lynden. I'll never forget that night as I went to my room and saw, through the open bedroom door, Jessie on her knees praying. I had never seen any of our parents or grandparents at prayer on their knees and this impressed me as very special.

Ever since Jake started flying the GII he heard rumblings from the pilots at work about their insecure jobs. The two pilots who were fired left for jobs in Saudi Arabia. Hans Fast, another pilot, quit at Kaiser to work for Ward Air Canada. Jake kept in touch with Hans, and then made an appointment for an interview with Ward Air. To our surprise, by the end of 1981, Jake got calls from Saudi. They were badly in need of pilots; would he consider coming? He said no.

Then on December 16, we awoke at 2:36 A.M. with another call from Saudi. Wally Kachur asked again if Jake would come to Saudi. When Jake came back to bed I asked, "You're not interested in that, are you?"

"No," he said, "but he wants us to come to B.C. when he gets back, just to talk about it. We can both go to see him and ask questions. He works for Bell Canada there."

I couldn't believe it. How often had I heard, "We'll just check out all the alternatives" and the choice I least wanted became reality. Usually it wasn't long after we moved to a new place that I began to wonder, *where will we move next?* We had been here less than two years. Would Jake really accept a job in Saudi Arabia? It was just too "far out," in more ways than one.

A few days later, we drove to Wally Kachur's house in B. C. I asked my questions. Will I be able to go there, too? Yes, he said, his wife had spent six months with him there. Where would we live? Anywhere we wanted to, here or Paris or England, anywhere in Europe, and Jake could commute! This mind-boggling news left me stunned and excited.

Jared's first reaction was negative. Janet was ecstatic about "all the Arabian horses." Jake said, "We won't move again unless all four of us are in favor."

On December 29, Jake took Jared along on a test flight of the new Gulfstream III (which he had flown from the factory in Savannah, Georgia to Los Angeles without paint or interior, where it underwent completion for six months.) Jared loved going with Jake and returned very excited.

"We flew 1000 miles in two hours, and did stalls and all kinds of neat things!" he exclaimed. This plane, a 19-passenger, very sophisticated business jet afforded Jared an adventure he could not have had at Hesston.

The next day, December 30, we had a surprise birthday party for Pastor James who turned 30. First, he and Tricia came for a turkey dinner. Then, as James played on the computer with Jared down in the family room, the whole church—55 people, including us—assembled. As all was in readiness, we sang "Happy Birthday." The house that God gave us resonated with happy chatter. Someone exclaimed, "The rooms just flow! The whole church fits in!" The Hollywoods and Pearl and Linferd Goertz lingered after everyone else had gone. We gathered around the piano and sang hymns and popular songs as Pearl played—the perfect ending to a great party.

It was also a lovely ending to the year.

Again we faced a momentous decision. For months a discontent that I could not shake had been growing inside me. Was God preparing me for another change? Jake was not ready to jump at the Saudi job because the schedule of two-months-gone, one-month-home posed a big hurdle. As I lay awake at night I wondered, *Will Jake take the job in Saudi Arabia? And will we really move to the other side of the world?* Perhaps. "My times are in thy hand" (Psa. 31:15). I knew that God's timing is perfect.

CHAPTER 32

A Monumental Decision

And the Lord will guide you continually, and
satisfy your desire with good things...
ISAIAH 58:11 (RSV)

1982

A brand new year dawned – 1982 – and I wondered what it might bring. We hadn't lived in our dream house for two years, but I sensed that we were on the edge of another move. I felt ready. However, the monumental decision we faced would affect the whole family more deeply than any previous move. If Jake took the job in Saudi Arabia – land of deserts, Islam, and oil – it would entail eight weeks on and four weeks off. This meant a two-month separation every three months.

Jake talked it over with the children and me and gathered information. We discussed it with the Hollywoods and other friends, with Dad, Jessie, and the family. Dad definitely did not want us to go. Others encouraged us.

On December 7, I bought *The Helper*, by Catherine Marshall, a book of daily devotionals on the Holy Spirit. The title had jumped off the shelf at me at the bookstore of a friend. I could not have imagined the important role it would play in my decision to move. I wanted to learn all I could about the Holy Spirit – Jesus' greatest gift to His church. This was the most exciting devotional book I had ever read. I savored one devotional each morning and could hardly wait to get up the next morning to read what God had for me. This daily tonic increased my confidence and boldness to take risks.

The children were negative at first and, later, ambivalent, as I felt at times. Jake vacillated greatly. The long periods away from the family gave him great concern.

On January 3, one of the pilots called from Switzerland and Jake asked questions. The next day, Felix Pole called from Ashbon Aviation, his London office. He urged Jake, "Call me by January 8 if you want the job."

Jake replied, "I need more time. How about if I call you on the 11th?"

"I'll wait to hear from you."

These phone calls from faraway places were exciting. The international nature of the job intrigued me. Twice that day Jake admitted, "I feel very frustrated about what to do now. Two months is too long to be gone from home, especially with the family in a new environment—a foreign country. Can you imagine what it would be like to be alone in a foreign country and not have anyone to talk to?"

"Don't worry," I reassured him. "We're not ready to make a decision yet. First we'll collect all the information and investigate tutoring possibilities for the children, and then we'll decide."

At breakfast that morning, Jake had read Jeremiah 29:11 for devotions, "I know the plans I have for you, plans for prosperity and not disaster." Later that day, that verse and *The Helper* reading inspired my prayers in my journal.

"Please, Father," I wrote, "do one for me this time. I've long desired to see Europe. You have shown me that what I once thought was impossible is possible – very possible – with YOU! Lord, I don't want this for me alone, but for the growth and development of our children, our whole family. But if it's not Your will, then block the way." That day I called Dad Friesen, Pearl Goertz, Trisha Hollywood, and Lynn Sloan to pray with us about the job. We needed intercessors!

One day Jake called his pilot friend Hans Fast about the Saudi offer. Hans revealed, "There's a mission boarding school – Black Forest Academy (BFA) – in Germany. My wife's sister and husband were dorm parents there for a year and loved it. We visited them there. If I took a job in Saudi I would move my family to Germany so our boys could attend that school. It sure is tempting!"

What an exciting answer and opportunity! Along with living in Europe there was a school for the children, the chance of a lifetime. It appeared that our children could attend a mission boarding school and live at home. Family conferences and more prayer ensued.

When Dad Friesen called one day he asked about the latest news and said, "I hope you don't move." We had enjoyed many good times together the past year and a half. We hated to disappoint him.

After Dad hung up, Jake said to us, "I wonder if Dad doesn't want us to go because he thinks he's going to die soon."

"He's so healthy," Jared chimed in, "it seems like he'll live 20 more years!" (In reality, he lived 18 more, to age 94!)

Jake set out two conditions for taking the Saudi job, as he told the children and me. "If Hans and Helene go with their two boys I'd consider it, because I don't want you to be alone in a foreign country. Second, Felix offered me a $48,000 salary. I'm going to ask for $55,000. If he agrees, and Fasts are going, I'll take it."

"That sounds like putting out the fleece, like Gideon," I said. The children knew the story.

By this time, Hans and Helene Fast were eager to join us, but Hans had to work things out with his company. When Helene learned we might go, she told me, "I'm jealous. Since we visited my sister and husband there as a family, I've always wished our boys could go to BFA." That sold me on the school.

On January 10, the Fasts invited us to their home in British Columbia. Their stories, slides, and contagious excitement about Europe and BFA inspired us. Our children learned to know their boys, Curtis and Andre. Janet would be in grade 12, Jared, grade 10, Curtis, 9, and Andre, 6. Hans wanted to quit his job and move in summer.

On youth Sunday in church, Janet read the Scripture very meaningfully. Tears of joy filled my eyes as she sang in a lovely trio, "Let's forget about ourselves and magnify the Lord and worship Him," and in the youth choir, "Give them all to Jesus." I was grateful for James Hollywood and his work with the youth. Janet's friendship with him and Tricia provided a positive influence.

One day James spoke to Janet's Great Religions class in school. She reported, "James did a choice job! All my Grace Baptist friends were there and he talked about how Mennonites and Baptists are alike and different. The Baptists in class agreed on the war and peace thing, but I don't agree with them on immersion and the rapture." She was proud of James as her pastor.

Jake got the *Mennonite Encyclopedia* (four large volumes which Jake had bought at seminary) and looked up some of the things she talked about, including "eternal security." It was not in the encyclopedia because Mennonites don't use the term or teach it. Jake told her, "Remember how King Saul hardened his heart?"

"Where is that?" she asked and wanted to read for herself the story in II Samuel. "James told us Mennonites are 'radical.' I liked that," she said.

Jake explained further how different the early Anabaptists were from other reformers, taking Jesus seriously about the Sermon on the Mount, peace and non-resistance, and adult baptism. He looked up certain issues and Janet copied down verses. James' talk sparked a wonderful, rare faith discussion between Janet and her father.

Later, as Jake and I talked about a possible move and our house, I said, "I think Christians should be radically different from non-Christians. Do you think we are?"

"Yes, I think we *are* radically different. I'm not tied to material things. I could give up this house any time if we have to. If it's a matter of choosing between this house and salvation, I'd choose salvation." Wow, a clear-cut commitment!

The day came when Jake seemed particularly troubled about taking the job. "I just don't know what to do," he admitted. "I hate being gone from the family for two whole months. But my job here could fold any time."

"I think you should take it," I encouraged, amazed at my own assurance. "It's a great opportunity for us as a family to live and travel in Europe. The mission school would be a unique experience. I believe it's an open door from the Lord and we should go. I'm ready!" Jake seemed relieved.

As the day approached for him to call Felix Pole, Jake told us, "I think I'll take the job even if I don't get $55,000. The salary is tax-free. In addition, I'll get housing and an all-expense-paid car in Saudi, including gas. I'll have free transportation back and forth to the States every eight weeks, and per diem, which is extra money every day for food" (far above what was necessary – and pilots kept what they did not spend).

"Then we're not putting out the fleece," Jared observed. When we were alone, he objected to me, "I only want to go for the summer, and we have to take Sparky and Harry" (his white cat). By this time, Jake and I had discussed staying for two years. What a turnaround for Jared. First he hated it here, and now he wanted to stay. More prayer needed! When tensions escalated, I had developed the habit of praying, "Lord, I need a 'word' from You!" I always found that word in the Bible and now, in addition, *The Helper* fortified me.

Janet sold Tico on January 14, believing a move was imminent. When the new owner came for him Janet was at school. After eight months with us, Tico was loath to leave. As the buyers walked down the road with him, he stopped, turned around, stood still and neighed. Jake had to walk along with him and the new owners. It saddened me to see how attached Tico had become to us, and his reluctance to leave. It was the first of a series of sad partings. But Janet told me later that Tico did that for her, too. "He's stubborn," she admitted. That helped make her parting with him easier.

That same day, only one month after the call in the night from Wally Kacher in Saudi, Felix Pole called from London and Jake accepted the job with Bell Canada Telephone Company. His starting date was set for February 16. He had notified John Caruso earlier of his plans to terminate with Kaiser.

When Jake hung up from this momentous call, I felt an emotional jolt. This moment of decision hit me hard, even though I was prepared for and wanted it. I felt butterflies in my stomach and, as Jake and I talked, I cried.

"What's wrong?" he asked. "Are you crying about Tico?"

"No. About the move—everything! There will be a lot of changes and it hit me all at once." Facing Jake's absence was the biggest. I asked the Lord to give me joy about the move as I prepared for Dad and Jessie's visit for supper. I had asked Jessie to come and make her special delicious "butter soup" (potato) for us and I had salmon, applesauce, cottage cheese and cinnamon buns. These times with Jake's parents were special.

Jake wrote a letter to Felix on January 20, laying out his terms. On January 23, Felix called from London saying he agreed to a salary of $52,000—good enough for Jake. In a letter, Felix listed terms and benefits as Jake had requested them. The next few weeks we made every day count; realizing the separation would not be easy. February 16 would come all too soon and I dreaded it. I had a heightened sense of the preciousness of family, and how much we depended on each other.

Three days later, Hans called Jake. "Guess what? I just got furloughed, so I don't have to quit. I'm free to go to Saudi!" Was God opening the doors, or what?

Later that day I called Helene to see what she was thinking. "We'll probably go!" she bubbled with excitement. "These are the last crucial hours!" I felt goose bumps.

With all details finalized, Jake planned to leave February 16. On my birthday, February 6, I told Jared, "I don't know if I can stand it for Dad to be gone two months."

Jared, who a year before complained bitterly about having Jake gone for a week, said, "If Lynn (Sloan) can stand to be gone from her husband for two years, you can stand it for two months!" Will wonders never cease? "Out of the mouths of babes." His perspective had changed and he had adjusted in spite of himself. Lynn and her three girls were like family to us and had lost husband and father to divorce. Our situation could hardly be compared with their devastating loss, but Jared's insight was gratifying. Janet seemed fine with the move.

The evening Jake left for Saudi, I took pictures of him with the children in front of the fireplace. Then we drove to the airport at Vancouver where we bravely said our goodbyes. As we kissed goodbye, my eyes filled with tears for a moment, then I turned away as Jake reminded, "Your parking meter will run out." As Janet and I rode down one escalator, Jared ran down – and up – and down – the empty "Up" escalator nearby so fast and looked so ridiculous that I laughed at the sight until my sides hurt. His antics eased the pain of parting. What a blessing children can be! (Several years later Janet admitted, "The day after Dad left for Saudi, I went into a restroom stall at school and cried." Not one to share her feelings and hurts easily, she suffered from Jake's absence.) Jared told me that he got used to Jake being gone now, so it "wasn't as bad as before."

The Helper devotionals, with daily reminders of the Spirit's presence, as well as encouragement from many friends, kept me motivated and joyful. Pearl requested that I teach a women's Bible study, so the week after Jake left, I began one in our home using *The Helper*. About eight women attended and the study and fellowship met a need for all of us.

The day after Jake left, he called at 4:00 P.M., midnight in London, so he could talk with the children after school. He said he was trying on uniforms and that he would wear the British Airways uniform. With gold stripes on the sleeves and a cap with gold stripes, he would look handsome and official.

God was gracious. Within ten days, Jake surprised me with a phone call and fantastic news, "I'm coming home for a week and a half while the plane is in the shop for maintenance!" We all rejoiced! This pattern continued for the duration of the job. Except for one time, he always got home for a week or more during the two months away.

While he was home, he talked with the children about moving to Germany and finally got Jared's consent. "Now we have to put our house up for sale," Jake said, and made an appointment with Realtor Ron. On Sunday, Hans and family came for dinner and we discussed our upcoming move. Having another family to go with relieved Jake's anxiety and made the move less intimidating and more fun.

Our first year in Washington, Jake traded the Mercedes for a Mazda 626 and occasionally Janet drove the Mazda to school. The day Jake returned to Saudi, Janet drove us to the Vancouver Airport while Jake and I sat in the back. We talked about how nice it was to have a daughter who could chauffeur us now, even on the freeway to Vancouver! She had turned 17 on January 27. Could it be possible?

Before long, our pastor, James Hollywood, had a decision for us. All the years Jake had lived in the States he never joined a church. I had my membership at Flatland, my home church at Quakertown. Jake requested his church letter from his Dad years before but would not join a church in the States. Now James asked, "How about joining Glendale, since the children are taking church membership class in preparation for baptism? Even though you're leaving in summer, I would strongly urge you to all join together." We talked it over as a family. Jake wanted to encourage the children in their step of faith and agreed. The children balked for a time, because we were moving. I told them our reasons, Jake wrote them a letter from Saudi, and they agreed with the wisdom of the decision.

Jake returned from Saudi on Saturday, May 1. On Sunday, his brother Peter and Mary joined us for worship and the day. Dad and Jessie also came for the baptism. What a special occasion and cause for rejoicing this was for me after being separated from our families for many years. Our move to the border – the 49th parallel – proved to be a rich spiritual blessing.

James called our family forward, asked a few questions, and then we knelt for prayer. His long prayer made it hard for me to concentrate as we knelt upright on the uncomfortable surface. In his very sincere fashion, he wanted to cover all the bases for his good friends. (James had confided to me earlier that he didn't know what he would do if we moved. I typed the bulletin for him and he brought it to me each week and stayed for coffee as we discussed theology and church matters.) We were greatly blessed and enjoyed the day of worship and dinner with Jake's family in our home.

In the two years at Lynden, many of Jake's family members came to visit: Friesens, Koops, Mulligans, Unraus, and Arlitts. We also made the trip to Schulzes in the interior. Margaret and Peter had raised their three children, Neil, Carol, and Laura, on the Island then moved to Lillooet. Carol was diagnosed with cancer at a young age and we were saddened when she lost that battle at age 30, on April 28, 1982. On May 3rd, we drove with Dad and Jessie to Lillooet for her funeral. I was thankful Jake got home in time to attend.

Carol was cremated and her ashes were taken to Carol Lake in Tweedsmuir Park out of Bella Coola in B. C. The Schulzes had toured the area when Carol was in her early teens and they met John Edwards, a guide there at the time. John decided to call the lake Carol Lake because she was the first young woman who had hiked there. It was named after her before she died. Carol's untimely death was a terrible blow to Margaret and Peter and the family.

While Jake was home, we turned our attention to selling the house. At first I worried, *How will we sell such an expensive house in time?* I committed it to the Lord and felt at peace. To my astonishment, before long Realtor Ron brought a widow, Mrs. G., who liked it and offered to buy with *cash*! Her husband had worked for Bell Telephone in Alaska and left her a grand sum. While Jake was home we finalized the sale. On May 10, Mrs. G. bought the house for $107,500! In less than two years we made $17,500 on it! We were amazed once again at God's leading and provision.

The downside was that Mrs. G. wanted to take possession as soon as possible so she could build a barn to raise beef cattle. We had to stall her off until the children were out of school and Jake was home in July to help with the move. We arranged to rent the house from her our last three months as she had a barn built. After Janet sold Tico, Mr. Crabtree had brought Bars back. So Bars was in the pasture, which didn't feel like ours anymore.

On May 14, Jake learned that Kaiser Resources in Vancouver had laid off their pilots. He had gotten out in time. The business slump continued until, after we moved to Germany, Kaiser declared bankruptcy. We were grateful that God used Kaiser to move us close to Dad for a time and then provided Jake with a good job well in advance of the layoffs and bankruptcy. I marveled again at God's timing. As we often heard, "God is never early and never late, but always on time."

The year before, on Janet's 16th birthday, I gave her a journal called, "This Is Your Life," with all the cute, funny, and sometimes exasperating things she did and said, and other interesting facts, gleaned from notebooks, slips of paper, and journals. Then on May 23, while Jake was home, I gave Jared his journal on his 14th birthday, unfinished, and kept adding to it until he was 16. Especially rewarding to me was the record of the children's spiritual development and progress. Jake left for Saudi the end of May, with plans to return the end of July for our move.

Ever since we moved to Washington, I had a desire to visit my family in Pennsylvania, and now we were ready to move again. We decided that Jared and I would fly out for a week in early July. Janet worked on a raspberry picker, took care of the animals, and spent time with friends. While there I visited my grandfather Landis who lived with Aunt Melba and Uncle Ivan, my mother's sister and brother. Aunt Melba gave me a postcard dated 1913 with a picture of a church, house, and barn with caption: "Oldest known Landis homestead, 1488 – Hirzel, Switzerland."

"We hope you can visit Hirzel while you're in Germany," Melba encouraged. I was delighted with this piece of history to help me get in touch with my family roots. The time "at home" sped by quickly, but I was grateful for quality time with each one of my family members.

Anna and John had moved back to Pennsylvania after 20 years in Chicago. They lived at Newtown and had the whole Herstine family over

Our trio: me, Millie, and Anna, July 1982.

to their house on July 11. I was happy Jared could be there, but sad that Janet was absent. Millie had brought a trio book along and she, Anna, and I sang "For All My Sin." Someone recorded it and took a picture. Anna sent me the tape and I had copies made for all of us. It is a joy to have this one recording—and we sound *good*! I am grateful for these reminders of our seven years of singing together.

Before our move we anticipated one more special event. We learned in spring that Bars was pregnant, due about July 10. Hoping we could all observe the birth, I wanted Jake to be home for it as well. I prayed that Bars would wait until Jake returned. Was this too trivial a thing to ask? Jake was due home July 23. Would Bars wait two weeks? I trusted that she would.

Jake returned from Saudi on *Friday evening*, and on *Saturday morning* at 8:00 Bars' labor began – two weeks late! God is so good! (I've read and experienced that God sometimes cares about the silliest little things, if I do.)

Janet put Bars in the back yard so we could see her at close range. On July 24, 1982, five days before we moved out of the house, we all watched from the break-

Janet, Michelle Fast, and Bars, July 1982.

fast table as Bars lay down. Soon the white sack began to show. I grabbed my camera and we went outside. I snapped pictures, one after another, as Bars delivered her colt in plain view in front of my flowers. They had bloomed early, in answer to my prayer that they would bloom before we moved! Jane Fast next door complained that hers still were not blooming.

I called the Hollywoods who were delighted to come and watch. What a treat to see the miracle of birth so close up. Even Sparky watched and walked inquisitively around the newborn colt. It lay on the ground until James lifted it up to stand on its gangly, wobbly legs. Soon it was walking and nuzzling its mother to nurse. We rejoiced at this unusual blessing to crown our stay in Washington.

The packers came to pack and the moving van loaded on July 29 to store our belongings in Bellingham. We loaned our piano to a friend, Doris Rempel, for her daughter to take lessons, stored our car in Pearl and Linferd's chicken barn, and sent our computer on loan to the Grabers at Hesston. We decided to give my little yellow Opel to the Bloomquists, since one of their cars had broken down and Barbara needed transportation to work. Jared agreed to give Harry the cat to Janet's friend who lived on a farm, and Peter and Mary on the Island agreed to take Sparky.

Our Lynden friends expressed sadness at seeing us go and wished us well with loving words. We had farewell meals with friends and with our "Supper Club" small group that Jake had instigated. They gave us a beautiful multi-colored egg made from Mount St. Helens ash, with which many unique and useful objects were crafted.

Finally, we took off to Nick and Margaret's in Canada for one night. The next day we rode the ferry with Dad and Jessie to Vancouver Island for time with Helen and Bert Arlitt and Peter, and Mary. A visit to Victoria and Butchart Gardens topped off our stay on the Island. We spent our last night with Nick and Margaret, Mark, and Garth, who were excited about our great opportunity.

The next afternoon we met James, Patricia, Pearl, and Linferd for dinner at a restaurant near the Vancouver Airport. They brought our eight boxes of household items, pots and pans, clothes, and other necessities. As we said our sad goodbyes, Pearl cried. Later Jared commented, "I feel sorry for Pearl." Trisha told me earlier, "It's hardest for those of us left behind." As part of a military family, she was used to moving and loved to travel. We had arrived in Lynden on August 3, and exactly two years later on August 3 we left Vancouver for Germany.

That night at 8:15 we flew to Seattle on the first leg of our nocturnal flight. There we boarded an awesome, nearly 500-passenger Boeing 747, my first such experience. We left at about 10 P.M. for our ten-hour flight to London over Greenland and Iceland – an exciting adventure! When I walked back in the cabin to the restroom, I was astonished at the sea of hundreds of faces – many East Indians and other nationalities – in that large "room." What an incredible flying machine! Many people were draped over the seats sleeping. We felt privileged to be up front in the more roomy business class, as Ashbon Aviation paid for the move and flight.

At 11:30 P.M. we had a wonderful dinner, and by 1:00 or 1:30 it began to get light as we traveled north over the land of the midnight sun. The fantastic movie, *Chariots of Fire*, kept us spellbound until 2:45 after which we slept until about 4:45. Before breakfast the flight attendant brought a hot washcloth to our seats. We felt like royalty with such service.

At 3:10 P.M. we touched down at Heathrow Airport, where Jake got a hotel room. Then we rode the tube (subway) to London. It sped like lightning, with many stops. Jake had flown to London numerous times and wanted to show us the sights. We walked to Buckingham Palace and saw the guards on duty. After supper at McDonalds, we walked to Westminster Abby and to Queen Marguerita's Church (the church of Chaucer, Milton, and where Churchill was married). We strolled past the parliament buildings and on to Westminster Bridge over the Thames.

By then our feet ached from walking many miles. Finding our way back to the hotel on the subway turned out to be a scary ordeal. Subways were numerous and confusing. We switched from one to another, often with lengthy waits. Once, as we got on the wrong one, Jake realized it just in time as the doors closed on his leg. He pulled them open with his hands and we jumped off. Subways were retired for the night and waits dragged on. At the airport, we missed the bus to our hotel. The terminal was deserted with no incoming flights and no cabs. Finally a bus arrived and at long last we dragged ourselves to our rooms.

After a short night we enjoyed a peaceful flight to Basel, Switzerland on Swiss Air. I was delighted to arrive in the land of my father's and Grandfather Landis's ancestors.

Helene Fast and boys arrived before us and she, along with the BFA business manager, Al Martens and his wife Edna, picked us up at the airport. After a 45-minute drive we arrived in Kandern, Germany where the school is located. Al showed us to our temporary apartment and spent time orienting us with all kinds of information, including a place to buy a car. The next day we bought an '81 Toyota for 9700 DM ($4000 U.S.). The friendly salesman had a sticker on his car, "Jesus Above Everything." After completing the sale he told Jake, "When you get in your car and take the wheel, let Jesus drive for you." Though Mr. Martens had told us he was a Christian, it was heartening to find an outspoken witness in a car salesman in mainly secular Germany.

World War II and Hitler had left an indelible imprint on my young mind. As I reflected on moving to Germany I was curious about the country. What would the people be like? What lingering signs of the war would we see? How did they feel toward Americans? How would we fare without knowing the language? An exciting year stretched before us and I hoped the children would adjust and be happy.

CHAPTER 33

Pleasant Fatherlands

*From one man (God) created all races of mankind and made them
live throughout the whole earth. He himself fixed beforehand the
exact times and the limits of the places where they would live.
He did this so that they would look for him, and perhaps find him.*

ACTS 17:26,27 (GNB)

1982

We soon realized our incredible good fortune of living in the famous Black
Forest area of Germany. God had transplanted us into the extreme southwestern corner of the country, a strategic location affording easy access to
France (20 minutes away across the Rhine River) and Switzerland and the
city of Basel (30 minutes away). The landscape was beautiful – gently rolling
hills, neat farms, and picturesque villages hundreds of years old. Cherry
orchards and vineyards covered miles of hillsides. The beauty and peace
of this nature-lover's paradise almost took my breath away. Not far away,
mountain ranges, peaks, and forests stretched for hundreds of miles.

Every day was a marvel of sights and places to see and explore. The first
Sunday afternoon the Fasts (except Hans) and we took a 12-kilometer hike
on trails walked by nature-loving Germans for centuries. The hilly terrain
through peaceful, lofty forests delighted the senses and challenged us unini-
tiated hikers. A large Black Forest *Wanderung* (wandering) map showed
hundreds of trails throughout the region and the Rhine River flowing for
almost 100 miles along the western edge of the Black Forest and Germany.

Since Daddy was of Pennsylvania Dutch/Swiss and German background,
Pappy Landis of Swiss, Grammy Landis of Dutch, and Jake's ancestors originally Dutch from Friesland – this continent held great meaning for us. I
had no information on my father's family. But I had a bound volume of the
Ackerman (Dutch) genealogy and a smaller booklet of the Landis (Swiss)
family, going back eight generations to the first Landis immigrants to

America. In addition to our early family members, our church fathers had lived in these lands. Many places beckoned us.

Jake wanted to show us the continent he had explored in 1957. After registering the three of us in the country (Jake was not required to, since he did not live there for three consecutive months), and buying our car, we left on August 10, a week after we arrived, for a whirlwind tour of countries to the north. We were all in good spirits and for me this was a dream come true.

We headed across the Rhine into France and drove north toward Strasbourg, taking in lovely farmlands and villages of ancient, quaint houses, many with barns attached. From France we crossed into Luxembourg, one of Europe's smallest and oldest independent countries. The capital and largest city, also Luxembourg, was so crowded that we could not find parking, so we drove on to Belgium. Late in the afternoon we saw our first thatched roof, typical of Holland. We looked for a hotel and found one in the middle of a forked road. Jake paid and told us, "They gave me change in guilders. I wonder why." A study of the map revealed we *were* in the Netherlands – land of Grammy Landis' and my ancestors. We had seen no signs at the Belgian border. This made our fifth country for the day, including Germany.

The next morning we came to the Dordrecht-Rotterdam area. At Kinderdijk, we saw 19 windmills, took a half-hour boat ride, and climbed up a five-story windmill with thatched roof. We stayed overnight at a bed and breakfast with a lovely retired couple, the van der Wals. Mr. van der Wal spoke English and Jake could also understand Dutch fairly well. He gave us a tour to the dyke and a windmill, explaining that people live in windmills and take care of them. He showed us where the water washed over the dyke in 1814 and made huge holes in the land, which became lakes. In 1953 the dykes overflowed again and 5000 people drowned. He also recounted how Hitler overran Holland and took all the men age 18 and older to Germany to work 12 hours a day, 6 days a week with meager food rations. Horrifying memories of the war were still etched in their minds. Seeing this land of extreme hardship, I was glad that Grammy's ancestors had moved to the United States.

Mr. van der Wal was a retired shipbuilder and an artist. He also played the organ in their home. As we visited, I asked if they knew of any Ackermans, since my great-grandfather was John Ackerman. They got out the phone book and showed us page after page of Ackermans! I felt right at home.

From there we went to Amsterdam where we took a one-hour boat ride on the canals. As we passed the post office, our guide said it was built on three artificial islands with 9000 wooden spires driven into the ground for the foundation. The oldest canals date back to the fourteenth century. An astounding 40 cars go into the canals every year! I can't recall if they fish them out, but surely they must or they would clog the canals.

On we went through the countryside from village to village. The drive through the beautiful, flat lush green farmlands was an experience in itself. The picturesque, serene landscape spoke of great love for and care of this beloved land. My heart rose up in praise to God for this place and for my Grammy Landis and her preacher father John Ackerman from the Church of the Brethren.

In Volendam Harbor, the 30-kilometer Barrier Dam—an awesome marvel of engineering—holds back the mighty North Sea from their precious land. This dyke is a monument to the indomitable spirit, persistence, and industry of the Dutch people who fought for centuries to hold back the sea. Two-fifths of their land lies below sea level, with the lowest point being 22 feet below sea level. The Causeway Dam highway joins North Holland and Friesland. Along the way we stopped at monuments telling of the tremendous courage and fortitude of the men who built this dyke under treacherous conditions. It was built between 1927 and 1933. In 1981, more than 8500 cars crossed the dyke daily, and 12,000 on Sundays.

We crossed over to Friesland, home of Jake's Friesen ancestors. It is also noted as the birthplace of Menno Simons at Witmarsum. There we found Menno Simons *Straite* (street) and a monument to him. Menno's followers in Holland were nicknamed *Mennists* or *"Mennonites."* Later the Swiss and German Anabaptists accepted his leadership as well. (Friesland and West Friesland are in Holland, but East Friesland was separated from Holland several times by war. It is now part of Germany.)

C. Henry Smith, in *Story of the Mennonites*, says, "Menno deserves a high rank among the great Reformers of the sixteenth century. Although he did not play as conspicuous a role as did his contemporaries—Luther, Zwingli, and Calvin—his real greatness cannot be measured by the more humble part he seemed to play in the religious arena of his time. His task...was much more difficult than that of the founders of the state churches...Menno rested his appeal upon the persuasive power of love and the simple truth of the gospel as sufficient to secure the permanency of the true church. He was centuries ahead of his day on many of the fundamentals of religious and civil liberty...religious toleration, separation of church and state, and the desirability of universal peace." (C. Henry Smith, *Story of the Mennonites.* [Newton, Kansas: Faith and Life Press, 1981], 71-72.)

From Witmarsum we drove through many towns on our way to Borculo where Janet had a friend, Ernie, a Dutch exchange student at Lynden the past school year. With enthusiasm, Ernie invited us in to see her "real Dutch house," as she said, a pleasant treat.

On the way to Denmark we went through East Friesland in Germany. In Denmark we enjoyed the sights in this land of Dag Hammerskold, United Nations Secretary General; famous author, Hans Christian Andersen; and Soren Kierkegaard, philosopher and Christian thinker, on whom I wrote a paper in seminary. Denmark is a land of small green farms and consists of a peninsula and 482 nearby islands! Twice we were surprised to see New Holland (Pennsylvania) farm machinery.

We got hotel rooms at Gredstedbro but ate supper in nearby Ribe, the oldest town in Denmark. Sunday morning we counted as a bell rang 77 times at 7:00, then ten single rings. "That's the 7 o'clock wakeup," Jake explained. That day we headed to Legoland at Billund, where we spent three wonderful hours seeing the awesome large displays made of Legos. Among my favorites was a realistic airport, complete with sound effects, NASA Space Center, and a lovely Dutch scene.

That night our hotel rooms overlooked the harbor in Sonderborg, with the date 1827 by the door. We learned that Europe's small towns and villages had many old quaint hotels and guesthouses with character, most of them with a restaurant. In our room was a picture of Soren Kierkegaard.

Monday we headed to Berlin, traveling through East Germany on one of three "corridors." What a different experience from the other countries. We had to fill out a paper for Janet, Jared, and me. We, along with our passports and car registration, were scrutinized thoroughly. Nearby stood an ugly tall double fence with three rows of barbed wire on top and a fence on both sides of the corridor, which spoke of the imprisonment of the East German people. We passed two large run-down churches with broken windows. This depressing militarized zone told us we were no longer free. Houses in the towns were a somber shade of brown and lacked colorful flowers and window boxes so abundant elsewhere in Europe.

When we came to Ludwigslust where we should have turned onto the main *Autobahn* (freeway) to Berlin, Jake kept going straight to see what would happen. We didn't have long to wait. Very soon a policeman stopped us, questioned Jake, examined our papers, fined Jake 30DM, and took a long time typing up a receipt on a typewriter in his car. (U.S./German exchange rate was $1.00 = 2.52DM. The exchange rate was broadcast on the radio each day.) Jake spoke English to the man who also knew English. Another policeman in the car used binoculars to look up and down the street. Jake was politely instructed to go back to the *Autobahn*.

When we got on the *Autobahn*, we were stopped immediately by another police car. Again one of them had binoculars. Jake showed our passports but they also wanted the car registration and took 20 to 30 minutes "to check that your papers are in order." Jake told us, "I think that other policeman phoned ahead for them to watch for us."

As we drove through the town of Wobblelin we were amazed to see a church with a sign on front that read, "Listen to God's Word." God had a witness here!

We continued to see police cars hidden on a hill beside a road or behind a sign or bushes. We felt paranoid. Janet especially hated the repressive atmosphere. We stopped beside the highway at a rest stop with no trees. An East German man was parked there who told Jake that the police stopped him because his brake light didn't work and he needed a wire but had none. Jake explained how he, too, had been stopped. The man rubbed his thumb and fingers together and said, "They want money from all the tourists."

I was glad Jake knew German and could converse with him. "Ask him if he's ever been out of the country," I coached. When the man said no, I pursued, "Ask him how he feels about that."

"When you've been in prison for 30 years, you don't know any better," was his sad reply. My heart went out to him. Communist repression became real to us that day. But the man seemed happy and was friendly. When a police car stopped at the entrance to the rest stop, we knew we'd better move on. We drove off as the man walked to the police car. From this brief encounter, I felt like we had a friend in East Germany. After four and one-half hours in East Germany we were relieved to arrive in Berlin where police with binoculars no longer patrolled the streets.

Berlin — with the Wall and museum at Checkpoint Charlie — was another experience that would take a book to describe. Before the Wall was built, three million people escaped from East Germany. On August 13, 1961 (just before we were married), 50,000 soldiers began constructing the wall during the night. The next day the people awoke to their terrible fate. Hundreds of pictures and stories lining the walls of the museum told the saga of tremendous suffering and of daring, ingenious escapes. We could only hope and pray that someday this evil repression would end and the Wall would come down. Little did we know that in less than a decade this miracle would come to pass.

We stayed overnight at Hotel Excellent on Kaiser Damm. Jake considered taking us into East Berlin but first asked an American soldier at the border about it. He warned, "They have very good museums but there are one or two places where you may not make a left turn and they are not marked. If you get stopped you are fined 1000DM ($400 U.S.). A man was caught recently and he didn't have enough money. They took all he had and put him in jail overnight." Who would risk that? We had seen and learned plenty and bought a book called *The Wall*, full of pictures and stories. This first-hand lesson on life behind the Iron Curtain made a deep impression on our children. We were exceedingly grateful for our freedom and sad for the millions still under Communism.

On Tuesday we headed back to Kandern. Janet could hardly wait to get through the East German corridor and back to "civilization." In eight days we had covered 3,700 kilometers through seven countries, including various parts of Germany.

Jake wanted to return a day early so we could shop and so he could show me how to take the *Autobahn* home from the airport. Instead, Helene informed Jake that he should call Riyadh, his home base in the capital of Saudi. They wanted him back the next day. It was hard to have him leave so soon, but I knew we could get along language-wise with Helene's fluency in German.

Because of an apartment mix-up, the Fasts and we had shared an apartment in Kandern since we arrived. Without enough bedrooms, the three boys had a pajama party every night, sleeping on many large sofa pillows on the floor in the living room.

Living with the Fasts provided good times of shopping, sightseeing, and walking around town to find stores and post office, or up on the beautiful hill above Kandern with a gorgeous view of the city and farmland below. We cooked and did chores in our shared living quarters and Helene and I talked about our lives with each other. She was born in present-day Poland, one hour south of Danzig, and had no birth certificate. (The first certificate said she died, and the second one was written in Polish. She had it translated a few years ago in Abu Dhabi, United Arab Emerites, where Hans later flew.) She and her mother, sister, and brother lived through the horror of World

War II in refugee camps. Between camps they walked many miles and hid often. They finally made it to freedom in the British zone of Germany.

Helene told me, "My father disappeared eight years prior to our time in Germany, while mother was still in the Ukraine. He managed to see her once before he disappeared. Just before we left Germany, we found out through the Red Cross that he was still alive. He was in prisoner-of-war camps and forced labor in a concentration camp in Russia and was almost executed three times. We were so glad that he escaped to Germany and was finally reunited with us in Canada." We empathized with each other in the hardships of our lives.

After hearing my story, Helene said, "You had a much harder life than I did. I had a very happy life growing up with my loving mother, and later father, in Canada. Mother and I did everything together." But I felt overwhelmed with all *she* had experienced – war, homelessness, hunger – with no word on her father. I could not imagine such an existence.

A wonderful part of BFA was the English BFA Christian Fellowship that met every Sunday at the school. The first Sunday the missionary speaker was from Washington state, near Victoria, B.C. That was a nice surprise and his sermon was excellent. The last hymn was "And Can It Be," the same one we sang our last Sunday at Lynden. I felt right at home. The owner of the well-stocked bookstore told me he brought his store from Beruit, Lebanon a year before. People were friendly, and soon I became part of a missionary wives Bible study.

Jake left for Saudi on August 18. He called on September 3 to wish me a happy anniversary and to give me a surprise. "Hans and I will be home Sunday (two days after our anniversary) because the plane will be in the shop in Basel for two weeks. So we'll celebrate then. We can stay in a hotel in Basel for a few days." I was ecstatic!

Jake decided we would get rooms for the children and us at the Basel Hilton. Then the Fasts decided to join us there. Curtis gave us a card that he spent most of the week making, which all four children had signed. The large colorful 4-page booklet had a "town crier" on the cover with tears coming out of his eyes, a bell in his hand, reading a script, "Attention! Attention! In the year of our Lord, 1982, the second (third, really) of September, be it known to alle! that Jane and Jake have been wed three score years." (Not really, they didn't know what a "score" was and thought it was seven.) The large "21" numbers covered one page with our faces, which he had drawn, showing through two holes. The last page had a large heart with drawings of Jake and me holding hands, and large words at the top, *"Die Frohliche, 'EINUNDZWANZIG' Ist Endlich Hier!"* Translated: "The Happy 21st Is Finally Here!" What fun! We marveled at such a unique and thoughtful card, which Helene obviously had a hand in creating. The children had a ball at the hotel, calling each other on the phone and planning harmless mischief.

The next day, Labor Day, we went to the airport for a test flight of the G II. The mechanic from England told me, "I've worked on G IIs for nine years. Once a year we take out the floorboards, panel by panel, the wing panels, and top of the plane and do a thorough check of each panel – not haphazard. Ten mechanics will work on this plane the first few days." I was so impressed and pleased to learn this and thanked him for taking good care of the plane. He brightened and responded with appreciation. I breathed a silent prayer to God, thanking Him for such wonderful mechanics.

Jared and I went along on the test flight but Janet declined, since at times she had a problem with motion sickness in small planes. But this was not a Cessna four-seater! As we sat sideways, on a sofa type seat, the plane took off like a shot from a gun. I had to hang on for dear life to keep my seat. Never had I experienced such a takeoff. Airliners seem to take forever lumbering down the runway. I suspected that Jake and Hans gunned the power that day to give us the thrill of our lives. However, Jake says the plane was lighter with only us on board, and a smaller jet always takes off faster than an airliner. Jake and I stayed two more nights at the Hilton since we were still living cramped in one apartment with the Fasts. During the day we came home to get our children to shop and sightsee. What we thought would be a lonely anniversary turned out to be very special.

While the men were home we moved into our house on September 9. I marveled again at God's perfect timing and was relieved that Jake could be there. It was great to have our own place again, even if there was an open stairway between the Fasts and us.

Our new home was in a little village called Oberegennen, about six miles from Kandern. Jake and Hans had looked at the house in June but it was not ready when we arrived. They decided that the Fasts would live upstairs because there was only an open doorway between two of the bedrooms, which became Curtis and Andre's. We got the downstairs with three bedrooms since we had a daughter. Our floor had a large living room and big kitchen; the Fasts, a small kitchen and small living room. Rentals were totally bare so Jake, Helene, and I shopped for necessities at used furniture stores. The kitchen had no cabinets. Wires hung from the ceiling, a strange custom in Germany. We bought light fixtures, kitchen cabinets, and appliances. Refrigerators were half the height of ours at home. We slept on mattresses on the floor, but the landlord had a single bed for Janet.

The children started school on Wednesday, September 15, a week after we moved. Much later I found out how difficult that was for Janet. The girls, having lived together in the dorm for years, were cliquish and left Janet alone at lunch. "They just disappeared outside," Janet said, "and I didn't know where they went." She cried in the restroom stall, missing her good friends at Lynden. But once the girls got to know her, Janet had many good friends. Jared did not complain as at Lynden. But he was quiet in class, probably a habit from the painful Lynden years. He and his best friends, Curtis and Andre, had good times together at home.

Helene helped me at the grocery store and often wrote me little notes if I went alone. Early on, Janet and I took an evening German class. Though I had a notebook full of notes and words, I never mastered the language. The Germans were very friendly and one always said, *"Guten Tag"* (Good day) to anyone on the street. My favorite words became *entschuldigen sie bitte* (please excuse me), a very useful phrase, and *ein und zwanzig* (twenty one) after our anniversary celebration. Each of them was a mouthful and gave the illusion that I had conquered the language! Janet's interest was French, which she had studied in junior high at Hesston and at BFA. (Later in college she took two more semesters.)

Jared took German at school and spoke so well that his teacher praised him for having no accent. Since we sent our computer on loan to Jim and Ruby Graber, Hans bought a computer for Curtis and Jared to use upstairs. The school did not have a computer but, upon learning of Jared's proficiency, they decided to get one and have Jared tutor students. This helped him learn to know the students more quickly. He also helped the principal set up a program for the canteen inventory.

Obereggenen (*Ober* means "upper") was a tiny village of 320, quaint and picturesque. (Our two families boosted the population to 328.) Barns were attached to houses, customary in many European countries. An old Lutheran state church had a small cemetery in back, beautiful with marble gravestones and colorful flowers decorating the graves. Graves are dug up every 20 years and bones placed in the church basement due to lack of space in the cemetery. Niedereggenen ("lower") village was a couple of miles away.

Our landlords, Mr. and Mrs. Braendle, lived in a new house next to ours. Very fussy about how we kept up the place, Mrs. Braendle explained to Helene that we must wash the small porch and steps every week and sweep the long driveway circling the house once a week. The gate by the road must be closed each night. Helene had pointed out to me the custom in town of housewives and shop owners washing their porch and steps every Saturday. They also hung their comforters out of the windows every day for airing.

Early on Helene had an unpleasant run-in with Mrs. Braendle. A plum tree loaded with fruit grew in our back yard. Helene understood that we could not go to the garden for anything but the plum tree. One day we were all outside when Helene told her boys, "Climb up in the tree and shake down the plums. We'll have a good feed." Curtis and Andre climbed up and shook to their hearts' content. Suddenly we heard loud yelling as Mrs. Braendle came running, scolding in German, and gesturing toward the tree. "This is *our* fruit!" Helene apologized profusely and felt terrible. She had totally misunderstood. Since I knew no German, Helene took full responsibility for all interactions with the Braendles.

Two days after school started, Helene was out sweeping the driveway when Mrs. B. came over to talk. Mr. B. had gone with Jake and Hans on a test flight of the plane and they were late returning. Mrs. B. was visibly agitated. They talked on the driveway for several hours. Mrs. B. said, "You have to be patient with us. We've been through the war..."

Helene responded, "We've been through the war, too. We lived in refugee camps here in Germany and did not have enough to eat. My brother and I searched through manure piles for potato and apple peels. My father was gone for eight years and we didn't know where he was." Mrs. B. listened with tears in her eyes. She saw that Helene really *did* understand.

When Helene told me this later, I saw how wonderful it was that the Lord led Helene to this house to share with Mrs. B. and they could empathize with each other over their sufferings from the war. This understanding softened Mrs. B. toward Helene and they became friends. I was praying for the Braendles and thanked the Lord for letting me be a small part of the drama that was unfolding in this tiny village. I continued to pray often for them. They had a son and a daughter still at home and owned a sawmill just down the street. Since Mrs. B.'s brother was killed in the war, she inherited her parents' mill. Large trout filled the fishponds at the sawmill. Once during that year, they invited each of our families separately to the mill for a fish dinner. We watched as Mr. B. scooped up a fish with a net, prepared it, wrapped it in foil with vegetables, and broiled it on a grill. We ate the delectable dinner at an outdoor table. This was a rare treat and I was glad Jake could converse with them in German.

One Saturday we took the children on another memorable excursion, this time south to Hirzel, Switzerland. Armed with the postcard of the "oldest known Landis homestead," I was happy to fulfill Aunt Melba's wish. It was a lovely drive on a gorgeous day.

When we arrived, we found a wedding party gracing the church lawn for picture taking in an idyllic setting. Jake went to the large house next door, also on the postcard. He spoke to a woman knitting on the porch, "Is this the oldest Landis homestead?" and showed her the picture.

She pointed up the hill and said, "Up there." The picture showed the wrong house! We walked on the path up the hill, exactly as on the postcard from 1913. Then we noticed that our time was the same as on the steeple clock on the postcard—2:40 P.M. How amazing was that! Time seemed to stand still and I felt a connection to the time when someone snapped that photo years ago. Sixty-nine years later, Jake snapped a picture of Janet and me there on the same path.

Janet and me, Hirzel, Switzerland, as on post card from 1913, same time on clock!

Up on the hill, the double house obviously had two different owners. One side was painted and well kept with flowers in pots and window boxes. The other half with peeling paint had no flowers. No one was home, so we walked around the back to a lush pasture overlooking a green valley below. Grazing cows wore huge cowbells that made a lovely sound as they moved. The scene seemed even more beautiful than my homeland in Pennsylvania.

We waited around and a teenage boy finally appeared. Upon seeing the post card, he said, "Many people come from America every year to see the homestead. We have a book in the house to write everyone's names in." He lived on the well-kept side, but he could not find the book. Then a woman and girl came. The woman said the girl was hers and the boy was a cousin of the girl. We were amazed to learn that the boy's father was Alvin Landis. My grandfather was Allen Landis. The woman's husband was Eric Landis. (She lived on the shabby side.) I showed her the postcard and she seemed amazed to see yet another one like so many they'd seen before.

"This is not the oldest homestead," she corrected. "The date on the card is wrong. The house was not built in 1488. Perhaps Landises moved here that year, since that's when the town started. All the Landises have moved to America. There are no young people left except the boy and my daughter." We concluded that a large number of cards were printed for a Landis reunion in Pennsylvania years ago, prompting many to come and visit. Even so, I was thrilled to find Landises still here.

Mrs. Landis showed us an old coat of arms dated "1412 Landis." On the back was a typed paper with a list of Landises and where they came from—Zurich and Luz—and where they had moved. I showed her Pappy's picture and she said, "He looks just like my husband's grandfather who died in the 1960s. He was in his 80s." How interesting! We took pictures of the three who seemed like distant relatives.

Hirzel had just a few houses on the top and sides of a few hills, but it was the most beautiful, peaceful place I had seen in a long time. Serenity and peace hung in the air like the scent of flowers on a spring day. Down at the church, the wedding party was gone, but we heard organ music floating out of the windows. A man with one eye told us to come in. In the simple, plain sanctuary, probably Swiss Reformed, we saw the pipe organ with very tall pipes. Again I felt a profound spirit of peace. At the cemetery with beautiful flowers and gravestones, we found only one Landis—Jakob.

After a little more than an hour in Hirzel, we joined with the Fasts and continued on to Zurich. There we enjoyed our picnic at a park near the Limmat River. Jake told everyone, "This is the river where hundreds of Anabaptists were drowned, including Felix Manz, the first martyr." In Zurich we visited Grossmunster Cathedral. Ulrich Zwingli became head pastor there in 1519. Founder of the Reformed Church, he was much more radical than Luther. He removed statues and paintings of the saints, opposed Swiss military participation in the armies of the Pope, and was strong on studying the Bible. However, other Catholic priests felt that Zwingli, like Luther, did not go far enough. These priests became leaders of a new movement, labeled *Anabaptism*. They believed the state should not dictate how people worship God, and that only adults can make a voluntary commitment to follow Christ in all of life. Therefore, they re-baptized each other. In an age of intolerance, this resulted in bitter persecution and martyrdom for thousands of humble believers. We walked inside the church briefly before it was locked for the day, but the dark events of history detracted from a sense of worship I might otherwise have felt.

Though these pleasant fatherlands were beautiful and peaceful, we knew how severely our forebears in past centuries had been persecuted. The *Martyrs Mirror* documents over 4000 stories of martyrs from the first century to the 16th, the bulk of whom are Anabaptists. Smith's *Story of the Mennonites* states that Hans Landis, an influential minister, was the last Mennonite martyr in Zurich, according to *Martyrs Mirror*. He was beheaded in 1614 for preaching and ministering, contrary to a decree of the Zurich Council, in effect for 84 years (Smith, p. 77). Dad Friesen gave us this enormous volume for Easter in 1979.

On the streets of Zurich we saw many youths with heads shaved, except for a strip of bright red hair down the middle, a red "Mohawk." We also saw purple and green spiked hair and strange clothes and behavior. Times had changed drastically from the era of persecution 500 years ago. All in all, for us it had been an educational, inspiring day.

Jake returned to Saudi the next day on a completely restored Gulfstream II. He came back unexpectedly on his birthday, September 29 and stayed until October 1. We had already celebrated it with the Fasts before he left, not knowing he'd be back so soon. I marveled at how often he got home and knew we had made the right decision to move there.

Now I looked forward to a visit from Sara Van Meter, my long-time friend from Vincennes. She and Sally had visited us in Lynden. After I drove Sara around our area on the country roads at Lynden, she exclaimed, "We saw many nice homes but yours is the most beautiful of all!" When we moved to Germany, we learned to our amazement that Larry was being transferred from the Philippines to the Frankfurt Social Security office. We lived a four-hour drive south of them. Sara wrote her great rejoicing in a letter and said she could come on the train for a visit. I took her on a drive through Black Forest country, which she loved. After that, when Sara wrote, she called herself "city mouse" and me, "country mouse," and the names stuck.

Jake returned from Saudi a few days later and we drove to Frankfurt for a special weekend with the children and Van Meters – Sara, Larry, and Sally. Laura and Chris were in college in the States. God was providing many "fringe benefits" with this job.

At times I wondered if I would find any Herstines in Europe. While Jake was home, we visited nearby towns, and found a Hertstein meat store. That was close. *Stein* means "stone" and *herr* means "lord, master, sir." It could mean that they lived by a stone or that they were makers of gravestones.

In November, the country celebrated Martin Luther Day, when Lutheran church members do penance at the cemetery. On November 30, Janet, a high school senior, received her letter of acceptance to Hesston College for the next year. We originally talked about staying two years, but as the months went by I leaned more and more toward returning to Hesston, since Janet would be going to college.

On a trip to France that winter, we came upon a surprise, the village of Friesenheim, which Jake translated as "Friesen home." Jake's knowledge of German helped greatly. This area, called the Palatinate, had changed hands between France and Germany many times due to wars.

For Christmas we headed to Frankfurt where Laura and Chris were home from college. On Christmas Eve we attended a meaningful, packed-out, candlelight service at the military chapel on the base near Van Meters' home. The delightful days with our friends passed all too quickly, but we must get home for another exciting trip.

Early in December Janet had come home from school with a request. "I want to go to the Missions '83 Conference on Evangelism in Lausanne, Switzerland. Can we go?" Jake was in Saudi but would be home during that time and agreed we could go for three days, including driving. I was grateful for the children's exposure to missions at BFA. Missionaries from various countries lived in the area and fellowshipped at BFA church. Some of the men went to Romania or other Iron Curtain countries, out of contact with their wives for months. Our women's Bible study regularly prayed for them in their dangerous work.

Driving to Lausanne, five hours away, we saw much snow in the mountains. When we arrived at the Exhibition Center, cars, busses, and people swarmed everywhere. With a crowd of 7000 attendees, we listened to challenging messages during the next two days and Janet got the tapes. We met many missionaries from various countries including David Winter from England who was on the planning board for Missions '83. He told us, "I'm an insurance salesman with Canada Life Insurance. It's a very good company and their salesmen become millionaires. I sell insurance one day a week and do mission work the other four. You can work five days a week and become a millionaire or work one and do missions!"

When he learned Jake was a pilot in Saudi he got excited. "There is a Christian magazine called *Magalla* (which means magazine) in Arabic sold on newsstands in Saudi," he explained. "It's very low key, all pictures and printed by Arabs. As an evangelism tool, it is truly a work of grace, a miracle in the Arab world."

We understood because Jake had told us how strict and closed Saudi was toward Christians. Even meetings in their compounds were strictly forbidden and a Christmas carol sing was cut short when it was discovered. Saudi women were completely veiled, with arms and legs covered. Consequently, Helene and I did not travel to Saudi.

Mr. Winter told Jake, "Go to the Magalla booth at the Exhibition Center and you can pick up a copy of the magazine." We went later and found Mr. Winter there, who introduced us to the man at the booth. He explained to Jake about their work and gave samples of the magazine and brochures. This surprising ministry to Muslims gave evidence that even in the most closed countries many young people were turning to Jesus. Our pastor James on our last Sunday at Glendale had prayed for Jake very specifically, "…for his witness, spoken or even unspoken in Saudi," and that God's Spirit would come upon us and use us with power. It was amazing to see thousands of people here filled with the Spirit, ministering in many nations.

One speaker who impressed me greatly was Virgilio Zapata, founder of Youth for Christ in Guatemala. After 100 years of Protestantism, since John Hill, Presbyterian missionary, took the Gospel there, Zapata said there are now 6000 churches in Guatemala. "Almost 50,000 accepted Christ in the last three years," he said. "God has given Christians three things: Life, Truth, and Love. No other group in the world has all this, which God has given us. When you're full of God, you are full of love. Jesus Christ is a powerful conforming power!"

Each day we met Christians of many nationalities: Chinese, English, French, Dutch – a foretaste of heaven. The last morning we met a Dutch girl who said there were 500 there from Holland. Christianity was alive and well in the far-flung corners of the earth. This was a rare opportunity for our children to experience a rich mosaic of believers committed to spreading the good news of Jesus.

Lausanne was a beautiful city but we could not tarry. We absorbed much in this three-day trip and first part of the conference. We took a different route home, through the beautiful Alps with quaint Alpine villages. We saw many funny little "barns" on stilts with round flat rocks between the stilt and the building. Jake thought they may be to keep mice out of the grain. Driving between the famous Matterhorn and Jungfrau peaks reminded me of teaching about them in my fourth grade class. How exciting to see them! Only 36 kilometers from the Matterhorn, we were in no shape to climb.

The road led through many tunnels. At one of them we drove onto a train car that carried us through. Our route also led through lovely Lucerne. It was like a tour through a storybook. Since reading *Heidi*, I loved Switzerland. Breathtaking beauty meets the eye at every turn. My one regret was lack of time to stop and explore the places we passed. Having left our hotel at 9:15 that morning, we drove through many miles of snow. With fog slowing us way down the last few hours it was a relief to be safely home by 7:30 P.M., back to the lovely *Schwarzwald* (Black Forest).

On New Year's Eve we invited the Fasts down for New Year's cookies, plump with raisins. After we watched fireworks outside, our landlords invited us all to their house from 12:00 until 2:00 A.M.! We played games, ate, and they all talked German. The boys shot off more fireworks outside. Eventually, the fast German chatter frustrated me almost to tears. A few times Hans or someone else took pity on me and interpreted. Then Helene noticed me and quipped, "Think of it as a song. My mother has to put up with this when our family gets together because we all talk English and she can't understand it. Though she probably understands more than you do German."

Not being a night owl, I knew I'd feel better after a good night's sleep. As I crawled into bed at last – in a brand new year – I asked God to forgive me for my grumpy attitude and counted my blessings. We had seen and done much in this land of Martin Luther, Mennonites, and the Reformation. Soon three of us must decide – will we stay another year or head back to Kansas? And, I wondered, before I drifted off to sleep, *Will Jake stay on in Saudi?*

CHAPTER 34

To Stay or To Leave

Praise the Lord, who carries our burdens day after day.
He is the God who saves us.
PSALM 68:19 (GNB)

1983

In the New Year we explored more interesting places near and far: castles, castle ruins, Roman ruins, shops with unique German wares or specialty baked goods. The Fasts raved about Ludwig's castles and other tourist sites they saw and urged us to see. Our children's horizons widened as they gained international experience through travel and study with students and teachers from various countries and backgrounds.

Black Forest Academy (BFA) had a Canadian curriculum, since the Janz Team brothers, founders of the school, were from western Canada. They came as missionaries, in the 1950s, and needed a school for their children. The school accepted ten percent of its enrollment from business, non-missionary families. Class work was challenging for Janet and Jared and both worked fairly hard for their grades, a great preparation for college in the States. They loved BFA and living in Germany.

From time to time a shepherd came to our village with his flock of sheep. We also saw shepherds go from village to village or one pasture to another. Our local shepherd had a donkey that carried his pack. At night, he put up a fence around the flock while he slept.

One day Jake and I drove to a large town to order a down comforter. As we left the store in Weil am Rhine, a great flock of sheep ambled by on the street. Where else but in Germany–a flock of sheep in a busy town! Another time, as we sat in our parked car by that store, the car rocked gently as a big flock of sheep walked by and brushed against it. It reminded me of David, the shepherd boy.

Jared and the Fast boys were good friends; they questioned him about whether we were staying another year. He spent hours with them upstairs at the computer and other fun games, and their laughter wafted down the open stairway. When Jake was home, we talked with the children about what to do but put off the inevitable decision.

In January 1983, Jake and I visited Bienenberg Bible School in Switzerland, a Mennonite school Jake had visited in 1957. We ate at the school restaurant and looked up Liesel Widmer, a relative of the Frei family in my home church. We found her in her secretary's office. What a fascinating person! She told us how she went to Goshen College in Indiana for a year as a Mennonite Central Committee trainee and worked for professor Harold Bender (our Mennonite history teacher). She worked in the historical archives on the *Mennonite Encyclopedia*, of which Harold was editor.

"When the year was over, Harold encouraged me to stay and become a student at the college," Liesel told us. "I said I would if I didn't have to take exams, since I wasn't fluent in English. He told me I wouldn't have to. I returned to Basel to get a student visa. When I went back to Goshen, Harold told me the faculty made clear to him that I *would* have to take exams. What a shock! So I had to get up at 5:00 every morning to study English." We were glad for her good English.

Liesel told us the history of Bienenberg. "The Mennonites bought the property when Mennonite World Conference met in Karlsruhe in 1957. The French, German, and Dutch Mennonites needed a Bible school to train students for the ministry."

"I remember that," Jake said. "I came for the conference and stayed here overnight. At that time it was a very big old barn where I slept."

"That's right. Later they built this building, about 1970, ten years ago. The restaurant, dorm rooms, and guest rooms above are all brand new." It was a lovely building with a wonderful restaurant.

Before we parted, we made plans to visit the French Mennonite church at Colmar together in the future. Later, the children accompanied us to Bienenberg. Janet loved the place and thought she would like to go to school there because they used French.

In February, Helene and I began tutoring high school students in English. For this we were called "missionaries," an interesting development. I had felt a call to mission work in my youth at camp, but never envisioned it in Germany. Janet sang in the girls' choir and Helene and I sewed 16 navy wrap-around skirts for them. After initial trials and frustration due to wrong pattern pieces, we sewed for weeks and each received a bouquet of flowers at the opening concert.

As the weeks came and went, the question of what to do at the end of the school year nagged at my mind. Janet was going back to Hesston College but said we could stay on. I leaned toward returning. The Fasts wanted us to stay and Curtis and Andre assumed we would. They wanted Jared around another year. I hated to disappoint them so mostly kept quiet. What should we do?

One day I asked for prayer in our women's Bible study for making the right decision. Another troubling concern haunted me. I had found a lump in my neck near the Adam's apple and also asked for prayer about that. One of the women was Mrs. Oldenberg, a sweet, devout wife of a missionary who spent long months behind the iron curtain in Romania. A feisty, outspoken person with a great sense of humor and strong Danish accent, she shared stories about great suffering and loneliness in her life. She sometimes called to see how I was doing with my husband gone so long, and asked me questions.

A few weeks after I shared my concern with the lump, Mrs. Oldenberg called and asked, "How is the lump in your neck?" I had actually forgotten about it, but now felt for it. To my amazement, it was gone. When I told her, Mrs. Oldenberg said, "I have been praying earnestly for the Lord to heal you. I told Him that you are in a foreign country and don't know the language and that is so hard. I told Him you don't need this to worry you. I am so glad He answered our prayers!" Overwhelmed, I thanked this dear sister for her caring and prayers and was struck again at God's personal care for me.

By March, Jared and I were in agreement about moving back. So one day we told the Fasts that we would probably go back to Hesston with Janet. Fasts said they would stay another year or more and applied pressure for Jared and me to stay on. Curtis and Andre badgered us with questions, especially Jared when he was upstairs with them. They could not understand why we would leave them there "alone."

"We'll be together at the high school next year," Curtis reminded Jared. At times I felt a tug-of-war inside, wanting to please the Fasts and feeling guilty for wanting to leave. The crux of the matter for me, which I didn't voice, was more separation of our family. Jake's long absences were hard enough, and I knew I would miss Janet greatly if she left too. While I loved being in Germany, I loved my family more.

In March we got the sad news that Pappy Landis had died at age 91. He had been pleased with my letter about our trip to Hirzel and the Landis homestead. Millie wrote me that at Pappy's funeral, his minister said of him,

"Allen loved music and reading and was a very mild-mannered man." That was how I remembered him, too, and as a blessing in my life.

Easter fell in early April. Since Jake got off work four days early and the children had a break, we joyously headed to Paris for four days through lovely countryside of lush farmland. In Paris we visited the Eiffel Tower and the Louvre museum, where we saw the Mona Lisa and Napoleon's loot. We took in a wax museum and the famous Notre Dame Cathedral, begun in 1163, where Napoleon was crowned ruler of France in 1804. The impressive Versailles Palace was closed but we enjoyed the magnificent park with formal gardens and fountains. Despite rainy weather, Paris was exciting. We sampled French pastry and rich coffee, foamy with milk. But we could not tarry since we were expecting special guests. We traveled home a different route through beautiful French mountains.

My father's Cousin Ethel had surprised me with a letter in January saying that she and daughters Carolyn and Charlotte were planning a trip to Germany. She had always wanted to see the land of her father's ancestors. Our being here provided the impetus for them. We had corresponded for years, and I was inspired by her strong faith. She was Daddy's only close relative. Charlotte and Carolyn were my second cousins who lived in western Pennsylvania, and whose dresses I had worn and loved as a girl. When I was five and Grace was a baby, we traveled the 300 miles to visit them only once, and Grace and I broke out with chicken pox while there. I had met Charlotte once at Anna and John's in Chicago but had not seen Carolyn since we were young.

The cousins arrived with hugs and laughter and we caught up on past years as we drove them around our beautiful area, up on nearby snow-topped Hochblauen Mountain, and through Black Forest villages. As we went toward Freiburg, Charlotte turned around to her mother and said, "If Grandfather Wehring was really born in Strasbourg, I think we should go there." Cousin Ethel was so pleased as she had not suggested this, thinking the girls were not interested.

"Yes," she responded, "my grandfather Wehring was born there and came to America at age 11. I would love to go! My brother Woody told me, 'You *have* to go to Strasbourg!'" Cousin Ethel's mother died when she was about one year old so she grew up with her Wehring grandparents. After a stop in Freiburg, Germany we headed to France. Cousin Ethel glowed with happiness as we toured Strasbourg.

Later, she and I enjoyed a late night, memorable, heart-to-heart visit. She said that after her three children were born, her husband drank all the time and they had no money. So she took the children and went home to her grandparents. "Grandmother Wehring was a very devout Christian. She influenced my life greatly," Cousin Ethel shared. "I later went back to Loyal (her husband) and lived with him 28 years in all." But again he drank too much and they separated. Their fourth child, David, was born with cystic fibrosis, incurable, and died when he was nine years old. He loved Jesus very much, and it comforted Ethel to know David was with Jesus.

"When we lived in Pittsburgh," she said, "I went to Kathryn Kuhlman's Bible study every Monday evening and to her miracle services every week. After moving to Washington (Pa.) I took the bus five times to hear her." Cousin Ethel's faith was strong and she remained faithful through many trials. I had heard Kathryn Kuhlman speak in Oklahoma, so we shared this in common. My time with Daddy's special cousin was a treasure. Since they had flown into Zurich, Switzerland and rented a car to sightsee on their own, we said our good-byes on Wednesday morning.

(A year later, our family visited overnight in Cousin Ethel's home in Pennsylvania. We continued writing until just before her death of a heart attack on December 31, 1984, her third within two weeks. Her family wrote, "She was cheerful, talkative, and smiling up to the final moment. She graduated into the presence of the Lord whom she deeply loved and was faithful to." I thank God for Cousin Ethel's life, for her love and interest in our whole family of Herstines.)

The day after the cousins left, we took advantage of the rest of the break for a trip south to Italy and the Mediterranean. We started off through Switzerland and tiny Liechtenstein, and through a 14-kilometer tunnel in Austria. Rain and low clouds prevailed all day. We stayed overnight at an ancient guesthouse, built in 1666, in Unken, Austria with walls one and one-half feet thick. The next day we headed to Eagle's Nest (near the border with Austria), Hitler's hideout during the war, but it was closed until May. At one point in Austria, Jared complained he was thirsty. We came upon a fast-moving mountain stream or river, with white-water rapids, near the road, so Jake pulled over and stopped. Jared, in bare feet, went down to the water's edge, lined with large rocks, scooped the cold, clear water into his hands and drank. No McDonald's or Burger King needed!

The Austrian Alps were magnificent. As we neared Yugoslavia, we drove up a very high steep mountain where the road became a natural roller coaster, then up more steep curving roads to the Austrian/Yugoslavian border. Jake told us, "I want to take you through a corner of Yugoslavia so you can experience a nicer Communist country than East Germany."

At the border, an official looked at our passports and asked if Jake had a visa. He did not. They simply issued him one at no charge and no problems. The beauty of the mountain scenery was offset somewhat by the poverty of the inhabitants.

We arrived at the Italian border at 5:15 P.M. on our second day. We drove around Trieste and got a hotel by 6:30 at Sistiana, overlooking the Adriatic Sea, where palm trees waved in the breeze along this arm of the Mediterranean. This was our first look at this famous, exotic sea—the ancient "great sea" of Bible times. Our hotel balconies facing the sea added a fun and exciting touch to our stay.

The next day in Venice, on a sunny but very hazy day, we maneuvered—walking—through swarms of tourists in the city center. We loved seeing this unique city of canals built on about 120 islands in the Adriatic Sea. Most of the houses along the canals are hundreds of years old. We took a "taxi" boat through the canals to an island where we watched artisans at a glass-blowing factory who fashioned creations out of the hot, liquid glass. A church and large cemetery filled another island we passed. We visited the famed, huge Cathedral of St. Mark (Roman Catholic) in Saint Mark's Square and walked on the famous footbridge that Jake said has been filmed in many movies. In four hours we got a good feel for this fascinating ancient city.

Leaving Venice on a warm, sunny afternoon we saw magnolias, japonicas, and orchards of pink-and-white-blossomed fruit trees along our route. Past Bologna, we got rooms at Chalet Delle Rose outside of Casalecchio. The beautiful evening complemented our ritzy accommodations, where we felt slightly out of place, but enjoyed nevertheless.

One of the most exciting stops on our trip—the leaning tower of Pisa—awaited us on Saturday. I had always loved the story of this marvel from grade-school geography. We climbed to the top, despite stories that the tower could fall any time. Adding to our sense of insecurity, walls or railings were nonexistent along the edge of each floor until we reached the top two. We learned that attempts to fortify the tower defied all modern engineering skill and know-how. The tower's colossal size and weight have deterred the most creative and bizarre plans, yet engineers still plot to save the treasure. An ancient Roman aqueduct, constructed with very high arches, and another Roman wall reminded us we were in the land of the great Roman Empire of Jesus' time. The bell tower (leaning tower), cathedral, and baptistery comprise one of the most famous groups of buildings in the world, and the tower is often called one of the "seven wonders of the world." We enjoyed pizza from a street vendor there before going on our way.

Heading toward France we drove through many tunnels drilled through the coastal mountains. I counted about 100 before Savona, then an incredible 180 more, some very short, by the time we reached the Italian/French border—which was in the middle of a tunnel! "Fingers" of mountains—perpendicular to the sea—reach into the edge of the sea for miles, challenging engineers who built this road. Between the tunnels were bridges over the water—tunnel, bridge, tunnel, bridge—making for a most unusual trip.

We arrived at Monaco at 5:40 in the afternoon. Wisteria and other lovely flowers bloomed in front of the world-famous casino. Though many wealthy people live there, Jake told us that citizens of the country may not gamble there—a wise ruling. Finding absolutely no parking space, we drove through the twisting, mountainous streets of the city. I told the children the sad story of Princess Grace Kelly (the Philadelphia actress who married Prince Ranier in 1953) who was killed on one of those streets as she drove with her daughter. Those treacherous, scary roads are host to the famed Grand Prix of Monte Carlo—an unbelievable 200-mile race! Our ten-minute stay in this decadent country of less than one square mile was time enough.

We had the good fortune to find a motel one-half block from the beautiful Mediterranean beach in Menton, France, next to Monte Carlo. Here we drank deeply of the fresh salt sea air. On Sunday morning after breakfast, we enjoyed a walk along the beach and took pictures. We all relished each day of this fabulous trip.

Much too soon—on Day 5 of our tour—we started back home through stunning French mountains. Another long old tunnel and snow beside us and in the valley below added to the beauty. Then we entered another mountainous arm of Italy. By 5:30 we reached the three and one-half mile tunnel at Great Saint Bernard Pass, which crosses the Alps on the border with Switzerland. Here we bought a postcard telling about the St. Bernard dog developed by Swiss monks to help find travelers lost in the snow, a moving story. We enjoyed the snowcapped mountains on this sunny warm day. I was in my sleeveless blouse and needed no heat in the car. As we entered southwestern Switzerland, spectacular scenery greeted us, with curving roads winding round and round on terraced hillsides, amazing us Kansas flatlanders.

One of my must-see places in Switzerland was L'Abri, since I had read and loved the book by Francis and Edith Schaeffer before coming to Europe. Meaning "shelter," L'Abri was begun in 1955 when the Schaeffers opened their home as a spiritual and intellectual "shelter," a place where people could be helped both to know and live biblical truth. Young people flocked there from all over the world to find or renew their faith. We found it southwest of Lausanne but did not have time to stop except for me to snap a few pictures.

The next weekend Jared accompanied us on a trip to castles at Stuttgart and nearby Ludwigsburg. Janet stayed home to do homework, including an anthology for English. We started out through the winding mountainous road east of us, deep into the Black Forest. Spectacular scenery and quaint mountain homes of craftsmen delighted us. Toys, cuckoo clocks, radios, and musical instruments were among crafts for sale. Old customs and traditions persist in this place of ancient German legends and fairy tales. Mineral springs have made the forest famous for its many health resorts.

After a couple of hours, we emerged from the peaceful rural scene onto the race-track-like Autobahn. I never got used to the speed and congestion of this freeway. We arrived at Ludwigsburg Castle, massive and impressive with its 18 buildings and 450 rooms. Tired after seeing 65 rooms—half of one floor—we enjoyed the beautiful gardens and children's fairy tale land with incredible flowers, trees, and birds. At Favorite Park we saw three kinds of deer and soaked up the peace and beauty of the park on a perfect, sunny day.

Sunday afternoon we took Curtis and Andre Fast along to the cave in Switzerland where Anabaptists hid from their persecutors at Wappenswil. Many Mennonites from the States and Canada, including college students on choir tours, visit this sobering site, remembering the price our forbears paid for their faith.

The next Saturday, Curtis and Andre went with us to visit a World War I battlefield at Hartmannsweilerkopf in France. There we found a large mountain full of tunnels and bunkers built by the French and Germans for fierce battles. The French wooden bunkers were crumbling, but the Germans' sturdy ones, built with concrete, were in good shape. Superior builders, as the Romans before them, they built even their bunkers to last. The boys had fun exploring these somber remains. On days like this the decision to return to the States was never far from my mind as I saw how much Curtis and Andre would miss Jared.

That Sunday, a more inspiring trip took us to France. Liesel Widmer, from Bienenberg, came to our home and went with us to the Mennonite Church in Colmar. As she directed us, she remarked that Colmar was in Alsace Lorraine, which went back and forth between Germany and France in many wars. At the church, we learned that they alternate every Sunday between the German and French languages. That day was French and I feared I would not understand until a young married woman, Valerie Wenger from the States, volunteered to translate for me. She was great and I took extensive notes.

A visiting Mennonite evangelist spoke first. Then a missionary, Miriam, told how the Lord called her to serve in an orphanage in Ivory Coast. Rev. Samuel Gerber, retiring long-time director of Bienenberg, reported on the school. Nine elderly workers, ages 67 to 70, were retiring at the same time, putting the school in dire need of replacements. Seventy-three students would graduate the end of May; ten had already left to go to work. Rev. Gerber expressed deep appreciation for the support of the French churches and stressed the need for prayer.

Rev. Gerber then preached the sermon on I Thessalonians 4 on the Second Coming of Christ. I thanked God for Valerie's translation. She told me later that her husband gets Christian films from the States and translates them into French to distribute all over France for an agency he started called, "Announce the Gospel to Men." Knowing how secular French society was, it blessed me to learn how zealously evangelistic these French Mennonites were.

After the service we had a wonderful dinner and fellowship at the home of Pastor Nussbaumer, Liesel's cousin, and pastor of the Colmar church. We had met Alan Maughlin at church, a young Voluntary Service worker from Newton, Kansas, who lived with Nussbaumers. He was happy to meet people from "home" as we had lived seven miles from him at Hesston. Alan said of the sermon, "Samuel Gerber spoke such good French, the best I've heard since I've been here."

Liesel added, "That's because he's Swiss. The Swiss are such perfectionists. They must speak the language just so!"

Over dinner, the subject of World War II came up and Pastor Nussbaumer told their story. "Fifty people were in our barn when U. S. planes bombed and destroyed our house. We were all praying and God spared us in the barn."

Liesel also had a war story. "When I was eight years old, I was with my family in the basement of our house when it was bombed. That day, 300 bombs fell on our village!" She grew up in the Palatinate, a part of Germany at the time, east of Strasbourg, France. She continued. "I'd rather die than live through another war. You hear about what the Germans and Russians did. You should hear what the Americans did!" I felt shame at our country's violence and could not imagine the terror of living through a war. Hearing these stories answered questions I had had about the war and I empathized with our new friends.

I asked Liesel about the name *Herstine*. "Herstine is Mennonite from the Palatinate," she said. "It is usually spelled *Hierstine* but it's the same name. There are many Herstines in the Palatinate where I grew up. They came to Germany from Switzerland during the persecution of the Anabaptists centuries ago." Finally I learned the origin of Daddy's name, which a Russian Mennonite in Kansas had told me was "not a Mennonite name." They just didn't know *Swiss* Mennos!

For our last trip in April, Jake and I drove nine hours north to Hamburg, Germany to visit a former seminary friend, Peter Foth, pastor of Hamburg Mennonite Church. Peter knew we were coming and was waiting for us on the street corner by his house. A spirited man, fluent in English, Peter was as happy to see us as we were to see him. We met Peter's wife Elke for the first time and enjoyed getting reacquainted with Peter. That afternoon we rested from four to six, in typical German fashion. Jake slept and I got up after an hour and went out into the hall. Peter saw me and called, "I'll show you what I'm working on – a slide set for catechism classes." I was delighted.

Especially excited about the verse in I Peter 3:21 on baptism, he explained, "One translation says, 'It (baptism) is that we may *have* a good conscience.' Another says, 'We *must ask God* for a good conscience.' I think that is the better translation – more correct." The New RSV in verse 20 talks about Noah and his family being saved through water, then in verse 21, "And baptism, which this prefigured – *as an appeal to God for a good conscience*, through the resurrection of Jesus Christ." His explanation amazed me.

That afternoon before I got up from my rest, I prayed that Peter would share with us what was important for us to know and that we would share what would be helpful to them. The past week I had struggled over my flaws, a recurring problem with my overly sensitive conscience. Why did I keep punishing myself, believing I was inferior and others were perfect?

Measuring myself by Christ's example and teachings I fell far short. A few minutes after I prayed, Peter explained the verse about the conscience and baptism. What a speedy answer to my prayer! I could *ask God* for a good conscience.

The Foths had three children, Dagmar, grade eight, who loved horses and riding. Birgit, grade ten, age 15, liked to read and play piano, and Kilean, grade five, preferred reading in his room. Peter's wife Elke was teaching German to a Turkish girl in Kilian's grade. Elke told me that Peter's father had been missing since Peter was two years old and then was said to be dead. The family never knew anything for sure. "My parents came from West Prussia and were not Mennonite," she said. "But my mother had a good friend, a Friesen, who was a Mennonite."

About the war, Peter reminded us, "Germany surrendered on May 8, 1945. The atomic bombs were meant for Germany, but were then used on Japan in August." This was news to us. Peter and Elke both felt that the Americans were not nearly as cruel as the Germans and Russians. "The Americans just wanted to get the war over with, so they bombed and bombed. It's like anything else," he observed, "the minister is not without one sin, the doctor is not completely healthy, and the political man thinks he needs just one more country to be safe. So he takes all he can. It's just how it is in our world."

Dutch Mennonites fled east to Germany during persecutions of the latter half of the sixteenth century and established churches there. Smith's *Story of the Mennonites* describes Peter's church and house as an elaborate, large church building with parish hall and parsonage built in 1914. The congregation of 400 moved here from nearby Altona. During the war, the old church in Altona was completely destroyed and the new church (Peter's) suffered damage. In July 1943, about 50 percent of the homes in Hamburg-Altona were destroyed in a few hours and Mennonites suffered in proportion. Peter became pastor there in 1968, having graduated from seminary with Jake and me in 1963.

The following day Peter took us next door to his chuch. Pictures of all former pastors, including Menno Simons, hung in a row on a wall, signifying that Menno had been in Hamburg. (Menno lived from 1496 to 1561.) Peter noted, "I think this is the original painting done by a local artist." I took a picture of it and of the high pulpit with semi-winding staircase. We were amazed that these pictures survived the war. We saw the cemetery with ancient stones and were impressed again with the tremendous sense of history and connection to our forefathers of faith. It was a joy to visit with Peter after 19 years and learn of his faith burning brightly. (Years later we were sad to learn that Peter died suddenly in April 2004.)

As the children and I talked about what to do after graduation, it became clear that Jared longed to go back to school with his Hesston classmates. In three years he had not forgotten them. Our desire to see Europe was largely satisfied by our travels. However, the Fasts were hoping we would change our minds. I asked God to help us work this out to avoid hurt feelings.

One day when Jared was upstairs the boys bombarded him with questions. He told them we were moving back. "We thought you were staying here two years. Then why are you going back?"

Jared answered, "We've already been gone from Hesston *three* years and we were going to go back after one year. Now it's already been three, and you've only been gone from home for *one* year." For Jared, returning to Hesston would be a dream-come-true and he "told it like it was."

"We thought you lived in Lynden a long time," Curtis said. Jared explained about the Hesston move from his point of view."

"I *hated* moving to Lynden and wanted to move back ever since we left Hesston!" Finally, it made sense to them. Though we would return, Jake planned to stay on in Saudi and commute; he and Hans would continue to fly together.

One day Jared looked at a little booklet from Hesston College and said, "I can hardly wait to go to Hesston College! It looks like so much fun!" He was glowing with one of his happy smiles that light up his whole face. For years he had said, "I'm not going to college. When I get out of school, that's enough." He had really disliked school. I could hardly believe the transformation from this year at BFA. Even *college* at Hesston now looked great!

The day Jake was to leave for Saudi, he and I drove to the town of Badenweiler, a famous health resort with mineral springs. We enjoyed lunch at a place with old country charm and delicious food, and then walked on the main street through a beautiful park to Roman ruins and a new convention center. By then it was 2:30, rest time, when the town closed down to cars. A man told Jake, "If you continue out of town, you'll be fined 30DM." Jake parked the car and we waited for 45 minutes. An entertaining book we bought in Germany, *These Strange German Ways*, explained it all.

That evening Jake left for his two-month stint in Saudi. He hoped to return in June for Janet's graduation and our move. This was hard for me, as many decisions must be made in his time away. The Psalms, and verses like Psalm 68:19, "Blessed be the Lord, who daily bears us up," sustained me.

Helene and I found a variety of things to do while the men were away. For Mother's Day, we went to Niedereggenen to the state church with the boys. When we arrived, the Obereggenen men's chorus was serenading the women on the street in beautiful harmony. The church was 1000 years old with foot-thick walls. Though I couldn't understand much, the service was lovely, with three young people playing guitars for singing, "He's Got the Whole World In His Hands." As the joyful young pastor preached, I often heard the words "Jesus Christ." Later Helene filled me in on the sermon. After church, the men were still singing outside. To Helene's great surprise, one of them walked to our car and recited a love poem to her. We returned to the church in the afternoon to hear an excellent chamber music concert.

On May's sunny days I relished walks on Obereggenen's hills, through the beautiful cherry orchards in glorious full bloom. Janet and I had a special walk one day in the grape vineyards on the hill behind our house. In nearby Holzen, storks sat on their nests atop steeples, attracting visitors armed with cameras, including me. Holzen also had a fine stork farm. Jeannie Glenn, daughter of seminary friends Jim and Irlene, arrived for a couple of days. I drove her to see the sights and baked her a cake for her 20th birthday. Jeannie was delighted with Hochblauen Mountain, with many hang gliders, storks in Holzen and Storkenblick, Black Forest drives, and walks through the cherry orchards. Sara Van Meter brought her parents down for two days and they loved the Black Forest tour. Never had I enjoyed so much the role of chauffeur and tour guide as I did these months in Germany.

One evening I took Jared out to let him drive, which Jake had done in April on the quiet country roads. He did very well. He turned 16 on May 23 and looked forward to driving with a permit in Kansas.

While Jake disliked being gone from home, he had interesting experiences in Saudi. Sometimes he flew Saudi princes, Bell Canada executives, and Dr. Kayal, Minister of Post, Telegraph and Telephone (MOPTT), who was on King Fahd bin Abdul Aziz's cabinet. One day the passengers invited the pilots to join them for lunch. They met in a tent where a whole goat had been cooked in a very large pot of rice. The men all sat around on the ground pulling off pieces and eating the goat and rice with their hands—Jake's initiation into Saudi culture. The country was booming with U.S. expertise in oil drilling and refining. Saudi claimed that no country in the world had changed so dramatically in so few years—from 1973 to 1981. Thousands of

Americans, Canadians, and other nationalities flooded into the country, working in every sector of society to modernize and build.

Large modern stores in Riyad, the capital, sold everything we had in the States. Jake brought us products we couldn't get in Germany, such as peanut butter and Noxema. Calculators, watches, tape players, and radios sold for a song. Jake bought inexpensive cassette tapes of all kinds of music: German folk and popular songs, classical by every imaginable composer, vocalists from many countries. He bought a radio/cassette player for our kitchen, where music brightened my days. The Fasts bought a TV but it was all in German. We learned that German TV never reports crimes like the U.S. media, a refreshing change.

Toward the end of our stay, I felt drawn to a certain faculty member and we met together and shared our lives, discovering that we had both had difficult stepmothers. One morning she confided, "You know, when the Fast-Friesen applications came in a year ago, they caused quite a stir among the staff. Everyone said we'd be flying free all over the world and they all wanted to be your friends. When I hear things like that, I withdraw," she said. "I don't want to be involved."

That helped explain the uncomfortable feeling I had had around some of the people our first months there. The staff people soon learned that neither they nor we were flying anywhere. My friend said, "That wasn't fair to you – how people judged you before you ever arrived. It's like James says, if a man comes into your assembly with a gold ring, don't show favoritism to him. It's not fair to you. We didn't really get to know you as you are." So that was the barrier I had felt. Now I knew why I was drawn to her. She had a heart of gold and I loved her for being honest with me.

I gave her my stepmother story, "God's Healing Love." She later told me, "After I finished reading your story, I had a good cry, then I made myself a cup of tea." I could hardly believe that she never told her husband about her hard life with her stepmother. She was older than I, part of the "silent generation." We felt each other's pain, and my heart was warmed with her empathy and caring.

Jake and Hans returned unexpectedly on June 9 for about a week, while the plane was in the shop. We all drove to Natzweiler, France to visit a concentration camp. This one was not for Jews but for Germany's intellectuals who opposed Hitler's ideology and war. After having read *East Wind*, which detailed life in such a camp, I could imagine the emaciated prisoners doing work described in the guidebook Jake read to us. We saw the cages where people were kept, gas chamber, the incinerator for the bodies, the experimental room, the museum with gruesome pictures of people like skeletons jammed together in a cage, and a room with urns of ashes to send to relatives for money. There was also a big empty hole in the ground where ashes had been dumped. After the war, the German people gave the ashes a proper burial. This camp was fairly small, with only a few buildings compared with Auschwitz (in Poland) and Dachau (ten miles from Munich in Germany). Yet too many people died here. (Auschwitz had four huge gas chambers where two and one-half million people – mostly Jews – were executed; 500,000 died of starvation.) Though French people living on farms nearby saw the smoke rising at times and smelled a foul odor, they never investigated. The horrors of war and man's inhumanity to man were made real to us that day.

The school year was winding down. Janet's graduation was set for June 24. To my relief and Janet's joy, Jake arrived home that morning. The inspiring service took place in a church in Kandern, with reception at the school. Janet wrote us a thank-you card expressing her heartfelt gratitude for all we had done for her that brought her to this day. We felt blessed to have such a wonderful daughter and for her experience at BFA.

It had been a great year in these pleasant fatherlands. Now we packed for our flight to the States in three days. We had farewell meals with friends and a "party" upstairs with the Fasts the night before we left. Helene, always the gracious hostess and wonderful cook, insisted on having us for breakfast before our four-hour drive to Frankfurt the next morning. She made individual pans of eggs for each of us. Her loving servant heart had blessed us all the past year.

Parting with the Fasts was sad, and Andre, the youngest of the children, cried when Janet and I hugged him goodbye. Then he ran beside the van taking us to Frankfurt, loath to see us leave. I was glad he had a friend there for the day, son of the couple who drove us to Frankfurt.

A long flight was before us – and then what? Jake had four weeks off. We would arrive in Vancouver, spend a few days in Lynden, and then make the 2500-mile trip back to Hesston. What awaited us there? How long would Jake continue in Saudi? Would he find work in Kansas? Many uncertainties and questions remained – but I anticipated the new chapter of our lives and another adventure.

CHAPTER 35

Ahh, Kansas! – Reprise

*The Lord, your God is in your midst…he will rejoice over you
with gladness, he will renew you in his love;
he will exult over you with loud singing.*
ZEPHANIAH 3:17 (RSV)

1983

Our eleven months in the beautiful Federal Republic of Germany came to a close on June 28, 1983. From Frankfurt, we flew the short hop to Amsterdam, left there at 2:30 P.M. that Tuesday with a stop at Edmonton, Alberta. After flying ten hours we arrived in Vancouver at 4:20 P.M., *still on Tuesday!*

We were met at the airport by Pearl and Linferd Goertz and Janet's friend Sue Miller and her parents. What a joyful reunion! Janet stayed with Sue, and Jake, Jared, and I at Goertz's lovely farm home where Pearl's beautiful paintings graced every room. Dad and Jessie invited us for supper and seemed as healthy as ever. We visited with Nick and Margaret and talked with other family members on the phone. At Glendale Church on Sunday, at the potluck following the service, many people assured us of their prayers as we returned to Hesston, especially that we would find a house quickly.

We started off on our three-day drive that Sunday afternoon. As we pulled onto the highway, Jared exclaimed, *"I'm so happy! I'm so happy we're going back to Hesston!"* He was finally realizing his heart's desire. He had grown in patience, wisdom, and in understanding that sometimes a circuitous route to one's dreams brings wonderful serendipities. I was grateful for answered prayer for Jared and all of us.

We slept that night near the Oregon border; the next night we arrived at Green River, Wyoming at midnight. We enjoyed our country's varied and beautiful scenery. I also relished Brother Andrew's *God's Smuggler*, about sneaking Bibles into communist countries.

On the third day we arrived at the Hesston Motel just after midnight, with Jared driving the last leg into town. He was one elated young man! Finally, he was *home*!

Jake wasted no time finding a house. At breakfast in a restaurant the next morning, we met realtor Murray Bandy who had sold our house on Amos and Weaver and our 11 acres. As at other times, I told the Lord that He knew which was the right house for us and asked Him to please lead us to it. At 11:00 we looked at a ranch style house at 103 College Drive, on a cul-de-sac. One look at it from the outside and Janet announced, "That house is *choice*!" Jared and I agreed. Next to a small children's park and the ballpark, it had been built by Vince Kraybill, former faculty member at the college. I had met at this house for our college wives' Bible study when Vince and Estelle lived there. Since then, they retired in Phoenix. After looking at every house for sale in town that morning, we all agreed on the "choice" one. In half a day we had our house!

That afternoon we met with Mary and Ervie Glick, the owners, to draw up a contract. At 3:30 we met again and signed the contract, 15 hours after we arrived. God was faithful and led us to the perfect house for us. It had a lovely back yard and garden, nice landscaping, and the college, Janet's new home, was a few blocks down the street. Built as a retirement home, our new house had a small living-dining room-kitchen, but adequate for us. Two bedrooms and bath up, a fully finished basement with bedroom, bath, office, storage room, and a large family room, made a nice compact homey place. After the huge house at Lynden, this one seemed just right. We earnestly thanked the Lord.

The house was only 13 years old, with 1187 square feet up and 1187 down. The price of $57,600 sounded wonderful after the Lynden $90,000! We knew it was well built and considered it a bargain. We paid $28,000 to the Glicks and owed $28,000 to Kraybills, since Glicks were paying them.

The next day Buetta Bontrager from our former small group called me and said, "You are God's angel, answering the Glick's prayers." It was mutual. Ervie Glick had taught at the college. He and Mary asked if we'd take their cat, P. J., since "cats are territorial creatures" and they were moving to Indiana. So Jared acquired a pretty gray and white cat. The Glicks had spent four years in Germany before their children were born and said they would love to go back. We understood.

The one drawback with the sale was that Glicks were not moving until July 18 — two weeks away, and Jake must leave for Saudi July 20. That was hard on Jake, but we made the best of it. We stayed at a small motel in town and almost every day of those two weeks we were invited for dinner with many friends. At Whitestone Church the first Sunday and our former church Inter-Mennonite the next, we were greeted with hugs and, "Welcome home!" It was good to be back.

Janet planned to live in the dorm and told us, "Since I'm going to be at the college, I'm going to go to the college church" (on campus). We were happy about that and decided we would go there, too. With friends at all three churches, we felt at home at all of them. (The other two had 250-300 members; the college church, Hesston Mennonite, 600.)

Over Sunday dinner with the Grabers, who raised sheep and farmed our land, we heard about their many setbacks the previous year. "It's been a very hard year," Jim said. "Fifty or so lambs were stolen, taking all our profit. The embargo on Poland stopped all wool and sheepskins from going in. This reduced prices drastically in one day." We hadn't realized the international nature of their business. I learned from Ruby that she was working in the fields until 11 or 12 at night, leaving two-year-old Troy with others. Fortunately, Jim's parents lived next door and his mother often provided childcare. My heart went out to them.

Later Jake told Jared, "You're 16 now and most kids your age have a job. You can work for Jim on the farm this summer." Jake helped Jim too as time permitted, one day working the land with Jared from 1–7 P.M. in blistering heat. Jared also drove a tractor the six miles to our land on the other side of town to pick up alfalfa bales, with Jim's dad sitting on the fender.

Janet helped by caring for Troy and working for Ruby. Janet and I shopped in Wichita for fabric and sewed clothes for Janet for school. Since my sewing machine was still in Washington, we sewed at Buetta's house.

Adjusting to the heat after Germany and Washington was rough. Jake had lived at times with 120 degrees in Saudi, in smaller segments – at the airport, shopping, and at their compound pool. But here, working out in the heat all day, Jake and Jared came home beat, covered with dust, and I wondered how the Grabers did it.

On July 12, Jared passed his written driver's exam and took the driving test. At the conclusion, the woman officer asked brusquely, "Didn't you notice the 20 mph speed limit sign? You drove too fast through there, you know!"

Surprised, Jared answered truthfully, "No, I didn't see it!"

"You'll need to be more observant," she advised. "It cost you your license, young man. Remember to watch for speed limit signs in the future. This is very important."

Disappointed, but determined to mend his ways, Jared returned the next day, passed easily, and got his license at age 16.

Jake, impatient to get into our house, helped Ervie Glick load their truck on July 18. Our moving van arrived on schedule the next morning. Jake helped unload, then took care of a multitude of details. The thermometer reached 100 degrees and we were glad for our first central air conditioning. Again we marveled at God's perfect timing. We made it into our house the day before Jake left. It was a fine house—the fourth one we owned and twentieth abode in 22 years of marriage. I was grateful that Jake was there for moving day but sorry he had to leave. I wondered, *How long will it take for him to find full-time work in Kansas?*

Making the transition easier for the children and me was our planned trip to Pennsylvania at the end of July for our "Bethlehem '83" church conference and to visit my family. Anna and John hosted a surprise 25th anniversary celebration for Millie and Ralph with all the family. Many of the children had blossomed into teenagers and Janet and Jared enjoyed getting reacquainted with their cousins.

We visited Aunt Melba and Uncle Ivan, who still lived at their parents' house. Melba gave me several of Pappy's old hymnbooks. A small thick one, without musical notation, contained hymns in English in the first half and German in the back. It is titled, *"Brethrens" Eng. And Ger. Hymn Book*, copyright 1867. Pappy often sang German solos and in quartets from this book. I told Melba and Ivan about our trip to Hirzel and the Landis homestead and showed pictures. I was glad we had represented the family for them.

The conference in Bethlehem was inspiring and I met old friends from college, seminary, and my home church. At this historic conference, both (Old) Mennonite Church and General Conference Mennonites met together for the first time, including Canadian Mennonites. Janet greatly enjoyed the youth convention. In a seminar led by noted historian and author John Ruth, I learned humorous stories about the "split" that occurred in 1847, and the un-charitable behavior of some "brethren." John Oberholtzer, leader of the new group, had copies of his constitution printed in Allentown. As they were being delivered to his home in Milford Square one night (a few houses down the street from Ralph and Janice), the stagecoach was hijacked and the 1000 constitutions stolen! Fortunately, Oberholtzer had a few copies still in his home.

Sister Ruth was remarried to Dave Ruch and they hosted a Herstine-Ruch reunion on the lawn at their mobile home. The whole family enjoyed this special time with Dave's brothers and families, Kenny, Marty and Scotty. Three of the four who were orphaned grew up at the Milton Hershey School. The children enjoyed the camaraderie of their cousins and I felt blessed that they could experience the love of our extended family.

Less than a month after Jake left, he called with good news, "I'm coming home for a week while the plane is in the shop!" His plane was due at 9:25 Sunday evening. I baked an orange cake, Jared iced it, and Janet wrote on it, "Welcome Home, Dad!" We all went to Wichita to get him. A big smile wreathed his face as we hugged our welcomes. Over the cake, we shared tidbits from our time apart. The week went by quickly with bike rides for Jake and me, drives, "shopping for nothing," and time with our children and friends. We took Jared to the Colonial House for breakfast one morning, a rare treat, had the Grabers for dinner for Troy's second birthday, and Jake took Jared to Ringling Brothers Circus at the Kansas Coliseum with free tickets from a friend.

As Jake prepared to return to Saudi, I fought the depression that often overtook me a day or two before he left. I told Jake, "I'm ready for you to stay home."

"But I need to find a job here first," he reminded. I bit my tongue. It was hard for him to give up the good salary in Saudi. But in three weeks he'd be home again.

The day Jared started to school as a junior, Dick Rempel called and asked me to work at my former job at Faith and Life Press. I agreed. On Saturday, September 3, our anniversary, Janet moved to the dorm. The house felt empty, but she was only three blocks away. It would have been a lonely day except for Jared's good cheer. We took a bike ride and looked at our slides of past years. Sunday morning we attended convocation at the college, and in the evening Janet invited us to a movie there, "Man From Snowy River." It felt good to be part of the college scene. Those first weeks, Janet came home for one reason or another almost every day. I was glad we had moved back with her instead of staying in Germany.

Later Dick Rempel called to ask if Jared and I would work on tallying a survey for our conference. We agreed. For weeks we went to Bethel College seven miles away to enter data into the computer. When the computer was down or the door to the room was locked, my frustration mounted. Sometimes we drove 25 miles to McPherson College to use their computer. We entered data, proofread, counted, repeating the process again and again. With 640 surveys to key in, the job looked endless. Sometimes when Jared was in school, I invited a few friends over to help with the tedious process of counting and proofreading. The computer's limitations hit us squarely between the eyes as it was down again and again. I spent precious time tracking down people at the college and at home for help. Jared worked faithfully and we even recruited his friend Phil Simpson at times. When Jake returned September 25, he helped enter the last 15 surveys at Bethel College. After that, we still had to proofread and make corrections.

One day Jared spouted off, "I'm not doing any more of those!" I couldn't blame him, but what would I do? At last, when I could find no one else, I talked him into helping and he agreed.

The next week at Bethel, the new computer was down with software problems. My frustration with computers had reached the limit. How would we ever finish? I found Professor Howard Snider, our advocate and encourager. He said, "Leave it with me and I'll find others to finish the job." Relief at last! He invited Jared and me to the coffee shop for a visit and remarked, "You two have had tremendous dedication to your job." He went on and on with his compliments until I felt overwhelmed. I was glad Jared had stuck it out and could hear this well-deserved praise.

Then he said, "Your husband is Jake."

"Yes."

He continued, "I know him from somewhere but I can't remember where."

"Well, he was at Bethel '59-'60, then at seminary three years, then MCC at Akron, and then in Mississippi two years."

"That's where I know him from—Mississippi! Esko Loewen and I took a group of Bethel students down at Easter break at the height of the unrest. As soon as we crossed the bridge into Mississippi I felt like I was in a foreign country." His face darkened as he said, "Medgar Evers was shot while we were there. Jake arranged a tour for us and for speakers at your community center. We slept at the center on bedrolls." How interesting to meet him again under different circumstances. I was glad Jared heard about Jake's work in Mississippi from another's perspective.

Howard told us, "I think you put in 100 to 150 hours on this job, and we really appreciate it." It took us less than a month, from September 9 to October 3, and we did get paid, though I'm not sure how much. Jared remembers that he got paid "a little." My introduction to the world of computer technology brought gratifying results and Dick Rempel was pleased.

In addition to his 11th grade classes, Jared took an aviation class at the college. When Jake got home for four weeks, he began giving Jared flying lessons. His first lesson in the plane was on October 7. Jake discovered it took some prodding to keep Jared motivated. But under pressure to return to Saudi for eight weeks, and anticipating bad weather the next time he got off in December, he pushed Jared to fly an hour a day. I struggled with anxiety about having not one, but two pilots in the family. Feeling not a little fearful and upset, I told Jake it was "a battle of the wills." But I resigned myself to it as I did to Jake's flying years ago.

Still, with ground school and Jared's other classes, it seemed like too much for him. A couple of times Jake got upset at me for talking and "influencing Jared" and they "wasted important flying time." Then the weather was bad a week straight. When they began again, only a week remained before Jake left for Saudi. On Wednesday of that week Jake told me, "I'm going to solo Jared before I leave on Sunday." Panic rose in me. Jared had only flown for nine hours!

"Aren't you pushing too hard?" I asked.

Jake finally sat me down and explained the procedure in detail. He drew a curve on paper and explained, "When students begin flying, their enthusiasm is good. Then they have a slump and want to quit just before soloing. After they solo they are enthused again and know they can do it. In a controlled program like college, they don't let them quit, but taking lessons on their own, some do. So it's very important to keep at it and solo." That sounded good for college students, but for my son? Yet I knew I must keep quiet now and pray.

After Friday's lesson Jake told me, "Jared did much better today. I think he's out of his slump. I congratulated him for doing well, even though he bumped hard on landing."

Saturday the weather changed – cool, cloudy, rain, and northeast winds forecast. The guys went to the airport and later came home for lunch. Jake was visibly disappointed. "We couldn't fly because the crosswinds were too bad for Jared to land," he told me.

In private I questioned Jake again about soloing. He pressed his point, "We never tell a student ahead of time that he's going to solo. When a guy is ready, the instructor simply gets out of the plane and tells the student to go around and land three times." Silently I cried out to God for help.

Though the 1:00 P.M. forecast said the weather would "probably not improve the rest of the day," they left again for the airport. I couldn't believe Jake's persistence in this. Still, he had experience with many students for more than eight years. Why didn't I trust him?

That afternoon, as I worked on laundry and a turkey dinner, the Lord spoke to me about my attitude. As I listened, God began to change my heart. I empathized with Jake. This was his last chance for two months to have Jared solo. I began praying, "Lord, please make the crosswinds stop, at least long enough for them to fly. And help Jared as he solos. Please keep him safe." Over and over I prayed those words. Finally, I just resigned the whole thing to the Lord and said, "It really doesn't matter, Lord. Your will be done!" With that I felt at peace.

About 3:30, as I took the wash off the line it began to drizzle. By the time I got inside, rain came down hard. The long delay, plus the rain, got to me as the clock ticked away. What was taking them so long?

At 4:00 I decided to call the airport, not expecting Jake to be there. But he was! "What's taking so long?" I inquired. "Have you flown?"

"The crosswinds were so bad," he answered, "that we went to the Corp hangar and hung out with Wayne Manske (mechanic). After a while I looked out and the weather had changed. So we went up and flew. Then I told Jared, 'I'll get out now and you go around three more times.' And he did it!" What a relief!

As Jake told me later, Jared kind of hemmed and hawed and said, "By *myself?*"

"Yes, you're ready. And it's much easier by yourself because the plane is lighter and flies better." He added to me, "There was rain all around the airport but none at the airport!" Amazing! A miracle! My heart leaped up in gratitude to God. He answered my prayer.

After nine hours of flying, Jared soloed—and survived! (I learned that nine hours to solo is normal.) I was thrilled it was over, and Jake was happy and relieved and could go to Saudi pleased with himself and Jared. I called Rose, our former next-door neighbor, who was in her 90s, and Jared's friend, Phil, to come for dinner to celebrate. I made a sign for the door, "Congratulations, Jared!" and we enjoyed a turkey dinner. I was grateful that Janet was home for the day and could join us.

The next week Jared flew with college instructor Dan Miller and passed his stage check ride. However, somewhat to Jake's consternation, after that Jared never flew again and did not get his license. "I'm too busy on the computer," he insisted. It had become his first love and he often had friends over in the basement family room to play games or explore the novelties of the technology. (Then 18 years later, he joined a flying club where he worked at Stan Roth's business in Wichita, took flying lessons and ground school over again, and got his private license. Jake taught him when we visited in Wichita, and Jared called Jake on the phone for help and advice. This time it was *his* choice.) During high school, Jared worked for Stan at Newton, polishing planes to earn some income.

Janet kept busy with her inductive Bible study on the book of Luke. She came home often when Jake was home and liked to pick his brain with questions such as, "Why did Jesus ask the disciples, 'Who do you say that I am?'" She was also trying to master the word processor and was frustrated almost to tears as Jared helped her.

Janet did very well in school and got all A's on her first report card except for a B in piano. "That's because I didn't practice an hour a day," she admitted. "I want to get an A in piano next report period." On her Bible paper, professor John Lederach wrote, "excellent answer," and her college writing prof told her, "I made no comments on your paper and that is quite unusual." She thought college was a "snap." Black Forest Academy had prepared her well. By the end of the year, she reached her goal of straight A's.

The next week I went with Jared to the college to register him for German for the second semester. His aviation teacher, Bob Harder, came to us and asked, "Did Jared tell you he got 98% on his FAA (Federal Aviation Administration) exam?" Jared had told me that in class Bob said, "Jared Friesen got the highest grade in the class, 98%." Bob continued to us, "I'm impressed!" Frankly, I was, too. I could hardly believe what happened to him the past year, after his seeming goof-off days in middle school. BFA had been good for him, too, and he was growing up. He also got an A in German at the college. I was proud of our two, hard-working, excellent students.

Jared came home one day in October and asked, "What would you like me to make in woodshop?"

"I've always wanted a round oak table. Do you think your teacher would let you make one?" He asked and got permission. He and I shopped for lumber at the Hesston Lumber Yard. I had a small catalog of tables to make from kits and he drew a design like one in a picture. His hard work produced a lovely large table with two extra boards and a fancy new type of metal extension track. The students and teacher, Mr. Petrocci, laughed as he worked on the lathe with the huge four-sided piece of wood for the fat pedestal.

December arrived and we were happy that Jake got home for Christmas. Dad and Jessie came on the 28th for a ten-day visit. We enjoyed touring them around and enjoyed family times with the children. On December 31, I whipped up a batch of Russian New Years' cookies and Dad and Jessie fried them in deep fat. Dad could not be without the plump raisin cakes. A new year was upon us, 1984, and Dad and Jessie's presence brought warmth and love to our time together. It was good to be back in Kansas.

However, a question often tugged at my mind, *How long will Jake stay on in Saudi?* I hated having him go back for two more months. *Oh, God, please let Jake find work in Kansas soon!*

CHAPTER 36

Together Again

*A man's steps are ordered by the Lord, how then can a man
understand his way?*
PROVERBS 20:24 (RSV)

1984–1985

Time marched on and Jake came and went, glad for extra time at home
whenever the plane went into the shop in Basel. I worked for the press and
kept up with the children's activities and friends. Life seemed almost back
to normal – except for Jake's long absences. I attended a prayer group with a
few women one morning a week before work. I also recorded a three-minute
"Moment of Inspiration" for Whitestone Church, which people dialed up by
phone. Jared helped with the recording at the church until I got the knack
of it. I attended Creative Writers Fellowship meetings and Jared did not
complain. Life was good, but Jake's absence left a big hole and I wanted him
home.

Janet stuck to her goal in piano, memorized a six-page piece, and did a
great job on it at the recital in May. She took riding lessons at a nearby stable;
for each $12.00 lesson she spent three hours working at the stable. By the
end of June she was giving riding lessons to students. Mrs. Burkhart, owner
of the stables, told her, "You have very gentle and good hands for the horses
and they respond well to you."

Jake received periodic bonuses and called one day to tell me, "The boss
says I'll get another big bonus if I stay on and sign a new contract." After two
and one-half years, I was very tired of this long-distance relationship and
told him frankly, "I don't care about bonuses anymore. I need you at home!"
Later I marveled at my own assertiveness.

He probably anticipated my response and readily agreed. "OK, I'll tell
them I'm quitting." On May 10, he telexed his letter of resignation to Ashbon
in London to quit on July 10. Hans Fast also planned to quit and move the

family back to Canada. Employment for Jake in Kansas did not worry me. Stan Roth sold refurbished business jets and told me in church one Sunday, "Tell Jake that when he comes back to stay, I'll have work for him."

In June 1984, on Jake's last month off before quitting, we left on a major road trip. My sisters and brothers planned a reunion and I wanted to be there. For years, Jake rarely went with me to Pennsylvania. It was time for all of us to go. I told him, "Our children have never been to New York City and Washington, D. C. While they are still with us, I want us all to go together. We can combine it with the visit to my family." He agreed, but Janet's reaction surprised me.

"I don't want to go to New York City!" she moaned. "We saw a movie at college about all the crime and muggings there. It's not safe!" She was terrified at the thought. "I'll stay home and water the plants." But I would not hear of it.

"We're going to a family reunion and you'll get to see all your cousins. And in New York we'll stay at the YMCA; we will trust God to take care of us." Reluctantly, she agreed.

On that trip we enjoyed supper and an overnight stay with Cousin Ethel at Washington in western Pennsylvania. The next day we toured the battlegrounds at Valley Forge and learned some Revolutionary War history. We arrived at Anna and John's in Newtown for an overnight stay and a family picnic the next day. All the Herstines came as well as Aunt Melba Landis and Cousin Bobby Moser. The 13 young cousins had a great time getting reacquainted: Brenda (Loux); Janet and Jared (Friesen); John, Jim, Amy, and Joel (Smith); Jeff, Wendy, and Janie (Herstine); April and Karlene (Ruch); and Michael (Herstine). On Sunday, Janet visited a BFA friend, Viola, at Hatfield. She had friends scattered far and wide in the world now and loved to visit them.

The first day in New York City we got a double room at the Vanderbilt YMCA. We toured the United Nations building, Rockefeller Plaza and observation deck on the 103rd floor, and Radio City Music Hall. We went to Times Square and the top of the Empire State Building (107th floor). Janet felt quite safe at the YMCA near the impressive U.N. building. The next day we took a bus to Lower Manhattan, then the Staten Island Ferry to the Statue of Liberty and Battery Park. Later we walked to Wall Street and saw the Stock Exchange from the gallery. We walked to the famous World Trade Center twin towers and ascended to the observation deck. What an awesome, breathtaking view from this great open roof! Jared took many pictures, including a unique one looking straight down, which captured the tips of his shoes and the street below.

We could not have imagined then the horrific end of these massive structures less than 20 years later. We brought home brochures with the bold heading: "The closest some of us will ever get to heaven." Ironic words. The shocking events of September 11, 2001 took many to their eternal destiny in an instant—or a slow, agonizing certainty that their end was near.)

In the evening Janet felt safe enough that she elected to stay in her room at the Y while Jake, Jared, and I went to Central Park, the New York Public Library, and we drove through Greenwich Village. Our last morning, we took a bus to the Museum of the City of New York, arriving too early. Since Central Park was across the street, Jared and I walked over to look around. An attractive Spanish-looking woman with a baby and a big smile asked, "Are you looking for something?" We asked about Central Park. She said, "The gate to the right goes to a conservatory of flowers given by the Vanderbilts." We were impressed with this outgoing woman, thanked her, and enjoyed a quick look at the conservatory.

After touring the museum, we took a bus back to Rockefeller Plaza. Jared and I decided to walk across the street to St. Patrick's Cathedral, when suddenly a friendly voice spoke, "Aren't you the same people I saw at Central Park?" We had just gotten off the same bus.

I turned and looked at her in surprise. "Yes," I smiled.

"Where are you from?" she asked. When I told her, she said, "New York must seem very different from Kansas!"

"It *is*," I responded, "but we lived in Europe for a year and got to London and Paris and many other cities."

"Oh," she exclaimed brightly, "I'm going to Spain this summer, to Barcelona. I won't take the baby along though. I'm an opera singer!"

That explained a lot about this very cultured, gracious lady. "You *are*?" I said. "What is your name?" She told us, but I could not remember it and often wished I had asked her to repeat it and written it down. I told her my name then, which sounded common after hearing her musical one. We wished each other a good trip and went on our way. That visit made my day! Jared and I were both blessed and amazed that we met her a second time. She was undoubtedly the friendliest person we met in New York City.

In contrast, however, a woman sitting behind me on a bus one day cautioned me about my gold necklace, "I think you better not wear that here in the city. It could disappear!" I thanked her for the warning. It was my name in Arabic that Jake had given me from Saudi, and I was amazed someone might steal it from off my neck! Janet's fears were not unfounded.

We concluded our time with a tour of NBC studios, drove in our car to Harlem past the Cathedral of St. John the Divine (where we had gone with Miss Guri on our seventh grade trip), past famous Riverside Church, through the Holland Tunnel, and onto the New Jersey Turnpike. Memories of these special days together would remain vivid for many years to come.

At Wilmington, Delaware we passed FlightSafety where Jake had his training for the Kaiser job. The date was June 20, and in Maryland we skirted around Elkton where my parents had eloped on June 25, 1932 – 52 years ago almost to the day.

Many poignant memories resurfaced for me on this East Coast tour and set me to reflecting. What was it like for my parents back then? Here they got their start in marriage, without family or a supportive church in attendance. I felt a mystical connection with them and that day many years ago, and praised God that I would one day meet them in heaven. Great tragedy struck five years after they were wed when my mother died after Baby Ralph was born, leaving Daddy with three preschoolers and a newborn. But God is a God of new beginnings. Here I was, 52 years later, remembering their wedding day and enjoying life with a wonderful family. Gratitude welled up within me for God's protection and constant care in my life and for my husband and children.

In Washington the next day we drove around the city, visited the Pentagon, Lincoln Memorial, Washington Monument, and Arlington Cemetery. At the White House, we gave up when we saw the long line waiting for tickets. In the midst of awesome monuments we realized that great poverty and crime also surround the splendor. Strolling on a sidewalk behind the White House, we passed a crazed woman screaming wild and obscene curses at no one in particular, a sad and troubling sight.

Driving on, we saw the Watergate Hotel, J.F.K. Center, and Library of Congress. On Friday we took a tourmobile to Arlington Cemetery where we saw Kennedy's gravesite and the Tomb of the Unknown Soldier, then on to the Lee Mansion. On the way back, we heard sirens and soon a motorcycle drove up. Our guide explained, "The President is coming!" We stopped and waited as the motorcade came by. I looked into the first limousine and saw no one. Then someone shouted, "There he is!" In the second car, I saw President Reagan turn and wave as they went by. Even with the dark glass and Reagan on the other side of the car, it was easy to tell it was he – my first and only sighting of a U.S. President in person. (We did not know then that in a few years Jake would fly former President Reagan on domestic and international speaking tours!)

At one point on our tour, we got separated onto two buses. Jake and Jared's double bus – with an accordion-like connection – collided with a VW Rabbit. The driver had tried to squeeze into the same lane and got smashed. More excitement! After getting another bus Jake somehow found us, a great relief. We visited the Air and Space Museum, the Capitol, and the FBI headquarters. We were awed by the giant dinosaurs at the Museum of Natural History and enjoyed the famous Smithsonian.

On Saturday, after a short visit to the Museum of American History, we left this amazing city. We passed the Iwo Jima Memorial and drove into Virginia via the beautiful George Washington Parkway. Crossing the Potomac into Maryland, we continued across West Virginia, Pennsylvania, and Ohio, to overnight in Columbus. Sunday we arrived at Findlay College, which had an equestrian program that Janet wanted to visit. Having decided to take equestrian science her last two years of college, she was checking out various schools. From there we drove the few miles to Bluffton where we visited the beautiful college campus, saw Clarence and Mary Ann Kooker, and the Buhlers from our Mississippi days. How exciting it was to show the children my alma mater and meet special people in this friendly town (population 3000) that I had called home for four years.

We arrived home happy from our 3,422-mile trip that took a mere 13 days. Two days later, Jake left for Saudi for the last time. We all rejoiced when he arrived home to stay on July 13, 1984! Having accumulated many frequent flyer mileage points from commuting back and forth, he asked me, "Where would you like to go for a vacation?"

I didn't have to think twice. "To Barbados!" (I had learned of it from my favorite TV teacher, Mary Goddard from British Columbia, who I watched at Lynden. She told about her ministry trips there and miracles through the power of the Holy Spirit.) I suggested, "Let's go in January, the coldest month in Kansas." Jake agreed.

In the meantime, we decided to buy 20 more acres of farmland for $24,500. Jim Graber agreed to farm it, along with the first 20.

Also that summer, Jake finally decided to become a U.S. citizen after living in the country for 25 years. On August 8, he and I drove to Kansas City for a naturalization meeting. Then on October 15, 1984, we went to the U.S. District Court in Wichita for an impressive ceremony with people from many countries, and Jake became a citizen. This made me very happy. But he refused to renounce his native land, as all new citizens are asked to do. He has dual citizenship, as do Janet and Jared, having been registered in Canada at their birth.

Jake returned to his former job teaching at FlightSafety International in Wichita part-time. Then on August 14, Stan Roth told Jake, "I'd like you to work for me half-time, flying demonstration flights with our customers. I'd also have work for you part-time in the office on the IBM computer. Jared could come along and learn the computer, too. What do you think?" Jake agreed and Jared tagged along to help at times.

Occasional trips for Hesston Corporation, Coleman, and Stan kept Jake in the cockpit. However, after flying the sophisticated, long-distance Gulfstream, he was not happy with this part-time work on Citations and Sabreliners. He talked of us going back to Saudi *together*. I was not enthused. My children were still home and I had no desire to move.

The old year was winding down and Dad and Jessie called before Christmas but decided to stay home. On the last day of the old year, Cousin Carolyn Smith called from Pennsylvania to say that Daddy's Cousin Ethel had died the night before. She had been a good friend to me through many letters, and I thanked God for her life and the good time we had together in Germany.

On January 11, 1985, on a cold, ten-degree day, Jake and I left for Oklahoma City to fly to Barbados. The night before we left, I was almost weepy about the long flight and leaving the children. I asked Jake a couple of times, "Is our will in order? And who will take care of the kids if something happens to us?" Jake thought it was funny, but to me it was serious. Jake's confidence shored up my sagging spirits and I had to commit the trip and the children to the Lord.

We had an absolutely fantastic time in a motel by the beach, with 70 to 80-plus degree weather the whole time. We walked along the beach to Bridgetown, rented an open roadster to drive around the 21-mile long island, and ate our meals outside on the terrace, where tiny birds joined us on our table, scavenging for sugar and bits of food. We took in a museum, a cave, a castle, and the Logos ship in the harbor, which traveled the world sharing the good news of Jesus. We tried to explore every nook and cranny of the island and just relaxed and soaked up the sun and healthful ocean breeze.

The people were extremely polite, friendly, and helpful, mostly blacks whose ancestors were brought as slaves by the British many years ago. The city of Bridgetown with stores and hotels had a decidedly British air and lovely British accents.

Back in Hesston, bitter cold assaulted us. Streets were packed with snow and ice. Relishing memories of sunny Barbados, we relived our exotic holiday with the children.

I was delighted to have Janet back home during her second year of college even though she spent a lot of time on campus. She majored in liberal arts and graduated in 1985 near the top of her class. Jared graduated from high school the same year and was in *Who's Who in American High Schools*. Their graduations were on the same Sunday, May 26. Janet graduated in the morning with a big crowd at Yost Center, which later emptied onto the surrounding lawn for picture taking, great camaraderie, and last goodbyes. Janet looked beautiful and joyful with her good friends who would soon scatter far and wide.

Jared graduated in the afternoon at the high school. Someone sang a touching solo of "Friends" by Michael W. Smith. It was a lovely sunny day with many warm and friendly faces of classmates together for the last time. Jake and I were proud of our children's accomplishments and happy we were back in this special town.

Before Jared's graduation, we had attended an awards night in the auditorium for students and their parents. At one point the computer teacher explained about the senior prank (a yearly occurrence at the end of the year), which set off the burglar alarm in the night.

It was a silent alarm system and the police responded. Students had rigged the alarm with the computer, using fishing line, which authorities followed to the computer. The police, administrators, and teachers were very angry about this false alarm. The principal asked the computer teacher, "Do you know someone who could do this?"

Mr. Banning assured him, "I most certainly do!"

At the awards ceremony, Mr. Banning held up a disk and said, "We didn't need to look far for proof. In the computer I found a disk with a name on it! No investigation was needed to find the culprit." At that point he said, "Jared, come up and claim your disk and your award for excellence in computer technology!"

Mr. Banning admitted it was an ingenious plan and Jared and team were forgiven. The place exploded with screams of delight as Jared went up to receive the award. His classmates' cheers were reward enough for his first lonely, miserable year at Lynden and he basked in the approval of his classmates. Jake and I finally realized why he and his friends had spent so much time in our family room at the computer the past few weeks. Mr. Banning had said that when students came to him with computer problems that stumped him, he sent them to Jared. Jake's foresight in buying the TRS-80 in Lynden, and Jared's helping students learn the computer in Germany, had paid off.

For his ten-year reunion booklet, Jared wrote about the prank: "We hooked up an old motor to an Apple II in the computer lab. We ran fishing line from the motor to an outside door and attached it to a loosened wire of the security system. I had written a program to turn on the motor during the night, setting off the alarm. It almost worked as planned, except after the alarm was set off, the fishing line broke at the motor, leaving a trail back to the computer. (The fishing line was supposed to wind up and be out of sight.) Unfortunately, I had left a disk in the drive with my name on it."

Over several years, Janet narrowed the field of "horse" schools and chose William Woods, a women's college in Fulton, Missouri, which she said had a fine equestrian program. During the school year, we accompanied her to attend meetings for prospective students and their parents. Though we were duly impressed with WWC, I was less than excited about her chosen field of study. But we had encouraged her interest in horses and she was already an excellent horsewoman.

In June of 1985, I was offered a job at our church when the secretary resigned in early June. The church board chairman called to ask if I would take the position. While still working as copy editor and proofreader, my heart was in church work and I had had a growing desire to work in the church office. Trepidation mingled with excitement as I thought and prayed about the matter. Not only was this a 600-member church, but for the first time ever I would be required to use a computer on the job. This in itself would be a challenge. Could I handle it?

The same day I received the job offer, I finished the first chapter of this family book on the computer. Even though I got sidetracked from serious work on it until 1997, it was a small beginning, and Jared was my great encourager in this project. He told me, "First make a list of chapters and then start writing."

In the meantime, I was glad for a few days away to relax, reflect, and pray about the job offer. We left with the children for five days to Stan Roth's vacation home in the Ozarks. We visited Silver Dollar City and Branson, Missouri where we saw the drama, "Shepherd of the Hills." Crossing the border to Eureka Springs, Arkansas we experienced the beautiful "Passion Play" of Jesus' life, which we had missed at Oberammergau in Germany.

It was wonderful to have Jake back home and enjoy these trips with the children. As we drove back to Hesston, I reflected on the last two good years in Kansas. Now big changes were ahead for all of us. I felt confident that the children were ready for the next chapter of their lives. The much-talked-about "empty nest" stared Jake and me in the face. I had prepared myself mentally for this, through reading and prayer, and determined that it need not be an unpleasant "syndrome."

But what was ahead for Jake and me—another move for Jake's job? If so, how soon? Should I take a new job with this possibility looming? I was reminded of Colossians 3:15, which helped me in the past: "The peace that Christ gives is to guide you in the decisions you make." Taking comfort in this promise, I resolved to trust God and enjoy whatever lay ahead.

CHAPTER 37

New Beginnings

I trust in You, O Lord; I say, "You are my God."
My times are in Your hand...

PSALM 31:14–15 (NKJ)

1985–1986

That fall I accepted the job as secretary at Hesston Mennonite Church (HMC) with some trepidation, trusting that the beginning computer class I took at the college would help. Dan Eigsti, who hired me, assured me I'd do fine.

My former job at Faith and Life Press was with the General Conference Mennonite Church (GC), in which Jake and I grew up. My new job at HMC took me into the larger Mennonite Church denomination (MC). Members of the two groups had worked together for years, and newer churches chose to have dual membership. The "split" in the church had occurred in my home district in 1847, when a progressive charismatic leader, John Oberholtzer, was excommunicated. Oberholtzer was pastor of my home church, along with other churches, from 1842-70. Numerous churches joined with him in Pennsylvania and Iowa, and from there the GC spread. Beginning in 1874, when the Russian Mennonites arrived on the Great Plains they chose to join the GCs, swelling their numbers. The MCs kept the traditional dress – prayer coverings and cape dresses for the women and plain coats (with no ties) for the men, while the GCs dropped them. At HMC, only a few older women wore the prayer covering. Differences had diminished over the years and talk of a merger of the two groups was ongoing and exciting to me. (This became a reality at the Nashville joint conference in 2001.)

On my new job, three half days of orientation with the former secretary seemed inadequate. At times that first week I felt alone and frustrated, especially meeting the bulletin deadline. Jared came to my rescue in the evenings, explaining the word processor. How grateful I was for his expertise and kindness. His unfailing patience amazed me.

Those first weeks were a trial and I trembled at my feelings of inadequacy. But I prayed, and help came in one form or another. I learned that on Monday mornings the offering must be counted and taken to the bank, a task I did not relish. A huge mailing to parishioners, spread out in boxes on the shelves behind my desk, screamed to be mailed. The secretary had said it should go out in a month. I saw no time in sight to do it. The monthly newsletter must be typed on that nerve-racking word processor. The phone rang plenty and people came in. The mail must be picked up at the college post office every morning, and the bulletin taken to the college print shop on time. On the big calendar on the wall I kept track of all activities in the fellowship hall or sanctuary and notified the janitor of events each day. The college, community, and church used the facility.

I cherished the summer with both children at home, aware that soon they would leave the nest. Janet enjoyed helping me with routine tasks in the office as she had time. Her presence and cheerfulness encouraged me. But she had two jobs during the day, plus babysitting, and friends were always a priority.

In June, a young Japanese woman arrived in Hesston for half a year. First, she stayed three months with the Dieners whose children were grown. We planned to keep her for three months in fall when Janet's room was empty. Mrs. Diener called and told me, "Kaoru is quite unhappy here with no young people in our home." I invited her for a meal occasionally or an activity with Janet and Jared and she loved our children. A much happier Mrs. Diener called again to say, "Janet is so outgoing and so good with Kaoru!" Kaoru later worked in the schools and tried to improve her English. She was a delightful person and we looked forward to her time with us.

Jared's summer job at the college included painting buildings inside and out, shampooing carpets, waxing floors, and a variety of other things, mostly in the heat. Janet worked at Burkhart stables in the mornings, then mowed and worked in the vegetable garden of an older couple in the afternoons. She came home beat. "I sure miss the cool climate in Washington and I hate this Kansas heat!" she complained.

Early in summer, she buttonholed Jake one day. "Can we go to Washington and B.C. in August before school starts? I really miss my friends there. *Please*?" Jared hated his job and wanted to quit.

Jake replied, "We can go on two conditions. First, if I don't have a full-time job by then and, second, we'll go if Jared doesn't quit his job."

"My job doesn't have anything to do with that," Jared squirmed.

"Yes, it does," Jake countered good-naturedly. "If you take on a responsibility, you should finish it. When you finish a job, you can give yourself a reward. The trip would be a reward for you," he smiled. Jared smiled too, convinced of his dad's wisdom.

"Ok, I'll stay with the job." A trip to the Northwest was a good reward, even to Jared. He relished seeing Curtis and Andre Fast again, his friends and housemates in Germany.

August came and Jake had no new job. I got time off work and we flew to Seattle August 7 for a week to visit Dad and Jessie, family on the mainland and Vancouver Island, as well as Lynden friends. We stayed overnight at Hans and Helene Fast's in B. C. one night, with Jared staying longer. Then Jake and I stayed with Pearl and Linferd Goertz at Lynden and Janet spent time with her Lynden friends.

On Saturday afternoon while at the home of Jake's brother Nick in Canada, we received a phone call from Pearl, which sent us back over the border. "I just got a call that Janet is in the hospital in Bellingham. She was riding Michele Fast's horse (our former next-door neighbor) and the horse reared up and fell backwards on top of her!" Fear rose within me. How badly was she hurt? Pearl did not know.

"*Oh, God,*" I prayed, "*please, take care of her!*" Immediately we drove to Cliff and Jane Fasts' at Lynden. Jane had called Cliff at work and he drove to the hospital, 13 miles south.

Jane, distraught over the accident, lamented, "We haven't had the horse very long and thought she was safe. I'm really sorry this happened."

Their son Jeff explained, "When Janet came this afternoon, Michele was gone picking berries. So I told Janet she could ride until Michele came home. I told her the horse was 'green broken.'" (Meaning, to the point where it would accept a rider on its back. Janet never turned down an offer like that). "Janet got on, but the horse reared up almost instantly, lost its balance, and fell over backwards." Janet was knocked unconscious and Jeff rushed to tell his mother to call the ambulance.

Cliff called home to say Janet was all right and he would bring her back. How glad we were for that news. The wait seemed interminable. Finally, it was a great relief to see Janet walking from the car – but *barely* walking. Jeff loaned her a pair of crutches for a few days. She felt badly to have caused us trouble, but we were concerned about her injuries.

"I'm very sore and bruised," she told us. "The doctor said I have internal injuries that will take about six months to heal." We were thankful there were no broken bones or serious head injuries. What a miracle!

Janet told us later that when she came to she could feel nothing from the waist down and thought she was paralyzed. Michele and her crew drove by the house on the way to another berry field when she saw the ambulance in her front yard. Alarmed, she asked the driver to let her out. Thus she accompanied Janet in the back of the ambulance to Bellingham.

Janet was very sore for weeks and received chiropractic treatments every day back in Kansas before leaving for college. We wondered how this would affect her riding program at school.

Jake had bought a small used Dodge pickup, which Janet could use for school. Our next-door neighbor, Karen, who had two sons, had become friends with Janet and, as Janet loaded the truck, Karen told Jake, "It's a sad day. Janet is leaving."

But Janet had become quite independent and was happy to strike out on her own. Before we said our goodbyes she told us, "I'll probably be home next weekend for Labor Day," and she headed off on the six-hour trip to William Woods. It appeared she did not want to break ties with home too drastically. She still loved it at home. Though I questioned her choice of majors, I decided to be happy that she could work toward her goal, whatever that was. It was great to have her back with her roommate the next weekend.

Now it was Jared's turn to pack. He moved to the college dorm and began classes on Labor Day. We had an empty nest, but Jared was close by, Kaoru had moved in, and I had a new and challenging job, which all helped ward off the empty nest syndrome. I marveled at how God had worked this out for me to work on campus while Jared was there.

Since I was not enthusiastic about Janet's equestrian choice, I began praying that she would change her mind. *Whatever will she do for a job with horses?* When she came home in late September for a chiropractic treatment, the doctor told her, "You should quit that riding class." She still did not have any muscle control to stay on the horse well, since she must hold on with her legs. So she quit the class but continued the non-riding equestrian classes.

Kaoru enjoyed Jared and they were like sister and brother. They spent time together at home on Saturdays or we all went to Wichita for the day. Sometimes Jared and a friend took her to special places, like the Cosmosphere at Hutchinson. Janet's weekend trips to the chiropractor afforded opportunities to bring friends home for a weekend and Kaoru enjoyed all their activities.

It was an extremely sad day for Kaoru at the end of November when she left to go back to Japan. The two evenings before we took her to the airport, she refused to come out of her room and join us. Later she tried to explain – it was just too emotional for her to leave her good friends.

By the end of 1985, Jake was quite unhappy with his part-time job situation and talked of moving to Seattle or going back to Saudi. He said to me one day, "If we'd go to Saudi now, I could work there ten more years." And I thought, *Ten years with no churches and no singing of Christmas carols allowed. I think I'd go crazy!* And then I told myself, *probably not, because God would be with me there.* What a different existence that would be! I could not envision it.

I told Jake, "I'm willing to move to Seattle," and mentally began packing and moving. What was ahead for us?

While Janet was home from William Woods for Christmas, she and I had a good talk. She told me, "I'm getting in really well with the equestrian teachers. They were so impressed with the paper I wrote on the Jack Brainard Clinic that they called me into their offices individually and commended me. They said, 'Anyone who gets that much out of a clinic should not be in beginning riding, but intermediate!'" She was a good student and loved her equestrian studies. She planned to take a short term riding class second semester. But I kept praying this would change.

On the last day of the year, Dad called. "Jessie went to the hospital on the 27th with flu and is very low." She had been frail for the past nine months, and we were not surprised when he called on January 4, 1986, to tell us she had died. Her two children were with her, as well as Peter and Mary's oldest daughter, Marlene. She had asked Dad to pray with her, which he did. When Marlene came, he said to her, "You better pray with Mom, too." So she prayed. Jessie told her daughter, Lila, "I'm going to die now," and Lila did not protest as she had earlier. Lila had never married and she and her mother were very close. Jessie was kind and loving and a great help to Dad, "both in her skill as a pianist and her hospitable spirit and loving ways with my children," as he wrote about her later. They had more than 15 years together and Dad missed her greatly.

In the church office, I worked first with Dan Johnston, former youth pastor who accepted the lead pastor role for a year when our pastor resigned under difficult circumstances. Young and dedicated, with a warm personality, Dan was a joy to work with. I sensed the burden he felt and prayed fervently for him with his heavy responsibilities. Our good relationship helped offset the frustrations of the routine work. Dan encouraged me to enlist others to do things I disliked, such as counting the large offering on Monday mornings. We hired Anna Ruth Beck, a former HMC secretary, who enjoyed doing the offering. Later, the church board bought a complicated computer program to enter all the members' statistics, and Anna Ruth relieved me of that also. Anna Ruth, an older, gracious woman, was a blessing in the office and we became good friends. I enjoyed learning to know the people who called and came in with needs and requests.

Pastor Dan talked with Jake and me about joining the church and we worked it out with the children. We all decided to transfer our membership from Glendale at Lynden. Janet came home with friends Joy and Ann in early March 1986, when we joined. After the service, Joy exclaimed, "You all looked so nice up there!" Ann, Joy, and Traci loved to come for weekends.

Pastor Dan left in July 1986, when Phil Bedsworth, a former pastor and head of the Pastoral Ministries Program at the college, began as lead pastor. Phil had preached for Dan quite often the past year and was a familiar, happy face around the office. He was a well-liked professor at the college, whom Janet and Jared had enjoyed. A few weeks later Carl Wiebe, just out of seminary, came as youth and associate pastor.

Early on, Phil told me, "You're more than a secretary. We are changing your title to Pastoral Assistant." I appreciated the affirmation. Paul Friesen, former pastor, and current art professor at Bethel and Hesston Colleges, was our part-time visitation pastor, and Orval Shoemaker, a retired psychologist, our counselor. Together with them I attended staff meetings each week and learned to know and appreciate each one. Their experience and wisdom, expertise and commitment impressed me and I was grateful for this stimulating and fulfilling job.

In the office one day, two weeks after Pastor Phil came, he asked me to serve as worship leader for the Sunday service. "This is Carl's first service and I want to ease him in gradually. He'll be teaching the youth class in Sunday school that morning. I'll be speaking at four sessions of conference that day and Paul Friesen will preach for me here. I don't want Carl to have full responsibility for worship leading. Will you do the Scripture reading and prayer?" Pastor Phil was definitely an encourager. When he had preached the past year he used women as worship leaders. They were good role models for me. I had never been worship leader at our former churches.

While in the past I hated doing things up front, I now felt a growing desire to lead worship, which helped overcome my fears. I prayed about it and agreed. Each of us on staff assured the others of our prayers. The service went well and I was overwhelmed by all the positive comments I received that day and throughout the week. John Koppenhaver, a retired pastor and former missionary, called to tell me that he and his wife thought I did a great job. I felt greatly encouraged.

After a year at William Woods, Janet and her roommate, Nancy, decided to go into Teen Mission for the summer of 1986. Janet took French at WWC and wanted to go to France. Nancy chose Africa. Raising $1800 support seemed prohibitive, but Janet garnered help from family and friends and collected the required amount. Their rigorous boot-camp training – running an obstacle course every morning, including climbing and teamwork activities in hot, steamy Florida – almost did Janet in, but she persisted. By contrast, she nearly froze in the frigid French mountains. Working with missionaries, learning masonry, she helped construct a mission building, using Jake's work boots from his construction jobs in northern B.C. The teens slept in tents and shivered in "showers" constructed from black plastic for "walls" around a hose dangling from a tree. Or they got a bucket of water from the stream, put it in the sun all day, and had the luxury of warm water by evening to wash up. The primitive conditions, work, witness, social activities, and discipline of regular devotions provided a challenging and rich growing experience for Janet.

Another challenge came for me when my friend, Lois Leinbach, asked me to tell my "stepmother story," or "spiritual journey," at their Whitestone Mennonite mother-daughter salad supper. I accepted and then agonized for weeks (and lost eight pounds) as I relived the painful years and wondered what to tell. At the supper, I shared about my mother's death, my stepmother's coming when I was four, and how I hated her. I related how the Lord taught me to love her, about my love for my father, his breakdown, the Tribute, Daddy's resolution of his fatherless childhood, and his death. After the talk, a stepmother and her stepdaughter came to me in tears. The girl's mother was my friend before she died of cancer, and I knew this girl had a difficult adjustment to her stepmother. I could identify and had prayed for them.

"I came here tonight expecting a relaxing evening," the woman said, "and your story tore me up!" But the Spirit used it and they could relate. I detected a change and softness in the daughter and praised the Lord in my heart that they had grown in love for each other.

In the fall I gave my "spiritual journey" again in our Sunday school class, with heartwarming affirmation. In the class were college professors, including psychology prof Phil Osborne. After he heard my story he asked me one day, "Would you be willing to tell your story to my Personal Growth Psych class?"

"I'm not sure," I hedged. "Jared is in that class and I'd have to talk with him about it." Jared had heard my story and said I could do it if I would take out the "psychology" and "interpretations"! Jake talked with Jared and encouraged him to let me tell it. In the end he agreed. I asked for his input on the "offensive" material and changed some of it to make it acceptable. I gave it in September and, unlike adult groups, the students hurried out of class without giving feedback.

Soon other adult Sunday school classes asked me to share my story then Pastor Carl asked me to give it in the youth class. The Lord kept opening doors for me. Betty Adkisson, my long-time friend and prayer partner, said, "The Lord is enlarging the place of your tent." God had impressed that verse on my heart at Vincennes, and I sensed that sharing my story brought me inner healing. I felt that the greatest thing I learned from losing my mother was the importance of leaning on God.

In June of 1986, we bought more land next to the 40 acres we already owned. It was 79.5 acres, surveyed. Our friend Jim Graber was happy for more land to farm.

Since our return to Kansas, we often heard the "Ahh, Kansas!" PR campaign on TV. Kansans were encouraged to sightsee in their own home state. We got a map with all the unusual places to visit. I loved the idea. When Jake was home we took Jared with us on several weekends to such places as Garden of Eden in western Kansas and Rock City north of Salina. Rock City is a park with huge round rocks – geological marvels that exist in only one other place on earth – India. These fun excursions helped relieve the stresses of our week and became a subject for sharing.

In August, Jake's Dad arrived for three weeks to help celebrate our 25th anniversary on September 3. Dad voiced surprise when he learned we had no reception planned at the church, which he said they always did at home. But

Jake is too private a person for such goings on. We greatly enjoyed taking Dad around the area again. We got together with friends and, on our anniversary, had a special dinner with Dad and Jared at the Colonial House. Jake blew me away with 25 red roses, and the children gave us a 25th anniversary plate and a beautiful cut glass pitcher.

At the church, Pastor Phil proposed an installation service of a five-member Pastoral Team, with three ordained–Phil, Carl and Paul–and two laypersons–our counselor Orval Shoemaker and me. God's gracious leading caused my heart to overflow with gratitude for this opportunity to serve with such a special team. "You're blue chip," Phil told me. "Don't hide your light under a bushel." I was often amazed at his sincere praise.

For the children's story at the installation service, Sue Gering introduced each of the five members of the team. She asked us ahead of time about a hobby we enjoyed doing together. I told her that we liked to tour the state and had a map especially for sightseeing. "That's unique!" she laughed. "You and Jake bring your map and he can tell about that." On Sunday as we stood on stage, Jake opened the map and said, quite seriously, "We use this map to travel around Kansas to see the sights." Knowing of his job in Saudi, flying all over the U.S., and our world travels, the congregation burst into laughter.

Thereafter, my name was listed with the other four in the newspaper's weekly listing for our church. I thought back to how intimidated I was when first moving to Hesston in 1973, afraid to take a job at the college. Instead, I worked at the Credit Union typing loan papers. But God kept working on me and giving me confidence and encouragement from others who discerned my gifts. An amazing change had occurred within me over the past 13 years.

Dad's presence at the installation service was an added blessing, along with his comment, "It was a good service." He told us many stories again about growing up in Russia and the hard times during and after the Revolution. He was pleased to give his life story one Sunday evening at our church.

With encouragement from the pastors, I took a seminary extension class at our church, "Preaching, Teaching, and Storytelling in the Church," as well as "Pastoral Identity" with the couples in the college Pastoral Ministries Program. Then I was asked to lead a women's group and used the book by Henri Nouwen, *The Way of the Heart*, on solitude, silence, and prayer. As I learned to know the women of the church, I was drawn into a ministry of listening and caring.

Though I rarely led worship, one Monday morning after I had, Wesley Jantz, chaplain of the retirement center in town, called to say, "I want to tell you how much I appreciated your worship leading, especially your reading of the Scripture. I felt like I could go home after that because I already had a sermon." The Scripture of David and Saul in the cave, when David could have killed Saul but instead cut off a piece of his robe to later show King Saul his loyalty, had greatly impressed me also. Again I was humbled and praised God for His Spirit at work.

The college had chapel twice a week in the sanctuary close to my office. I sometimes attended as time permitted. One day after chapel a student came to my office. "Hi, I'm Daniel," he smiled. "I'd like to interview you for my business class sometime."

"Sure, right now is fine," and I offered him a seat.

He sat down and got right to the point, "I wanted to stay after psych class that day and talk with you about losing a parent, but I couldn't. My mother died when I was born because she lost too much blood."

"That's just like my mother and brother! And my brother is coming from Pennsylvania tomorrow!" I was amazed at Daniel's timing. Jean Walker's words to me in Vincennes came back to me, "These things are not coincidence!" I called them "God's incidents." Ralph and Janice had their 25th anniversary in June and decided to drive out and celebrate with us belatedly.

Daniel continued, "I've often felt guilty about her death – that it was my fault."

"That's exactly how my brother has felt. Would you like to meet him?"

"Yes!" he agreed, his bright eyes shining. I was glad Jared had let me tell my story in his class, and grateful that it touched someone's heart.

Ralph and Janice arrived the next day. Anna and John, Ralph and Janice, and Jake and I were married the summer of 1961. Ralph and Janice were commissioned to bring us the family's gift, a lovely pewter lamp.

On Thursday morning I took them to chapel at the college, where Pastor Phil spoke. Later we met Daniel for a brief visit that blessed both Ralph and Daniel. They shared about their experience in common and acknowledged that life is good. Daniel's openness to share gave Ralph a warm serendipity on his arrival in Kansas.

Through the years, Ralph has shared with me information about our mother and her family since he lived with them and continued in their church. He knows that any new nuggets and stories from people who knew our mother are exciting to me. For over 40 years, starting in 1966, Ralph worked at Friendly Sales warehouse in Quakertown, which sells Scripture greeting cards. A long-time member of the Springfield Church of the Brethren, Leroy Cramer, still worked at Friendly Sales part time at age 84. One day he told Ralph, "I remember being in your mother's Sunday school class as a young lad. In order to inspire us to learn the books of the Bible, she had a contest for the one who found verses the fastest. The prize was a baseball catcher's mitt. At first I wasn't very interested in looking up verses. But then an evangelist came to church and he had the children look up verses, too. I really wanted that catcher's mitt and I practiced a lot and got much quicker at finding verses. But by the time the evangelist left, the contest was over and another boy won the prize."

With a big smile and a twinkle in his eyes, Leroy recalled, "Even though I didn't win the contest I've come to realize that I was a winner, too, since your mother gave us that challenge and a prize far more valuable than a catcher's mitt. She sparked my interest and gave me the gift of a lifelong love for the Scriptures, which began in her class." What a precious memory of our mother to cherish!

25th anniversary, Hesston, KS, Ralph, Janice, Jake and me, 1986.

Ralph and Janice delighted in the unusual sights and places of Kansas – flat farmland as far as one could see, roads straight as an arrow – a contrast to eastern Pennsylvania. They met wonderful people and we enjoyed family stories and reminiscing. Ralph loved getting better acquainted with Jake and he was impressed with my position on the pastoral team. I was amazed when shy, quiet Ralph told me he became a deacon five years after they were married, at age 28. At their church, deacons serve for life. He also taught Sunday school, played piano for worship, and typed the church bulletin for many years. His wife, Janice, has been a faithful supporter and helpmate to him, active in the church, and a good friend to me. When their visit was over, we hated to part, and wished for fewer miles between us.

Another special event on our 25th anniversary, September 3, was the wedding of my younger brother, Tom, to Debby on St. Thomas Island. How romantic, to be married on an island bearing one's name! His name is Thomas Martin and they also visited nearby St. Martin Island. We were happy that Tom found a new mate, and regularly had visits with his son Mike from his first marriage of several years.

For a hobby and diversion, I decided to take an evening quilting class offered at the middle school. Each of us made a "country sampler" with twelve 12-inch pieced blocks of different designs. I sewed mine by hand, except for the border, and worked on it slowly over several more years, lap quilting with a large round hoop. I loved putting in every stitch and called it our "25th anniversary quilt." Aunt Naomi told me that my mother and her siblings, even the boys, helped stitch quilts during the winters as they were growing up.

While Jake still chomped at the bit about the job situation in Kansas, he spent a week in recurrency classes at FlightSafety in St. Louis in June 1986. There he met a pilot who changed the course of our lives. Phil worked for American Continental Corporation (ACC) in Phoenix and gave Jake a glowing report of the company.

Jake came home excited and hopeful with the news. "I met Phil Calvert, a pilot for a fantastic company in Phoenix. He said they've had quite a turn-over of pilots the past year and I should apply. He thinks they could use me as a relief pilot." Phoenix! That sounded exciting.

Jake applied immediately and for the next four months he made frequent calls to the director of the flight department of ACC, with no trips. I prayed and waited and wondered. Questions swirled through my mind and onto my journal pages. *Will Phoenix be our next move? Am I ready to leave this job, church, loving friends, and – for the first time – the children?* Janet loved to come home with friends occasionally on weekends. How long will we have to wait? The verse, "My times are in Your hand," came to mind. God knew. That was enough.

CHAPTER 38

Crisis!

He forgives all my sins and heals all my diseases.
PSALM 103:3 (GNB)

1986–1987

As Jake waited and hoped for a job in Phoenix, Hesston Mennonite Church faced a huge challenge. On October 3, 1986, Pastor Phil dropped a bombshell. He and his wife Joyce came to my office early that morning looking grim. "Get the Kleenex box," Phil said. Puzzled, I wondered what could be so sad. Phil had been to the doctor the day before and blurted out, "My blood count should be 10,000 and it's 250,000! I have leukemia!"

I was stunned and could hardly absorb the news. We talked briefly and Joyce asked me to make a phone call to Dan from the church board to give him the news.

"I can't believe this!" I stammered. As they rose to leave, I got up and walked around my desk to give Phil a hug. He began to cry. Joyce was already at the door, and turned around. I reached out to include her in the embrace and she confessed, "We spent most of the night crying."

Together they broke the news to the church the next Sunday morning and explained what lay ahead for Phil. Shock and grief gripped the congregation as they faced another uncertainty without a lead pastor.

The next day, October 6, Phil "celebrated" his 36th birthday, wondering if he would make it to his 40th. Friends made a pizza-size birthday cookie and their Sunday school class decorated their front lawn with luminaries placed to form a giant 36. His best birthday present, he said, was a note from Milo Kauffman, president emeritus of Hesston College, in which he wrote that Christ was telling them that they were His chosen vessels for short-term, special service. It may be as witnesses of Christ's healing power or to His all-sufficient grace in affliction and suffering. He reminded them that the trying of their faith would be more precious than an ordinary life of service would be. [Philip and Joyce Bedsworth, *Fight the Good Fight* (Scottdale, Pennsylvania: Herald Press, 1991), 26.]

The next weeks and months became a time of adjustments as we all shared responsibilities. Phil had many doctor appointments and he and Joyce spent hours researching bone marrow transplants. One day Phil told me, "I'm at peace, but I will need to cry once in a while." That day I wrote in my journal, "Father, it is so sad to be with him in the office, yet I have not felt a heaviness, just an awareness of a very somber verdict."

Herb Minnich, pastor of Inter-Mennonite Church, visited Phil in their home and gave him a verse, Psalm 118:17, *"I shall not die, but live to tell the goodness of the Lord!"* Knowing of Herb's charismatic ministry, I had felt strongly that he could help bring healing to Phil and prayed God would use him. His verse was a "word of knowledge" that ignited Phil's faith and I rejoiced when Phil told me of Herb's visit. But as we all prayed earnestly, we wondered, *Will he be healed?*

In the midst of this swirl of events, Jake, undaunted by the four-month silence from American Continental, surprised me with pleasant news. "I want to visit Steve, head of aviation at ACC. You and I can fly out to Phoenix together for a weekend. How would you like that?" I loved it! We left on October 16 and I fell in love with Phoenix at first sight–the "Valley of the Sun" and Sonora Desert. We took a side trip to Sedona in the stunning red rock mountains, which Steve recommended. It was an unusual and exotic state, with perfect weather! *Might we really move here?*

On Sunday we went to Trinity Mennonite Church in Glendale, where our Pastor Carl's father, Peter Wiebe, was pastor. Vince and Estelle Kraybill, who built our house, met us after the service. "Are you looking for a house?" Estelle asked.

"No," I said. "Jake doesn't have a job here yet."

"Well, maybe when you're ready to move we'll be moving to the retirement center and you can buy our house. Come over this afternoon for a visit and see it." She gave the address and directions. Their house and yard were charming, with a lovely little flower garden in front. But I hardly dared think we could ever live there. We returned home excited about prospects. Months went by with no trips for ACC. Jake tried to be patient.

Janet continued coming home some weekends during her second year at WWC. It was nice to know she missed us. On October 24, 1986, Jake called her at school and they visited quite a while. Then it was my turn. A few minutes into the conversation she said, "Oh, I have some big news for you. Are you sitting down?" I was.

"I quit equestrian!" I nearly fell off my chair! God had answered my prayer! She continued, "I just hated going to riding class anymore and I kept finding excuses not to go. In Hunt Seat we had to jump fences and the new teacher made us jump with our arms straight out at our sides. Girls were falling off and landing in the hospital and I sure didn't want to fall again!

"Remember when I was home I met with Ron? (Her former Bible prof at Hesston College.) Well, I told him I wanted to quit but I was afraid you and Dad would be angry because it cost so much and you'd be out of that money. But he told me to just quit and tell you!" There! It was out.

"Angry?" I replied with gusto. "I'm *delighted!* That's great news to me, and I doubt that Dad will care. I've been praying you'd change your major!"

"You have?" Now it was her turn to be surprised.

Often when she was home, she got together for "coffee" at the Colonial House with Professor Ron Guengerich. I praised the Lord for him and his fine mentoring.

Janet went on, "I changed my major to psychology and I'll get a minor in religion. The Bible classes are at Westminster College, a couple of blocks away. Ron told me, 'I think you should go to seminary,' and I told him, 'My mom tells me that, too.' He said, 'I'm not going to stop telling you!'" Music to my ears. She was one of Ron's star pupils in Bible at the college.

Several years later she admitted to me one day, "I wanted to be a jockey, and race horses someday, but then I got too big and I knew I could never be a jockey, so I lost interest. Jockeys are almost always under 5 feet and under 100 pounds." She was 5 feet 4 inches and hefty compared to small-boned me. So that was what had motivated her all these years. I confess I had a jaundiced view of such frivolity. She had kept her secret well, but God had other plans for her. First, the fall in Washington slowed her down. Then girls falling off their horses at school clinched her decision. Sometimes God moves in not-so-mysterious ways to accomplish His purposes.

Her second year at WCC, Janet was president of her dorm, and took on the daunting challenge of leading a Bible Study, called BASIC, Brothers And Sisters In Christ. It was open to Westminster students (men) as well, and sometimes 30 students came, "because we prayed a lot!" A few times she called to tell me that her closest friends came to the meeting intoxicated and acted out to disrupt the meeting. She shared her distress and I prayed for her with a heavy heart, glad when the situation improved. How pleased we were at her words in a letter, "We have an awesome family!" She met many girls who did not grow up with a church or Christ in their lives.

In the months following Phil's diagnosis, he and Joyce rejoiced to find a bone marrow match in his sister Betsy. They also had the grueling task of locating the best transplant center for him. Only 500 bone marrow transplants were done annually by 1986. There was a 25-30% chance of death occurring during the transplant process, but a 45-50% chance of a cure. After much research and visiting two centers, Phil and Joyce chose the University of Iowa Hospitals and Clinics at Iowa City, the largest teaching hospital in the U.S. They received a tip that a Mennonite physician, Roger Gingrich, managed the bone marrow center there. In addition, their survival rate was better than other centers they checked. The president of the board of Hesston College lived in Iowa City and he and his wife offered their home as a place for Joyce to stay. Pastor Carl Wiebe and his wife Mary offered to move into Bedsworth's home to take care of Sara and Steven while Phil and Joyce were gone. Others volunteered to take care of a host of needs and details to support Carl and Mary and the Bedsworths.

In December, Phil had his spleen removed in Wichita. He lost four units of blood and required a second surgery for the bleeding problems. He was seriously ill and this setback postponed the transplant for a month. Though Phil understood the risky nature of the procedure, as he faced the transplant in Iowa City he assured the congregation confidently, "I plan to be back to preach on Easter, April 19!" His favorite verse was Psalm 103:3, "He forgives all my sins and heals all my diseases." We hoped and prayed this would all come to pass.

But sometimes I felt helpless, small, and weak in the face of Phil's ongoing struggle. Grief dogged my days and nights, even though I prayed. Parishioners came into the office with their questions and concerns. Typically, in the past, I grew speechless in the face of deep grief or death. Was this a carry-over from long years of silence about my own mother's death when I was too little to understand or speak?

One day, as people came in, I felt tongue-tied, not knowing what to say when they spoke of Phil's illness. Then I realized I didn't need to speak. Anna Ruth was there, a fountain of beautiful, eloquent words of faith and trust. "I'm praying for whatever will bring the most honor and glory to God," she'd say, "whether through Phil's healing or his death." I felt humbled and rebuked by such mature trust, and enormously grateful for her presence. Amazed at her cheerful fluency, I saw how God had put her in the office "for such a time as this," to help me in more ways than clerical work.

In January in Iowa, Phil began heavy chemotherapy doses and became gravely ill. As I wrote him a letter at home one evening, I broke down and wept. Janet was home and held and comforted me gently. Gratitude for a dear, empathetic daughter welled up in me.

The church board decided to hire an interim pastor until Phil was back, and I couldn't be more delighted with the choice – Jacob T. Friesen, my former pastor at Bluffton College. From nearby Newton, he began on January 4 and remained for seven months. I had often typed and run his church bulletins at Bluffton – and babysat their children – and this renewed association blessed us both.

Phil wrote a letter to the church the day of the transplant in which he said that this was "the day of my new life." He thanked everyone for their prayers and verses in cards. He mentioned especially, "When you pass through the waters, I will be with you." Strong words of faith filled his mind as he submitted to the dangerous procedure.

Phil had the transplant on January 15, and – miraculously – survived. It grieved him that several others died who had the procedure at the same time. Among his many complications were no immunity and little strength. Mary Wiebe told me in the office three days after the transplant, "I talked with Joyce Sunday night and she said Phil still has no fever [fever is common after a transplant], he rides his bike in his room an hour a day, and works on his computer!" What incredibly good news! God was answering the prayers of His people.

While not out of the woods, Phil and Joyce hung onto hope tenaciously. Joyce, a nurse, insisted on the best treatment for Phil and that he do his daily exercises even though his strength was spent. His life depended on it. Sara was in third grade, Steven in first, and it was Phil's hope that he would live to see them graduate from high school.

Phil's survival and courageous fight buoyed me up. The end of January, in a flash of inspiration, I wrote him an acrostic poem, which was printed in a church paper and the college newsletter. I cannot recall what "B-Man" stood for, perhaps "Bionic Man," a nickname he called himself.

To a Jolly Good Fellow: B-Man

P is for Phil, our pastor and pro,
H is for Househusband, a good one, we know.
I is for Ill – a real blow life gave you,
L is for Life you've been given anew.
I for Intention to preach Easter Day,
P – Philadelphia, childhood home far away.

B is for Betsy who shared of her life,
E for Eternally grateful – your wife.
D is for Dove of peace resting on you,
S for God's Spirit, your hope to renew.
W is for Wonderful answers to prayer,
O for Our Father who watches with care.
R is for Riding your bike in your room,
T for Triumphant, our faith in full bloom.
H is for Health and strength from God above,
And all of us here send you our love.

After months of uncertainty and excruciating trials, Phil did indeed come home to preach on Easter Sunday. The church was packed with over 600 present. What a cause for rejoicing and praise to God! Joyce had carried a single yellow long-stemmed gladiola at their wedding. On Easter Sunday morning, they gave a gladiola bulb to each of us as we left the sanctuary to signify Phil's new life. We got four bulbs for our family and I got four extra from the leftovers in the office. Thus began years of growing beautiful tall glads, my first experience with this exquisite flower. (I brought the bulbs along when we moved to Phoenix where they grow unusually tall.)

Phil returned to Iowa City after Easter. From there he called me a week later and exulted, "I'm cured!" No sign of leukemia! However, complications persisted, and his grueling walk every day, outside or in the college gym, left him beat. Though he came home, he regularly returned to Iowa City for checkups. In June, Jake flew him and Joyce to Iowa in Stan Roth's plane.

For now, it seemed, the crisis was over. Phil was on the road to recovery in answer to many prayers. His miraculous recovery gave everyone hope. We prayed God would strengthen him and add many years to his life. But the question remained, *How long could he serve as our pastor in his weakened condition?*

CHAPTER 39

Expanding Horizons

I'm staying on Your trail; I'm putting one foot in front of the other.
I'm not giving up.
PSALM 17:4–5 (THE MESSAGE)

1987–1988

In the spring of 1987, I took a Spiritual Direction class at Frances Newman College (Catholic) in Wichita with several others from church. For centuries, spiritual directors have had a wonderful ministry in the Catholic Church. Our teacher, Sister Mary Kevin, told us, "I have had the same spiritual director for 20 years and it is a real gift. In counseling, there are only two people present, the counselor and counselee. But in spiritual direction there are three people–the director, the counselee, and God. We learn to take God into every area of life, the next-door neighbor we can't stand or a problem with a spouse. I want each of you to find a spiritual director for the duration of the class and I'd encourage you to continue thereafter."

Phil was recuperating at home and since I took his mail over to the house, I asked him about taking on this role. He consented and was eager to hear about what we learned. He said he had taught similar things in his class at the college. One day I shared some concerns about Janet and a couple of suicidal, demanding college friends who caused her much distress. One had attempted suicide several times, and Janet knew the other one had a plan. She told Janet, "If you don't do what I want, I'll kill myself!" The year Janet lived at home I found her sick in bed one day. Sensing something more serious was amiss I questioned her and learned of this frightening situation. I insisted she talk with a professor, which she did. He gave her good counsel on how to deal with the girl's threats and a book on how to say NO. That relationship was never easy.

Phil's assured me, "Janet has chosen you as her role model. That is the highest compliment anyone can give you. She likes to help you in the office

454

because she enjoys being with you." What a comforting thought. When the class ended, so as not to tax Phil's fragile strength, I asked Jacob T. Friesen if he would be my spiritual director for a short period. He agreed and this was also a good experience.

Jared lived at home his second year of college and had jobs in the media services department, videoing soccer and basketball games, setting up projectors for classes, and showing campus movies. He was also a computer lab monitor and got minimum wage for both jobs. His good friends, Bill, Jerry, Harold, and Dave spent many evenings with him in our family room. Dave Andre especially loved Jared and coming to our house, often for a meal. He sometimes brought his girlfriend, Candi, a student from his hometown in Massachusetts.

On May 6, 1987, Janet graduated magna cum laude from William Woods. We drove to Missouri with Jared for her special day. Through two difficult but rewarding years she had grown and matured in many ways.

A week later, Jared graduated from Hesston College. His name had appeared in the newspaper a number of times as an honor roll student. The gym was packed for a wonderful service and rousing address on being "required persons." The African-American speaker, having conducted funerals for 17 murders the past eight years, reminded the graduates how bad the world is out there. He challenged them to meet God's requirement: "What does the Lord require of thee, but to seek justice, love mercy, and walk humbly with your God" (Micah 6:8).

We would miss the happy faces of Jared's friends around the house. In addition to his jobs in media services and the computer lab at school, Jared had worked for Stan Roth in off hours and during the summer. Now Stan hired him full time to network all their computers. It was good to have him at home another year.

Jake was in Alberta, Canada, on Father's Day, to return home that evening. So I took Janet and Jared to Eden Mennonite near Moundridge for something special. Memories of my first visit to this church in the '50s – and how astounded I was by its enormity and the powerful preaching – had lingered through the years. I was not disappointed. We heard an excellent sermon on parenting and fathers. At home later, Janet's words astonished me, "I was thinking during the sermon that you and Dad have done a really good job of parenting." When I looked at her in surprise and disbelief, she reaffirmed,

"You really have! The way so many young people are these days..." I could hardly believe my ears. (This was the girl who at Lynden told me one day, "I can hardly wait till I'm 18 so I can move out and get my own apartment!" She felt too restricted.) These timely words from her were like "apples of gold in a setting of silver" (Prov. 25:11, NRSV) and warmed me to my toes. Sometimes my faults and insecurities clobbered me flat and only God and my journal knew how I struggled. Such praise was mightily reassuring. Jake returned that evening and was warmed, too, by Janet's words.

Janet decided to go into Mennonite Voluntary Service (MVS) for a two-year term in Beatrice, Nebraska. In church one Sunday in June, she was interviewed for the children's story time. Asked to explain what VS was, she asked the children, "Do you know what a volunteer is? Are you all going to Bible school?" They said yes. "All the people who help with Bible school are volunteers—that means they work without getting paid. VS is short for Voluntary Service. And in VS you work without getting paid much." Then she said, "I once saw a bumper sticker that said, 'Jesus was a volunteer.'"

"How did you decide to go into VS?" the interviewer asked.

The children listened intently as Janet answered, "When I was very little—littler than most of you—my parents went into VS. I was too little to remember it but I heard stories about it through the years. When I went to Hesston College, I learned that some of my teachers had been in VS. Then one day a man came from Newton and talked to our class about VS and I thought that would be a worthwhile thing to do."

Then she was asked, "What will you do in VS?"

"I'll be a Child Protective Service Worker. Sometimes people don't take care of their children very well—either they don't have enough money or they don't treat them very well," Janet explained. "So I'll go into their homes and find out what's happening and see if we can help." Janet's degree in psychology qualified her for this position at the courthouse in Beatrice. Her salary would go to MVS and she would get an allowance of $75.00 a month for her basic needs. VSers lived in a VS house with room and board provided. After a week of orientation in Colorado in June, Janet prepared to move to Beatrice. I nearly choked up as I prayed for her at the table. Before she left, Jake read Psalm 121, the "Traveler's Psalm." As he began she said, "That's the Psalm I used at our last worship time at orientation," and she quoted along with him in the King James Version. She would be only four hours away compared with six at college.

On June 29, 1987, Janet began her new job. Intense and grueling, the work with parents, children, police, and sometimes testifying in court, took its toll on her mentally and emotionally. The appalling treatment and neglect of children angered and moved her deeply. She was grateful for the two Mennonite churches there and became good friends with one of the pastors, Preston Goering and his family, where she also babysat. Preston prayed her through some extremely tough times and he and his wife became long-time friends to her.

I volunteered to teach the eighth grade Sunday school class and used part of each period to interview a "mystery guest:" a college professor, student, sometimes a parent. One Sunday I interviewed Janet and she told of her work with abused children and their parents. It was quite an eye opener for those eighth graders. One day a student asked me after class, "Why did all the mystery guests have something bad happen to them?"

"That's life!" I responded. "And that's why we need Jesus as our Savior to help us through the hard times, because sooner or later hard times come to most of us."

When Janet entered VS, I felt awed about her call to work with abused children, as if I were walking on holy ground. After coming back from Germany, I was astounded at the barrage of child abuse cases reported regularly on Wichita TV news. Many a night I went to bed with a heavy heart and cried out to God for these children. When Janet took that position, I felt it was God's answer for me personally, in a small way, to relieve the suffering of God's helpless, innocent ones.

Jake still waited for a call from Phoenix and a job with American Continental. I wondered if another move was in the offing that would take us away from the children.

In February 1987, Jake met Phil Calvert again at FlightSafety in St. Louis. While there, Jake got a call for his first trip with ACC for the next week. After badgering the company a year for a job, success tasted sweet. On February 18-19 he flew Charles Keating's son-in-law to Flagstaff and stayed overnight in a hotel. Jake called to tell me about it. "The crew was invited for breakfast at Keating's daughter's home, and his son-in-law prayed at the table. They're Christians!" I was delighted and impressed.

That summer, over July 4th weekend, 1987, Jared and I accompanied Jake on a trip for Stan Roth, delivering a King Aire plane to Phoenix. Jared and I relaxed at the pool and Jacuzzi at a lovely hotel, with graceful queen palms and pink oleander in abundance. Our stay was paid for by Keating's company since the aviation head wanted to spend time meeting with Jake. On the Fourth of July, with one flashlight, we climbed a small mountain after dark with friends Joanne and Nelson Kilmer, also from Hesston, and others to observe fireworks around the Valley. The Arizona heat was unbearable, even at 10 P.M.! It made Kansas' climate look moderate. Would Jake ever land a full-time job with Keating? With his persistence, it would probably happen sooner than later.

As Jake continued to fly occasionally as relief pilot for ACC I felt in my bones that the move was imminent. In August, a surprising phone call came from Phoenix – for *me*! The mellow voice on the other end said, "This is David Mann, pastor of Sunnyslope Mennonite Church in Phoenix. We need a coordinator at our church and wondered if you would accept the position?" I could hardly believe my ears. I was offered a job in Phoenix before Jake!

"We're not moving to Phoenix," I replied, "because my husband doesn't have a job there. He just flies part time for a company there." Later, Pastor Carl told me one day, "My dad (Peter Wiebe, pastor of Trinity Mennonite in Glendale, next door to Phoenix) asked if you would be their secretary. The present one is pregnant and they're looking for someone."

"But we're not moving to Phoenix!" I repeated. "Jake doesn't have a full-time job there." Having been offered *two* jobs before Jake landed a full-time job made me feel *good*! I felt grateful for their trust in me since I knew neither of these men. But Carl had praised me to his dad and told him that Jake was flying for a Phoenix company. Moreover, Peter and David Mann were good friends and colleagues in Phoenix.

Carl was ordained on August 16, 1987, and Peter and Rheta Mae came from Phoenix. For Carl's birthday on Friday, I baked a coffee cake (as I did for all staff birthdays) and his parents joined my office full of well-wishers. I met them for the first time and found Peter to be warm and outgoing. Having been pastor at HMC for 13 years in the '60s, he knew the town and people well. When we were alone he quizzed me on what was most important to me in my job.

"Communication," I answered quickly. "I like to understand why things must be done." He had heard similar sentiments from other pastors' secretaries. I was impressed by his sensitivity and interest.

On Sunday, through Peter's energetic part in the service I saw his inspiring, humorous, and loving pastor heart, and his great pride in his son. After the service, a reception for Carl was held in the Fellowship Hall, just off the hall by my office. Jake was in Ireland, Janet in Beatrice, and Jared off somewhere, and suddenly I felt very alone. Usually I took Jake's absences in stride. But as I entered the Fellowship Hall and observed the warmth and camaraderie of friends greeting Carl and Mary and Peter and Rheta Mae, a tidal wave of unexpected loneliness and grief swept over me. Tears sprang to my eyes and I hurried to the office to regain my composure.

I was happy for Carl and Mary, but in my mind's eye I saw Jake and me as we started out at seminary, like Carl and Mary. I had dreams of having a spiritual journey similar to theirs, but it was not to be. Jake had chosen aviation. The longings and guilt of the years crashed in on me. Our experience stood out in sharp contrast with the joy of the Wiebe family. I sobbed from my depths as I grieved for what might have been and cried out to the Lord for help. His Spirit comforted and strengthened me. I dried my eyes—and remembered my upcoming trip! That afternoon, Jared took me to the airport for a 2:44 flight from Wichita to Pennsylvania. My sadness evaporated and the blessings of the next ten days with my family left me rejuvenated.

New Year's Day 1988 came and went with Jake still waiting for a full-time job. His big break came on February 11, two years after his initial contact with American Continental. His voice was animated when he called from New York City on a trip for ACC. "Steve phoned me from Phoenix and asked if I was still interested in a job. I said yes. So he said, 'When you get back Monday, come into my office. We'll talk about it and about flying your family down here.'"

The next day he called with more news. "The company fired two pilots. They'll replace them with two new ones—including me, it looks like." This same thing had happened before Jake was hired for the Kaiser job. I felt sad for the men who lost their jobs so my husband could have one, but happy for Jake. It felt like déjà vu. My distaste for corporation culture grew with each new experience with these multimillion-dollar giants. But with Jake's aviation career track with the Gulfstream, our dependence on them grew. Steve had told Jake, "If you pass your medical, the job is yours." I was sure it was in the bag. Though I was in the middle of a preaching class in the college Pastoral Ministries Program, it would be a relief to be rescued from that. I sensed this was not my calling. My place was with my husband.

I flew to Phoenix February 19-23 to meet Jake as he returned from New York. On the flight, I read an article by someone who moved from the lush green state of Kentucky to Arizona and was enthralled by the beauty of the desert. The detailed word pictures prepared me for anticipating living in brown desert after having grown up in the green state of Pennsylvania. During our visit to Phoenix, every day was sunny, with a perfect 75 degree high – paradise on earth. We had dinner with Steve and wife Chris at a steak house. Steve pelted Jake with questions, then asked how I felt about the move. "We work our pilots hard," he told me, "but try not to have them fly more than 21 days a month. What will you do here while he's gone?"

"I've already had two job offers at churches here," I told him, "and it won't take me long to get involved in a church. By now I'm used to corporate flying and having Jake gone." Steve appeared satisfied. His wife talked about her Sunday school teaching and I felt at ease with her.

Monday, Jake met Charles Keating for the first time when he flew him on a short trip to Tucson. Jake learned that he is Catholic, was responsible for getting the Pope to Phoenix, contributed millions to Mother Teresa, and fought pornography for 30 years. He sounded like a good man. I went with Jake to the doctor's office for his medical exam. Then he stayed on in Phoenix and I flew home. He still had to sign a contract but was certain the job was his.

I wondered who would take my job in the church office and prayed for a replacement. Anna Ruth suggested Barbara Martin. With mounting excitement, and a tinge of sadness, I turned in my resignation, effective in a week or two, and gave Barbara's name. She was delighted to have the position. I praised the Lord and thanked Anna Ruth.

Poor Phil's kidneys had given out and he needed a transplant. He had no energy and told me he was often confused. The church board decided to give him another six-month leave of absence and Carl took over as lead pastor. Carl's delight showed. Many changes the past year left only two of the five members of our pastoral team.

Carl and I had worked together well and had become good friends as we filled in for Pastor Phil. His sense of humor helped keep things light and his sincere appreciation for my work helped immensely. One day after I shared with him about appointments I had with two women on Saturday, and work I had taken home from the office, he stated, "You should be a pastor for two reasons – you have a pastor's heart and also, you don't keep track of your time like pastors do!" He made me feel so important on that job. But I was ready to let it go, pain or no pain. I cancelled my preaching class with no regrets and repaid the money to the church.

On Monday, February 29, leap-year day, the church staff and others surprised me with a farewell party. Twice in the past two years they had a birthday party for me. This year—on my fifty-third—Paul Friesen, well-known potter and sculptor, had made me a teapot and eight lovely cups. I was amazed that he did this for me. Now they gave me a going-away party. What a wonderful group of people God had blessed me with there. I loved them, each one. God had seen my trembling inadequacy in this office at times and used these people to pour out on me more praise and appreciation than I had ever received on a job. It would be sad to leave them. In the two-year interim while Jake waited for full-time employment, God had blessed me with the most fulfilling job of my life. God's timing is perfect.

The day after the party, on March 1, Jake signed the contract with American Continental. They paid for packing and moving. Everything happened so fast. I cried to the Lord to help me get through the next weeks. Convinced that God had opened this door for Jake, I rejoiced that the move was to Phoenix and not to Saudi Arabia. My excitement was tempered by the keen realization that for the first time, we would move without our children.

Jake stayed in Phoenix until March 4 and found an apartment for us. Friends called or came to say goodbye. In this cyclone of events, I felt a deep peace and calm at my center. God had promised, "I am with you and will keep you in all places, wherever you go." Sensing His leading, I was not afraid.

But what would life in Arizona be like? After the pressures and demands of the past several years, I felt like an eagle ready to soar free. But how would I fare facing the wrenching separations still to come? I'd have to rest in the Lord and cross that bridge when I got there.

PART VI

ADVENTURES AND BLESSINGS

CHAPTER 40

Retirement Job?

The harbor was not a good one to spend the winter in;
so most of the men were in favor of...trying to reach Phoenix...
in order to spend the winter there.
ACTS 27:12 (TEV)

1988

While Phoenix beckoned, separations loomed ahead. I cherished times with Jared who had taken a year off from college to work for Stan Roth at Executive Aircraft in Newton. We would miss Janet and her VS friends, but she could visit us in Phoenix. I refused to let sadness or regrets spoil this latest adventure of a move to the beautiful and amazing desert of the "Valley of the Sun."

Jake arrived home the day before our last Sunday at church. ACC kept its projection of "working their pilots hard—21 days a month" as Jake had only one day at home in the last three weeks. Phone calls helped us keep pace with each other. I had the house appraised, and Jake found us an apartment near the airport in Phoenix. My last day of work was Friday, March 4. We planned to leave on Tuesday, March 9. Jared could live in the house until the end of May when we would return to finalize the sale and move the furniture.

That last Sunday in church with Jake, Jared, Janet and a VS friend, Rosanne, mixed emotions rose within me. Pastor Phil was preparing for a kidney transplant. I listened with sadness and hope as he preached for the last time and called the congregation to love, unity, and forgiveness.

Pastor Phil was encouraged to rest, spend time with his family, and drop in at the church office whenever he desired as he waited for a kidney. Carl led the elders in prayer as they laid hands on Phil and Joyce. (As it turned out, Phil's recovery was so slow that he later resigned as pastor. He eventually recovered and directed the college's Pastoral Ministries Program for eight years, when he died of a heart attack. With characteristic good cheer, faith, and humor, Phil cherished every day with his family and friends.)

When we called Janet in Beatrice the morning of our departure she said, "I want to come to Phoenix March 17." We planned to arrive March 11. As it turned out, she was very sick for two weeks, and her visit was delayed until Easter break.

Jake and I started our leisurely drive to Tucumcari, New Mexico. From there we called Jared and learned that a young couple from church was there to see our house. Two days later, they agreed to buy it – a speedy sale, like our two former houses.

On our third day we drove through spectacular scenery at Salt River Canyon, east of Phoenix. Driving down steep, winding curves almost took my breath away. Though dizzying, the drive opened up a panoramic view of this incredible canyon. Our introduction to the fantastic Southwest of canyons, mountains, and deserts piqued my desire to explore Arizona.

We arrived in Phoenix at 10:45 that morning. At 2:55, at the American Continental hangar, Jake talked on the phone with the buyer of our house and they agreed on the price of $55,500.

The first Sunday we went to church at Trinity we met Vince and Estelle Kraybill who had built our Hesston house. "Are you looking for a house?" Estelle asked. "We're planning to put a "For Sale" sign out tomorrow morning."

"Yes!" I answered excitedly. "Jake was hired full time and we moved here this week." What amazing timing! They told us about it two years ago and God saved it for us. We went to look at the house that week and I loved it as before. With three bedrooms, two bathrooms, living room and kitchen/dining/family room, it was perfect for the two of us. A large outside laundry room off the back patio had plenty of storage space. We agreed to buy it for $75,000.

Vince told us, "We bought it at auction and got it for a low price. The woman who lived here had 13 cats and it was in bad shape. I'm not looking to make a profit, just to get out of it what I put into it." He had done a beautiful remodeling job.

Jake had trips to California, Detroit, and Miami that week. Between trips we made arrangements to buy the house, with closing date the end of May. Jake's busy schedule those first weeks left me alone in the apartment for days on end. Though I felt detached from people, I wrote letters, journaled, read, and quilted. I found an inspiring 24-hour Christian TV station from California and watched as I worked on my quilt.

I loved taking walks, sometimes to the strip mall a mile away. The incredible climate lifted my spirits, blue skies with not a cloud in sight, temperatures in the 70s, and 7% humidity. I praised God for bringing us to this amazing place. Two and a half million people lived in the vibrant sprawl of the metropolis, comprised of 17 joined cities. I learned that Phoenix has sunshine 86% of the time, with rainy, cloudy weather 14%.

I eagerly awaited Easter and Janet and Jared's visits. Janet, arriving a day before Jared, loved Phoenix from the minute she stepped off the plane. "This is neat!" she exclaimed, "I saw a palm tree! It seems like a tropical climate, different from any place I've ever been!" (She forgot our short visit to the Mediterranean coast of France.) She exuded over the balmy weather, palms, and varieties of trees. Never in our travels around the country, Canada, or Europe had I seen her so excited about a place. She was extremely happy to be "home" with her family, despite the small apartment.

On Saturday, we went to see our new house-to-be at Vince and Estelle's. At first sight of it, Jared complained to me, "This house is too small. You'll have to buy another one in a year or so. You'll never get all our furniture in. You should have a bigger house. You deserve it!"

I couldn't believe this foolish talk and replied, "I *like* this house! And our furniture will fit in fine." Our large Lynden house and the two floors at Hesston had spoiled him. He forgot *he* wouldn't be living here! Actually, I was surprised and touched by his fierce defense of his mother, his concern of wanting the best for me. He was a dear son.

After we left, Janet said, "The house is really nice. I like it." Her more mature assessment and approval blessed me.

We showed the children the sights of the big city and surrounding towns, such as Carefree where Hugh Downs and other famous people lived. The fancy malls, the unfinished Phoenician Resort and the elegant ACC hangar, the cacti, all duly impressed them. We drove up Scottsdale Road past the Arabian horse farms for Janet's benefit. And we dined atop the hill at Rustler's Roost, overlooking Sky Harbor Airport.

When the children and Jake left, I felt lonely and isolated in the apartment. I looked forward to a trip to my family in Pennsylvania in April and a stay with Jared at Hesston. Jake had a two-day trip to Florida and got home in time for us to have a special evening together before my trip. He took me to the Marriott Hotel for dinner outside by the pool. This rare date in the beautiful climate seemed an enchanted evening. The next afternoon, Sunday, he left for St. Louis, to return on Thursday evening, the day of my flight to Pennsylvania.

The morning I left, the taxi picked me up at 6:50 for the 12-minute ride to the airport. I would be gone two weeks, so we'd have a three-week separation this time. It reminded me of the Saudi job. Jake had time alone in the apartment and complained to me on the phone about his time off. "I thought you liked having time off," I said. "It's like being retired!"

His words warmed my heart, "I like being off when you're *here*, but not when you're gone!" Those were my sentiments exactly; the shoe was on the other foot.

My time in Quakertown afforded wonderful visits with family, Mrs. Renninger, and people from church. I visited Frank and Helena Milz, my former Sunday school teachers, and told them our family history, beginning with Daddy's birth to an unwed mother, and our growing up with Mom. Mom had told us "Don't go over to the church and talk about me." So we didn't, and they knew almost nothing about our life with her.

Frank was a small man, caring and tenderhearted. As I spoke, he fought back tears at times and his emotions showed on his face. They both were interested and asked questions. They also shared about themselves and their daughter. When I left, Frank stood near the door and I hugged him. He kissed me and looked as though he would cry. This empathy from someone I had loved and respected as a model believer touched me deeply. All the time we were growing up, we three girls suffered alone. No one outside the house knew of our plight, except Mom's family and perhaps a few others, as they visited and observed. Our loving church family had provided an oasis of support, kindness, and encouragement that we sorely needed. This devout couple's listening and understanding was a blessing. Visits with each sibling and their families brought me up to date with them and I relished this time at "home." I felt I had an advantage over the others in the family because they rarely visited each other, except for quarterly gatherings with the whole family, which I often missed. When I came home I liked to visit each one, often one-on-one.

From Pennsylvania I flew to Hesston for a good week with Jared and friends. Jared and I drove to Kansas State University in Manhattan where he registered for the fall term and signed up to stay at House of Shalom, a Mennonite dorm. Hearing an address by Speaker of the House Jim Wright added spice to our day. I left Hesston knowing I'd be back in two weeks to pack, clean, and move out of the house. Five years full of living here and the children's college experiences were tucked away in our memories.

When I returned to Phoenix, Jake was in New York City. A taxi took me to the empty apartment. How my life had changed! I was grateful for Jake's good job of keeping in touch by phone. He was concerned about not being off for the Hesston move.

Jake took me to the airport on May 12. The next weeks were busy with sorting and packing special and fragile things and time with Jared. When I told him about my trip to Pennsylvania he said, "We should go there again. We always have so much fun out there!" His wish did not materialize for many years.

Fortunately, Jake was free for the last weekend at the house. Janet and Rosanne came from Beatrice. We attended the college graduations of Jared's friends – Dave Andre and Candi Fiorillo from Massachusetts. Dave's mother and Candi's parents came for the occasion and visited in our home on Sunday. They were grateful for the home away from home we had provided for Dave and Candi. Later, Dave and his mother helped celebrate Jared's birthday with us, enjoying a sweet chocolate pie. (After we moved to Phoenix, Dave told Jared he dreamed about my pies.)

Jake helped greatly with wrapping things up at the house before leaving on Sunday. On Monday, three women came to pack – on Jared's 21st birthday, May 23. Tuesday morning excitement mounted when the huge moving van pulled up to the curb. Jared moved his belongings to the basement apartment of college professor Hugo Boschmann, where he lived for the summer. That afternoon, my seminary friend, Estelle Enns from Ontario, came to town. Jared picked her up at 5:30 as the truck was loaded, ready to go. Estelle and I had dinner at the Colonial House and returned to Newton. That evening Jared and I organized his apartment. Before I drifted off to sleep on my sleeping bag, I was gripped by a deep feeling of gratitude to God for this house and the wonderful friends we had in this special town.

The next day Jared took me to the airport after work. I arrived in Phoenix at 6:40 and took a taxi. Jake returned from his trip a couple of hours later. What a life! While wanting my husband at home, I was forced to be independent whether I liked it or not.

But if I thought my lot in life was bad, Jake's was worse. He wearily broke the news to me. "I have to leave tomorrow morning for Memorial Day weekend to fly the Keating family to Traverse City, Michigan and wait there with the plane, in case something happens. Sunday night a relief pilot will fly in for me and I'll take an airliner to Savannah for a week at FlightSafety on the Gulfstream. I won't get back until June 4, after you're in the house!" He was extremely disappointed that he'd miss the moving van and I would move into the house alone. It became clear that summer and holidays would be Jake's times away because Charlie Keating and family liked to get out of HOT Phoenix.

"Then I'll have about a week at home before I leave for Europe for three weeks!" Jake finished dejectedly.

"Will things ever slow down for you?" I asked. Then remembered, "I'm sure glad Jared is coming the end of June for two weeks. He's really anxious to come out again." I wondered how long Jake would be happy with this job and being gone when the family got together. We packed all we could in the apartment for me to take to the house the next day.

One of the many Gulfstream business jets Jake flew for 25 years worldwide.

After Jake left the next morning I took a carload to the house and then shopped for a refrigerator, washer, and dryer. Jake helped by phone with my selections. On Friday, May 27, I emptied the apartment and moved to the house with the things we had brought in our car. A sleeping bag was my bed the first few nights.

For weeks I had dreaded moving in alone, since we had only a carport, and the door into the house had a window in the top half. Watching local TV news with break-ins, rapes, and murders sent shivers down my spine. That small window made me feel vulnerable. Jake agreed we could enclose the carport. However, God had prepared me to trust Him through testimonies of God's faithfulness on TV. People shared about visions, angels, and incredible answers to prayer that bolstered my faith.

The night I moved in, I was not afraid. As I lay down in my sleeping bag, I asked God to put His angels at the four corners of the house. The strong impression came clearly: *My angels are at the four corners of this house!* Overcome with awe, I repeated the beautiful words over and over and prayed the angels would be there all night. Thanking God again and again for His protection, I *knew* with absolute certainty the angels were there, and I slept like a baby.

Those first days, with Jake gone, I loved the early morning hours on the back patio, drinking in the beauty of this little piece of God's earth He had given us to enjoy. Birds sang and hummingbirds darted back and forth to the feeder the Kraybills had left by the patio. We were three blocks from a main thoroughfare but the neighborhood was so quiet I hardly knew this was Phoenix.

On Monday, Memorial Day, the moving van driver called that he had arrived in Phoenix and would come the next day. Tuesday morning I was greatly encouraged when Vince Kraybill arrived to help. His cheerfulness made the day enjoyable as we put things in place. God had provided. When Jake returned, he asked David Hostetler from church to enclose the carport, with many cupboards for storage. Jake helped as time permitted. And Jared was right—our furniture did not all fit in, but we didn't need it all and sold it or gave it away.

This was the twenty-first place we lived in during 27 years of marriage. I was thrilled that we lived on Augusta Avenue, my grandmother Herstine's name. I had never met anyone except Cousin Ethel who knew Augusta. But brother Ralph told me that Mary Geissinger (whose daughter I knew) knew our father and grandmother. I wrote to Mary at her retirement home. In June her letter came. She wrote: "I read your article in *Window to Mission*, with your picture. You look just like your grandmother Augusta. I have seen all of your sisters and you are the only one who looks like your grandmother. Look in the mirror and you will see what she looked like."

How interesting to learn this from someone who knew Grandmother Augusta who died before I was born. I was amazed that God revealed to me something I never dreamed I could know. God had led us to the perfect house on the right street.

But what would I do with all my time here while Jake was away? I prayed God would show me and make His will clear. I was 53, with many good years ahead to serve God. And Arizona was just waiting to be explored!

CHAPTER 41

An Abrupt End

Come to Me, all you who labor and are heavy laden,
and I will give you rest.
MATTHEW 11:28-29 (NKJ)

1988–1989

When Jake returned from Savannah, we unpacked and organized in earnest. Jake was happy that the trip to Europe was postponed a week. On June 21, he took off to Switzerland, Yugoslavia, France, and Syria. He called me from Damascus one evening, ready to leave for Geneva. Meanwhile at home a big storm blew in that evening after a 108-degree day. My first monsoon season had begun!

Jared came on June 25 and while Jake relaxed at the beautiful beaches at Nice on the Mediterranean coast, Jared and I traveled around the valley and north to Sedona red rock country. We went to pools at gorgeous resorts, since our neighbor told me, "No one comes here in summer and the resorts like people to come and swim. My son and I go there." I felt out of place, but Jared loved the cool pools. One night we hadn't walked a block before he complained, "It's too hot out here!" We headed back and checked the thermometer–90 degrees at 10:00! That July proved to be the hottest on record in Phoenix. (On June 26, 1991, a record 122 degrees shut down the airport.)

Jared sorted through his boxes and I showed him some of my writing from my correspondence course. He appreciated the graders' glowing comments with superlatives to describe my stories, and the comment, "Don't let anyone change your style!" His enjoyment and affirmation blessed me. He was a good companion with his unassuming nature, sense of humor, and quiet interest.

Jake flew on to London, then Ireland, and arrived back the day Jared was to leave. We picked him up at the Keating hangar. I will never forget the look on Jake's face as he exited the Gulfstream. He greeted us with the most dazzling smile I had ever seen on his face. I shook hands with Mrs. Keating and saw Charlie for the first time. Jake had missed Jared's two-week visit, but relished a few good hours with him that day.

In July Jake and I took a two-day trip to the Grand Canyon for the first time and visited Montezuma's Castle near Flagstaff, with Indian ruins high in a cliff. These wonders of God's creation and ancient Indian peoples amazed us.

Later that summer, Jared prepared to move to K-State in Manhattan on August 19. Janet was four hours from Hesston in Nebraska. We were a thousand miles away, and I felt for Jared starting off alone. The morning of the 18th, Jake called me from the hangar. "I'm leaving for a trip to Wichita overnight. I'll drive up to Hesston to be with Jared before he leaves for school tomorrow." Father and son had lunch together the next day then Jake helped Jared pack his apartment and saw him off. I marveled again at God's leading and perfect timing.

Our church was a few short blocks from our house and I felt like we were living in its "shadow," the way I grew up at home—a comfort in this big metropolis. Church work had been my life and over the years I enjoyed working with more than 20 pastors and church administrators. At Trinity, I agreed to lead a women's Bible study in the fall and serve on the Sunday night committee. This group decided to have persons share their spiritual journeys and asked me to be first. After that I also gave it at Sunnyslope Mennonite Church in Phoenix and at the women's prayer breakfast at Glencroft Retirement Center.

While I did my little bit at the church, Jake was up to his neck with Charlie Keating's company. The more I heard about the company—the lavish spending and gigantic real estate ventures—the more I wondered where he got all his money. In August, Jake got a copy of the oversized *Tucson City Magazine* with a huge picture of Keating on the cover, sitting at his desk with a wide smile. The long article described in detail the man, his extravagant lifestyle, and company. He was called "the biggest player Tucson has seen since Howard Hughes;" "maybe the biggest tycoon in Arizona, building the world's fanciest hotel;" "at war with the federal bureaucracy." He owned Lincoln Savings and Loan (S&L) in California, which fed his building projects, and his flight department boasted a BAC 1-11 (British airliner), a Gulfstream II, a Sabreliner, and a helicopter.

Keating provided support for many commendable activities: flying and funding Mother Teresa, getting the Pope to Phoenix (Jake was in Phoenix at the time, and saw the Pope's entourage go by), and the $500 a plate Children's Ball each Christmas to raise money for the fight against pornography. (The article stated that his passion for fighting pornography stemmed from the fact that one of his five daughters was kidnapped at gunpoint and brutally raped in broad daylight in Cincinnati in the early 1970s.) Jake had flown several trips to Yugoslavia to the church and site where, for several years, children saw sightings of the Virgin Mary. As Catholics, the Keating family loved to visit this sacred place.

At the same time, this powerful man fought with Washington regulators who tried to catch him on shady financial deals and junk bonds with Lincoln S&L. After Reagan's deregulation of S&Ls, federal officials worked to tighten the rules and Keating fought ferociously. The "feds" began a lengthy examination of Lincoln in 1987. According to the article, they "took one look and had the bureaucratic equivalent of a coronary." In May of 1988, as Jake was flying him around the world, Keating won the "biggest victory in memory of a banker over the watchdogs." But the watchdogs did not give up.

Keating hired people with a positive attitude—young, attractive, "wholesome all-American types," who followed his instructions perfectly. If they didn't work out, he fired them *fast*.

In the midst of the turmoil with the company, my sister Ruth called me in early August, very excited. "We found a house in Slatington (from where my stepmother hailed) and we'll be moving in a few weeks. Come and help us move!" I didn't need to think twice.

"Okay! I'd love to!" Ruth and Dave were living in a small cabin in the Pocono Mountains with their daughter, Karlene, and wanted to move back to civilization. I flew out and had a great week. Others in the family came to help on moving day.

Later that week, Jake called. "I have a trip to Newark tomorrow and may come to Slatington. Give me directions to Ruth's house." He arrived the next afternoon. He and I took a walk at the small Slatington Airport, across the street and down a short lane from their house. Ruth's daughter April was married to Mike DelBorello and we visited them, as well as brother Tom and Debby. Then Jake left for Newark. Another serendipity!

Home in Phoenix, we attended a "sneak preview" and cookout at the Phoenician Resort, which Keating was building on the side of Camelback Mountain. He had a side of the mountain blown off so his lavish, 600-room, $300 million hotel could be nestled into it. In Phoenix, on Camelback Road – with a more prestigious Scottsdale address that Keating requested – it was due to open in October of 1988, but was behind schedule.

On September 11, Charlie hosted a giant hamburger fry on the unfinished front lawn of the hotel for about 1000 employees. We attended along with the other pilot couples. After the cookout, attractive young employees acted as tour guides and took us through the hotel, the casitas (apartments), grand ballroom, multimedia theatre, and much more. We learned that all the rooms had 100% wool carpets since wool is fire retardant. Rooms cost $200-300 a night. The presidential suites went for $2500 a night. (Charlie had his headquarters in one.) Our guide escorted us around the grounds, through the amazing cactus garden behind the hotel, to the necklace lagoon, the five pools, and explained and answered questions. It seemed that no question was off limits. Having heard rumors, I asked, "Is American Continental the sole owner of the Phoenician?" The pert young woman answered, "No, Kuwait owns 51%!" Kuwait! Charlie was a high flyer and knew how to cut a deal.

Furnishings in the hotel were from Mexico and Europe, where Jake had flown Mrs. Keating, her daughters, and the interior decorator. Two marble grand staircases came from Italy, plus Italian chandeliers with 1000 tiny lights in each. The grounds and landscaping, already finished, were beautiful, with queen and other palms and bright red bougainvillea. Jake had flown a palm tree nursery supervisor and his family from Florida to Phoenix several times, as orders were placed for the palms. More than five hundred tall palms were hauled on semis all the way from Florida.

In addition to the Phoenician, Keating was building Estrella, a development for 200,000 southwest of Phoenix, which he believed would fill up with Californians eager to flee their crowded, unsafe state of gangs, riots, fires, and earthquakes. We had taken the children to Estrella to see the lakes lined with beautiful queen palms waving in the breeze. Houses were just being built. Keating also had major development plans in Tucson. It seemed excessive and obscene. But the great beauty and opulence of the Phoenician mesmerized me and in years to come I gave our out-of-state guests the "grand tour."

While Jake kept busy flying Mr. Keating, I received a new assignment. Jake's father called to say, "I'm working on my second book and wondered if you would type it for me again?" I began in mid-October, a pleasant diversion from which I learned more of Jake's family history.

Since coming to Phoenix, I admired the queen palms with their long, arched fronds. I wanted some for our house and we planted two in October, where they graced our front lawn, adding a Southwest touch.

We regularly kept in touch with our children and were glad Jared was enjoying K-State with no complaints. Janet's grueling VS job with sexually abused and neglected children became more harrowing when her co-worker was fired on trumped-up charges. Janet was devastated. As if her work wasn't tough enough, investigating and testifying for children, she now had to testify in court on behalf of her friend. When the day came, she waited from 1:00 until 6:00 P.M. then testified for ten minutes. She was the only one to testify. Her friend was exonerated, but after her unfair treatment, she resigned. Janet missed her greatly. In December, Janet applied to the University of Missouri to work on her master's degree in counseling psychology when her two years of VS ended in summer.

By December, things were heating up for Charlie Keating. Jake flew him on many trips to California. On December 12, *Forbes Magazine* published an article that accused American Continental of being $100 million in the red, despite Charlie's claims that all was well. On December 19, the day Janet and Jared arrived home for Christmas, Jake left for California at 11:30 P.M. and returned at 2:30 in the morning. The next day he learned that Keating had sold Lincoln S&L and the Fiesta Mall in Mesa—alarming news to the pilots. That day, instead of the usual generous Christmas bonus, the pilots received a $100 gift certificate for the Mary Elaine French Restaurant at the Phoenician. The pilots knew the company was in trouble. God was showing us the folly of materialism, wealth, and greed.

The Mary Elaine Restaurant on the top floor of the hotel was named for Keating's wife. Before the hotel and restaurant opened, they served dinners to groups of "guinea pigs" to insure perfection. The pilots and wives were invited for dinner on December 1, and what an elegant setting and dinner that was! Waiters in black tuxes and ties served us whatever we desired at no charge. The six at our table rang up a bill of $425! I ordered duck at $22, and we shared five desserts around the table. A $100 gift certificate to this place was fine with me. We treated Janet and Jared at Christmas, beginning with soup and ending with dessert. Jake had to fork over $50, but the children enjoyed the exotic experience. It was a joy to have them home, and for seven whole days, Jake did not have a trip.

On Christmas Eve we called Jake's dad and all of us talked with him. He was happy that his book was ready three days before Christmas.

Jake spent the last four days of 1988 in New York City. Then on January 3, he told me that Keating had sold Estrella, another huge blow to the company and its employees. From then on, Keating kept a maddening schedule for the pilots as he fought furiously to save his company. Jake left for Europe January 15 and was gone 24 days straight, mostly in Nice, France, and in London, where Keating tried to secure financing from wealthy Arabs.

On March 2, Jake called from a trip to Dallas and Washington D.C. to say that Keating was being investigated for fraud. For 18 days straight Jake was gone – flying back and forth across the country from California to New York and Washington – where Keating battled the regulators.

On April 11, Jake was scheduled for a trip to Cincinnati and Washington. Instead he returned from Cincinnati. That evening, Steve, the aviation manager, told Jake, "An announcement is coming." The next day, the bombshell hit: American Continental had filed for bankruptcy. TV stations quickly spread the news of Charlie's misfortunes. We watched for days to learn the latest developments.

Jake called John Caruso, his former boss at Kaiser in Vancouver. Kaiser had a company in Oakland, California where Jake phoned and got an appointment for April 21. Though he had not officially lost his job, he wanted to check things out in case the company collapsed. At the ACC hangar a grim-faced Steve called Jake into the office. "It doesn't look good. Things could happen a lot faster than we think." Jake told him about the Oakland appointment and Steve said, "Go for it!"

We drove to Oakland where Jake saw the chief pilot and filled out an application. That afternoon, Jake called the hangar in Phoenix. The secretary broke the news, "The pilots all received their last paycheck today, except for Dave and Mike who have the most seniority. They will stay on a while longer for the Sabreliner. CIII (Keating's son) was in the hangar Wednesday morning and shook hands with all the pilots. He looked very down." She finished, "I'm sorry, but you no longer have a job."

What a blow! Jake's dream "retirement job" had come to an abrupt end. It lasted exactly one year, one month, and six days. So what would we do now? What was God trying to tell us?

One report said that Arizona was the top in employment in the country in 1987. Now, a year later, it was second from the bottom. The real estate market had crashed, adding to Keating's woes. The national unemployment rate was 5%, Phoenix, 6%.

Jake continued going to the ACC hangar to talk with Steve and the other pilots until April 28. That morning when he came out for breakfast, he said to me, "Well, this is the end – my last day at the hangar. They're changing all the locks on the doors today."

"What will you do with yourself all day without a job?" I queried.

"I'll make a call every day and listen to my motivation tapes every day…" He went on with a long list he had in mind. He would not rest until he found a job.

Keating held on to his two hotels, the Phoenician and Crescent, for several more months as the investigation continued. Then on November 16, 1989, federal agents seized the hotels at 2:00 A.M. while the guests slept, oblivious to the changeover. Keating's financial empire had totally collapsed. Nine months later, on August 24, 1990, Keating made news again when he and five aides resigned from American Continental Corporation. He announced that he would defend himself against the charges. A year later, his trial concluded on December 4, 1991. He was found guilty on 17 of 18 state and federal charges of racketeering, fraud, and conspiracy.

The collapse of Lincoln Savings and Loan in California left many investors in ruin. Heartbreaking stories of elderly people who lost their life savings enraged the public. In April 1992, Keating was sentenced to ten years in prison, a sad ending to his illustrious career.

While he was in prison his lawyers battled for his release. Jake and Steve, former aviation head, visited him in prison in Tucson. Keating seemed as upbeat as ever, confident his lawyers would get him off. Other reports indicated he was very depressed. In 1996, after more than four years behind bars, the convictions were overturned and Keating was free on his 74th birthday. However, he still faced a $3 billion civil judgment against him. Undaunted, he began new business ventures, including seminars advising Certified Public Accountants and investors where to put their money – in microchips.

Now Jake was without a job. I prayed that if the Lord wanted us in Oakland I'd be willing to move there, but if it was not His will, He would shut the door. The door closed. Thus began a long wait, with no health insurance or income, while Jake called and applied to any and all leads. Our good health was a blessing.

After the first difficult months, part-time flying jobs kept us afloat, but Jake could not be happy for long just getting by. Knowing that our security is not in a job, but in God, I prayed for Jake and hoped something would turn up. Tycoon Charlie Keating had given Jake, and thousands of other people, a very hard landing. The fallout would continue for a long time. Where would Jake find work now?

CHAPTER 42

A Remarkable Guest

The righteous shall flourish like the palm tree...
they still bring forth fruit in old age.
PSALM 92:12,14 (RSV)

1988–1989

During our first year in Phoenix, we sometimes had guests during Jake's frequent, lengthy absences. Though Jake missed time with them I thrived on their company. Early on, someone at church told us "Family and acquaintances will all come to visit you here the first year." How true. Phoenix was definitely a tourist attraction. In November, Sara and Larry Van Meter came from Vincennes as well as Jake's boyhood friend, Jake Koop and wife Ursula, from British Columbia. I was grateful that Jake was home for most of their visits.

In early January 1989, while Jake still worked for Keating, Jim and Ruby Graber came from Hesston, with Troy and Baby Sara. Seven-year-old Troy wanted to see the desert and loved everything he saw and did. We climbed part way up 2300-foot Squaw Peak (now Piestewa), and took them to parks, resorts, the sand castles at a mall, and the Phoenician. Jake was home for most of that enjoyable time.

The end of January I was thrilled when my niece Brenda, Millie and Ralph's daughter, came. Jake missed her visit but she and I had a great time seeing sights around the Valley. She enjoyed the amazing sandcastles and we shopped at Metro Center. We climbed Squaw Peak to the top where we met Mennonite girls, distinguished by their prayer coverings, and I had one of them take our picture. Feeling like a guide myself since the sneak preview, I gave Brenda the grand tour of the Phoenician where she took many pictures. I snapped wherever she did and got beautiful shots.

Brenda appreciated a favorite place of mine, Canaan in the Desert, retreat center and prayer garden of the Evangelical Sisterhood of Mary, a Lutheran group from Germany. As an evangelical outreach, it has similar centers in 25 locations worldwide. We visited Sedona, and at Fountain Hills we saw the tall fountain in the lake with colored lights by night. We ate out and on our patio and had great sharing times and laughter. I also enjoyed taking her to our church. Before she left, Brenda gave me *Gift From the Sea* by Anne Morrow Lindbergh. In it she wrote, "I enjoyed everything we did and talked about." We missed Jake, who was stuck in London the whole time.

Brenda and me at church, January 1989.

Jake got back from 24 days in Europe the day his brother Peter and wife Mary came. Perfect timing! He had several days with them, celebrating Peter's and my birthdays and their anniversary. They enjoyed the sights and the posh Phoenician, especially the extensive cactus garden and handsome Indian sculptures gracing the grounds. One day when Jake was gone, Peter climbed Squaw Peak and met Amish men in black garb and broad-brimmed hats, women in long dresses, climbing as well. As they came down the mountain, Mary and I watched the unusual sight of our "cousins" in the faith enjoying the same outdoor recreation that we do. Peter and Mary taught us new games, which we played with many a hearty laugh.

On March 6, while Jake was gone to Dallas and Washington, D.C., his father arrived for three weeks. Not knowing what to expect, I had asked the Bible study group to pray for me as I spent time with Dad. I needed wisdom to know what to say about things he shared since we would spend considerable time together. Jake and I had six parents between us, and Dad was the last one left. Since I typed his two books, he was special to me and I looked forward to his visit.

Jake called me with Dad's flight information. "His flight number is 606," he said.

"That's exciting! Praise the Lord!" Jake knew what I meant because 606 was the hymnal number for the long version of "Praise God From Whom All Blessings Flow." Known as "the Mennonite hymn" and short for "Praise the Lord" I took that as a good sign.

However, I was totally unprepared for the man I met getting off the plane. The flight number had done him no good. His face was dour and his demeanor depressed. A normally friendly man and pleasant to me, he did not smile. This was so uncharacteristic that I wondered if Dad was upset that Jake wasn't there and he was stuck with me. But never mind, I gave him a hug and told him I was glad to see him, which I was. But my heart rose up in a cry, *"Help!"*

As we drove home, he complained bitterly, "I often wonder why I'm still here. I outlived two wives and I think God should have taken me, too." He seemed downright angry. I could hardly believe his sour mood and prayed fervently for him and for God's help. He definitely was not himself. I remembered that it is not uncommon for ministers to become depressed in their older retired years. Dad needed a lot of tender loving care.

Later that day, I took from the shelf Henri Nouwen's book, *The Way of The Heart*, and gave it to him. "This is a really good book," I said. "A Hesston College professor has all his students read it." He loved to read and I knew it would do his heart good. He started on it that same day and I prayed the Lord would speak to him through it.

I genuinely loved my father-in-law and from his two books I felt I understood him quite well. Through the years, I had learned to accept his critical insinuations and prayed for God to forgive him and help me forgive him. He had lived through tremendous heartbreaks and overwhelming trials, yet his faith had brought him through. With his enviable record of over 50 years in ministry and evangelistic work all over British Columbia and beyond, I knew he had led many people to the Lord. But now, a few weeks from turning 88 (on April 15), he felt useless.

I showed Dad around our house, the patio, and yard. He spotted the old rocking chair on the patio. "I have so much pain in my legs," he said. "I think I'll sit here in the sun a while." That became one of his favorite places to sit every day, where he drank in the peace and beauty of our back yard and watched the hummingbirds. There the sun did its healing work on his legs.

In two days Jake got home, but only for a day. He mowed the lawn, tried to catch up on things and spent time with Dad. We were all grateful for this time with each other. Then Jake flew back to Washington, where he practically lived these days.

Dad had a habit of regular Bible reading and prayer and so I wanted to include him in my devotions at breakfast. One of us read the devotional book and one the Bible passage and we took turns praying at each meal. I prayed for Dad's health, for Jake and the children, and Dad's family. He brought his fervent requests to the Lord as well. This became a time of rich fellowship and sharing and he opened up about family concerns that were on his heart. God's presence seemed to hover over us like a mantle. How grateful I was that, as the days went by, Dad lightened up.

A week after he arrived, with a big smile on his face, Dad held up Nouwen's little book and said, *"Now I know why I'm still here! I can still counsel people!"* What a joy it was to hear those words! I was positive the book would have that effect on him because it told about the desert fathers in the early centuries who lived in isolation for 20 years, then reentered society with a powerful counseling and healing ministry. Dad had counseled people for years and could see himself in these ancient saints. It was a wonderful answer to prayer and a miraculous transformation. My heart lifted to God in praise and thanksgiving.

Aunt Melba Landis had given me several of Pappy Landis' German devotional books and hymnbooks, which I showed to Dad. He loved them and often sat taking notes from them. It blessed me to think he appreciated my grandfather's books.

It was fun getting out of the house with Dad and showing him around. We saw the unique storybook sandcastles and went to Canaan in the Desert, which he loved. He enjoyed talking with the workers in German and seeing videos of the miraculous way God had led in building the first center in Germany, after WWII, and the ministry's impact around the world.

On a couple of days we visited people, including Peter and Myrtle Friesen, whom he remembered from Hesston. A favorite activity was going to parks, which we did often during those three weeks. Dad especially enjoyed Saguaro Park with the peacocks. One day I packed a picnic lunch. As we ate, the peacocks felt invited and climbed onto our table! Dad laughed and I got good pictures.

On a day at the zoo we had a leisurely stroll and 30-minute train ride on a beautiful March day. Then we ate lunch at another park. That evening our small group from church met at our house and Dad enjoyed meeting the people and participating. Later, as he was ready to go to bed, he stopped in the kitchen. He looked at me with a broad smile and said, *"You shove new life into me!"* Then he added with a twinkle in his eye, "I'll be spoiled after I leave here."

I could hardly believe these words coming from this reserved man. I gave him a hug and said, "I really enjoy doing things with you, Dad, and am so glad you came. You're good company when Jake is gone." We got along famously and I praised the Lord for blessing me beyond measure with a fine father-in-law. With my love of the church, pastors, and evangelists, we had much in common.

Since Jake was gone and the grass needed cutting every week, it grew quite long so I hired a young fellow from church to mow. From the time we lived in Vincennes, a grass allergy kept me inside on mowing days. Dad watched as the young man mowed and commented, "Jake mows very fast and this boy very slowly." Almost everything Jake did was at top speed. (Later I wrote a poem called "My Jet-Speed Husband.") Plus, the grass was so tall that it slowed this fellow down.

Dad missed Jake and the children and said one day, "I have really been thinking about Janet and Jared today."

I said, "Doesn't it seem like they should be here?"

"Yes," he said, "I've been thinking of them so much. Can you get me cards for them and I'll send them each one."

Jake called to say he'd probably be home on the weekend. Dad said at suppertime, "I've really been thinking of Jake today and that he has to stay there all week alone." We were delighted when he came Friday night. On Saturday we toured the Phoenician and went to visit Dad's second wife's relatives, Russell and Leona Ward, from Canada, who were staying in Mesa. Leona told us, "Someone said they were so astonished at how backward Canada was when they came from Russia in the twenties." Dad and Mother Friesen had come in 1925 to the barren prairies of Saskatchewan and experienced harsh pioneer conditions, plus ridicule about their language. Their faith was severely tested.

On Sunday morning, Jake attended church and a chili dinner there with us. Then he left for New York City and Washington, D. C. with Mr. Keating. The next week I invited the Wards for lunch and great fellowship.

One morning at breakfast Dad said, "People used to get so angry at me for pushing English in the church. Other churches in Langley filled up with

Mennonites who spoke English and we lost a lot of people." Jake had told me that Dad was progressive in this way.

Dad continued, "I figure the English are way ahead of the Germans. They learned how to say 'Excuse me' and 'I'm sorry.' We never learned how to do that." *What a shame*, I thought, *to never learn common courtesies*. His confession and acknowledgement of this weakness impressed me.

Another time he surprised me with his candor. "The older I get the stingier I get. I want to save everything for missions. Even though God told me, 'This is all love,' I thought I would always feel loving, but I don't. I'm still tempted sometimes not to love someone."

"I think this is common to everyone," I empathized. He was hard on himself because he was a minister and therefore also hard on others.

"I've been too critical," he admitted. "Some people don't want to see me or talk to me when they see me coming because they know I'll talk to them about the Lord."

One Sunday night we went to prayer meeting at church. Our Pastor, Peter Wiebe, gave a meditation and Maribeth Troyer, the church secretary, was worship leader. There was time for anyone to share or pray. Dad stood up and told about his life and hardships and gave a testimony. He also said some nice things about me, which warmed my heart.

Later at home Dad asked, "Who was that woman in charge? Was she the minister's wife?" I was surprised because she was a young woman and Pastor Wiebe an older man.

My response nearly blew him away. "No, she's the church secretary." This was unheard of in his church. Maribeth had led the meeting with such ease, prayed a beautiful prayer, and spoke of Jesus with such love and reverence. Dad could hardly believe it.

"I still have too much to do with tradition," he admitted. That was understandable from his background, and a statement he had often made to me.

At the women's Bible study that week, one woman said, "I thought it was so neat how your father-in-law shared in church on Sunday night. That was a real tribute to you." The others agreed and I felt blessed. They had prayed for me and then saw the answer to all of our prayers.

Several times those weeks Dad told about women back home that he prays with and how he tells them they need to pray. "They refuse," he told me. "They say, 'I can't.' In Russia they were told not to share their faith and now they can't." What a tragedy. Czarina Catherine the Great had invited the expert Mennonite farmers to come and farm, provided they did not proselytize. They promised they would not. This heart-wrenching fact about the Mennonite era in Russia took a heavy toll on the faith and joy of these believers.

Jake called every day to let us know of his whereabouts and to see how we were doing. He had only been home two and one-half days so far. While we waited and hoped for him to come home, he called from New York one day and said, "I'm being transferred to the Antigua trip." I learned that was in the Caribbean. What an exotic spot! Jake explained, "Dave (the other pilot) was sent back to the BAC 1-11 (British airliner) in NYC and Steve doesn't trust one of the pilots on the Gulfstream because he talks too much to the passengers. That's the 'good news.' But the bad news is, I'll be gone possibly till Easter, maybe even until Monday when Dad leaves." Dad would not be happy.

While I groaned inwardly, I was prepared for anything. I explained to Dad. Later I wrote in my journal, "Father, I've had the feeling that You have some purpose in allowing Jake to be gone so long this time." As Dad had said thoughtfully, "It's nobody's fault."

But when Dad got up the next morning – a week before he left – he said, "I didn't sleep very well last night. I really want Jake to get home before I go back. I want to have a prayer with you both before I go home. You better pray that he gets back!" It was a command and he was not smiling. I was beginning to think this was my fault! But that was nonsense. We both continued to pray Jake would be home soon.

Dad talked constantly about money – wasting money, spending too much money, and being stingy. He could be very negative about many things. I prayed for grace to overlook these irritants. He said, "I see now that I grew up as an orphan." His mother had died when he was four, as mine had when I was three. We had this in common. Later he had a stepmother, then his father sent him to live with his step aunt and uncle when he was ten years old. There he was made to work in the fields *in bare feet* and the stubble cut and bloodied them. He cried and cried from pain, but also because the horses were too big for him to manage. Yet his uncle drove him, saying at meal times, "Eat now, chew later!" My heart ached for the little boy in him that still hurt.

Dad shared other painful memories. "I buried two wives and I never held their hands when they were dying. It would have helped them so much if I had held their hands!" (I wondered if he learned that from *The Blessing*, by Gary Smalley, which we had given him some time before.) He had many regrets. His life had been extremely hard, but in spite of that God gave him an amazing, fruitful ministry. Dad had detailed it all in his two books – the Revolution in Russia, the anguished early years in Canada, and more.

One day he said, "I'm alone so much that sometimes when I start talking to someone or to a group, I can't stop. (He *had* talked a long time at our Sunday evening prayer meeting.) I figure it's old age. When I'm alone I think of all the things I've done and how the Lord used me in the lives of so many, to get them into the kingdom." He told me story after story of people saved and influenced by his ministry. He was overwhelmed with it all and marveled, "I wonder how I could have done all that!" He admitted his insecurity about his lack of theological training, adding, "I'm glad I got to be in the small group twice. It helped me to see that even if you have education you still have problems."

One day, a week before Dad left, he said, "Maybe I shouldn't say this, but there is jealousy in a big family and some of the children are jealous. They want me to like them the best. Since I'm here I feel like I've been to the hospital and was made well again!" What a wonderful work God was doing in him. "Sitting in the sun has really helped my legs," he said, "my pain is gone." I could have leaped for joy! I gave these blessings back to the Lord and praised Him for all He had done. The Valley of the Sun had had its effect.

"When I came I wasn't interested in anything," he confided. "I just wanted to rest, I was so burned out. I've really been encouraged by the Christian TV we watched and the videos." I had gotten videos at the Christian bookstore of Sandi Patti and Larnel Harris in the Holy Land, one on Steve Greene, and one on D. L. Moody. We both loved them.

In the end, Jake was gone 16 days straight, including the day Dad left. He had been home less than three days.

But in three weeks, I had learned much about Jake and the family from a different culture that had often been a mystery. Dad was honest and open and I felt the Lord put us together to enlarge my understanding about this family into which I had married. He was a good sport about leaving with Jake gone. He rejoiced that he felt so much better and thanked me for everything. Two days later, Jake returned.

Dad called a couple of weeks later and said, "I wish I were there. The weather here doesn't agree with me. It's so rainy. I should have come for five weeks. I can't sing long in church like I did there. My heart hurts when I sing." Was it the pain of being alone?

Soon after, when Jake called Dad, he said, "I recuperated there and I'm still fine." Jake was grateful and happy for the change in his Dad from his time here and sorry he couldn't enjoy more of it with us. But we told Dad he had to come again and he looked forward to that.

As I reflected on the man who arrived on March 6 and the great privilege I had to listen to his heart and his stories, his great enjoyment of the things we did, my heart overflowed with praise to the Lord for this unique man. I felt as though I had walked on holy ground in the presence of a man greatly used of the Lord. I stood amazed at the transformation I saw before my eyes, from depression to joy and delight, from pain to healing. Only the Spirit of the Lord could perform this. I thanked God for this miracle and for my remarkable guest.

Dad Friesen, March, 1989.

CHAPTER 43

A Silver Lining

If God gives a man wealth and property and lets him enjoy them,
he should be grateful and enjoy what he has worked for.
It is a gift from God.
ECCLESIASTES 5:19 (RSV)

1989–2005

The year after Jake lost his job, our mettle to endure in the metropolis of Phoenix was tested. The first three months, he flew ten days total as relief pilot for various companies. August and September saw no trips at all. Jake applied for unemployment, discouragement dogging his days. After years of flying jets, he had accumulated a list of pilots and companies with planes. Networking was the name of the game, but with a glut of pilots, jobs were scarce. Jake persisted in making phone calls. In October 1989, he began flying part-time for the owner of the Philadelphia Flyers hockey team. We were grateful for every trip.

In November that year we rejoiced over the news that the Berlin Wall had opened up. Millions of people, including Jake's dad, had prayed for years for the fall of Communism and the Wall. Thousands of East Germans were protesting, demanding freedom to leave. Thirteen thousand escaped through Hungary to Austria. While many gave credit to Reagan and Gorbachev, God was at work behind the scenes.

In Leipzig, East Germany, St. Nicholas' Church, founded 1165, played an astonishing role in the collapse of the 45-year dictatorship. My chiropractor, Dr. Lelia Schlabach and husband, visited the church and she gave me a pamphlet documenting the events. [A May 1, 2009 article on Deutch Welle website (http://www.dw-world.de/dw/article/0,,3805080,00.html), also tells the story: "Peace Prayers Helped Bring Down the Wall," quoting Christian Fuehrer, pastor of St. Nicholas Church at the time.]

Every Monday evening since 1982, more than 2,000 people, Christians and non-Christians, gathered at the church to pray for peace. Authorities exerted great pressure to stop the meetings. Beginning in May 1989, police blocked driveways to the church and arrested and brutalized many protesters. But attendance grew, the peaceful attitude spread, and thousands more came from all over the country to pray at the church.

Then on October 7, 1989, the 40th anniversary of the German Democratic Republic (GDR), police battered defenseless people for ten long hours and hauled them away on trucks. The next day, a newspaper article stated that the authorities would crush the "counter revolution" on Monday, October 9, "with whatever means necessary."

For weeks, many policemen attended the meetings and heard messages on peace and love. On October 9, 1,000 policemen were ordered to attend the prayer service to investigate. Beneath the outspread arms of the crucified and resurrected Jesus and a painting of an angel of peace above the altar, police listened in rapt attention to messages on the Sermon on the Mount and Beatitudes, many for the first time. They heard Jesus' words, *"Blessed are the poor"* and *"Love your enemies."*

That night, 6,000 to 8,000 people crammed into central Leipzig churches and 70,000 more waited outside with candles in their hands and the miracle occurred. Jesus' spirit of non-violence seized the masses and became a peaceful power. Police planned for everything but candles, for which two hands are needed – one to hold the candle, the other to protect it from the wind. No stones were thrown and the tanks did not move forward. Military troops and police were drawn in, engaged in conversations, then withdrew. It was an evening in the spirit of Jesus, ending with a tremendous feeling of relief. Pastor Fuehrer explains that the Bible taught thousands of young people the power of peaceful protest, and "the Sermon on the Mount was condensed into two words: *no violence.*"

One month later, on November 8, the Wall collapsed and the Cold War ended. Pastor Fuehrer firmly believes that the GDR would not have collapsed and the Wall would not have come down without the peace prayers. Things happened in Leipzig that happened nowhere else in the country. "In the fullness of time," God answered prayer. Our family's visit to the Wall had been somber. Now we rejoiced with the people of the Eastern bloc countries who were freed. However, on the negative side, a vacuum was created and new problems arose in a country where so many did not know Christ.

On a more personal note, Jake's brother-in-law Bert Arlitt was born in Berlin and has vivid memories of the horrors of living through that war. He left Germany in 1952, moved to Vancouver Island in 1962, and later married Jake's youngest sister Helen. In 1989, they visited Berlin with their daughter Phelia and got pictures of Bert's former homes and school. Bert had three sisters living there, and two live there at present (2009). In 2008 Bert and Helen returned to Berlin with Phelia and their son Terry. It was an emotional time for Bert and a time of healing of some memories as he shared them with his children.

In December our children came for three wonderful weeks. Dad Friesen arrived on December 31 to see in the New Year. He enjoyed seeing the children but, unfortunately, Jake had a trip the next day.

After several dry months, 1990 started well for Jake. He left on a trip to Houston, Dallas, New York, and California. Another call came for a trip to Europe in mid-January. Then the Flyers' chief pilot called to schedule a trip to the Super Bowl the end of January, followed by another with Frank Sinatra.

Jake got home for part of a day with Dad and left the next morning to Wichita. From there, he accompanied a German owner of a new Cessna Citation for ten days as they flew around Europe. What a windfall of trips for Jake! After many lean months the New Year had a silver lining.

While Jake was gone, we visited, played games, and went sightseeing with the children. Dad stayed so happy that one morning he said, "I feel happy-go-lucky!" I took him to Canaan in the Desert where he visited with Sister Ruth and told her about his two books. She exclaimed, "You made my day! May I have a copy of your books?" Dad was pleased to oblige.

The evening before the children left we enjoyed a fondue supper and surprised Janet with an early birthday celebration with her Opa Friesen. He gave her $100, showing his approval of her service in VS. The next day Janet left for Nebraska and Jared headed to Kansas, cold northland states.

We were thankful that Jake had five days at home before Dad left. On his last night, he prayed with us and then we enjoyed lemon meringue pie made with lemons from our tree. The next day he packed oranges and lemons from our trees in his suitcase. As we left for the airport Dad grinned, "I feel fine again, healthy and strong. And I gained back the ten pounds I lost!" Later, on April 2, he moved into the Menno Retirement Home in Abbotsford, B.C.

and loved it. The family breathed easier, as he often complained of pain at his heart.

Jake called Jared one day and he complained, "I *hate* Manhattan now! It's so cold and gray here!" He missed the Arizona sun, warmth of family, and the good times in our beautiful valley. Also, it was back to the daily grind of school. Some time later he reported, on a better note, "I got my grades today: four A's and one B. My grade point average is 3.8. I'm in the top 10% of my class." I commended him.

In late January, Jake enjoyed the trip to the Super Bowl in New Orleans and flying Frank Sinatra from Ft. Lauderdale to Albany, New York for the opening of a new stadium, managed by the owner of the Flyers. Old "blue eyes" was a sociable passenger who liked conversing with the pilots. In fact, he rarely sat down on a trip, but paced back and forth, peering over the pilot's shoulders. Sinatra explained that he had "walked all the way home from Australia." His restlessness probably stemmed from his mother's tragic death in a plane crash.

February, with no trips at all, was a huge letdown for Jake. He wanted a full-time job. Phil Calvert, former Keating pilot, had gone to Saudi Arabia and called Jake about their urgent need for pilots.

"I may take a job there again," Jake told me. "You could go with me this time," he grinned. This was no grinning matter! On the one hand, it was exciting to think of living in this strange land, where I would be isolated and could write to my heart's content. But I could not envision a move so far from the children – and no Christian church.

Meekly, I voiced my objection. "I prefer to stay in this country where my children are." Nevertheless, he applied. He learned on February 7 that his application was approved. My heart skipped a few beats. On February 19, Phil's wife (in the U.S.) called with the news, "Phil said to tell you 'Don't come! The wives can't stay.'" And she listed other reasons that made the job prohibitive. I was relieved.

In April Jake had his first trip for The Air Group of Van Nuys, California. Then from April 6-19, he flew for them to Acapulco, St. Martens Island, Miami, Orlando, back to Acapulco and Van Nuys. We hoped they would hire him full time, and I prayed this would happen.

However, Jake had seriously followed up on the Saudi job. While he was in Acapulco, his airline ticket to Saudi came. My heart sank. After telling Jake about it on the phone, I asked the Lord to please shut the door on this one. When he returned, he immediately sent the ticket back! "I'm not ready to accept just yet and I don't want to be pushed," he said. It appeared that he would take the Saudi job as a last resort.

The past year, I had gotten more involved at church, mentoring women who requested it. Pastor Wiebe also asked me to visit several women with special needs. Having worked with Carl at Hesston, I enjoyed learning to know his father and we shared mutual concerns about the church. One day I told him about the Saudi job. Concern clouded his face. He offered to pray with me and poured out his heartfelt request to the Lord. "Father, please lead and guide in this decision. And please let someone else tell Jake that he should not move to Saudi Arabia again, so we won't have to tell him." I was struck by his specific, brilliant request. As he prayed, a confidence and faith that I did not possess grew within me. I thanked him and left his office rejoicing, knowing that God had heard.

When Jake returned on May 31, I listened in amazement as he explained, "*The pilot I flew with told me I should not go to Saudi!* He said by the time I got back I'd be too old to find a job here. He's a retired airline pilot and he has a hard time finding work." (After mandatory retirement with the airlines at age 60, pilots may still fly corporate and charter flights.) I rejoiced and thanked God that Jake took this advice seriously. He canceled his Saudi application, a great relief for me, and our pastor.

Throughout the summer, Jake flew many trips for The Air Group. We wondered and hoped and prayed. Finally, on August 15, 1990, he called me from Savannah, Georgia with the news. "*After my interview this morning I was hired full time,* so they sent me down here to Gulfstream school." Over the phone I could sense his beaming smile.

A year and four months after losing the Keating job, Jake had a full-time job. The Air Group managed planes owned by various corporations. When not in use by the owner, others chartered them. Thus began a string of flights with famous people, including several trips with former President Ronald Reagan. Jake flew movie stars, vocalists, and rock groups unfamiliar to us. (Jared read of a documentary about the Van Nuys Airport—the busiest general aviation [non-commercial] airport in the world—home to 100 Gulfstreams plus other business jets, which are chartered by stars and other jetsetters.)

Jake flew Ronald Reagan to Tokyo, Mexico, and on an eventful trip to Las Vegas on April 13, 1992. On that trip, Jake called and told me to watch the TV news because Reagan was attacked while giving a speech. It turned out that a harmless anti-nuclear activist had rushed the stage, grabbed and smashed the crystal eagle statue Reagan had just received. He tried to make a statement but was hustled away and, a few minutes later, Reagan continued his speech to the National Association of Broadcasters. The pilots did not need to make a fast getaway as they had been alerted.

For the next 14 years, Jake flew for several Van Nuys and Scottsdale companies, full or part time, until he was 70 – in 2005. His aviation physical expired and he decided not to renew it. Known for his overseas experience and expertise, he had flown part time for many companies when one job folded or an owner sold his plane. The exotic sites and countries he flew to boggled my mind. While most people saw it as a glamorous job, flying had its down side, literally – hours of waiting for passengers, demanding, tiring schedules across many time zones, long periods away from home. He often came home exhausted or sick from 18 or more hours of flying back from Europe, Africa, Asia, Australia. Nevertheless, he loved to fly and while I objected loudly at times, he seldom complained. "Up, up and away" was the place for him.

Over the years, Jake flew such celebrities as Prince Andrew, the Duke of York; Prince Faisal of Saudi Arabia; Justice Sandra Day O'Conner of Arizona and the U.S. Supreme Court, Whoopie Goldberg; televangelist Pat Robertson; from Britain: Andrew Lloyd Weber of "Jesus Christ Superstar" and "Cats" fame; golf pros Phil Mickelson, Tom Weiskopf, and Jack Nicklaus; basketball greats Michael Jordan and Charles Barkley; Hollywood stars or singers Frank Sinatra, Sean Penn, Sylvester Stallone, Neil Diamond, Neil Young, Lionel Richie, Janet Jackson, Dolly Parton and more. He also took Elton John on a tour of all South American capitals.

Having read Jake's class prophecy from Canadian Mennonite Bible College (now University, CMU) in 1959 by President Henry Poettcker, I should not have been surprised by Jake's aviation career. The prophecy states: "Jake Friesen, of course, was the world traveler. Paris, London, Rome, Altona, or St. Catharines. Name the place and he would have been there. Mature for his years in many ways while he was in college, he nevertheless proved once again that boys will be boys." The stunning fulfillment of those words often struck me through the years. (Of course, Mr. Poettcker knew of Jake's summer of traveling around Europe and made a brilliant deduction.)

While Jake was gone for days and weeks at a time, I kept busy at the things I did best – church work, working with people, writing, and keeping close to my children and family. I was often amazed at the exciting, fulfilling relationships, events, and answers to specific prayers that filled my days. The presence and work of Christ through the Holy Spirit became more real to me than ever before.

Pastor Wiebe, knowing of my nocturnal habit of journaling, woke me with a call one Sunday morning at 7:00. (We were concerned about a certain matter that was to be aired in church that morning.) "Do you have a prayer for me this morning?" he inquired. Surprised, and still groggy, I tried to recall what happened during the night. Then I remembered.

"Yes," I said, "I was up at 3:00 and journaled a prayer for the service. Do you want me to read it to you?"

"Please." After I read it, he requested, "Would you please type that up and bring it to the service this morning?" I did, and he used part of it in his morning prayer. I was astonished that he had called me for a prayer, but even more so later when he told me, "I was so amazed at your prayer! It was *publishable!*" Peter's thoughtful, beautiful pastoral prayers had blessed *me* many times.

After VS in Nebraska, Janet moved to Columbia, Missouri to work on her Master's degree. The fall of 1990, she invited me to visit. I said, "I'd love to come when the fall colors are at their best." I flew to Kansas City in October. Jared picked me up to spend the weekend with us.

Early Saturday morning Janet took me to a stable with 24 horses where she cleaned stalls and exercised horses. On that beautiful morning I watched as she rode, glad to see her happier since leaving her stressful job. She attended a small fellowship of Mennonite and Church of the Brethren people with a fellowship meal each Sunday. There she met John Brejda, a "very tall, handsome" young man that she had told me she "could be interested in." He had taken her along on a trip to Hesston for his MCC Bangladesh reunion so she could visit friends. She wanted me to meet him. John wanted to know if she got to see her family much. She told him, "At Christmas and summer vacations and sometimes in between. But my mom is coming to see me in October because she likes the fall colors."

"Then let's go on a hike in the woods when she comes," he suggested. I was intrigued.

"He likes to hike, too." Janet told me. "He grew up Catholic, but he's not Catholic anymore. He was in MCC in Bangladesh for three years in agricultural work and hiked a lot in the mountains in Asia. I told him you climb mountains in Phoenix and about your VS in Mississippi. He wants to hear about it."

That Saturday, John drove us to a park where we had a noon picnic, with John's favorite—ranch style beans. He cooked them over a fire for us. I was impressed. We all enjoyed the hike through a lovely wooded area full of autumn color. The fresh air, red and burnished leaves, and wafting scent of fall in the forest intoxicated the senses. John pointed out things in nature and told us names of trees and plants.

John had become a Christian when he was at Arizona State University (ASU) and was part of a men's Bible study. "He loves Oswald Chambers," Janet told me, knowing that I did, too. I felt a bond with John since I had used *My Utmost for His Highest* for years.

"Also," she said excitedly, "when he was at ASU he looked up Mennonite churches in the phone book and found one at Chandler. He went to Koinonia and loved the pastor, Don Yoder, and his wife, Bonnie." Well, that was exciting and very interesting. We knew Don Yoder, founding pastor of our church, Trinity Mennonite. It appeared that Janet and John had a number of things in common.

Later that week, John called me while Janet was gone. "I'd like to take you out to dinner with Janet this week," he offered. "I want to hear about your MCC work in Mississippi." We set a date and had a delightful time. Impressed with John's dazzling smile, relaxed manner, and intense interest in our MCC experience, I sensed that he was in love with my daughter. And I could see why she was taken with him.

When Janet arrived home for Christmas that year, she glowed with excitement. Starry-eyed, she showed me an opal ring John gave her with two small diamonds. "I'm not sure what it all means," she beamed, "but I think it's a promise ring." It was obvious she hoped this was the real thing. I wondered *What big changes are ahead for her, and how soon?* Our heavenly Father knew, and I committed her and the matter to Him.

CHAPTER 44

Wedding

Jesus and his disciples (were) also invited to the wedding.
Jesus performed (his) first miracle in Cana in Galilee; there he
revealed his glory, and his disciples believed in him.

JOHN 2:2,11 (GNB)

1992

On the first day of spring, March 21, 1992, Janet was wed to John Joseph Brejda in Hesston, Kansas. John's name matched the other Js in the family: Jacob John, Jane, Janet, and Jared John. He added one new name: "Joseph." Janet and John both mean "God's gracious gift," as does Jane. With Jake's and Jared's "John," all five of us were blessed with that meaning.

But I'm getting ahead of my story. In February I flew to Missouri to be with Janet in Columbia. Two whole weeks with my daughter as a single girl were a luxury. Janet wanted me to help make her dress of polyester taffeta, fully lined, with a train, long sleeves, and a large bow in back. We worked for hours cutting out the pattern pieces and were ready to sew.

The first morning after she left for work, as I sat at the machine, anxiety at my inexperience overwhelmed me and I felt paralyzed. I cried to the Lord for help and knew what I must do. I dialed my friend Lois Leinbach in Hesston, who had inspired and helped me sew many things the Hesston years.

"You can do it!" she said then offered, "I'll sew any troublesome part when Janet comes on February 28 if she needs me to. She can keep her dress here and I'll iron it for her before the wedding." What a blessing from the Lord was this friend of 28 years – since our MCC days at Akron and 12 years in Hesston. When I hung up, I was ready to proceed. In the evenings Janet and I took turns at the machine.

On my 57th birthday, February 6, surprises abounded. Janet stayed home from work in the morning and cooked breakfast for me. Then she told me we were going to the Career Planning and Placement Center (CPPC) where she worked as a program director for Student Career Services.

At 10:30, Janet and her jovial co-worker, Rob, an especially good friend, delighted everyone with a party. Rob had brought chocolate cake and Janet supplied orange juice. The student career assistants gathered round and one of them, Mark, sang "Happy Birthday" to me in Danish. He had spent a year in Denmark after high school. I enjoyed the friendly students. After their "coffee break," they went back to work in the center, and I sat down to read in a corner. One after another, the students came to me to chat and wish me a happy birthday. It was obvious they loved Janet. Never had I received so much respectful, genuine attention from strangers on my birthday. I loved it and praised God for Janet and her kind friends.

At noon Janet glowed as she told me, "Rob and I are taking you out for lunch." I was amazed and enjoyed the conversation over lunch at Denny's. Rob shared, "I often feel like an alien in this world." Though not a Christian, he seemed to feel like one. Having been torn up over two painful divorces, he appreciated Janet's cheery personality and excellent help in the center. I was blessed to see how the Lord honored Janet with this incredible job. That day, she loved having her mom soak it all up with her. To thank Rob for the birthday cake and lunch, I wrote him on the last page of a tablet on which was printed, "Letter from a friend – Jesus." I knew Rob needed Jesus as his friend. Janet told me that he was "deeply impressed" by it.

That night, John took us out to eat at Alexander's Steak House, where he cooked our steaks. As we ate, I asked him, "How did you become acquainted with *My Utmost for His Highest*?"

"After my three years with MCC in Bangladesh, I was in Tempe at ASU, looking for work. A couple of friends and I met together once a week at a Christian bookstore to pray for the university. One day, one of the guys read from Chambers' book and I was impressed, so I bought a copy."

Jake called that evening and a lovely card in the mail from him left me teary-eyed. In a card from John's mother she wrote what a sweet girl Janet was, and added, "I'm impressed that Janet is sewing her gown." Sister Grace wrote, "I'm coming for the wedding and then plan to stay a week with you in Phoenix." Super! Brother Ralph called and said that he and Janice were driving out to Hesston, bringing Millie and Ralph along. I was ecstatic.

Sunday was another special day. John had asked me to preach for him at their "church." Since it was a small fellowship with no pastor, a Shepherd Group of four took turns preaching. Janet and John were part of the Shepherd Group. Weeks before I came, John called me to say he had a trip out of state that weekend and wanted me to preach. I protested, but he insisted,

"You've been to seminary and you can do it." With his words of affirmation, I agreed.

Jared drove to Columbia for the weekend. I told the group, "I don't 'preach,' I just share." My topic was "The Kingdom of God – Christ In You," on the parables of Jesus in Matthew 13, emphasizing Jesus as the "Pearl of Great Price." After the service as we drove home, I asked Janet and Jared what they thought of it. Both were enthusiastic. "It was *very good!*" they said. A young man, Darren, had told me, "I really appreciated your message. Matthew 13 is my favorite chapter in the Bible, with the Kingdom of Heaven parables." I had not been nervous and praised God for the good experience.

Janet and I loved having Jared there and we three took in the movie, *Father of the Bride*, which Jake and I had seen at Janet's insistence. It was so hilarious that I didn't mind seeing it a second time. Then Jared took us to the Olive Garden to celebrate my birthday and Janet's – ten days before mine.

A month later found me in Hesston, preparing for the wedding a week in advance. The sewing went well and the finished product pleased the bride. Janet planned the entire wedding service, mindful of John's Catholic background. Having gone to Mass with him in Oklahoma City, she observed little touches she could add to the service from his tradition. One such: the priest says, "The Lord be with you" and the congregation responds, "And also with you." She had asked for a copy of our wedding bulletin and chose to use the hymn, "Joyful, Joyful," Jake's favorite, and I Corinthians 13, which we had used.

The rehearsal dinner was planned for the Colonial House, which Jake had managed for several years. Three weeks before the wedding, she called and asked, "Are you sitting down? The Colonial House burned down! It started in the kitchen at about 2:00 A.M. while the manager was in the basement office." What a loss to Hesston and disappointment for us. We planned to have a dinner for family and close friends after the reception at the church, so we moved the rehearsal dinner there as well.

Excitement mounted as Janice and Ralph and Millie and Ralph arrived and Jake flew in from Phoenix. Janet's wedding party helped decorate the fellowship hall. Friday night of the rehearsal dinner, Grace was late coming from Pennsylvania. I waited and watched for her to arrive from Wichita in a rental car. As time dragged on, I prayed and watched at the door. Finally she breezed in, full of talk.

"You didn't tell me the Colonial House burned down!" she chided. "I drove into town and saw no one in sight and almost no cars on the streets. I never saw such a dead town! I drove up Main Street to where you said it should be and didn't see anything. I went to the end of the street, turned around and came back down and still couldn't find it. Finally, I saw a man walking on the sidewalk. I stopped and rolled down my window and said, 'Excuse me, but could you tell me where the Colonial House is?' He smiled a funny smile and said, 'Well, three weeks ago it was down there,' pointing back down the street, 'but it burned down.' I couldn't believe it! And I didn't know where you were."

As the light dawned, I felt terrible. How could I have forgotten to tell her? I apologized and hugged her again. "How did you find us?"

"I drove to the address you gave where I am to stay overnight (at Dean and Betty Adkisson's). Dean was just driving into their driveway. I told him my predicament and he said you were probably at the church and he led me here."

The morning of the wedding, our family met for breakfast with Janet at a restaurant. As we ate, the song, "Morning Has Broken," came over the airwaves, which Janet's pianist, Connie Esau, chose for the processional. It added a special touch to our time together.

Janet's two attendants, Wendy and Rosanne–both Canadians, were former VSers from her days in Beatrice. Wendy was matron of honor and Rosanne sang. John's best man, Steve, was his professor at the University of Nebraska in Lincoln who had told him about MCC work overseas. A radiant, caring person, his attention to John was unusually supportive. He smiled and patted John throughout the ceremony.

As the congregation stood and read I Corinthians 13 in unison, tears ran down my face. It was a beautiful moment, full of God's overpowering love. I recalled how I memorized this chapter so I could learn to love Mom, and how we used it at our wedding. I felt the Spirit's presence and my heart filled with gratitude for God's goodness and care for Janet.

Later, at the reception, a friend told me, "That was such a worshipful service." Another woman said, "There was so much love at the wedding. I've never been at a wedding with so much love."

I praised God for pouring out His great love on Janet and John and our family.

Janet and John Brejda, March 21, 1992.   October 1993.

Sunday morning we flew to Phoenix, as did Janet and John and Grace, on different flights. From my window seat, as we neared Phoenix above the clouds, I noticed a rainbow in the cloud. Then I saw it was a circle, and another circle, one inside the other. Jake asked if the circle had a dot in the center. It did, and the light dawned. "It's the 'glory,' isn't it?" I asked. I knew about it from the book, *Into the Glory.*

"Yes," he said, "it's formed when the plane is between the sun and the clouds, a circle of light surrounding the plane's shadow." (It's also called a "round rainbow," because rainbows are round and if you're looking down from an airplane, there is no horizon to break the circle.) It was exciting to see it for the first time.

At noon we had a small reception in our home with our small group and Pastor Peter and Rheta Mae. Ruth Yoder decorated the house and everyone brought food. Ramona Yoder's daughter Kristin, eight years old, had sung a solo in church, "I Wonder How It Felt," (to be various Bible characters) and I asked her to sing it for us. Someone gave her a spoon to hold as a microphone. She sang about being a child, having one's life before her, waiting and trusting to see what God has for her. Janet's new life was before her and she was deeply moved by the song.

Earlier, John had asked Jake if he could get a better price on reservations for their honeymoon to Mexico where they planned to use his parents' timeshare. Jake did – $200 cheaper. He also got them routed through Phoenix on the way out, and overnight on the way back. When they returned from

500

Mazatlan, I took them to our bedroom (with our 25th anniversary quilt on the bed) and said, with a sweep of my hand, "The honeymoon suite." It was small but looked lovely.

John protested, "This is the master bedroom?"

"Yes," I said, "we want you to have it."

He looked incredulous and remarked, "You two continue to amaze me!"

Grace was with us in the guest room and Jake and I slept on the sofa bed in the family room. We all enjoyed the brief visit with bride and groom. All too soon we said our goodbyes and they were off to their new life in Columbia, Missouri.

I knew that Janet at 27 and John, 34, would have adjustments and prayed earnestly that they would stay close to each other and to Christ in the years ahead.

CHAPTER 45

Trips and Ministry Opportunities

Whenever you possibly can, do good to those who need it. Never tell your neighbor to wait until tomorrow if you can help him now.
PROVERBS 3:27-28 (GNB)

1990–2010

After the Keating job, while Jake searched for full-time work, our pastor called me into his office one day (July 1990) and asked if I would come on staff one-quarter time and be licensed to work with women. I was already mentoring and visiting with a number of women. I had mixed feelings and said I would pray about it and talk it over with Jake.

Jake advised, "I don't think you should be tied down since I don't have a full-time job. We might be moving, depending on where I find a job. Maybe we should just plan as though we're going to Saudi!" I was shocked that he still wanted to return to Saudi Arabia. I declined the position but told the pastor I would continue my work with women on a volunteer basis. He seemed disappointed and I felt torn. I was thankful when the Saudi job did not materialize.

In 1990 I began writing stories about people in our church, which were published in *Christian Living* magazine. On July 4, 1992, I attended my first meeting of Phoenix Christian Writers Fellowship, a rich experience, as with the Kansas group. The leader, Vic Kelly, had at least one book to his credit and others had books and articles published. They shared prayer requests, told of writings published, and read and critiqued each other's writing. In awe of these competent writers, I hesitated to speak, but loved listening and learning. After several months, I took some things to read. When I read my "stepmother poems," the positive comments surprised me. None amazed me more than the leader's: "You can tell these were not written by someone who just writes verse. *This writer writes poetry!* Everyone really connects with it [from the amount of comments]. There's a sense of tremendous maturity between the poems – *Lament* and *Song of Praise*."

Another time as we went around the circle reporting, I said, "I'm just journaling all the exciting things God is doing for me in my life right now, and the exciting things God is doing all over the world and in many people I know."

Vic became excited and said, "The journaling is a seed plot, tremendously valuable. It will pay off some day. Keep at it. They are going through Mark Twain's diaries and journals now and pulling things out. The journal will shape mind and heart of the person doing it." What an encouragement!

From 1990 to 1997, I had nine articles published, unusual stories of local Mennonites. My three Mississippi articles appeared in 1997. When Dad visited us after Christmas, I interviewed him for an article for *The Mennonite*. In 1998 my article about our new church columbarium, "Practical Funeral Plans," was published in the Mennonite Mutual Aid magazine, *Sharing*.

For years I had neglected my book. Being in the writers' group inspired me to return to it. I loved interviewing people for articles and made new friends in the process, but by 1997, I was ready to give that up and concentrate on my book. By now I had over 80 large journals recording our lives the past 30 some years. Prayers filled many pages, with answers often recorded immediately after. Praise and thanksgiving had become a habit. Researching journals and many smaller notebooks, writing, and checking details with family and friends became my passion and hobby.

In August 1990, I was pleased to have a rare visit from brother Ralph and Janice and sister Ruth and Dave Ruch. We went sightseeing and enjoyed family stories. Jake was in Alaska so I toured them through the Valley from Carefree and Fountain Hills to South Mountain and the Christown Sand Castles. When we picked Jake up at the airport, Dave videoed him getting off the commercial plane behind Senator Dennis Deconcini, but Jake was cut off on the video. The new tunnel on I-10 in downtown Phoenix opened up that week. Dave videoed the tunnel later when we took Jake to the airport for a trip to Aspen. Early Saturday morning, Ralph, Janice and I took a slow climb up Squaw Peak (now Piestewa), too rigorous for the out-of-shape. While they were here, Dave's brother Marty and son Bobby stopped by with their 18-wheeler for a first-time visit on their way back East. I enjoyed this relaxing breather and welcome connection to family.

Remembering my humble roots in that house on Thatcher Road in Pennsylvania, where God became real to me as a young child crying for my mother, I realized that God had transformed my suffering into a ministry of compassion for others. Paul's words in I Corinthians 1:3-7 give understanding: "Blessed be the God and Father of our Lord Jesus Christ, the... God of all comfort, who comforts us in all our (sufferings) *that we may be able to comfort those who are in any trouble with the comfort with which we ourselves are comforted by God*" (italics mine). I could never forget how God by His Spirit comforted me on my bed in the night.

During this time, the Lord drew me to those dying of cancer, first a friend, pastor and chaplain John Oyer, who died about a year after we first met him and his wife Ellen. We had enjoyed good times with them and were shocked at his sudden recurrence of cancer and death in October 1989. A church friend, Marcille Davidhizar, was struggling with cancer at the same time and grew very weak by October 1990. She asked if I would have the invocation at her memorial service and, when I asked, she agreed that Jake could do it with me.

In the meantime, Jake brought me good news one day after the Keating job ended. "From that one year of staying at Marriott Hotels, and saving points, we have three free trips of four nights each, and a free car. You can choose where you'd like to go." I could hardly believe my good fortune.

Since Jake was flying for The Air Group in Van Nuys, California, I chose the nearby Marriott at Century City for our first trip. We drove out October 31 and visited the sights around Hollywood, Avenue of the Stars, Beverly Hills, Santa Monica beach, toured Universal Studios, and drove along the beautiful coast. Our opulent hotel with valet service left me feeling lowly and intimidated. One day, armed guards and secret service personnel made us wonder if President George H. W. Bush (41st president) was staying there. (Bush was once in the hotel where Jake stayed in Istanbul. Guests were notified to be cautious and not display American spirit, due to demonstrations.)

One day we drove to San Diego to visit our former pastor, James Hollywood, wife Tricia, and girls, for a great catch-up time. He was now a chaplain in the Navy, remembering with gratitude that a military chaplain had led him to Christ in Vietnam. On Sunday we visited the Crystal Cathedral at Garden Grove, and met two women from our church.

It was a great getaway except that I couldn't forget Marcille suffering back home. In our hotel room in the middle of the night, I prayed and planned and journaled in the bathroom. Aware of Jake's trip scheduled for Europe,

November 6 to 13, and wanting him to be with me at her service, I prayed fervently that Marcille would not die until he returned.

Back at home I visited Marcille for the last time on November 12. She died the next evening. That same night Jake called me at 9:45 to pick him up at the airport at 12:15. God had answered my prayer!

Later, at the memorial service, I read from Psalm 46 and Jake prayed. He concluded his prayer in a strong, booming voice beside me, "In the Name of our Resurrected Lord, Amen." It was an incredible moment of Jesus' power and comfort for me. After the service, a man came to us with a look of admiration on his face and in his eyes. He spoke warmly, "That was wonderful! You both really have a gift!" I gave this unexpected compliment back to the Lord and thanked Him for helping me through a difficult assignment.

Then I spoke to Marcille's daughter and told her, "I prayed that your mother wouldn't die until Jake returned from his trip."

She looked at me in amazement and cried, "So, *you're* the one!"

I asked, "What do you mean?"

"Our family had all released Mother and we couldn't understand why she hung on. That explains everything!" I felt rather sheepish about my selfish prayer, but I was grateful for Jake's strong presence beside me in front of that church full of people.

In addition to my church ministry, I became involved with a neighbor who had surgery for a recurrence of cancer. She struggled in her marriage with an angry, emotionally ill husband. In March of 1991 he forbade her parents to visit her. Her mother came to me in tears, pleading for me to make the carrot and green juices for her daughter, which she had been doing. At 4:00, 6:00 and 8:00 P.M. that day, I made the juices for the first time. Four times a day I went to wash and juice carrots, greens, and apples.

At times I invited my neighbor (a former missionary and Lancaster County Mennonite) to my home and we spent hours visiting. We prayed together and I read Hebrews 11 to her, her favorite chapter. She was concerned about her 12-year-old son whom she had home schooled. Phil Bedsworth's gladiolas had multiplied, with up to 100 gorgeous blooms in our front garden. My friend loved the long stemmed pink ones I gave her, which she called *exquisite*. Throughout that year my involvement with and burden for the family increased. Daily I cried to the Lord for them and for myself. Having smarted a bit at not accepting the licensing at church, one morning I sensed Jesus' presence very near and a verse seemed blazoned on my mind: "You have not chosen me, but I have chosen you and *ordained you* to go and bring forth fruit..." (John 15:16). I knew I did not need to be ordained to do God's will and I rejoiced in His approval and strength for my task. And I marveled at how God supplied my needs in unexpected ways, including trips that helped restore me. (In my absence, a friend from my neighbor's church helped her.)

The end of March I flew to Pennsylvania for a surprise 50th birthday party for sister Ruth at Grace's house. Ruth had a big surprise when she opened the large box tied with ribbon and large bow, where Grace had hid me. I wrote a praise poem for Ruth, which my siblings and I read. A pink gorilla showed up with balloons and a boom box and danced and sang. It was good to enjoy this time with the family, especially since Ruth had feared she would not make it to 50, because Mom died at 48. Earlier, when she wept about this on the phone, I assured her that she could outlive Mom and prayed with her. (In 2010 she turned an amazing 69!) God has answered many prayers for her.

From time to time Pastor Wiebe asked me to visit women who were depressed, three in close succession, just out of the hospital. As I juggled regular meetings with them and my neighbor, mentored others, interviewed people for articles, and wrote, Jake said to me with a smile one day, "You have a lot of full-time jobs!" "It does feel like it," I agreed, pleased and grateful that he noticed and understood.

In April 1991, Jake and I left on our second free trip, this time to Amsterdam—another gift from the Lord. We arrived at our Marriott Hotel in the center of Amsterdam with our free rental car the end of April. With tulips at their best, we visited a tulip garden where we saw thousands of blooms bursting with colors of every hue. We then took a two-day jaunt to Germany to see Jake's relatives, recently arrived from Russia. Dad Friesen's three sisters enjoyed freedom to live out their senior years in peace after the fall of Communism, due to Glasnost under Gorbachev. They and their families welcomed us warmly. The older women in babushkas, the German language and food took us into another world. Charming five-year-old twin boys, Peter and Rudolf Tissen, stood on their heads for us.

Through Jake, I asked questions and he interpreted for me. Dad's sisters told heartbreaking stories of Russia and their exile to Siberia after the Revolution. The oldest, Anna, short and round, with a wrinkled face, sweet crooked smile, and twinkling eyes told us, "It took 17 days by freight car to

506

get to Siberia. Sometimes the train sat on the track for two days. We took turns sleeping in bunk beds. If you had three children under nine, you could stay home. If you were 55 or older you didn't have to go, but I was 54. We had to pack our own food to take."

"How long were you there?" I asked.

"I worked in Siberia for six years until I was 60. I walked 1000 miles back home, with no food. I ate bark from the trees to stay alive. Now we have bread to eat and are happy again."

Sara, 85, tall and strongly built, told us, "I had one daughter and had to leave her with relatives. In Siberia, I helped build factories. My husband and I worked for 21 years in the coal mines. We pushed coal on the tracks in baskets on cars. We had only thin soup and hard bread to eat, and meat once a month." We marveled that they survived at all with such harsh conditions.

The third sister, Lena (Helen), told us, "I had three children under nine so I could stay. But women left at home had it just as hard. There were no men to help work, so we had all the farm work, plus taking care of the children and home. It was a very hard life." These sturdy women of Dutch stock had survived near starvation and tremendous suffering. They lived in a big apartment building and had freedom to worship. We stayed overnight in the home where we had dinner and I was deeply impressed by all the love I felt that day.

One of Jake's first cousins, Katherina Tissen and her husband Wilhelm, gave us a tour of the new home they were building. With ten children, including the twins, the whole family worked on the house. After years of deprivation, they had prospered. In Russia, only the Baptist church was registered with the government so they had become Baptists.

Anna was the first to migrate to Germany in September 1990, with Sara and Helen soon to follow with their families. After a 65-year separation (except for a couple of visits to Russia), Dad was anxious to visit his sisters. He planned a three-week trip that December with his son-in-law Bert Arlitt, who grew up in Berlin. The day of their departure, Jake had a trip to Vancouver, with the surprise of meeting Dad and Bert at the airport. We never expected to meet any of Dad's family on this earth, but Dad encouraged us to go. We loved our time with them.

(Sixteen years later, in 2007, Peter Tissen, one of the twins, came to the U.S. to do Voluntary Service in Baltimore in lieu of military training in Germany. He visited us twice and Jared flew out to Arizona to spend time with his second cousin. While those in the military in Germany serve only a year, with pay, Conscientious Objectors who leave the country must serve 18 months and pay their own way. Peter is a committed Christian from a church of 400, a strong, close-knit community where divorce is unheard of.)

On May 10, I flew to Kansas City to attend Janet's graduation from the University of Missouri the next day. Jared picked me up at the airport and took me to Columbia. It was an exciting time amidst that great crowd of graduates, to see Janet walk across the stage to receive her Master's degree in Educational and Counseling Psychology.

That week we spent time at Manhattan with Jared and with friends in Hesston. The next Saturday, on May 18, Janet and I attended Jared's graduation from K-State with a Bachelor of Science degree in Information Systems. We missed Jake, who was on a trip to Hawaii and Europe. That day, Janet and I flew to Phoenix. Jake returned the next day, and Jared joined us on May 22, the day before his 24th birthday, for ten days.

Jared worked on his resume with Jake and mailed ten copies. One day he flew to San Francisco for an interview with Chevron. He already had job offers from Mutual of Omaha and Dillard's Department Stores. On May 31, he accepted the job at Dillard's headquarters in Little Rock. He worked at Executive Aircraft at Newton until he moved to Arkansas on July 26. Janet left earlier and was also applying for a job. Our children were moving into the world of the employed.

On October 6, I flew to Little Rock for my first visit with Jared. I loved the city with many trees, a golf course for walking near Jared's apartment, a small shady canyon where we hiked, and his Southern Baptist church. He gave me a tour of Dillard's headquarters and showed me his cubicle where he worked as a computer programmer/analyst. Those ten days he often had meetings and was required to work in every department in the store, including women's dresses and lingerie, to learn all aspects of the business. He had decided to work five years for a Fortune 500 company. Living alone was a tough adjustment after college but he soon made friends and joined a Bible study with co-workers.

In early September 1991, Jake and I took our last free trip, celebrating our 30th anniversary with a fantastic vacation in Hong Kong. We flew from Seattle with a stopover in Korea.

Hundreds of skyscrapers and high-rise apartment buildings, lit up like Christmas trees all around the harbor, greeted us as our plane landed in Hong Kong at 9:30 at night (6:30 A.M. Phoenix time). Jake had flown into the city before and told me, "It's a difficult airport to fly into, surrounded by mountains, buildings, and the harbor." (A new airport opened in 1998, built to withstand severe typhoons on an enlarged island off the coast, for $20 billion, the most expensive airport ever built, according to *Guinness Book of World Records*. The old Kai Tak Airport, begun in 1925, had one runway, extending into the harbor, and the mushrooming city grew up around it, making landings notoriously difficult.) I thanked the Lord for a safe landing for us and for Jake on previous trips.

The next day we saw swarms of Chinese people, thousands of small stores and gaudy signs, buses, cars and bikes crowding the streets—a mass of humanity. What an astonishing world, and I enjoyed it all immensely. I felt like a queen far above the city at our high-rise Marriott. Jake was familiar with famous Victoria Peak on top of which we strolled along a beautiful trail with a breathtaking view of the city. We shopped a bit and we walked till we dropped. One day we took a four-hour bus tour to the New Territories and China border. At a visit to a temple I felt grieved over the many people with sad faces worshiping and offering bowls of food to grotesque idols—a stark reminder that despair abounds without Christ.

Among highlights of the trip were visits with missionaries from our seminary and Hesston days. We met Carolyn and Junior Kauffman (son of Milo, former president of Hesston College during the Depression) in their apartment. Their living quarters were 500 square feet, 3 bedrooms with bath, and cost $3000 a month. We enjoyed hearing about their work. Another day we had lunch and a delightful time with long-time missionaries, Hugh and Janet Sprunger, whom we knew at seminary.

On the way home, we had a brief stopover in Tokyo, lost a day, and had two Sundays flying back. Mileage was 7,800 one way, 15,600 round trip. It amazed me that Jake did this for a job, crossing time zones and cruising the world—for free, and getting paid for it!

When we arrived home on September 8, my neighbor was in a greatly weakened condition. (Her juicer had broken down earlier so we had bought one and I made the juices at home.) Three days later, when I took her juice that evening, her gown was open over her chest revealing the huge scab from radiation. She had told me it went around her side and to her back. The loud rattle in her lungs and gasps for air unnerved me. I hated seeing her like this. But with a beautiful smile, and face radiating peace and joy, she thanked me graciously for everything, as she always did. Though I often felt helpless and inadequate, she and her mother called me an angel. Her needs were heavy on my heart day and night, and I often wondered how she could hang on. We had rejoiced together earlier when she told me that her husband had apologized for his treatment of her and asked her forgiveness. I was comforted to learn that he relented and allowed her mother to visit and stay with her for the night for her last days on earth.

At home, knowing that her end was near, I prayed fervently for the Lord to take her. Then I stayed up and read *Only One Year* by Stalin's daughter Svetlana Alliluyeva. Reading of her tragic life with a ruthless dictator father helped divert my mind from the suffering of my friend.

The next morning, the Hospice nurse came to tell me my friend had died peacefully after her mother left. Her husband was alone with her when she breathed her last. He told me that she and their son had exchanged loving words and big smiles that morning before he went to school. Our hearts had been knit together in love and I was grateful she was finally at peace with the Lord she loved so dearly. She was 53 years old.

Over the next years, I served on commissions and the church board, taught children and adult Sunday school classes, served on committees, then as secretary for our California/Arizona conference, Pacific Southwest. I traveled to California for board meetings and became involved with Native Americans, both Hopi and Navajo. The Lord gave me a special Hopi friend, Nadenia Myron, a pastor who was licensed when her husband Elmer was ordained. At their ordination/licensing service, out of the blue she asked if I would mentor her. We had precious times of prayer and sharing our hearts with each other. Nadenia always wept as she cried out to the Lord for her Hopi people to come to know Jesus. Nadenia, Elmer, my Hesston friend Betty, and I also traveled to a Vineyard Conference in Anaheim and heard John Wimber, Vineyard founder, and inspiring speakers from London.

In mid October 1995, Jake joined me for my namesake Janie Herstine's wedding to Tom Mann. After a trip with Led Zeppelin rock group to Ames, Iowa, and Chicago, he was given leave to fly to Allentown where he met me at the airport. We enjoyed an overnight stay at Ruth and Dave's. I was sorry I had missed other nieces and nephew's weddings. That Saturday, as we sat with my siblings near the front of the Quakertown Church of the Brethren, I was overcome with emotion—deep joy and gratitude at being here with Jake. Overwhelmed with the warmth of family, the tears flowed. I asked the Lord to turn them off and He did. It was a lovely wedding with Aunts Naomi and Melba, Uncle John and Aunt Dottie, and cousin Bobby Moser present.

After dinner at the fire hall, for the first time in my life I danced at a wedding (Jake declined!) with brother Ralph and sister Ruth. During one fast dance Ruth, several times my size, suddenly picked me up, laughing, as she spun round and round. While I stayed on with the family, Jake left Sunday morning to Chicago to continue the Led Zepplin nine-day tour, returning with a $1000 tip!

The end of April 1998, I flew to Pennsylvania to attend the wedding at Pittsburgh of Anna and John's youngest, Joel, to Kara. I was pleased to experience this wedding of a nephew and the stunning wedding party. Then I stayed several days with Ruth, while Dave was ill in the hospital, and had time with Millie and Ralph and brother Ralph and Janice. When I visited Uncle John and Aunt Dottie Landis, John told me two stories of my mother that I treasure.

"Your mother came sledding down the hill across the street from our house one day and as she neared the street, a car was coming," he recounted. "Her sled hit the back tire of the car and bounced off and she was unhurt." I was amazed and grateful for God's protection that day.

"And Grace taught herself to play the pump organ in our home. The younger ones liked to lay on the floor and pump the pedals for her, for fun," he said with a grin. I loved these stories of my mother and hearing them from Uncle John was a special treat.

Back home in Phoenix, Jake and I kept a busy schedule. In addition to flying, Jake found time for service. We served together on Outreach (Mission) Commission and the Marriage Listening Committee. Jake served on the church board and took mediation classes for VORP (Victim Offender Reconciliation Program). For several years he mediated numerous cases between offenders and victims, bringing them together for reconciliation. Offenders made restitution to victims, thus avoiding probation or incarceration.

We also served on the Refugee Committee, where Jake played a huge role in resettling two refugees, Belay Tuccu from Ethiopia and David (later changed to Carlo because of threats on his life), an Iraqi Kurd. Both came in

1991 and became a part of our family. Belay returned to Ethiopia to marry Emebet in June of 2004. After a year of paperwork, his lovely wife, "Emmy," joined him in Phoenix and we enjoy meals and games together. When Carlo married an Iraqi girl, Zhian, her family of 11, new in the U.S., moved in with them. I tutored the women and girls in English several times a week and taught them songs, like "Jesus Loves Me." Later most of her family moved to San Diego, where Carlo, Zhian and their three children followed later. The two couples' phone calls and visits are full of loving words and hugs. Our friendship with these dear ones from other cultures has greatly enriched our lives.

We moved to Sun City in 1999. Jake became treasurer of our association after the former one died suddenly. Then in 2003, while Jake was on a ten-day trip to Figi, he was elected as one of 11 Directors of the Condominium Owners Association. After serving two terms, he served on the Home Owners Association Enforcement Committee. He served on the Ten Thousand Villages board for several years and was chairman of our church Leadership Team. With so many board meetings for years, I began calling him the "most bored person" I knew!

Since retiring, Jake has clerked in the Ten Thousand Villages store at times and helps unpack boxes. A "mystery shopper" makes periodic visits and writes a report for the manager. One day the manager called to tell Jake that he got a 100% score from the mystery shopper! She said no one else ever got such a high mark. The shopper found Jake to be friendly, courteous, knowledgeable about products, and he took time to chat about things other than business. Jake's broad experience with the public in a myriad of jobs has made him a natural with people from all races and walks of life.

In 2004, I served on the Pastor Search Committee for a lead pastor for our church. After many meetings and much prayer, we decided to call Shane Hipps, a new graduate of Fuller Seminary in Pasadena. (His amazing resume had given me a strong sense that he was our next pastor.) Only 30 years old, from non-Mennonite background, Shane had had a Mennonite pastor, James Brenneman, as his mentor during seminary, attended Pasadena Mennonite, and embraced Anabaptist/Mennonite beliefs. His five years at Trinity Mennonite brought an influx of new members and revived the congregation's understanding of and appreciation for our 500-year heritage. His sermons enlightened and astonished listeners in our church as well as across the nation and in many denominations via our website. We were saddened when he resigned to become teaching pastor at a large church in Grand Rapids. Many grieved the loss of Shane, his wife Andrea, and young daughters, Harper and Hadley, in May 2010.

But God graciously provided a new pastor "before we called." Hal Shrader came to us in 2007 from missionary work in Chile. Having learned about Shane and our church through a friend and our website, Hal, his wife Chrisie, and daughters, Mollie and Madison, moved to Phoenix to attend our church, even without jobs. Hal's remarkable gifts for ministry soon became apparent and he later became part-time Pastor of Student Ministry and Adult Spiritual Formation. As a pastor in southern California for 10 years, his ministry was heavily informed by Anabaptist theology and he was "drawn to this unique approach to following Jesus." Hal has led mission trips to Mexico, Chile, Argentina, Peru, Ecuador, Colombia, Spain, Turkey, Morocco, and Iraq, and led a group of college students on a fact-finding trip to Thailand. He and Chrisie visited his missionary aunt in India on this trip. Hal loves people, is an excellent Bible teacher and preacher, and is passionate about communicating the Gospel to those who are open to our Anabaptist "third-way faith." Shane and Hal had worked well together and we were grateful for this seamless transition in leadership.

Ron Faus, our associate pastor, is an excellent pastor as well, from Church of the Brethren background in Pennsylvania, something I have in common with him from my mother's family. My brother Ralph is still a member and deacon at my mother's home church.

In 2006, we were asked to buy a house for Goldensun Peace Ministries for developmentally disabled adults. Three young men live in the house, along with a staff member and at times VS'ers as well. Ours was the third house in the program, situated close to our church in Glendale. The first house has three women residents; the second is for men. Three more houses have been added to the program. Parents of residents are deeply grateful for a Christian home with a family atmosphere for their children. Support from the state helps pay residents' rent, which in turn pays for the mortgages on the homes. Goldensun is a Mennonite Central Committee (MCC) initiated program. Jake is privileged to serve on the Goldensun board and our church is blessed with these special people in our community.

During these years, God's marvelous grace and leading filled our lives with abundant blessings of family and friends. However, we were saddened to realize that a special person's life was drawing to a close.

CHAPTER 46

Dad Friesen's Homegoing

And God will wipe away every tear from their eyes; there shall be
no more death, nor sorrow, nor crying. There shall be no more pain,
for the former things have passed away.
REVELATION 21:4 (NKJ)

1990–1995

Jake's father moved into the Menno Home in Clearbrook, British Columbia, on April 1, 1990 and loved it. Still going strong, he ministered to others in the home. One day he told me on the phone, "I woke at 5:00 as usual and was praying. I cried for joy because I'm so happy at the Menno Home." We were grateful he was happy, surrounded by caring people.

As he grew older, he became emotional about many things. He enjoyed a little "game" that he told me about: "When I have three hiccoughs and the phone rings, I know it's you." Or he would call and say, "I wondered if you prayed for me because I had three hiccoughs." He called on his 89th birthday, April 15, 1990, and again in May saying, "I had hiccoughs, so I had to call. I'm doing great."

A year later, he called before Easter, sounding sad. He spoke quietly, "I couldn't sleep, and I cried that I can't send Easter cards anymore."

"You were on my mind this morning," I told him.

He laughed and said, "You're *always* on my mind – every day!" What a father-in-law the Lord gave me! His love warmed my heart and filled me with joy. "I'll be calling the other children, too," he added. He was used to Jake being gone and often called to talk to me.

My article in *The Mennonite*, "Happy 90th Birthday, N. N.," was published in April 1991, before his birthday. (His first name was Nickolai and he added another Nickolai since he lacked a middle name. He usually went by N. N.) Earlier he had protested, "You should not publish it, I'm afraid it will make me proud." He was serious. But after it was out he got wonderful phone calls and letters and called to share his excitement. One morning in May, he phoned and exclaimed, "I'm so excited!"

"Why?"

"I got a letter from Hilke De Jong. He said he got saved in a meeting where I preached. He called about Jake and said he went to Canadian Mennonite Bible College with him." (Dad wrote in his book how Hilke prayed first in High German and then switched to his native Dutch when he gave his life to Christ. He came back the next night to tell Dad how happy he was and to thank him.) "I told you not to publish the article," he reminded, "because it's too much like bragging. Now I know it was of the Lord because I'm getting all these letters. I pushed evangelism hard, and they don't do that anymore. I figure it's a sign of the times. But many agree now that my work was good. So I know the Lord was leading you and I want to thank you." He repeated this often when we talked on the phone.

Alone in his room in the Menno Home, Dad reflected on the past. He called me a year later and said, "I didn't want you to write that article. The devil got me cornered one time and I almost took my life after we came to Canada and life was so hard. I was going to hang myself. I had lost $150 a month and didn't see how we could make it." But the Lord was gracious and prevented the tragedy. As he wrote in one account of this incident, "A loud voice shouted, 'Don't do it! I have work for you in Canada. I *need* you!' And He did. Glory to His Name again and again!"

"I had a lot of opposition to my evangelism," he continued on the phone. "But since your article, I had a letter from New Brunswick. I got ten letters similar to that from people who got saved through my preaching. I put the letters in a box and Peter read them."

With joy he exclaimed, "I'm willing to live ten more years now." How astonishing!

He continued, "I got a letter from Russia. A niece wrote, 'You are my uncle and you were at my place in 1978, 14 years ago. You prayed in our home. I asked you to pray before the meal and you prayed that God would bless this house and the people. Now I have two sons who are ministers. You are the first one who prayed the blessing in our house and over our home.'" They had to become Baptists, and Dad told me, "There are no Mennonites or Baptists in heaven, only Christians."

As time went on, Dad began to change. Sometimes when we called he was confused and didn't know us. Once he told me, "I lost my voice for a week."

Another time he was disoriented and couldn't talk. Jake called a few days later and he was better. He reported, "I was sick for a week and couldn't think in the mornings." He kept a record of daily events and visitors.

Later, he explained on the phone, "In September, I was in a wheelchair all the time. I told the Lord, 'I'll do anything you want me to do but you'll have to help me because I can't do it by myself.' The next morning I was healed."

Jake's brother Peter confirmed it when he called, "Dad got rid of his cane and walks fine!" It was amazing how often he reported such healings.

Ever since Dad said he was healed at our house, he wanted to move in with us. In 1993, he lamented to Jake twice in phone calls, "I'm sorry I didn't come and stay with you." He talked with his children by phone and they visited him more than we could. Helen wrote us, "All Dad talks about is wanting to move there with you."

Through the years Dad often told me, "I always ask people to pray for me that I stay humble." Once when he called he repeated that phrase and confided, "I always thought I was better than everyone else." He could finally admit this weakness.

For Christmas one year we gave Dad *The Blessing* by Gary Smalley and John Trent. Later he confessed to me, "This book makes me feel so guilty. I failed often with the children. I wasn't there when they were growing up and I didn't help them with their spiritual problems."

Dad had by necessity learned to be independent. He had lost his mother when he was four, lived with his step-grandparents from age seven to eleven, and saw his family only once in those four years. After that visit, he secretly cried and had a longing to go home. Then he was wrenched from his homeland and family against his will at age 24 when he was the only one to immigrate to Canada. In that strange land he worked hard from sunup to sundown to ward off poverty, with little time for the children. Later, his demanding ministry kept him away from home. After he lost two wives, he shed many tears and suffered remorse over his failings.

Through all the letters, phone calls, respect and affirmation from church colleagues who had openly disagreed with his methods of evangelism, the Lord had humbled him. God answered the prayer of his heart and lifted the burden of guilt he had carried.

Jake's mother's life as a Mennonite minister's wife was hard. Their children were aware and saw their mother's suffering. Some resented Dad's insensitive treatment of Mother. At least one of them openly told him of her feelings. "Dad was the boss," she told me. How sad to learn our lessons too late. He cried many tears until finally the Lord brought forgiveness, healing, joy, and *love* so overpowering that Dad felt he could not contain it.

By the spring of 1994, I felt a strong urgency that we should visit Dad. He was 93 and I wondered how much longer he would be with us. Jake saw no need to go and did not want to miss work. So I told him I could go by myself and visit our friends, Pearl and Linferd Goertz at Lynden. Dad was a few miles over the border from them. When I shared my desire with Pastor Wiebe, he strongly encouraged me and prayed fervently for me and for Dad. He remembered his good visit with Dad alone in our home and their prayer time together. Dad and Pastor Peter were both strong men of prayer.

Jake got reservations for me to Bellingham, Washington for May 14-18. There I rented a car and drove to the Goertzes. I enjoyed my time catching up with Pearl and Linferd and spent many hours each day with Dad. I also had a delightful visit with Jake's niece, Marlene, and husband, John Unrau, at Surrey, B.C. where I stayed one night. They had been involved in Marriage Encounter (ME) and Marlene recommended me for editor of the ME newsletter, which I accepted for several years. John and Marlene had also attended seminary at Elkhart, so we had much in common.

Dad seemed fine to me and carried on good conversations. However, one day a man came into his room to visit and told me his name. When he left, Dad looked at me with a wide grin and a twinkle in his eyes and announced, "He has the same name as me!" It was then that I realized his mind played tricks on him. The man's name was totally different.

The nurses and administrator said he was confused and had been very paranoid, but was much better recently. They reassured me that he did not "bother" the other people by visiting them, contrary to some reports we heard. He performed a needed ministry at the Menno Home for several years, visiting, counseling, and leading people to the Lord. (He had told me on the phone one day, "I led two men to the Lord in one week. One is a Dutch man.")

Dad and I prayed together every day when I was there. On the last day I was deeply moved as he prayed, "Father, bless and reward Jane for coming, and help her to be *loaded down with the Spirit*." Wow! Three times he asked that I be kept safe. He was definitely not confused when he prayed!

Later that year, I phoned Dad one morning and he did not know me. A sad feeling came over me as he talked on and on in German. As his phone calls stopped, Jake and I felt cut off from him.

In February 1995, Peter's wife, Mary, planned a surprise party for Peter's 70th birthday on Vancouver Island. The family had not been together for a long time. Jake wanted to drive. In the Northland winter, snow slowed us down for many miles on the freeways in Oregon and Washington.

An added bonus of this trip was a visit to Dad. We arrived at the Menno Home in Abbotsford as dinner was being served. When we found Dad, a helper who was feeding him told Jake that he could take over. Dad was in a wheelchair so the woman wheeled him to a table where we could be alone. I watched with an array of emotions as Jake fed him bite by bite. Dad did not speak. He looked at us with interest, but his mind seemed blank. I asked if he remembered Janet and Jared. He replied, "Yes." That was all, and I doubted that he did.

What a poignant scene, watching my husband feed his father as his father had surely fed him when he was a small boy. I recalled Dad telling me how he held the children on his lap at the table. Now the roles were reversed. It was the last time we saw Dad alive. When we parted, he gave us a big smile and said, "Good luck!" How different he was from my visit the year before, and how thankful I was that I had come.

Anticipating the party, we joined a vanload of relatives the next morning and took the ferry to Vancouver Island. Jake's nieces, Marlene and Barbara, with their husbands and three children apiece were lively conversationalists. We had great discussions on various topics, from spanking children to counseling. Marlene was a counselor and her husband John a pastor and chaplain.

It was a treat to be with the family to surprise Peter. He thoroughly enjoyed the celebration with his two brothers and three sisters and spouses, and Peter and Mary's three children, their spouses, and the grandchildren. After dinner, a program of hilarious skits, readings, and touching letters from Peter's children with their "memories of Dad" entertained us. It was good to be together, but I was aware of Dad's absence. Mary said to me later, "It was sad that Dad couldn't be with us."

At Peter's 70th birthday party, Vancouver Island, 1995. Back: Peter, Helen Arlitt, Nick; Front: Margaret Schulz, Mary Ann Mulligan, Jake.

The next morning at Peter and Mary's lovely new bed and breakfast, we awoke to a beautiful sight – six inches of snow. Many family members came for breakfast and more visiting. Then we took off to the ferry on snow-covered roads, and to Goertzes at Lynden for the night.

A three-day drive lay ahead of us. The third night as we drove the last hundred miles from Parker to Phoenix, a beautiful full moon rose in the eastern sky. Then lightning flashed in great thunderclouds on both sides of the highway in a magnificent display for miles and miles. The fantastic billowing clouds lit up from the inside and I told Jake, "I think God is blessing us with these fireworks." I had never seen anything like it before and sensed the majesty of God's power. Many people must have been impressed with the display in the heavens that night. Still, it seemed as though this awesome show was just for us, flashing fiery pillars of benediction on the close of Dad's life, a reminder that God is with us and would lead us forward. It was a memorable 3456-mile trip, not counting the ride to the Island.

On the morning of September 28, 1995, the day before he turned 60, Jake called me to pick him up from Sky Harbor Airport, as I had done count-less times. We got home about 10:00. When we sat down for lunch about 12:00, I felt led to pray for Dad, "Father, please give Dad peace and take care of him."

About 45 minutes later the phone rang. It was Jake's brother, Peter, with the news, "Dad died today—around noon." He was 94.

I was amazed and wondered if my prayer had just preceded his home going. Though it was sad to know he had left this earth, we knew he was rejoicing that at long last he got his wish to "go home."

Over the years I had wondered how it would be when Dad died—would Jake be home or off on a trip? I prayed he would be home and committed the matter to the Lord. I was immensely grateful that Jake was home that day to get the message and call the children: "God's perfect timing."

Later that day, Jake called Peter. The funeral was set for October 6. Next, Jake called Jared who planned to check airline rates. Then he called Janet. She had a conference on the 6th and a doctor appointment the 7th. My niece, Brenda Loux, was arriving in two days for vacation, so I knew I couldn't go. That felt fine with me because I had talked often with Dad on the phone and had that good visit with him in May a year ago. God had given me the gift of that four-day visit while Dad could still talk. That's how I would remember him. God is so good!

Early Saturday morning Jake left for a trip to Santa Fe, Denver, Los Angeles, and Scottsdale. Brenda arrived that evening and Jake returned at 3:00 A.M. Sunday morning Jake slept in and I took Brenda to the church designed by Frank Lloyd Wright—First Christian, in nearby Phoenix. We were duly impressed with the magnificent church and the uplifting service of praise and worship. That afternoon Jake drove us south to Biosphere 2, built between 1987 and 1991 at Oracle. On a two-hour tour of the expansive glass buildings we saw where eight people lived for two years, engaged in an amazingly successful scientific mission to increase one's lifespan through nutrition.

On Monday Jake left for a three-day trip to Chicago, Teeterboro (NJ), and Dallas, continuing to Seattle on Thursday where he met Jared en route to the funeral.

While Jake was gone, Brenda and I left Tuesday morning at 5:15 for Monument Valley on the Navajo Reservation in northeast Arizona and Utah border. At Kayenta we had a rest stop at Burger King. Jake and I had followed the incredible O. J. Simpson murder trial on TV and the jury verdict was to be announced that morning at 7:30. With no radio reception on the reservation, Brenda and I felt cut off from the outside world and were curious about what happened. At Burger King, a man informed me, "Unfortunately, he was acquitted!" The high-suspense courtroom drama left many angry and dismayed.

We arrived at Monument Valley at 10:00, amazed at the awesome spires and rock formations – "Big Mitten," "Little Mitten," "Three Sisters," and more – dotting the desert landscape for many miles. From there we drove to beautiful Canyon de Chelly (pronounced Shay), still in Navajo country. Indians cultivate crops in the valley where magnificent sheer rock cliffs rise above them. The stunning "White House" Indian ruins are nestled in a large crevice of the cliff.

After dark, we drove to the Hopi Cultural Center and motel, where we stayed for the night. The next day in Hopiland we visited Second Mesa, Hopi Mission School, and Oraibi Mennonite Church, where we talked with Hopi women gathered there. (The Hopi Reservation is a small island within the Navajo Reservation, the largest Indian reservation in the U.S. General Conference missionaries started the Hopi Mission School in the 1950s. We had learned about the school from Hopi missionaries in missions class at Men-O-Lan in my youth.) On the way home we spent time at the Grand Canyon overlooks where Brenda added to her photo collection.

On other days, Brenda and I visited the new state-of-the-art, nine-story Phoenix Library, the Heard Indian Museum, and Sonora Desert Museum near Tucson with desert animals, plants, cacti, and a cave with precious stones and minerals. As we were leaving, a coyote walked near us on the parking lot, adding an exciting touch to our day in the desert. We enjoyed eating out, shopping, and were nearly late for church as we chatted over blueberry muffins and coffee on our patio. We laughed a lot and got better acquainted and I was deeply grateful for the blessing of Brenda's good company during this time of Dad's home going.

When Jake flew to Seattle for the funeral, whom should he meet on the plane but James Hollywood, our former pastor at Lynden, Washington. After that pleasant visit, he met Jared at Seattle where they went sightseeing and spent the night.

The day of the funeral was rainy. Jared served as pallbearer with his cousins. I was glad for the tape of the service that Jake brought home.

Several ministers spoke, with Rev. George Groening giving the final message. He said, "N.N. was a man of vision. He said we must provide English services because many of the young people no longer spoke German. In that he was a forerunner. N.N. also had a love for missions, whether at home or abroad, and he never lost sight of that goal." Groening stressed that N. N. had finished the race, just as a marathon runner would burst into Athens during Paul's time crying, "Rejoice! We have triumphed!" Rev. Groening ended, "His prayer for you as a family was that each of you would fix your eyes upon Jesus, for He'll be waiting for you at the finish line."

A men's quartet and women's duet provided music. Laura More, a grand-daughter of N. N., read the loving obituary of his life. It mentioned that the separation from his family in Russia was very difficult and he often spoke of his loneliness and loss. It told of his dream of someday owning a black stallion and that this dream came true. Games of crokinole with the grandchildren and teaching some of them how to make sausage were special memories. It also stated that N.N.'s wife, Elizabeth, was the backbone of the family and the church, and without her, he would not have been able to do the work he did. He had 15 grandchildren, 15 great-grandchildren and 2 step-grandchildren, and was survived by one sister, Helen, in Germany. Mention was made of his "hearty bass voice." The reading concluded with, "We rejoice with him that he is home at last." Laura was especially close to her grandfather and read with loving expression.

In 1980, Dad started a book with lists of guests who visited him up until 1993. The half-inch thick book was filled almost to the end with the many people who visited him every day. The last years, he also recorded healings and events, such as the day he moved into Menno Home and when he got his pacemaker and walker.

On February 17, 1992, he wrote, "I sent money to Janet Friesen," probably for her upcoming wedding a month later.

On February 29, 1992, he wrote with red ink, signifying the importance of the entry: "The last 10 days in February '92 I had wonderful dreams. In the first one, Jesus himself, with a nice suit, slept beside me. As I looked and looked to see Him, He was gone.

"The next night I was in a most holy place; everything I saw looked holy. A couple of nights later, I woke up at 6:06. As I sat up in bed, I started to cry. The question was *Why does God love me so much?* I am not worthy of it. After 30 minutes, someone opened the door. I called, 'Come to my bed.' The nurse said, 'Why are you crying.' I told her, 'I don't know why God loves me so much.' She said, 'You know, we can't thank Him enough for all His grace.'"

He kept wondering, "Why these special dreams?" as he wrote in his account of them. "I looked in the Bible. In Joel 2:28,29 and Acts 2:17,18, it says:

> And afterward, I will pour out my Spirit on all people,
> Your sons and daughters will prophesy,
> your old men will dream dreams,
> your young men will see visions.
> Even on my servants, both men and women,
> I will pour out my Spirit in those days.

Dad wrote, "I spoke to some pastors and Christian nurses. The Joel prophecy was fulfilled on the day of Pentecost and God's Spirit has been poured out on mankind ever since, on those who are open and willing to receive Him."

On the last pages he reverted to his native German language, which Jake translated. He wrote about physical problems and healings, of hours of sleeplessness, as he lay awake crying and praying, with sorrow over family members and loved ones who were not ready to meet the Lord. He wrote of his two sisters, Sara and Helen, in Germany. The last entry is February 4, 1994: "I fell flat on my back. I will long feel pain (but broke no bones). Your letter (whose?) has given me much courage. Then…" It trails off, with an unfinished sentence.

It is certain that hundreds of people will be rejoicing in heaven because of Dad's faithfulness to his call as a young man on his sick bed, "Go and preach…of the great love of God." His faithfulness to the end surely brought him a great reward. He had finished his course.

CHAPTER 47

Heartbreak and Hope

And great multitudes followed Him (Jesus), and He healed them all.
MATTHEW 12:15 (NKJ)

1993–1996

In 1993, Janet and John moved from Columbia, Missouri to Lincoln, Nebraska where John worked on a Ph.D. in Agronomy. Janet worked as Career Placement Specialist in Career Services at the University of Nebraska and as Career Counselor at Southeast Community College. By the spring of 1995, they decided to begin a family. Janet had no trouble getting pregnant.

Unfortunately, in October 1995 she miscarried. She was ten weeks along and the fetus had died at six weeks. She also learned that her uterus was heart-shaped, which can complicate pregnancies. What devastating news! Janet had a feeling the baby was a girl and named her Jamie.

Before long, Janet was delighted to learn she was pregnant again. But in December, that pregnancy also ended prematurely. I grieved with her as we talked on the phone but reminded her that if a pregnancy is aborted it is probably for a good reason, as she knew. I added, "Don't worry, God knows the best time for you to get pregnant, so we will trust Him." She agreed.

On January 25, 1996, she called to say she was one month pregnant. Her due date was September 20. Before I ever had news of her third miscarriage, I cried out to the Lord at 4:45 A.M. on Valentine's Day (in my journal) and told Him Janet was in trouble. "She has trouble with her womb and needs healing. Whatever the cause, Lord, she's in trouble and discouraged. Please help her! Three miscarriages in five months would be too much.

"Lord, you reminded me this morning about healings I experienced as I read the Psalms as a youth. I'd claim my healing as I talked with You and while I 'walked by the way' to work (at the hatchery). And I *knew* You were my Healer. We need to claim Exodus 23:25, 'I will take sickness away from thee.'" I prayed, "Lord, whatever her problem, whatever the cause, you *can* remove it – and You have given me faith this morning to believe that you can and *will* remove it from her…Jesus Christ is LORD, Healer, Victor…!"

That very evening, Janet called to report the unthinkable. I could tell she had been crying. "I had another miscarriage! I cried all afternoon. I'm so discouraged." It was heartbreaking. I tried to comfort and reassure her. She told me, "John came home from work and spent the afternoon with me." I was comforted by his care for her.

The next morning, at 4:40 A.M., I wrote in my journal about our sorrow and asked God to heal Janet and let her find the problem and correct it. As I waited on the Lord in quietness, a calm came over my spirit. I knew God was in charge and that nothing is impossible for Him.

On February 17, Janet said doctors gave encouraging news: her uterus looked good and there was no permanent damage from her fall off the horse in Washington. The hospital had a special ceremony for everyone who had lost a baby due to miscarriage or stillbirth. The service was deeply meaningful and comforting to Janet.

The evening of February 29, I called Janet before taking off on a three-week trip. She said, "The test came back on the fetus and it was a normal baby girl." She and John now had three babies in heaven whom Janet had named Jamie, Bethany, and Rachel. She said, "I had a feeling that the second one was a girl too." Her next news made me happy. "We're leaving for four days at a cabin for our anniversary. At the marriage conference they said couples need to get away for a weekend, and those who don't do it need it the most."

"John is a wonderful husband!" I responded, grateful he would take time off.

We both rejoiced that her midwife Joanne encouraged her, "Despite the heart-shaped uterus, you should be able to carry a child to term." She sounded happy again and hope rose within me as I prepared to leave on a very special trip.

For months I had planned a trip to the Holy Land and Egypt, a long-time dream come true. Jake was not interested in visiting the Holy Land, saying, "I've flown into Tel Aviv." That was not good enough for me.

The summer before, my friend Sara Van Meter visited and gave us the book *Blood Brothers* by Elias Chacour, whom she and Larry had heard speak. Elias was a bridge builder between Palestinians and Israelis with a school in

Galilee for all children. One day, as I read about Elias' ministry in Nazareth and Galilee I got so inspired that I told Jake, "I want to go to Nazareth!"

He said, "Look in the *Mennonite Weekly (Review)* and call Menno Travel for a tour."

In the current issue, I was amazed to find a tour of Egypt and the Holy Land for March 1-20, 1996. I hesitated spending that much money on myself, but when our wheat check came from our Kansas land the fall of '95, it was almost exactly the cost of my trip. Jim Graber had told us, "Your wheat did better than most of the other farmers in Kansas." I thanked God from my heart for blessing us so I could take the trip guilt-free. Through Sara's gift, God had inspired me to go, Jake encouraged, and God provided the means, through Jake's work and the farm. I was ecstatic.

On March 1, 1996, I flew to New York City where I met our tour group and leader. From there we flew to Cairo and were met by missionaries Jon and Jacqueline Hoover who accompanied us on our tour. My friendly roommate was Priscilla Huyard from Lancaster County, Pennsylvania. We saw the pyramids, rode on a camel, visited the tombs of the queens and some pharaohs, had a cruise and dinner on the Nile, saw the oldest church in Cairo on the spot where Mary and Joseph supposedly had visited when they fled with Jesus, and a very large Coptic Christian Church. We took a bus to Mt. Sinai, where some in our group climbed the snowy path to the top, and we spent two wonderful days by the warm beach along the Red Sea. Here as I was beachcombing, I found a perfect little heart-shaped piece of coral, a special sign to me of Jesus' presence and love.

Back at our hotel in Cairo, at Heliopolis, dinners were superb, with always a delicious creamed soup before the entree. Breakfasts were delectable, with potato salad and cucumber and tomato salad every morning, in addition to a variety of other foods.

For several days Jake tried to reach me at the hotel but the staff misunderstood my name. Finally Jake got through and told me of two men who died suddenly, one of them our good friend Vince Kraybill. The other was Elmer Miller, founder of House of Refuge Sunnyslope (HRS) for homeless men. Elmer and I had had a long conversation by phone before I left and he said he would like Jake and me to help at HRS. What a shock to learn these two were gone!

Before we left Cairo, we heard that many people were killed in a bus bombing in Jerusalem. This raised concerns for those of us continuing on to Israel. Jon Hoover assured us that "Israel takes very good care of its tourists." I knew that tourist buses were also hit at times, but trusted the Lord for protection.

After 13 days in Egypt, I flew to Tel Aviv to join the Israel tour group for seven days. Bonnie, our friendly Jewish guide, made a point of explaining that she and our congenial Palestinian bus driver were good friends. We visited Joppa, Caesarea – where we saw Herod's enormous amphitheater, uncovered in the 1960s, where the Apostle Paul was tried – and many sites in northern Galilee. But my greatest interests were Nazareth and the Sea of Galilee. At Nazareth on March 13, we visited the beautiful Church of the Annunciation, with huge depictions of Jesus by artists from around the world gracing the walls. At a fascinating museum under the church we viewed ancient artifacts dating from the time of Christ, such as tear bottles and pottery. We entered the grotto where the holy family could have lived, with two rooms, the one in back for animals. Nazareth is situated on a high hill, and as our bus descended on the dangerous, curving road, I cringed as I recalled the incident about enraged villagers wanting to throw Jesus off the cliff.

In Nazareth I had asked Bonnie about Elias Chacour and his book and wondered about visiting his school. Imagine my surprise when she retorted, "He's a liar and his book is full of lies!" I was taken aback, then realized that his book put Jews in a bad light since he reported the killing of Palestinians and taking over their villages when Israel became a nation in 1948. I felt sad that we had to miss Elias and the school, and sad about Bonnie's attitude toward such a compassionate man.

That night we got our rooms at Ma'Agan Kibbutz (tourist center) at the southern tip of the Sea of Galilee. There I walked on the small sandy beach where the waves washed gently on shore and felt as though I was on holy ground. A sense of awe filled my being at this beautiful place and our great God who created it, and who came down to live here 2000 years ago in the form of man.

The next morning I awoke with the hymn, "Fairest Lord Jesus," on my mind. A feeling of praise and excitement gripped me. It was March 14, Mom's birthday! (She had died 31 years ago – the year Janet was born.) I was overcome with gratitude for the special providence of God in my life and how He led me here to remember her birthday and fill me with joy. I walked on the beach and, finding no shells, I picked up small stones. My eyes lit on a beautiful, tiny heart-shaped stone – another sign to me of Jesus' presence and love. What a miracle to find a heart-shaped piece of coral at the Red Sea and a heart-shaped stone here! To me, this was not coincidence.

On this adventure-filled day, we took a two-hour boat ride on the sea, where Bonnie (a Jew!) taught a class on Jesus' rich ministry around this famous sea. A crewmember gave a demonstration of Peter the fisherman throwing a net into the sea. Reveling in the beautiful warm sunny day on this calm and peaceful lake, I felt God's presence and love–and Mom's–surrounding me. All hurtful memories seemed washed away, replaced by an unbelievably deep sense of *shalom*–health and wholeness. I thought of Janet and lifted her up to Jesus' healing presence.

After disembarking, we went to the Church of the Beatitudes on the famous hillside of the Sermon on the Mount, where I signed a guest book by mistake. A nun came running and cried, "That's only for the priests!" I apologized, inwardly amused, sensing Jesus there with me, with whom there is no hierarchy and no favorites. For lunch some of our group had "Peter's fish" by the seaside; then on to the impressive ruins of Capernaum, Jesus' hometown during his three-year ministry. We saw ruins of the synagogue and were reminded of the many references to Jesus having lived and ministered in this place. From there, we drove to the Golan Heights border between Syria and Israel, where I had my picture taken with a young guard. Here 550 Austrians, 350 Poles, plus Japanese and Canadians, guarded the 50-mile border along the foot of Mount Hermon, believed to be the site of Jesus' transfiguration. We stopped by the archeological site of Herod's shops and ruins at Caesarea Philippi, place of Peter's confession, "Thou art the Christ, the Son of the living God!" What a memorable day!

Before we retired for the night, our spiritual leader for the tour, retired Lutheran pastor John Sholz of Oregon, asked us to meet on the beach by the sea in the morning. I slept so peacefully and awoke with a song of praise in my heart. I told the Lord, *"I would like to have prayer for Janet here by this sea where You healed so many thousands of people!"* Then I told my roommate, Rosemarie Oldenberg from Oregon, the same thing. I prayed for Janet every day, as well as Jake, Jared and John.

Outside, warm rays of the morning sun shone on the beach where ripling waves lapped ashore. Jesus seemed so near as I recalled how special this place was to Him. As all were gathered, Pastor Sholz said, "I'd like to have a time of prayer this morning for any requests you may have. We can't do this on the bus, so this is a good place for it. Who has a request?"

I blurted, "I'd like prayer for my daughter, Janet. She has had three miscarriages in the past months and is grieving over this. Please pray for the healing of her womb." Though for an older man that seemed a bold request, I knew that's what Janet needed. As others gave requests, Pastor Sholz wrote them down. Then he read his list, "For Janet, the healing of her hurting *heart*."

I was disappointed. He couldn't say the word *womb*? Not wanting to embarrass him, I kept quiet. Then his wife, sitting next to me, spoke up loudly, "Pray for the healing of her *womb*!" Enormously grateful to her, I chuckled inwardly.

Pastor Sholz's prayer stirred faith within me. I *knew* that God had heard and felt assured that Jesus would answer.

Leaving that beautiful seaside, we drove to the head of the Jordan River, just below the Sea of Galilee, where thousands of Christians have been baptized for years. The water was too cold for me, but some of our group were immersed. At this site I met Jean and Jane who were traveling with a large group from Calvary Church in Phoenix. I was surprised to meet another Jane I had met at the Druze village, so we had our picture taken together.

We continued south to ruins of a huge Roman gladiator amphitheater built 5000 years ago, which Jesus would likely have passed through. From there we drove along the famed Jordan River to Jericho, where we saw an archeological site (part of the wall of Jericho, made of bricks, supposedly "sunk into the ground by angels"), and a large sycamore tree like Zacchaeus climbed. Later we came back to the Dead Sea, but for now we were off to Bethlehem and Jerusalem.

I loved driving through the shepherds' fields to Bethlehem and buying olive wood items in the shops there. The ornate church, built over the supposed site of the stable of Jesus' birth, was full of groups of worshipers, whose devotion was more impressive to me than the building.

In Jerusalem, it was sobering to contemplate the crucifixion at Calvary, but exciting to recall resurrection morning at the empty tomb. Nearby, we celebrated Communion in the beautiful garden. At the Mount of Olives, Bonnie led us in singing, "I Come to the Garden Alone," as we walked the path lined with ancient olive trees to the church with the rock where it is believed Jesus prayed. At the Temple mount, I stuck a rolled up paper with a prayer I wrote into a crack in the Wailing Wall, along with hundreds of other prayers. I was touched to see Orthodox Jews praying and wailing over the loss of the Temple. Along the Temple steps, an abundance of rosemary bloomed with tiny blue flowers. The archeological dig below the Temple of the main street—where we were told Jesus must have walked many times—inspired me with awe. Here we met the chief Israeli and U. S. archeologists, a friendly, happy team. At the dark and somber Holocaust Museum, the names of the six million Jews who died are read continuously.

By contrast, the Upper Room where Jesus supposedly ate the Last Supper and where the Holy Spirit fell on the 120 praying believers was bright, with windows and arches. A group of Pentecostals joined us in another part of the spacious room. They sang, "We are standing on Holy Ground," and "Sweet Holy Spirit," two songs I love. Our guide Bonnie became greatly excited as they began praying in tongues.

"That's the first time I've ever heard that here," she exclaimed, "and I've been coming here for 17 years!" Feeling enormously privileged, I was transported back 2000 years to the Day of Pentecost. So much biblical history had come alive for me over the past seven days in this land of the Messiah.

At our hotel one evening, a Mennonite Central Committee worker spoke to us about the work of MCC in Israel and the West Bank. He told inspiring stories of efforts by Israeli and Palestinian Christians to build bridges of understanding and love between all people.

I flew back to New York tired but greatly inspired by all I had seen and experienced. Jesus' life and presence came alive for me in new ways and was more precious shared with believers from many countries. In addition, my hope for a grandchild had taken wings with the prayers to Jesus, the Healer. I couldn't wait to call Janet with the good news of the prayer for her womb by the Sea of Galilee.

CHAPTER 48

Exciting News!

Lord, you have been our dwelling place in all generations.
PSALM 90:1 (NKJ)

1996

The year 1996 was a year of trips for me. As Jake traveled for his job to exotic and ho-hum places, I often traveled alone to see my family in Pennsylvania or to visit our children. But this year was different. After my trip to the Holy Land and Egypt, we anticipated a first-ever family reunion with Jake's mother's family in July at Mayfair, Saskatchewan, where he was born. We were delighted that Janet, John and Jared could come too.

On our flight from Phoenix to Minneapolis, I was so inspired about the reunion and Jake's background that I wrote a list of 45 things we have in common! At the Minneapolis airport we met Janet and John and together visited the famous, humongous Mall of America where we found a restaurant. Janet was in a particularly happy mood and no sooner had we sat down, when she blurted out across the table, *"We're going to have a baby in March!"*

"You are?!" I fairly flew out of my chair and ran around the table to give her a hug. The men enjoyed our exuberance and we all laughed together about this joyful news. Janet's confidence and faith were striking after her three demoralizing losses. It had been almost three months since the prayer at the Sea of Galilee, which reinvigorated our faith.

The happy glow on John's face testified to his excitement as well. After all, he was the one who told Janet before they were married that he wanted *12 children!* Later he pared that down to six. Janet had hesitated to get pregnant at all, saying, "I'm not into pain."

John expressed his concern to me on one of my visits to them. I encouraged, "We have to pray about it and in time she will be ready." What a joy to see them happy together at the prospect of a baby.

The reunion with Jake's sisters, Margaret and Peter and Mary Ann and Dave, and brother Peter and Mary, aunts, uncles, and cousins, was a memorable occasion. At Saskatoon we had a day of storytelling by Jake's siblings and relatives with much laughter and some tears, recalling the sorrows of the move to Canada and tremendous hardships their parents had endured – poverty, language barrier, backbreaking work, loss of crops.

Jake's mother's only living sibling, Uncle Peter, was weak and frail so his daughter Olga read his story, with tears of grief and love. Peter and Jake's mother had been very close and Uncle Peter's remarks began with her. "Elizabeth was very loving, giving, and extremely hardworking. She ran the farm single-handedly with N. N. gone so much. Women were not recognized back then. She was an excellent pastor's wife and carried many burdens. She was the backbone of the family and church in her quiet way. In addition to all the farm work, she helped much in the church and community. They were very poor."

Uncle Peter wept as Olga continued, "Elizabeth was loved by all. She had great concern for others. She did not show disrespect to her husband. She was a loving and dynamic mother – strong, well, and tireless."

Recovering his composure, Uncle Peter mustered his strength to tell a story about Jake's older brother Peter. "One day when Peter was small, he killed or strangled seven young ducklings, then went to his mother and told her they were all sleeping. She must have been very disappointed." Uncle Peter ended with a regret: "I should have given her much more recognition and appreciation when I was young."

After the meetings at Saskatoon, we drove to Mayfair, Jake's birthplace, listed as "SEC23 TP46 RGE12 W3RD CAN" (Section, Township, Range, Ward) on his birth certificate. Here Jake's grandfather Duerksen helped to start a church when they arrived from Russia in the 1920s. A service was held in the small church, with family members taking leadership. Janet was recruited as song leader, John read the Scripture, and Bob Zayonc, Olga's son and a sharp young minister, gave a dynamic message. After the service, we went outside where a plaque commemorating the Duerksen family as founding members was unveiled on a rock in front of the church.

After the service, we drove to the homestead of Grandfather P. G. Duerksen. The log house was in serious disrepair, but the very large barn was in good shape. We visited the site where Jake's parents' house once stood, close to the railroad track. Other log homes were in various stages of dilapidation. Janet and John and Jared enjoyed this excursion with aunts and uncles and seeing where their dad was born and lived until age four. Much humor and laughter added spice and a light touch to the weekend. We reveled in the stories and lives of Jake's unusual "Russian" relatives on this truly wonderful family vacation.

In my family that year, Grace began dating a man she was very excited about and called to tell me about Philip. It was obvious that the feeling was mutual, so I wasn't surprised when on May 17, 1996, after 18 years of single life, Grace married Philip Covelli, whom she met through a good friend. Grace had changed her name back to *Herstine* and decided to keep her maiden name. Philip teaches classical guitar and other instruments at his home studio and at a branch of the Settlement Music Schools of Philadelphia. At the time, Grace worked for the American Baptist Foundation at Valley Forge and lived in nearby Phoenixville.

Janet and her pregnancy were often in my thoughts and prayers. On August 7, after an ultrasound, she called me with surprising news, "The baby is due *March 14!*"

"March 14?" I repeated in disbelief. "That was my stepmother's birthday! It's the day I was on the Sea of Galilee and felt Jesus' love and hers—and mine for her—so strongly. I felt total peace and forgiveness toward her; and the next morning the pastor and our whole group prayed for you for the healing of your womb. This is incredible! What a blessing and miracle!"

She agreed and I reminded, "We know that babies don't always arrive on their due date—like you were ten days early—but God can do anything!"

"Yes," Janet replied. "John and I saw the fetus on the ultrasound. The person who did the ultrasound was so excited, and so was Joanne (nurse midwife) when she saw it. I saw the heartbeat, which is twice as fast as the mother's. It squiggled around a lot and Joanne said that shows that it has a good blood supply." I had specifically prayed for that, since one of the other fetuses was in the top of one side of the "heart" where it lacked blood supply. We rejoiced together.

Late that afternoon I called her back. "Did you dedicate the baby to the Lord?" I asked.

"Yes!" she answered.

"I did, too." We would wait and pray in expectation until March 14th.

My next trip in August was a total surprise and I love surprises. Jake worked for a Scottsdale company that flew charters, sometimes for famous people. He told me, "Next week I'll be taking Michael Jordan and his family for a three-week vacation to Hawaii."

"Three weeks? This time I want to go!" Since the company had gotten reservations for me once before to fly to Hawaii when Jake was there, and that time didn't work out because the passenger didn't stay put on one island, I didn't hesitate this time. I was ready!

Jake told the office staff at Scottsdale and they got me a ticket to fly commercially. We had 11 glorious days *free* at a Marriott Hotel on Maui. Since our 35th anniversary was coming up on September 3, I called it our 35th anniversary trip.

We rented a car and drove on the 52-mile famous road to Hana with its 617 curves and 56 bridges, most of them one lane. Beautiful scenery through rain forest with alternating rain and sunshine, waterfalls, flowers, and birds delighted us. We drove up Mt. Haleakala, the 10,000-foot volcano which scientists claim has had 800,000 years of fiery existence. Labeled dormant but not extinct, its last eruption was in 1790. The view was magnificent but the cold wind soon sent us on our way.

On the trip down we found a restaurant with a fantastic view. As we finished our meal, a man I had noticed by the window I was facing came to our table and said, "I'd like to buy you dessert. I've been watching you and you were so sweet, just glowing, and I couldn't resist. I wanted to be drawn in!" What an unusual compliment! How could we deny him? We offered him a seat and ordered key lime pie. For the next 30 to 40 minutes he told us tales of adventures, work and family—from around the world and the country. He called himself "Father" Kelly, a priest of sorts that we couldn't figure out, and said his family lived nearby and he had a wonderful wife and children. Yet he had looked so lonely and forlorn sitting by himself earlier. We later wondered if his tales were too tall to be credible and what his life was really like.

At Lahina, a coastal town close to our hotel, we saw the powerful movie *A Time To Kill*, filmed in Canton, Mississippi where we had lived. We enjoyed walking around Lahina, where enormous banyan trees graced the town square, explored a whale museum and fishing ship, and ate at a restaurant that protruded partly over the water's edge.

Before I joined him, Jake had told me about a worship service on the beach Sunday morning. He knew I'd want to go. That Sunday morning, I woke at 4:30, as I often did, and began to pray. I prayed for the service and the speaker and that we would have a message from the Word.

The service could not have been more inspiring. The speaker, a layman from the Baptist Church in Lahina, told about the miraculous ways of God in his life, and his call ten years ago to preach on the beach at this Mormon hotel. His sermon on worry was filled with positive faith and admonitions from Scripture. He said, "Worry creates stress and does no good at all." His father left his mother when he was two, and he often wondered, "Would I be different if I had a father who would do things with me? Twelve years ago, I realized I had a Father all the time – the Lord Jesus Christ!"

After the moving story of his conversion, he said, "Do we have any prayer requests? I want to pray for you. We should always bring our requests to God."

As in Galilee, I was the first to speak. "I want to praise God that our daughter is pregnant again for the fourth time after three miscarriages. My request is that she will carry this baby full term." After the other requests, he prayed a fervent, faith-filled prayer, and I felt lifted to the throne of heaven. For Janet he prayed, "For the one who is pregnant after the miscarriages, Lord God, you do miracles. Do a miracle in that life." Other warm hearts around us from various nationalities affirmed the prayer with "Amen" or other audible expressions. In my heart I believed it was done.

After the service I spoke to the leader and thanked him for his sermon and prayer for Janet. I told him, "When I awoke at 4:30 this morning I was praying for people and I prayed for you and the service and that we'd have a message from the Word."

He responded, "I felt different this morning. I was on fire! I felt so free." I was incredibly grateful for God's blessing and gift of hope through this man of God, Richard Murray, on another beach. I could never have imagined these prayer times for Janet on two beaches separated by thousands of miles: Galilee in Israel, and Maui in Hawaii. God is the God who does wonders!

I also marveled that this fantastic vacation in Hawaii didn't cost us a cent. Every morning we enjoyed scrumptious brunches at the hotel with tropical fruits, eggs, potatoes, meats, and pastries. The open restaurant by the beach with its balmy climate provided the perfect setting. We drove all over the island in a free rental car. (Jake told me that it probably cost Michael Jordan $8000 a day for not releasing the Gulfstream for other trips.) We were thrilled to have this relaxing time together to enjoy the beautiful green island, tropical flowers, and endless fields of pineapple. The native Hawaiian people blessed me with their humble, quiet, and sweet spirits.

After we returned, Jake received a big raise, and a week later the crew all got a $5000 bonus. However, Jake was extremely unhappy with the job because the other pilot did not comply with FAA regulations and the owner of the plane didn't care. Jake was ready to quit.

Exactly a week later, after a huge ruckus and upset, Jake came home with a big smile and said, "I was fired today!" Unbelievable! But he was elated. The constant haggling and stress related to the other pilot and the owner's volatile personality and crazy lifestyle had gotten to Jake. He had stood his ground and took the rap for it. He was ready for a breather and some time off.

Now we looked forward to a trip to visit our children. Jared had bought a '94 Saturn that he liked really well and that fall of 1996 we decided to buy a year-old one like it. Janet and John needed a larger four-door car for the baby, so we decided to sell them our Nissan. When I talked with John on the phone he sounded very happy about the baby and exclaimed, "Janet walks a foot off the floor!"

In October, we drove through Colorado on our way to Janet and John's to deliver our car to them. We had a delightful overnight stop to visit niece Amy and husband Tim near Denver. I had been privileged to attend Amy's lovely wedding to Tim Udager on August 27, 1994 in Pennsylvania when Anna and John lived at Newtown. (Tim and Amy later moved to Tim's hometown, Rapid City, South Dakota, where they live with their three sons. In August 2007, our family enjoyed a good time with Amy and boys at Mt. Rushmore Campground, where the cousins swam, played, and got acquainted.)

Janet was a career counselor at the University of Nebraska and the day we arrived in Lincoln she was involved in a Career Day, which we attended. She was dressed up and looked so professional and attractive. I was very proud of her. There we met a lawyer from Meridian, Mississippi who told us he was the only black lawyer in east Mississippi. It was good to hear there was at least one!

After a good time with Janet and John we flew from Lincoln to Little Rock, Arkansas, where Jared lived. From there we drove with Jared to Jackson, Mississippi to show him the hospital where he was born and a bit of the city; then drove north to where we had lived at Valley View near Canton. Jared was interested in seeing his first hometown.

I had an assignment to write three articles on our MCC VS experience in Mississippi in 1965-67 for *Christian Living* magazine. The first article was due out in the October/November issue. Research in my diaries and files refreshed my memory on those days and was good preparation for this trip.

Returning after 30 years, we were amazed at the changes everywhere. Instead of dilapidated unpainted shacks, we saw nice brick homes. What a transformation! Jared enjoyed meeting many of the people we had known 30 years ago, very poor back then but now prosperous with good jobs. Jessie McCullough had been elected County Supervisor. He gave us a tour and took us to see the movie set from *A Time to Kill*, in a huge building with the interior of the courthouse inside. He was an "extra" in the movie and enjoyed watching the filming. Though his wife was gone, he invited us for breakfast at his home one morning.

Shirley Simmons, Jake's former young secretary at the Community Center, was now president of the Madison County School Board and proudly told us she was often on TV and in newspapers. We enjoyed breakfast in a restaurant with Shirley and her husband, Princeton, and another black couple. We were surprised to meet Mr. J. T. Shaw who had owned the tiny store in a shack next to our house; now he was proprietor, with his son, of a spanking new gas station in Canton. We returned to Little Rock inspired by the changes in Mississippi and the success of our friends.

As I looked back over the year I was amazed at God's goodness and leading through all the trips: Egypt and the Holy Land by myself; Hawaii and Colorado with Jake; and Saskatchewan, Lincoln, Little Rock and Canton with the children. My heart overflowed with gratitude.

Now we anticipated the birth of our grandchild.

CHAPTER 49

A Blessing Heaven-Sent

For this child I prayed.
1 SAMUEL 1:27 (KJV)

1996–1997

Jared went to Dillard's in Little Rock in 1991 as a computer programmer/analyst, with a goal of staying about five years. "It will give me good experience to work for a Fortune 500 company," he told us, "but I don't want to work for a big corporation all my life. So I'll stay at Dillard's five years."

I loved visiting him at Little Rock about once a year, and sometimes Jake went with me. We enjoyed exploring the city of the Clintons and I took daily walks on the nearby golf course. Jared took us to the wooded canyon in the city to hike and to Hot Springs and Pinnacle Mountain. He introduced us to the intricacies of department store buying, sales and inside stories. Jake and I were impressed with his Southern Baptist church, which had an excellent preacher. On one of my visits he encouraged me to get busy on my book. He was excited about what I had written and I was grateful for his enthusiasm about the project. I needed a push.

True to his word, Jared moved back to Kansas in October 1996, to work for his former employer, Stan Roth, at Executive Aircraft. While applying for other jobs, he had called Stan to ask for a reference. Stan told him, "I just told my people that I need to hire someone to fix up our computer systems. I'd like you to visit us to talk about it." Jared flew to Wichita for a weekend and talked with Stan and other employees. Stan asked about his salary at Dillard's and, much to Jared's surprise, Stan said, "I can match that amount." Jared thought it over and accepted the offer.

Jared found an apartment in Wichita and hunted for a house. Like his dad, he is frugal and a saver. He decided on one of the first houses he had looked at – a great house and location in a development in the far northwest corner of the city. He called us often to discuss negotiations. It was listed at $90,000, the price we had paid in Lynden for our dream home 17 years earlier, but his was a smaller place. He made a counter offer of $83,000, they countered with $87,000 and settled on his offer of $86,500.

The 1080 sq. ft. main level had two bedrooms, two baths, living/dining room with fireplace, vaulted ceilings, and kitchen. The fully-finished basement with another 1080 sq. ft. had carpet throughout, a large game room for a ping-pong table, bathroom, utility room, small bedroom, and a good-sized room that he used for his office. An oak banister by the open stairway matched the oak kitchen cabinets. The former owner had built a large attractive deck in back with benches all around. The back yard bordered a wooded area, and wooden fences on either side of the yard gave privacy.

Jared's moving weekend was January 24-25, 1997. Jake was conveniently there on a trip so he and Jared picked me up at the airport. The next day, Jake helped at Jared's apartment before leaving on a trip with Lone Star Steak House to North Carolina, Tennessee, Wilmington and other cities. I packed and cleaned. Janet and John arrived from Lincoln that evening. We worked like troopers, loading a U-Haul and our car, then unloading at 12123 West 19th Street, Jared's new address. The bitter cold and wind killed the leaves on his beautiful indoor ficus tree, but its lovely green foliage grew back within the year.

Jake called to say that he would be back by about 3:00 a.m. so Jared and I waited up for him, unpacking, cleaning, and organizing. By 1:00 we were exhausted when the doorbell rang. Jake was early! On Saturday, the three men finished moving so Janet and I unpacked. It was fun getting Jared settled in his first house.

Since Janet would turn 32 on January 27, we celebrated with the Grabers at the German buffet, The Breadbasket, at Newton. Ruby was bubbly with all kinds of good news on their family and we were excited together about Janet's successful pregnancy. She was feeling great, with seven weeks to go till March 14.

On March 13 at 6:45 a.m. Janet called with excited voice, "We're ready to leave for the hospital. My water broke and contractions are starting." I assured her we'd be praying and we hung up. Would the baby be born on the 14th? We waited and wondered and waited some more. No word. By evening we were getting anxious. Why hadn't we heard? Disappointed that this happened on the 13th, I realized that the delay could mean the baby would be born exactly as predicted. Nevertheless, we became more and more concerned when we heard nothing.

Finally I called St. Elizabeth's Hospital in Lincoln. The receptionist could not give information on the phone, so I asked for Janet's room in the birthing suite. "I'm sorry, but they are not taking calls."

I was devastated. Why could we not reach them? What could possibly be wrong? I called my sister Anna and she tried to reassure me and told about Amy's delivery story when her son was born in January. I called Jared. He said, "Call the hospital back and ask a nurse to give a message to Janet and have the nurse call you back." But somehow I couldn't. I told him, "The hospital has rules!" But I should have taken his advice.

I *had* to keep faith and told Jake, "We have to *pray!*" Aloud I lifted Janet up, *Please, Father, protect Janet and the baby and keep them safe!* We went to bed hoping for the best.

Sleep eluded me as I wondered what was happening. Hadn't we prayed at the Sea of Galilee and in Hawaii? Hadn't God answered the prayers in Galilee for the healing of her womb? Yes. Hadn't He answered the prayers in Hawaii for her to carry the baby full term? Yes. But there was one more thing—the special date—March 14th! I remembered my own long labor with Janet from morning on the 26th until 2:02 a.m. on the 27th. I prayed, *"Father, I don't understand You, but I trust You,"* and drifted off to sleep. (I learned this meaningful prayer from the prayer garden at Canaan in the Desert in Phoenix.)

The next morning the phone rang about 8:00 and John gave us the long-awaited news: *"We have a baby boy, Joel Jacob, named for his Opa, Jake!* He weighs 8 pounds 7 ounces and was born at 2:25 this morning. There were complications, and things didn't progress well. Janet had a C-section after hours of labor. She's doing fine and can tell you more later. Joel definitely has good lungs!" We congratulated John and praised the Lord for this wonderful news.

Then I realized, *Joel's birth date was right on target—March 14!* He was a gift of love to me on Mom's birthday, as predicted, and I marveled again at our great and loving God.

Janet called about 7:00 that evening and told about the exhausting 22 hours of labor. But she sounded so happy for her baby and said, "This is the life!" She felt like a queen, getting waited on and just holding and nursing her beautiful son.

Janet explained, "His head was turned and Joanne, the midwife, was hoping it would turn. She had me *run* up and down the hall. That was hard. John ran with me, and the baby turned his head. Then she had me squat for 30 minutes, but I was tired so I sat in a rocking chair and his head turned back. I could have run the hall again but Joanne was concerned I'd be too exhausted, so I rested in bed for several hours. Eventually all the monitors went off because his head was pushing down against the umbilical cord. So Joanne had to reach in and push his head back. She made the decision to do a C-section, since by then I was too worn out to push. I had no painkiller until 10:00, then got an epidural at 2:00 or just before the C-section." How thankful I was that God kept mother and baby safe through this trying ordeal.

Though I planned to fly to Lincoln to help Janet, I was hit hard with an allergy attack. After my second trip to the doctor, she blamed it on our two mulberry trees in the back yard and ordered, "You go home and get rid of them *today!*" Jake was on a trip and I felt helpless. I called him and he said he'd chop them down when he returned in a day or so. Removing the huge trees was backbreaking work. How I hated losing the beautiful tree that shaded our back patio. Our Iraqi Kurd friend Carlo helped; then Jake dug out the enormous stumps by hand.

Due to congestion and a bad cough, I slept on the big chair in the living room for two weeks. I wanted desperately to help Janet and see Joel but I was too sick. Janet warned, "The doctor says not to let anyone near him who is sick or has a cough." I would comply.

Janet soon reported struggling with breastfeeding, Joel's continual crying, and her lack of sleep. This broke my heart. I wept when I got off the phone with her; then wept tears of joy when Jake finally made my reservations to fly out on March 25. Jake planned to join me soon, since John had graduated with a Ph.D. in Agronomy and accepted a post-doc position at Ames, Iowa. They were getting ready to move and we could help them.

Janet met me at the airport in Omaha with her precious "bundle" – our grandson Joel, 11 days old. He was so quiet and sweet. He looked into my eyes the same way Janet had the first time I held her. What a special moment! I held our "miracle baby" at last!

As Janet drove to the university to show Joel to her coworkers, Joel began to fuss in the back seat. Then he screamed so loudly that it tore me up. Due to my late arrival his feeding time was delayed and he was upset.

"Stop the car!" I demanded. "I want to hold him."

"He's OK," she insisted. "He does that all the time. He cried like that day and night for three days before I went to the breastfeeding clinic. Since I'm supplementing with formula he's been much happier." That was little comfort to me as he screamed at the top of his lungs for 15 minutes. I could hardly bear to hear this dear little helpless one in so much distress. We hurried him into a small room at the university where Janet fed him and he was content.

How I enjoyed Joel, holding and loving him. I packed and cleaned cupboards and their apartment in preparation for the move. Jake arrived two days later and was quite taken with his little namesake. It was wonderful to be "Oma" and "Opa" to this tiny boy. Two days later, on Saturday, March 29, Jared came from Wichita. He also enjoyed holding and getting acquainted with his nephew.

That day, our loaded caravan headed for Ames. Jake drove the U-Haul, John his pickup, and I drove their Nissan with Janet in front and 15-day-old Joel in back. Jared trailed behind in his car. After my initial car ride with Baby Joel, I was concerned about this four-hour trip and prayed earnestly for him to stay peaceful. The Lord answered wonderfully and after one brief, hard crying spell, Joel was quiet the whole four hours.

At Ames, we got things settled into their nice two-bedroom apartment. The next day, Easter Sunday, we celebrated Jesus' resurrection at the Evangelical Free Church. Joel was mostly quiet. A very cold strong wind blew snow in our faces, but Joel was safely covered with a blanket in his car seat. Jake and Jared returned home the next day. I loved staying on for two and a half more weeks.

I kept occupied cleaning cupboards, unpacking, and cooking as Janet took care of Joel and tried to catch up on sleep. Breastfeeding was a challenge and I helped with bottle-feeding when I could. I was delighted to take the nighttime feeding at 2:25 when he was four weeks old—the exact time of his birth one month earlier. Janet slept through this night feeding for the first time in a month. John loved to hold his little boy and helped where he could.

On April 3 I recorded, "Joel smiled a lot today!" That Saturday I babysat him while Janet and John went on a date for lunch, a movie, and shopping. I relished this time alone with my grandson. After I fed him, he was completely quiet and peaceful as I held and talked to him. When he fell asleep, I stood up with him and he smiled and made noises. Then he smiled another big smile and laughed out loud – in his sleep! It was so precious. How I praised the Lord for this wonderful gift – a blessing heaven-sent.

One day when I talked to Joel he looked at me intelligently and bright-faced and started "talking" back to me. Janet captured us on camera with his mouth open, speaking. I told his parents, "Joel is precocious!"

On April 19, John and Janet took me to the airport at Des Moines. As we ate at a restaurant, John gave me gifts: a book by Aldo Leopold, *A Sand County Almanac* (one of John's favorite authors and books from his studies on conservation and nature in Wisconsin), a lovely silver hummingbird pin, and a framed certificate, "For Being An Awesome Grandmother," signed by "Joel Jacob Brejda." I was deeply touched as John lovingly expressed their appreciation and gratitude for my help the past weeks.

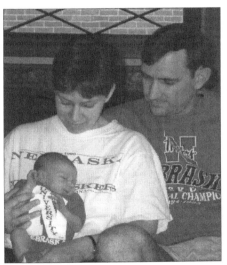 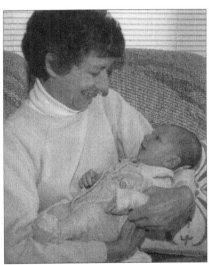

Janet, John, Joel Jacob Brejda, 1 week old. March 21, 1997.

Joel "talking" to me, "Oma," at 4 weeks old.

Later, as my plane lifted off into the sky, my heart was heavy for Janet and I wished we were closer so that I could help her more. I was comforted by the memory of John holding Joel on one arm and the Bible in the other hand, as he stood and read the devotions before breakfast one morning. How John loved his little son whom he called "Big Guy," and was very attentive to him.

When I called Janet on Sunday afternoon, she burst into tears and cried, *"He misses you!"* I was absolutely heartbroken as I listened to her anguished tale and wanted to fly right back.

"I think *you* miss me!" I said, and she agreed. And I sorely missed them both.

"He was so fussy during the night, kept losing his pacifier, and in the afternoon he kept waking and fussing and I couldn't sleep. I'm so tired!"

I had kept Joel so quiet when she slept that I knew it would be hard when I left. The next day when I called, she was much better and on top of things. "I just changed him," she said; and I heard him cooing.

"Give him a kiss for me," I said, and she reported, "He smiled when I kissed him."

"Let me talk to him." She put the receiver to his ear as I spoke.

"He really listened!" she exclaimed happily. "He's so cuddly at night, so soft and sweet." I remembered well how he was like a warm, relaxed cuddly kitten—but so much more wonderful. The old Janet was back and I praised God for giving her joy and delight in her precious son.

When I visited them in May, Janet told me about a study done with babies. "The study said that by one year babies engage adults. You can't ignore them." Her eyes shone as she said, "Joel is so engaging with his smile and the look in his eyes and face!" My sentiments exactly!

In July, I returned to Ames and we drove to Anna and John's in Cuba City, Wisconsin. Amy was there with her son Brennen and she and Janet enjoyed catching up with each other. It was good to be with family, and I loved seeing Joel's progress and development and bonded with him again.

In August we drove to Jared's with a used pickup Jake had bought, loaded down with Janet and Jared's boxes, which we had stored for them. Jared had room for them now. (Later, when Janet and John bought a house in Lincoln, they were only five hours from Jared, and Janet retrieved her loot.) We drove back to Phoenix straight through in 17 hours.

In October we again drove to Wichita, continuing on to Janet and John's in Ames. From there we all drove to Anna and John's in Wisconsin, where Ralph and Janice and Ruth and Dave had come from Pennsylvania. Anna and John's house bulged with this mini reunion of Herstines, where we enjoyed a rousing good time.

What a great year 1997 turned out to be with our heaven-sent blessing! I prayed Joel would grow up to love Jesus and know the God who does wonders—and performed the miracle of his birth.

CHAPTER 50

A Second Blessing

You are the God who works miracles.
PSALM 77:14 (GNB)

1998–1999

In May of 1998, I flew to Iowa for Mother's Day and Joel's dedication. Due to the large number of babies to be dedicated, a separate service was held after the worship service. After calling parents to the stage and opening remarks, the pastor asked John to pray. He prayed a passionate, eloquent prayer for the children and that the parents would raise them in the admonition of the Lord. He spoke of the dangers in the world and prayed for protection from harm and evil. I was deeply touched and comforted as John poured out his heart for our grandson and all those present. Several people thanked John later and commented on his moving prayer.

In November, Jake's brother Peter and wife Mary came for Thanksgiving. One day I said to Jake, "Let's take Peter and Mary to see where we want to live in Sun City." We had friends living there and I had told Jake I would like to move there sometime. For years he had talked about buying a condo so he wouldn't have yard work to contend with after trips. We drove past our friends' house on Sandstone Drive then turned the corner onto Shasta, where a sign greeted us: "For Sale – Open House."

Mary cried, "Let's go in and take a look!" We did and liked what we saw. Mary raved about the new Berber carpet throughout, and the realtor said the walls were freshly painted. He noted, "The woman who bought the place was coming out on a flight from Denver and died an hour into the flight. The plane turned around and took her back." She had planned to join her children here. As a result, the house stood empty for two years.

We liked that area of Sun City with a green belt of winter grass (rye), no walls enclosing the yards, and many trees. Before the week was out, we decided to buy the duplex at 9542 Shasta Drive, with closing in January. Our children were less than enthused, thinking we were too young for Sun City!

In early December when I talked with Janet, she reported, "Joel is so focused. When we were at a friend's house, he put tapes in and out of their stereo for hours and then screamed when it was time to leave!" He loved books, as I had predicted because, during his first months, his little basket bed was placed in front of a bookcase in the living room. He stared intently at those shelves of colorful paperbacks and book jackets for hours, while listening to classical and Christian music on the stereo. Janet and John read to him at a young age and he became absorbed in books. His first favorite was *Goodnight Moon* by Margaret Wise Brown and Clement Hurd.

At Christmastime our family came to our Phoenix house for the last time. We all enjoyed Joel immensely. When I held him and danced around the room to music, he squealed with delight. Most days the weather was perfect and Joel enjoyed playing outside on the patio with toys and croquet balls. Jake liked to pick an orange from our tree and hold it while Joel sucked on it.

For Christmas, Joel gave me an envelope with a picture of himself holding baby Charlie, Janet's friend's baby. On the card was written, *"Practicing for when I'm a big brother in August!"* What special news!

When Janet got home, she called on January 5 to say, "I was just to the doctor and we have a heartbeat!" My heart rejoiced that all was well.

On Saturday, January 16, 1999, our small group helped us move to Sun City, about 13 miles to the northwest. We were blessed with two beautiful pink camellia shrubs blooming at the back of our house and gorgeous roses on the east side.

We had put a "For Sale" sign out on Augusta Avenue on January 5 and several people came to look. The evening we moved, a woman across the street on Augusta said she was interested. When she saw it she exclaimed, "I love this house! I love this house! I've always loved this house!" Outside on the patio she cried, "This is my favorite part of the house! I love this back yard!" We had our buyer. We bought it 11 years earlier for $75,000. She agreed to $106,300 and bought it the next day, four days after our move. The new house cost us $83,500. We marveled at God's guidance and help.

One day on the phone, Janet said that they pray at the table with Joel for people at church and related a heartwarming story. "When I took Joel to the pediatrician for his two-year checkup, as we left the clinic a woman I had seen at church came toward us with a boy and a baby. She was crying. I asked her what was wrong. She said that they had another son who was just diagnosed with a disease that starts at the feet and moves up the legs and paralyzes as it goes, if not caught in time. I gave her a hug and told her I'd pray for him."

"Guillain-Barré Syndrome," I told Janet. "An 80-year-old woman at our church was recently diagnosed with it. Once it reaches the lungs, it paralyzes them and the patient can't breathe."

Janet added, "A friend told me that sometimes they don't recover." Yes, I knew it could be fatal.

Janet continued, "As we walked to the car I told Joel, 'Her boy is sick. We need to pray for him.' We did. Several times that day, Joel said to me, 'Her boy is sick. We need to pray for him.' So we stopped and prayed together. Joel repeated that for the next three days, so we kept on praying. A few days later I heard that the boy was out of the hospital. Doctors were amazed that he recovered so quickly. The next time I saw the boy's mother, I told her about Joel's reminders and how we prayed."

Several months later, Janet told me the boy was well. What a spiritually sensitive child Joel was at two years of age, having learned to pray by his parents' example. Later I learned that Guillain-Barré Syndrome is treatable if it is diagnosed in time, and children recover more quickly than adults. Even so, I believe that God answered the simple prayers of a child who had complete trust in God to hear and answer (as well as many other prayers for that boy).

As the end of John's two-year job loomed ahead, he applied for other jobs and had interviews but nothing worked out. Janet longed to go back to Lincoln so she could have the baby with nurse midwife Joanne. In May of 1999, Janet learned that their insurance would not cover the delivery, and John still needed a job. When she told him about the insurance he said, "Then we need to tell as many people as we can to pray for us." Two days later, John received word that he had another post-doc position back at Lincoln. Janet was ecstatic. Joanne could deliver the baby in August.

Before leaving Ames, Janet and John wanted to visit my sister Anna and John in Wisconsin one more time. Joel remembered them from his previous visit. Later when I talked with Anna on the phone she exclaimed, "Joel looks so much like you!" I had thought at times that he favors the Herstines and it was sweet of Anna to tell me that.

Janet and John moved to Lincoln over the 4th of July 1999. The timing was perfect since the baby was due August 16. Jake and I flew to Omaha, rented a car and drove to Ames to help pack and load the truck on Friday. Saturday we drove to Lincoln, and Jared drove up from Wichita. Janet and John had rented a three-bedroom house with a basement apartment below. The new place was a block from a park and had nice streets for stroller rides, one of my favorite activities with Joel. I stayed on to help get them settled.

Janet took the task of preparing Joel for his new brother very seriously, explaining things and letting him feel her tummy. During her previous pregnancy, Joanne showed her a rubber doll each month and told her, "This is how big your baby is now." With this pregnancy, Joanne did the same thing.

One day when Janet and John were in her office, Joanne got out the rubber doll. Joel said, "Joel want to rock the baby." Joanne gave him the doll and he sat down on the floor. He held it and looked at it intently, checking out its eyes and fingers.

John, impressed, said, "He's really into this! Let him rock the baby." Joel held and rocked the baby. They hoped this would help him accept his new brother.

Janet's pregnancy went well. She was taking progesterone for the first trimester, as she had with Joel. After three miscarriages, the midwife knew that's what was lacking. God had answered our prayers with this simple solution. This time I flew out *before* the birth. I arrived on her due date, but this baby decided to take its time – a whole week more.

On the morning of August 23, I awoke at 4:14 and heard noises, then saw light under my door and got up to investigate.

"We're leaving for the hospital," Janet said. "Contractions started around 3:30." We all hoped she could deliver this one naturally, with no complications. She gave me last minute instructions for Joel. I looked forward to caring for him, now two years and five months old.

John called at 7:45. "We're making progress. Contractions are about a minute and a half apart. Joanne is here now." It felt good to be kept informed this time.

When Joel got up around 8:00 he said, "Where's Dad?" Then, "Where's Daddy?"

I said, "I have a surprise to tell you."

"What is the surprise you have for me?"

"Mommy and Daddy are at the hos..." and he finished it, "pital!" He was well prepared and was quite the talker.

John called while we were at the park. At 11:15 he called again to report, "Josiah John was born at 10:48! He was born in just under six hours of labor, with no forceps. Janet pushed him out!" He weighed 7 pounds, 6 ounces. What great news! She had told me that after one has had a C-section, doctors don't often advise a natural birth; midwives do more often. What a wonderful answer to prayer!

That afternoon before supper, Joel asked me to read his *God Loves Me Bible*. As I opened it, he asked, "Where's the one about the disciples?" I found it and he said, "Read it." This story with an illustration of Jesus' 12 followers was his favorite. His interest in Jesus and the Bible blessed me.

That afternoon John came home so I could go to see Janet and hold Josiah. He was very red and cried and looked like Joel. What joy to hold my grandson the very day he was born!

That evening we took Joel to see his mommy and baby brother. Josiah was in the nursery to give Janet time with Joel. Later John and I took Joel to the nursery to get Josiah. When we got there, the nurse stuck Josiah's heel with a needle to draw blood. He screamed and cried loudly. Joel let out a wail, upset that the nurse had hurt his baby brother. John hurried Joel away as he wailed. After that he was very protective of Josiah whenever a nurse came into the room. (Even later when they were at church or a store and someone wanted to look at Josiah, Joel became agitated and tried to block them and said he didn't want them to hurt his baby brother.) Later, when the boys were calmed down, Joel held Josiah with Janet on the bed as I took pictures.

Josiah was born on Monday, August 23, and they came home on Wednesday. Joel was not a happy camper. He wanted his Mommy to himself. That evening he cried a long time, feeling displaced by a wee baby. Janet held and rocked and soothed him. He slept and woke up crying again. Janet empathized: "He's heartbroken." The first days Joel took long naps and woke up screaming. I took him for many walks in the stroller, which he loved, and I helped with Josiah as much as possible. By Friday Joel had a fever of 102 degrees. He needed time to adjust. In a week he seemed much better and accepted Josiah well, at least for a day!

As Janet and I ate ice cream before bed on Jake's and my 38th anniversary, Janet shared about Josiah's birth. "Josiah's birth experience was so different from Joel's. I got to the hospital about 5:00, started pushing at 9:00 and he was born at 10:48. I held Josiah on top of me and John said, 'I want to cut the cord,' and Joanne said, 'You *can!*' So he did. Josiah didn't cry much at all. Then Joanne put Josiah in the Jaccuzi with me and bathed him. We were in about 30 minutes." This sounded so much better than Joel's birth.

Joel, 2½, holding one-month-old Josiah, September 1999.

Joel, 5, and Josiah, 2½, March 2002.

Josiah was an exceptionally good baby and slept through the night except for one feeding. I was delighted with the name Josiah, a favorite Old Testament king. Janet chose it when Joel was six months old. She told John that was her choice, but saved it for a surprise. John also liked the name, as he loved reading the Bible and liked Bible names. Josiah John had his Daddy's name, as well as Jake and Jared's middle name.

Jake flew out for the next weekend and Jared drove up from Wichita to celebrate the new baby. Now we were a family of seven. Jake read Joel's thick Bible book to him all the way through. Joel never tired of the stories from the Old and New Testaments.

John's job required travel to various states close by as well as Nebraska to study legumes for research. He was gone for a week and when he came home as we sat down to eat pie before bed he said, "Josiah has gotten a lot fatter. And Joel changes so much when I'm gone. He seems older and more independent, has a better vocabulary and talks better."

I stayed on two and a half more weeks, glad to relieve Janet so she could sleep or get out at times. My leaving was hard for all of us and I hated the many miles between us. Joel had been our miracle baby, but Josiah was just as much of a miracle—a second blessing from heaven.

While I was gone, Jake and a carpenter from church were enclosing our back patio to make an all-purpose Arizona room. At a used furniture store, we found a beautiful sofa bed like new. We added a couple of chairs and, at the other end of the long

Josiah, 5, and Joel, 7, December 2005.

room, a nice dinette set from a thrift shop. With double-paned windows all around and a heater/cooler in the wall, it was perfect. Jake did a great job and now we had another bedroom, plus dining and playroom, for when the whole family came.

At Christmas that year, I flew to Wichita. John and Janet stopped overnight and went on the next day to John's parents in Oklahoma City. After Christmas, they returned to celebrate with our family. Jake arrived on Christmas Day. We flew back home January 3 after a great time of seeing the boys, reading to Joel, caring for Josiah, enjoying a good family time. Jake and I were grateful for our family and our two little heaven-sent blessings.

A year after Joel's birth, a new "family member" had joined us. But that's another story.

CHAPTER 51

A New Brother

He who refreshes others will himself be refreshed.
PROVERBS 11:25 (NIV)

1998–2010

Jared enjoyed his job at Executive Aircraft Corporation (EAC) in Wichita, where he began in October 1996. However, two years later, tragedy struck. EAC's owner, Stan Roth, was killed in a plane crash near Peabody, Kansas, in July 1998. Stan was instructing his older brother, Jim, in the Sabreliner jet and tragically took his brother to his death with him. Because we have a number of Hesston people in our church, we heard the shocking news on Sunday morning, the day after the accident. Jared was on vacation in Los Angeles and learned of the crash that Sunday noon. It was a devastating blow to the families, friends, and the company.

Stan's wife, Jan, took over the company as owner and chair, and hired an acquaintance as president. But by 2000, Jan decided to sell. In October 2002, the company filed for Chapter 11 bankruptcy. Stan had worked the phones constantly to buy and sell planes, but since his death and the September 11 attacks, the company took a nosedive. The sagging economy made things tough.

These developments impacted Jared's job security. His workload increased due to all the changes – and layoffs, including his assistant. Emerging from bankruptcy with a new company name was not enough. In 2005, the business was up for sale again. Whereas EAC had nearly 200 employees at one time, about 60 remained, with others leaving or laid off as months went by. Jared's job was secure for the present but he wondered if a new company would keep him.

A flying club for employees had been formed at EAC and a plane made available. Jared joined, took flying lessons again (after 18 years), and got his license in 2000. When we visited him, he sometimes took us up for a ride, often over our land at Hesston, where Jake took pictures. One day he flew us to the refurbished Beaumont Hotel in Kansas for lunch. The 11-room hotel, originally built in 1879, had been a favorite dinner or overnight stop for pilots for many years. Landing on a grass strip, we taxied down a gravel lane, up to the grass parking lot across from the hotel, where we enjoyed lunch and conversation with the manager.

Jake and Jared with Piper Warrior at Beaumont, Kansas, 2002.

Dillard's in Little Rock wanted Jared to come back. When he worked there, his manager wrote in his evaluation: "Jared takes on every challenge with an excellent attitude, dedicated work ethic, and self-motivated drive. He possesses the knowledge and pride that always delivers the desired results. Of all the exceptional people in my group, Jared's growth has impressed me the most."

Jared's team leader, John, wrote in a letter of recommendation: "Jared exhibited strong programming abilities and was able to discern what the users needed and produce a friendly interface to the data needed for marketing and check verification. Jared was well liked by all who were involved on the project, users and data processing staff alike. Jared is a team player who knows how to make sure his part is reliable and completed on time...There are few men who are as capable and dedicated as he." (John led a Bible study for employees; later he left with his wife and small child to serve as a missionary in a Middle East country.)

Jared's evaluations at EAC were equally as impressive. But since the company lost much of its business in the four years following September 11, 2001, Jared looked in vain for work in Wichita. Thousands of workers had been laid off. Since his colleagues in Little Rock persisted, he went down for an interview in 2005, but declined their offer. He did not want to leave

Wichita and his house, church, and friends. Plus, for the past six years (since 1999), he had another good reason to stay where he was—a "little brother."

Jared had lost track of most of his high school and college classmates. He was still in touch with Hesston friends, Phil Simpson and Merv Bitikofer (who also attended KSU in Manhattan), and made new friends at work. He found First Mennonite Brethren Church in Wichita to be a good fit.

One day a woman at work suggested, "You should get a little brother from the Big Brothers/Big Sisters program." Jared followed up and in April 1999, he first met his new "brother," nine-year-old Jose Ging. He got together with him about once a week. Big Brothers' monthly activities such as visits to the zoo and museums or barbecues provided times to get acquainted. In addition, Jared took Jose to parks or to his house to play games. He used his creativity and love of gadgets and fun to make rockets to shoot off, build a robot, or by remote control sail a boat on a lake.

Over the years, Jared took Jose to church and got him involved in Jr High Youth group (JrMBY). Once Jared drove a carload of lively youths to a weekend retreat; another time Jose joined the group in feeding the homeless in downtown Wichita. He also enjoyed the JrMBY parties. For a masquerade party, Jose dressed in a large navy rain poncho and sported two heads. The extra one was his grandma's mannequin for her wig, which Jared helped him fasten onto a piece of Styrofoam to fit on his shoulder. This costume won praise from his peers. When his church hosted a youth conference for the district, Jared had eight people from Kansas City at his home for two nights (six youths and two sponsors). They greatly appreciated his hospitality and had a rousing good time. Jose loved it and said, "We should do that again!" In 2005, Jose attended church camp with the JrMBY group.

Canoe camping trips to Oklahoma, skiing in Colorado, and trips to Janet and John's in Lincoln provided new adventures for Jose. He liked to come to Jared's house when the family visited, to play games and enjoy home-cooked meals.

After Jared got his private pilot's license in 2000, he took Jose up for rides and flew him to Oklahoma to eat at an airport restaurant. Jose often slept over at Jared's house, insisting on using a sleeping bag on the floor in Jared's room, sometimes with his little sister Melissa. Finally, as he grew older and felt more secure, he agreed to sleep in the guest room.

An important part of the relationship for Jared has been helping Jose keep up with schoolwork, which became a challenge. He enlisted teachers' help with phone calls, e-mails, and by attending parent teacher conferences with

Jose and his mother. Jose became a good reader by collecting cards with much writing on them for a game. His favorite table game is "Life," from our children's youth. Jared has also bought him a Bible and subscribed to an exciting Christian magazine for teenage boys.

Jared was amazed to learn that Wichita is the largest Big Brothers/ Big Sisters program in the nation, larger than New York City or Los Angeles. In spite of that, 1000 "at risk" children are still on the waiting list in Wichita.

Jose Ging (age 13) and Jared, September 2002.

Jared served on the Big Ambition Campaign to raise funds for a new building, where he enjoyed meeting city leaders. His faithfulness at Big Brothers events, the campaign, and service projects won him a place on the "Big League" activity committee.

From a shy quiet boy of nine, Jose blossomed by age 15 to the extent that others in the program were amazed and commented on this to Jared. Jose spoke freely to the leaders and his caseworker as friends, astonishing even Jared. Jared thoroughly enjoys Jose and has won the trust and friendship of Jose's family. His mother, Rita, told me at a barbecue she hosted, "Jared is the only person I can trust. I can tell him everything." She has five children, two of them from the same father. Jose enjoyed the peace and quiet and good organization of Jared's home; he has helped Jared cook and bake occasionally, and at times mows the lawn for spending money. His family comes to Jared's for parties and has the run of the house for "hide and seek," ping pong, and other games. Jared has also flown Jose, his sister Melissa, and his friend Joaquin to Ponca City, Oklahoma for dinner, impressing Joaquin's mother.

Since Joel and Josiah have been old enough to walk and talk, Jose has enjoyed them and loved when their family came to visit. The boys loved Jose in return and liked to play with him. Jared bought a used hot tub for his back yard beside the deck. This has given many hours of fun to Jose, Joel and Josiah, as well as Jared's friends. One year for his birthday, Jose wanted a trampoline, so Jared bought a large one for his back yard. Jose, his family, and Joaquin have had great fun on that, along with Joel and Josiah when they visit. Joaquin's continuous back flips astonished us all. Joel and Josiah think their "Unky" is the greatest, and Josiah called him "the funniest guy." The rest of us take a back seat when Uncle Jared is around.

In 2005, a Herstine family reunion was planned for July 17. Jared told Jose, "I'm going to a family reunion in Pennsylvania," and Jose said, "I want to go to Transylvania!"

Jared laughed, "Not *Transylvania, Penns*ylvania!"

Jose insisted, "I still want to go!" Jared bought him a ticket to fly with him to Philly. Jose wanted to see Philadelphia and in the process of planning, Jared mentioned Washington, D. C. as a possibility. Jose got excited, exclaiming, "I learned about Washington at school!"

Jared and Jose had seen the movie, *National Treasure*, an action film of two sets of people racing to find clues to the location of a "great treasure." They wanted to visit some of those places. (Part of the film was set in Independence Hall in Philadelphia. Adding to the intrigue, some clues were written on the back of the Declaration of Independence, which was on display in the National Archives in Washington, D. C.)

Jose's first commercial plane flight turned into a 15-hour ordeal. Instead of a 1:15 departure, after an hour on the plane, they deplaned and waited four more hours because of storms in Atlanta. When they arrived, they were relieved to find their loaded plane waiting for them. In Philly at 12:30 midnight, after a long wait they learned their luggage did not arrive. In more long lines they reported the missing luggage, waited for a car rental shuttle, and finally for the rental car – a Chrysler Sebring convertible that Jared had reserved. They started off on the 55-minute drive to Quakertown. Even that seemed jinxed. As they drove up to the ticket booth of the Pennsylvania Turnpike, they found the ticket vending machines all out of order, then waited with a growing line of cars for an attendant. One driver informed Jared, "If you drive off without a ticket, you'll pay $25.00 at the other end."

Finally, tired but safe, they arrived at my brother Ralph and Janice's house at Milford Square at 3:38 in the morning. Even so, they looked fresh as the morning. Jose greeted us with a big smile. The delays had not dampened his spirits for his great adventure.

The missing luggage came the next day, and Jared's friends, Pat and Denise, arrived from New York. The four of them drove in the convertible to Valley Forge, where Jose relished getting a taste of history and photos for his album.

Jose thoroughly enjoyed the sights at Quakertown. In school he learned about the Underground Railroad, which helped former slaves from the south in their escape to Canada. We saw the large stone double house (two-family dwelling, common in the east), formerly owned by a Quaker who hid blacks in his basement and helped over 600 escape to freedom.

Not far from the house, we drove by the stately Quaker meetinghouse for which the town is named. A stone wall surrounds the park-like grounds, with large trees and old cemetery, located near the highway between Philadelphia and Allentown. We also saw the replica of the Liberty Bell in front of a small stone house. It is believed that the Liberty Bell was brought from Philadelphia and hidden under straw behind the house during the Revolutionary War. Along with the famous bell, all the church bells and other valuables were brought on 700 wagons to a Lutheran Church in Allentown, 13 miles north of Quakertown. (In 2005, a history of Quakertown was written for the 150th anniversary of the incorporation of the town in 1855 and includes these details with pictures.) We then took Jose the couple of miles to my beloved childhood neighborhood where Jose showed delight as I pointed out my home, church, and school in close proximity.

At the reunion, Jose participated in a baseball game for all ages. The game went on through two heavy downpours. Jose also played kick ball, and enjoyed the spread of scrumptious picnic fare. On the way back to my brother's house, Jose drove the convertible on a parking lot, quite a heady experience!

Jared planned to visit Philadelphia on Monday with his Aunt Grace as guide. He took Jake and me to the airport for our flight to Phoenix and returned the rental car. Grace met them and took them to downtown Philly via New Jersey (on a wrong bridge) by mistake. They toured the U. S. Mint, saw Independence Hall, the Liberty Bell, the Betsy Ross House, and many historic buildings. They saw the cemetery where Benjamin Franklin is buried (from an action scene in *National Treasure*). After lunch, Grace dropped them off at the Amtrak station. To Jose's delight, the train went through two more states, Delaware and Maryland, on the way to D.C.. Excitement mounted as they planned sites to see that Jose learned about in the movie. Jared's travel log gives the rundown of places visited:

At Washington we took the Metro (subway) and walked to our motel. Swam, ate pizza, went to the National Archives, where we saw the Declaration of Independence on display, walked to the Washington Monument in the dark, past the Environmental Protection Agency (EPA) where we saw rats, past the IRS, Justice Department, Smithsonian, Department of Labor, WW II Memorial, then to the Lincoln Memorial, went by the Vietnam Wall and Einstein Memorial, past the State Department and George Washington University. Went to our motel and to bed.

Tuesday: Ate at Sunoco Gas Station, took the Metro to the Capitol, walked past Library of Congress. First we had to go to Representative Todd Tiahrt's office to get tickets and got lost in the office building. Back at the Capitol, we saw the House and Senate chambers. Saw Joe Lieberman, Patrick Leahy, Pat Roberts and many other senators in the chamber. Walked down Pennsylvania Avenue and found a place to eat. Past the Federal Trade Commission, the FBI and Canadian Embassy. Went past the U. S. Treasury building to the White House. Saw an Australian motorcade and news crews at the White House because Bush was announcing the Supreme Court nominee tonight. Back at motel, we swam and ordered pizza and watched, *Day After Tomorrow.*

Wednesday: Took the Metro at 9:00 A.M. Our tickets weren't good until 9:30 but the ticket agent let us on early and called the exit for us. Went to the Bureau of Engraving and Printing, got tickets for 5:45 P.M. Toured the Holocaust Museum, ate at their café, then to the International Spy Museum where Jose bought a shirt. Went to Library of Congress and Supreme Court, past the Federal Aviation Administration (FAA) building. Went to Air and Space Smithsonian briefly, ate at McDonald's/Boston Market there. Toured Bureau of Engraving and Printing and bought shredded money and a dollar ring. Back to motel, swam, and watched TV and typed this.

Thursday: Got up, jumped on the beds. Checked out and took the Metro to Virginia to National Airport. Saw Pentagon from the Metro. Took airport shuttle to our terminal. Left just a few minutes late and had no problems in Atlanta.

Aunt Grace's mistaken route into New Jersey turned into a plus for Jose. He was happy to add six new states to his list of those he already visited: Pennsylvania, New Jersey; Delaware and Maryland on the train; Virginia and Georgia (at airports); plus the District of Columbia. What an educational experience, which Jared also relished. Jared always loved home and family, fun, play, and travel, and is still a child at heart. In December 2006, he received the well-deserved "Big Brother of the Year" award for Sedgwick County for his outstanding brothering of Jose for seven years.

In December 2005, Jared was offered a job, with no effort on his part, at SecureNet Alarm Systems. They were looking for someone to develop a data backup system for businesses and individuals to store computer data and a friend who worked there recommended Jared. A new building was constructed about five minutes' drive from his home. The computer "safe room" has one-foot thick walls and ceiling, made of reinforced concrete, to protect data from natural disasters, such as tornadoes, fires, floods, and other misfortunes. We visited him in October as he was in the process of connecting 300 cables in the computer room. The cables hung from one corner of the ceiling where a tile had been removed – quite an impressive sight to his parents. (A bonus for me is that, at Jared's urging, a copy of my book is stored automatically in the safe room once a week – a technological marvel I could never have imagined when I began this project.)

Jared also masterminded the company's move from the airport building to the new one in Maize, a suburb of northwest Wichita. His employer was amazed at how smoothly the move went. At a dinner for the managers Friday after work, they all cheered for Jared when he walked in a bit late. The boss could not stop talking about Jared's terrific job and asked, "What do you want, Jared, a trip or a car or a bonus?" Jared said he didn't know, but later received a nice bonus. Jared has proved he can handle whatever comes along, with confidence, professionalism, and class.

In early October 2006, Janet, Jared and I planned a surprise Open House for Jake's 70th birthday at Jared's home. Jose documented the event on video camera and loved being with the family and friends. Then in June 2007, we surprised Jared with a 40th birthday party at his house. Jose brought his friend Joaquin, and as they arrived at the house with Jared before the party, Jose called out his characteristic greeting, "I'M HOME!" His enthusiasm for life and our family warms and blesses my heart.

Jose has an older sister, Victoria, who was the first in her extended family to graduate from high school. After the graduation, at a party at her mother's house, Victoria and her mother cried for joy at this accomplishment. Victoria is married to Lupe and they have five little daughters – Esmeralda, Isabella, Maria Victoria, Lolita, and LLuli (pronounced Yuli). They are also a part of Jared's life. Once Victoria asked Jared if she could have a garage sale at his house; he consented even though he was gone that weekend to Denver to help a friend move back to Wichita. The family had the run of the house, as usual. Jose's older brother Oscar was next to graduate from high school. In addition to Melissa, Jose has a little sister, Maria, who was six in 2010. (With the hot debate over immigration in 2010, Lupe went to Mexico and was approved as a permanent resident, a proud day and great relief for him and Victoria. They own a lawn service business. He is a hard worker and has contracts for city properties to mow parks and cemeteries.)

When Jose was 15, Jared made a video with pictures of Jose's life since he's known him, with family members included. He used the song, "Friends" (written by Deborah and Michael W. Smith) for background music. When Jose's mother watched it for the first time, she was moved to tears. On Jose's 18th birthday, September 18, 2007, Jared again had a party for him with all of his family and a few of Jose's friends there.

As a result of Jose's experience with Jared at many BBBS events, as well as great times with Jared's family and friends, Jose told Jared he would like to be a Big Brother. In reality, he *has been* – to a whole neighborhood of children younger than himself. Others comment about how he is always playing with the younger children, and has brought some of them to Jared's house. He has also spent many hours babysitting his little sister Maria. He has become a blessing to his home and neighborhood, and a delightful "little brother" to Jared. And Jared has grown and matured through sharing his life and house in this commendable responsibility and ministry.

In June 2008, when Janet and boys came down during wheat harvest, our family and Jose went to the Kauffman (Mennonite) Museum, with and old house and barn, at North Newton. Our next stop was Hesston College where the boys played and rode their scooters, and we saw the new church. At Newton the boys played at Athletic Park near the dried-up river where we saw huge machines dredging the bottom. Dinner at our favorite "Breadbasket" restaurant completed our enjoyable excursion, which Jose relished as well.

In 2009, Jose graduated from high school, a major accomplishment for him, giving his family and Jared much pride. In the fall of 2009, Jose entered Job Corps at Manhattan, Kansas, to study plumbing. Jose likes coming home for holidays and an occasional weekend, by bus or with his mother or Jared. Once Jared flew up to get him. Though Jose's official participation in Big Brothers ended with his graduation, Jared will continue to enjoy this special friendship with his "brother" Jose for years to come. Jared's hope is that Jose will find something to do in life that he enjoys.

For almost a year, Jared was without an official "little brother." Then in 2010, he was matched with a new "brother," Esteban, and enjoys activities with him. These "brothers" enrich Jared's life as he has enriched theirs. The blessings grow and multiply as our "double-rainbow family" expands.

CHAPTER 52

Miracles and Healings

He sent his word and healed them.
PSALM 107:20 (KJV)

1993–2010

In July of 1993, Janet and I had two weeks together in a Spiritual Formation class at the Elkhart seminary where Jake and I met 33 years ago. In the early sixties it was Mennonite Biblical Seminary, but now Associated Mennonite Biblical Seminary (AMBS), since the Goshen and Elkhart seminaries merged. I flew to St. Louis where Janet picked me up. The Mississippi River was swollen out of its banks in an historic flood; the raging torrent below us was a scary sight from the long bridge into Illinois.

On campus we stayed in a two-bedroom apartment, far bigger than the studio apartment Jake and I shared when we started our marriage there 32 years ago. Janet fell in love with the place and told me, "I hope John and I can come here to study. I already have our furniture all arranged in this apartment in my mind." I hoped they could, too. (They did take a class there the next summer, and she took one class online later.) Janet audited another class in addition to the one we took together.

Stimulating classes, inspiring chapels, and challenging homework filled our days. Visits with current and former professors were invigorating, and we enjoyed learning to know the students. One day in the library Janet was pleased to find Jake's and my seminary papers on Kierkegaard, and I showed her our seminary transcripts. We laughed a lot, shared new insights, and our love of learning and for Jesus. Janet's meaningful reading of Scripture in chapel one day brought tears to my eyes. We greatly enjoyed a side trip to Menno-Hof, a unique Mennonite museum in the Amish/Mennonite town of Shipshewana.

Our class had used the texts *Fashion Me A People* by Maria Harris and *Christian Spiritual Formation in the Church and Classroom* by Susanne

Johnson. As we drove back to Missouri, Janet put in a tape and said, "This is my favorite song – 'He Has Formed Me,' by Second Chapter of Acts." The powerful words seemed right out of our texts and discussions. We made a stop at Atherton Park at the University of Illinois to see the beautiful formal English gardens. Janet had gone there for meetings and knew I'd love the gardens.

On July 31, Janet and John moved from Columbia, Missouri to Lincoln, Nebraska where John began a three-year program for a Ph.D. in Agronomy. Janet left behind many good friends and a wonderful job. Soon she had two part-time jobs: placement specialist at the University of Nebraska Lincoln and career counselor at Southeast Community College. She also taught a class at both places.

In August that year, Jake and I received unwelcome news after his routine aviation physical. He learned that he had a polyp in the rectum. Surgery was scheduled, the beginning of a confusing emotional roller coaster. The doctor told Jake, "Just the benign polyp will be removed, nothing else." That sounded hopeful. After the half-hour outpatient surgery on September 16, the nurse showed me the polyp and described it as "big." She advised that Jake rest that evening and eat soup. Instead, Jake insisted on keeping our dinner date with our small group at a Chinese restaurant. He looked sick and struggled to get down two small spoons of soup.

When we got home, Jake announced, "I'm taking the trip to Calgary and Vancouver tomorrow" (for several days). I protested, but he declared, "I'm fine and I can do it." The next morning we left for the airport at 6:00. Trying not to show anxiety, as he said goodbye, I prayed, *"Father, please take care of him."* That day, a man from our small group called to say, "I was really angry at Jake for coming to the restaurant last night. He looked terrible!" But that's Jake. His strength and determination to not let anything keep him down amazed me. He continued on the trip with no problems.

Four days later, while Jake was in Vancouver, the doctor called with shocking news. The polyp was malignant. He also called Jake on his cell phone at Calgary. *How can this be?* I called Janet with the news, then Jared, our pastor, family, and friends, and asked them to pray.

Later the doctor assured Jake, "You have the 'best kind' of cancer. We'll do another surgery to remove the tumor. It's similar to what President Reagan had and he came through just fine."

On Thursday of that week Jared arrived to work at the Phoenix Dillard's store. His job often took him to other cities to help open stores or work on their computer programs. The timing couldn't have been better. What a comfort it was to have him with us for a few days and a joy to celebrate Jake's 58th birthday together early. That Sunday, Jake's request for prayer in church helped calm me.

Jake underwent the second surgery on October 2, after which he had excruciating pain in his legs from the anesthesia and being in a stationary position so long. The doctor had warned about this. I called Jake's chiropractor sister, Mary Ann, in Canada and she called him at the hospital to encourage him.

Four days later the doctor told him the cancer was gone and he needed no follow-up treatment. What a relief! While Jake and I had both faced cancer in our parents—Jake's mother and my father—we hadn't expected to face it personally. We were grateful to God and our praying family and friends.

Jake asked the doctor what causes these polyps. "Red meat," he replied. Previously, Jake had said to me at times, "I think I should become vegetarian."

In spring of 1994 we read an article about vegetarian M.D. and psychiatrist Neal Barnard, president of Physicians for Responsible Medicine, with over 10,000 members. The article told of his books, *The Power of Your Plate* and *Food for Life*, which Jake ordered. The books made clear the relationship of diet and disease. Jake decided, "I'm going to be vegetarian." Not wanting to cook two ways, I chose to do the same. Reading testimonies of people with terminal illness who became well, with robust good health by changing their diet and lifestyle, convinced us. We learned much from our growing library of inspiring vegetarian books.

A year later, I had a mammogram on November 28, 1994, expecting it to be routine. That evening my doctor called. "Your mammogram showed calcium deposits in the left breast, which could mean cancer. You will need to have a biopsy and possibly a mastectomy." I was stunned. The biopsy report came back negative and I was greatly relieved.

However, after my surgeon returned from a two-week vacation, at my follow-up appointment, his first words were, "Did you come alone?" Warning bells went off.

"Yes," I said. "Why?"

"There's been some mistake. I'm sorry, but the biopsy *was* malignant."
I was shocked and asked how this could be. He showed me a diagram and
made long explanations about calcium deposits. He said the area was small
and I could probably get by with a lumpectomy and radiation. Or I could
have a moderate radical mastectomy with treatment to follow, if required. I
felt sick. How could they have made such a mistake? The next day Jake went
with me to see the surgeon. I needed time to decide what to do.

My family and church friends prayed and supported. I struggled and
prayed. A friend, Donna Smoker, loaned me her book, *Cancer Battle Plan* by
Anne E. and David Frahm. Judy Bontrager gave me an eye-opening article
from *Reader's Digest* that said one should take time to research and study
before rushing to cancer surgery. It said, in effect, "It's your body and you
need to take charge of your treatment." Inez Unruh from church had the
same surgery two months before and gave wonderful support.

Still uncertain, I called Jake's sister Mary Ann for counsel. Having dealt
with patients in a similar situation she advised, "I'd say get rid of it. Then
you'll have peace of mind and won't have to wonder if they got it all." I didn't
want radiation so decided on the mastectomy.

Memorable phone calls, visits, and prayers from loving friends and family
sustained me. Two phone calls stand out. Belay Tuccu, the Ethiopian young
man whom our church sponsored and who often had meals in our home,
surprised me with a call. He expressed concern and advised, "Read the book
of Philippians." I was deeply touched by his faith and thoughtfulness.

"I love Philippians!" I told him. "I memorized most of it as a youth. It's
the book of joy."

"Yes," he agreed.

"That is a very good suggestion and I surely will read it now. Thank you
so much."

The other call was from Janet. Her concern moved me to tears and her
loving words strengthened me just before surgery. What a special bond I felt
with my much-loved daughter. I knew she was praying.

Our small group and Spiritual Life Commission laid hands on me and
prayed. Four close friends called and prayed for me on the phone and I felt
like the paralytic who was let down on a pallet in front of Jesus.

Before surgery, on December 1, our pastor and his wife, Peter and Rheta
Mae, came to the hospital to pray with me. As Peter prayed, my tears flowed.
"Why are you crying?" he asked, concerned.

"That was so beautiful," I reassured him. "I felt overwhelmed with love." He had been like a spiritual father to me in prayer, counsel, and friendship, and I was moved by his heartfelt petition. Peace flooded my being. Jake was with me too, of course, as I would not have had the surgery without him present.

Then a male attendant came to wheel me on my bed to the operating room. As Jake walked along in the hall, we learned that this nurse had graduated from Hesston College! What a small world indeed, that he should attend me in this huge metropolis of Phoenix. Again I felt God's loving care.

Fifteen lymph nodes tested negative and the area around the small malignant area tested negative as well. A lumpectomy with no follow-up treatment would have sufficed, but the doctor would have insisted on radiation. (My own reading, and news reports years later, revealed that many doctors were "cutting off breasts needlessly" for years, making huge amounts of money on mastectomies and breast implants.) I was grateful that all was well. It was an easy recovery with little pain. Jake was a wonderful help and cheerfully made meals the first few days. Verda Albrecht from church came to change my dressings. Jake and I were both grateful that we survived cancer with no follow-up treatment.

Then a surprising phone call from my Aunt Melba blessed me. She reported that she had just finished taking Tamoxifen for five years following her mastectomy. (She has done well and turned 89 in 2010.) I declined to take Tamoxifen since I learned that it increases the risk of cancer of the uterus. When I told the oncologist I wanted to use a healthy diet instead, he laughed at me. Jake stepped in and told him we had read books by medical doctors that supported certain diets for overcoming disease. Taken aback, the doctor grew serious and listened with respect. We began juicing carrots, greens, and an apple regularly. Later, we sometimes bought a 50-pound bag of organic carrots for $7.00 to split with our friends, Merv and Berniece Nafziger. These hiking buddies and we enjoyed climbing the Phoenix mountains together for more than ten years, once a week, when Jake was in town – a pleasant way to keep in shape and enjoy great fellowship.

SISTER MILLIE

Being separated from my family by thousands of miles for many years greatly endeared them to me. If I knew someone was struggling or hurting, I tried to keep in touch to encourage. Millie's lingering, intermittent depression for more than 35 years concerned me and I phoned her more than my other siblings. At times I asked God, *How long will Millie suffer this way? Will she ever be healed?*

One day when I called her from Phoenix she was very down. Nothing I said made a difference. I felt like a helpless failure and chided myself. *If I had faith as a mustard seed, this mountain of despair should move.* What a frustrating, heartbreaking dilemma! But I knew that "God moves in mysterious ways," and He is "the God who does wonders." It would take a miracle to help Millie, and I had to leave her in God's hands.

That summer, I led a women's group at church using videos of psychologist John Bradshaw on dysfunctional families. On July 28, we viewed the video on "Spiritual Child Abuse." Bradshaw defined this as churches and Christians who force negative doctrine and hell-fire sermons down children's throats, causing fear, guilt, and self-condemnation long into adulthood. Recounting my camp experience as a ten-year-old, I asked the group if they thought that fit the description. They agreed it did. That set me wondering. *Was this the root of Millie's depression and fear?*

The very next Sunday in church, a young man, Todd Murray, stood to his feet during sharing time. "I have been disobedient," he confessed. "I had a vision about three weeks ago and didn't share it." Holding his Bible he read from Acts chapter 2, quoting Joel chapter 2, about the coming of the Holy Spirit. "In the last days…God declares, I will pour out my Spirit upon all flesh, and your sons and your daughters shall prophesy, your young men shall see visions and your old men shall dream dreams…"

He closed his Bible and continued, "In the vision, Jesus and I were walking down the aisle toward the back where we saw a hurting person crying. I believe this vision is for someone sitting here who is hurting, or it could apply to several people. If you think it's for you, please see me or one of the pastors after the service." I was strangely moved.

That evening after the praise service, as I walked near Todd I heard him explain the vision in greater detail. "Jesus and I entered the sanctuary and walked up the aisle and on the back bench was a little girl, about seven to ten years old, in a nightie. She was bent over sobbing."

Instantly, my mind flashed back to my first night at camp, the hell-fire sermon, and my inconsolable weeping. In awe, I said, "I wonder if that could have been me?"

Todd turned to me and asked me to explain. "I went to camp when I was ten and at campfire the first night there was a blazing campfire and a hell-fire sermon. The minister explained how we were all sinners and sinners will go to hell and burn forever. But because of our sin, God sent Jesus to die for us so we wouldn't have to go to hell." Todd listened intently. "He said if we accepted Jesus as our Savior we would be saved from hell. But by then he lost me. I was terrified and so upset that God made Jesus die and was going to send everyone to hell if they didn't accept Jesus. I couldn't believe it! I went forward at the invitation because I was so afraid of hell!"

"Then what happened?" Todd asked.

"I cried hard as the minister prayed for us and I cried on the walk through the dark woods back to the cabin. I kept crying as I got ready for bed, so the counselor told me to get in bed with my older sister Millie. She didn't like that, and it was a narrow bed, but I crawled in with her."

Todd is a very tall six foot six. He looked at me with great tenderness and said, "I'm sure that vision was for *you*! The girl on the back bench crying had on a long nightie, sort of shabby, with a wide ruffle at the bottom." That sounded strangely familiar. It seemed I could remember such a nightgown.

He added, "While you were talking, I could see the path back to the cabin. And then inside the cabin it was dark, with just one light bulb hanging from the ceiling."

"Yes!" I responded. How amazing!

"Another thing," he added, *"I saw Jesus there in the cabin, weeping with you!"* I was overwhelmed at this wonderful thought.

Todd looked at me earnestly. "Do you mind if I pray with you?" I agreed, and we sat down on a bench in back. His wife Janis had joined us and he took my hands and began to pray. He walked me through the camp experience, with Jesus by my side, and prayed for healing of the memories. What an absolutely inspired prayer—full of Jesus' love! When he said "Amen" and I looked up, I was struck by his eyes, filled with deep compassion.

I marveled and remarked, "Your eyes look like Jesus' eyes – so compassionate."

Todd encouraged, "Be like the little child you were before that hurtful experience at camp." We had warm hugs all around and I felt wonderfully free and loved.

When I got home, I wondered about the experience. I told Jake about it and recorded it in my journal. But I questioned why I needed this healing. I had often shared about my time at camp as I did with the Bible study women. I had had prayer a number of times previously for healing of memories. And I understood that the pastor at camp meant well. I had also come to understand God's love in Christ. So why did I need the vision?

Then I remembered Millie. Millie needed this healing! Suddenly I realized—that very day that I heard the vision was August 9—Millie's 59th birthday! In my excitement, I *knew* what I must do. I could hardly wait until morning to call her.

That Monday, after I wished Millie a happy birthday, she said cheerfully, "I had the best day yet yesterday. Brenda (their daughter) invited us to her apartment for supper and we had such a good time." That made me happy.

As we talked, I asked, "What do you remember about going to camp the first time?"

"Well," she answered, "there was a sermon on hell."

"Of *course* there was!" I interjected. "There *always* was!" I prodded, "Do you think about that sometimes?"

"Yes, *I think about it all the time.*" I groaned inwardly.

She continued, "I didn't go forward at the invitation and then I was afraid when I got back to the cabin. I told a girl about it and she told the counselor. She took me outside and we sat down on the steps of the cabin. She explained the plan of salvation again and prayed with me. Then she asked, "Where is Jesus now?" and I said, "In heaven.'"

"The counselor said, 'He's in your heart now, isn't He?'"

"Did it feel like He was in your heart, and did you feel joy?" I asked.

"No," her sad voice came through the receiver, "I didn't really understand it." Thus she had doubted ever after for 48 years, and continued to condemn herself. "I think about how I didn't go forward, and I didn't know Jesus was in my heart." The full weight of her grief hit me as the picture of her doubt and fear from camp came into sharp focus. She felt like a failure.

I ached for her and pointed out, "This is child abuse, with inappropriate use of the Bible with young children, and *at bedtime*—such an upsetting story *at bedtime!* Don't you see it?"

"Yes," she agreed, "and I remember how Mom read *The Titanic* to us at bedtime."

Yes, Mom did a lot of inappropriate things. This treatment opened the door for us to be too conscientious and submissive in everything we were told—and guilt—oh, the guilt!

Eagerly, I told Millie about the vision and Todd's beautiful prayer. "You need someone there to pray for you," I advised. But after I got off the phone, I wondered who would do it, plus, Millie was too reserved to ask.

I sensed the Spirit saying, "*You* pray for her."

Of course! Those were the days when I made long-distance calls only on night or weekend rates, so I waited till the next morning. Too bad I made her suffer one more day, wondering what to do.

When I called her Tuesday morning and explained that I would pray for her, she was ready. Walking her through the camp experience with Jesus, as Todd had done with me, I sensed the Spirit guiding as the words flowed forth. *"Father, please forgive any resentment Millie has had toward others, and thank You for Your forgiveness, Lord Jesus. Thank You that You love Millie as Your little sheep, and that You are the Good Shepherd. Thank You that You love us more than the most loving person we can think of. Father, help Millie to lay down these burdens and memories now at Jesus' feet. Heal, Millie, Father, body, soul, and spirit. Lord Jesus, be very present with Millie today; caress her head and love her and hold her in the palm of your hand. In the mighty Name of Jesus, Amen and Amen."* I tried to cover all the bases, but this was the gist of it.

When I finished praying, she said sweetly, "I cried."

"Tears of joy?"

"Yes."

"Oh, good. And the vision was for *you*! God gave it to Todd to share *on your birthday!* What a fantastic birthday gift! God is so good and He loves you and wants you to let go of the guilt. Let joy flood your soul today as you go about your work." She was grateful and I hung up with a song in my heart.

Then I had to call Todd. He was absolutely dumbfounded that his vision had reached and healed someone almost 3000 miles away in Pennsylvania. We rejoiced together in God's goodness and guidance.

A month later when I talked with Millie and asked how she was doing she said, "Fine."

"Do you think that was a spiritual healing a month ago?"

"Yes, I do, because I hardly ever think of it (camp and hell) anymore." God had done His work deep within her. I could not thank God enough for this miracle.

About 17 years later in 2010, I shared this experience in my Sunday school class and told how the vision was for Millie since I thought I had worked through the trauma from camp. Chuck Fondse, former pastor and chaplain, pointed out that the vision was probably for me, because I needed healing *first* before I could pray for my sister. He felt that I was probably the girl sobbing on the bench in the vision. He also grew up with the fear of hell and God's anger and said, "You and I have a common need for that healing from spiritual abuse; when you were talking I felt that common need with you."

As I reflected on this, I recalled that for several years before the vision, I felt like a failure. I grieved and cried inside about something deep within that I could not put my finger on. Perhaps it was this subconscious fear, and great sadness and concern for Millie, whom I loved deeply but could not help.

I called Millie then and told her that Chuck felt I needed the vision and healing first. She was glad and said, "I think our image of God came also from Mom, her anger and wrath at us, rather than love."

"Yes," I agreed, "discipline was swift and severe." I reminded her that Mom's sister, Aunt Ruth, once told me fiercely, *"Your mother was not a mother to you girls!"*

Millie and I agreed that Auntie Ruth was a good mother to cousins Betty and Wally, and we loved her. But we knew Mom had a hard life and we forgave her. She gave us Grace and Ruth and Tom to make our family complete. We loved our siblings and were grateful for the healing and growth that God had brought about in each one of us.

CHAPTER 53

Siblings Update

*You have changed my sadness into a joyful dance; you have taken
away my sorrow and surrounded me with joy...
Lord, you are my God; I will give you thanks forever.*
PSALM 30:11-12 (GNB)

Through 2010

My stepmother wrote to me on Sunday, March 8, 1964 (to Akron, Pa.): "Well, it was 25 years on Saturday that I live here (March 7, 1939). Millie was saying that she can't wait until she doesn't have to put leggings on Brenda (age five) and I told her, 'Now you can see how little you all were when I came.' But it doesn't seem that long."

That December, she and Daddy celebrated their 25ᵗʰ wedding anniversary with an open house that Grace planned at her church. It was a happy occasion with all of us there. A sweet picture of the two of them is a reminder of their commitment to each other through many hard times.

Jean and Ralph at their 25ᵗʰ wedding anniversary, December 1964.

Yes, we were very little when she came—Millie was five, I was four, and Anna, two. Ralph was one year old and living with the Landis grandparents.

Twenty-three year old Jean became our mother nine months later. She bore Grace and Ruth to Daddy, and Tom 14 years after Ruth.

While I know it's impossible to sum up the lives of my brothers and sisters, I'd like to share a bit about each one. That's difficult to do in a few lines, but my life has been intertwined with theirs and each one is a treasure to me.

MILLIE

Millie has had a ministry of her own through many years—as church organist, Sunday school and vacation Bible school teacher, and as host to a Backyard Kid's Bible Club at their home. Ralph has taught adult Sunday school and Bible studies and does substitute preaching. Their times with Brenda are a special delight. In April 2004, Millie, Ralph and Brenda drove out from Pennsylvania to visit us in Sun City, a great adventure for them and a wonderful treat for all of us. We visited local sights and the Grand Canyon, and invited Todd, Janis, and Janis's mother Leanna Miller for an evening of dinner, fellowship, and a game of Mexican train with dominoes.

Millie, a conscientious homemaker, especially loved working out-of-doors in their large lawn with flowers and vegetable garden. She'd tell Ralph, "This is God's Garden of Eden for us to take care of for Him." But eventually the yard work became a burden.

Millie, Ralph, and Brenda Loux, August 2008.

In July 2005, Millie and Ralph moved to Fairmount Homes Retirement Community in rural Ephrata. They are enjoying retirement to the full, with new friends and ministries. It's hard to find words to describe the change from their life in Quakertown to their happiness at Fairmount.

Brenda agrees. She wrote, "You're right, it *is* hard to find words...I try to describe it whenever anyone asks how my parents are doing. I really admire and appreciate their decision to sell the house in Quakertown and move to Fairmount. I know it wasn't easy, and it was a lot of hard work, but they took responsibility for their future and made a wonderful decision. By contrast, I know people who abdicate that responsibility and descend into a passive life, the result being that others are forced to take care of their business. I appreciate what Mom and Dad are doing on at least two levels: first, they set their own course and didn't leave it to me (which always turns out to be harder for everyone); and second, they set me a good example to follow as I grow older."

Millie and Ralph are very grateful to Brenda for her tremendous help with the move. Instead of hiring a moving truck, Brenda came every day after work for a week, loaded her Honda CR-V with boxes and small furniture and hauled it to their new home, an hour's drive away. (They bought new big items in Ephrata, which made the move easier.)

God is blessing Millie and Ralph beyond measure in their golden years in a loving Christian environment. They in turn bless our families as we visit in their home and enjoy their hospitality, as well as the beauty and bounty of Lancaster County with its large concentration of Amish and Mennonites. The shops, crafts, restaurants, and humble Christian service and spirit of these "plain people" are a constant source of amazement and joy to Millie and Ralph. We are all grateful for God's provision for them far beyond what they could ask or think.

A special event took us to Pennsylvania in August 2008: Millie and Ralph's 50th anniversary celebration at our home church. All seven siblings were present. Brenda hosted the event with help from friends and family. Pictures of Millie, Ralph, and Brenda's life brought back memories. Our former pastor's wife Bertie Denlinger (now deceased) was a special guest who showed much love and interest in us girls. Her husband, also deceased, had married Jake and me. She wanted Millie, Anna, and me to sing a trio, but lack of practice had taken its toll and, try as we might, we could not "get our pitch." Great food, and wonderful visits with former neighbors, Richard, his wife Joanne, and James Renninger, the Frei families, and many others made for a perfect day, blessing Millie, Ralph, and Brenda immensely.

Millie and Ralph's wedding party at their 50th anniversary celebration: Grace, Anna, me, Millie, Ralph, Bill Dinkler, and brother Ralph, August 2008.

ANNA

Anna was 14 months old when our mother died. In her late 60s she was delighted to learn that she was at our mother's funeral. She told me, "I've always noticed babies who are 14 months old and think *That's how old I was when our mother died!* I see that I really didn't know anything that was going on." As a mother of four, Anna grieved over the thought of such a small child losing its mother. Twice when Anna was asked to baby-sit a 14-month-old baby while the parents went on a trip she was scared. She didn't want to do it and felt a mother should not leave a child that young. In each case, she had no way out. Anna was amazed when the babies did fine and were happy in her home.

"This was an eye opener for me," Anna says. "I think God allowed that so I could see how well Heidi and our grandson Graham did apart from their mothers. It was a healing for me." Anna was 68 at the time of the first experience with baby Heidi.

Anna is a prayer warrior and has lived her life in the Word of God, resulting in a strong and vital faith. She is a beloved wife of John, mother of four, and grandmother of 12. She is the first to be blessed with a great-grandchild, Isaiah. They love keeping their grandchildren in their home for days or a week at a time.

Anna and John restored several houses they bought in Chicago. More recently she helped restore and decorate an old farmhouse in Cuba City, Wisconsin into a beautiful home. John and their sons helped, but Anna was the "idea girl," as John calls her, and put in many hours of hard physical labor.

John spent years in mission work in Chicago and Dubuque, Iowa. Anna and John have served many people in the churches they've attended and are dearly loved by family and friends. Their children are John and wife Melissa, James and wife Allison, Amy and husband Tim, and Joel and wife Kara. In March 2005, Anna was diagnosed with stage IV ovarian cancer, a terrible blow to the family. After surgery at University of Iowa Hospital and chemo at Dubuque, a change in diet, and much prayer by family and friends far and wide, Anna made a remarkable recovery and was "cancer free" for two and one-half years. In August 2009, Anna had a recurrence and four more chemotherapy treatments. In December, they drove to Zion, Illinois to Cancer Treatment Centers of America for tests and evaluation. Scans and tests showed the cancer is once again in remission.

We are so thankful to God for Anna's comeback from a devastating prognosis four years ago. In spite of the recurrence, Anna enjoyed gardening in summer, growing and harvesting vegetables and berries, and helping to dig up 120 pounds of potatoes!

Anna's caring ways, strong faith, and ready laughter draw people in and make them feel at home. She is a blessing to many people – lifelong friends, family, and people in their neighborhood and church.

Anna, John Sr., Amy, John Jr., Joel, and Jim, Newtown, Pennsylvania, 1983.

RALPH

Though Ralph didn't grow up in our home, he has special memories of Daddy. "I remember his special, tender love for me – and the cigar smell," he laughed as he told me. Daddy loved his children dearly and I'm thankful that Ralph experienced that also.

Ralph explained, "Everywhere I went with Grammy and Pappy as a young boy, I heard them explain, 'This is our grandson, Ralph. His mother died when he was born and we're taking care of him.' I didn't think anything of it until one day, when I was older, I realized, *I could have died instead of her!*"

"I had a wonderful mother," he says. "Grammy was kind and caring and she baked me wonderful birthday cakes."

When our mother died, Grammy cried her heart out, according to Aunt Melba. Then she poured her love into her beloved daughter's only son. As he grew older, when he had something that was hard to do, he wished that he had died instead of our mother. His lifelong commitment as deacon and Sunday school teacher produced much stress. This went on for years until one time he told me, "I've had a real change in attitude toward life, especially regarding church work, and I know it is only by God's grace. I see Him working on my behalf and feel as if I now understand what the Bible means when it says, 'The Lord turned the captivity of Job.' After a long time of what felt like a 'captivity,' things are changing for the better." He receives many compliments on his teaching and now accepts and enjoys his gift of teaching.

Ralph married Janice Weisel on June 24, 1961. Janice joined the Church of the Brethren and has been a faithful worker alongside Ralph. As they got acquainted, they were surprised to learn that Ralph's Great Aunt Hattie served as midwife for both of their mothers when they were born. Sister Ruth and Janice were high school friends and it was Ruth who introduced Ralph to Janice. She says, "I thought he would make a good husband for her."

Ralph and Janice, Jeff, Wendy, and Janie, April 2010.

As a couple, Ralph and Janice have a unique place in our family. Their marriage has been a bridge between the older family and the younger one–between our mother's and our stepmother's children. Janice is still Ruth's best friend. Janice and Ralph visit Ruth regularly on Fridays to play their favorite game, Parcheesi, amid lots of laughs. God has blessed our family with this providential "bridge."

Since Millie and Ralph left Quakertown, where I often stayed when I went "home" alone, Jake and I have been hosted by Ralph and Janice and have enjoyed many good times in their home. Ralph's hobby is driving on the beautiful country roads; he loves showing us local sights and scenery when we visit. In springtime the abundant pink and white dogwood trees create a stunning display in lawns and woods. In this Ralph is like Daddy, who took the family on rides as a regular pastime to enjoy the beauty of God's creation.

Ralph and Janice live in Milford Square and keep busy with their three children, Jeff and wife Deb, Wendy and husband Walt, Janie and husband Tom, and seven lively, talented grandchildren.

GRACE

Over the years, Grace worked at a variety of jobs: for lawyer Freed at Quakertown, a Souderton bank, *The Reporter* newspaper in Lansdale, and later Gannett Company, Inc. In 1972, she began college classes and later transferred all credits to Temple University where she graduated with a B.A. degree in Communications in 1984. With Gannett she lived in Rochester, New York, then Arlington, Virginia. She resigned in 1986 and returned to Pennsylvania.

Through her pastor, Grace found a position as Communications Director at the American Baptist Foundation at Valley Forge. Later she transferred to their seminary, Eastern Baptist Theological, as Planned Giving Director. When the seminary merged with Eastern College, she began at American Baptist USA International Ministries. As development officer of their Foreign Mission Board, her travels brought her to Phoenix at times and she stayed with us while visiting clients.

Grace's last years of work brought great fulfillment and opportunities for travel to supporters of the ministries. On a mission trip to Africa, she experienced inspiring worship, gracious hospitality, and warm love of local pastors and churches. She was deeply impressed by their joy and love for Jesus in the midst of poverty.

Grace Herstine and Philip Covelli, wedding day, May 17, 1996.

In 1994 Grace moved to Phoenixville and later married Philip Covelli. Though Philip doesn't enjoy traveling, Grace continues to enjoy the hobby she loves. She has traveled to Canada, Mexico, England (3 times), Ireland (2), Wales (2), France (4), Italy, Germany, Austria, Greece, Turkey, Spain, Ghana (Africa), Thailand, Columbia, and Peru. She also enjoyed a three-week "Majestic National Parks" tour in the USA. She enjoys her many nieces and nephews, and keeps in touch with Olive, the woman with whom she lived from nine months until age five. (In 2010, Olive turned 87 years old. She lives in New York with her son Chuck.) Grace loves to hike, and has gone on many peace walks from Nazareth to Bethlehem, Pennsylvania at Christmas time.

During her time at American Baptist Foundation, Grace was asked to write a devotional for the book, *Miles Ahead* (Carol Spargo Pierskalla (editor), *Miles Ahead* [Valley Forge, PA: Judson Press], 37-39). In it, she wrote: "God has gifted me with life so that I may greet each day as an opportunity to create a blessing. I don't always succeed. But God is patient and good." Grace does create many blessings for her family and friends, by giving of herself and being there in good times and bad, appreciating and sharing the fullness of life.

RUTH

When Anna worked as a practical nurse at Yingst Nursing Home in Quakertown she got Ruth a job as a nurse's aide. In Mom's letters to me at college, she often wrote that she was waiting up for Ruth on the 3:00 to 11:00 P.M. shift. Ruth married and has two beautiful daughters, April and Karlene.

Unfortunately, Ruth's marriage did not last. Later she married Dave Ruch. Ruth enrolled her girls in the elementary school at Faith Baptist Church and drove bus for the school. There the girls accepted Christ as their Savior, as Ruth and Dave had done. Ruth drove school bus for church and school districts for about 30 years. Remarkably, she has never had an accident with car or bus, not even a ticket for a traffic violation, for which she is rightfully proud.

After a lengthy illness, Dave died in the University of Pennsylvania Hospital in Philadelphia on January 11, 2000. After five years living alone in her mobile home, Ruth rented April and Mike's former house, down a short lane from them, near Tamaqua. She is fortunate to live close to April and Mike and the children, Matthew, Mitchell, and Alyssa. Karlene is married to Steve Kohler and they live in Allentown.

April, Karlene, and Ruth, May 2010.

In spring, 2009, Karlene learned she was pregnant, along with the heart-breaking diagnosis of leukemia. With limited treatment during the pregnancy, she did amazingly well until after Ethan was born on October 28. Then, after about a year of ineffective chemotherapy, a bone marrow transplant was indicated. Though there was less than a 3% chance, April was found to be a perfect match – a miracle! As of this writing, the transplant is set for March 24, 2011. Many prayers ascended during Karlene's pregnancy; especially fervent were the prayers of Ethan's cousins, Matthew, Mitchell, and Alyssa, who long had desired a cousin. Now again, prayers are being offered for a successful transplant and for a miracle. Karlene knows *our God is a God of miracles!*

Ruth has been greatly blessed through her two daughters. She is a family person and relishes Herstine get-togethers and hosting the extended family at her home. Ruth thrives on making beautiful counted cross-stitch creations for family and friends. Her daughters bought her a special light to use for creating her masterpieces. The highlight of Ruth's week is Friday, when Ralph and Janice come to play Parcheesi and enjoy fellowship.

Ruth is closest to Tom in age and geographically. They enjoy phone chats and are good friends. Tom's visits brighten Ruth's days as they share things in common and their enthusiasm for Penn State football.

TOM

Grace took major responsibility for Tom in the years after I left home before he was two. She says, "Tom's experience of our family was different from all of us in one significant way. Because of the time lag before his birth, he never really got to experience being part of a group of siblings." A few years later when Mom developed diabetes, with complications, she was often hospitalized and had a leg amputated in 1962 when Tom was seven. With the rest of his siblings living away from home, and Grace and Ruth taking over much of his care giving, Tom felt confused as to his role in the family. Grace observed, "Losing his mother at age ten, living alone with an older father for several years, and then, in seventh grade, moving to the city of Chicago to live with his sister Anna and her family were all difficult transitions. It's remarkable that he has turned out to be the hardworking and caring person that he is."

Tom and Debby were married on St. Thomas Island on September 3, 1986, the same day that we celebrated our 25th anniversary in Hesston. Since Debby worked long hours for H & R Block for many years over the dinner hour, Tom enjoyed doing the cooking.

Tom worked for a furniture company for years and then drove a milk truck. For seven years he was janitor at his church and on the Property Committee for many years. He currently works for the township of Upper Saucon and lives near Center Valley with his wife, Debby, and daughters Jenna and Megan who are now in college at Kutztown University. Jenna is studying psychology, and Megan, elementary education. Tom and Debby are very proud of their daughters.

Tom has grown into a fine man who enjoys life and loves his family. He appreciated learning gardening from Mrs. Renninger. He grows vegetables and keeps the lawn and pool in shape in summer. He and the family relish camping and trips to the seashore. At Christmas time he decorates their home so beautifully that one year he was surprised when he saw his house on

TV. He went outside and found the Allentown reporter filming it!

In 2007, through a co-worker, Tom got in touch with his son Mike, from his first marriage. They had a wonderful hour-long visit on the phone. Tom learned that Mike is an Emergency Medical Technician (EMT) in Allentown and his wife

Jenna, Tom, Debby and Megan, October 2003.

is a nurse at a hospital. In addition to this news, Tom learned that he would soon become a grandfather. Mike's wife Melissa delivered a healthy baby boy on April 18, 2008, whom they named Jacob Michael Eschleman. This was good news to Tom.

Brother Ralph told me on the phone about Tom's news and added, "I prayed every week that Tom and Mike would get together." I was amazed at his faithfulness in praying for his brother. The rest of us have followed Mike with our prayers over the years, and are happy they've been reunited.

Tom told me on the phone that he said to Mike, "I love you now as much as I did the day you were born. I always paid child support and was never late." To me he added, "I told people for years that Mike and I would get together again sometime." He had great faith and acknowledges that God has taken care of him and loves him. As a family, we rejoiced with Tom in this reunion.

Then on December 10, 2009, a daughter was born to Mike and Melissa, and Tom enjoyed meeting his "cute" granddaughter, Ana Elizabeth Eschleman. Jacob is a toddler, walking and beginning to talk, and Tom has great joy in his grandchildren.

God has been gracious to each one in our family, guiding and blessing us. I pray our lives will show forth God's goodness and grace to others around us and bless them as He has blessed us.

CHAPTER 54

Rainbows in the Desert

He has made everything beautiful in its time.
Also He has put eternity in their hearts.
ECCLESIASTES 3:11 (NKJ)

1995–2005

During our first years on Augusta Avenue, monsoon storms with drenching rain descended without warning during July and August, creating a river in the street in front of our house. Rain is scarce in Phoenix and the Sonora Desert where we live–seven inches a year contrasted with eastern Pennsylvania's 44-52 inches. As a result, we rarely see rainbows. But to my delight, a rainbow often appeared after storms and I'd grab my camera. Sometimes I prayed for a *double* rainbow, and it appeared, giving me great joy.

On August 4, 1995, I got up and journaled from 3-5:00 A.M. about our childhood suffering and God's goodness. I felt God near as I wrote, "Lord, you are *transmuting* Mom and Daddy's and my mistakes and failures and *transforming* our family's pain into something beautiful. You are showing me your love, guidance, and providence in our lives. Lord, you are indeed transmuting and transforming our family into a beautiful rainbow of many colors. Each one in our family is a different hue of the rainbow–seven children, seven colors."

Then I checked "rainbow" in *World Book* and there it was–seven colors! The spectacular double-rainbow photo showed a Sonora Desert scene with tall saguaro cactus. All excited, I went back to bed as Jake woke for his trip to Tucson.

"I was writing my book," I exclaimed.

He stretched and yawned, "Good. Write all night and sleep all day."

"A rainbow has seven colors."

"Sometimes it's 14," he reminded sleepily.

"A *double rainbow*!" I cried. "Seven is the perfect number. There were seven in my family and seven in yours...a *double* rainbow! *Our families make a double rainbow!*"

Suddenly, I knew I had my title. I jumped up to write it down. My book would be *Double-Rainbow Family*! I loved it and joyfully thanked the Lord from whom all good ideas come.

Memories of double rainbows came to mind: one I snapped through Millie and Ralph's kitchen window; one Jared shot at the parsonage at Lynden; the brilliant one we saw on the ferry from Vancouver Island to the mainland after Jake's sister Elizabeth died in 1964 at age 36; another on our last visit with Peter and Mary at their Quail Place Bed and Breakfast. On a walk with them along the bay we marveled at how the brilliant double rainbow in the east touched the earth on both ends just beyond us; it remained for our entire walk. Others greeted us along the footpath and commented on it. One woman exclaimed, "I have never seen such a brilliant rainbow in all my years on the Island!" I was amazed, and sorry I didn't have my camera. Visits with Jake's family were rare, and we felt a special bond with Peter, the oldest and spiritual leader of the clan. I marveled at the rainbow's timing and sensed God's loving presence and blessing on us.

Unfortunately, not all of life is sunshine and rainbows. On August 13, 2002, we received sad news. Jake's brother Peter called to say that he had incurable cancer. He and Mary were just getting settled in their new condominium in Comox on the Island when his pains began. Over the next weeks, Jake and I had several good phone conversations with Peter. He said, "I'm just praising the Lord every day. The grandchildren stop in all the time."

My thoughts returned to our last visit with Peter and Mary, in August 2001, and the amazing rainbow as we walked and heard the tide rushing into the bay. We had also hiked in a forest by Miracle Beach where Jake played as a boy. That day, Peter gave me his inspiring excerpts on the cross from a devotional book by Selwyn Hughes. He said the book answered his question about why God made or allowed evil and he didn't have a problem with it anymore. Another day, Jake and I drove with Peter to the top of Mt. Washington where we hiked six miles among tall firs and Peter and I fed "blue jays" from our hands. We enjoyed a fine dinner visit at a restaurant with siblings, Helen and husband Bert and Nick and wife Margaret.

We left on a trip to Jared's at Wichita, then to Janet and John's in Lincoln for Jake's 67th birthday. There, Jake received a call from his sister Mary Ann that Peter had died the day before, September 24. He was 77. From the time he called us with the diagnosis he lived six weeks. Jake flew out for the funeral, scheduled on Jake's birthday. That Sunday, September 29, before the funeral, his sister Helen had the whole family over for a surprise birthday lunch for Jake. He enjoyed catching up with his family over lunch, at the memorial service at his boyhood church, and later at Mary's new condo.

Peter was well loved by his family and grandchildren. Some of the grandchildren stayed in Peter's bedroom his last days, and even took turns sleeping with him. Peter loved and laughed with his family to the end. He had almost completed his memoirs, which his children later had printed for the family. He also pre-planned his entire memorial service.

Besides their three children—Marlene, Barbara, and Raymond—Peter and Mary had given a home to over 30 foster children, and adopted Glenn. For years, Peter was part of an interfaith men's group, a wonderful spiritual support to him, as he was to them. He served others and the church in many ways and befriended men who had no church. Many of these asked him to conduct their funeral service when they knew their end was near.

Peter and Mary visited us a number of times—at Hesston, Lynden, and Phoenix. They helped find our house in Sun City and visited us there once. During our enjoyable visits to their home, Peter's inspiring prayers and devotions at breakfast revealed his humble faith and love for God. His newsy, personal letters showed deep affection for our family. He taught us many new games and his life sparkled with humor, faith, and love.

Two years after Peter's death, Jake's brother Nick died of cancer on November 18, 2004, on Vancouver Island. He was 73. His wife Margaret and their sons, Mark, still living at home, and Garth and family in Florida survived him. Mark wrote a glowing obituary for the Victoria, B.C. newspaper in which he described his dad as a "gentle father and the most devoted of husbands." He told of Nick's life as a Provincial Judge of British Columbia and his retirement in 2001 at age 70 "after 30 stellar years on the bench." A year later, Nick's wife Margaret died of cancer, and Mark moved to Tallahassee, Florida, to begin law school, following in his father's footsteps. There he is closer to his brother Garth and Jeannie and their three children. Jake had sought Nick's advice on jobs and other matters, and we got together with his family when we lived at Lynden. The deaths of his two brothers left a big hole in Jake's life.

On April 22, 2004, from Sun City, we acquired another piece of farmland at Hesston. Jim Graber called to tell Jake of an auction coming up.

"It's a choice location near Hesston Corporation," Jim said, "and I'll be happy to farm it for you." Jake asked Jared to attend the auction with Jim and told him the maximum amount to bid. At the auction, Jared stayed on the phone with Jake in Sun City as the bidding progressed. I listened in on the excitement. One man bid higher and higher, but Jared finally clinched the deal. Jim said, "It was funny because people wondered who this young bidder was that no one knew." We now had 127 more acres for Jim to farm.

Jake decided to use income from crops on this land for a trust fund for our grandsons to attend Hesston College. The fund grows, sometimes with a double crop–wheat in June and soybeans in October. At times the land lies fallow for a season. For years Joel and Josiah have known that their mom and uncle attended Hesston and their Opa taught aviation there, and they've enjoyed romping on the campus. They attended the college's 100th anniversary with us in 2009 where they learned a lot of history and heard a powerful message by our former pastor, Peter Wiebe, who served as interim president there for two years. He asked the boys if they were coming to Hesston and facetiously told them to pick out their room and choose their rug color. For years, when Joel was asked where he's going to go to college he'd say, "Hesston." We hope our dream may become a reality for our grandsons.

Joyous Reunions

In September 2003, I flew to Pennsylvania for a festive reunion of one-room schools in our township. My former teacher, Miss Eleanor Guri, now Mrs. Charles Hester, came from Oregon as guest speaker. I wrote a poem for the occasion and went with Millie, Ralph and Brenda. We met on the lawn of a one-room-school museum, where I saw classmates I had not seen in over 50 years. Among other speakers, Mrs. Hester shared her memories of teaching, I read my poem, which moved her to tears, and school children sang for us. Great visits with former neighbors, Richard and James Renninger, Richard's wife JoAnne, my friend, Janice (Mann) Fendrick, as well as Mrs. Hester, made the day exhilarating.

(Mrs. Hester taught for 50 years, 29 in public schools, 21 teaching adults who couldn't read or wanted to learn English. Her love of teaching and for her students blessed many lives, including my sisters and me; Millie and I are still blessed by her loving letters at Christmas. Eleanor and Charles were married on the *Bride and Groom* TV show, and celebrated their 60th anniversary in 2009.)

One month later, in October, Jake flew with me for my 50th high school reunion. In conversation with our former high school music teacher, Henrietta Landis Jahnsen, I learned she was a Landis relative. A delightful person, she told me that our ancestor, George Landis, started the Flatland Church where I grew up, and was its first minister from 1837-57. Rewarding visits with classmates and hearing each one's sharing of their lives brought us up to date. Meeting Doris Lindberg Sheridan again led to our wonderful meeting in Phoenix a few years later.

Before the reunion, Jake and I spent a couple of days in Amish country in Lancaster County. From our Mennonite-owned motel with fine restaurant at Bird-in-Hand, we went on a small tour bus with a former "Amish girl" as driver and guide through the countryside to shops in Amish homes. At a quilt shop I bought a beautiful Amish appliquéd quilt called "Country Love of Roses." We took in two Bible dramas at Sight & Sound in Strasburg: the tender *Abraham and Sara* at the smaller Living Waters Theatre, and the awesome *Daniel* at the enormous Millennium Theatre.

Herstine Mennonite Churches

From Amish country, on our way to the high school reunion, I wanted to find the Herstine Mennonite Church in Montgomery County that someone at seminary told me about years ago. How could it be that I had never heard of another Mennonite named "Herstine" outside of our family, let alone a church by our name? After a lengthy search on winding roads, we found a red brick church with a sign, "Hersteins Mennonite Church," built in 1966. Not very old and the spelling was different, though I knew it was a variation of our name. Still, I took pictures of our exciting find.

Herstine Chapel, on Neiffer Road at Bragg Road, Schwenksville, Pa. Me at sign, October 3, 2003, 200 years after the chapel's founding.

Thinking that was it, we drove on down the road about a mile when we came upon a little white church with a sign that read *"Herstine Chapel 1803."* Such a tremendous surprise! We stopped at the chapel where I felt a strong connection with history. Ancient stones with mostly illegible writing filled the cemetery. I wondered, *What was the connection of my family with the founder of this church? With my grandmother Augusta Herstine's ancestors?* Would I ever know more about them? (It took four more years to solve this mystery.) I was glad to have pictures from our find for our family reunion the next day.

On Saturday, October 4, our family gathered for a Herstine reunion near our childhood church. A new church had been built directly across the street from the house where we girls grew up. Thirty-six people attended, including all seven siblings. I had written a poem for Millie and Ralph's anniversary and one for Jake's birthday. As I read of Jake's life and family hardships in his poem, memories paraded across my mind: of life across the street, my life with Jake, and separations from family due to his aviation career. Overcome with emotion, I stopped—too choked up to read. Time stood still with racing flashbacks and memories condensed into seconds. "I don't know if I can finish this," I whimpered.

Then—in a "grace moment"—niece Wendy Weaver (Ralph and Janice's daughter) called out, *"You can do it, Aunt Jane!"* Encouraged by this surprise, I recovered and read to the end.

Thirty-six family members at Herstine reunion, October 2003.

While growing up in our house across the street had been crazy and fun, it was also traumatic, especially for little sister Anna. Years later, Anna and her daughter Amy experienced a time of healing together. As a teen, Amy wondered about her mother's growing up years and asked Anna, "Why don't you talk about your childhood like your sisters do?" Anna's answer: "I can't remember." Amy instinctively felt her mother's pain at being motherless. She became obsessed with the desire to know.

In February 1998, Amy, who was married and had a baby son, wrote me in an email: "When I was in my late teens and early twenties, I was drawn to your old house on Thatcher Road. Sometimes I would drive out just to look at it and wonder about everything that happened there. I remember sitting there thinking about all of you as little kids, and crying for you. It still makes me cry to think about it. It amazes me how blood ties seem to run so much deeper than anything we can see or understand. I look forward to reading your book, and Mom is looking forward to reading the first three chapters." I was deeply moved by Amy's sensitive spirit.

Earlier I had sent the first chapters to my siblings to read. At times I checked to see if Anna had read them. She hadn't. I suspected that it was too painful for her. Then in July of 1998, Amy was visiting her parents when Anna got out my chapters. The two of them read about our mother's death, our stepmother's coming, and her harsh treatment of Anna. Finally, Amy *saw.* Amy empathized, "When your mother died, so many lives were touched." Anna began to cry. That day, mother and daughter cried together in anguish. Memories surfaced and Anna finally found release and healing as she cried with her loving daughter.

Anna called me then and thanked me for helping her face the bad memories and find healing. She said, "I never had a grateful heart. I'd often look at the picture of our mother and Daddy on the bureau in the bedroom and ask God, *'Why did you let our mother die?'* I thought I was the only one who suffered. Your chapters helped me to see from others' point of view, to see *their* suffering—like Daddy's, Grace's, and yours." Joy and gratitude to God welled up within me for Anna and Amy's healing, and for that wonderful phone call from my dear sister who had suffered for many years.

At our reunion in 2003, we celebrated the joys of family and being together.

Two years later, in 2005, Jake and I reached an impressive milestone—we both turned 70. Now it was Jake's turn for his 50ᵗʰ high school reunion in July. (I am eight months older than he, and he had grade 13 in high school, equivalent to first year of college.) We planned a visit to all of his family in British Columbia. In the meantime, another Herstine reunion came up unexpectedly, also in July, when all the Smiths—Anna and John and their four children, with their families, from Wisconsin, Illinois, and South Dakota—planned to be in Pennsylvania for a wedding. This meant we could see Jake's and my families in the same year, within weeks of each other, a first-ever occurrence.

We flew to Pennsylvania on our first trip. We missed Janet and family but were glad that Jared and Jose attended. All the rest of the grandchildren and great-grandchildren of Jean and Ralph were present. Brother Tom found us the perfect spot, a beautiful park at Center Valley. A special guest was present, Aunt Melba Landis (my mother's sister), who turned 84 the day before. Cousin Bobby Moser, as well as Mom's niece and our cousin, Betty Blose, attended. Sixty-two family members met on Sunday, July 17, for food, games, and fellowship. A memorable softball game continued during two lovely, hard downpours, with pictures taken of the soaked athletes.

Back: John Smith (father of Smith clan), Steve Kohler, Jose Ging, Brenda Loux, Zachary Herstine, Melissa Smith, Keondra Smith, John Smith Jr., Matthew and Mike DelBorello, Amanda Smith, Shelby Herstine. Front: John Smith III, Sara and Benjamin Smith, Mitchell DelBorello..

Many years had passed since our growing-up days in the house on Thatcher Road. I decided to write a poem for the occasion and, as is my custom, I asked the Lord to help me. Early one morning, inspiration hit and the words flowed forth. This time I chose not to read the poem myself. Jared read it for me and I treasure a snapshot showing him reading with a smile.

The Herstine Family

In June of 1932,
Ralph and Grace were wed,
They made a lovely couple,
As everybody said.

Then Millie joined the family
In 1933,
She's the smallest of the clan
But sweet as she can be.

In February '35
Jane Ellen came along.
Daddy called her "Janie Lee,"
She's happy as a song.

Anna Kathryn next was born
In '36, November,
Sweet and kind and giving,
A loving family member.

Ralph Landis joined his sisters
Early in '38,
And how his sisters loved him,
Thought that he was great!

But Mother Grace took wings that day
To God the Father's throne,
Now Jesus cares for each of us,
Until He calls us home.

Then Ralph and Jean were married,
In 1939,
And Grace Elizabeth was born,
Beautiful, sublime.

But God had one more girl to give
To make the number five.
Ruth Ethel came in '41,
Jolliest girl alive.

The family still was not complete,
We needed one more son,
For 14 years we waited,
For Tom, the special one.

How blest we are as Herstines,
Though tested much, and tried,
We've grown and wed and multiplied,
We've scattered far and wide.

And now we number sixty-six,*
What a family tree!
How greatly God has blessed us,
Let's praise Him, you and me.

Our hearts are filled with gratitude,
As we gather here today,
For love and faith and joy in life,
Let's trust God, come what may.

We praise God for each husband,
We praise Him for each wife,
We praise Him for the children
We thank Him for each life.

May Jesus draw you closer,
And keep you ever near.
And may God bless and prosper
Each one of you so dear.

by Jane Herstine Friesen
July 4, 2005

*Includes Mike (Herstine) Eschelman, Dave Ruch and Jose Ging, and the three parents.

For our second big trip in July, we went by car to Yosemite National Park, the Redwood Forest, and the Oregon coast. Our leisurely two-day drive brought us to Bellingham, Washington for the night then to Jake's high school reunion – Mennonite Educational Institute (MEI). Cedar Springs Retreat Center in Sumas, Washington, close to the Canadian border, sported tall cedars, lush colorful flower gardens, ponds, hanging gardens, green lawns with walking paths. This, plus the beautiful Northwest weather, provided a perfect setting for our weekend of fellowship.

The former classmates told of their lives as missionaries, pastors, teachers, musicians, and other professions. Marriage counselors, Bill and Charlotte Dyck impressed me with their great role playing, transparency, and wisdom. Hank Spenst told of 20 years as a linguist with Wycliffe Bible Translators in Bolivia, coordinating two major translation projects. The Ketcheni (Indian) language Bible was dedicated to him and I saw his copy with the inscription. Former teachers, including principal Bill Wiebe, shared memories; humorous stories abounded, with anecdotes, jokes, songs, and hymns, often in the Low German language.

Following the reunion we visited Jake's family on Vancouver Island. Helen and Bert hosted a picnic at their home at Black Creek where we met nieces and nephews and great nieces and nephews. We felt for the two sisters-in-law who recently lost a spouse. On the mainland we stayed at Marlene and John Unruh's new home and enjoyed seeing their family. Then we drove through the mountains to see Mary Ann and Dave Mulligan at Creston, where sister Margaret and Peter Schulz joined us. We were fed and treated royally and I was pleased to gain several pounds, which I could not do at home.

These wonderful reunions with family and long-ago classmates were gifts from God to us, along with good health and safe travels. Before long, we would head to a somewhat unexpected reunion with our family of seven, our double-rainbow family, including our two grandsons, Joel, 7, and Josiah, 5. Our lives overflowed with God's goodness.

591

CHAPTER 55

Mississippi Revisited

Write down for the coming generation what the Lord has done,
so that people not yet born will praise him.
PSALM 102:18 (GNB)

2006

In July 2006, a special event brought together our family of seven: Janet, John, Joel and Josiah, Jared, Jake and me with the people we knew in Mississippi and the university work camp students from the summer of 1966. We never dreamed we'd see these students again.

Bill Winfield, of Madison, Wisconsin, former work camper, searched the Internet and found sociology professor Paul Murray of Sienna College in New York; then Paul found us. We talked with Paul by phone and learned that he was writing a book on his Mississippi experience. I told him I had written three articles on our two years there, so we traded writings. Paul, Bill and Jake began to plan for a reunion at Canton where the students had worked for eight weeks. Paul searched the web. He found all but three of the students, most of whom enthusiastically encouraged the reunion.

Since Jake, Jared, and I had been to Mississippi in 1996, we had recent contacts, addresses, and phone numbers for black people we had worked with there. Paul made contacts and Shirley Simmons, Jake's former secretary at the center, became reunion coordinator in Mississippi.

From July 14-16, we gathered with eight of the thirteen students plus a few spouses for a joyful time. Our friends, now in various professions, came from all over the U.S. and Japan. Paul brought copies of reports the students had written 40 years ago for the American Friends Service Committee in Philadelphia, Pennsylvania, their sponsoring agency. The students' most vivid memory was of their arrest and subsequent jailing after they participated in a civil rights demonstration in Canton. Before the students arrived that summer of 1966, Jake had reassured the sheriff that they would not be involved in demonstrations. The students were informed likewise. However, as a result of the tear-gassing of people at the James Meredith March, just before the students came, blacks decided to boycott white businesses in Canton. When the students learned of it, they decided to participate in a march around the courthouse the Saturday after they arrived. All 13 were arrested and jailed. When the sheriff learned that the students were from Valley View, he was furious.

The students shared at the reunion about their frightening experiences in jail and release late that night when our landlord, Rev. McCullough, put a lien on his property for their bail. They also recalled the harrowing days following their release when the sheriff insisted they must leave the state. Jake and others negotiated for many hours with the sheriff. Finally he agreed that if their leaders, a young couple from Philadelphia, went home, the rest could stay. Then it was up to the students to decide if they would stay or leave. They chose to stay, with Jake and me as their leaders.

At the reunion, there was much humor, laughter, and emotion as the students recalled with fondness and great appreciation their time at Valley View. Many said that the experience changed their lives and impacted their career choices.

Paul Murray brought a college student with him to video-record the event and Paul interviewed each person. When interviewing Jake and me, he asked why Jake volunteered to move to Mississippi. Jake told of his travel to the state for MCC the winter before we moved, where he saw the poverty and need. He said, "I fell in love with the people and wanted to help."

We visited homes of some of the black people, sites of the early freedom movement in Canton, and the Canton Chamber of Commerce, where we received a gracious and warm welcome from three women, two white and one black, who worked there. This welcome was in striking contrast to our secretive, low-key arrival in 1965, knowing we were *not* welcome.

At the Chamber of Commerce, we were given a stack of newspapers with an article about the reunion. Another surprise! We visited the jail where the men were kept 40 years earlier. No longer in use, it was locked and very small, but the men could see through the bars, and Jared took pictures. Then one of the women from the Chamber of Commerce escorted us to the women's jail, now a museum. The large, attractive building camouflaged the ugly two-story room inside with a row of cells along one wall and an upstairs balcony with more cells. Women told their poignant memories of spending hours in jail. A young Valley View girl, Stella, had resisted arrest. Terrified and alone in a cell, she moaned for several hours and the sympathetic work campers could not go to her.

On Saturday afternoon we drove to Jesse McCullough's house, our former landlord's son, for a delightful visit. He showed us his book, *On the Mississippi Road*, published by Vantage Press, which Jake had bought and read before the reunion. After losing his teaching job due to his civil rights activities in the 1960s, years later Jesse was elected County Supervisor of roads. His significant contributions included building many bridges and improving roads; but he was most proud of his work "to get the hospital to deliver babies again," a boon for all of Madison County.

Our group enjoyed special dinners together on Friday and Saturday nights. On Friday, Shirley and Princeton Simmons joined us, and "Prince" offered a moving prayer and blessing on our group before the meal, expressing love and deep gratitude to God for all of us.

On Saturday evening, a 40th anniversary celebration of Head Start was held at an elementary school, where a number of eloquent black leaders spoke. Head Start began in 1966, the year Jake helped open the school at our community center. An exuberant female lawyer said, "I got my start in Head Start and now I'm a judge and I'm very proud of that." Many people were honored and remembered for their help over the years, including the students and Jake. When called on to speak, Jake made a brief but emotional statement. He choked back tears, overwhelmed at how the movement had grown and spread and brought great progress to blacks. Everyone was invited to church the next morning at St. John's Missionary Baptist, closest to the center and our former house. The evening concluded with an amazing buffet of fried chicken, sandwiches, cookies and rich desserts. The people went all out to show their appreciation.

The Sunday morning service was another highlight. St. John's had been bombed or burned down and then rebuilt by Quakers from the north before we arrived in the fall of 1965. The pastor praised the students' work of 40 years ago. Sinnie Nichols, 18 years old in 1966, welcomed us and introduced our group. She sang with a loud joyful voice in the "choir" of about six people. The pastor preached a fine message and introduced by name the many visitors from other churches who were present for the occasion. At the conclusion, he asked Dr. Paul Murray to call on the former students one by one to speak. Then Paul called on Jake, who in his brief remarks again struggled to control his emotions. Though he had spent the most time in Valley View, working with the people for two years, he had the least to say.

After the service, a lovely buffet dinner was served at the community center. Princeton Simmons sang "Just A Closer Walk With Thee." Several people made remarks, some thanking everyone for what they did years ago and for coming back. Jake kept his seat.

Then Bill Winfield stood and insisted, "Jake, you *have* to say something. You did more here than all the rest of us put together! If you hadn't been here, none of the rest of us would have come." It was an accurate statement. Overwhelmed, Jake stood to speak a few words. The weekend events and praise had focused mostly on the former students' work. Bill's recognition of Jake's contribution and exemplary role touched a deep emotional nerve in Jake. He gave credit to Rev. McCullough and said, "He was like a father to me." Two of McCullough's sons, Jesse and Clarence, were present at the church and dinner.

The work campers commended Jake and me several times on our well-behaved grandsons, Joel and Josiah. We had also observed this and were proud of them.

We made our way outside for pictures of our group in front of the community center, and one of our family of seven across the street near where our house had stood 40 years ago. It was burned down by arson a couple of years after we left, while Jesse McCullough lived there. The lot was transformed from a field of weeds as Jake, Jared and I last saw it in 1996, into an estate of lush lawn, with pillars by the road and a long asphalt lane up to a knoll. On the hill stood a beautiful house with a pond in front and lovely landscaping. It belonged to Clarence McCullough's niece and her husband. Clarence wanted to show us the house even though they were not home. We were impressed with the beauty of rooms and furnishings, including a large white open stairway at the entrance, and a grand piano. The niece's husband was a retired military man with a son and daughter. Their daughter was an accomplished pianist.

Again I was struck by the dramatic change in this community. Instead of tumbledown shacks and shy, fearful people, we saw sturdy homes and confident productive people who had come into the 21st century. From seeds sown 40 years ago and the dedication and sacrifice of thousands of people, we saw a rich harvest. Jake's obedience to God's call helped change a community and the lives of the work campers who participated with us for a summer.

Back: Jared, Janet and John Brejda, Jake, me. Front: Joel and Josiah Brejda. Valley View, Mississippi, July 2006.

Paul Murray wrote a brief report of the reunion for the American Friends Service Committee's newsletter, *Quaker Action*, Fall, 2006. Here are excerpts, used with his permission:

> Asked if he regretted his arrest, Ken Zeserson replied, "Absolutely not. I never felt the need to apologize for being arrested for demonstrating for civil rights."
>
> Masafumi Nagao traveled from Japan where he is a professor at Hiroshima University. As a student at Carleton College, he signed up for the work camp to see a different facet of American society. His Mississippi experience helped prepare him for his current project developing educational programs in South Africa.
>
> Bill Winfield observed, "More important than the buildings we worked on are the friendships that have endured."

Paul also wrote of conditions faced by civil rights workers in Madison County in the 1960s, as described in Anne Moody's biography, *Coming of Age in Mississippi*:

Madison County was considered a place with a possible future for Negroes. In addition to the fact that our records showed that there was a population of twenty-nine thousand Negroes as against nine thousand whites, Negroes owned over 40% of the land in the county. However, there were only one hundred and fifty to two hundred registered to vote... Of this number, less than half were actually voting."

Four weeks after federal registrars came to the state in 1965, 6000 blacks were registered, and the progress continued. The students contributed to that progress in our county in 1966, and were astonished now to see blacks in leadership and enjoying a better way of life.

After the reunion we took Jared to the Jackson airport for his flight back to Wichita. Janet and family stayed on for a day of sightseeing in the area. At our motel near Jackson, the boys enjoyed swimming, with the temperature close to 100 degrees. On Monday we visited a petrified forest, a rarity east of the Mississippi, and a museum of agriculture, aviation, and forestry. Tuesday morning we left for home, grateful for the wonderful family time and that our children, grandchildren, and John got to meet our good friends from the summer of 1966.

Our life with Jesus was full of adventures, along with the quiet days of enjoying our retirement together. Would the year ahead hold more adventures and discoveries? We were about to find out.

CHAPTER 56

Double-Rainbow Family

O God, you have taught me from my earliest childhood…
Now that I am old and gray, do not abandon me, O God.
Let me proclaim your power to this new generation,
your mighty miracles to all who come after me.
PSALM 71:17-18 (NLT)

2007-2010

In the year 2007, Jake and I made gratifying discoveries about our ancestors. Jake's family has a Friesen genealogy and a Duerksen one of his mother's side going back several generations. Likewise, I have a brief Landis and extensive Ackerman genealogy on my mother's side. But on my father's Herstine line we had not a shred of information. My grandmother Augusta's gravestone reveals that she was born in 1881. Other than that, we knew nothing, not even the names of our great-grandparents. In 2007, we unexpectedly began to bridge that gap. Brother Ralph and Janice led the way.

First Herstine Ancestor in America

In early May of that year, Jake and I flew to Pennsylvania to visit my family. Months before, Janice told me on the phone, "When you come we want to take you to the Mennonite Heritage Center at Harleysville. My sister Dawn was a volunteer there for years. It's so interesting and you'll love it!" Indeed I did.

A 20-minute video compressed centuries of southeastern Pennsylvania Mennonite history into a fascinating story. We browsed through giant wall displays. A stunning blowup of a large group of Sunday school members covered one whole wall. What a joy to recognize the fieldstone church of my childhood, Flatland Mennonite, taken many years before my time. That Sunday school blessed my sisters and me tremendously 100 years later.

As if that weren't enough, when we met curator/librarian Joel Alderfer he noted, *"Your first ancestor in America was Johannes Herrstein. He was an interesting character and an important leader. I don't hear the name Herstine very often. There aren't many of them around."*

Ralph and I were astonished to learn that Joel knew of our ancestor. He explained, "Johannes Herstein gave land for the Herstine Meeting and is buried in that cemetery. I know where his gravestone is."

"Jake and I found the chapel and church four years ago," I enthused, "in 2003."

Joel offered, "I can show you Johannes's gravestone when you have more time."

He continued, "Back then, most Mennonites never returned to Europe once they got here. But Johannes paid his own way back to Germany. He went with another man, and had a book of sermons reprinted. The pastor there, Jacob Denner, had a thick book of his sermons. Johannes had a copy of that book, took it back to Germany, and had copies reprinted. He brought them to Pennsylvania and sold them to new ministers who were chosen by lot. Since they had no training, some got into the pulpit and cried because they didn't know what to say. For many years, ministers read sermons from that book."

We were blessed to hear of our ancestor's ministry to struggling, untrained preachers. I could hardly believe I was learning about my first ancestor to Pennsylvania in my 72nd year. It was like finding one of the last missing pieces of the puzzle of my life.

Joel took us to the library and brought out two very old copies of the Denner Sermon Book, each about five inches thick, from the archives. He showed us the original book with the pastor's picture in front, then one of the reprints Johannes Herstein had done. "We have numerous copies of the reprinted book," he noted.

I told Joel, "We don't know much at all about our Herstine ancestors since our father took his mother's name – *Herstine*. We don't even know her parents' names."

"When you have more time, if you come back I'll help you look up more of your relatives. It's not that hard. We can find them in church or cemetery records or in census reports. We have a subscription to the census records." Ralph agreed to follow up.

Later I contacted Joel and he referred me to www.RootsWeb.com. He told me that *Johannes' wife* was *Catharine Schantz*. Jake and I found many

Herstines on the Internet with different spellings. Jake also found a family tree for Johannes, which has his name Americanized to John Herstein, born March 10, 1754, died, February 17, 1829. The Herstine Chapel was built in 1803, when John would have been about 49 years old. He died at age 75. His wife Catharine was born March 12, 1757; they were married on May 10, 1780. After she died, Johannes married Eva Reiff.

The family tree lists two sons and five daughters: John, Magdalena, Jacob, Susanna, Catharine, Esther, and Elizabeth.

On August 4, Ralph and Janice went back to the center where Joel searched census records and learned the names of grandmother Augusta's parents. For the first time, we knew the names of our great-grandparents on Daddy's mother's side—Samuel and Emma!

Ralph told me on the phone, "It was exciting. I'm going to write a book now!" He was kidding, but he was delighted to have found Daddy and his mother Augusta in the census records.

The 1880 census lists *Samuel and Emma Herstine* with *Hannah, born 1879, one year old*. Hannah was Augusta's older sister. (Augusta was born in 1881, 127 years after Johannes was born).

The 1890 census has almost nothing left, as records were lost in a fire. Augusta would have been 9 years old.

In 1900, no Augusta was listed.

The 1910 census lists *Augusta for the first time*. They found her and *Daddy, age five, living with Jacob Bryan in Bedminster Township*. Joel said he knows where that house is. This was not new to me since I asked Daddy to drive me there with Janet and Jared when we visited him in 1976, the Bicentennial year. I took a picture of the house at that time.

The 1920 census lists my grandmother *"Gusta" as a "servant,"* with *Ralph, age 15, living with James Weaver*. Evidently, Augusta and Jim were not yet married; we have no date for their marriage. We have been unable to trace Augusta back to Johannes, but what we found was rewarding.

Ralph was intrigued with the census records, handwritten in cursive. On each form, Pennsylvania was spelled out, all the way down the page. Census takers went door-to-door, writing down every person in each household. These records are not preserved on microfilm.

As a family, we are indebted to Joel Alderfer for his kindness, taking the time to do this research for us, to Janice Herstine for wanting to take us to the Heritage Center, and to Ralph and Janice for returning to gather the research.

In 2010, I did further research on the book of sermons brought by Johannes Herstein from Germany. The sermons, preached by Pastor Jakob Denner at Altona (near Hamburg), were printed in two volumes (1706, 1707), which he later combined into a 1,718 page book (1730). In an article on *Hamburg*, Denner is described as a "greatly gifted preacher." (*The Mennonite Encyclopedia*, Vol. II [Scottdale Pa., The Mennonite Publishing House, 1956], 640).

The article on *Jakob Denner*, states that his sermons were "strongly emotional and pietistic," his delivery "gentle and sincere" and his personality "charming and pleasant." He was ordained in 1684 and preached for many decades. People from all denominations, even "pious Catholics," flocked to hear him. The nobility of Denmark and Holstein associated with him and a later king of Sweden frequently came to hear him preach. His book of sermons had five German, two Dutch editions, and one in Philadelphia in 1860. It is not surprising then that Johannes Herstein knew of this book and its "tremendous influence in and beyond the Mennonite church," and saw the need for it in the Pennsylvania churches.

In the article on preacher Denner, I found our ancestor Johannes Herstein, an exciting discovery. It says the 1792 edition of sermons is of particular note as Johannes Herstein "undertook . . . the hardship of a voyage across the Atlantic to Germany for the sole purpose of procuring an edition of the big book for the brethren of their conference." Another layman, Johannes Schmutz, accompanied him. The 500 copies brought from Germany quickly sold out (Wenger, *Franconia*, 323). Curator Joel Alderfer told me they found Johannes Herstein on the ship's list, arriving back to Philadelphia on September 22, 1792.

Johannes immigrated to the U.S. in 1773 at age 38; Denner died in 1746 at age 87. Denner's writings "did much to promote pietistic tendencies among Mennonites." The book was still in many Mennonite homes in the Palatinate of Germany, in Pennsylvania, and in the prairie states in 1956. (*The Mennonite Encyclopedia*, Vol. II, 36, 37).

The more than 500 copies of Denner's book in circulation must have had a widespread impact for decades in southeastern Pennsylvania and beyond, a blessing made possible through the vision and perseverance of our ancestor, Johannes Herstein. I am deeply grateful for this story and for his life.

Visit to the Ukraine

From September 27 to October 12 of that same year, Jake and I had the trip of our life – The Mennonite Heritage Cruise in Ukraine, down the Dnieper River in the land of Jake's ancestors – part of the former Soviet Union. When Jake learned that George and Edna Dyck, former classmates from Canadian Mennonite Bible College days, were going for a second time, he wanted to go. He invited his sister Mary Ann and husband Dave Mulligan and they signed up as well.

While changing planes in Vienna, Austria, we met the first couple from our tour group, John and Agnes Peters from Abbotsford, British Columbia. When they learned Jake's father was N. N., Agnes exclaimed, "Your father baptized me! I always loved N. N. Friesen. He was a great man. I came to the Lord through one of his messages. He made the Gospel so clear. He reminded me of Santa Claus with his round face and twinkling eyes." It was a joy to meet and visit with them. From Vienna we flew two hours to Kiev, capital of Ukraine. I enjoyed visiting with our seatmate, Victor Wiebe, whom we learned was also baptized by Jake's dad at the Vancouver Mennonite Mission. Another serendipity!

When we landed at Kiev airport, the weather was sunny and warm in the mid to high 70s. This "Indian summer" continued, for most of the next 13 days – "the best weather of any cruise in the last 12 years," our leader stated. From the airport we traveled by bus to our ship on a six-lane boulevard with a lovely median and beautiful forests lining both sides of the road. In the city I was awed by miles of incredible high-rise buildings – hundreds of apartments built in Soviet times – jammed along both sides of the street. Our guide explained, "They are very tiny – two small rooms, and tiny kitchen and bathroom. They were free under Communism, but now are very expensive." With no elevators in these tall buildings, the elderly and even pregnant women must carry groceries up many flights of stairs.

After getting settled in our small cabin, Jake and I explored the ship. We ate dinner at our assigned restaurant, the Yalta, while another group ate in the Kiev. In the coming days we alternated between the two.

The next day, the 29th, was Jake's 72nd birthday. In the wee hours of the morning I looked out of our window, thrilled to see a spectacular brilliant star – the "morning star," probably Venus. I often saw that star on dark mornings in Phoenix and praised God for Jesus, the "bright Morning Star" (Rev. 22:16).

That Saturday morning, a free day, we took a walk past McDonald's on an old main street to find water and a place to exchange money. We strolled by the river near our dock to a tiny chapel surrounded by a balcony with benches. Close by, a humongous Chinese restaurant dwarfed the little chapel.

Mary Ann and Dave's arrival that afternoon generated much excitement. On this beautiful day we walked up a tall hill to a ritzy underground mall. With no party, cake or song, Jake's birthday was extra special on this cruise with Mary Ann and Dave. That evening we enjoyed dinner with them and their Creston, B. C., friends Sharon and Dave, who added much fun to our lively table. After dinner, we met in a large room on the top deck of the ship where our tour leaders and the ship's captain brought greetings. To top off the day, the Horlysta Folk Ensemble entertained us with lively singing, dancing, and many instruments.

Sunday was Election Day in Ukraine and our first official day of the cruise. Our group of 188, mostly from Canada, toured the city in five buses. We saw magnificent Orthodox churches with spires and domes of gold or green. St. Andrews Church was named for the Apostle Andrew who it is believed brought the Gospel to Ukraine. Later the Greeks brought the Greek Orthodox Church; Kiev became the center of the church for 1000 years. It was a joy to meet some of these devout believers.

Next we visited a sobering Holocaust Memorial to 100,000 Jews (and some others) who were murdered in Kiev during the German occupation. The worst massacre occurred on September 29-30, 1941. Under the guise of resettlement, Jews were told to gather at a location outside the city and bring their possessions. They were ruthlessly stripped naked, robbed of their wealth, then herded by groups to the edge of a deep ravine and shot. Nearly 34,000 men, women, and children were killed in two days, and 500,000 in all. A sculpture on a high knoll depicted figures of children and adults falling into the ravine known as Babi Yar. Near the ravine was a memorial site with menorah, pictures, and flowers. Here we read a litany written by a Jewish rabbi in Winnipeg for Mennonites to use. Many world leaders have come to this somber place to pay respects.

Impressive Saint-Sophia Cathedral had 40 buildings where 1000 monks once lived. Seventy years of atheism had taken their toll; in 2007, there were only 130. We observed two wedding parties here and frescoes wonderfully preserved for a millennium.

We took time to stroll on a street lined on both sides with craft and souvenir stands. As we browsed, Jake said, "Look at that car when it turns." The driver of the flashy black convertible maneuvered in a tight space. Then I saw the license plate proclaiming, *Pennsylvania*! Amazing! Jake mused, "It's probably one of the *oligarchs*...or maybe he's mafia!"

The oligarchs were the corrupt rich who lived in huge houses built on historic land in a valley where building was prohibited. Our guide pointed them out from where we stood on top of a high cliff and said, "Corruption is rampant in the country, from the highest levels and every level of society, police included. The citizens are outraged, but what can we do?" The country is losing population due to deaths from suicide, alcoholism, and depression. Young people leave the country; many who stay don't have children. The government gives 8000 *grivna* to each couple on the birth of a baby as an incentive to increase the population.

In the afternoon we visited the most historic of all Orthodox monasteries, the Pechersky Lavra, with eerie, narrow underground catacombs with mummified monks on display. Our guide, a tour guide all her life, told us, "These grounds are considered very holy to the Greek Orthodox. They say when you are here you are cleansed of sins." With a big smile she said, *"So you are all free of your sin!"* This remarkable statement coming from a guide from the former Soviet Union surprised and blessed me. God could not be stamped out during 70 years of atheism.

That evening excitement grew as we waited on deck for the ship to depart at 7:00. Our group gathered on the stern, while many on shore above us waved goodbyes. After dinner, as we floated toward the Black Sea, we had our first lecture. For 12 years the cruise has been known as the "Floating Mennonite University," with ten lectures on Russian Mennonite history, genealogy, and architecture given by professors from the U.S. and Canada. The gripping topics included "The Promise and Perils of the Mennonite Story," "Pathos and Tragedy," and "Paradox and Irony in the Russian Story."

(The Revolution of 1917 set off a reign of terror in southern and eastern Russia. Thousands of Mennonites died and thousands more escaped to the U.S., Canada, Paraguay, and Mexico over several decades. [From 1923-30, more than 21,000 were brought to Canada under the auspices of the Canadian Mennonite Board of Colonization, according to the article on David Toews in *The Mennonite Encyclopedia*, Vol. 4, 1959, 735.] A film, *Through the Red Gate* documents the persecution of Mennonites in Siberia by the Gulag, the penal system of the U.S.S.R., with a network of labor camps. After *perestroika* with Gorbachev, beginning in 1987, approximately two million Mennonites migrated from Russia to Germany. This included three sisters of Jake's father and their families. The German government paid for them to resettle and gave generous subsidies.)

All Sunday night and all day Monday we floated down the river, at times going through locks, great fun to watch. Sometimes the river was so wide we could not see the shore outside our window. On Tuesday morning, we woke about 3:30, looked out the window, and shared the excitement of docking at our first city.

That day we toured the beautiful city of Dnepropetrovsk, with two million people. A century ago it was Ekaterinoslav, named after Catherine the Great. We learned about the large number of Mennonite businesses in the city and visited a huge former flour mill and the impressive city hall (*duma*), built by Mennonite Mayor Johannes Esau. He was mayor from 1904-9, then re-elected. Now the hall is a ballet school; a class performed for us in the ornate room where the city council once met. Esau laid out the wide city streets, parks, and the trolley system (after visiting the California trolleys), unchanged since he built it. At a museum we saw a memorial room to honor all who perished under Communism. The large former hospital built by Esau stands in disrepair across the street from the enormous former KGB (secret police) building. Esau had been in charge of the Red Cross for all of South Russia (now Ukraine). Hundreds of Mennonite nurses and male medics took care of the wounded during the war.

That evening at 8:30 we began sailing to Zaporozhye, a city of 800,000. From there we fanned out on field trips the next day, Wednesday, learning first about the city as we drove through. Five buses went in different directions; private tours were available to selected locations for those in search of ancestors' villages. We left at 8:30 with Mary Ann and Dave to Molotschna North and East villages in the former South Russia, two hours away. Bag lunches and water were provided. Relief stops were in the bush along the road – "men on one side, women on the other, and no peeking." I determined to drink as little as possible and avoided these stops.

As we drove, our leaders gave history lectures. At long last we saw the villages we had studied in Mennonite History class years ago. Some villages had been destroyed, one had ruins of a large church, another had only the train station left from the Mennonite era. From that station, Mennonites were herded away to exile or death during WWII. There, while awaiting their fate, they always sang, "Take Thou My Hand, O Father," a favorite, comforting hymn.

At 12:30, at Waldheim, we saw a sign stating that Mennonites founded the village. We visited a hospital built by a Mennonite woman doctor in 1908, still in use. Since many women died in childbirth back then, Mrs. Warkentin, moved with compassion, went to Germany to study midwifery and returned to build the hospital. With 15 beds, it serves 5000 people from surrounding villages—in primitive conditions by our standards. A doctor and therapist spoke to our group. Free medications are given to the poor. The hospital is supported by Mennonite Centre, which we had yet to visit.

A highlight of the trip was visiting the villages of Jake's grandparents. That afternoon we visited Landskrone where his grandfather Peter G. Duerksen was born in 1877. The former church had collapsed a few years before, with only the foundation remaining. At this special place, Jake and Mary Ann got small pieces of brick as souvenirs. Grandfather Duerksen later moved with his family to Ishalka, Neu Samara, Russia, some 800 miles east of Moscow. There he met and married Maria Wedel and they migrated to Canada in the early 1920s. (Jake and Mary Ann knew their grandfather well and our children and I met him in Canada. He was 96 when he died in 1973.)

Our group was deeply impressed with the Mennonite Centre in the former village of Halbstadt (now Molochansk), "power base of Molotschna" in 1803. Before the war, wealthy Mennonites thrived here with successful farms, businesses, and schools. After the war, with Mennonites gone, peasants moved into the village. Now crushing needs and malnourished people abound, as in many rural villages. A century ago, a girls' school flourished in the beautiful building. After *perestroika*, Mennonites from Canada began to visit and found the school empty and deteriorated. They came with funds and skilled labor to restore and update the school. For the past six years they have funded and directed varied programs: a kindergarten, senior programs with lunches, youth activities, education, and a group study of *The Purpose-Driven Life* by Rick Warren. The village people have come to trust the Mennonites who serve with love and kindness. The center supports the local hospital, supplying a doctor and providing food for patients. They also built a sports school where children and youth excel in gymnastics. Center staff work too with Baptist and Orthodox churches. Many passengers from the yearly cruise bring an extra suitcase with clothing, shoes, health and first aid supplies, and toys to be distributed. The center is a lighthouse to villages in a wide area, where the lonely and depressed come to understand Jesus' love.

That day, we visited or saw about 16 villages and arrived back at the ship by 7:30 for a late dinner, tired but inspired by all we had seen.

On Thursday, we left again to Molotschna, this time to the South and East. On this long drive we visited or saw about 13 villages, two of which were of special interest. In the morning, we stopped at Gnadenfeld, where Jake's grandmother Maria Wedel Duerksen was born in 1875 and lived until her teens. She then moved with her family to Ishalka. (Jake remembers her well and her death on Vancouver Island on November 20, 1941. He was six years old and recalls playing in the yard while Grandpa Duerksen built her coffin.)

In the afternoon we visited Marienthal, village of Jake's grandfather, Nickolai Johann Friesen, born May 31, 1875. (He died June 11, 1950 in Ishalka, Neu Samara. In 1907 he was a director of a forestry area with conscientious objectors at Scherebkovo, near Odessa. In 1912 he began teaching and farming in Ishalka). A highlight for me in this village was meeting an old peasant woman who spoke to us through our interpreter. Sitting on a bench at the front of her home, she said she remembered the Mennonites and how they were herded together one day in 1943 and taken to the train station to be sent to the mountains or killed. A man in our group showed her a picture of his father and grandfather's house in her village, with relatives standing near a gate in front. When the woman saw it, she cried as she spoke.

"I remember that gate! There were two gates like it in the village. The Mennonites were such good people and gave us bread and crackers to eat when we were hungry." Her memories were vivid 54 years later.

My heart went out to her and I asked through the interpreter, "How old were you when the Mennonites were taken away?"

"Sixteen."

"And how old are you now?"

"Eighty."

Then her face brightened with a smile. "I have a brick that I saved from a Mennonite fireplace. I kept it to give to someone who lived here, if they ever came back." To Ted Rempel who had the picture she said, "I want you to have it." She walked with crutches to the side of the house to get the brick. It was like a heavy cement block, which Ted accepted reluctantly at her insistence. She smiled broadly as he took it. Deeply touched by her story, I lingered behind as the others were leaving and gave her a hug and a kiss on her pink cheek. She was heavyset, reminding me of my stepmother. She wore a royal blue cap and had teeth missing, but she was sweet and beautiful to me, a living connection to Jake's ancestors who had lived there. Her deep love for the Mennonites had created a keen sense of loss within her and I empathized with her grief.

Jake and Mary Ann with the woman in Marienthal, Ukraine.

Villages were more numerous than we could possibly see in two days. (Many were burned down during the war.) We enjoyed the great adventure of reliving life on the steppes (vast level, treeless tracts of land), which the Mennonites had caused to bloom and flourish with wheat fields, flour mills, thriving businesses, factories, schools, and churches.

On the ship, a genealogy professor made appointments with individuals who wanted help with family genealogies. Mary Ann and Jake met with him to give their family information for the professor's program and to gather information. His program is called *GRANDMA: Genealogical Registry and Database of Mennonite Ancestry*. Over 1,100,000 names, mostly with Russian Mennonite ancestry, are in this database.

Jake and I caught colds, like many other passengers, so I didn't go out on a couple days of breezy cool weather. But Jake attended the picnic on Fisherman's Island and saw the daredevil stunt show of Cossacks on fast-moving horses.

On days I stayed in, I re-read Dad Friesen's book, relishing his stories from this land of Jake's ancestors and from Canada. (I had an extra copy along and gave it to Agnes Peters who was baptized by Dad and she was thrilled.) I read of his Easter Monday in 1987 when he spent the day reading the Bible. Three times he was "driven to his knees to thank God for His great love." As he continued reading, the third time he felt a Presence in the room. He looked up and saw many angels. Dad had numerous unusual experiences with God. I was richly blessed reading again of his devotion and testimonies.

We sailed on south to the Crimea and the Black Sea to the city of Sevastopol. Jake went on the tour to ancient Greek and Roman ruins. He related that his tour guide, head guide in the city, was funny and told them, "I like Mennonites because I don't smoke, and everyone in our office smokes. I never drank, I danced a little bit, and I was baptized at age 21. So I could be a Mennonite and I like taking Mennonites on tours!" In the evening, Jake went with our group to hear the Black Sea Fleet ensemble of song and dance and bought me a DVD. We had three days in Sevastopol where our miracle weather returned. One day Jake and I walked up town past McDonald's to check emails and write to our children at a place with computers. Then we browsed through interesting shops on this beautiful old street.

From Sevastopol, we left at 1:00 P.M. to cross the Black Sea. Rough seas prevailed all night. Each time I awoke, I felt the ship rocking from side to side, but I slept well. We docked in the cold, windy harbor at Odessa for our last day.

That evening we enjoyed a gala captain's dinner with our whole group. A reception line with the captain and our leaders greeted us as we entered the Kiev Restaurant. We shared a table with Mary Ann, Dave, Sharon and Dave, our usual dinner partners. Caviar canapes, seafood salad, and a delicious turkey dinner preceded the giving of Certificates of Academic Achievement from the Mennonite Floating University.

Dessert was listed as a "surprise;" the lights went out as we waited. Waiters and waitresses brought in trays with lit candles and red liquid under them. Then a waiter brought in a large cake with blazing candles. Soon the center candle flamed up high and nearly reached the ceiling as people cheered. The baked Alaska was taken to the kitchen to cut and serve. It was a lovely ending to our romantic, exhilarating cruise. We said goodbyes and, from Odessa, Mary Ann and Dave took a bus back to Kiev and Jake and I flew to Austria and home.

Fast forward to 2010 when I discovered the connection of Grandpa Duerksen with relatives in Kansas who loaned the $300 for ship tickets for Jake's parents to immigrate to Canada ($146 per person). Grandpa Duerksen's book, *Reminicenses*, and a story from Buhler, Kansas provided the missing links. Grandpa wrote:

> By God's leading, we got to know a Doukhobor widow in Marcelin (Canada) and moved in with her. I went to Rosthern (Sask.) to talk to the Mennonite Board of Colonization about bringing our other children from Russia. I was asked by a dear Bishop, David Toews, where we were planning to get the money for tickets. *I said that my dear wife had an aunt in Buhler, Kansas, a Mrs. Tobias Dirks.* (Italics mine). We were going to see if she could help us. Bishop Toews said, "She won't help you right away, but have patience. They have the means and will help eventually. I know her. I will be seeing her shortly and will make a plea for you. She immigrated together with me from Russia via Turkestan and China some years ago."
>
> *My wife's aunt, Mrs. (Tobias) Dirks from the States, eventually loaned us $300* (Italics mine), and the Doukhobor widow loaned us another $300. Now, with the help of the Mennonite Board of Colonization, our children were able to come to Canada. For this, all I can do is thank the dear Lord and dear Bishop David Toews (chairman of the board).
>
> This was in 1925. Next we got a letter from the Mennonite Board of Colonization saying that our married daughter Elizabeth in Russia had a son, so they needed an additional $5.00 for the child's fare. We immediately sent $5.00 to the Board.
>
> …My wife's uncle was a doctor. Some of her uncles and aunts remained in Turkestan. Others went further east to China and some of these made it to the States. Mrs. Tobias Dirks was in this group She was the generous person who lent us the $300 which, with God's help, we were able to repay. The final payment was not made until after my dear wife's death (1941, 16 years later). [*Reminiscences*, P. G. Duerksen, 1949.]

Also in 2010, we learned of Keith Dirks from Buhler whose grandfather was born on a harrowing journey in Asia. When I heard his amazing story, I decided to find out if Keith was related to Jake and gave him a call. He said that his family left Russia with a group of Mennonites bound for the U.S. via China. The group traveled east, south of the Caspian Sea, in Turkestan, hiring guides along the way. When they ran short of money they stopped to work, sometimes for long periods. They endured severe hardships, bitter cold and blizzards, and extreme heat in summer. After five years of this, one group decided to turn back, including Keith's great-grandparents. They traveled with a camel caravan across the Kara Kum Desert. Rugged mountains were ahead and as winter approached, the guide wanted to hurry since snow made the mountains impassable.

Women, especially pregnant women, rode on a platform built on top of a camel. As they were approaching the Amu Darya River, Keith's grandmother, Eva Dirks, was about to deliver her baby. Her husband Tobias asked the guide to stop so the camel could get on its knees. The man refused, insisting, "We must keep going!"

A skirmish broke out and, in desperation, Tobias Dirks slashed off part of the guide's ear with his whip. He stopped then and grudgingly agreed, "Only for ten minutes!"

The camel got on its knees so someone could assist; the baby was born on the platform, and they hurried on. That baby was Keith's grandfather, Abraham Dirks. The group and baby made it to a train and later boarded a ship bound for the U.S. Tobias and his wife Eva, with baby Abraham, later settled in Buhler. Keith added to me, "They took a barrel of roasted zwieback with them on the ship – clear full to the top – their food for the trip!" Abraham T. Dirks was born Sept. 27, 1881 near Bukhara, Uzbekistan, and was two years old when the family arrived in Kansas, according to a family history written by Joy Dirks Imel (unpublished), page 46.

From Grandpa's book, we learned that Mrs. Tobias Dirks was Keith's great-grandmother Eva. Finally, here was the connection between the Duerksen/Friesen family and the Dirks family through Mrs. Tobias (Eva Wedel) Dirks and Grandma Maria (Wedel) Duerksen. Mrs. Dirks delivered her baby on a camel in Asia and later in the U.S. loaned Jake's grandfather the $300 for Jake's parents' trip across the Atlantic.

What a different life Jake would have had if his parents had remained in Russia, to say nothing of *my* life!

(For history buffs, the account of the migration from Russia across Turkestan into China is documented in a book: Fred Richard Belk, *The Great Trek of the Russian Mennonites to Central Asia, 1880-1884* [Scottsdale, Pennnsylvania: Herald Press, 1976]. Jake's great-great-grandfather Johann Wedel appears on pages 101 and 224.)

In closing, I must get back to our trips to the Mennonite Heritage Center in Pennsylvania and to the Ukraine. Jake and I both came full circle in 2007. Jake visited the villages of his two grandfathers and a grandmother in Ukraine, former south Russia. I learned about Johannes Herstein, saw the church he founded and the cemetery where he is buried. For the first time, I learned my Herstine grandparents' names. God had led us on our "double-rainbow family" adventures to these discoveries.

Our families of seven each – plus parents, grandparents, aunts, uncles, cousins, nieces and nephews – have overarched our family of seven like a beautiful double rainbow, giving support, prayer, warmth, and love.

As a child, I, along with Millie, Anna, and Ralph, sometimes felt abandoned by our mother and by God. As we grew older and wiser, our perspective changed. It is my belief that God has answered the prayers at my mother's funeral and ongoing, offered by hearts that loved, grieved, and cared. God was with us! Along with the trials, we have been a family of music and song. God has given us much happiness and success in all we have done (Psalm 90:14,17). We are greatly blessed with children and grandchildren.

It is my hope and prayer that our descendants and each reader may know God's constant love and salvation in and through Jesus Christ. Our salvation through Christ is the source of our joy. An article I once read (and, sadly, lost track of) called *The Indestructible Joy of Jesus*, contains this compelling line, "...*The light of Jesus' joy makes a rainbow in the tears on his face.*" What a beautiful description of our Savior, "who for the joy that was set before Him, endured the cross, despising the shame, and is set down at the right hand of the throne of God" (Heb. 12:2 KJV). The Good News Bible says: "Let us keep our eyes fixed on Jesus, on whom our faith depends from beginning to end. He did not give up because of the cross! On the contrary, because of the joy that was waiting for him, he thought nothing of the disgrace of dying on the cross, and he is now seated at the right side of God's throne." I praise and thank God in Christ for all He has done for me, for our family, and our world.

May we all see God's awesome deeds, and experience His salvation, with happiness, singing, blessing, and success in all we do. May we serve God and others all the days of our lives until we come into His glorious presence and hear His "Well done, good and faithful servant;...Enter into the joy of your Lord" (Matt. 25:21).

The significant friendship of Jesus has blessed me all my life. He is our infinite, eternal Friend, and His name is LOVE. Jesus says in Mark 5:19 (GNB), "Go back home to your family and tell them how much the Lord has done for you and how kind he has been to you." That is my hope for this book. To God be the glory.

My siblings at Millie's 60ᵗʰ birthday dinner: Millie, Tom, Ruth, Anna, Ralph, Grace. August 1993, Quakertown, Pennsylvania.

Double-Rainbow Family

Even an ordinary life can be epic as shown in Jane Herstine Friesen's autobiography *Double-Rainbow Family*. Jane was born into a poor family in Pennsylvania in 1935. Her father, Ralph, weathered the Depression working at a bakery shop. After her mother's tragic death, a domineering stepmother entered Jane's life. She vacillated between hate and love for Jean, her new mother. A surprise opportunity led her to a new life of challenge and planting seeds of reconciliation with her stepmother.

Jane recounts her romance and marriage to Jake Friesen, from a radically different Canadian Mennonite family. Together the couple served in the South during the Civil Rights movement of the sixties, after which Jake began an exciting career in aviation. When the family settled into life in a Mid-western town, Jane found a new vocation. The story sparkles with her children's eventful, often painful, growing up years. Jake's jobs moved the family to exotic places, and he flew many famous people, including Ronald Reagan, Frank Sinatra, and Michael Jordan.

Jane's tribute to her father changed his life dramatically in his last months. Though thousands of miles from their families, Jane kept in touch with them and developed an unexpected and heartwarming relationship with her father-in-law. This fascinating tale recounts reconciliation, reunions and excursions, and Jane solves mysteries as she uncovers family histories.

About the Author

Jane Herstine Friesen

Jane Herstine Friesen grew up in a family of seven near Quakertown, Pennsylvania. She has been a teacher and copy editor, and has had devotionals and numerous articles published as a free-lance writer. She served with her husband, Jake, with Mennonite Central Committee in community development in an impoverished rural area in Mississippi during the Civil Rights movement of the sixties. She has led women's Bible studies, mentored women, and worked in various capacities in churches and educational institutions in Pennsylvania, Ohio, Indiana, Kansas, Washington, Germany, and Arizona.

Jane's hobbies include reading and traveling with her husband, especially to visit their daughter and son and two grandsons in Kansas and Nebraska. She loves networking with family and friends, old and new. She enjoyed making a country sampler quilt by hand. A nature lover, Jane grows beautiful flowers, which she photographs. She has relished hiking the Phoenix mountain parks in the Valley of the Sun with her husband and friends. Jane resides with her husband in Sun City, Arizona and is a member of Trinity Mennonite Church in Glendale. The couple anticipates celebrating their 50th wedding anniversary in September 2011.

Visit her website at www.doublerainbowfamily.com.

Published with CreateSpace.com

7800781R0

Made in the USA
Charleston, SC
10 April 2011